Organizations
Management Without Control

Howard P. Greenwald
University of Southern California

SAGE Publications
Los Angeles • London • New Delhi • Singapore

For information:

Sage Publications, Inc.
2455 Teller Road
Thousand Oaks, California 91320
E-mail: order@sagepub.com

Sage Publications India Pvt. Ltd.
B 1/I 1 Mohan Cooperative
Industrial Area
Mathura Road, New Delhi 110 044
India

Sage Publications Ltd.
1 Oliver's Yard
55 City Road
London, EC1Y 1SP
United Kingdom

Sage Publications Asia-Pacific Pte. Ltd.
33 Pekin Street #02-01
Far East Square
Singapore 048763

Printed in the United States of America

Library of Congress Cataloging-in-Publication Data

Greenwald, Howard P.
Organizations: Management without control/Howard P. Greenwald.
     p. cm.
Includes bibliographical references and index.
ISBN 978-1-4129-4247-8 (pbk.)
   1. Organizational sociology—Textbooks. I. Title.

HM786.G74 2008
302.3'5—dc22   2006102693

This book is printed on acid-free paper.

07   08   09   10   11   10   9   8   7   6   5   4   3   2   1

Acquisitions Editor:	Al Bruckner
Associate Editor:	Deya Saoud
Editorial Assistant:	MaryAnn Vail
Production Editor:	Diane S. Foster
Copy Editor:	Halim Dunsky
Typesetter:	C&M Digitals (P) Ltd.
Cover Designer:	Candice Harman
Marketing Manager:	Nichole M. Angress

Organizations

To Phoebe and Jared

Brief Contents

Detailed Contents

List of Abbreviations

CBO: Community-Based Organization

CEO: Chief Executive Officer

EAP: Employee Assistance Program

HQ: Headquarters

IRB: Institutional Review Board

MBO: Management by Objective

MNC: Multinational Corporation

R&D: Research and Development

TQM: Total Quality Management

Preface

This is a textbook about formal organizations and the issues they raise for members, managers, and society. Formal organizations may be understood as frameworks for focusing the efforts of many individuals on common, recognizable objectives. Organizations of this kind include armies, churches, political parties, community improvement societies, many clubs, and most business firms of consequence.

Many types of formal organizations exist. But most have characteristics that make them easy to recognize. These characteristics include (a) assignment of specific jobs to individual members, (b) operation of mechanisms to ensure that everyone performs his or her function at an acceptable level, and (c) linking of individual functions to achieve objectives. Formal organizations follow routines. They have membership rosters, hold meetings, and occupy recognized physical space. They have the power, to a greater or lesser extent, to reward and punish members. Many have dress codes (explicitly stated or assumed) and sometimes uniforms. Features such as these cause people to behave differently than they might in other settings, creating challenges for members, managers, and society as a whole.

The formal organization may be thought of as a *technology* capable of coordinating the thinking and energy of millions of human beings. Formal organization has helped humankind achieve mastery of nature. Monumental achievements ranging from 19th-century railroads to 21st-century space travel have depended on formal organization. The theater, the opera, television, the World Series, and the Super Bowl would be unthinkable without formal organization. The most personal of resources, from a bottle of prescription drugs to an investment account, are made available only by formal organizations.

Everyone reading this book has had significant experience in formal organizations. They constitute an essential element of life in the modern world. The chapters to follow will help readers achieve an improved understanding of the organizations in which they find themselves or that they may join in the future. This book provides vocabulary to help people communicate with each other regarding their experience in organizations. It provides "handles" by which people may grasp the problems that inevitably occur in organizations and suggests steps toward their solution.

This book pays special attention to practical interests and applications. While it introduces and explains basic terms and concepts, it makes only limited use of technical language and jargon. Formal theories on organization are introduced in an early chapter. Rather than extensively debating the merits of each theory, however, the chapter draws basic implications from several. These are presented as three "analytical perspectives": organizational function, environment, and conflict. Although they in no way exhaust the conceptual approaches to organizations, these perspectives occur in several widely cited theories and are linked with classical ideas in the social sciences. Practically, these perspectives help explain the resources upon which organizations depend, the challenges organizations face, and the trade-offs involved in management decisions.

Along with these perspectives, this book is based on a belief that organizations never fully control the thinking and actions of their members; hence, the book's subtitle. This proposition raises challenges for managers and members alike. Seldom if ever can managers succeed by simply giving orders to their subordinates. Likewise, members cannot fully attribute frustration of personal goals to the organization, nor can they fully blame the organization should they engage in unethical, unlawful, or socially destructive behavior.

The book is divided into five parts. Part I introduces the concept of the formal organization and compares it with the group and the family. Capacities offered by formal organizations can (but do not always) help both members and outsiders to accomplish more, feel happier, and live longer (Chapter 1). Chapter 2 highlights the organization's "milieu," encompassing phenomena internal to the organization (such as individual personalities and group dynamics), outside influences on individual members, and the broader social environment. These factors represent both challenges and assets to the organization. Chapter 3 introduces a range of theories about the formal organization and links the analytical perspectives of function, environment, and conflict with these theories.

Part II explores the means by which organizations meet the challenges they encounter and make use of the assets available to them. Organizations attempt to direct individual efforts toward their objectives by assigning roles and establishing structure. Roles (Chapter 4) instruct individuals to carry out specific sets of tasks and to conduct their behavior within an acceptable range. Structure (Chapter 5) arranges roles into a matrix that, ideally, ensures that each role reinforces the contributions made by other roles to the organization's objectives. Though they may be considered the stable core of an organization, roles and structure are subject to continuous modification.

Part II also addresses the question of why people adhere to roles and structure. Organizations depend on resources that induce members to carry out their roles within acceptable limits of deviation and to accept, if only superficially, the direction of others. For this task, organizations utilize mechanisms such as rewards, imperative forces, and organizational culture. Organizational reward systems (Chapter 6) allocate personally gratifying resources (such as money) to people in exchange for accepting and adequately performing their roles. Organizations back up reward-based motivation with imperative forces (Chapter 7), such as power and authority. When effectively exercised, both power and authority cause an organization's members to set aside their personal judgments and needs, at least temporarily, in the interest of organizational objectives.

Organizational culture (Chapter 8) helps capture the members' "hearts and minds." Culture is visible in the myths, symbols, artifacts, and rituals found in perhaps every organization. In an organization, the dominant culture justifies reward systems, legitimizes power and authority, and focuses the individual's attention on the organization's desired outcomes. Reward systems, imperative forces, and organizational culture reinforce each other's hold on the individual.

Part III explores a series of dynamic forces in organizations. These forces arise from interplay of actual human beings. Roles and structure may promote stability in an organization, but human action constitutes its life. Dynamic forces are important in every organization. Leadership, for example, is of concern almost everywhere. Chapter 9 explores the basis for leadership and the methods by which it is exercised. This chapter also inquires into the reception of leaders by their followers, an important though often-overlooked concern. Chapter 10 examines organizational communication and decision making, "intelligence processes" within organizations that can lead in some instances to outstanding success or in others to disaster. Politics, conflict, and change, the subjects of Chapter 11, are interwoven processes highly pertinent to the success of individuals and ultimately to the organization's survival.

Part IV addresses the future, asking whether large-scale human organization can work differently and better than it does today. Chapter 12 deals with bureaucracy. Unlike in many textbooks, treatment of bureaucracy in this book occurs late rather than early in the succession of chapters. It is placed here because bureaucracy, as the most "formal" of structures found in formal organizations, represents a crystallization of the features of organizations addressed earlier. A term used as much for pejorative as for descriptive purposes, *bureaucracy* embodies a possibly irresistible trend among modern, formal organizations. Bureaucracy, though, has more attractive features for the individual member than are often recognized. Chapter 13 reviews specific steps people have taken to change the nature of human relations in formal organizations. These steps represent efforts to make bureaucracy more efficient and more rewarding for its members, as well as a search for alternatives to bureaucracy itself.

Part V intensifies the book's emphasis on limits in the formal organization's power over individuals. Chapter 14 provides guidelines to assist the individual in assessing the organization's suitability to his or her personal goals and deciding upon steps to achieve them. Of equal importance, Chapter 14 addresses features present in many organizations that place members at risk of unethical, unlawful, or socially destructive behavior. Chapter 15 offers a perspective on the impact organizations have had on the societies within which they operate. The multinational corporation receives attention here, with particular consideration given to the degree of dominance these organizations may someday achieve over world politics and economics.

Each chapter concludes with several sections intended to aid the reader's understanding of the topics it covers. A section entitled *Issues and Applications* demonstrates relevance of the foregoing material to practical dilemmas and challenges. A brief concluding section, entitled *Chapter Review and Major Themes*, is also provided. This section summarizes the chapter's main points. It also connects the subject of the chapter with the analytical perspectives described above and the theme of personal independence and choice within organizations.

A section containing discussion questions also follows each chapter. These are particularly useful in seminar and classroom settings. Discussion questions have been designed to stimulate ideas, controversy, and synthesis of fact and theory. They concentrate on drawing issues from the text rather than serving primarily as means of review.

Finally, each chapter concludes with references keyed to bibliographic notes in the preceding text. Each reference indicates a book or article in a social science or management journal from which material in the text has been drawn; sometimes, reference is made to journalistic sources as well. For the curious or skeptical, these references provide an opportunity to see whether assertions in the text are backed up with systematic research.

More important, the references in each chapter should promote awareness among readers of the vast world of research, writing, and thinking by both professional researchers and practitioners regarding organizations. Academic journals from a number of fields are frequently cited, such as *American Sociological Review, Administrative Science Quarterly, Journal of Management,* and *Public Administration Review.* More familiar to many readers will be publications such as the *Wall Street Journal, The New York Times,* and *Harvard Business Review.* Material from journalistic sources such as these may be less systematically documented than that found in academic journals. At the same time, news stories and magazine articles are usually more current and directly relevant to the reader's immediate experience. Some statistics have been taken from a primary source, the 2002 *National Organizations Survey.* This database is referenced as *NOS* in the text.[1]

As a whole, this book aims at alerting the reader to the variety, depth, and power of forces at work in organizations today. Even the highest-level managers often exercise at best imperfect control over these forces. This perspective promotes understanding of the typical organization not as a unified monolith but as a dynamic array of shifting roles, flexible structures, imperfect communication, and conflict among individuals, groups, and specialized internal units. From this background can come an understanding of how organizations work, how they can be helped to work better, and how they can be prevented from doing harm.

The book discusses management tools such as negotiation, progressive discipline, conflict resolution, exercise of authority, and leadership. But it does not prescribe formulas for problem solving. Actual challenges faced by managers have highly specific character and context, both of which change with the flux of organizations and their environments. Thus, this book emphasizes background and perspective as the best preparation for management in the years to come.

Reference

1.   Smith, T. W., Kallberg, A. L., & Marsden, P. V. (2002). *National organizations survey* (computer file). ICPSR04074-v1. Chicago: National Opinion Research Center (producer), 2003. Ann Arbor: Inter-university Consortium for Political and Social Research (distributor), 2004.

Acknowledgments

A number of individuals deserve special recognition for contributing to the inception and development of this book. The initial project was suggested to me by my friend and teacher, Edgar F. Borgatta of the University of Washington, who provided inspiration and encouragement at every stage. My colleague Carl Milofsky of Bucknell deserves special recognition for reading manuscripts, assigning drafts to his classes, and making important suggestions. It was Professor Milofsky who helped crystallize the book's principal theme, as reflected in its subtitle. Professor Milofsky's wisdom was reinforced by that of James Begun of the University of Minnesota, who encouraged me to deviate from conventional thinking in organizational behavior and theory.

Colleagues at the University of Southern California made valuable contributions to successive drafts by reviewing material in their areas of specialization. In particular, I wish to thank Professors Gerald Caiden, Michael Moody, Peter Robertson, and David Lopez-Lee. A large number of students in master's and doctoral classes at USC served as test audiences for various drafts. These students, many of whom had significant career experience in organizations of all kinds, helped correct academic misimpressions of the world of the corporation, government agency, and nonprofit. I am grateful as well to my colleagues and friends at the Group Health Community Foundation in Seattle for enabling me to live life in the corporate world, and thus to experience its issues and challenges directly. Deborah A. Dickstein and Gabriel Kabakov provided invaluable critiques at various stages of manuscript development.

Richard W. Beesen, adviser to the president, Globexbank, Moscow, and former vice president, Bankers Trust Company and Deutsche Bank, New York and London, deserves special thanks for providing insights on multinational corporations in banking, finance, and several other industries.

I am grateful to a number of reviewers who helped guide revisions and provided important suggestions. In addition to Carl Milofsky, these are Mary E. Guy, Florida State University; Abbas S. Mehdi, St. Cloud State University; Shibu Pal, Carleton University; W. W. Riggs, Texas A&M International University; Eugene S. Schneller, Arizona State University; Victor N. Shaw, California State University–Northridge; Peter F. Sorensen, Benedictine University; and Blue Wooldridge, Virginia Commonwealth University. Heidi Merrifield deserves thanks for producing graphics for the book. Few, I'm sure, have thanked Alaska and Southwest airlines for delayed flights, but I shall; over the years, delays at LAX provided the opportunity to work on the manuscript in an atmosphere of managed chaos, a description applicable to at least a few organizations.

Most of all, I thank my family. My wife, Romalee Davis, provided the necessary ingredients of patience and encouragement. My children, Phoebe and Jared, contributed laughter and distraction, which I occasionally had the sense to receive with gratitude. It is to these children that the book is dedicated. To my family in its entirety, I owe my personal education in "management without control."

To the Student

S ome students will find this book easy reading, addressing as it does numerous everyday experiences and problems familiar to people used to life in formal organizations. Others may experience challenges due to new concepts and unfamiliar vocabulary. A number of special sections are included in each chapter that will be valuable to all. These sections underscore major themes, connect content with personal and management issues, and encourage development of independent perspectives.

Each chapter begins with an item entitled *Learning Objective*. Under this title is a sentence-length statement of the chapter's main concern. This item is followed by a statement of about one page on individual principles to be covered in the chapter. Learning objectives and chapter principles are intended as signposts to help the student maintain awareness of each chapter's key issues and messages. In themselves, these signposts provide bare outlines of the material to follow. Reading them alone is insufficient to attain full understanding. But checking back on these items can be invaluable to the student who finds him- or herself lost in a chapter's details.

As noted above, each chapter concludes with a series of sections titled *Issues and Applications, Chapter Review and Major Themes,* and *Discussion Questions*. These sections constitute signposts leading from the details presented in the chapter back to major ideas and messages.

The *Issues and Applications* section provides concrete examples of events and dilemmas related to the chapter's subject matter. They connect abstract principles and theories with the world of human experience.

The *Chapter Review and Major Themes* section restates the chapter's messages. In addition, this section applies the book's key analytical perspectives—function, environment, and conflict—to the specialized area addressed by the chapter. In most chapters, graphics are provided to illustrate how these perspectives apply. In addition, the *Chapter Review and Major Themes* sections periodically revisit the theme that resources at the organization's disposal, although capable of promoting cohesion and coordination among individuals, do not result in absolute control over them.

The *Discussion Questions* section at the end of each chapter offers an important opportunity for learning. These questions provide a structure for review of material presented in the chapter. Review, however, is of secondary importance. More significantly, the questions provide students with an opportunity to deal with issues emerging from the text. They invite the student to apply material encountered in the chapter to his or her own life, to think independently, and to compare his or her interpretations with those of others. They promote sharing among students of individual experience. For any question, a number of different answers may be equally correct, depending on the facts and theories upon which the student chooses to focus. This mirrors situations often found in analysis and management of organizations, where the broad context of an organization's functioning is crucial.

Although the student will regularly encounter the theme of imperfect control by organizations over their members, this theme is not intended to dominate the text. Many more things are important to learn about organizations. Imperfect control does not imply that chaos prevails in organizations. Organizations have resources that generally keep relationships orderly and activities focused on a day-to-day basis. But the understanding that objectives are best reached through willing cooperation rather than control enables managers to excel at their craft. An understanding by members that the organization does not fully control their thinking and actions enables them to remain true to their individual interests and those of society.

PART I

Understanding Organizations

The French philosopher Jean-Jacques Rousseau (1712–1778) once wrote, "Man is born free and he is everywhere in chains." These words express the thought that people are by nature independent beings, but live under the constraint of social expectations and duties. This state of affairs may have a positive outcome. Participation in society enables the individual to attain his or her full potential as a moral and civilized human being. Still, Rousseau implies that conflict between individual freedom and social constraint never loses relevance. Generations that followed looked to Rousseau for justification of social protest and revolution.

Formal organizations—arrangements devised to achieve objectives by assigning responsibilities and promoting their fulfillment—reflect Rousseau's seeming paradox in today's world. The formal organization channels human energy and behavior in a manner often experienced as constraining. Yet formal organizations can do much to enhance the individual's accomplishments, advance his or her personal goals, and enable him or her to participate more fully in the broader human community.

A prosperous, democratic society requires formal organizations. Industrial production, science, and government operations today require organization to take place on a very large scale. Properties associated with formal organizations make them particularly well adapted to carrying out large-scale jobs such as these better than informally organized groups of families.

A successful organization must operate in a manner compatible with the basic needs of its members. Organizations, though, often require people to perform duties and accept rules inconsistent with the personal inclinations of their members and their responsibilities outside the organization. Seldom if ever can organizations contain the resulting conflict by exercising full control over members' thinking and actions. In addition, organizations must deal effectively with potential conflict with the broader society.

Despite the positive contributions they often make, organizations cannot be counted upon to operate effectively or benefit their members and the broader society. The manner in which organizations address their members' needs and relate to broader social forces helps determine their effectiveness and longevity. These factors also influence the public's perception of the organization as favorable or unfavorable.

Social and management scientists have formulated many theories about organizations. Some have focused on organizations as mechanisms rationally designed to accomplish tasks. Others have highlighted the organization's environment, including its economic, technological, and legal dimensions. Still others have concentrated on the presence of conflict: among members of organizations, between members and the organization itself, and between the organization and the surrounding society. Several theories focusing on other dimensions have made important contributions as well.

CHAPTER 1

Let's Get Organized!

Learning Objective

To understand the nature and importance of organizations.

Principles

○ An organization may be thought of as a body of individuals working under a stable system of rules, assignments, procedures, and relationships designed to achieve identifiable goals. By promoting coordination and cohesion, organizations have enabled humankind to attain its greatest material achievements.

○ Examples of organizations include clubs, business firms, government agencies, political parties, and armies.

○ Organizations differ in important respects from informal groups and families and perform functions that groups and families generally do not. Organizations are better able to focus on specific purposes and to persevere in their pursuit. Organizations make possible a high degree of individual specialization. Organizations enable individuals with diverse backgrounds and changing needs to work together in an atmosphere of stability and trust. Due to these features, organizations make it possible for large numbers of people to pursue defined goals over long periods of time.

○ Although organizations have the capacity to benefit their members and the surrounding society, this capacity is not always realized. Highly organized systems do not always operate effectively. Organizations, moreover, are capable of doing harm as well as good.

The Importance of Organization

Let's get organized!

How many times have we heard this said?

Combining the efforts of many people to achieve a successful result requires organization. In competitive situations, people who are well organized usually triumph over those who are not. This principle is as valid in business and politics as it is in sports and warfare.

Consider a contest between two teams in a recreational soccer league, the "Wombats" and the "Sharks." The Wombats have athletic ability that is average at best. Several members have never participated in competitive sports. But even though the league is informal, the Wombats proceed to select a captain and assign everyone a definite position. Team members meet to develop a few simple plays and take time to practice them.

The Sharks have considerable talent. Most members played competitively in high school. Two were star athletes. This team trusts in the individual gifts and prior experience of its members. Early recruits call their friends to fill out the team roster. It is agreed that positions will be assigned at the playing field, where several of the Sharks will meet for the first time.

The season's first game pits the Sharks against the Wombats. The Wombats score early, thanks to a prearranged, well-drilled routine. The Sharks strike back, easily outrunning and outmaneuvering the Wombats.

But the Sharks perform unevenly. Intending to pass the ball, a Shark hesitates as he looks for a teammate and is tackled. Later, the two one-time high school stars on the Shark team quarrel over who will be goalkeeper. The Sharks are hampered by the fact that several of their team members failed to show up.

Throughout the season, the Wombats suffer much humiliation and many bruises. But they win more games than they lose. They become used to their assigned positions. They take advantage of the talents of their teammates and compensate for each other's shortcomings. They know how to communicate with one another. While the Sharks experience clashes among egos, the Wombats develop team spirit and friendship. They also have a good time.

Most real-world situations are more complicated, but the principle is clear: organization promotes success.

People who are not organized face great uncertainty. Individual human beings harbor an endless variety of needs, objectives, and values. Some of these arise from basic survival functions common to all animals. Others stem from the rich mixture of family and cultural influences, as well as economic pressures and personal commitments of an ideological or spiritual nature.

Without organization, cooperation is always in doubt. Individual human motives, values, and loyalties are seldom completely consistent with the needs of the group. Moreover, individuals tend to change their minds rapidly and unexpectedly. Change takes place more quickly today than ever before. The pace with which people switch jobs, political allegiances, homes, and marriage partners illustrates this fact.

But people who are well organized can count on each other's cooperation. People organized to perform a specific activity often feel distinct from others and develop team spirit. They share ties of mutual obligation. They know what to do when they require each other's assistance. They recognize their supervisors and subordinates. They learn to expect rewards for certain behavior. Organization strongly influences individuals. When people realize that they live in a world of stable, continuing relationships, they plan their entire lives around them.

The Process of Organization

Organization is a process by which people coordinate their activity though prearranged agreements or mutually accepted understanding. Steps in organization include assigning jobs, setting schedules, evaluating performance, allocating rewards, and administering punishment. Ideally, the process of organization enables human beings to carry out collective action in an efficient manner.

Organization is one of humankind's basic survival skills. As a human achievement, organization is no less important than the ability to use fire and invent tools. People throughout history have recognized leaders, assigned each other duties, distributed rewards, and applied punishment to achieve collective goals. Organization increases the ability of people and groups to meet their needs.

Organization is the principal concern of top business executives and government officials. These executives are responsible for making sure that large numbers of people work together effectively. Organization is equally important to people in small businesses who train and monitor the performance of a few employees, or the residents of a community hoping to reduce neighborhood crime, improve schools, and elect officeholders responsive to their needs.

Human organization takes an endless variety of forms. It is often spontaneous and informal. A few friends may meet regularly to drive to work, play golf, drink beer, or shop. Under such arrangements, each individual may have a specialized function. One may arrange a meeting time, another may volunteer to drive, and a third may select the destination. As time goes by, outsiders recognize the comrades as people who seem to belong together.

Organization may be much more concrete and regularized in nature. The people involved may be required to swear oaths, pay dues, or take tests in order to participate. They may have definite, even written rules that govern their behavior. They may wear insignias or uniforms. They may receive pay or resources such as housing as rewards for membership. Once people have joined they may not be free to leave. Membership itself may be coerced or legally required rather than voluntary.

People working, playing, or simply spending time together within spontaneously developed, fluid frameworks of expectations and agreements can be said to possess organization. But only people who act under an enduring system of more or less explicit principles governing their relationships belong to *an organization*. The features, benefits, and problems associated with an organization conceived in this fashion, often designated as a *formal organization*, are the concerns of this book.

The Nature of Formal Organizations

Organizations Defined

The chapters to follow will discuss a wide variety of organizations. But a core of common features tends to distinguish organizations from the other frameworks under which human relationships take place. First, human relations within organizations, to a greater or lesser degree, are *formal* in nature. As used here, the word *formal* refers to behavior rather than dress. People in organizations generally work and communicate with each other according to standardized patterns recognizable by everyone.

Members of organizations are typically aware of their formal characteristics and boundaries. Most members can describe, with some accuracy, what constitutes acceptable and unacceptable behavior. Everyone in an organization can identify specific qualifications for membership. People in organizations can describe definite procedures for seeking entry. They can specify who has supervisory responsibilities. They can tell an outsider who has the right to initiate communication with a particular supervisor. People in most organizations can indicate what is acceptable attire, and many organizations have written dress codes. To some degree, everyone can explain how these arrangements are related to the organization's objectives.

Second, organizations can be seen as primarily *instrumental* in nature; that is, as tools for accomplishing identifiable tasks. Individuals may feel affection for organizations such as the Army or Navy. But it is easy to argue that these organizations exist in order to provide for national defense, just as a regional telephone company exists to operate communication services and the Internal Revenue Service exists to collect taxes.

Much has been written about organizations, and many definitions have been put forward.[1-4] In fact, organizations are highly diverse—varying, for example, in mission, size, and degree of formality. Recognizing this range of differences, the chapters to follow will use the term *organization* to signify

a body of individuals working under a defined system of rules, assignments, procedures, and relationships designed to achieve identifiable objectives and goals.

The Human Experience in Organizations

However organizations may be defined in textbooks, people can almost always recognize them. The daily experience of countless men and women illustrates key characteristics of formal organizations. The example below, though fictional, contains elements recognizable to almost everyone who has lived in a modern city:

Beginning his workweek, a man enters the downtown office building owned by his company. A guard in the lobby requests his identification badge. He quickly clips the badge onto his lapel and steps into the elevator. Exiting at his floor, he hurries to a conference room for the weekly meeting of his unit, the Corporate Sales Department. Gathered around a table are a dozen men and women in dark blue or gray suits. A large chair at the head of the table remains unoccupied.

After a few moments, a woman in early middle age arrives, the unit director who holds the title of vice president. Conversation dies down as she takes the vacant chair. She greets her subordinates and is handed a sheaf of papers by her secretary. Items for discussion and action are introduced according to their order on a written agenda.

Of interest today is the plan to hire a senior credit analyst for the unit. Despite the long-realized necessity of such a specialist, no position of this kind has existed before. With a note of gratification, the director announces that a higher-level officer has approved the position, and everyone applauds. She circulates a job description drafted by her executive assistant. A few of those present suggest revisions, and these are noted by the secretary. The director comments that the final language will have to be approved by the Human Resources Department, after which the position will be officially posted and advertised.

The meeting adjourns at 10:00, although two items remain on the agenda. These will be dealt with at next Monday's departmental meeting. The conference room empties.

Explicit rules governing behavior, titles, and adherence to schedules are hallmarks of modern formal organizations. Contrast the surroundings just described with those of men and women relaxing at a tavern after work or ministering to their children at home. Outside formal organizations, activities are seldom conducted according to agendas, clothing is usually varied in color and style, and work or play is tied less firmly to the clock.

The experience illustrated in the above example may seem uncomfortable and unappealing. Yet it is difficult to imagine that people outside a formal organization might achieve enough coordination and obtain sufficient financing to own an office building or carry out large-scale operations. Activity less overtly formal than the business situation described above may still bear the mark of formal organization. Participants in an archaeological dig, for example, may dress in dusty khakis and address each other by first names. Yet the expedition runs according to an explicit schedule, meetings occur regularly to discuss findings and progress, a project director assigns tasks to subordinates, and an institute, museum, or university assumes legal accountability for the funds.

Even at the level of casual observation, organizations stand out from other forms of human association. Closer examination makes the distinguishing features of organizations more explicit. Clarification of these features, in turn, helps identify the *function* of formal organizations, namely the "payoff" they can provide, which, in many instances, justifies the resources required for their maintenance and the constraint experienced by their members.

It is useful to begin by comparing organizations with informal groups and families. A comparison of this kind helps identify some characteristics that are common to many organizations. Each of these characteristics, in turn, can be connected with a contribution to performing tasks and accomplishing objectives.

Informal Collectivities and Formal Organizations

Arguably, the most basic frameworks of human relationships are not formal organizations, but groups and families. An awareness of the features of groups and families is important for understanding how organizations operate in the real world. A great deal more will be said about this in chapters to come.

In contrast to formal organizations, groups and families may be thought of as *informal collectivities.* Members of a collectivity are familiar with each other and engage in continual communication. Informal collectivities are thus distinguished from formal organizations because they lack explicit rules and procedures. Informal collectivities are also distinguished from mere numbers of individuals whose proximity is accidental and temporary, like passengers on a city bus or a crowd competing for bargains at a department store. Neither the passengers nor the bargain hunters possess internal organization of any kind.

The Group

The group has long commanded special attention from sociologists and psychologists.[5–7] A group comprises a number of people who feel a sense of common purpose or interest, clearly distinguish themselves from people outside the group, and can, when necessary, identify leaders to speak for the group or help direct its actions. Unlike organizations, which people design and construct to accomplish specific purposes, most groups arise spontaneously. Groups may act in a consistent manner from day to day, but they seldom have definite routines that all members are required to follow. Although they often have identifiable leaders, leadership requires no specific qualification and is subject to challenge.

The groups that appear most basic to human organization are those that address a broad range of their members' needs. One hundred years ago, an observer named Charles H. Cooley coined the term *primary group* to signify groups whose members know each other in great depth.[8] Such familiarity can arise only through long personal acquaintance, as among people who have grown up in the same neighborhood or worked together for extended periods of time. Primary relationships, involving frequent face-to-face communication, are said to prevail within primary groups.

Groups are very powerful forces in the lives of individuals. Strong emotional ties often prevail among group members. This is particularly true among members of primary groups. Feelings such as familiarity, friendship, loyalty, and agreement in basic outlook bind individuals to each other in a powerful and enduring fashion. A series of experiments conducted decades ago, now recognized as classic, has demonstrated the considerable power that groups exercise over their members.[2–4] Repeatedly, these experiments indicated a tendency among individuals to discard their own perceptions of reality and conform to those of the group.

An early study by William F. Whyte alerted many for the first time to the ever-presence and importance of spontaneously formed groups in society.[9] Living in an Italian immigrant neighborhood in the 1930s, Whyte attained personal familiarity with street and community life. As expected, he observed several formal organizations, such as the Democratic Party and the Catholic Church, to be important in the lives of residents.

But social life on the street was dominated by informal groups of young men. Each "gang"—a word then used in a more benign sense than today—was associated with a particular street corner. Definite leaders and hierarchies were observed. Groups and cliques of this kind helped give structure to the community as a whole. They provided the coordination and personnel needed to get things done. As an example, Whyte described a vote fraud scheme carried out by gang members to help win a local contest. The city's politicians knew to whom to turn when they needed something done on the street.

The Family

The family may be humankind's most enduring and versatile form of social organization. Until very recently in human history, families constituted the primary means by which individual human beings were linked with one another. As does the group, the family comprises a system of primary relationships. Like the group, the family has commanded much attention from social scientists.[10–12]

The importance of the family in raising children helps account for the fact that the institution is present in nearly all societies. Much psychological evidence suggests that children reared by formal organizations such as hospitals and orphanages risk developmental impairment.[13] Attempts to replace the family have had very limited success. For many years, for example, the Israeli *kibbutz* required that children live outside their parents' dwelling.[14] Though the practice continued without apparent harm for a few generations, it has almost been abandoned today.

The ability of families to conduct actions of worldwide importance attests to the strength of this type of collectivity. Family businesses provide one example. As a large, extended family, the Rothschilds have conducted international business for hundreds of years. In North America, the Bechtel, Bronfman, and Pritzker families have operated huge business empires for generations. On a more everyday scale, thousands of small businesses and professional practices continue from generation to generation within the same family. No subject better illustrates the potential strength of the family as a form of organization than politics, as exemplified by the lineage of Presidents Bush (father and son) and the Kennedy clan.[15]

Informal Collectivities and Formal Organizations: Distinctions in Characteristics and Functions

A detailed comparison of informal collectivities and formal organizations helps explain why each is better at meeting different human needs. Table 1.1, on page 10, contrasts formal organizations and informal collectivities according to specific characteristics often associated with each. Each characteristic enables the formal organization to do something less readily done in an informal collectivity, and vice versa. Although informal collectivities and formal organizations differ according to many other dimensions, the five to follow provide illustration.

Table 1.1   Informal Collectivities Versus Organizations: Characteristics and Their Effects

Characteristic	Informal collectivities are . . .	which promotes	Formal organizations are . . .	which promotes
Origin	Spontaneous	Responsiveness	Deliberate	Commitment
Purpose	Indistinct	Gratification	Specific	Focus
Behavior	Flexible	Accommodation	Standardized	Coordination
Leadership	Personal	Acceptance	Impersonal	Stability
Longevity	Transitory	Relevance	Perpetual	Perseverance

Origins

Formal organizations and informal collectivities differ in their origins and paths of development. Typically, groups develop spontaneously. They often form among casual acquaintances without anyone's planning. In their modern form, families come into being on the basis of mutual attraction by potential spouses, usually a spontaneous process. Less spontaneity occurs in established families, which operate within a framework of traditional expectations and laws.

Formal organizations, though, are deliberately created. A group of tennis players decides to form a club. Three hairstylists decide to set up a small business corporation so that they may rent space for their own shop. The government mandates establishment of a new agency to enforce environmental protection laws. Creation of an organization involves commitment of resources for a particular purpose. Instruments such as bylaws, corporate charters, and legislative mandates reinforce such commitment.

Formal organizations are often likened to machines, which are intentionally designed by people to do specific things. Ideally, they are instruments for pursuing definite ends. Informal collectivities are more like plants and animals. Their members coalesce in response to surrounding conditions and needs, without commitment to any particular task or outcome.

Because they are not established to serve as instruments for specific goals, informal collectivities can often be more responsive to the changing needs and interests of their members. A group of men in their 40s may readily choose to change their preferred pastime from basketball to golf. Even within an established family, husband and wife can readily respond to an unenjoyable home life by divorcing.

Purpose

Formal organizations and informal collectivities typically differ in their purposes, recognizable as *goals* and *objectives.* Typically, organizations articulate goals that are definable and widely recognized, though often neither specific nor concrete. Examples of goals include becoming the preferred national provider of a certain good or service, developing better pharmaceuticals, or protecting American values and freedoms. An organization's objectives are typically more specific and immediate. These may include building the bridge, raising the funds, developing the cures, electing the candidate, winning the war. The presence of specific goals and objectives promotes the focusing of attention and resources on those purposes.

In contrast, the purposes of informal collectivities tend to be mixed, corresponding to the multiple needs of members. This mixture includes two distinct types of goals that the sociologist Robert Bales once called *instrumental* and *socioemotional*.[16] Instrumental goals involve performance of concrete tasks, the area in which formal organizations may be said to specialize. Socioemotional goals focus on gratifying the needs of the individual. These include emotional support, encouragement, companionship, and affection.

Families may have instrumental goals, such as paying off a home mortgage and educating children. But the family does not exist exclusively for the purpose of achieving such goals. The modern family is expected to provide its members with stable, intimate companionship. A family that concentrated on concrete goals and objectives, but provided little affection, would today be considered "dysfunctional." A group or family's mixture of purposes seems more likely to result in overall satisfaction than the productivity-oriented organization.

Behavior

In the formal organization, individual behavior tends to follow a set pattern, which is stable over extended periods of time. A person may sell stamps at the post office for three or four decades. Mechanization may improve and prices may change. But the job continues to focus on communicating with customers, accepting requests for postal goods and services, receiving letters and packages across the counter, and taking payment.

Standardization of behavior enables the actions of one person to be highly coordinated with those of others. Such coordination is the basis for industrial production, in which the work of individuals is highly specialized. In a well-functioning organization, standardization of behavior helps generate value for outsiders. Well-coordinated actions by specialized individuals produce more efficient public service for citizens, better products for consumers, and higher profits for stockholders.

Behavior patterns in informal collectivities are more flexible and changeable. Family life provides examples. Depending on his or her mood, a parent may treat a child with varying degrees of patience. As children mature, parents treat them differently, allowing more privilege and liberty. The needs and capacities of all family members may change over time. Family members need different things from each other as the years go by.

Informal collectivities tend to accommodate the idiosyncratic and changing needs of their members and have the flexibility to do so. But, at least in industrial society, they are not as well adapted to producing things of value to outsiders.

Leadership

People ordinarily become leaders in formal organizations through concrete, widely recognized means. Often, leaders in formal organizations achieve their positions by demonstrating a particular level of training and skills. In public agencies, many people move up the ladder largely because they have spent a number of years within the organization.

Objectively recognizable qualifications for leadership are observable in many types of organizations. Organizations whose work is based on science and engineering, such as Boeing and Pacific Gas and Electric, typically offer top management positions to engineers. Executives in any field who run profitable units may be recruited into top management. Nobel Prize-winning scientists become chiefs of large institutes or university presidents. Most public agencies require success at promotion examinations to move up in the ranks. A graduate management degree can advance an employee's prospects for leadership.

Leadership in formal organizations is said to be *impersonal*. People accept the leader's directives because of his or her job title. People typically obey, even if they do not respect the leader personally or feel that he or she deserves the job. In military organizations, soldiers are instructed to "salute the uniform," giving the same level of allegiance and respect to whoever occupies the office.

This "automatic" feature of leadership promotes stability in key positions. Leaders in all organizations come and go: individuals are removed by higher-ups, terms expire, coups d'état take place. But leadership change is an occasional rather than a regular phenomenon.

Informal collectivities select their leaders through more personal means. Group members identify leaders for whom they have personal affection or loyalty. Leaders are selected according to whether they can please group members or solve problems directly relevant to their lives. As conditions and preferences change, so do leaders.

Longevity

It is possible to find examples of both formal organizations and informal collectivities that have lasted a very long time. But generally, formal organizations have a longer lifespan. Many business firms fail after a few years of operation. But the ones that survive this critical period may last for many decades.

Government agencies are especially long-lived. Once the government establishes a department or bureau for some specialized purpose, its elimination is very difficult. Government agencies change their names, divide into separate units, or become absorbed in larger departments. In the 1970s, for example, the federal Department of Health, Education, and Welfare was split into independent halves: the Department of Health and Human Services and the Department of Education. But actual demise of an established governmental unit is unusual. Zealous efforts by the newly elected Congress of 1994 to dismantle 250 federal departments, agencies, and bureaus were almost completely unsuccessful.

Informal collectivities, though, tend to come and go regularly. Families, historically the most stable of informal collectivities, today frequently dissolve due to divorce. Even families that remain intact disappear after children move away and spouses die. A generation or two later, no evidence may remain that a family once existed other than legal records of interest only to genealogists.

Formal organizations have much greater staying power. They are well adapted to recruiting new people to replace individuals who retire, die, or move up the ladder. Individuals beginning work in formal organizations tend to perform their activities similarly to those who formerly occupied their slots. Business corporations are said to have "perpetual life."

The tendency of informal collectivities to form and dissolve rapidly (at least relative to organizations) contributes to their relevance in their members' lives. They serve emotional and recreational needs and disappear when their members move to a new stage of life. The formal organization, though, maintains the resources—human and material—needed to continue and improve on its achievements year after year.

Informal Collectivities and Formal Organizations: Similarities

The differences between organizations and informal collectivities summarized above should not be overemphasized. Informal collectivities and organization share several core features, although these may be developed, expressed, and experienced in different ways. Within actual organizations, characteristics associated with the informal collectivity may be found intermixed.

Core features common to both informal collectivities and organizations include

- A feeling of personal identification by members
- A sense of solidarity within the group as a whole
- Maintenance of boundaries between members and nonmembers

Personal identification is a process by which people come to believe that the collectivity reflects their most prized beliefs about themselves. When personal identification is strong, individuals feel happy that others identify them as members of either the group or the organization. They share the values, objectives, and tastes of others within the collectivity, and believe the collectivity's actions personally benefit them.

Solidarity indicates a sense of mutual commitment and support among members of organizations and groups. Support may take an emotional form, such as people encouraging others to achieve a goal or recover from a setback. Support can also have a material nature, such as individuals lending each other money or helping each other complete work assignments. Solidarity means "one for all and all for one."

Boundary maintenance signifies the placement of boundaries between people who are in the collectivity and people who are not. In groups, this feature may be quite informal yet very meaningful. Group members may develop a common jargon or a stock of "in-jokes" that are meaningless to outsiders. They may invite each other to parties and gatherings that are closed to others. They may engage in business relationships that are closed and invisible to the outside world. Boundary maintenance is more explicit in formal organizations, visible every day as guards check identification cards at the doors of office buildings.

Contrasts between formal organizations and informal collectivities, as identified in the table above, are often muted within actual organizations. For some members of a formal organization, the "official" goals may become subordinated to socio-emotional ones. A church, for example, may become more important to its members as a place to meet friends and chat than as a place of organized worship.

The distinctions between leaders in formal organizations and informal collectivities are also blurrier in real life than in theory. Many formal organizations select their leaders according to instrumental qualifications. But leaders in formal organizations may also attain such rank with the aid of personal warmth, social connections, and political savvy.

It is likely that no formal organization exists anywhere in which informal social interaction is absent. Members exchange personal opinions about the organization as well as private matters. They form networks to exchange secrets. They get together on the outside to play, worship, and perform public service. They flirt, have affairs, and marry. Still, the basic features summarized in the table above distinguish formal organizations and help explain their importance.

Social Structure: Formal and Informal

The concept of social structure helps summarize the differences between informal collectivities and formal organizations described above.

The idea of social structure is central to a number of social sciences. Social structure comprises a pattern of relationships, expectations, and transactions. Differences in social structure may be observed among nations, organizations, and informal collectivities.

Formal organization in general is distinguished from other frameworks of human relationships by *formal structure*. Formal structure is characterized by explicit criteria for boundary crossing (such as membership qualifications and initiation procedures); rules governing access of some individuals to others; defined procedures for requesting and giving of help and exchanging resources; definite gradations of power and authority across hierarchical levels; and recognizable pathways to promotion.

Informal collectivities, too, have structure. Clear patterns and expectations, as well as power and authority, characterize many families and groups. But these elements are less explicit than they are in formal organizations. For example, members of a group of youths might have commonly held ideas about how their leader should behave toward them. But these may be vague and the subject of recurrent dispute.

In the chapters to come, a great deal more will be said about formal structure and differences in structure among individual organizations.

Features and Functions of Organizations: A Historical View

Table 1.1 illustrates characteristics and related functions of formal organizations that have clear connections with performance of specific tasks. The idea of formal structure draws these characteristics together into a single concept. Formal structure itself makes possible additional capacities of a more far-reaching kind. Several historical examples provide illustration. It is tempting to think of the formal organization as characteristic of modern society. Indeed, standardization of behavior and other features of formal organization have served the requirements of industrial production well. But, as documented by Max Weber, one of the founding figures of modern social science, organizations have been important in many economic systems and past eras.[17]

Case Studies Throughout History

Case 1: Tribal Herdsmen

The first example is not a formal organization at all, but a Northeast African tribe known as the Karimojong. Historically, this tribe engaged in practices unusual among premodern peoples. These practices provide clues about the functional capacities observable in organizations today.

Roaming a semidesert in northeastern Africa,[18] the Karimojong farmed and herded cattle. They occupied an environment poor in grass and water, resources crucial for maintaining cattle herds. In Karimojong country, water was found only in scattered, unpredictable locations. Waterholes varied in size, some capable of supporting several hundred head of cattle, others only a few. Karimojong tribesmen were thus forced to herd in small numbers rather than in the large, family-based groups common among native herders elsewhere.

In the search for water, tribesmen often encountered herding groups whose members they had never met before. When pockets of abundant water and grass were found, several herding groups, usually from different home areas and families, rapidly occupied them. The Karimojong had a proverb to describe the resulting propinquity of strangers: "the sun mixes us together."

On the range, disputes inevitably arose over the sparse resources. These almost always took place among tribesmen who were not each other's kin. At these times, elder individuals would be convened from all the families present and constituted as a council to render judgment. If a disputant refused to accept the elders' judgment, the elders would render a curse upon him. If that proved ineffective, they would order all the youths present to beat the dissident with sticks. Compliance was typically forthcoming.

It is useful to think of the Karimojong council of elders as an elementary manifestation of formal structure. The convening of a council whenever necessary was a standardized procedure carried out by people who did not otherwise interact. The availability of this mechanism involved a cost, as elders were presumably less vigorous herders than the younger men. In a sense, the elders represented "administrative overhead."

But without the elders' councils, herding in Karimojong country would have been impossible. The need to opportunistically search for water required peaceful relationships among bands encountering each other as strangers. It is noteworthy that nearby tribes such as the Nuer, whose members farmed and herded primarily as family units,[19] had no such councils.

Organizations in modern society can be said to share an important feature with the Karimojong.[20] In the modern world, formal organization makes it possible to sustain activity among people who have no preexisting family or primary group ties. Formal structure, it may be inferred, enables strangers to work together, a crucial capacity in today's society.

Case 2: Freemasons and Patriots

Research on early voluntary societies in Europe helps bring to light another basic function provided by formal organizations: separation of specialized activity from general social life. Organizations provide a "protected space," both literal and figurative, in which individuals may pursue activities and advance objectives not shared by others in their personal lives or society at large.

According to Alfred Kieser,[21] voluntary organizations began to appear in Germany in the late 1700s. A great many of these organizations were Freemasons' lodges and patriotic societies. These organizations had become extremely popular by 1800.

(Continued)

(Continued)

At this time, most of Germany had not yet begun to industrialize. A great many people lived on agrarian estates owned by feudal lords; a smaller number lived in small cities, as lifelong members of craft guilds or merchant communities. People lived their lives in a seamless web of human relations, encountering the same individuals at home, at work, and in worship. Little opportunity existed for independent expression or visible breach of tradition.

Change began as the ideas of the Enlightenment spread from France. Enlightenment thinking emphasized the independence of the individual and questioned the right of lords and kings to undisputed rule. The Freemasons embraced these ideas, as did patriotic societies seeking to advance a modernized and progressive Germany.

Some key characteristics of the Freemason lodges resembled those of many modern organizations. Boundary maintenance was strict, enforced by ritual secrecy. This was necessitated by a political system hostile to progressive thinking. Formal structure was apparent, with hierarchy, rules, and rituals intended to sustain values and discipline. The structure and practices of these voluntary organizations were in fact adopted in the military and industrial sectors as they developed in the early 1800s.

The maintenance of a protected space behind organizational boundaries remains an important function of the formal organization today. Some organizations still maintain their boundaries through ritual. Secrecy is the rule in many government agencies and in industries such as banking and health care. Security guards and identification cards are rapidly becoming the rule. As in the 18th century, some modern organizations use their protected space to examine ideas unacceptable within the broader society. But more often, protected space enables organizations of many kinds to maintain records, supervise employees, and build corporate culture, free, at least in normal times, from outside interference.

Case 3: British Speculators

Promotion of an atmosphere of confidence and reliability among participants appears to be another broad contribution of formal organization. This principle is illustrated by an organization historically specializing in the management of risk.

Dating from the 1600s, Lloyd's of London is one of the longest-functioning business organizations in the world today. One of the world's foremost insurance companies, Lloyd's is famous for insuring items ranging from supertankers to pianists' fingers. The firm's origins are traced to a London coffeehouse in which unaffiliated individuals met for the purpose of pooling funds to insure sailing ships. Business was extremely speculative, and a gambling spirit prevailed: participants not only wrote insurance policies but made wagers on future events of any kind. The assemblage attracted its share of unscrupulous players.

Lloyd's developed into a formal organization in the century to follow. Stages in this process included establishment of a formal "society," open only to the better-established coffeehouse congregants. Dues were charged, and the society instituted a system of inspection and reporting on the conditions of ships. The society successfully lobbied Parliament for favorable treatment of its business and obtained physical premises devoted entirely to insurance activity.[22] A centralized system of rules governing membership and brokerage was developed.

Today, Lloyd's bears the mark of its origins, with considerable independence prevailing among brokers and underwriters. But the process of formal organization consolidated diverse participants and standardized practice under a set of distinct rules. This system builds confidence among outside investors and promotes public trust.

To summarize, the basic features of formal organizations adapt them well to performance of specific tasks. But organizations contribute broader capacities, too. They make it possible for people lacking preexisting ties to work together. They enable activity to take place in a manner protected from public scrutiny and safe from outside interference. They foster an environment of sufficient confidence and reliability to induce individuals who would otherwise remain independent to share resources and collaborate.

Organizations: Ideal and Actual

Parts of this chapter may seem to characterize organizations as tight, smooth-running collectivities that are beneficial to both their members and society at large. In fact, the connection between the characteristics of formal organizations emphasized in this chapter and effective pursuit of objectives applies unevenly among actual organizations. Organizations in which boundaries are weak, goals indistinct, and behavior patterns inconsistent can sometimes be effective. Organizations that possess the characteristics emphasized in this chapter, moreover, sometimes serve their members and outside constituents poorly.

The description of organizations that predominates in this chapter in fact represents an *ideal type*. A frequently encountered component of modern social analysis,[23] ideal types are concepts that synthesize features of many actual cases but describe few, if any, concretely observable ones. In an example appearing early in this chapter, a man going to work in a downtown office building encounters a clearly defined structure and he, himself, exhibits a formalized pattern of behavior. This example may accurately reflect the large, 21st-century profit-seeking organization in the United States. But such organizations, and the ideal type to which they closely correspond, differ from many viable forms.

Other organizations look quite different. Community-based organizations concerned with mobilizing local residents to improve the quality and well-being of their neighborhoods provide an illustration.[24] In these organizations, leaders tend to depend on persuasion rather than command. The boundaries of these organizations are considerably less distinct than those of the large business concern. Satisfaction with social relationships may achieve greater emphasis than goal attainment. Goals may themselves readily shift. Although factors conducive to inefficiency are apparent, forces affecting the organization restrict its ability to more closely approximate the ideal type. These forces will receive detailed attention in the chapters to come.

Close resemblance to the ideal type, moreover, does not necessarily enhance the benefits the organization delivers. Recall the example with which this chapter began, concerning a recreational soccer team calling itself the Wombats. Though possessing at best average ability, the Wombats held their own against more talented teams due to superior organization. They achieved a winning record and had a good time.

Consider, however, the possibility that the team may evolve into a different type of collectivity. Over time, the Wombats place increasing value on winning games. Open participation and good feelings among team members become subordinated to consistently skillful play. Formal tryouts for team membership are instituted. Dues are imposed. Consistent with its newly emerging purpose, the team more closely conforms to the definition of a formal organization.

But for many, the new order is likely to be negative. The numerous formal procedures, the "bureaucracy," seem likely to be off-putting to many. In addition, less-skilled but no less enthusiastic members may spend most of the game time on the bench. The team's record may improve, but for many, it is no longer fun.

For the majority of members, the Wombats have become dysfunctional as an organization. Interpersonal conflict may result, as team meetings become heated exchanges over the organization's purpose. If their grievances are not addressed, a significant proportion of members are likely to terminate membership, leaving even the skilled newcomers with diminished support. The organization as a whole may disband.

Focusing on the modern business organization, social critics have raised issues that are considerably more profound. Consolidation of activity within a reliable system of rules and expectations, as in the Lloyd's of London example, appears constructive. According to sociologist Charles Perrow, however, organized consolidation on a significantly larger scale can have quite adverse effects. Although formal organizations were few and small at the time of the American Revolution, the vast majority of American workers had become employees of large organizations by 1900.[25] According to Perrow, these large and dominant organizations (both profit-seeking and nonprofit) weakened local communities. Lacking commitment to the well-being of the locales where they operated, consolidated business organizations polluted environments and eventually moved plants and jobs abroad. Perrow asserts that a less organized system of independent local and regional companies might have produced the same economic benefits with lower social costs.

Next Steps

This chapter has introduced the concept of the formal organization. Emphasis has been placed on organizations as mechanisms for coordinating individual efforts that, in turn, produce benefits for both members and outsiders. Prominence has been given to the functions performed by organizations.

Organizations, though, are not simply integral mechanisms that autonomously channel the efforts of individuals. The members of an organization never simply become its tools. People have highly diverse characteristics, orientations, and needs. These do not disappear when the individual enters an organization. The potential for conflict is always present in organizations, as individuals may not fully accept the mechanisms used by the organization to coordinate and focus their efforts. Conflict between an organization and the broader society often occurs as well.

The chapter to follow addresses the importance of factors outside the organization's sphere of operations. Although they are necessary to the organization's existence, these factors and their consequences constitute key challenges to organizations. Some of the most important tasks of management arise in connection with these challenges.

Issues and Applications

This chapter has focused on the characteristics, contributions, and costs of formal organization. Among people deciding how best to accomplish tasks and pursue objectives, dilemmas constantly arise regarding formal versus informal mechanisms. Here are two examples.

- A group of engineers has been perfecting an invention they hope will make them wealthy. The group has regularly assembled in one member's basement to assemble equipment, perform test runs, and brainstorm technical problems. After perhaps two years, sufficient progress has occurred for a patent application to be submitted. Should the group now transform itself into an organization? What costs may be incurred in terms of procedures, bylaws, and legal fees? Will the process be detrimental to the atmosphere of friendship and spontaneity that has prevailed? What risks would the group face were the step not taken? The group will have to weigh multiple risks and potential advantages.

- A nonprofit community clinic has received a foundation grant to promote health and safety in the surrounding neighborhood. Prior to receiving the grant, the organization simply housed a small staff of physicians and nurses who treated patients on a sliding scale. Monthly, a management group of clinic personnel met in private to allocate resources and make strategic decisions. However, the new grant calls for community participation in decision-making. Should steering committee meetings now be open to laypeople from the community? Should the goals of the organization be made more fluid? Having accepted the grant, the organization may need to depart from the formal model.

Chapter Review and Major Themes

In contrast to groups and families, organizations are deliberately created to pursue identifiable goals. Organizations have characteristics that enable them to coordinate and focus the efforts of large numbers of people over long periods of time. These include an emphasis on instrumental goals, standardized behavior patterns, and impersonal qualifications for leadership. Unlike primary groups and families, organizations are capable of ensuring peaceful cooperation among strangers. Organizations promote the establishment of separate physical and social space for specialized activity and the consolidation of diverse individuals and groups within centralized systems. Individuals and societies engage in a trade-off of costs and benefits associated with formal organization.

Many of the features of organizations seem to imply a surrender of individual liberty to the organization's needs. Features such as boundaries, formal structure, and impersonal leadership seem cold and controlling. In fact, organizations may be thought of as battlegrounds between efforts at coordination and assertion of individual desires and objectives. As the next chapter will illustrate, even people with the least official power in an organization often resist being controlled by the organization's structure and management. Ultimately, a free society allows people to select the organizations they join and to leave them at will.

Discussion Questions

1. The establishment and operation of formal organizations involve trade-offs between costs and benefits. What are these costs? What are the benefits?

2. Which tasks may be best done by formal organizations, and which ones are best done by informal groups?

3. Are there clear differences between formal organizations and informal collectivities in the level of comfort and fulfillment experienced by their members?

4. Think of an activity in which you have been involved that could have been more effectively organized. How could organization of that activity have been improved? Were barriers to improved organization present?

5. Does the tension between organizational objectives and individual needs ultimately help or harm the organization?

References

1. Bernard, C. I. (1938). *The functions of the executive.* Cambridge, MA: Harvard University Press.

2. Blau, P., & Scott, P. R. (1962). *Formal organizations: A comparative approach.* New York: John Wiley & Sons.

3. Katz, D., & Kahn, R. L. (1966). *Social psychology of organizations.* New York: John Wiley & Sons.

4. Luhman, R. (2001). *The sociological outlook.* San Diego: Collegiate Press.

5. Shepard, C. R. (1954). *Small groups.* San Francisco: Chandler.

6. Summers, I., & Horton, R. E. (1988). Work group cohesion. *Psychological Reports, 63,* 627–636.

7. Forsyth, D. (1990). *Group dynamics.* Pacific Grove, CA: Brooks/Cole.

8. Cooley, C. H. (1909). *Social organization.* New York: Scribner.

9. Whyte, W. F. (1961). *Street corner society.* Chicago: University of Chicago Press.

10. Duda, K. (Ed.). (2003). *The American family.* New York: H. W. Wilson.

11. Allen, G. (Ed.). (1999). *Sociology of the family: A reader.* Malden, MA: Blackwell.

12. Skolnick, A. S., & Skolnick, J. H. (2003). *Family in transition.* Boston: Allyn & Bacon.

13. Bithoney, W. G., & Newberger, E. H. (1987). Child and family attributes of failure-to-thrive. *Journal of Deviant Behavioral Pediatrics, 8,* 32–36.

14. Spiro, M. E. (1959). *Children of the kibbutz.* Cambridge, MA: Harvard University Press.

15. Goodwin, D. K. (1986). *The Fitzgeralds and the Kennedys: An American saga.* New York: Simon & Schuster.

16. Bales, R. F. (1958). Task roles and social roles in problem-solving groups. In E. E. Maccoby, T. M. Newcomb, & T. M. Hartley (Eds.), *Readings in social psychology.* New York: Holt, Rinehart and Winston.

17. Weber, M. (1946). The meaning of discipline. In H. H. Gerth & C. W. Mills (Eds.), *From Max Weber: Essays in sociology.* New York: Oxford University Press.

18. Dyson-Hudson, N. (1966). *Karimojong politics.* Oxford, UK: Clarendon.

19. Evans-Pritchard, E. E. (1965). *The Nuer.* Oxford, UK: Clarendon.

20. Greenwald, H. P. (1972). Patterns of authority in two herding societies: An ecological approach. *Administrative Science Quarterly, 17*(2), 207–217.

21. Kieser, A. (1998). From Freemasons to industrious patriots: Organizing and disciplining in 18th century Germany. *Organization Studies, 19*(1), 47–71.

22. Lane, N. (1957). The origins of Lloyd's. *History Today, 7*(12), 848–853.

23. Coser, L. A. (1977). *Masters of sociological thought: Ideas in historical and social context.* New York: Harcourt Brace Jovanovich.

24. Milofsky, C. (1988). Structure and process in community self-help organizations. In C. Milofsky (Ed.), *Community organizations: Studies in resource mobilization and exchange,* Chapter 9, 183–216. New York: Oxford University Press.

25. Perrow, C. (2002). *Organizing America: Wealth, power, and the origins of corporate capitalism.* Princeton, NJ: Princeton University Press.

CHAPTER 2

The Organizational Milieu

Learning Objective

To understand the importance to organizations of factors beyond their direct control.

Principles

- As powerful and long-lasting as organizations may be, they do not develop and operate with complete autonomy. Organizations are confronted by the needs and values of people within them; by naturally occurring social ties among their members; and by the broader forces of society.

- Even within organizations, the individual's web of informal social relationships affects his or her thinking and actions. These relationships may span organizational boundaries or take place entirely within organizations.

- Broader social forces include contemporary lifestyles as well as long-established patterns of thought and behavior. In the United States today, social change has affected organizations by transforming the characteristics and expectations of key population segments.

- Every organization functions within a matrix of other organizations; organizations in the same field or with similar goals affect each other's operations through a wide variety of competitive and collaborative relationships.

- The organizational milieu contains a multiplicity of challenges as well as potential sources of support in the organization's efforts at attaining its goals.

Organizations, Individuals, and Social Forces

Chapter 1 characterized organizations as structures especially adapted to the pursuit of goals. Excessive attention to the goal-attainment function of organizations, though, would neglect a key factor in their development and operation: the matrix of influences, constraints, and potential sources of support in which they are embedded. Rather than independent, goal-pursuing actors, organizations are participants in a continuous process of accommodation, confrontation, and exchange.

The manner in which organizations respond to these challenges and opportunities is crucial. How the organization responds helps determine the efficacy with which it pursues objectives. The organization's response to these factors influences whether collaboration or conflict will predominate in its pursuit of goals.

The *organizational milieu* includes a broad range of factors beyond the organization's immediate or direct control. These include

- Psychological characteristics of the organization's own members, which typically develop outside the control of any individual organization
- Natural or extra-organizational ties among members, some extending beyond the organization's boundaries, others involving spontaneous primary relationships within the organization
- Social forces, such as lifestyle, culture, political economy, institutions, and social change
- Other organizations

The organizational milieu helps explain day-to-day decisions by leaders and managers of organizations and frames the strategic dilemmas that organizations face. An understanding of the organizational milieu lays the groundwork for broad perspectives on why organizations exist and how they work.

A Manager's Story

To many, emphasis on the formal organization as a mechanism for achieving goals would seem natural and obvious. Organizations exist to do a job, as mandated by owners, managers, or taxpayers. But actual organizations seldom function in so mechanical a fashion. Ultimately, the organization's success depends on the willingness of individual members to contribute to a shared plan of action. A manager's story about his experience at a small, experimental plant involved in the manufacture of a new synthetic fuel underscores this point. The multinational corporation that owned the facility sought to impose changes. But the employees had other ideas.

Frank Peace, an experienced executive, was assigned the job of making the plant into a profitable fuel factory. A highly skilled engineer, Peace was well prepared for the scientific demands of the job. He had significant leadership experience as well. Earlier assignments had included supervision of a large chemical plant.

But the experimental facility was different. Unlike the chemical plant he managed, the experimental unit had only a few hundred employees. The chemical plant carried out a well-established process and produced familiar products. The experimental unit was attempting something completely new. Scientists and highly skilled technicians predominated among its employees, people who had expected to do innovative, creative work.

As he told his story in the *Harvard Business Review*,[1] Peace began his assignment with his customary management routine. He called his second-level managers together and informed them of the corporation's decision. He distributed his plan of action to the subordinates. Each received a schedule for reaching specific milestones.

But the employees did not accept the new system. Many assignments were carried out with little enthusiasm. Some were completely ignored. Serious conflicts arose between managers and employees. Arguments took place in the plant. Managers who pushed their subordinates to accomplish Peace's objectives were harassed. Tires were slashed in the plant parking lot.

Peace realized success would require more than orders and schedules. He began by holding group meetings. Some groups included only managers, some only workers, some a mixture. At the meetings, everyone was encouraged to share his or her personal views. People were free to air misgivings over objectives and plans.

Gradually, the talks helped Peace understand the reasons for resistance to the corporation's plan. Due to their scientific training, many employees valued scientific achievement over commercial success. Employees resisted the movement away from the relaxed, creative atmosphere that often prevails in research settings.

Peace's meetings with subordinates allowed them to come to terms with these conflicts. The process made employees feel that they were valued colleagues. A structure evolved that was looser than the one Peace had originally envisaged.

Stories such as this illustrate the fact that forces other than official objectives play an important part in organizations. In this case, the expectations and values of subordinates initially crippled an effort at change. The conscious or unconscious thinking of an organization's members strongly affects the character and effectiveness of the organization. Individuals may "belong to" an organization and yet be only imperfectly subject to its control.

Individual Psychology: Some Brief Perspectives

The most elementary features of an organization's milieu are the thinking and feelings of the individuals inside it. Examination of the individual members raises a paradox in the study of organizations. Individuals are "inside" the organization. Yet, their personalities and many of their interests and attitudes originate outside and remain tied to outside forces. Business executives are fond of saying that their organizations are "only people." But much of what these people think and their most important concerns may have little to do with the organization and its objectives.

Psychologists have developed hundreds of concepts and terms to describe specific aspects of human mental functioning. A few examples include needs, values, and disposition. Exploration of these basic properties of the human individual suggests substantial independence from organizational purposes and structures.

Needs

Needs are urges felt by individuals to fulfill the requirements of survival, reproduction, and personal gratification. Abraham Maslow, a psychologist of the mid-20th century, developed a theory of human needs often cited by people who study organizations.[2] A recent study covering people in many nations has confirmed his early thinking.[3] Maslow wrote that fulfillment of basic, biological needs enabled people to seek satisfaction of needs that were specifically human. This theory is known as the *hierarchy of needs.*

Maslow's Hierarchy of Needs

Self-Actualization

Esteem

Belongingness and Love

Safety

Physiological needs

Physiological needs are filled by biological necessities, such as food, drink, and sex. Once physiological needs are met, people can turn their attention to "safety" needs. Today, people seek safety in well-maintained dwellings and crime-free neighborhoods. Needs related to "belongingness and love" follow safety. Maslow writes, "If both the physiological and the safety needs are fairly well gratified . . . the person will feel keenly, as never before, the absence of friends, or a sweetheart, or a wife, or children."

Next come "esteem needs." When people have solved the problems of physiological needs, safety, and belongingness and love, their thinking often turns to issues of esteem. Self-confidence and gratification with the products of one's work contribute to a person's "self-esteem." Esteem from others is also a human need, as seen by the widespread desire for distinguished-sounding titles, offices in the executive suite, and prestigious consumer goods. The need for "self-actualization" occupies the apex of Maslow's hierarchy. Self-actualization refers to people's desire to make real (actualize) what they perceive to be their potential.

Psychologists have identified other, particularly human needs. The so-called "need for achievement" (abbreviated as *n-achievement*), which impels some individuals to continuously pursue higher goals, has received much attention. Scholars have identified need for achievement as an ingredient in economic growth and industrial development.

Values

Psychologist Milton Rokeach has defined a "value" as an individual's preference for a "specific mode of conduct or end-state of existence."[4] Values, then, go much deeper than day-to-day choices. They guide an individual through his or her entire life, influencing goals at work, choice of friends and mates, rearing of children, and participation in the community. They may determine whether an individual plans his or her life around attaining fame, serving the public, working in friendly surroundings, or avoiding difficult or tension-provoking duties.

Religion provides many vivid illustrations of the importance of values. One of the most famous studies of values is sociologist Max Weber's book *The Protestant Ethic and the Spirit of Capitalism.*[5] In this book, Weber explained the great cultural and economic achievements of Europe on the basis of values widely held among Europeans between 1500 and 1800. Three values formed the core of the "Protestant Ethic." These included selecting and becoming expert at a definite occupation (calling), working hard, and saving money.

Values of individuals in the United States today constitute elements of mental life that influence a broad range of behavior. Many of these values stem from the surrounding cultural system. "Democracy" and "equality" are widely shared values. Due to these values, Americans respond positively to openness in decision making by authorities in government or the workplace. Most Americans strongly oppose racial bigotry.

Disposition

Disposition refers to general outlook on life and interpretation of surroundings. People are said to have dispositions that are positive, negative, friendly, hostile, trusting, suspicious, "sour," or "sweet." An individual's disposition includes a set of *attitudes,* positive or negative receptions of specific stimuli.

Disposition presents challenges to formal organizations. Persistently negative attitudes among some members can have a depressing effect on others and threaten the organization's well-being. Managers of work organizations today expend significant resources redesigning jobs to promote better feelings among workers and offer counseling to individual employees.

Among scientists who study organizations, controversy has arisen regarding disposition. Some maintain that the individual's experience in an organization—his or her job situation, for example—determines his or her disposition. This interpretation is known as the *situational theory.* Contrary to this theory, other observers believe that people develop basic dispositions as children and keep them throughout life. The position of these observers is called the *dispositional* theory.

Although this debate remains active, a study in California has provided evidence to support the dispositional theory.[6] Psychologists in the 1920s and 1930s interviewed children as young as 10 years old. The psychologists evaluated each child according to positive and negative emotional predisposition. Later generations of psychologists reevaluated these individuals at successive stages of their lives. It was found that individuals who evidenced a negative disposition in adolescence tended to evidence a negative disposition in adulthood. Most strikingly, people with negative dispositions in their teens or even earlier were more likely than others to have negative job attitudes in late adulthood.

Limits of Organizational Influence

Organizations are often concerned with the needs, values, and personalities of their members. In recruiting new personnel, business and military organizations have taken personality into serious consideration. Personality tests such as the Minnesota Multiphasic Personality Inventory (MMPI)[7] and the Myers-Briggs Type Indicator[8] (MBTI) have been part of the personnel specialist's tool kit for generations. Some theories suggest that behavioral scripts,[9] potentially created by organizations, strongly influence individual personality.

Still, any organization's ability to dictate the mental lives of its members (or to recruit members who have mental characteristics they consider desirable) is incomplete. The influence of outside forces, ranging from genetic heritage to childhood experience, is manifested within the minds of the organization's members. Of potentially greater importance to organizations, though, is the influence of informal social ties on individuals.

Why People Can't Be "Programmed"

It is tempting to think that people, like computers, can be programmed. When computers are programmed, they carry out interconnected sequences of explicit instructions. People may act as though they, too, are programmed. This is particularly true in organizations. Employees at all levels may carry out their tasks in stereotyped ways year after year, unless instructed to do otherwise. People of strong values and established habits may explain their behavior with the comment, "I've been programmed that way."

The forces that impel people to act as they do, though, fundamentally differ from codes written by computer programmers. The process of socialization is much more complex. In early life, people receive numerous messages about how to think and act. These messages may be indefinite. They may come from different sources—parents and friends, for example—and be mutually contradictory. Each individual puts the pieces together for him- or herself. Each of us develops his or her own slant on life. People have a biological capacity that enables them to interpret and respond to stimuli in a unique manner.

Most important, people never lose the capacity for deliberate change. Reflecting on his or her needs, values, and patterns of behavior, a person can elect to acknowledge some and suppress others. Young people reject the ideas of their parents. Individuals "reinvent themselves," forsaking accustomed lifestyles and occupations to pursue new, untried directions.

Informal Ties Within Organizations

Some of the most important relationships among members of an organization are neither purposely promoted by the organization nor under its control. Relationships of this kind are *primary* in nature: they involve individuals familiar with each other, acquainted for an extended period of time, and able to communicate about personal interests and private matters.

Chapter 1 discusses primary relationships as characteristic of informal collectivities, which, in turn, are contrasted with the formal organization. Nevertheless, primary relationships occur within formal organizations. Members of organizations belong to informal collectivities outside. Full-fledged informal collectivities, moreover, develop and function within formal organizations.

Informal ties with outsiders are of obvious importance. Individuals often place greater importance on the obligations claimed by parents, spouses, and children than on those of any organization to which they belong. The sense of obligation that prevails among individuals in primary relationships often contradicts the priorities of formal organizations. In modern corporations, employees often refuse transfers to distant cities if a spouse objects. They may put obligations to formal organizations aside to care for ailing children and aged parents. They may hesitate to carry out tasks that contradict the values prevailing in their communities.

Direct, interpersonal relationships affect people's choices about which organizations they join. People often join churches and fraternal societies to demonstrate solidarity with those with whom they have developed informal social ties. These ties facilitate entry into organizations with well-guarded boundaries, as when members of exclusive clubs lobby for admission of their friends.

Informal ties within organizations are numerous and varied. They include the cliques, cabals, and networks found in every college and work organization. Within this area, the group and the family have classically attracted the attention of social scientists.

Groups Within Organizations

Although groups are often freestanding, many are organization dependent. Such groups develop among individuals that a formal organization has brought together. Many would disappear if the organizations that surrounded them were dismantled. Work and military organizations provide examples.

People at work. Most work today takes place within formal organizations. Yet, on factory floors and inside city skyscrapers, primary groups may strongly affect motivation and productivity. Researchers seeking ways to improve productivity of electrical equipment workers several decades ago were among the first to realize this.[10]

Conducting experiments at a plant in Hawthorne, Illinois, the researchers thought they could encourage the workers by paying extra for exceptionally high productivity. These workers wired transformers that were used in the telephone systems of the time. Although the men shared the same worktable, each man's performance was monitored separately. Each worker was required to complete a minimum number of transformers per workday to earn the basic wage. He received a bonus proportional to the number of transformers he completed above the minimum.

The researchers expected that a higher rate of pay for units produced above the minimum would result in higher productivity—that is, a greater number of transformers being completed per day. It did not. Total output remained stable when an incentive of this kind was added. The research team observed the work site and interviewed the men to learn why greater rewards for extra productivity failed to produce the desired result.

The workers, it turned out, had developed and stuck to their own production schedule. They worked rapidly in the morning, building up a stock of completed transformers. In the afternoon, they would slow their pace, ending the day with the minimum number of units, or perhaps a few more. They kept close watch on each other to see that no one produced significantly more than anyone else. Stories were told about how men who had produced extra units were punished. Men who worked too fast received light punches on the arm from their neighbors. Producing more units than necessary was derided as "rate-busting."

Workers at the Hawthorne plant were clearly not isolated individuals. They formed a group, one of whose functions was moderating the pace of work to reduce fatigue and stress. Solidarity appeared to be high, as the men molded their behavior patterns to suit the needs of others. The men clearly seemed to identify more with their work group than with the experimenters or management. Strong boundary maintenance could be assumed to prevail on normal workdays. Had the researchers not been there, managers would never have learned of the workers' secret practices for limiting production.

Soldiers at war. Some of the most valuable observations of groups within formal organizations have been made in wartime. War places individuals under conditions of deprivation and peril. Temptation would appear ever-present among soldiers to desert or surrender. Few soldiers in fact do so.

The most visible motivations for soldiers to remain at their posts would appear to be patriotism and conviction to a cause. But research has revealed that day-to-day motivation among soldiers depends little on patriotism or even fear of punishment. Time and again, studies of military organizations have demonstrated that personal relationships within small groups of soldiers account in large part for a unit's effectiveness and tenacity.

Evidence for the importance of the primary groups in military life may be drawn from the American Civil War (1860–1865). The war began with great rhetorical flourish about freedom and honor. But, according to writings left by soldiers, patriotic and moral fervor diminished as the drudgery of war continued year after year. In place of their original motivations, Civil War soldiers resisted temptation to desert or shirk in battle for fear of letting their comrades down.[10] Increasingly, soldiers fought to protect and share the burden of war with men they knew and with whom they ate and tented.

Another example of the importance of primary groups has been drawn from World War II (1940–1945). Hitler's army proved an extremely tenacious force. Germany's defeat seemed certain by early 1945. Still, Allied forces had great difficulty in securing surrender of German military units. Small bands of soldiers continued to resist even after being cut off from upper levels of command.

U.S. Army intelligence officers later traced this staying power to group life in the German army. Each individual had served in the same group of five through the entire war. Each soldier encouraged his comrades to stand firm, less for concern with Germany or the army than with the small group in which he fought.[11]

Observation of conflicts as historically distant as the Civil War and World War II provide examples of informal group behavior within large, formal organizations.

Unlike the electrical workers chronicled in the Hawthorne studies, these examples contributed to persistence and effectiveness of the surrounding organizations. Some observers of the United States Army in the Vietnam War reported low levels of solidarity among soldiers and poor group relationships. Assignment of soldiers to units with which they had trained was not a universal practice. It appears possible that promotion of stable primary groups within the United States Army might have led to a different outcome of that conflict.

Families and organizations. Chapter 1 recognized the importance of families in enterprises large and small. As noted above, family ties can counteract the influence of organizations. But families also function as organizational allies.

The business world provides numerous illustrations of interdependence between organizations and families. In their hiring practices, businesses often prefer to hire sons, daughters, and siblings of current employees rather than applicants responding to newspaper or Internet ads or sent by employment agencies. Even very large firms often look with favor on relatives of current employees. Steel firms in the American Midwest and utilities such as California's Pacific Gas and Electric have followed this practice for generations.

Reliance on families by organizations may go much further than recruitment. Schools provide a familiar example. Parents use persuasion, rewards, and punishments to motivate their children to support the schools in their mission of education.

In rural parts of the United States, a supervisor may seek help in solving a discipline or absenteeism problem from the employee's parent or spouse.

The potential importance of ties between organizations and families is strikingly illustrated by sociologist Robert Cole's observations in modern Japan.[12] In post-World War II Japan, about one-third of all employees obtained their jobs through friends, family members, and "family patrons"—individuals who have helped the family over the years in exchange for loyalty, support, and service in time of need. Friends, family members, and patrons introduce new workers into the firms at which they are employed.

Interpersonal ties used in recruitment are important in maintaining motivation and discipline as well. Executives and workers alike often prefer informal methods of supervision to formal procedures and rules. Cole provides the example of a young automobile parts worker:

> His father's friend, a white-collar employee at the auto parts firm, had secured him the job. He explained that he felt obliged to this individual neither to cause any trouble in the company nor to quit. In the past, he had had some quarrels on the shop floor, after which his supervisor went directly to his patron, who stopped off at his house the same night. There, the patron consulted with the father and the young worker to resolve the problems. This course was taken rather than the supervisor directly approaching the worker on the shop floor to deal with the matter. The young worker saw nothing unusual about this procedure and appreciated having his father's friend look after his interests. (p. 192)

Informal ties between work organizations and family members have been credited (or blamed) for the weakness of unions in Japan. Cole cites examples of companies pressuring workers to persuade their siblings not to participate in union activity. Informal relations involving mutual obligation, it may be argued, have traditionally encouraged the Japanese to work hard for low wages. Such behavior has contributed to the rise of Japan as a major industrial power. Although not as readily apparent, informal social ties also play an important part in recruitment, discipline, and motivation among workers in the United States.

Social Forces

Above and beyond primary relationships among individuals, broad social forces affect very large numbers of people simultaneously. These forces communicate to individuals patterns of behavior considered desirable or mandatory. Social forces help mold individual values. Since they permeate the numerous sectors of society, they affect not only an organization's rank and file, but its leadership as well.

Among the many social forces that can be observed, the following provide illustration:

- *Lifestyles:* Visible, internally consistent patterns of thinking, behavior, and consumption associated with distinct categories of people
- *Culture:* Symbolic representation of traditional values, patterns of behavior, and interpretation of natural and social events
- *Laws:* Statements identifying mandatory public duties, acts, or practices enforced by public officials, and rights protected by society
- *Political Economy:* Principles governing ownership of property, political power, and the rights of citizens
- *Institutions:* Traditional forms, models, and practices that guide the manner in which society carries out its most important functions and in which individuals live their lives

Lifestyles

Among social forces affecting organizations in the contemporary United States, lifestyles are perhaps the most visible. Researchers at the business-consulting firm SRI International have provided a useful perspective on lifestyles. These investigators continually survey thousands of Americans to identify lifestyles and how they change. Analysis of these surveys has recognized a total of nine distinct lifestyles in the United States.[13, 14]

The researchers have named one of the lifestyles the *belongers.* Belongers tend to focus their attention on home, family, and job. They believe it is important to "fit in." They are socially conservative, reluctant to take risks, and respectful of leaders. They read magazines, buy greeting cards, and find interest in cooking and do-it-yourself jobs at home.

As a contrasting lifestyle, the researchers have described the *experientials*. Experientials are younger than belongers. They are less likely to work full-time, but they are still savvy about money and their careers. They tend to be socially permissive and express relatively little confidence in leaders. They prefer foreign to American-manufactured cars and are more likely than average to consume sugar-free soft drinks and eat Mexican or Chinese food.

Within organizations, belongers would be more likely to make stable employees or well-disciplined soldiers. Experientials, by contrast, would be better suited to invention, product development, or assignments requiring creativity or risk. Belongers may be more readily counted on to support an organization's leadership, but they are also more susceptible to *groupthink,* a process by which an organization can blunder into a disastrous course of action because of its members' disinclination to disagree.[15]

Challenges arise when organizations cannot recruit people with the lifestyle they desire. Conservative organizations in banking and insurance, for example, may prefer to hire belongers. But individuals of this description are not always sufficiently available, as when job seekers are in short supply or lifestyles that challenge convention are popular, as they were in the era of "hippies" or "punks." Under these conditions, organizations may adapt by relaxing dress codes, welcoming people with unconventional attitudes, and modifying jobs to provide opportunities for variety and creativity.

Culture

As a social force, culture is arguably more important than lifestyle. In the United States, lifestyle is a matter of personal choice. Culture, though, has a more mandatory quality and affects everyone.

Although there are no universally accepted definitions of culture, a classical conception formulated by anthropologists A. L. Kroeber and C. Kluckhohn[16] describes culture as an essential core of "traditional ideas and values . . . transmitted by symbols." Culture is transmitted and received continuously, through childhood socialization, formal education, and both elite and mass media. Culture provides individuals with information about which behavior is desirable and which is not. It is easy to see how culture helps determine the values of individuals.

Many values supported by American culture are relevant to organizations. Culturally sustained values such as industriousness, loyalty, team spirit, and fair play support the efforts of organizations to achieve cohesion and attain goals. Other values promoted by the broader culture may be problematic in some organizational contexts. Personal independence and freedom of thought, for example, may mesh imperfectly with the routines of organizations making standardized products or delivering services of a uniform kind.

Challenges to organizations arise when their *internal* values contradict those of the broader culture. Organizations such as law firms, hospitals, and universities, for example, require young professionals to spend many evenings and weekends at work during their first years of employment. Industriousness is a value clearly endorsed by American culture. But this value, reinforced by *professional* culture, contradicts the value of establishing a family. In a more striking example, anti-bigotry elements in American culture have limited the success of the Ku Klux Klan, an organization once prominent in American life.

Because the messages of culture are not always consistent, individuals often experience *conflicts of values.* The valuation of success can lead to corner cutting and malfeasance in business organizations. But the value placed on honesty limits such practices in most individuals.

Laws

Laws are among the clearest of the social forces affecting organizations. Organizations pay extraordinary attention to the law and its implications. The resources organizations allocate to legal services illustrate the importance of laws. Nearly every university degree program in management requires at least one course in law.

Ideally, laws should represent social *norms,* prescriptions for action based on values, in written form. The foundation of business law is the contract. A contract is an agreement whose provisions can be enforced by legal authorities if necessary. Agreements must have specific properties to constitute legal contracts. But the idea of a legally enforceable contract is merely an extension of the widely respected cultural norm: "A deal's a deal."

Law exerts a powerful hold on individuals. People resist temptation to break the law, of course, for fear of punishment. But most people also believe in the law. They have sympathy for the motivation of legislators regarding laws, or at least a conviction that the process by which laws are made is legitimate. Most people obey laws even when they experience temptation to transgress and when they have little chance of being caught. Taxation in the United States is a good example. Temptation to underreport income or exaggerate deductions is widespread. But still, most people pay approximately what they owe.[17]

Ordinarily, people bring a basic support for lawful behavior with them into organizational life. Organizations cannot expect most members to readily transgress laws. The law, moreover, offers protection to "whistleblowers," people who report transgressions by organizations for which they work to outside authorities.

Law also constrains the operation of the organization as a whole. Organizations in the United States today, for example, can neither hold slaves nor, except under highly specific conditions, employ children. Organizations cannot keep employees on their premises by force. Battery laws prohibit employers (or officials in organizations of any description) from using physical force as a method of discipline. Labor law guarantees the right of employees to form unions and bargain collectively. Legal codes and government regulations affect working conditions related to health and safety.

Political Economy

Political economy is the most comprehensive of social forces. This term designates the basic principles about the way in which a society functions. Societies have different rules and conventions governing production and distribution of goods and services. They also have conventions and rules determining how key political decisions are made. Social scientists use the term *political economy* because mechanisms governing economic and political matters must be compatible with one another.

Political economy reflects some elements of culture but is more concrete in its development. For example, in the United States the dominance of corporations over many aspects of life was established through legislative struggles and landmark court decisions.[18] But political economy also reflects cultural precepts about how things should be.

Political economy in the United States today may be characterized as *democratic welfare capitalism*. Capitalism rests on the principles of private enterprise and profit making. But because these principles can foster poverty as well as wealth, the United States maintains a system of social welfare. Workers contribute to an unemployment insurance program and receive benefits if they lose their jobs. Workers also contribute to the Social Security system, which pays benefits when they retire.

Many argue that capitalism today would be impossible if it did not coexist with a welfare system. Competition among capitalists may create a better economy. But many individuals get hurt in the process. The welfare system acts as a safety net for these individuals. The welfare system lowers public anxiety and promotes acceptance of capitalism despite its problems.

The other essential element of American political economy is democracy. Political decision makers are elected and are assumed to make laws and set policies in the interest of the public. Political leaders receive massive support from large-scale capitalists. But elected officials must ultimately satisfy the broader public.

A country's political economy directly affects every formal organization operating within its borders. The profit-seeking corporation would be unthinkable within a system that prohibited private ownership of capital. Many nonprofit organizations could not exist or would find their operations restricted in the absence of democratic principles such as freedom of assembly and freedom of speech. The democratic process limits the power of government agencies and makes their actions visible to the public.

Political economy also helps shape expectations of an organization's members. This is clearly visible in relationships between employers and employees. In the United States, people generally believe in an employer's right to make a profit. But this right is accompanied by numerous duties and responsibilities. Americans feel that profits are legitimate only for those who produce desirable goods and create jobs.

Institutions

The last of the social forces to be considered here is that of *institutions*. Institutions comprise widely approved and valued methods of handling the challenges facing individuals and society as a whole. Institutions may be thought of as concrete applications of culture and values.

"Marriage," for example, is widely acclaimed as an institution. Marriage provides a form according to which people pair up, carry on sexual relations, and initiate family life. It is a widely approved and legally supported pattern of behavior.

A Capitalist Villain

The Story of "Chainsaw Al"

The story of Albert J. Dunlap, who headed several major U.S. corporations in the 1990s, illustrates how organizational leadership may clash with national culture and political economy.

Dunlap grew up in the slums of Hoboken, N.J., the son of a shipyard worker. He played football in high school and graduated from West Point. Later in life, he recalled being "a nothing kid from the slums . . . trying to prove he was worth something."

Dunlap made himself famous for turning financially troubled companies into moneymakers. He did this by closing plants, cutting executive staff, and laying off workers. At timber company Crown-Zellerbach, he eliminated 11,000 jobs, a third of the payroll. He achieved his greatest fame at the Sunbeam Corporation, where he slashed half the company's jobs.

His relentless drive to close factories and eliminate jobs earned Dunlap the nickname "Chainsaw Al."

Dunlap's downfall came when he was fired from Sunbeam. Despite drastic economies, the company failed to earn the profits he had promised.

Management experts view Dunlap as a villain because he weakened the bond of trust between employees and their bosses. Americans do not believe employers owe them a job. But the political economy of welfare capitalism leads people to expect employers to be concerned with their well-being.

Americans believe that productivity requires people working together for common goals. Chainsaw Al didn't work this way.[19, 20]

Alternative practices have become the object of widespread usage and experimentation. But most, if not all, societies depend primarily on marriage to regulate and manage sexuality and childrearing.

Other institutions include the practice of educating children in government-operated organizations outside the home; holding town meetings to discuss community issues; and soliciting charitable donations for community causes.

An institution important to millions of workers is the practice by employers of providing employee health care benefits. In most of the United States, employers are not legally required to do so. In other countries, health care is usually financed through government taxation. Not all companies in the United States offer health benefits, but those that do not are looked down upon. In the abstract, large corporations that have provided health benefits for generations could discontinue the practice. But few if any have done so, despite the immense cost of such programs.

In a practical sense, institutions require formal organizations to sustain themselves and order society. Marriages require registration machinery. Democratic decision making requires election bureaus and legislatures. Private charity requires organizations such as the United Way. The degree to which institutions serve society often depends on the effectiveness and efficiency of the organizations through which they operate.

* * *

Broad social forces such as those described here clearly comprise both challenges and assets to organizations. All these forces place their stamp upon the thinking and behavior of organization members. Sometimes, the resulting values and orientations contribute positively to an organization; at other times, they cause problems. Laws, political economy, and institutions limit management options but also serve as resources for the pursuit of objectives.

The full impact of factors outside an organization's direct control can be seen most clearly when they are in a state of change. Modern American history illustrates this principle.

Social Change: A Great American Transformation

Major social change occurred in the United States over the latter half of the 20th century, with crucial consequences for organizations. Shifts in the distribution of races and age-groups within the population contributed to this change. Changes in the way people thought about themselves and their place in society contributed as well.

A stereotype of American life at midcentury was illustrated by one of the era's most popular television programs: *Father Knows Best*. The program depicted a White family living on a tree-lined street. The middle-aged father, the family's sole breadwinner, sold insurance. Upon returning from work, he would shut the door, take off his hat, and announce his arrival by calling, "I'm home!" This image was duplicated in a dozen other popular television serials.

Not all American families conformed to this stereotype. The United States was also home to Blacks, Hispanics, Asians, and other racial minorities, although these were seldom seen on television. Not everyone was stably married or heterosexual. Within stable families, male heads of households could lose their jobs. Many women held paying positions outside the home. Marriages broke up and women headed families.

Changes in society between 1950 and 2000 gave people once considered marginal not only faces, but voices demanding participation and equality. Traditionally mainstream Americans, moreover, adopted new ways of life— sometimes, but not always, by choice. Three forces helped bring about these developments: *liberation, immigration,* and *economic change.*

Liberation

Liberation refers to the achievement of freedom. Prior to the 1960s, many Americans lived under social conditions they considered almost unbearable. Most women, for example, had significantly less choice over how to live their lives than they enjoy today. Many a stay-at-home wife secretly desired a career of her own. Many had children not because they wanted them but because they felt compelled by society's expectations. Many desired to exit an affectionless marriage, but could not due to the social stigma and high cost associated with divorce.

Both male and female homosexuals experienced oppression in the pre-1960s era. Same-sex couples were tolerated almost nowhere. Untold numbers of people hid their sexual preferences from others and denied them to themselves. The number of people attracted only to members of the same sex who lived lives of discomfort in heterosexual marriages will never be known.

Members of all racial and religious minority groups faced manifest bigotry and discrimination before midcentury. It was uncommon to find Black or Hispanic Americans in any of the professions. Jewish people faced quotas for admission to universities and professional schools and were barred from living in certain neighborhoods.

Even White, heterosexual men were affected by the narrowness of choice open to them. Not all wanted to be husbands, fathers, and breadwinners. But powerful social expectations compelled most to conform.

Challenges to these conditions began to appear by the mid-1950s. In urban centers, the "Beat Generation" allowed people to live as nonconformists, at least in style. In 1954, Blacks in Montgomery, Alabama, challenged segregation on city buses, a campaign that proved the opening salvo in the struggle for equal rights. By the mid-1960s, the unpopular war in Vietnam was creating hostility against both government and big business. In a challenge to once unassailable authority, men began refusing involuntary military service.

A "sexual revolution" accompanied these political events. Divorce laws were liberalized. Convenient and reliable methods of contraception became available. The "Women's Liberation" movement followed rapidly behind the sexual revolution. Mainstream Americans no longer needed to marry in order to gratify sexual needs. At the same time, homosexual men and women asserted their rights to associate in public and live together openly.

Concrete achievements of these movements had profound implications for organizations of all kinds. Federal legislation was passed that prohibited discrimination against minorities and women in employment. The federal government instituted a policy of *affirmative action,* which encouraged increased hiring of minorities and their admission to colleges and universities.

Immigration

Immigration has always been a powerful force in the United States. In America today, close to 20% of the population is foreign-born. Federal officials estimate that immigration adds 900,000 people to the United States population each year. High levels of immigration are expected to continue indefinitely.[21]

A low birthrate among people born in the United States has increased the impact of immigration. Without immigration, the U.S. population would soon stabilize and might even decrease. American women in the 1990s had an average of 2.1 children. This average is close to the *replacement rate,* that is, the rate by which those who die are replaced by newborns. Immigrants and the children of immigrants are expected to add 70 million to the U.S. population by 2040. This figure includes 25 million immigrants, plus their 45 million children. People who immigrate are usually healthy and of prime childbearing age, and the cultures of many immigrant groups encourage larger families.

Immigration has profoundly changed America's demographics. The United States today has many more young people than it would have had if immigration had been less extensive in the late 20th century. Waves of immigrants have greatly raised the proportion of Americans who are non-White. Many people reared outside the Judeo-Christian tradition joined the American mix during these years. Many immigrants still prefer their native language over English even after years of residence in the United States.

Economic Change

According to critics, the principal social change now occurring in the United States involves a decline in the fortunes of working people. Commentators of yesteryear believed that unfettered economic competition would drive working and middle-class people into poverty and misery. Nothing like this has happened in the United States since the Great Depression (1929–1940). But compared with middle-class people in the 1950s, the lives of today's Americans are less secure and of lower quality according to several criteria.

Among the most important demographic shifts in the past half-century has been the increase in job-holding by women with children. By 1997, 64% of women with children under six held jobs outside the home. Less than 20% of women with children under six held jobs in 1960.[21] Most single-adult families (16% of all American families in 1993) are maintained by women. The vast majority of these women support their families by working outside the home.

Some social scientists argue that many women in married-couple families work outside the home by choice. These observers contend that many women seek their own careers in order to achieve personal fulfillment and independence. N-achievement among women increased substantially between 1957 and 1976.[22] But most women work for reasons other than personal ambition. Typically, women head one-parent families. Women are the sole income earners in two-thirds of the families in the United States maintained by a single person. In 1993, such families composed 16% of all families in America, up from 12% in 1980.[21]

A large part of the economic transformation experienced by both genders is traceable to *globalization*. Expanding worldwide trade has reduced opportunities traditionally available to American heads of households. *Technology* has contributed to the declining fortunes of some workers, drastically reducing if not eliminating jobs for people as diverse as middle managers, draftsmen, and machinists. Advances in communications and software enabled both private firms and public agencies to "export" white-collar work to English-speaking, low-wage countries. Deregulation, the movement to eliminate legal restrictions on competition in industries such as airlines and trucking, has also eliminated jobs.[23]

Impact on Organizations

The long-term effects of these social changes are impossible to determine at this time. But challenges and benefits for organizations are already evident. These are perhaps most apparent in work organizations. Table 2.1 provides some examples.

Table 2.1   America's Transformation and 21st-Century Work Organizations

Dimension of Social Change	Changes in Workforce	Issue for Work Organizations
Liberation, economic change	More single heads of households and female workers	Competition between work and family responsibilities Schedule conflicts
Liberation, economic change	More working spouses	Decreased willingness of workers to relocate
Liberation	Assertion of rights by the physically challenged	Need to improve physical access, reschedule and redesign jobs
Liberation	Decreased loyalty to employers	Retaining valued employees Maintaining motivation Controlling conflict
Immigration	Greater racial, ethnic, and cultural diversity	Socialization and acculturation of newcomers Development of language skills and cultural competence
Economic change	More workers over 65 years of age	Accommodating the needs of elders Integrating different generations

The clearest outcomes of the changes described above are alterations in the workforce, which in turn challenge work organization. Women with children, a rapidly growing workforce segment, are more likely than men to leave work unexpectedly to care for an ill or injured child. Women with young families may less readily accept overtime work or consent to extended business travel. Despite recent social change, women today retain primary responsibility for child care and household tasks. Problems faced by working women and the organizations that employ them are more acute in single-parent families, most of which are headed by women.

Family responsibilities have proven a challenge to many women seeking career advancement. Successful careers in business and the professions require extraordinarily long hours in the early stages. Women with children are often reluctant or unable to rise on management ladders with such requirements and often choose positions requiring less time in the office but providing less advancement potential. Modern commentators have dubbed such positions the "mommie track."[24] Managers of work organizations face the problem of retaining valued female workers and maximizing their productivity.

Liberation and economic change have affected the relationships of both men and women to their work organizations. Ties between workers and their organizations have become weaker, as employees expect to hold their jobs for fewer years than in the past.[21] Men are no longer as free as they once were to accept a transfer to another city. In the past, many men made relocation decisions without having to consider jobs held by their wives. But movement of women into desirable careers has ended the age of the "trailing spouse."

Immigration has presented the work organization with the need to teach new-comers about American customs and expectations. Newcomers from some cultures may require encouragement to accept the authority of female supervisors. Employees born in the United States may need encouragement to accept the use of languages they do not understand. Executives may have to overcome scheduling problems associated with practice of religions outside the Judeo-Christian tradition. Organizations, furthermore, cannot depend on an overburdened public education system to teach language and reading skills to newly arrived workers. Many organizations today develop their own education programs.

The aging of the American workforce raises additional issues. The average age of working people is rising due to demographic factors such as low birthrates and longer life expectancy. Economic factors are also beginning to raise average workers' ages, as support from pensions becomes less reliable. Federal legislation has protected older workers as well, making it illegal in nearly all industries to compel their retirement.

The presence of numerous older workers raises the possibility that conflict among generations may develop. Young people may exclude elders from conversation. Elders may become suspicious of younger people and look down upon them due to their inexperience. Elders are often more conservative than youths and may accommodate themselves less readily to changes in rules, expectations, and office rearrangement.

Social change has significantly altered the American workforce and thus created challenges for work organizations. Opportunities have emerged as well. The availability of women and minorities, and their access to key positions, has brought previously untapped talent into organizations of all kinds. The presence of individuals fluent in Spanish and Chinese, and with cultural ties to countries such as Mexico and China, has increased the capacity of organizations to profit from globalization.

Relationships Among Organizations

Every organization is surrounded by an array of other organizations. The presence of other organizations in an organization's milieu can have great influence on whether and how it achieves its objectives. Like other elements over which an organization has no direct control, other organizations can pose challenges as well as assets to it.

The impact of organizations on each other has attracted significant attention among students of organizations. A number of models and theories systematically address interorganizational relationships. On an elementary level, organizations concerned with each other's actions may either compete with each other or establish relationships of interdependence.

Competition

In everyday life, people talk often about competition. This is true in many business sectors. Businesses compete for raw materials, inventory, and sales. But competition occurs among organizations in many other fields. Nonprofits compete for charitable donations and grants. Clubs compete for members. Universities compete for students. Political campaigns compete for voters.

Many books offer advice to businesspeople on how to compete in marketing and sales. These books provide insights into how the competitive environment may influence decision making in an organization. Business executives are told to think like military strategists, acting according to principles such as the "flanking attack," avoiding engagement with "superior forces," and "attacking at the enemy's strength."[25] Alternative business strategies may include chipping away at rivals' product lines that are weak (the flanking attack) or concentrating development effort on an item of obvious superiority to a rival's premier product (attacking at the enemy's strength).

Interdependence

While competition among organizations may be readily visible, relationships of mutual dependence and benefit are equally frequent. Many industries, for example, operate through elaborate systems of mutual interrelations. In these situations, "alliances" are more prominent than "enemies."

Uzzi's description of the clothing industry in New York provides an example of a community of interrelated business organizations.[26] Clothing "manufacturers" have recognized labels and operate showrooms. But these manufacturers do not directly control production of the garments they offer. The manufacturer conceives the product line and orders designs and patterns from other firms. Raw textile is ordered from another separate firm. Cutting and stitching are performed under contract by still other firms. Additional organizations, from boutiques to department stores, purchase finished garments from the manufacturer and sell them to retail customers.

Each of the interconnections in alliances of this kind requires time and other resources for cultivation and maintenance. But most participants would have neither sufficient funds nor expertise to operate independently. The concept of *social capital* is frequently applied to alliances of this kind.[27] Social capital refers to networks of interrelationships among individuals and organizations that, by promoting mutual assistance, benefit both individual participants and the community as a whole.

The concept of social capital is often applied to communities, neighborhoods, and other venues of informal social relationships. Though separate, firms in the alliances described above are linked by relationships of trust built up over many years. Such ties promote a degree of flexibility that helps maintain the network. A manufacturer will tolerate delay in delivery of product from a business associate of long standing, and the same business associate may exercise patience in the receipt of payment by the manufacturer in difficult times. Intermarriage and association within Chinese, Jewish, Hispanic, or other ethnic communities significant in the clothing trades help promote and maintain these ties.

Relationships of mutual support and dependence occur in the nonprofit world as well. Hospitals provide a brief though comprehensive example. The "community nonprofit" hospital predominates in the United States hospital industry. Significant competition for patients, physician participation, and insurance dollars prevails among hospitals in any given locality. But each hospital operates within a matrix of interdependent organizations. Each hospital requires licensure, accreditation, and certification from a vast array of public and private organizations, ranging from national accreditation bodies to the local fire marshal's office. Well-managed hospitals communicate continually with each of these agencies to provide required information and project a favorable image. Dependence is indeed mutual, as accrediting, certification, and licensing agencies depend on the fees paid by hospitals and the political support of the hospital industry.

Among organizations of all kinds, a wide variety of linkages can be described.[28] These include relationships that leave the boundaries of each organization unaltered, as when organizations simply exchange resources. Relationships among organizations may also involve penetration of each other's boundaries. When business organizations join a trade group that sets standards for their industry, for example, they may incur the obligation to abide by the standards it sets.

The Impact of Organizational Milieu

This chapter began by noting that organizations cannot be viewed simply as independent systems single-mindedly pursuing explicit objectives. Several key factors beyond the organization's direct control affect its functioning. Internal factors of this kind include the values of individual members and the groups and networks members spontaneously form. Factors beyond the organization's control in its external environment include social forces, social change, and other organizations.

The values and personality features of individuals, internal interpersonal relationships, and the external environment constitute the milieu in which organizations operate. Organizations may respond to these forces through procedures ranging from accommodation to opposition. Sometimes, accommodation alone is possible. Examples include the need to adapt to a changing labor force and to develop relationships of collaboration and trust with other organizations. Later chapters will provide more specifics on the impact on organizations of internal factors such as the personalities of leaders and environmental features such as technology.

It is important to note that the organization's relationship to forces beyond its control often involves conflict. Business competition amounts to conflict among organizations, even though it is usually conducted without violence and within the law. Competition among political organizations in the United States is readily observable. Attempts by organizations to override the values and needs of members may result in malfunctions ranging from restriction of productivity to sabotage.

Issues and Applications

Far from operating as independent entities, organizations experience challenges from both outside and inside. Challenges from the outside may arise from social change. Challenges from the inside may stem from basic individual psychology and relationships among individuals. Here are a few examples:

- A young woman, recently graduated with honors from a prestigious college, begins a job at a state agency administering air quality regulations. She works well and feels comfortable with her coworkers. She concentrates on her assignments, stays late to make sure her deadlines are met, and feels proud of her performance. However, her supervisor treats her coolly and minutely criticizes her work. In return, the young woman is haughty and sarcastic in meetings with the supervisor. The relationship steadily deteriorates. The young woman receives an unfavorable review at the end of her probationary period. A clash of personalities may be at fault. In the language of transactional analysis, the supervisor's punitive parent ego state confronts the young woman's defiant child. A vicious cycle of mutually reinforcing ill will results.

- Reflecting immigration trends, a church in a long-stable White neighborhood finds its congregation becoming predominantly Filipino. Responding to the needs of the new members, the pastor hires assistant clergymen who speak Tagalog, the Filipino native tongue. A number of special services are instituted in that language. Long-standing church members, including several who provide significant financial support, begin expressing discomfort. Some leave the church to attend services outside the neighborhood. The organization must seek a balance between the needs of its traditional members and those of the newcomers.

- A software company needs experienced technical professionals and offers exceptional salaries to attract such employees. However, large numbers of employees regularly depart for positions in firms paying even higher salaries. Salaries are raised but the frequent turnover continues. Management must consider the possibility that frequent layoffs during past periods of industry slack have weakened the feelings of loyalty and obligation that prevailed in earlier times.

Chapter Review and Major Themes

This chapter highlights the importance of the organizational milieu. Key features of the organizational milieu include the thinking and behavior of individuals; informal personal ties both inside and outside the organization; broader social forces (such as lifestyle, culture, and institutions); and other organizations. Social scientists usually refer to the matrix of outside forces within which individual organizations are embedded as the *organizational environment.*

Organizations should not be viewed simply as agencies involved in the deliberate pursuit of objectives. Rather, they carry on their operations within a dynamic array of forces beyond their control responding sometimes through accommodation, and at other times through opposition. Figure 2.1, below, illustrates the place of the organization within this milieu.

In Figure 2.1, the shaded area represents organizational functioning, taking place with the aid of structure, rewards, and a number of other factors to be addressed in later chapters. A realm of interpersonal functioning exists within this shaded area, comprising personalities of members, spontaneously formed groups, and informal networks. Outside the area of organizational functioning is the environment. Factors such as technology, politics, and the field of other organizations have immediate effects on the functioning and strategy of most organizations. More remote factors such as demography, culture, and institutions may have less immediate but still profound effects on the organization's internal functioning and ultimate success.

A number of themes in this chapter highlight the limited ability of organizations to control their members or the outside environment. This is not to say that organizations are powerless or chaotic. However, a continual dynamic, strong and evident in some organizations and subtle and hidden in others, takes place between the organization's purposes and those of individuals or outside forces.

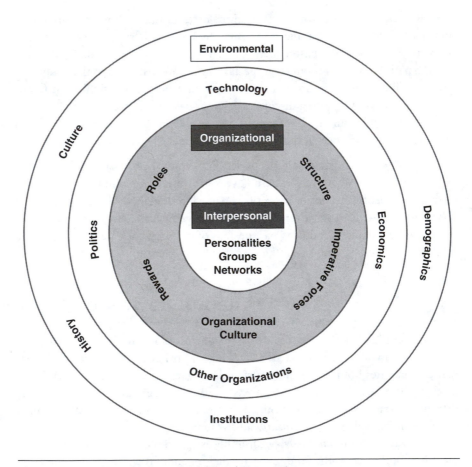

Figure 2.1   Organizations: A Multilevel Perspective

Discussion Questions

1. Are the close linkages between work organizations and families observed in Japan desirable from the point of view of the worker? Are they desirable from the point of view of the employer?

2. The political economy of the United States has been characterized as *democratic welfare capitalism.* What challenges or benefits does this political economy present to organizations?

3. A number of distinct "lifestyles" have been described in this chapter. Does your own lifestyle affect how well you work in the organizations in which you participate? If so, how?

4. If the social forces described in this chapter intensify over the decades to come, how will this affect organizations?

5. To what extent does the "organizational milieu" restrict or enhance the tools available to an organization for promoting coordination and cohesion?

References

1. Peace, F. (1986). I thought I knew what good management was. *Harvard Business Review, 64,* 59–65.
2. Maslow, A. H. (1996). A theory of human motivation. In J. S. Ott (Ed.), *Classic readings in organizational behavior.* Belmont, CA: Wadsworth.
3. Lester, D. (1990). Maslow's hierarchy of needs and personality. *Personality and Individual Differences, 11,* 1187–1188.
4. Rokeach, M. (1973). *The nature of human values.* New York: Free Press.
5. Weber, M. (1998). *The Protestant ethic and the spirit of capitalism.* Los Angeles: Roxbury Press.
6. Staw, B. M., Bell, N. E., & Clausen, J. A. (1986). The dispositional approach to job attitudes: A lifetime longitudinal test. *Administrative Science Quarterly, 31,* 56–77.
7. Dalhstrom, W. G., & Welsh, J. S. (1960). *An MMPI handbook: A guide to use in clinical practice and research.* Minneapolis: University of Minnesota.
8. Briggs, K. C., & Myers, I. B. (1976). *Myers-Briggs type indicator—Form F.* Palo Alto, CA: Consulting Psychologists Press.
9. Agnew, N. M., & Brown, J. L. (1989). Foundations for a model of knowing: 1. Constructing reality. *Canadian Psychology, 30,* 152–167.
10. Gallagher, G. W. (1997). *The confederate war.* Cambridge, MA: Harvard University Press.
11. Shils, E. A., & Janowitz, M. (1948). Cohesion and disintegration in the Wehrmacht in World War II. *Public Opinion Quarterly, 12,* 280–315.
12. Cole, R. E. (1971). *Japanese blue collar: The changing tradition.* Berkeley: University of California Press.
13. Mitchell, A. (1984). *The nine American lifestyles.* New York: Warner Books.
14. Holt, D. B. (1997). Poststructuralist lifestyle analysis: Conceptualizing the social patterning of consumption in postmodernity. *Journal of Consumer Research, 23,* 326–350.
15. Janis, I. L. (1982). *Groupthink.* Boston: Houghton Mifflin.

16. Kroeber, A. L., & Kluckhohn, C. (1963). *Culture: A critical review of concepts and definitions*. New York: Vintage Books.

17. Scholz, J. T., & Lubell, M. (1998). Trust and taxpaying: Testing the heuristic approach to collective action. *American Journal of Political Science, 42*, 398–417.

18. Knoke, D. (2001). *Changing organizations: Business networks in the new political economy*. Boulder, CO: Westview Press.

19. Brannigan, A. J., & Hagerty, J. R. (1998, June 15). Sunbeam, its prospects looking ever worse, fires CEO Dunlap. *Wall Street Journal*, p. A1.

20. Deogun, N., & Schellhardt, T. D. (1998, June 23). Some lessons learned from two who felt the ax of Al Dunlap. *Wall Street Journal*, p. B1.

21. Judy, R. W., & D'Amico, C. (1997). *Workforce 2020*. Indianapolis, IN: Hudson Institute.

22. Veroff, J., Depner, K., Kulka, R., & Douvan, E. (1980). Comparison of American motivations: 1957 vs. 1976. *Journal of Personality and Social Psychology, 39*, 1249–1262.

23. Budros, A. (1997). The new capitalism and organizational rationality: The adoption of downsizing programs. *Social Forces, 76*, 229–249.

24. Jacobs, D. L. (1994, October 9). Back from the mommy track. *New York Times*, sec. 3, p. 1.

25. Reis, A., & Trout, J. (1986). *Marketing warfare*. New York: McGraw-Hill.

26. Uzzi, B. (1997). Social structure and competition in interfirm networks: The paradox of embeddedness for economic performance of organizations. *Administrative Science Quarterly, 42*, 35–67.

27. Knoke, D. (1999). Organizational networks and corporate social capital. In R. Leenders & S. M. Gabbay (Eds.), *Corporate social capital and liability* (pp. 17–42). Boston: Kluwer Academic.

28. Child, J., & Faulkner, D. (1998). *Strategies of cooperation: Managing alliances, networks, and joint ventures*. New York: Oxford University Press.

CHAPTER 3

Organizational Theories and Perspectives

Learning Objective

To become aware of alternative conceptual approaches to understanding organizations.

Principles

Multiple theories help explain why organizations exist, how they function, and what influences affect them. Key theories include

○ Transaction cost theory, which justifies the existence of organizations by their ability to reduce the costs of individual-to-individual economic relations

○ Rational systems theory, which thinks of organizations as tools to achieve specific goals

○ Contingency theory, which highlights the effects of purpose, technology, and environment on organizations

○ Institutional theory, which emphasizes the organization's need to attain legitimacy and stability within a potentially disruptive social environment

○ Network theory, which explains thinking and action within an organization on the basis of the place that the organization occupies in an array of organizations involved in related activities

○ Critical theory, which stresses competition over resources and the use of organizational means by elites to dominate workers and society as a whole

○ Humanistic theory, which emphasizes the importance of reconciling the needs of individual members with those of the organization

N o theory offers a complete understanding of the formal organization. Each has special value in explaining some features of organizations and the challenges they face. As starting points for understanding, the major theories suggest attention to function, environment, and conflict.

Why Theory?

It would be impossible to make sense of the world without theory. A theory is a set of interrelated statements about some feature of reality. Without theories, people would have only disconnected observations of phenomena in the physical or social world. At its core, a theory contains (or implies) a fundamental, central belief. Theories help the observer understand limited or brief observations as part of a big picture. Theories also help observers ask questions and solve problems.

People of practical bent may deny the importance of theory. Some scientists and philosophers, those subscribing to the schools of empiricism and phenomenology,[1–2] are also so inclined. Yet, even people who reject the idea of theory often have theories they do not recognize as such. Implicit theories of this kind may not be elaborate or even written down. They are developed as the individual observes events and consciously or unconsciously links these observations.

Theory is particularly important in the study of organizations. Organizations are complicated. They are difficult to observe in their entirety. Organizations take many different forms. Only through theory can a grasp of the phenomenon as a whole be attempted.

Theory has a practical value. It helps the individual recognize the effects of organizational phenomena on his or her life. Within an organization, an individual may experience frustration with the structure or distress over lack of opportunity. An understanding of the way an organization works and why it exists can explain the individual's experience. Such an explanation can help the individual recognize that the problems are not solely of his or her making. This understanding can serve as a basis of action, either to make life in the organization more gratifying or to leave the organization.

Social scientists have developed numerous distinct theories about formal organizations. They attempt to explain why organizations exist; how they function internally; and how they reflect, respond to, or influence their environments. These theories all have value in promoting comprehensive understanding. In addition, they can help link features of organizations with issues applicable to society as a whole.

Major Theoretical Perspectives

Transaction Cost Theory

Transaction cost theory emerged from an attempt by economists to explain the existence of organizations. Traditional economics, it may be argued, has no place for organizations. Economics focuses on the exchange of valued items among individuals.

If human relationships are based on such exchanges, it is difficult to identify a valid function for the organization. Implicit in classical economics is the myth of spontaneous exchange. This myth envisages stone-age human beings spontaneously exchanging primitive commodities, such as flint and salt. No third party need be interested, nor have reason to interfere, in such a transaction, which is driven by the desire of the two principals to exchange items of obvious and equal value.

It seems likely that economists have always realized that real exchanges were more complex. This realization appeared in the thinking of Fredrick Hayek in the mid-20th century.[3] According to Hayek, two types of human interaction occurred. These were, first, spontaneous interchange of valuable items. Second, human interaction could include contracts and agreements that addressed rules governing exchange.

The Nobel laureate Coase[4] advanced this idea by commenting that transaction costs could be greater outside than inside a system of stable social relations. Transaction costs might include effort required to find a trading partner, ensure the good faith of traders, and guarantee the safety of the transaction. More recently, Williamson[5] contrasted settings under which transactions might take place: spontaneously versus under supervision. He characterized these two settings as "markets" versus "hierarchies." Two management scientists[6] summarize his formulation as follows:

> In general, [markets] rely on prices, competition, and contracts to keep all parties to an exchange informed of their rights and responsibilities. Hierarchical forms of governance, on the other hand, bring parties to an exchange under the direct control of a third party (typically called "the boss"). This authoritative third party then attempts to keep all parties to an exchange informed of their rights and responsibilities. Moreover, this third party has the right to directly resolve any conflicts that might emerge in an exchange. (p. 117)

In the opinion of Williamson, markets face important limits in enabling exchanges to take place. Contracts could not be written that would anticipate all possible mishaps. There would be insufficient safeguards against fraud and abuse. The individual, then, cannot act with the pure rationality that traditional economics assumes. He or she must pay the price of organization.

This theory has intuitive appeal. It is, after all, unrealistic to imagine complex economic activity taking place merely as a series of exchanges between individuals. It is difficult to visualize, let us say, the assembly of an automobile based on sale by individual fabricators to others of bolts, bushings, and pistons. Whatever might be the cost of housing the fabricators in an industrial facility, adjudicating what disputes may arise among them, and paying for their eventual retirement, it would be less than that associated with the spontaneous exchange of auto components. Indeed, the cost of such a procedure would preclude production of even a single auto.

The "economic theory" of organization has contributed interesting ideas to explain the existence of organizations. Yet the value of this theory for understanding actual organizations seems uncertain. Questions can be raised about the theory's main principle. For example, the cost of maintaining "hierarchies"—this word should be understood simply as "organizations"—can itself be high. Large organizations incur high overheads due, in part, to the need to pay people not directly involved in production of goods or services. Items such as salaries for executives, maintenance of buildings, planning for the future, and operating the company cafeteria all contribute to overhead.

In response, some organizations today appear to be moving away from the large, high-overhead model. Downsizing, formation of autonomous divisions, and divestiture of units are illustrative examples. Profit-seeking firms, private nonprofits, and government agencies today outsource functions from long-term strategic planning to janitorial services.

Rational Systems Theory

Rational systems theory is perhaps the oldest and most straightforward of the theories about organizations. Under this theory, organizations are considered mechanisms for achieving goals. The relevance to rational systems theory of identifying functions of organizational components and practices is easy to see. Under rational systems theory, every component of the organization should directly or indirectly contribute to its survival and the attainment of its goals.

In characterizing this theory, the word *rational* connotes the fitting together of components into a consistent whole, configured in a fashion favorable to achievement of specific goals. Parts of an organization conforming to this template would be rational in the same sense as a legal system, as described in Chapter 2. Ideally, individual laws fit together into a consistent whole and promote a just society according to prevailing social norms and values.

In addition, the theory suggests that structure should dominate the organization. Rationality is reflected in the structure. People in the organization, it is implied, would operate under a system of rules severely restricting their independent decision making.

Among approaches to organizations, rational systems theory may be the most time-honored. It is consistent with some of the thinking of Max Weber,[7] whose work in the early 20th century helped establish the field of sociology. As is true of many great thinkers, Weber's work has also contributed to theories about organizations quite different from rational systems. Much more will be said about the contributions of Weber later in this text.

Many researchers and commentators have questioned rational systems theory, at least in its traditional form. The study of groups and informal relationships in organizations, as described in Chapter 1, suggests a potential shortcoming. Even in organizations where numerous and tightly enforced rules prevail, individuals maintain substantial control over their behavior.

Critics have commented that new types of organizations are evolving, and that the rational system provides insufficient help in understanding these organizations. In these new types of organizations, it is argued, coordination of members is looser and cohesion within organizational boundaries is less important than in the past. Forces outside the organization, they argue, have become more important than those inside.

In addition, critics contend that while rational systems theory considers goals the focus of an organization's effort, goals in organizations are often unclear. Multiple and competing goals may exist. Members of organizations do not merely receive goals from some outside force; they develop goals through internal processes. More will be said about this, too, in a later chapter.

Nevertheless, rational systems theory has the advantage of focusing on the most concrete and immediately visible features of an organization. Despite criticism from several quarters and the formulation of competing theories, rational systems theory remains a necessary and beneficial resource for the study of organizations. Rational systems theory is straightforward. In a wide variety of organizations, it is readily applicable for understanding and problem solving in many organizations. Many researchers on organizations who have concentrated on other approaches are today rediscovering rational systems theory as an important tool.[8]

To summarize, the central principle of rational systems theory is that deliberate pursuit of a goal determines the configuration of social relations and other resources in an organization. Such a configuration may develop spontaneously, result from plans formulated by members, or be mandated by managers.

Contingency Theory

The word *contingency* connotes the existence of a wide variety of possibilities, any one of which might be unexpectedly realized. The rational model, in its simplest form, assumes that organizations require stable relationships and task assignments among members. In reality, the conditions in an organization's environment can change rapidly. Organizations must respond to changes in markets, funding opportunities, politics, technology, and public values.

The instability of organizational environments implies the key provision of contingency theory: there is no one best way of arranging activity within an organization. Different principles for assigning responsibilities and channeling effort will work best in organizations engaged in similar tasks, challenged by similar forces, and pursuing similar goals.

According to contingency theory, uncertainty and information play a key role in determining how an organization should be configured.[9,10] Some organizations enjoy high levels of certainty, knowing that their requirements will remain constant over time. In such organizations, members need very little information to do their work: a fixed set of instructions is adequate. In organizations whose tasks are changing, members need a great deal of information. No simple set of instructions will work. Members need to be given the liberty to make personal judgments among alternatives, often in a rapid-response manner.

The contingency model helps explain variations within as well as between organizations. Human relationships, management practices, and culture can differ from department to department. Even in a small firm, for example, the accounting department is likely to be more formal than the marketing department, the employee fitness room, or the child care center.

The contingency theory can be seen as complementing rather than contradicting the rational systems theory. At least one author has referred to a "rational-contingency" theory.[11] Under this formulation, organizations pursue definite goals, but do so in a manner that is sensitive to specific characteristics of their environments.

Thus, electric utilities located in urban Massachusetts and rural Utah would be likely to operate differently in some respects. The Massachusetts company would probably expend more of its resources on pollution abatement and public relations.

The central principle of contingency theory is that constraints on the "free will" of the organization determine the configuration of social relations and allocation of resources within it. These constraints can be environmental, or they can grow out of the technology used by the organization to pursue its goals.

This book makes use of contingency theory as a useful adjunct to rational systems theory. Applications are to be seen in the forthcoming sections on the influence of technology on organizational structure and on the qualities essential for leadership at different times and in different situations.

Institutional Theory

In comparison with the theories summarized thus far, institutional theory places minor emphasis on the organization's direct efforts at goal achievement. Instead, institutional theory focuses on organizational characteristics that arise from its history and place in society. As applied by some, institutional theory seeks explanations of an organization's development and action in the influence of external stakeholders. In the hands of others, this theory looks at the way organizations respond to the influence of major social institutions.

An important study of the Tennessee Valley Authority (TVA) by sociologist Philip Selznick helped propel institutional theory to prominence.[12] Still functioning today, the TVA is a government-supported agency involved in dam and power plant management on a system of rivers that runs through a number of states in the Southeastern United States. The agency, begun during the Depression, was intended to help people of modest means by controlling floods, generating inexpensive electricity, and providing much-needed jobs. As the project took shape, however, it became clear that well-organized, well-connected, and well-funded groups outside influenced the organization's development. Electricity was sold at favorable rates to large industries. Some agency resources were diverted to the manufacture of fertilizer, of use mainly to large farming interests. In an effort obtain the support of these large interests, the agency bypassed some of its original goals.

In the language of modern theorists, organizations acquire similar forms and methods due to the influence of "organizational fields." An organizational field compoises a set of organizations that together form a "segment of institutional life." Concretely, an organizational field encompasses all organizations involved in a particular activity, such as education, health care, or government. Over time, organizations composing the organizational field develop shared expectations regarding how business should be conducted. Often, these expectations mirror those of the broader society.

Theorists today emphasize that the organizational field acts as a homogenizing influence on the organizations belonging to it. According to some contemporary observers, the organizational field transmits elaborate rules and requirements to which individual organizations must conform.[13] Organizations that do not conform to such norms may never find full acceptance by the broader society. A tendency of organizations involved in similar economic sectors to appear similar in form is known as *institutional isomorphism.*

Concretely, institutional isomorphism develops in a number of ways.[14] One organization may mimic another's structure and practices in hopes of emulating that organization's success. Recurrent exchange of personnel among organizations results in a sharing of values and expectations among individuals throughout an organizational field. As in the case of the TVA, the dominance of key stakeholders such as important purchasers of goods or centers of political power can drive organizations toward adopting common practices.

Today's institutional theorists often emphasize the significance of external influences on organizations. But the fundamental theory recognizes the importance of internal processes as well. These may include evolutionary development of symbolism and culture.[15]

Institutional theory recognizes that organizations develop structures and carry out practices not clearly related to their internal goals. Such features develop and continue because members and leadership value them or believe they are necessary for survival. While some practices in fact promote an organization's capacity to achieve objectives (an organization cannot pursue goals if it does not physically survive), not all practices are functional in this sense.

Network Theory

Like the institutional approach, network theory pays special attention to phenomena outside organizational boundaries. To explain the actions of organizations, network theory examines the "larger structural networks within which they are embedded."[16] Most obviously, these networks are made up of other organizations, all of whom share a niche or area of specialization.

According to network theory, organizations that occupy similar positions in a network should act similarly. All organizations that depend on a single agency for a vital resource, for example, should have similar sets of departments and rules. All medical schools in the United States, for example, are dependent on the American Association of Medical Colleges (AAMC) for accreditation. In response, all have similar faculty expertise and require their students to take similar courses. Businesses dependent on investment banks adopt similar financial reporting procedures.

Networks do not always comprise systems of dependency. These sets of interrelationships may be based on exchanges of information and resources. Some networks are based on mutual "boundary penetrations," as members of different organizations sit on each other's governing boards and engage in collaborative projects. Some networks among organizations are founded upon long-term trust, as organizations collaborate with each other repeatedly over many years.

Network theory is particularly attractive because of its breadth. Network theory can offer an explanation for the form and actions of a group of organizations. In addition, the theory is useful in explaining relations between departments or even individuals within an organization. Individuals within organizations, for example, occupy different positions within communication networks. Relatively isolated members of an organization can be readily observed to think differently from those at the center of conversation among peers or who communicate directly with superiors. Network theory may generate worldwide perspective, as clusters of organizations in different countries are more and more frequently linked with each other as globalization increases.

A great deal has been written about the practical value of networks and networking. People tied in to a vigorous system of interpersonal communication and assistance possess important advantages in finding jobs and advancing in their careers.[17] Interpersonal networks within organizations have value for the organization itself as they facilitate communication and collaboration.[18]

Many observers of organizations find network theory particularly attractive because it applies uniform principles to settings ranging from interpersonal to worldwide. The theory also lends itself to the quantification that characterizes all fields widely accepted as "science." A number of researchers have developed mathematical techniques and software to identify networks according to the interaction patterns of organizations.[19, 20]

Critical Theory

Critical theory is most readily associated with the Marxist critique of modern society. Under this theory, the central concern of humankind is the exploitation of some people by others. Many Marxist thinkers believe in the existence of a worldwide ruling class that controls industry, government, and culture. Corporations pay workers enough to stay healthy and motivated, but not nearly as much as their services are worth. Since the ruling class controls the media, workers remain ignorant of their exploitation.

For 100 years after the death of Marx in 1883, Marxist thought spawned workers' movements that advocated revolution. Since the fall of the Soviet Union in the late 20th century, the heritage of Marx has been carried on largely by intellectuals. According to critical theory, the modern ruling class utilizes more sophisticated methods of exploitation than its predecessors. Rather than assaulting factory workers with truncheons, today's ruling class tempts clerks and professionals with consumer goods and unattainable cultural ideals.[21,22]

Modern critical theory teaches that formal organizations cloak manipulative and exploitative practices in the guise of technical efficiency. Organizations of paid employees take over functions once performed by families and communities. People lose control of greater and greater portions of their lives to large, formal organizations. It is argued that social relations within the modern, formal organization mirror patterns of oppression in the broader society. These include the presence of hierarchy, the marginalization of women and minorities, the encouragement of passivity in most organizational participants, and the sacrificing of nature and the quality of life to development and ever-larger profits.[23,24]

Critical theory clearly implies a political program. It assumes that increased awareness and control by workers would reduce the negative impact organizations have on their members and the wider society. In the form it takes today, the theory is neither necessarily antimanagement nor anticapitalist. Rather than condemn profit making, for example, it implies that profit seeking should be balanced with more human concerns.

The basis of critical theory is open to question. Since Marx, many have argued that what has been condemned as exploitation is actually legitimate reward for entrepreneurship.[25] In addition, it is not certain whether a worldwide ruling class exists. Institutional theory suggests that the oppressive practices of the broader society should naturally be reproduced within organizational boundaries. Yet, political figures in the Marxist tradition have embraced the hierarchical, formal organization as a means to achieve their ends.

Although critical theory is rightly associated with the Marxist tradition, elements of this theory receive attention and support from thinkers who are decidedly non-Marxist. Weber, for example, criticized the Marxist principle that history is driven by struggles over material advantage. He recognized, however, the importance of competition in society. Many of Weber's writings concerned the means by which individuals exercise dominance over others. Some of his most important works address competition by social classes, "status groups" (such as educated elites), and political parties over the resources and allegiance of society at large.[26] An important group of scholars, the so-called Frankfurt School, integrated the Marxist ideas with a variety of more modern concepts. Writers even more remote from Marxist ideology than Weber focus strongly on competition for material resources, power, and influence. The German scholar Ralf Dahrendorf,[27] for example, emphasized new complexities of class conflict in post–World War II Europe, while American Robert Wuthnow concentrated on the development of religious ideas as objects of conflict.[28]

Humanistic Theory

A number of important researchers and commentators, active from the 1930s onward, contributed what may be called *humanistic organization theory*.[29] These scholars, sometimes called the *human relations school*, concentrated on the fit (or lack thereof) between the needs of the organization and those of the individual. Contributors to this approach included those who conducted the Hawthorne studies. The development of humanistic organization theory is sometimes explained as a reaction to rational systems theory. It is easy to interpret some versions of rational systems theory as reducing human beings to components in a machine. Humanistic organization theory, on the contrary, pays close attention to the needs of the individual.

In the world of organization theories, humanistic theory has taken a backseat to macroscopic (rather than person-focused) formulations. But humanistic theory still permeates the practical world of organizations. Popular management books highlight solutions consistent with humanistic theory.[30] Problem solvers such as human resources personnel, often trained in the tradition of humanistic theory, daily seek ways to help individuals fit in better with the needs of the organization, and vice versa. Worker-oriented innovations over the last century, from health benefits to ergonomics, have received support from humanistic theory.

Despite their concern for society's downtrodden, researchers and commentators identified with critical theory have strongly criticized the humanistic approach.[31] Critics in this tradition have characterized innovations formulated under humanistic thinking as superficial. Accordingly, humanistic reform is seen as lacking real value because it does not change the so-called exploitative relationship between organizations and their workers.

Because this book emphasizes factors above and beyond the individual (such as organizational structure and macrosocial forces), humanistic organization theory receives limited attention here. However, this body of thinking has focused on individual behavior and group process in greater detail than any other. It has inspired significant efforts to reconcile the needs of the organization with those of its members. Chapter 13 will devote detailed attention to organizational experiments and innovations consistent with the concerns raised by this school of thought.

Other Approaches

Other theories, concepts, and perspectives relevant to organizations abound. *Agency theory,* for example, raises questions about the benefits that formal organizations actually provide to those they are intended to serve.[32] This theory highlights the fact that modern organizations are managed by individuals other than those to whom they are ultimately responsible. Thus, corporate officers manage firms owned by stockholders, and government officials manage agencies supported by taxpayers. The risk of conflict of interest is always present, as recurring corporate scandal and government corruption illustrate. *Sociobiology,*[33] which applies observation of the natural world to human relationships, can be seen as interpreting formal organization as species adaptation.

Postmodernism and related thinking[34,35] deserve special attention. This developing body of theory comprises a broad-ranging critique of cultural and economic life, and, like critical theory, sees the modern, formal organization as a repository of oppressiveness and obfuscation. Postmodernism emphasizes the role of human ideas in the domination of some groups over others within particular eras, civilizations, and social structures. Postmodernism may in part be seen as a response to *devolution* of dominant organizations. Instances of such devolution occur when a major firm transforms former departments into independent companies or a large government agency hires contractors to perform its functions. Postmodernism, in addition, can be interpreted as a response to the blunting of traditional focuses of conflict (such as labor versus management) and the emergence of new conflicts (such as those based on gender and ethnicity). Should these trends become more pronounced in the coming years, so will the relevance of postmodernism to organization theory.

Common Themes

Several of the theories summarized above, although distinct in specific focus, share common elements. The functional nature of organizations—their ability to provide value to their members and the broader society—is clear in transaction cost theory and rational systems theory. Both these theories emphasize the payoff obtained from formal organization. Transaction cost theory recognizes value in reduced cost associated with business dealings. Rational systems theory fundamentally conceives of organizations as functional tools, arrays of components logically interconnected in a manner consistent with the needs of task performance.

A number of the theories discussed above can be placed within the category of *open systems* theory. The concept of open systems recognizes that organizations cannot function in a manner independent of their surroundings. Interaction with the external environment takes place continuously. The open systems concept appears most clearly in contingency, institutional, and network theory. Contingency theory attributes importance to the organization's specific goals in determining its structure. Yet this theory also takes note of factors in the surrounding society, such as technological development and political climate. Institutional theory recognizes the importance of an organization's internal history, which gives rise to practices valued in themselves rather than for clearly functional purposes. But institutional theory also highlights the importance of external stakeholders. Network theory is most explicitly oriented toward an open systems outlook. This theory sees the organization's internal thinking and structure as strongly influenced by its relationships with other organizations.

Followers of both critical and humanistic theory are concerned with conflict. However, each theory's approach to conflict is different. Critical theory believes that employees have interests fundamentally opposed to those of owners and managers. Humanistic theory believes potential conflicts to be avoidable through recognition of the worker's personal needs and adjustment of the organization's practices to these needs. While the critical theorist looks to fundamental reform if not revolution as a solution to conflict, humanistic theory looks to the benefits specialist and industrial psychologist.

Analytical Perspectives

Despite its value, the elaborate and abstract nature of theory can inhibit its practical application. But most if not all theories of organization support themes introduced in Chapters 1 and 2: function, environment, and conflict. As basic *analytical perspectives,* these themes should serve as the beginning points for understanding organizations. Each receives support not only from major theories of organization, but from the classics of social thought.

Organizational Function

The concept of function is one of the oldest in the social sciences[36] and retains the interest of social scientists in many specialties.[37,38] The concept is consistent with the emphasis placed in Chapter 1 on contributions made by formal organizations to the achievement of collective goals. Using the perspective of organizational function, a person observing an organization asks what benefit the organization might obtain from a particular structural feature, practice, or individual.

Of the theories discussed above, transaction cost theory and rational systems theory place the most emphasis on organizational function. Under both theories, organizations may be characterized as existing for an explicit purpose. Closely associated with this is the implication that all features and processes within an organization contribute to some dimension of its functioning.

In the history of social analysis, the search for function is often connected with Emile Durkheim, who, like Weber, contributed to the founding of sociology. Examining aboriginal societies at the end of the 19th century, Durkheim interpreted myths, symbols, and religious formulations as contributing to a society's basic self-conception and internal solidarity.[39] Religion, then, had a concrete function above and beyond the spiritual message it contained.

Focusing primarily on the search for function as a tool of social analysis has been given the label *functionalism*. It is possible to think of Durkheim himself as an adherent of this school. Functionalism became the dominant approach to social analysis among American social scientists in the 1950s and 1960s. Talcott Parsons of Harvard University, whose writings schematized society's diverse elements into cleanly interlocking categories, was perhaps the leading exponent of this approach.[40] The theory fit well with the quiescent and socially conservative era in which it was formulated. According to this perspective, most, if not all, practices carried out in society could be interpreted as meeting an identifiable need.

Discovering the function of a particular practice in an organization is often straightforward. In the Karimojong herding organization cited in Chapter 1, for example, the practice of bringing elders on long treks may be economically inefficient. But their presence serves the crucial function of managing disputes among strangers.

Modern social scientists address the question of social function with caution and are often critical of functionalism. Their criticism is based, in part, on a belief that functionalism fosters acceptance of undesirable practices. Most people today would disapprove of a woman's receiving lower compensation than a man receives for the same work. Yet such a practice may be interpreted as functional, allowing products or services to be offered to consumers at a lower cost. The practice, of course, would be dysfunctional for the women and their families.

At its core, the modern critique of functionalism asserts that "one can always find a function for anything."[41] Within an organization, a practice may be found functional not for the organization as a whole, but, for example, for management at the expense of workers, or directors at the expense of stockholders. Practices functional within an organization, furthermore, may be costly to the outside society, as when an inefficient government agency provides its employees with stable jobs but offers substandard service to the public. Critics comment, furthermore, that functionalism obscures injustice and conflict within an organization.

Still, seeking to identify the function of practices observed in an organization can help explain why they take place. In the sense that it is used here, organizational function is intended as a guide to asking questions about an organization. To identify a function is not to justify a practice. But asking what the function of a practice may be can promote understanding.

Environment

Like theories that emphasize the identification of function, perspectives emphasizing the environment in which organizations develop and operate enjoy a long and distinguished history. Environment in this sense includes historical, social, economic, and political dimensions, and perhaps others as well. The concept of organizations as open systems, consistent with contingency, institutional, and network theory, has been used by organizational researchers for many years.[42]

That organizations need human and material resources from outside their boundaries and provide goods and services to the outside community is obvious. Less obvious, however, is the degree to which outside forces influence the internal features and processes of the organization. The preceding chapter of this book hinted at the open system perspective. It explored the influence of interpersonal relationships spanning the organization's boundaries. It identified effects of broader social forces. It paid special attention to the mental life of an organization's members. Although the individuals concerned are "within" the organization, their needs, values, and dispositions are shaped by forces in the broader environment.

Researchers have commented that organizations require flexibility to deal with environmental pressures.[43] This perspective finds application among students of government who report that the politics and the values of administrators on the state level affect the actions of federal agencies.[44] Studies provide numerous examples of the effect of environmental factors on organizational change.[45] Of immediate significance, the contextual or open systems perspective serves as a tool for understanding the impact of readily available electronic communication among work groups and across organizational boundaries.[46]

Organizations, then, bear the mark of history and structure themselves in a manner consistent with the values and economics of the surrounding society. But the manner in which an organization relates to its environment is not merely one of response. Many organizations take an active role in modifying or even determining the politics, economics, and historical development of the society that surrounds them.

Conflict

While many, and perhaps most, characteristics of an organization may in fact contribute to cohesion, coordination, and task accomplishment, organizations are seldom simply venues of productive harmony. Cohesion and coordination may be the rationale of formal organization. But organizations are also places where ill will, competition, and struggle may almost always be expected.

Conflict of an interpersonal nature is familiar to almost everyone. Individuals lock horns over office space, personnel, and money. Disagreements arise over how best to do a job or solve a problem. Conflicts within organizations may involve disputes between departments and units. Technically trained individuals may chronically differ in outlook from business-oriented personnel.

Yet, *interpersonal* conflict may be neither the most basic nor the most significant form of conflict observable in an organization. Gender and ethnicity may become the focus of conflict, as women and minorities are excluded from leadership positions. Individuals stuck in positions that do not utilize their talents and skills, or who experience the organizational climate as hopeless or "dehumanizing," feel themselves in conflict with the structure that surrounds them. Individuals exposed to adverse stimuli from these sources experience conflict not with other members, but with the organization itself.

The most profound conflict within an organization arises from competition for control of the use to which an organization, in whole or in part, is put. An organization's leadership may develop interests different from those of the rank and file, and restrict their followers' input and access to information. Elites, whether members of the formal leadership or not, may seek to utilize the organization's resources for purposes they alone favor. High-level executives and members of governing boards may channel profits into their own pockets rather than those of either workers or stockholders. Zealous and skilled subgroups may capture a union or environmental organization and employ its assets to support a candidate or movement disliked by most members.

Applying Theories and Perspectives

A very broad range of thinking has been applied in theorizing about organizations. It is conceivable that every human discipline might contribute to understanding in this field. In addition to the traditional social sciences, disciplines such as applied mathematics and cybernetics have added their voice.

It is important to understand that each of the theories described here has explanatory power in a particular area. Table 3.1, above, summarizes the central contribution of each. Rational systems theory does a good job at explaining the organization's fundamental, static features. Both contingency and institutional theory help explain the differences among organizations and the importance of the organization's environment. Transaction cost theory provides historical perspective. Critical theory emphasizes the possibility that today's formal organizations exact costs that, while usually overlooked, can be great indeed.

Rather than attempting to identify the strongest theory of organization, it often makes sense to use individual theories on a selective basis. Specific theories may be profitably applied, in situations where they seem to have their greatest explanatory power. For some readers, this picking-and-choosing approach may seem intellectually unsatisfying. Yet, theories capable of explaining everything in a comprehensive manner are wanting, not only in the social sciences but in the natural and physical sciences as well.

Alternatively, a number of theories may have equally valid applicability to a given situation or problem. In such instances, different theories may complement each other. Social situations are by nature complex. The applicability of multiple theories and diverse perspectives illustrates this complexity.

Recall, for example, the experience of Frank Peace, presented in Chapter 2. Peace had extensive experience and skill as a manager. But he encountered stiff resistance in his attempt to manage an experimental synthetic fuel facility.

Contingency theory offers an explanation. In earlier assignments, Peace had managed highly standardized production, where explicit direction of all personnel made sense. Achievement of the experimental plant's objectives, however, presented workers with the need to independently assess and solve problems. Institutional theory contributes a second interpretation. Employees had developed expectations and values over time that had attained high legitimacy. Peace's order-giving style was perceived as incompatible with the workers' expectations of being able to exercise independence and creativity. The presence of scientists and engineers lends itself to an application of

Table 3.1   A Summary of Major Theories of Organization

Theory	Central Concern	Key Application Area
Transaction Cost	Efficiency of economic transactions	Business organizations
Rational System	Goal attainment	Stable, purposive organizations
Contingency	Environmental uncertainty	Organizations in changing environments
Institutional	Internal climate and social environment	Organizations needing legitimacy, accommodation with outside forces
Network	Exchange of information and resources	Systems of interlinked organizations
Critical	Social conflict	Social dominance in and by organizations
Humanistic	Compatibility of individual and organizational needs	Labor-intensive organizations

network theory. These personnel doubtless belonged to networks of other professionals and shared their valuation of independent scientific reasoning. Critical theorists might add that Peace's initial regime merely reflected a society-wide tendency to "disempower" or "deprofessionalize"[47] a traditionally elite category of employees. Finally, Peace's ultimate solution—a program of direct communication between himself and his subordinates—lies squarely in the camp of the humanistic school.

In a similar manner, multiple theories might be used to explain a great many of the examples and situations presented in the chapters to come. Many readers, though, may find the actual workings of organizations, opportunities to improve organizational operations, and effects of organizations on individual lives of greater interest. This book, in fact, focuses on concrete questions of this nature. Still, theory is necessary for truly understanding any given organization. Because the three analytical perspectives presented above capture common themes of several distinct theories, they provide a convenient means for adding a theoretical overview to discussions of specific organizational mechanisms and issues. Many of the following chapters conclude with an application of these analytical perspectives. Beyond this, readers are encouraged to identify individual theories that apply to the concrete material that follows and to draw lessons from them.

Issues and Applications

Knowledge of theory can help a person better understand his or her experience in an organization. Consistent with the perspective of this book, theory can help broaden an individual's understanding of his or her personal challenges. Theory promotes this understanding by suggesting realities that transcend individual organizations.

- Dedicated to helping people with emotional problems, a young man obtains a master's degree in psychiatric social work. After five years in the field, however, he feels he has never been sufficiently effective. Although he has worked for three public mental health agencies, this feeling has dogged him from job to job. The young man should consider the likelihood that most, if not all, public mental health agencies suffer from similar challenges: insufficient and unsteady funding, high case-loads, and turnover of professional staff. Homogeneity among these organizations—and hence in the young man's experience—likely results from the fact that the organizations all belong to the same network of public mental health agencies.

- A woman pursues a finance degree, expecting to find high-paying work in a large corporation. Upon graduation, she is able to find openings in small consulting firms. Large corporations have found it too expensive to hire in-house personnel in her field, since "transaction costs" such as hiring and direct supervision have become too high.

- Among administrative agencies of a large state government, corrections officers in the state prison system receive steady increases in pay and benefits, while personnel elsewhere face pay freezes and cutbacks. One explanation of this observation might argue that the corrections officers' favored treatment performs a function for the state, attracting and retaining personnel for disagreeable and dangerous work. Alternatively, conflict theory might argue that the corrections officers have merely applied effective pressure on decision makers through their union and their lobbyists. According to the conflict perspective, the corrections officers' success has come at a cost to other state employees as well as the state's taxpayers.

Chapter Review and Major Themes

Theory, though often dismissed as impractical, has value for both the researcher and the practitioner. Theories are sets of consistent, mutually reinforcing statements about a phenomenon that include or imply a central principle or concern. Theories help observers grasp the big picture and ask appropriate questions. This chapter focuses on seven major theories, each of which has value in explaining a different set of facts and problems. Analytical perspectives such as organizational function, environment, and conflict are not theories themselves. But, reflecting key theoretical contributions, they readily lend themselves to numerous applications. Although no theory offers a complete explanation of organizations, all can contribute to the observer's understanding.

Discussion Questions

1. Of the major theories summarized in this chapter, which would be the most valuable in explaining the operations and challenges of organizations with which you are most familiar?

2. To what degree are the issues raised by critical theory valid today?

3. Are there important organizational issues that none of the theories considered here adequately address?

4. How useful are theories of organization to the concerns of managers in actual organizations? Illustrate with examples.

5. To what extent does organization theory explain the individual's acceptance of or resistance to the constraints imposed by organizations?

References

1. Williams, J., & Parkman, S. (2003). On humans and the environment. *Human Studies, 26*(4), 449–460.

2. Schlossberg, D. (1998). Researching the pluralist universe. *Political Research Quarterly, 51*(3), 583–615.

3. Ioannides, S. (2003). Keynesian comparative economics. *American Journal of Economics and Sociology, 62*(3), 533–566.

4. Coase, R. H. (1937). The nature of the firm. *Economica, 4*, 386–405.

5. Williamson, O. E. (1975). *Markets and hierarchies: Analysis and antitrust implications.* New York: Free Press.

6. Barney, J. B., & Hesterly, W. (1996). Organizational economics: Understanding the relationship between organizations and economic analysis. In S. R. Clegg, C. Hardy, & W. R. Nord (Eds.), *Handbook of organization studies* (pp. 115–147). London: Sage.

7. Weber, M. (1972). Bureaucracy. In H. H. Gerth & C. W. Mills (Eds.), *From Max Weber: Essays in sociology* (pp. 196–244). New York: Oxford University Press.

8. Reed, M. (1996). Organizational theory: A historically contested terrain. In S. R. Clegg, C. Hardy, & W. R. Nord (Eds.), *Handbook of organization studies* (pp. 31–66). London: Sage.

9. Lawrence, P. R., & Lorsch, J. W. (1967). *Organization and environment: Managing differentiation and integration.* Boston: Graduate School of Business Administration, Harvard University.

10. Galbraith, J. (1977). *Organization design.* Reading, MA: Addison-Wesley.

11. Hall, R. H. (1987). *Organizations: Structure, process, and outcomes.* Englewood Cliffs, NJ: Prentice Hall.

12. Selznick, P. (1949). *TVA and the grass roots.* Berkeley: University of California Press.

13. Doreian, P., & Woodard, K. L. (1999). Local and global institutional processes. In S. B. Bacharach, S. B. Andrews, & D. Knoke (Eds.), *Research in the sociology of organizations: Networks in and around organizations.* Stamford, CT: JAI Press.

14. DiMaggio, Powell W. (1983). The iron cage revisited: Institutional isomorphism and collective rationality in organizational fields. *American Sociological Review, 48*, 147–160.

15. Selznick, P. (1992). *The moral commonwealth*. Berkeley: University of California Press.

16. Knoke, D. (2001). *Changing organizations: Business networks in the new political economy*. Boulder, CO: Westview Press.

17. Krackhardt, D., & Hanson, J. R. (1993). Informal networks: The company behind the chart. *Harvard Business Review*, July–August: 104–111.

18. Cross, R., & Prusak, L. (2002). The people who make organizations go—or stop. *Harvard Business Review, 80*(6), 104–112.

19. Burt, R. (1976). Positions in social networks. *Social Forces, 55,* 93–112.

20. Batagelj, V. (1997). Notes on block modeling. *Social Networks, 19,* 143–155.

21. Marcuse, H. (1991). *One dimensional man: Studies in the ideology of advanced industrial society*. Boston: Beacon Press.

22. Habermas, J. (1987). *The theory of communicative action* (Vol. 2: *Lifeworld and system*) (T. McCarthy, Trans.). Boston: Beacon Press.

23. Deetz, S. (1994). The new politics of the workplace: Ideology and other unobtrusive controls. In H. Simons & M. Billings (Eds.), *After postmodernism: Restructuring ideology critique* (pp. 172–199). Thousand Oaks, CA: Sage.

24. Alvesson, M., & Willmott, H. (1996). *Making sense of management*. London: Sage.

25. Schumpeter, J. A. (1978). *Can capitalism survive?* New York: Harper & Row.

26. Weber, M. 1997. *The theory of social and economic organization*. New York: Free Press.

27. Dahrendorf, R. (1959). *Class and class conflict in industrial society*. Stanford, CA: Stanford University Press.

28. Wuthnow, R. (1989). *Communities of discourse: Ideology and social structure in the Reformation, the Enlightenment, and European socialism*. Cambridge, MA: Harvard University Press.

29. Jex, S. M. (2002). *Organizational psychology: A scientist-practitioner approach*. New York: John Wiley & Sons.

30. Ghoshal, S., & Bartlett, C. A. (1997). *The individualized corporation*. New York: HarperBusiness.

31. Braverman, H. (1974). *Labor and monopoly capital: The degradation of work in the 20th century*. New York: Monthly Review Press.

32. Bird, A., & Wiersema, M. F. (1996). Underlying assumptions of agency theory for non-US settings. In P. A. Bamberger, M. Erez, & S. B. Bacharach (Eds.), *Research in the sociology of organizations: Cross-cultural analysis of organizations*. Greenwich, CT: JAI Press.

33. Wilson, E. O. (1975). *Sociobiology: The new synthesis*. Cambridge, MA: Harvard University Press.

34. Lounsbury, M., & Ventresca, M. (2003). The new structuralism in organizational theory. *Organization, 10*(3), 457–480.

35. Mills, T. L., Boylstein, C. A., & Lorean, S. (2001). Doing organizational culture in the Saturn Corporation. *Organization Studies, 22*(1), 117–143.

36. Merton, R. K. (1968). *Social theory and social structure*. New York: Free Press.

37. Demerath, J. N. (1996). Who now debates functionalism? From systems, change, and conflict to "culture, choice, and praxis." *Sociological Forum, 11*(2), 333–345.

38. Burrows, C. P. (1996). From functionalism to cultural studies: Manifest ruptures and latent continuities. *Communication Theory, 6*(1), 88–103.

39. Durkheim, E. (2001). *Elementary forms of religious life*. New York: Oxford University Press.

40. Parsons, T. (1951). *The social system*. Glencoe, IL: Free Press.

41. Collins, R. (1994). *Four sociological traditions.* New York: Oxford University Press.
42. Scott, W. R. (1987). *Organizations: Rational, natural, and open systems.* Englewood Cliffs, NJ: Prentice Hall.
43. Quinn, R. E., & Rohrbaugh, J. (1983). A special model of effectiveness criteria: Toward a competing values approach to organizational analysis. *Management Science, 28,* 363–377.
44. Keiser, L. R., & Soss, J. (1998). What good cause: Bureaucratic discretion and the politics of child support enforcement. *American Journal of Political Science, 42*(4), 1133–1156.
45. Yan, A. M., & Louis, M. R. (1999). The migration of organizational functions to the work unit: Buffering, spanning, and bringing up boundaries. *Human Relations, 52*(1), 25–47.
46. Kiesler, S., & Sproull, L. (1992). Group decision making and communication technology. *Organizational Behavior and Human Decision Processes, 52,* 96–123.
47. Haug, M. R. (1975). The deprofessionalization of everyone. *Sociological Focus, 8*(3), 197–213.

PART II

Means of Cohesion and Coordination

Key functions of organizations include (a) promoting social cohesion among members and (b) coordinating the efforts of multiple individuals in a manner capable of achieving objectives. Observers and managers of organizations require an understanding of how organizations achieve the required cohesion and coordination.

Two basic mechanisms are important in enabling organizations to do this. The first mechanism is a system of roles. Adopting the familiar theatrical term, social scientists designate as a *social role* the acts, communication linkages, and ways of thinking a person is expected to adopt in a primary group or organization. Behavior that takes place according to social roles ensures that functions required for the organization's objectives are carried out.

The second mechanism is known as *organizational structure*. Organizational structure refers to a pattern of linkages among roles. Occupants of any given role are expected to provide (or receive) communications and resources only from occupants of certain other roles. Coordination of roles in this manner helps achieve the organization's objectives.

Both roles and structure can be experienced as constraints on individual thinking and behavior. Organizations must possess means for inducing people to put up with these constraints. Such means include (a) *rewards*, (b) *imperative force*, and (c) *organizational culture*.

Rewards comprise resources capable of enabling members of an organization to meet their personal needs. Rewards may include salary, benefits, prestige, and opportunities for personal growth. Punishment constitutes *negative* reward, the withholding or withdrawal of personally valued resources or conditions. Organizations reward their members for appropriate role performance and adherence to structure.

Unlike rewards, imperative forces impel individuals to set aside their personal needs and preferences in favor of the will of others. Imperative forces include primarily power and authority, and more rarely discipline and coercion. Supervisors in all organizations issue orders and subordinates are expected to obey irrespective of the supervisor's ability to allocate positive or negative rewards for each act.

Organizational culture, finally, includes beliefs and values shared widely throughout the organization. These beliefs and values help members accept their roles, the surrounding structure, and the organization's system of rewards, punishment, and imperative force. Organizational culture helps members identify actions that, though not specified in their roles, promote the organization's objectives. Rituals, symbols, and myths are visible in most formal organizations. These artifacts and practices express, reinforce, and perpetuate underlying beliefs and values.

Ideally, roles, structure, rewards, imperative forces, and organizational culture reinforce each other. All these mechanisms should act in a consistent manner to influence the individual's thinking and actions in the organization. However, such seamless consistency seldom occurs in actual organizations. The analytical perspectives of environment, function, and conflict help explain both the positive contributions and the challenges that means of cohesion and coordination present to organizations.

An understanding of how organizations achieve cohesion and coordination underscores the fact that such seemingly concrete entities as roles and structure exist largely in members' minds. Modern organizations seldom employ physical constraint or motivate cooperation through coercive threats. Voluntary collaboration, encouraged and channeled through appropriate mechanisms, is ultimately stronger and more stable.

The means used by organizations to achieve cohesion and coordination, finally, are imperfect. Although individuals may outwardly conform, they remain free to question, accept, or reject their roles, the organization's structure, and the forces that support them. Individuals and groups find ways to limit the organization's control over them and to press for advantages within it.

CHAPTER 4

Social Roles in Organizations

Learning Objective

To understand the social role as a means for directing individual capacities and efforts toward achieving organizational objectives.

Principles

○ An organization's principal challenge is to coordinate the actions of individual human beings. The organization promotes coordination by assigning *roles* to its members. Roles are prescriptions for thinking and behavior. These prescriptions involve both duties and a range of acceptable behavior.

○ Roles in organizations are directly or indirectly linked. In a well-functioning organization, an individual's performance of his or her role contributes to performance of all other roles. Ideally, all roles help achieve the organization's objectives.

○ Neither assignment nor performance of roles within organizations takes place automatically or with complete reliability. The organization faces a challenge in effectively transmitting roles to individual members. Often, individual members attempt to adapt the roles they receive to their own needs and objectives.

○ It is often the case that individuals need to balance their role performance against personal values, objectives, and interests outside the organization's boundaries.

The Need for Roles

Chapters 2 and 3 of this book have described a large number of influences on the thinking and behavior of individuals. These chapters have emphasized two major categories: mental life and social forces. Neither set of influences originates primarily within the boundaries of an organization. The basic thinking of individual human beings, then, is not necessarily consistent with the needs of the organizations to which they belong. The predispositions and orientations of individuals, in fact, may contradict the needs of their organizations.

Key elements of mental life may undermine the purposes of an organization. According to Maslow, people have a natural need for safety and security. Some organizations, however, depend on their members' willingness to expose themselves to risk. Such organizations, of course, include armies. More mainstream examples include firms that trade financial instruments (bonds, futures, etc.) for internal profit. These firms encourage the traders they employ to take risks and reward those who are successful.

Social forces often contradict the needs of organizations. Many Americans, for example, subscribe to the "experiential" lifestyle described in Chapter 3. This lifestyle encourages suspicion of big organizations. People under its influence shun mainstream styles and entertainment. Still, experientials often take jobs in highly conventional companies, impelled to do so by the need to earn a salary. Large numbers of conventionally oriented business and government agencies have staffs that include many individuals who are, in their basic thinking, rebellious.

It is often said that no two people are exactly alike. The same may be true of any two members selected at random within an organization. Mental life is unique to each individual: no two people have precisely the same needs, traits, and values. Although social forces affect large numbers of people in similar ways, it is unusual to find two individuals whose interpretation of the culture and institutions around them is identical. Superficially, people in an organization may look and dress alike; they may take the same oaths and recite the same slogans. But they are ultimately diverse in their thinking and divergent in their objectives.

In modern society, people seem more likely to move off in widely different directions than to act in concert toward a commonly held goal. How, then, do organizations focus the energy of numerous individuals on achieving a set of organizational objectives? The practice in organizations of assigning *roles* to their members provides part of the explanation.

The Concept of Social Role

Roles in Society

The use of the term *role* by social scientists strongly resembles its use in everyday language. Roles reflect, in part, what people see as the expectations others have of them in a group, family, or organization. At the same time, roles embody the way individuals themselves believe they should act and feel. An individual's role takes shape in his or her mind by responding to social cues or emulating the behavior of significant individuals in their lives. Both classical and contemporary sociologists identify the individual's role or roles as crucial elements of the individual's self-definition.[1,2]

An individual's social role is much like a role played by an actor in the theater. The actor receives a script containing lines to recite. The script implies the personality of the character the role portrays. The actor or actress creates this personality on stage. Theatrical roles are subject to significant interpretation by individual actors, and the speech patterns and mannerisms associated with most are likely to vary from production to production.

Similarly, ordinary people adopt the words and gestures prescribed by their roles. Like thespians, people in their day-to-day roles wear costumes consistent with their roles: suits for businesspeople, white coats for health professionals, uniforms for police officers, bus drivers, and soldiers. As often happens in the theater, ordinary people tend to carry out their roles in the manner they consider most personally advantageous.

The concept of role is widely employed by people concerned with broad social issues. In such applications, role is often conceived as something imposed on individuals rather than voluntarily adopted. *Sex roles,* for example, have received interpretations of this kind from social scientists. Despite their newfound independence and assertiveness, it is reported, women much more often than men express a willingness to adjust career aspirations to family needs.[3]

Roles in Organizations

Within organizations, roles assigned to the membership constitute a principal mechanism for promoting coordination of effort. In comparison with roles in broader society, the script associated with an organizational role may at first appear highly explicit. When taking a job, for example, the employee may receive a written job description, listing the specific duties for which the jobholder is responsible. Typically, work organizations develop job descriptions for use in recruiting applicants for the position. Managers in large organizations draw up job descriptions specifying the duties associated with new positions. Often, these descriptions are developed for approval by staff specialists or higher-level executives. The law requires most public agencies to develop job descriptions for every position. Union contracts often specify duties required (and excluded) from every occupational title cited in their contracts.

Typically, though, an individual's role extends far beyond a listing of his or her job duties. An organizational role suggests, and may specify, the people with whom the role-holder (sometimes called the *incumbent* or *focal person*) is allowed to initiate contact. Military personnel are usually prohibited from initiating contact with officers more than one level above them in rank. Similarly, an employee in a business firm or public agency goes "over the head" of his or her supervisor only at great personal risk.

A role may suggest, or even explicitly specify, the manner in which the focal person addresses others or is addressed by them. In court, lawyers address the judge as "your honor." Modern police officers and welfare agency personnel are instructed to address members of the public as "Ms. Jones" and "Mr. Green" rather than "Sandra" or "Willie." Subordinates are expected to address executives as "Mr." or "Ms.," or, in less formal settings, by their initials. Secretaries, food service personnel, and maintenance workers are almost always addressed by their first names.

Perhaps more for cultural than for organizational reasons, roles are often associated with the personalities and appearance of their incumbents. Drill sergeants, traffic policemen, and construction foremen are expected to conduct business in a stern manner. Psychotherapists, anthropology professors, and retail salespeople are supposed to be friendly and interested in the needs of others. Bankers are expected to look prosperous. Cooks shouldn't be too thin.

Generally, a role provides the focal person with the orientation, information, and resources required to carry out a function required by the organization. Many role incumbents receive explicit instructions regarding their expected performance. But such instructions usually focus on concrete task performance. Even here they may be incomplete. The incumbent fully learns of his or her responsibilities through informal as well as formal means. The trappings of role-related behavior (self-presentation, clothing) are almost always acquired informally. The people with whom the focal person may initiate contact and to whom he or she is expected to respond are not always specified in a job description.

People often learn about roles well before they take them on. Future incumbents of a role observe its present incumbents. Mentors and sponsors grooming junior colleagues for leadership roles point out aspects of such roles not known to outsiders.

Roles in organizations may change over time. As new people come into an organization, for example, the mix of skills among them may change. A role incumbent may be asked to take on new responsibilities or be relieved of old ones. Some role incumbents may seek ways to expand their range of responsibilities and contacts. Such augmentation often reflects a strategy for increasing influence and promoting future opportunity. Other role incumbents may try to reduce their range of duties. Reduction of this kind decreases the effort required for job performance.

Roles People Play: Three Days in the Life of George F. Nolan

To illustrate the operation of roles in an organization, consider Mr. George F. Nolan, assistant principal of the Hamilton Middle School in Los Mesas, a small city in California. Both the city and the assistant principal's name are fictitious. But though fictional, the story that follows illustrates tasks and challenges known to occur among actual school administrators.[4]

Mr. Nolan arrives at his office at 8:00 a.m. on a Monday morning. He begins his work by preparing several documents. First, he prepares a list of announcements to be made to pupils at the morning assembly. Second, he prepares an agenda for a faculty meeting scheduled for the lunch hour. Third, he prepares a memorandum for the principal on an expected budget shortfall for the current year.

At 10:00 a.m., Nolan goes to the school auditorium. He stands solemnly as the kids salute the flag and sing the National Anthem. Then he walks erectly to the podium. He waits for complete silence and clears his throat. "Good morning, boys and girls," he begins.

Nolan congratulates the soccer team for a recent victory. He notes an increase in dress code violations and reminds the audience that violators will be "severely penalized." He announces a summer science program for which some of the kids may be eligible. Then he introduces Lieutenant Plunkett, school liaison officer from the Los Mesas Police Department, who will present a lecture and slide show on the dangers of drug abuse.

After the lights dim Nolan quietly leaves the auditorium and returns to his office.

This vignette illustrates several elements of Nolan's role. His job description, as published by the Los Mesas School District, lists several concrete responsibilities. The assistant principal's job description includes preparing budget reports for the principal and the school district: hence the memorandum on the fiscal shortfall. The job description also includes responsibility for student discipline. This explains Nolan's comments at the assembly on dress code violations.

Other elements of the role Nolan is carrying out this morning do not appear in his job description. Officially, Mr. Ludlow, the principal, is required to convene faculty meetings. This includes developing agendas. But Ludlow's Rotary Club meets at noon on the first Monday of each month, the time when faculty meetings are regularly scheduled. Shortly after Nolan's appointment as assistant principal two years ago, Mr. Ludlow asked him to convene and chair the faculty meetings. The principal confided that he does not like to meet with the faculty as a group.

Nolan got the idea that he should open the proceedings at assembly by watching the person who held the job before him. Before his first assembly as assistant principal, Mr. Nolan checked with the music teacher who led the singing of the National Anthem. She raised no issue regarding his appearance on the podium immediately following the Anthem's last bar. Several previous assistant principals had followed this procedure, she said.

Nolan also knew that he could slip away as soon as the formal program started by watching his predecessor. The preceding assistant principal had exited quietly, through a side door, as soon as the next event began. So Nolan took the opportunity to return to his office and catch up on paperwork.

Back at his desk, Nolan receives a call from downtown. It is Mr. Ludlow, who is attending a school board meeting. This board, whose members are elected by the city's voters, sets policy for the school district. Ludlow needs disenrollment figures for the previous school year. Nolan promises to fax them immediately.

The faculty meeting begins at noon. Nolan acts as chair. The principal's secretary takes notes. Nolan announces a new procedure for teacher evaluation. For the first time, evaluation of teacher performance will be "results-based." Teachers will be evaluated on the basis of students' standardized test scores in reading and mathematics.

"I don't think that's very fair," comments a woman teacher.

"You give me all the problem kids and then . . ." grumbles a man.

"This may represent a violation of the work rules provisions of our contract!" declares another teacher, the union representative. She draws a cellular phone from her purse and stalks out.

"Yeah," mumble a few others.

"Remember," says Nolan, "Neither Mr. Ludlow not I make the rules. Our hands are tied by the school district. I will be scheduling personal meetings with all faculty."

Other business is routine. The United Way campaign is announced. Short discussions take place regarding responsibility for cleaning the microwave oven in the teachers' lounge and ordering bottled water. The meeting adjourns at 1:00.

Ludlow returns at 2:00 and Nolan goes to his office. Nolan gives him the budget documents and explains details.

"OK," says Ludlow, "I'll take these downtown," meaning that he will discuss the figures personally with the superintendent of schools, the top official responsible for managing the school system.

(Continued)

(Continued)

> *Then Ludlow says, "Oh, George, are you still interested in the Citizens' Advisory Commission meeting tonight?"*
>
> *"Sure," answers Nolan.*
>
> *"Thanks, man," says Ludlow. "That gets me out of a jam. I need to go to a Civic Club function. And we need an official at the Commission."*
>
> *Back in his office, Nolan receives a visit from the union representative. She brings a copy of the contract with some passages underlined. Nolan scans the pages and says, "I don't think I have the authority to handle this. Let me call Human Resources."*
>
> *Nolan calls the Director of Human Resources at the Las Mesas School District who says that, indeed, his office is handling grievances over the new teacher evaluation scheme. Relieved, Nolan writes a memo to the union representative.*
>
> *Late that afternoon, Nolan calls home. His 11-year old daughter answers. He says, "Please tell your mother that I won't be home 'til late tonight."*
>
> *"Oh, Dad, but you promised!" whines the girl. "My dance recital is tonight!"*
>
> *She calls her mother to the phone, who says, exasperated,*
>
> *"Oh, George! Not again!"*

These events illustrate dynamic features of Nolan's role as assistant principal. His formal job description included reporting on attendance figures. But the job description had not included chairing faculty meetings. Principals before Ludlow had done that themselves. Ludlow, however, had asked Nolan to take it over.

Nolan's job description had said nothing about working with the teacher's union. This morning's flap made him worry. Interested in future career advancement, Nolan was eager to take on additional responsibility. But work with the union representative would have taken a lot of time. The new, results-based teacher evaluation process might give rise to significant conflict. Nolan didn't want to be in the middle. He was relieved when the school board's personnel man said he would handle the matter.

Nolan's desire to take on additional responsibility had caused some conflict with Ludlow in the past. A year or so earlier, Nolan had called the superintendent of schools to talk about a budget matter. He hadn't reached the superintendent, succeeding only in leaving a message with his secretary.

But Ludlow had been furious. The superintendent had called him upon seeing Nolan's message. Raising his voice and pounding on his desk, Ludlow made it plain that only he was to communicate with the superintendent. Thereafter, Nolan merely brought budget matters to Ludlow's attention.

Likewise, only Ludlow attended school board meetings. On several occasions, Nolan had volunteered to take his place. But Ludlow had always said something like, "I think I'd better go this time."

Nolan realized that visibility was essential for career advancement. Having your name known around town was more important than willingness to take on new assignments. But Ludlow, also eager for advancement, jealously guarded his contacts.

Ludlow, though, asked Nolan to represent him at the Citizens' Advisory Commission. The Commission, established a few years earlier, was instituted to encourage citizen involvement in education and to help make the schools more responsive to local communities. Prominent citizens sometimes attended. The meeting might provide an opportunity for all-important exposure. To Nolan, this opportunity was important enough to justify disappointing his family.

> *After school, Nolan goes to a fast-food outlet for a quick dinner and then to the Citizens' Advisory Commission meeting. The meeting room is packed. School safety is the major agenda item. Nolan takes a seat in the front row.*

Open to the public, Commission meetings are the place where complaints are heard about the school system. All attendees are allowed 30 seconds to ask a question, raise an issue, or make a comment. A crosswalk accident has prompted tonight's interest in safety. A succession of parents take the microphone.

Someone with a child at Hamilton Middle School takes the rostrum. She demands to know why the school now has only one crossing guard. Years ago, she says, the school had three such guards.

Mr. Nolan answers that funding for crossing guards comes from the school's discretionary budget. A "discretionary budget," he explains, is a pool of funds from which each school may draw to meet local needs. In the past few years, parents have requested increased resources for the Arts and Dramatics program, leaving less money for crossing guards.

The parent mumbles something and sits down. Nolan is relieved. He is not called upon again. At 10:00 the meeting adjourns.

The next day, Nolan meets with a parent who demands that his daughter be placed in the Arts and Dramatics program. Nolan explains that all children take the standard Arts and Dramatics Aptitude Test, and the ones who score highest are invited to participate. The parent remarks that his daughter doesn't do well in testing situations and asks whether something can be done. Nolan says he will discuss this with the principal.

Later, a teacher ushers an 11-year-old girl into Nolan's office. The girl has regularly violated the dress code by wearing lipstick to class. Nolan tells her that lipstick is inappropriate for schoolgirls and will not be tolerated at Hamilton Middle School. Next time, she will be sent home.

That afternoon, Nolan asks Ludlow about the Arts and Dramatics program. Ludlow asks who the parent was. He thinks awhile and says, "OK, we'll let her in." Ludlow telephones the parent to tell him the good news.

It is easy to see why Ludlow asked Nolan to attend the Citizens' Advisory Commission meeting in his place. The Commission has no real power. It makes recommendations to the school board but cannot enforce them. School officials are expected to participate. But for many school officials, there is little to be gained personally. Comments expressed at the Commission meetings have little effect on the way the schools run. At these meetings, school officials risk "looking bad" if they say something unpopular with the public. They sound like "bureaucrats" when they refer to rules and regulations.

Nolan expected that an additional pupil or two could be admitted to the Arts and Dramatics Program. But he realized that such decisions were Ludlow's. He had been criticized in the past for giving special consideration. Ludlow reserves the privilege of handing out favors for himself and does not hesitate to accept credit.

Giving the lipstick-wearing 11-year-old a talking-to about the school dress code is clearly part of Nolan's role. His formal job description includes the area of student discipline. Enforcement of dress and behavior codes constitutes a humdrum part of the assistant principal's job.

Nolan goes home on Tuesday evening. Over dinner, his wife comments that he is spending too many evenings away. His daughter asks why he didn't attend the dance recital. "Everyone else's father was there," she complains.

On Wednesday morning, Nolan is off to work. He pauses to say goodbye to his wife and children. The children, already dressed for school, are eating breakfast. He notices that his daughter is wearing lipstick. He realizes that every school's dress code prohibits the cosmetic. Maybe he should tell her to remove it. He opens his mouth to speak. Then, reconsidering, he turns and walks out to his car.

(Continued)

(Continued)

Analysis of Mr. Nolan's Role

Mr. Nolan has brought to his job a variety of individual needs and objectives. But the role he accepts in the work organization channels his activity into directions that contribute to that organization's mission. Since the organization is a school, it may be assumed that its mission is education. But the organization has additional objectives. These include keeping parents satisfied, a necessity for protecting faculty and administrators from disruptive criticism. This explains the importance to officials of attending public meetings and occasionally distributing favors.

In addition, some of the organization's resources are directed toward the personal needs of its leadership and staff. The leaders and functionaries of most organizations redirect at least part of the organization's focus toward their needs. The principal's desire to maintain connections with important segments of the community and to make himself look good, then, have importance for the organization as a whole. Teachers, of course, see the school as the source of their livelihood. Hence, the union, which represents them, is sensitive to changes in the organization's functioning and its management practices regarding teachers.

Every feature of Nolan's role contributes to achievement of the school's diverse objectives. The function of Nolan's managing budgets, monitoring attendance, and carrying out disciplinary procedures is to ensure stable, routine operation within the school building. "Taking the heat" for the principal at the Citizens' Advisory Commission meetings helps the principal avoid challenges to his public image.

As in Nolan's story, the features of a role are dynamic. The basic content of a role may be formally specified, but actual responsibilities and patterns of action are established over time. A process of negotiation determines the content of many roles. With partial success, Nolan has negotiated for expansion of his role to allow visibility outside the school. Through successful negotiation, Ludlow has induced Nolan to accept the risky assignment as representative to the Commission.

Negotiation of Roles

Negotiation is an essential feature of exchange in human life. It is another word for "bargaining." More broadly speaking, negotiation is a process in which two individuals communicate to each other about what each is willing to do to help achieve a mutual objective.

The most familiar form of negotiation occurs in economic exchange. In this instance, each party states how much money he is willing to pay or accept. Each party shares a desire to close the sale.

Negotiation also takes place among incumbents of roles that require them to work together. One person states what he or she expects of the other, and the other responds negatively or affirmatively. Often, negotiation takes place without words. A superior, for example, may imply that certain actions would be appreciated and others not.

Table 4.1   Analysis of a Social Role: The Assistant Principal of a Middle School

Formal Role	Negotiated Role	Core Functions
Administer school budget	Attend Citizens' Advisory Committee meetings (+)	Administer school operations
Monitor attendance	Manage faculty affairs (+)	Protect the school from criticism
Carry out discipline procedures	Manage union contract (–)	Make the boss look good
Assist principal as needed	Interface with school board (–) Distribute special favors (–)	

Note on Column 2: (+) denotes element of role sought and added through negotiation; (–) denotes element of role sought through negotiation but not added.

Negotiation also takes place through experimentation. An individual seeking to alter his or her role merely alters his or her behavior. If the change is tolerated or encouraged by incumbents of other roles, the negotiation has been successful.

The table below provides an analysis of the features and dynamics of the social role in a formal organization. The table uses Nolan's role as assistant principal at Hamilton Middle School as an illustration. The *formal role* comprises officially assigned duties, actions, and areas of responsibility. On entry, people in formal organizations ordinarily see only formal roles, their own as well as those of others. The *negotiated role* includes a set of responsibilities and actions that are added to or subtracted from the formal role over time. Elements of the negotiated role are often deliberately sought by the focal person or incumbents of other roles.

Core function expresses the essential contribution people make to an organization through role-scripted activity. As described in Chapter 1, "function" constitutes the manner in which a person or practice helps an organization to operate, continue over time, and achieve objectives. Identifying the core function that a role serves for an organization provides an understanding of the role as a whole and the underlying rationale for its existence.

Core function can be difficult to identify through direct observation. Formal and negotiated roles are recognizable as concrete, observable actions by their incumbents. Core function must be inferred indirectly by watching people carry out their roles over time.

Different types of functions may be associated with a given role. Some functions can be characterized as manifest. *Manifest functions* are those that are visible, explicitly recognized, and official. Alternatively, many roles have *latent functions*. These are often invisible, ignored, or purposely kept secret. But latent functions are often more important than manifest ones.[5]

The core function of Assistant Principal Nolan's role includes both manifest and latent aspects. The manifest function of this role is to ensure that routine operations at Hamilton Middle School take place in a reliable manner. This role supports that of the principal, freeing him to concentrate on vital outside agencies. The assistant principal's role has latent functions as well. The core latent function may be to safeguard the principal's public image, advancing his career prospects.

It is not uncommon for employees in a work organization to encounter an executive whose function they cannot identify. Such an individual may have a title suggesting a formal role associated with a specific function, say, "director of market planning." But the individual in fact does nothing that resembles market planning. He or she dresses well, attends top management meetings, arrives at the office late, and leaves early.

Employees speculate that the executive is merely a close relative of the chief executive officer (CEO). But in fact, the executive has a personal network of great value to the firm. Whenever a problem with credit or government regulation arises, this executive knows whom to call. Although this executive has no identifiable role or function in the formal sense, his implicitly recognized role and latent function are of great value to the firm. His role may be characterized as that of "fixer."

In a fictional account of a manufacturing firm, Ritti and Funkhouser[6] describe an executive named Ted Shelby who continuously assumes responsibility for new and risky projects. Nearly all his projects fail. Employees wonder how an individual with such a questionable track record can keep from being fired. But Ritti and Funkhouser point out that Shelby's role is as a risk taker, hustler, and irritant. In the fictional account, an experienced organization member explains the latent features of Shelby's role:

> It is always easier to find a dozen reasons why something can't be done than to find one good way to do it. I don't know why this should be so but it is. . . . But one will never do anything unless he tries, so someone is necessary to get things stirred up—a shaker, a mover, an irritant. (**p. 150**)

When Shelby's projects fail, as they usually do, the company does not fire, but promotes him. According to the experienced observer, this confirms the importance of Shelby's role, no matter how invisible it may be to an outside observer:

> (T)here are certain projects that, from the perspective of top management, are too important not to take a crack at. That is where the value of a Shelby must be appreciated. Make no mistake, Ted knows how to bring people together and get the ball rolling. And yes, I know that he isn't so good at following through, but there are others to do that. You need someone who is willing and ready to take risks, to bet on the long shots—and also, you must protect him from the consequences of his failures.
>
> So when you find someone like Shelby with, say, a certain flair for getting risky projects underway, you protect him. . . . He's too valuable to go down with the ship. (**p. 153**)

Boundaries are an important feature of most social roles..Roles prohibit as well as mandate certain actions. In addition, the focal person plays his or her role only in connection with a limited array of others. Nolan, for example, does not challenge the principal's insistence that he alone maintain contact with the school board. Neither does he play his "assistant principal" role outside of school. Although he has just disciplined an 11-year-old for disobeying the dress code, he ignores a potential infraction by his daughter. Exercising school discipline at home would cause ill feelings. Such discipline is part of the role of the assistant principal of the school attended by Nolan's daughter.

Theoretical Perspectives on Roles

Observers of organizations have developed concepts useful in recognizing and analyzing roles. Acquaintance with associated terms and concepts helps people in organizations recognize the importance of roles in their own lives. Terms and concepts also provide a vocabulary to help people in organizations communicate about problems related to roles and formulate solutions.

Katz and Kahn, two social psychologists, have collected and published a widely used set of concepts and definitions of great value in understanding organizations.[7] They have defined roles in organizations as "mutually dependent prescriptions for behavior". They describe behavior occurring within roles as "recurring actions of an individual, appropriately interrelated with the repetitive activities of others so as to yield a predicable outcome". Katz and Kahn emphasize regularity of action within roles and interdependency among them.

The fictional case study of Hamilton Middle School focused on a single role, that of the assistant principal. Everyone else in the school occupies a role as well. Like the assistant principal's, the other roles prescribe regular, recurring actions and responsibilities, both assigned and negotiated.

Any two roles at the middle school may be seen as dependent on each other. Principal Ludlow's role performance depends on the role performance by the assistant principal. The principal could not attend to the outside liaison work in which he specializes without the assistant principal's management of the school's day-to-day operation in a routine, predictable manner. Likewise, the assistant principal counts on the principal to obtain needed resources, such as supplementary funding in the event of budget shortfalls.

It is easy to see why all roles in a school must be interdependent, extending through the teaching ranks and down to secretaries and maintenance personnel. Everyone in the building has his or her personal style and way of doing things. Some people try to expand their scope of works; others seek to reduce theirs. But the greater part of everyone's actions is scripted in a manner that (1) supports the actions of others and (2) protects others from interference and potential conflict. Generally, people know the actions expected of them on a day-to-day basis and the activities and interactions from which they are expected to refrain.

Beyond the basic idea of the organizational role, several concepts provide tools for understanding conditions and developments in actual organizations. These include role set, role expectations, role sending, received role, role episode, role ambiguity, the role episode, and role orientation.

Role Set

The concept of *role set* promotes an understanding of the manner in which roles fit together in an organization. *Role set* is defined as the set of role incumbents with whom the focal person interacts. Members of the focal person's role set are sometimes referred to as his or her *role others*.

Relationships at Hamilton Middle School illustrate the concept of role set. The assistant principal's role set includes teachers, secretaries, students, and Citizens' Advisory Board members. As made clear earlier, his role set does not include the school board's elected members, who make decisions for the school district, or the school board's top staff. The principal's role set includes school board members and staff, but neither students nor teachers.

Everyday life in organizations illustrates the importance of role set. The individual's position in an organization strongly influences the people with whom he or she is able to establish direct contact. The range of individuals with whom a focal person normally communicates is one of the "prescriptions for behavior" that define social roles.

Violations of this role prescription are potential causes of conflict. Recall the instance in which Assistant Principal Nolan placed a call to the superintendent of schools regarding a budget matter. He received stern instruction to refrain from such contact in the future. Nolan, the subordinate, learned that he might contact one of Ludlow's superiors only at the risk of being thought to have "gone over the boss's head." This is considered a serious infraction in many organizations.

Roles also impose limitations on the behavior of supervisors. The school board or superintendent would be unlikely to carry out performance reviews of individual teachers. Such actions would be considered "micromanagement," a practice frowned upon by modern administrators. Similarly, principals and assistant principals are hesitant to interfere with the day-to-day practice of individual teachers, as long as standard procedure is generally followed in their classrooms.

Role Expectations

Within the focal person's role set there is a general belief about what actions the role requires and where it is situated in the chain of communication. Typically, people form a consensus regarding proper actions and communication behavior for the incumbent of any given role. This consensus expresses role expectations. *Role expectations* in this sense are not those of the focal person. Rather, role expectations are what others expect of the person occupying a role.

In the Hamilton Middle School example, everyone in Nolan's role set expects him to discipline students, prepare statistical reports, and carry on faculty reviews. No one who knows the system (least of all his superior) expects him to communicate directly with the school board or superintendent of schools.

Role Sending

Role sending refers to the process by which members of a role set transmit their expectations to the focal person. Some of these instructions are transmitted via written directives. Written documents, such as a worker's job description or the bylaws of a club, may contain instructions of this kind. Often, people are given such documents when entering an organization and instructed to read and act consistently with them.

But communication in forms other than writing often plays a more important part in role sending. People directly instruct others on how to carry out their roles. They send information about their expectations by setting examples. These can be negative, as when a teacher or officer "makes an example" of a pupil or a soldier, exercising discipline for the instruction of other pupils or soldiers.

Successful incumbents of roles set positive examples for new occupants of the same or similar roles. Newcomers are likely to imitate the behavior of long-term occupants of their roles if these individuals have received visible rewards from the organization. Newcomers, furthermore, are likely to imitate people whose behavior appeals to their values. The term *role model*, which has evolved in everyday conversation, expresses the importance of imitation in the process of role sending.

Some of the most effective role sending takes place through informal mechanisms. Role sending, for example, may take place through humor or ridicule. The sociologist Smigel[8] provides an example from a Wall Street law firm. In this example, a young associate assumes that the firm's dark suit and necktie dress code will be relaxed on Fridays, as it is in many business settings. Appearing in sport jacket and slacks, the associate became the butt of jokes about "beginning the weekend early."

A feminist tells the story of a young woman beginning work in a foundry, historically an exclusively male work setting. The men in the shop instructed her to wear insulated gloves for an operation involving a hot metal object. She did as instructed but was scorched nevertheless. Though not injured, she experienced discomfort, as well as horselaughs from the men. "You're supposed to wear two pair for that procedure," they joked.

It is easy enough to assume that the men were ridiculing the woman because she invaded their preserve. But is it as likely that generations of men have also experienced instruction through this means. Never again would a man or woman ignore the need to take proper precautions against hot metal. In addition, the procedure undoubtedly serves as an initiation ritual for the work group.

Received Role

The *received role* denotes the role as perceived by the focal person based on information transmitted by the role set. This information includes responsibilities, activities, behavioral style, and role set itself. It is important to note that the received role does not duplicate the role as sent by others. Every individual interprets role information sent to him or her in an individual way. Information sent by others is interpreted in a manner influenced by the receiver's own personality, assumptions, and desires. It is reasonable to conclude that no two received roles are entirely alike.

Role Episode

The concept of *role episode* is particularly important among theoretical ideas and perspectives about roles. The role episode highlights the dynamic nature of roles. It also underscores the nature of the role incumbent as a thinking, active participant rather than a passive object.

Conduct of the role episode. Technically, a role episode is a feedback loop between the behavior of the focal person and the role set. The role episode feedback loop operates as follows:

1. *The focal person acts.* The role incumbent carries out actions as prescribed under his or her received role. He or she assesses the permissible range of action applicable to a given situation and selects an alternative. Note that permissible alternatives include the decision not to act.

2. *Members of the role set respond.* Role others may respond positively or negatively, thus letting the focal person know whether he or she has fulfilled the applicable role expectations. Response by the role set constitutes an instance of role sending, involving messages such as "Yes, that's the way," or "No, why don't you read your manual?"

3. *The focal person adjusts and redefines his or her received role.* The focal person feels gratified at the positive response of the role others or licks his or her emotional wounds. He or she reconsiders what constitutes appropriate actions in the situation just experienced and makes mental notes for future reference. The focal person may take concrete action to define his or her received role, such as writing a memo to file specifying the feedback he or she has received.

Thus, role episodes are dynamic. First, they involve communication of ideas between the focal person and the role set. This communication can change the focal person's received role. A single role episode can produce small- or large-scale changes in the focal person's received role. Changes in the focal person's conception of his or her role can be small, as when an action produces expressions of discomfort among role others. A single role episode can also produce major changes in the received role. Feedback such as a formal reprimand to the focal person for transgressing the boundaries of his or her role, for example, can have a major impact.

Role episodes as negotiations. The importance of a negotiation process regarding roles is illustrated earlier in this chapter. Both Nolan, the assistant principal, and his boss have personal career agendas. Each tries to nudge the other into permitting or performing actions that will advance his interests. The terminology of role episode merely presents a schematic layout of the negotiation process.

The part played by negotiation underscores the reciprocal nature of role sending. The focal person is not necessarily a passive receiver of definitions and operating instructions. The person occupying a role independently interprets inputs from others. The focal person often attempts to tailor the received role to his or her own interests, talents, values, and ambitions.

Successive role episodes amount to a series of experiments by the focal person. In most cases, the role incumbent acts according to information transmitted regarding provisions of the role. He or she receives expressions of approval or routine corrective messages from the role set in response. In rarer instances, the focal person initiates action primarily according to his or her personal needs and objectives. If feedback from the role set is positive, neutral, or only mildly negative, the role incumbent will continue acting in the same manner, having successfully revised the role.

Sequences of role episodes amount to negotiation between the person in the role and members of the role set. Usually, this negotiation involves small details in the specifics of performance. People may wish to avoid aspects of their roles that they find emotionally difficult. Some physicians, for example, have trouble telling patients bad news about their health or life expectancy. These doctors may delegate such communication to specialists more comfortable with the task.[9] Individuals also seek to expand or reduce the extent of their roles depending on how hard they want to work. Negotiation via series of role episodes typically takes place silently rather than through verbalized requests. People continually test their role set to see what works or what they can get away with.

Over time, successive role episodes reduce or increase opportunities for the incumbent. A person who negotiates for a smaller and smaller scope of work may be viewed as dispensable at the next cutback. A person who negotiates for a larger scope of work or a more extensive role set may be viewed as particularly valuable. Alternatively, such a person may come to be seen as an "empire builder" and let go when an opportunity to take such action becomes available.

The career of public-sector tycoon Robert Moses illustrates the breadth to which role expansion can take place.[10] Over the middle decades of the 20th century, Moses became the head of 18 separate public agencies in the states of New York, New Jersey, and Connecticut. He did this by persuading legislators to include small-scale provisions in budget bills that gave him additional authority. Each increment may be seen as a role episode on a very large scale. Moses became the most important development official in the northeastern United States, dictating the layout of roads, bridges, parks, and buildings among which millions lived.

The world of medicine furnishes a more everyday example. In the atmosphere of short staffing and intensity that often characterizes medical work, nurses may gravitate toward "upskilling," or performing tasks traditionally covered by physicians. The process likely takes the form of recurring requests and assents. Negotiation by nurses out of their traditional role is made more acceptable to physicians by the conception that the physician still "owns" the delegated work and can take it back at any time.[11] Similarly, Assistant Principal Nolan's superior knows that he can resume attending the meetings he has allowed Nolan to attend if it becomes in his interests to do so. Still, Nolan's effective role, like that of the nurses, has expanded.

The mechanics and outcomes of the role episode underscore the dynamic nature of roles. Both role expectations and boundaries evolve along with changes in the surrounding society, culture, and economic conditions.[12] Over time, individual role episodes and negotiations help enable such changes to take place.

The Role Orientation

Over and above the specific expectations associated with a role, all roles can be thought of as having different basic *orientations.* In different organizations, for example, roles with a particular type of orientation may predominate. Differences of this kind are recognized as particularly important across national boundaries and cultures.[13] An understanding of differences in role orientations can be essential for success in international business as well as diplomacy. But role orientations differ among organizations within one country, and potentially, within the same organization.

Classifying Role Expectations and Orientations

Social scientists have developed many formulations regarding role orientations. A schema formulated by sociologist Talcott Parsons in the 1950s is still widely applied today. The schema highlights five distinctions in role orientation. Known as "pattern variables," these include the following:[14]

- *Affective Versus Affective Neutrality*: The degree to which emotions are involved
- *Self-Orientation Versus Collectivity Orientation*: The degree to which individual role behavior directly benefits the focal person versus other members of the organization
- *Universalism Versus Particularism*: The degree to which thinking regarding others is based on abstract principles versus personal relationships
- *Achievement Versus Ascription*: The degree to which people are viewed in terms of their concrete capabilities and level of effort
- *Specificity Versus Diffuseness*: The degree to which actions are focused on a narrowly defined set of concerns and objectives

Affective Versus Affective Neutrality

Expectations regarding actions in some roles prescribe that they be "affective." In other roles, actions are expected to be "affectively neutral." Usually, the term *affective* is used to denote emotion. Some roles encourage their holders to feel and exhibit emotion, meeting either their own emotional needs, those of others in the collectivity, or both. The pattern orientation associated with such roles is "affective." In other roles, the incumbent is expected to think and act in a matter-of-fact way, performing technical functions without emotional expression or response to others. This orientation is "affectively neutral."

Role orientations in collectivities such as friendship groups and families are typically affective. Those in modern, formal organizations are often affectively neutral. But it is possible to find exceptions. Most clergy perform affectively neutral administrative functions in religious organizations. Yet they also serve as confessors and confidants of their parishioners. Their duties may include counseling and social work in an instrumental sense. But they also transmit the moral teachings of the faith, a clearly affective feature of the role.

Self-Orientation Versus Collectivity Orientation

This pair of alternative role expectations is again familiar in content. Some roles are naturally self-oriented. These include many business functions, particularly those related to sales. Salespeople are typically paid on commission. Their income depends directly on the volume of sales they make. Performance of their role brings personal benefits, but of course benefits the firm as a whole. There is no need for the organization to discourage a self-orientation in role performance. But there is no expectation that the individual salesperson's success directly promotes the success of other salespeople.

Professionals working for large organizations usually have a collectivity orientation. An engineer performing a routine design task does not benefit himself or herself in any special way by completing his or her work successfully. But the small design feature toiled over by one technical professional affects the success of projects combining the efforts of thousands of people: airplanes, hydroelectric power plants, large-scale software packages. Every professional role involves some degree of collectivity orientation, since professionals often think of themselves as members of a community of similarly trained colleagues.

Universalism Versus Particularism

Some roles call for the treatment of individuals according to rules and principles applicable to all. Favoritism of any kind is prohibited. This role orientation is known as "universalism."

Government agencies in modern, democratic societies are often cited as models of universalism. Internally, government employees expect each other to act according to rules that apply equally to all. Salary increments and promotion decisions are determined by criteria applied to all, regardless of personal characteristics such as race, gender, or popularity in the workplace. Likewise, every citizen expects services of equal quality and timeliness.

Roles in families have a particularistic orientation. Parents protect and nurture their children not because they are "children" but because they are "theirs." A relationship with the particular child (biological or adopted) determines thinking and behavior in the parent role. Roles in friendship groups are particularistic. People are admitted and assigned leadership roles according to highly personal criteria.

Roles and orientations in some formal organizations are particularistic as well. Some business firms promote only engineers or lawyers into top management, although abstract reasoning might suggest that people with other training would make better executives. People in some roles in business organizations and government agencies have a particularistic orientation. An example is a person with hiring authority who chooses friends or relatives over other job applicants.

Achievement Versus Ascription

Recognition of an individual's achievement is a key American value. "Achievement" in this sense reflects the combination of an individual's innate capabilities and level of effort in developing skills and performing well on the job. In an organization whose role orientation emphasizes achievement, managers hire and reward workers based on what they have made of themselves.

"Ascription" as a role orientation has a much longer history than "achievement." Whereas achievement orientation meshes well with modern, democratic values, ascription harks back to medieval times. Ascendancy of a prince to the throne due to his father's royal status reflects assignment of a role on the basis of ascriptive criteria. Family-based formal organizations today also harbor ascriptive role orientations. Family members may receive the best jobs, and employees pay special attention to ensuring satisfaction among family members, their friends, and those they have designated as meriting special attention.

Public and private sector programs designed to increase recruitment and advancement of minority group members into desirable jobs represents a modern form of "ascription." People, of course, do not "achieve" membership in a minority group. Much public criticism of preferences for minorities stems from a long-standing value on advancement due to achievement.

Specificity Versus Diffuseness

The specificity-diffuseness distinction classifies role orientations according to their scope of action. Roles high on the specificity dimension involve narrow ranges of duties and technical skill. Roles with high degrees of specificity tend to predominate in unionized workplaces. Union contracts foster development of very narrow job descriptions. Thus, a "machinist" would not be permitted to change a defective light bulb if this function were, under union contract, restricted to the "maintenance worker." Technical specialization in professional fields has a similar effect. Pediatricians, for example, do not feel competent to treat adults.

Diffuse roles tend to predominate in informal collectivities and less-formal organizations. The parent role, again, typically involves that of both teacher and healer of children. Diffuse roles exist in formal organizations as well. The executive "troubleshooter," for example, may be brought in to solve whatever atypical issue comes up. Senior individuals in law firms and universities, although possessing definite technical specialties, also serve as "mentors" for newer people. In this role, they provide information on pathways to success and insights into the organization's history and values. These mentors benefit the organization by helping newcomers learn their roles and become familiar with the organization's mission. Among formal organizations, those that are small seem more likely to foster diffuse roles. At a small high school, the science teacher may double as the basketball coach and may hold counseling responsibilities as well.

It is important to emphasize that distinctions between patterns of role expectations are matters of degree. No role orientation, for example, is devoid of affect. Professional roles are supposed to be carried out with emotional detachment, as when a physician examines a patient's laboratory tests. But few physicians retain complete emotional disinterest when faced with the necessity of giving the patient particularly good or bad news.

Individual Challenges

As the preceding material illustrates, people may develop and revise roles in a manner consistent with their interests and needs. But people seldom, if ever, design their own roles. Roles are created by collectivities either deliberately or through evolutionary trial and error. It is not unusual for individuals to experience discomfort due to the roles they occupy. The fact that individuals have multiple social ties contributes to such possibilities. A few of many possible instances are illustrated below.

Multiple Roles

Occupation of multiple roles creates a risk of conflict.

A hypothetical employee in a business firm illustrates the presence of multiple roles in individual lives. Assume that he is a teller in a downtown bank. During the workday, he has little opportunity to initiate communication. Customers request service and he provides it in a standardized manner. His role set is restricted to colleagues from whom he must occasionally request assistance and the superior to whom he reports.

After working hours the employee steps into his role as president of a motorcycle club. He trades his white shirt and necktie for leathers. He rides at the head of the pack as he and his buddies roar out to the countryside.

As president of the club he carries out many routine functions. Like the bank where he works, the club is an organization. He chairs meetings and convenes working groups. He sees that a mailing list is maintained and that the monthly newsletter is sent out.

In the club, though, his role set is more diverse than at the bank. He is free to initiate contact with any club member. In this organization, his role set is much larger and more varied than the role set associated with his employment. As president, he is active in initiating contact and at one time or another initiates contact with every club member.

Occupancy of several distinct roles is the norm in most societies. People holding an employee role may also be members of voluntary organizations (such as the motorcycle club just described), families, and informal groups. Roles associated with each collectivity may have different requirements.

It is useful to recall Assistant Principal Nolan's response to his daughter's use of lipstick. In his work role, he has just reprimanded a girl of his daughter's age for wearing it. In his role as a father, he decides to overlook the behavior. This is true even though he knows his daughter is bound for school, and that her school has the same rules as his. "Let the assistant principal of *her* school take care of it," he reasons.

Not all individuals are as capable of separating their multiple roles as our assistant principal, however. Researchers have reported a "spillover effect" from family roles into organizational roles. A 12-year study of married couples, for example, found that dissatisfaction and discord in the marriage tended to produce a similar effect in the work role.[15]

Role Ambiguity

Not all role sets are equally efficient in the process of role sending. Some role sets transmit messages regarding what people within the roles are supposed to do or with whom these role incumbents are supposed to interact. Faulty role sending causes *role ambiguity,* that is, uncertainty by the focal person about his or her duties, place in the organization, and expected contribution to the organization's goals.

Role ambiguity may result from several factors. First, members of the role set may be unskilled at transmitting information. They may have limited talents at verbal or written communication. They may themselves be unclear about the goals of the organization or duties of incumbents in specific roles. Management itself may have designed job descriptions with unclear or overlapping duties.

Political or emotional factors may also contribute to role ambiguity. Those responsible for orienting and instructing new members may be reluctant to communicate the true facts. They may be reluctant to send unambiguous information about a role that is mundane or risky or that involves potentially dishonest behavior with customers or clients.

Features of the process by which people are recruited into an organization may promote role ambiguity. Managers seeking new employees often exaggerate the features of the job that are interesting and provide opportunities for upward mobility. The new employee may come to realize that key features of the job he or she has accepted were not made clear in the recruitment process. The employee may be left to discover the true nature of his or her role over time, assembling bits and pieces through verbal communication and responses to his or her actions.

Research suggests that role ambiguity can create a good deal of dissatisfaction in organizations. Role ambiguity, for example, appears related to job turnover.[16] The presence of role ambiguity is inconsistent with the human need for clarity and consistency.

Role Conflict and Its Management

The Problem of Role Conflict

Although they may be functional for organizations, roles often cause discomfort for the people who occupy them. The experience of multiple demands associated with one or more roles is frequent in the modern world. Perceived inconsistency in role expectations is known as *role conflict.*

Role conflict in organizations arises from the human element. People engage in thinking independent of that dictated through the provisions of their roles. People carry out the task of role sending imperfectly. People usually occupy multiple roles, the expectations of which are not necessarily compatible. The fact that people are seldom dominated by a single role presents an ever-present risk of role conflict.

Specific causes of role conflict include

- Holding of multiple roles
- Inconsistency among task elements required for performing a role
- Faulty communication, or role sending, by people involved in a role
- Personality and prior history of people in roles

Multiple Roles

Occupation of multiple roles creates a risk of conflict. Differences between an individual's role in a formal organization and his or her role in an informal collectivity illustrate this risk. Patterns of role expectations within an organization tend to emphasize universalism, specificity, and affective neutrality. Role expectations in an informal collectivity tend to be affective, diffuse, and particularistic. People regularly shuttle between such roles without always adjusting to their differences.

Consider, for example, the role of mother. On a given Sunday, she may be expected to manage household finances, chauffer her daughter to a soccer game, and then help with homework. The mothering role is also affective. On that Sunday, the mother is expected to offer comfort in the event of disappointment or injury at the soccer game and encouragement for completion of the school assignment (affective actions). Of course, the mother's role is one rich in particularism, the actions described above being taken toward a particular child, not children as an abstract class.

Imagine that on Monday the same mother returns to work as a teacher of English in our familiar Hamilton Middle School. Her role expectations there are universalistic, discouraging her from showing favoritism toward any given child. They are affectively neutral, discouraging emotional expressions of dissatisfaction with her pupils or displays of affection.

Role conflict results from contradictions between two roles held by the same person. Placement of the teacher's daughter in her mother's classroom would result in extreme role conflict. Both mother and daughter would experience discomfort, never fully accepting the need to abandon their family roles. A wise administrator would ensure that the daughter would never be placed in a class taught by her mother. Even so, the teacher may have trouble slipping back into her professional role on Monday. People do not switch easily and automatically from one set of expectations to another.

The teacher's role described here, finally, is highly specific. On seeing a maintenance person struggling with the task of moving supplies, for example, she may experience a strong desire to help. But formal provisions prohibit this. The Teacher's Union bars instructional personnel from performing maintenance tasks. And the maintenance workers' contract specifies that only they may do maintenance work.

Conflict also arises from roles that individuals occupy in different formal organizations. The motorcycle club president described above, for example, may meet a bank executive at a club activity or function. As club president, the individual can claim social equality or even superior standing to the executive. Yet the work role demands deference. The two men are likely to feel uncomfortable with each other when they meet outside the bank.

Even within one organization people have different roles with expectations that can be in conflict. A team leader's role expectations may emphasize encouragement and task sharing with his or her subordinates. Yet the same individual's membership on the management team may require him or her to inform team members of their termination at times of corporate downsizing.

Allocation of time is often the most visible symptom of role conflict resulting from multiple roles. Assistant Principal Nolan's attendance at the school board (part of his executive role) makes him unable to spend evenings at home or attend functions at his daughter's school (acts required in his family role). This symptom is familiar to many of today's executives and professionals. But time allocation problems due to multiple roles occur among many other people. Students who become involved in volunteering and campus politics experience similar challenges, as demands of the "student" and "activist" roles vie for their time.

Task-Related Conflicts

Even within a single role some elements may contradict others. Many such conflicts arise because a single role involves diverse tasks. Examples abound in the lives of professionals, whose work often involves tasks that are multifaceted and complex.

The work of an architect, for example, involves design of buildings. But such work requires consideration of multiple objectives. The architect, for example, is responsible for producing practical designs, that is, plans for buildings that are inexpensive and structurally stable. He or she also feels responsible for designing aesthetically attractive structures. Few if any architects would attempt to persuade a client to accept a design that was structurally unsound. But many might induce their clients to adopt artistic design features that they might not initially want.

Psychotherapists also experience role conflict due to inconsistencies in the tasks they perform. Part of the therapist's task is to provide emotional support to clients experiencing stress, depression, or other problems. Actually performing therapy is another part of the task. Performing therapy may require skills very different from providing emotional support. Therapeutic procedures often present clients with emotionally difficult challenges, as they are forced to confront uncomfortable feelings and change comfortable (yet dysfunctional) patterns of behavior. Psychotherapists may confront this role conflict during every therapeutic session. They must maintain the client at a sufficient level of comfort to ensure that he or she will not discontinue therapy. Yet, they must apply sufficient emotional pressure to induce the client to make favorable changes.

Role conflict is a familiar phenomenon among college and university faculty. The faculty member's tasks include teaching, research, and, increasingly, raising money through grants and contracts. Most faculty members must perform significant research to keep their jobs. Research draws time and energy away from course preparation and attention to students. Fundraising takes time from both teaching and research. But employment of many faculty members today requires continuous preparation of applications for funding from the government, private foundations, and corporations. Most people who become college and university professors do so because they desire to teach. But the other task demands facing instructors in higher education present those committed to teaching with serious conflict.

Faulty Role Sending

Expectations from members of the role set may be communicated in a faulty manner. People whose responsibilities include instructing the focal person in a role may unintentionally distort the role expectations. People may engage in such distortion in their haste to hire a person into a vacant slot. Thus, the opportunities and authority associated with a role may be exaggerated. The individual who accepts the role will find out about its true expectations soon enough. Conflict occurs within the person taking the role as the true expectations of others are seen to contradict the expectations he or she was given to believe earlier.

People in an organization can intentionally send incorrect messages to role incumbents in an attempt to cause them difficulties. They may want the given role to be filled inappropriately. Alternatively, they may want the person occupying the role to perform his or her job ineffectively, thus ensuring his or her termination.

Sending of different messages by individual role others may also result in role conflict. People in different parts of an organization have different conceptions of what individuals in a given role should be thinking and doing. Inconsistent or contradictory instructions are likely to cause confusion and discomfort in the focal person's mind.

Role others give different messages at different times. Most people act and think in a manner that is not entirely consistent. The individual in an organizational role, then, may encounter confusion and discomfort as inconsistent and even contradictory role expectations are perceived.

History and Personality

An individual's personal history, disposition, and values can potentially cause role conflict. Personal history provides striking examples. When assuming a new role, for example, many people still feel responsible for carrying out the expectations of the role they held before. This causes internal discomfort and conflict with colleagues.

Researchers have been performing studies on this form of role conflict for generations. Classic examples include the factory foreman. Promoted from among the operatives, foremen supervise individuals whose work they formerly shared. Foremen, then, experience feelings of divided loyalty. They desire to succeed in their new management roles. At the same time, they may feel reluctant to criticize their former buddies. Similar observations have been made about sergeants in military units. As noncommissioned officers, they are members of "management," but they originate from the ranks and many have difficulty making a clean break. Mr. Nolan, the fictitious assistant principal at Hamilton Middle School, is a former classroom teacher. Normally, he would experience some degree of discomfort administering the teacher evaluation procedure to people who were recently his colleagues.

Modern, real-world examples include physicians who enter management positions in hospital or health care systems.[17] These executives have received intense and lengthy training in the profession of medicine. Along with this training come personal ties with other doctors as well as jealousy over the physician's right to make decisions independently. As an executive, though, a physician occupying a position such as vice president for medical affairs owes primary responsibility to stockholders, trustees, and other managers. Most of his or her management colleagues will have business and management rather than medical backgrounds. The physician-executive is expected to represent management's position to clinicians, potentially questioning their decisions due to fiscal and administrative concerns. It is easy to see why feelings of personal discomfort may ensue.

People also experience conflict when their role expectations contradict basic elements of their personalities. Introverted persons, for example, may feel uncomfortable in roles involving sales. Introverts try to avoid such roles. Yet many accept them in order to make a living, reconciling themselves to acting in a manner inconsistent with their basic inclinations. People are resourceful and adaptable, often finding ways to do jobs for which they are not naturally suited.

Mechanisms of Role Conflict Management

Many people experience some degree of role conflict. Widespread role conflict arises from the fact that most people in modern society occupy multiple roles and that many people move rapidly from one role to another. People employ both conscious and unconscious methods for reducing role conflict or avoiding its consequences.

Role Segregation

Among the causes of role conflict listed above, difficulties resulting from multiple roles appear to be the most frequent. In modern society, nearly everyone occupies multiple roles. Other forms of role conflict are likely to diminish as an individual becomes more accustomed to them. Natural social and mental processes tend to reduce role conflict. Despite faulty role sending, people eventually figure out the range of actions expected of them. Past history becomes less important as a person gets used to a new role and spends more and more time with members of the new role set. The foreman, for example, spends less time with his old friends and more time with other foremen.

But time does not diminish the viability of a distinct role. The process of role sending and reinforcement through punishments and rewards continues as time goes by. People who occupy more than one distinct role, then, are at risk of experiencing continuing conflict. Mr. Nolan, the assistant principal, will continue to experience conflict between his role as a family member and as an executive with the school system.

Role segregation is a social process that helps manage conflict caused by multiple roles. The process occurs when people occupying two or more distinct roles keep them strictly separate. This means, for example, that an individual will not act according to the same role orientation in a work as in a family role. Goals that receive emphasis in one role will be unimportant in another. The fact that many roles are associated with particular buildings, rooms, and other locations helps maintain role segregation.

Multiple roles occupied by police officers have received attention from researchers as causes of conflict.[18] Detecting crime and arresting offenders are the most visible acts associated with the police officer role. The police officer role has been cited as difficult to reconcile with the role of "neighbor." Nearly everyone does things that are technically illegal on a day-to-day basis, such as parking in prohibited spaces, having unlicensed pets, and setting off firecrackers on the Fourth of July. Having a neighbor who possesses the power to arrest or give citations causes discomfort.

It would seem that police officers would do well to act as little like police as possible when they are off duty. But in reality they are seldom completely away from the job. Many carry their service weapons when they are out of uniform. Role segregation, though potentially beneficial, is difficult to achieve.

Generally, role segregation helps maintain commitment to individual roles. People who do not "bring their jobs home" are said to make the best workers and the best family members. Role segregation reduces role conflict that may make adherence to either the work or family role less comfortable.

The Dictator and His Family: A Case of Role Segregation

An international student told the following story to illustrate the principle of role segregation.

His father was a leading general in the military junta that controlled a Central American country. Media in the United States had reported that the junta maintained its rule by suppressing dissent through intimidation, imprisonment, and torture. The generals had personal reputations of being both tough and cruel.

The student, though, had no such impression of his father. "He never wore his uniform at home," the student remarked. Recalling his family life, the student commented that his father had been "the nicest, sweetest person you could ever imagine."

Achievement of Cognitive Consonance

Factors related to history and personality also cause a good deal of role conflict. As noted earlier, people enter organizations with already-formed commitments and values. Their role expectations may include items that contradict the values they have brought with them. In their organizational roles, people receive encouragement to do things that contradict their personal values. Elements of their mental life register these expectations as both good and bad. Perception of contradictory pieces of information is known to social psychologists as *cognitive dissonance*.

The human mind does not live comfortably with cognitive dissonance. The mind's homeostatic mechanism attempts at all times to reconcile contradictory stimuli. Psychologists have performed experiments to demonstrate the mind's attempts to achieve cognitive consonance. An uninformed experimental subject, for example, was placed in room along with 12 other individuals and shown a point of light on a movie screen. All were asked, in turn, to estimate the number of inches the light moved. The uninformed subject was made to answer last. In reality, the light was stationary. But after the 12 others (who had been so instructed by the experimenter) each said the point moved between six inches and one foot, the uninformed subject answered similarly.

An attempt to achieve cognitive consistency might occur on a more conscious level as well. Consider a recent graduate from a city-planning program who has a long-standing conviction that urban, high-rise development should be strictly limited. She takes a job in a real estate development firm and is assigned to a project involving demolition of small homes and erection of office buildings and condos. As time goes by, the planner reconciles her personal values with role expectations at work. She convinces herself that development in the city will prevent suburban sprawl from inundating natural areas in the countryside. This formulation allows the planner to consider her work with the development firm as compatible with her basic values. It thus reduces role conflict.

Issues and Applications

Assignment of roles constitutes a crucial component of an organization's capacity to coordinate the efforts of highly diverse individuals. Each role has one or more functions. Abstractly, organizations may seem to comprise arrays of clearly formulated roles. However, uncertainty and conflict may accompany the taking and enactment of roles, as these examples illustrate.

• A promising student in public policy receives a coveted summer internship. He moves to the state capital to join the staff of a leading legislator. His first day finds the young man, in coat and tie, awaiting instructions. After a brief introduction, the legislator takes a coin from his pocket and hands it to the young man, saying, "Son, get me a coke." Feeling demeaned, the intern sulks to the coke machine. Perhaps without conscious intent, the legislator has engaged in role sending, letting the young man know that performing personal tasks for the boss is a component of the staffer's role.

• After early career service at a government agency, an economist takes a job on Wall Street as a securities analyst. He is assigned the task of assessing investor risk associated with a forthcoming bond issue underwritten by the firm. Upon reading his draft findings, a superior asks him to revise certain language to make risks associated with the issue less apparent. The analyst carries out his superior's instructions, resulting in language more beneficial to the firm's clients. Discomfort experienced by the analyst reflects role conflict arising from inconsistency between business needs and professional values—a dilemma he will have to resolve by changing his way of thinking or leaving the job.

- The president of a sports club calls a meeting to order. Members continue to converse, happily exchanging stories of team events and personal notes. The president checks the agenda and glances toward the clock. How long should she allow the chatter to continue? Should she emphasize the "specificity" dimension of her role and insist that the meeting begin on time? However, facilitation of informal communication and affective exchange are clearly organizational objectives. She might think of her role as "diffuse," and participate in the banter a few more moments before sounding the gavel.

Chapter Review and Major Themes

Organizations may be thought of as systems of roles. Each role is a prescription for individual behavior. The role occupied by an individual informs him or her of actions to carry out or avoid in a given situation. Concretely, roles are socially determined, recurring actions taken by an individual. In an organization, each individual's role is interrelated with the roles of other individuals. Actions carried out by individuals according to their roles are presumed to advance the objectives of the organization as a whole.

Formulation and assignment of roles is a key method by which organizations promote coordination and pursue their objectives. Ideally, roles ensure that the behavior of each individual contributes to the work of all others, day after day, year after year. In this way, organizations concentrate the efforts of hundreds, thousands, and even millions of individuals on achieving a specific outcome. Roles promote coordination and focus on the organization's objectives even among individuals with widely diverse values, needs, and personal goals.

Roles are neither rigid nor static. No two "received roles" are exactly alike. Even people with identical job descriptions may define their roles differently. Role sending is a recurring process, in which participants experiment until an acceptable role is determined. Ideally, roles stabilize in a fashion consistent with the organization's needs. But the organization cannot fully control the manner in which individuals receive their roles or choose to restrict or expand them. Except perhaps in the most rigid of organizations, then, individuals have some degree of choice over how they carry out the roles assigned to them.

The analytical perspectives described in Chapter 3 are useful for understanding how roles contribute to organizations and in some respect present challenges. Figure 4.1 presents a schematic diagram of how the organization's environment may help shape roles, and the implications of roles for function and conflict. In the diagram, the broad arrows represent visible and generally expectable effects. The slender arrows represent less usually observed but potentially important effects. Signs (+ or −) associated with each arrow indicate a positive versus negative effect on function or conflict.

Roles would appear to contribute substantially and positively to function within organizations, certainly within those generally regarded as successful. At least some roles, though, are potentially dysfunctional. Examples include instances in which incumbents expand or restrict their roles to too great a degree, or in which incumbents find their organizational roles seriously conflicting with the roles they occupy outside. It would appear that roles usually reduce conflict in an organization, by specifying each member's responsibilities and access to communication channels. But roles may contribute to conflict in instances where one individual expands his or her role into another's "territory." Alternatively, important functions may be neglected because existing roles direct no one's effort toward them, and individuals refuse to expand or act outside their roles.

In most organizations, environment contributes to roles in an indirect fashion. Labor market conditions, union demands, and laws, for example, affect the kinds of responsibilities that may be assigned and the breadth of individual roles. Licensure and accreditation requirements encourage the presence of specific roles in organizations such as hospitals and universities.

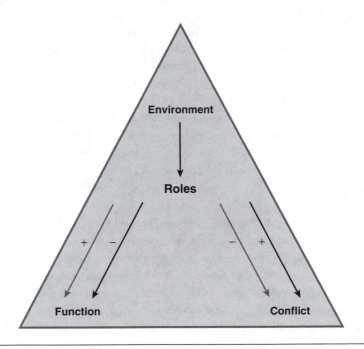

Figure 4.1   Analytical Perspectives Applied to Roles

Discussion Questions

1. Nearly all large corporations or public agencies have "job descriptions" covering the responsibilities of individual employees. How does the employee's job description differ from his or her "role"?

2. Think of an organization in which you have been involved. How would you characterize your role in that organization? How did you identify the requirements and limitations of your role? How might this process have been improved?

3. How might the individual's liberty to negotiate his or her role differ in different types of organizations? What differences might be noticeable among (a) large business firms; (b) moderate-sized government agencies; (c) small voluntary organizations?

4. The phenomenon described here as "role segregation" is sometimes viewed as personal dishonesty, as individuals relate differently to others depending on the setting, for example, at "the office" versus at home. Is this true?

5. All things considered, how effective is a system of roles in promoting coordination among individuals in the "average" organization?

References

1. Mead, J. H. (1934). *Mind, self, and society.* Chicago: University of Chicago Press.
2. Zurcher, L. A. (1983). *Social roles: Conformity, conflict, and creativity.* Beverley Hills, CA: Sage.
3. Konrad, A. M. (2003). Family demands and job attribute preferences: A 4-year longitudinal study of women and men. *Sex Roles, 49,* 35–46.
4. Heck, R., & Hallinger, P. (1999). Next generation methods for study of leadership and school improvement. In J. Murphy and K. S. Louis (Eds.), *Handbook of research on educational administration* (2nd ed.). San Francisco: Jossey-Bass.
5. Merton, R. K. (1964). *Social theory and social structure* (9th ed.). New York: Free Press.
6. Ritti, R. R., & Funkhouser, G. R. (1994). *The ropes to skip and the ropes to know.* New York: John Wiley & Sons.
7. Katz, D., & Kahn, R. L. (1978). *The social psychology of organizations* (2nd ed.). New York: John Wiley & Sons.
8. Smigel, E. O. (1973). *The Wall Street lawyer: Professional organization man?* Bloomington: Indiana University Press.
9. Greenwald, H. P., & Nevitt, M. C. (1982). Physician attitudes toward communication with cancer patients. *Social Science and Medicine, 6,* 591–594.
10. Caro, R. A. (1975). *Power broker: Robert Moses and the fall of New York.* New York: Vintage.
11. Harvey, J. (1995). Upskilling and the intensification of work: The extended role in intensive care nursing and midwifery. *Sociological Review, 43,* 765–781.
12. Turner, R. H. (1990). Role change. In W. R. Scott & J. Blake (Eds.), *Annual review of sociology* (Vol. 16). Palo Alto, CA: Annual Reviews.

13. Hampden-Turner, C. M., & Tropennaars, F. (2000). *Building cross-cultural competence.* New Haven, CT: Yale University Press.

14. Parsons, T. (1965). *The social system.* New York: Free Press.

15. Weitz, J. (1956). Job expectancy and survival. *Journal of Applied Psychology, 40,* 245–247.

16. Rogers, S. J., & May, D. C. (2003). Spillover between marital quality and job satisfaction: Long-term patterns and gender differences. *Journal of Marriage and the Family, 65,* 482–495.

17. Schneller, E. S., Greenwald, H. P., Richardson, M. L., & Ott, J. (1997). The physician executive: Role in the adaptation of American medicine. *Health Care Management Review, 22,* 90–96.

18. Skolnick, J. (1975). *Justice without trial: Law enforcement in democratic society.* New York: John Wiley & Sons.

CHAPTER 5

The Rule of Structure

Learning Objective

To understand the importance and operation of organizational structure.

Principles

- While roles guide the thinking and action of individuals, structure co-ordinates the roles. The structure of a well-functioning organization helps focus individual roles on the organization's objectives. Structure constitutes the organization's stable core.

- Organizational structure is sometimes deliberately created by entrepreneurs and planners. Sometimes, however, structure evolves through spontaneous human action.

- Structure varies among organizations. Organizational structures differ in characteristics such as hierarchy, centralization, and complexity.

- A variety of factors account for structural differences among organizations. These include size, technology, age, environment, and leadership. The organization's environment often influences its structure.

- While an essential part of every organization, structure poses challenges in many instances. An organization's existing structure, for example, may not be the type best fitted to its objectives.

The Importance of Structure

Earlier in this book, social structure was characterized as an enduring framework that guides the behavior of individuals toward each other. Ideally, social structure ensures that each role reinforces the contributions made by other roles to the achievement of objectives. Formal structure, which characterizes organizations, is distinguished by greater stability and explicitness of relationships relative to informal collectivities.

According to a definition put forward by Rodolfo Alvarez and Leah Robin, organizational structure comprises a set of interrelationships, or social bonds, between positions in the organization.[1] Through such interrelationships, incumbents of individual roles are linked, directly or indirectly, with all others in the organization. People who do dissimilar work or occupy unequal levels in an organization may not knowingly adjust the performance of their roles to each other's needs. But, ideally, structural linkages extend from the highest to the lowest levels of an organization. This property of formal organizations counteracts the potential entropy of individual members that is promoted by the uniqueness of mental life and the pull of external social forces.

Despite its importance, organizational structure is not always immediately visible, as are the structures of buildings or bridges. But it can be discerned by observing the behavior of people in an organization. Interviewing people about their perceptions and thoughts yields insights into structure. So does studying organizational documents such as bylaws, organizational charts, and records. The humble telephone directory may be better than the official organizational chart, listing thousands of personnel and offices under the names of the unit heads to which they report. Structure constitutes the stable core of the formal organization, molding the activities and lives of individuals generation after generation.

Even in organizations that have written bylaws, operating procedures, and internal legal codes, actual relations between "roles" or "positions" may remain obscure. Yet, the absence or deterioration of structure is readily observable. Consider the following example from the post-Vietnam War film *Apocalypse Now*.

The dispirited United States Army was clearly losing in Vietnam. A senior officer defected from the army, accompanied by a band of followers. The officer did not desert the American cause, however. Operating from a remote jungle base, he continued to fight the war "his own way."

The rogue officer attributed America's setbacks in Vietnam to the command's reluctance to use sufficiently aggressive tactics. He had witnessed acts of unparalleled terror by the Communist guerillas. America could not win, he concluded, unless it adopted equally brutal methods.

Knowing he would never convince his superiors, the officer broke from the ranks. He established himself in the jungle and launched brutal attacks against the enemy. He initiated no contact with his superiors and took no orders. He was "off the grid."

Back at headquarters, command staff knew what was going on. A force was sent to seek out and destroy the renegade. Those at the top felt that the rogue's exploits, no matter how successful, could compromise diplomatic efforts. His independent action, moreover, might weaken the regular army's system of command.

This story illustrates how an individual can carry out a role but do so outside organizational structure. Here, the focal person wears the uniform he was issued. He performs the actions of an army officer: he plans strategy, lives in a military camp, and goes out on operations. But no force ensures coordination of his actions with units of the larger military organization.

Though this example is fictional, real events illustrating the principle abound. Legendary infantrymen of the Imperial Japanese Army kept their arms, hiding in the jungle for years after the end of official hostilities.

Throughout history, disenchanted members of established religions, both lay and clergy, have opposed direction from the main organization. Some have chosen to live in isolation, becoming religious hermits. Others have preached messages at variance with the hierarchy's instructions. Established religious organizations have done their best to punish these defectors, using methods ranging from defrocking to immolation at the stake.

Less heroic examples are easy to find. Consider the political appointee to a government agency who reads newspapers, conducts personal business, leaves early, and yet receives no criticism from his superior. Or think of the unscrupulous person who, nearing retirement, no longer fears discipline or termination. Having "retired on the job," he goes through the motions of his position but pays little attention to communications from superiors, changes in procedure, or complaints from clients.

The rogue soldier, political appointee, and unscrupulous employee all carry out actions within their expected roles. But they perform these actions outside the information network and chain of command, key dimensions of organizational structure. Disconnection of this kind places them outside the grid of communication and direction required to coordinate their actions with those of others. Even if they carry out the functions of their roles in a technically acceptable manner, their actions are, at best, poorly coordinated with the efforts of others.

A structure that is both well maintained and appropriate to an organization's purpose is necessary for its survival and the attainment of its goals. This chapter examines the wide variety of forms that may constitute appropriate structures for different organizations. It explores the manner in which organizational structure originates and develops. Organizational structure raises practical issues for members at all levels. An organization's structure, even if long-standing, cannot be presumed to support the organization's objectives better than an alternative one.

Roles, Purpose, and Organizational Structure

A reexamination of some concepts and terminology already introduced helps lay the groundwork for understanding and analysis of organizational structure: roles, objectives, and goals.

Another Look at Roles: Joining Roles and Structure

As in the examples of rogues and renegades provided above, roles may be carried out in a manner detached from structure. But such situations are unusual and unstable. In well-functioning organizations, role and structure are firmly linked. Role expectations, as discussed in the preceding chapter, provide the linking mechanism.

To understand how roles are linked into surrounding organizational structure, it is useful to review the concept of role expectations. As discussed in the preceding chapter, role expectations constitute what others expect of the person occupying a role. Role expectations address many features of the individual's role. Of course, these include concrete task performance. But they also include expectations regarding relationships with the rest of the organization.

Role expectations, in fact, may be thought of as two types: *internal* and *relational*. Internal role expectations prescribe behavior regarding job performance, personal comportment, dress, and manner of communication with customers or clients. Relational role expectations prescribe relationships between roles in the organization. These expectations include rules stipulating with whom the focal person may initiate contact and from whom he or she must accept supervision.

Internal role expectations tell the individual what to do at his or her desk, machine, or drawing board. They enable the organization to carry on routine business. Relational role expectations link roles with one another. They tell people whom they may talk with and when, whom to obey, how good actions will be rewarded, and to what level they may aspire. Relational role expectations arrange individual behavior according to predictable patterns of initiation, subordination, and mobility within the organization.

Organizational Purpose

Assessment of an organizational structure's appropriateness requires a grasp of the organization's purpose. However, identifying organizational purpose represents a challenge in itself. Mission statements, formulated and widely disseminated by numerous organizations, are notoriously vague.

In the preceding pages, organizational purpose has been expressed in terms of "objectives" and "goals." While they have been used interchangeably above, they are different. The distinction between objectives and goals illustrates the challenge of identifying an organization's actual purpose.

The term *objective* denotes the hoped-for result from a finite set of actions. Objectives are concrete and often measurable: development of a reusable space vehicle; sale of 250,000 units of a certain automobile; building a church and holding services. All organizations have definable objectives.

Goals are less tangible and take far longer to achieve than objectives. Goals are large in scale and abstract in nature: solving the mysteries of outer space; dominating the domestic automobile market; achieving humankind's salvation. Still, if asked, most people in an organization can identify a purpose broader than that achievable through visible, near-term efforts.

Objectives make greater practical sense than goals in defining an organization's purpose. Researchers have difficulty specifying procedures for identifying an organization's true goals. Operating managers often encounter frustration in understanding (much less pursuing) goals stated by the top leadership. It is easier for analysis of structure to focus on objectives.

Yet it would be an error to ignore goals. An organization can achieve numerous, near-term, measurable objectives, and at the same time miss its deeper, longer-term goals. Railroading in the United States has been cited as an example. In the 1950s, it is argued, railroads focused on the objective of operating trains. However, they ignored the broader goal of providing economical service to the traveling public. According to some, railroad companies lost the chance to become diversified providers of transportation. Many such firms went bankrupt as trucking, long-distance buses, and airlines became dominant.

Though difficult, assessment of the appropriateness of an organization's structure—the degree to which it is functional—requires attention to both objectives and goals. When the following discussion refers to objectives, the reader should be thinking "goals," and vice versa. Practically, different individuals in an organization are likely to focus on objectives and on goals. Although some members, then, may consider existing structure appropriate, others may not. In reality, an existing structure may be functional for some members of an organization and dysfunctional for others. One of the functions of leadership is to promote a balanced view.

Roles and Structure: Design or Evolution?

How does organizational structure come into being?

It is tempting to begin an explanation of an organization's structure by saying, "this organization is designed to . . ." Such language assumes deliberate formulation of roles, structures, and other organizational components. Chapter 1 characterized organizations as deliberate in origin. Indeed, organizations are often created as tools for accomplishing some concrete purpose. But this does not mean organizational structure is always, or even usually, the product of human invention.

An organization's structure can emerge through either design or evolution. The first process is one of deliberate formulation by executives and planners. The second process is one of groping and experimentation, under which roles emerge through patterns of action and interaction arising spontaneously in crucial situations. Both processes seem to play a part in determining roles in formal organizations.

As the simplest component of organizations, roles provide clues to the characteristics of organizations themselves. Examination of the ways in which roles are created helps explain the processes that create the organizational structures in which they are embedded.

Deliberate Development of Roles

Deliberate planning and formulation of roles has clearly taken place on a very large scale in modern formal organizations. Focus of efforts by many individuals on an explicit goal is one of the essential characteristics of formal organizations. It seems natural that executives and technical specialists would design a set of roles rationally focused on the desired outcome, as engineers design the parts of a machine.

One of the most important management principles of the 20th century emphasized the need for just such a process of design. Frederick Winslow Taylor, active at the turn of the century, is the most famous proponent of this approach.[2] Taylor saw every human element involved in the process of production as capable of improvement through rational design. For this reason, the movement he launched was called "scientific management."

Taylorism, as this approach was also called, dictated meticulous design of every function in the productive enterprise. At a production plant, for example, Taylorism called for deliberate design of each tool and specification of how the operative was to use it. Taylorism went so far as to dictate the postures operatives were to assume in performing their functions and the amount of time each operation (such as lifting a shovel of coal or stamping out a metal part) should take.

Out of Taylorism came the image of a technician with a clipboard and stopwatch observing men and women at work. Even in his time, Taylor received criticism for limiting the creativity of individual human beings and ending centuries-old traditions of craftsmanship. But Taylor countered that his methods increased productivity while reducing drudgery and fatigue in the worker's life. The Russian revolutionary V. I. Lenin may have opposed most capitalist practices but he embraced Taylorism, calling for its adoption within the Communist state he founded.

The logic of Taylorism remains important today. Development of job descriptions for new positions is a major management responsibility. Researchers in fields such as human factors engineering and operations management continuously develop and perfect techniques for designing jobs.[3] Experts use mathematical models to set up positions on assembly lines. In a process called "assembly line balancing," these techniques enable managers to adjust the time required to complete a particular task to the time required for each additional assembly task down the line. Databases available to managers and planners include information on actual time required by workers to carry out motions such as bending and reaching. The federal government and a private organization known as the Motion Time Management (MTM) Society maintain these databases.

Deliberate job design continues to occupy an important place in the management of organizations. But this process is more complex than it was in the early 20th century. Employees today are more likely to do "brain work" than they are the physical labor performed by their ancestors. Managers more often need to balance the skills required in each position than they do the time required to complete an individual task. With increased training and discretion, employees are more likely than ever to invent ways, overt or covert, to modify their task performance in a manner that better meets personal needs.

It must be remembered that an individual's job description is not the same as his or her role. But a large part of many roles is concerned with concrete operations similar to those of Taylor's industrial employees. Among people who work with either their hands or their brains, patterns of task performance strongly influence patterns of social relations.

Evolution of Roles

Deliberate design of jobs is one process that helps to create roles in organizations, but researchers who study organizations have also documented spontaneous development of roles. One such instance, among a group of radiologists and radiology technicians, is described by Barley.[4] Radiologists are physicians who specialize in obtaining and analyzing images of internal body structures. Before the late 20th century, radiologists spent most of their time taking and reading x-rays.

At the time of Barley's study, new technology was being introduced in the form of computerized tomography (CT) and ultrasound devices and methods. Barley observed that this era was one in which role expectations were quite fluid. No one had sufficient experience to call himself or herself an expert in CT or ultrasound. Much mutual teaching took place by both physicians and technicians. Older radiologists, who continued to rely on x-ray technology, became isolated from those adopting the new technology.

Barley's study suggests that patterns by which people *interact* develop into roles within the organization and influence its structure. The term *interact* as used here refers to reciprocal communications and action by individuals on a continuing basis. In the community Barley describes, it appears likely that roles will develop with expectations permitting initiation of contact and mutual requests for assistances by both superiors (radiologists) and subordinates (technicians). Among the late adopters of new technology (radiologists and technicians who continued to rely on x-rays), strong relationships of subordination seem likely to continue.

Observations by these researchers and others[5] indicate that social roles emerge from *group dynamics,* that is, spontaneous, face-to-face interaction of people as individuals or within small groups. Changes in technology can stimulate these dynamics. So can emergence of new challenges for an organization. Under either condition, the process of role formation takes place outside the realm of deliberate planning by managers and experts. Workers observed in the Hawthorne study (see Chapter 1) also provide evidence for the importance of group dynamics in forming role expectations. Despite the efforts of management, these workers developed their own expectations regarding pace of work, norms of production, and practice of discipline.

As the fundamental units of formal organizations, roles must be compatible with the organizational structure by which they are linked. Structure is undoubtedly influenced by the characteristics of roles. But structure also limits the influence of microsocial dynamics.

Organizational structures and roles appear to emerge through both deliberate design and spontaneous evolution. This process may occur in the same organization. Managers, for example, may set up a work unit whose roles will later be modified through informal evolution. Singly or together, design and evolution produce organizational structures of many different types.

The manner in which an organizational structure originates does not determine whether that structure is appropriate or inappropriate for the organization's objectives. Only one thing can be assumed about the structure of an existing organization: it keeps the organization "alive." Judging the structure's appropriateness for accomplishing the organization's stated objectives is another matter. This is a key concern of both managers and analysts. Such judgment requires an understanding of the dimensions along which organizations differ. But first, it is essential to understand structure as an operating mechanism.

How Structure Works

Traditionally, organizational structure has been depicted as an array of interconnected boxes. This is the "chart" familiar to most people who have participated in organizations. Such a chart is illustrated in Figure 5.1, which presents, in abbreviated form, official reporting relationships within the National Aeronautics and Space Administration (NASA). Highly simplified, this chart omits support units such as the comptroller's office, budget, and accounting. Of NASA's many operational facilities, the chart includes only the Kennedy Space Center. Likewise, the chart omits the numerous subunits and individual member roles subordinate to the key executives.

The anatomical nature of an organizational chart suggests that structure operates primarily as a "chain of command." Structure, though, is expressed and maintained through several forms of human interaction. These may include

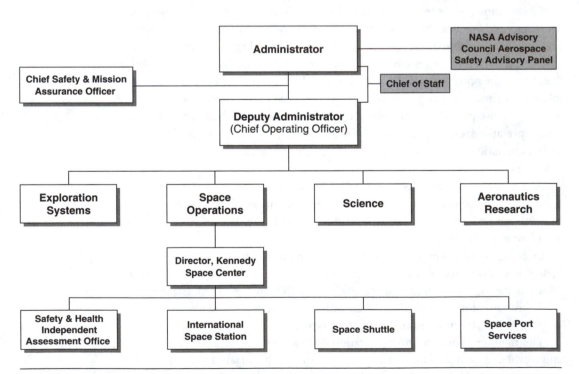

Figure 5.1   National Aeronautics and Space Administration (NASA) and Kennedy Space Center Organizational Chart (Greatly Simplified)

off-the-record conversations between individuals. At other times, structure may exert its influence through a written memorandum prepared by an organization subunit operating under highly formalized rules. Actual processes may occur along these lines:

- Instruction
- Correction
- Information
- Resource allocation

Instruction

Instruction is an easily observed process through which organizations assign tasks and monitor their performance. People receive instructions through written and oral means, explicit or implicit according to the formalization of the organization. Incumbents of some roles are empowered to instruct incumbents of certain other roles.

Structure becomes clearly visible in assigning of objectives. Annual procedures for this purpose have become widespread within the management and professional ranks of organizations. In a procedure sometimes called management by objectives (MBO), supervisors negotiate with subordinates for objectives to be accomplished during the coming year. These subordinates carry out a similar negotiation process with people working under them. This pattern of instruction illustrates structure as a successive series of initiative steps.

Correction

Organizational structure also operates by informing people when they are working in an unacceptable manner. Correction may take the form of informal words couched in persuasive language. It may also occur through formal reprimands prepared by semi-judicial bodies in organizations.

It is important to note that structures other than formal hierarchies can undertake corrective processes. Formal organizations of "peers" carry out corrective communications with each other. Physicians in a medical group, for example, often identify a practice by one of their colleagues that they consider inappropriate, dangerous, or excessively expensive. In such instances, a physician of equal rank delivers the message, either on his or her own initiative or as a representative of the group.

Information

The giving and receiving of information is a crucial organizational process. Organizational structure affects human behavior in part by influencing the flow of information. Information includes facts ranging in importance from curiosities to crucial knowledge of opportunities for advancement, interests of top managers, and forthcoming hirings and firings. The volume of information transmitted and received varies according to the organization's degree of integration.

Information often induces action. Transmission of facts, for example, may substitute for direct orders. Knowledge of what an influential manager wants, for example, may be sufficient to change the behavior of ambitious subordinates.

Access to information reflects standing in the organizational structure. The person on the bottom is usually the "last to know" about important developments. In decentralized organizations, though, the CEO may receive information about a distant operating unit long after lower-level, on-site managers.

On an interpersonal level, an individual's place in the information network helps shape roles. The roles with which people can and cannot communicate shape the manner in which they work. Who does and who does not return one's telephone calls and e-mail is an indication of structure. If the holder of a certain role never responds, the holder of another role cannot coordinate his or her work with this individual. The roles of each have no direct, structural linkage.

Resource Allocation

Organizational structure determines the manner in which resources are allocated. Resources include, of course, monetary compensation, which will receive major attention in the next chapter. Other resources have important effects on how roles are carried out. These resources include

- Number and quality of personnel assigned to an individual manager
- Capital budget, covering buildings, machinery, office furniture, computers
- Amenities, including size and location of office, travel budget, access to company cars, club memberships normally given to executives

Sometimes the process of resource allocation may seem informal. But over time it forms a definite pattern. In many organizations, the levels of organizational structure are clearly visible on an office-building floor. Secretaries sit at open desks. Staff without supervisory responsibility—those at the bottom of the organizational chart—occupy windowless cubicles. Personnel who exercise first-line supervision have offices with windows and doors. The department manager occupies the fabled "corner office," which is served by a personal secretary/receptionist and endowed with amenities such as conference tables and upholstered couches.

Varieties of Organizational Structure

The most easily observed fact about organizations is that no two are exactly alike. Business organizations "feel" different from public agencies. The "flavor" of a sports club is different from that of a political club. Even organizations involved in the same line of work seem different.

It is often possible, moreover, to detect differences from organization to organization in the roles played by people with similar job descriptions or titles. Teachers in one school, for example, may assign extra homework as punishment for bad behavior. Teachers in another school may let unruly kids off with a warning.

One of the classic studies of behavior in organizations provides numerous examples of structural variation. In the 1950s, Burns and Stalker's *Management of Innovation*[6] compared organization in firms concerned with several different types of product.

One of the operations studied by Burns and Stalker was a rayon factory. In the plant, job duties were strictly defined. There were several levels of supervision. There seemed to be a rule for every aspect of the operation. To solve problems, workers and managers often referred to an operating manual known as the "factory Bible."

Another firm that Burns and Stalker described manufactured electronic equipment. Both manufacturing and research and development took place at the same site. In parts of the operation, the responsibilities of one individual often seemed to merge with those of another. There were only a few levels of management. Subordinates interacted freely with their supervisors, and the top administrator's door was always open. Solutions to problems were sought through discussion by small groups of engineers and managers.

Differences in the overall picture presented by these organizations reflect differences in structure. In turn, differences in structure account for differences in patterns of thinking and behavior among role incumbents of different organizations. A basic understanding of organizations requires a grasp of why structure differs from organization to organization.

A review of various organizations' differences in structure helps illustrate the relationship of structure to observable patterns of role behavior. People who study organizational structures most often distinguish them according to the dimensions of *formalization, centralization, hierarchy, complexity,* and *integration.* Other potentially important structural distinctions among organizations include *locus of initiative, flexibility, accessibility,* and *opportunity ladders.*

Formalization

Formalization denotes the degree of formality of a formal organization. Recall from Chapter 1 that a formal organization is defined as one in which behavior takes place according to standardized patterns recognizable to everyone. All organizations are "formal" in that they have specific procedures for doing things, qualifications for entry, criteria for advancement, and often rules governing dress, including army uniforms and civilian dress codes.

Some organizations are more formal than others. Organizations with the highest degree of formality have the most rules. Responsibilities in these organizations tend to be highly defined. The boundaries between roles are readily perceived and widely understood. Problems are solved by reference to technical manuals and codes of regulations.

Organizations with lower levels of formalization permit more spontaneous action. People can substitute for each other (assume each other's roles) when necessary. Problems are solved through discussion among the people whose interests are involved. Solutions to problems may take the form of inventive, new types of action rather than standard procedures.

Organizations with a high degree of formalization resemble the rayon factory described by Burns and Stalker. Organizations with relatively low levels of formalization resemble the electronics plant.

Observers aiming to assess degree of formalization can use several convenient markers. In a work organization, the number and length of job descriptions per 100 employees is an indicator of formalization. Amount of paperwork required for carrying out a given procedure is another indicator. A college or university that requires completion of a long, complex application form is more highly formalized than one that requires an application form of only a few pages.

Centralization

Centralization denotes the degree to which decision making in an organization is concentrated in only a few hands. Roles in highly centralized organizations have little discretion. Except for the top leaders, few individuals make major decisions. Geographically dispersed units of a centralized organization look to the "home office" for instructions despite their geographic remoteness.

Government and politics furnish good examples of highly centralized organizations. The Communist Party of V. I. Lenin carried centralization to an extreme. Major decisions affecting not only the Soviet Union but also Communist activity worldwide were made by a small, secretive body of party leaders in Moscow.

The national government of modern, democratic France, though, is also a highly centralized organization. Major decisions are made in ministries in Paris and carried out in all French "departments," the equivalent of our states. A famous story illustrates centralization in French government. According to the 19th-century historian Hippolyte Taine, the minister of education prided himself on being able to announce, just by consulting his watch, the page of Virgil to which all the schoolboys of France were turning at that exact moment.[7]

It is notable that government in the United States is highly decentralized by comparison. Part of the United States Constitution known as the "reserve clause" ensures that states retain independent power in any area not specifically delegated to the federal government. Independent state legislatures have developed a wide variety of criminal and civil codes and systems of taxation.

Large business firms offer both highly centralized and decentralized examples. In his study of the 50 largest United States companies, business historian A. D. Chandler[8] describes transition from centralized to decentralized structures. Early in the 20th century, these businesses were quite centralized. A single body of top managers at "headquarters" made decisions regarding investment, production, and marketing for hundreds of products and plants located throughout the world.

By the middle of the century, though, the majority of these firms had undergone a major process of decentralization. Headquarters no longer made operating decisions. These decisions were delegated to managers running separate, independent divisions. Each division manager now had the power to decide how raw materials were to be obtained, what goods were to be produced, what volumes were to be manufactured, and how products were to be sold. Management at the firm's home office confined its function largely to monitoring profitability of the divisions and providing them with capital.

Hierarchy

Hierarchy is the most visible dimension of organizational structure. Hierarchy comprises a system of successive levels of supervision within an organization. Typically, hierarchies are depicted in the form of a pyramid. A single "boss" or top echelon makes the major decisions. Middle managers are required to act in a manner consistent with these decisions, and so on down to line managers, foremen, clerical personnel, factory operatives, and foot soldiers.

Hierarchy is a highly visible part of military organizations and some organized religions. Armies and navies have generals and admirals at the top, who give orders to colonels and captains, and so on. Catholic priests work under the supervision of prelates such as bishops and cardinals, and everyone is required to accept the dictates of the Pope.

Most organizations have some kind of hierarchy. It is difficult to conceive of an organization of any size without one. But organizations differ in the number of levels of their hierarchies. Organizational structures are often characterized as "tall" versus "flat." A tall organizational structure has many levels of decision-making and supervision between the top manager and the operative. A flat organizational structure has very few levels of hierarchy. Researchers have observed that large manufacturing firms, such as steel and automobiles, tend to have tall hierarchies. Research and development organizations as well as start-up firms tend to be flat.

While people often refer to the hierarchy in their organizations as a chain of command, this is not always accurate. Supervisors may issue guidelines or define objectives rather than issuing detailed instructions or direct orders. The degree to which directives from a supervisor to a subordinate actually resemble commands depends on the organization's degree of formalization.

Complexity

The dimension of *complexity* refers to the *number* of hierarchies or other foci of communication and control in an organization. Traditionally, organizations have only one hierarchy. Organizations with a single, identifiable hierarchy are characterized as *monarchic*. Inspection of the organizational landscape reveals exceptions to the monarchic model.

Hospitals are traditionally regarded as having multiple hierarchies. All such organizations have an administrative structure forming the traditional, tall pyramid. An "administrator" resides on top, directly supervising department heads in areas such as finance, operations, and marketing. Each department head supervises several managers, who in turn supervise operatives such as bookkeepers, salespeople, and maintenance workers.

Health care professionals, though, have traditionally operated outside the management hierarchy. Physicians, for example, operated outside the hospital management hierarchy through most of the 20th century. The top administrator of a hospital could not direct the most junior physician in matters regarding patient care. Rather, physicians maintained their own hierarchy.

A physician who had completed his or her training exercised supervision over residents. Senior residents supervised junior residents. Less formally, the most senior and widely esteemed doctors reviewed and commented on the work of junior colleagues.

A similar structure prevails in modern universities. The university president and his or her assistants directly supervise chains of middle managers and office staff. But teaching faculty maintain a separate and independent hierarchy, with tenured, senior faculty (full and associate professors) reviewing the performance of assistant professors.

Less traditional institutions often have structural complexity of a different form. The so-called *matrix organization,* for example, departs form the monarchic model. In these organizations, people work under several different supervisors, moving back and forth as the needs of the organization change.

Highly complex organizations seem more appealing than the single hierarchy monolith. But management decisions are harder to make in the more complex setting. Decision making in complex organizations requires negotiation and compromise among independent executives. Implementation of decisions requires effective action in several chains of supervision.

Integration

The concept of integration in an organization refers to the degree of coordination and interdependence among diverse parts. Integration of various degrees may be observed in relationships among people and among organizational roles. In highly integrated organizations, occupants of each role have accurate knowledge of the expectations governing other roles. People in a given role know what those in other roles need in order to do their jobs well.

The concept of integration also applies to organizational units (divisions and departments) and subunits (special purpose work groups within departments). Separate units in an organization can operate with a surprisingly low degree of integration. They may know little about each other's operations, or they may even work at cross-purposes. Business researchers, for example, have reported cases of poor integration between manufacturing and marketing units. The marketing unit seeks to maximize sales, while the manufacturing unit seeks to limit production to restrain costs and safeguard quality.

Integration may seem to be a natural feature of organizations. Actually, it is high in some organizations and low in others. It is not unusual for an employee, customer, or client to remark that "the right hand doesn't know what the left hand is doing," an indication of poor integration in an organization providing goods or services.

High levels of integration prevail in firms referenced in the business press as "integrated oil companies." These firms, including giants such as Chevron and Arco, explore for petroleum, pump crude oil, produce refined commodities (heating oil, diesel fuel, and gasoline of various grades), ship crude and refined products, and carry out large-scale marketing (including market research, advertising, and the operation of gas stations). Insufficient organization would result in problems such as shipments from the oil fields in excess of storage and refining capacity and market demand.

Some government agencies are also models of integration. The Internal Revenue Services (IRS), for example, attempts to apply the same interpretation of tax code in units located throughout the United States. Government units performing less standardized tasks, such as school boards, may operate with a lower level of integration.

Organizations concerned with the delivery of health care are among the least integrated. Firms like Tenet, Healthnet, and Columbia/HCA operate numerous hospitals and contract with thousands of physicians to provide patient care. But health professionals often perform their day-to-day tasks with little understanding of the challenges facing hospital administrators. Difference in technical background and rewards sought from work make integration difficult.

Observers can estimate an organization's level of integration by counting the number of *liaison devices* it uses. Liaison devices include documents such as interoffice memos and circulars. Interoffice memos are designed to inform people in diverse roles of each other's actions and needs. Circulars inform role incumbents of management policy and directives. Other than documents, liaison devices include meetings, retreats, and certain forms of in-service training. The percentage of an organization's personnel slots dedicated to liaison-related work is also an indicator of integration.

Locus of Initiative

Comparisons among organizations reveal differences in the liberty of lower-level people to initiate action or make suggestions to upper-level managers. People sometimes refer to this distinction as "top-down" versus "bottom-up." Role expectations in organizations reflect the approved locus of initiative. Instructions on whether the individual is expected to initiate contact, provide information, or make suggestions to a higher-up is "wired into" his or her consciousness via relational role expectations.

The locus of initiative in "membership organizations" is typically "bottom-up." Membership organizations are dues-supported, formal collectivities designed to provide direct service to members. Members may be individual people or other organizations such as clubs. Recreational clubs are included in this category. So are professional societies such as the American Medical Association and industry groups such as the National Association of Manufacturers. These organizations depend on the desires of their members. Members are often included in decision making through participation in standing committees and task forces.

An entity of the type known as the community-based organization (CBO) places special emphasis on maintaining a bottom-up structure. CBOs aim at improving quality of life in the neighborhoods in which they are located. They have attempted to improve health, safety, and employment opportunities in their localities. A high proportion of CBOs serve communities with many poor and minority residents. Many receive financial support from charitable foundations.

CBOs are presumed to represent the needs of the community. To accomplish this purpose, they include community residents on their governing boards. The foundations that support CBOs continuously encourage this representation. Lower-level staff, often community residents themselves, are encouraged to participate in decision making.

Not all organizations dedicated to public service are bottom-up. Major nonprofit organizations such as the American Cancer Society and the Braille Institute have reputations for being top-down. Goals are set by high-level staff, public figures, and technical specialists. Large numbers of volunteers carry out fundraising activities, but receive no formal encouragement to participate in decision making.

It is tempting to think of locus of initiative and hierarchy as more or less the same. The presence of hierarchy, some might think, is synonymous with top-down organization. But organizations relatively free from hierarchy may be top-down. Such organizations include small and start-up businesses where the boss (often the founder) insists on controlling everything. Organizations with several levels of hierarchy, on the other hand, may do their best to maintain an "open-door policy."

Flexibility

Flexibility in an organization refers to the ease with which rules and procedures may be applied or changed. Some organizations allow participants a great deal of discretion. As mentioned earlier, discretion signifies the degree to which a role incumbent has choice of action. A role with a great deal of discretion allows the incumbent to decide among options in response to a given situation.

The ease or difficulty of changing rules within an organization is the best indication of its flexibility. At one extreme, a large public agency may need to ask Congress or the state legislature for action to change any significant procedure. At the other extreme, management may habitually respond to changing conditions and make the required changes.

It is tempting to think of flexibility (or lack thereof) as no different from formalization. Yet an organization with a high level of formalization may be more flexible than one with low formalization. It is always possible to change the rules in a large, public agency through executive orders or legislation. An organization without as much paperwork or formal procedure may have less flexibility. No effort to change rules and procedures in a small, family-dominated firm may work, at least until top executives and their heirs have passed from the scene.

Accessibility

Accessibility signifies two important structural characteristics of organizations:

- The ability of outsiders to utilize the resources of an organization or affect its operations
- The ability of people outside an organization to enter one of its roles through processes such as hiring, nomination, or election

The degree to which an organization is accessible to outsiders in this fashion may be thought of as the organization's "shell." Some organizations have thicker shells than others. An accessible organization promotes ease of contact and entry. The mechanisms that promote or restrict access are rooted in individual roles and sustained by structure.

Organizations offer varying degrees of accessibility to customers or clients. Full-service retail businesses are by nature accessible to customers. In these organizations, salespeople are numerous and receive instructions and incentives to help customers. Inexpensive ethnic restaurants typically keep their doors open late, depending on walk-in clientele and low-paid employees.

Other organizations purposely restrict access. A high-prestige restaurant, for example, requires advance reservations. Business is based on high revenue from a relatively few customers, with personnel and scheduling arranged accordingly.

Health maintenance organizations (HMOs) are often charged with purposely restricting access. These organizations provide health services to people whose bills have been paid in advance. Typically, an employer makes a contract with an HMO to cover its employees. The HMO receives no additional money if it provides an unexpectedly high volume of service. HMOs, then, have incentives for avoiding client service whenever this can be done without serious risk to the client's health. HMOs restrict access by employing relatively small numbers of receptionists and physicians in specialties such as urology and psychiatry. Some clients give up and elect to do without; others seek care from private doctors.

Organizations provide varying degrees of access to people seeking to become members. The most selective discourage applications by requiring significant paperwork and test taking prior to consideration. They may also set very high standards for admission. Selective universities and some government agencies build such mechanisms into their structure through the above-described formal procedures and instructions to employees in personnel or admissions.

Less-selective organizations may have simple, easily completed application procedures. Application forms are typically brief and technical standards low. The organization often allocates large numbers of people to recruitment-related positions. At various times in the late 20th century, the United States Army could be viewed as an organization of the "less-selective" type. Large state colleges and expensive, nonelite private universities are also of the less-selective variety.

For these organizations, low selectivity may be determined originally by external factors. In times of peace and prosperity, the army is unable to benefit from feelings of patriotism and lack of job alternatives that have historically brought applicants to its ranks. Some state universities are required to admit all qualified state residents who apply, limiting their selectivity. Private universities are typically tuition-driven. It should be noted that less-selective organizations often prune newcomers to ensure that only those with adequate performance capabilities are retained long-term. This process is sometimes called "selection after admission."

Opportunity Ladders

Organizations also differ in the degree of opportunity they offer their members to move into new, more desirable roles. Opportunity ladders, the pathways by which people move into more desirable roles, represent a form of accessibility limited to insiders. This form of accessibility reflects the ability of a member to enter roles other than the one he or she initially assumed. This dimension of structure strongly affects the member's personal fortunes, and hence his or her actions and thinking.

The opportunity for people to enter new roles with higher status and material benefits is an important feature of organizational structure. Structural features of work organizations that allow people to move up are known as *job ladders*. A job ladder is a sequence of positions with interrelated skills. Mastery of skills on the entry level of the ladder qualifies an employee for entry onto the next step and then higher as his or her skills and experience grow.

Social scientists describe an individual's move upward in status and income as *social mobility,* and the sequence of jobs he or she holds as his or her *career*. The structure of an organization clearly has implications for both. Some organizations are relatively rich in job ladders while others are relatively poor. Those with numerous job ladders of multiple rungs are said to have strong *internal labor markets*. An organization rich in job ladders offers more opportunity for long-term employment and social mobility than one poor in job ladders.

The organization offering the greatest opportunity will be one in which every entry position is part of a job ladder. This is true of many organizations. Technically, it is possible for any seaman in the United States Navy to rise to the level of rear admiral. At the close of the 20th century, all 15 of the top executives at United Parcel Service of America, Inc. (UPS) were individuals who had begun their careers sorting packages.[9] In many operations, though, technical personnel and factory operatives have no opportunity to rise beyond first-level supervisor. Technical and assembly-type manufacturing skills do not directly build management qualifications.

The presence of job ladders, and the length of those ladders, has important implications for individuals' performance in their roles. Perception of access to successively higher positions promotes motivation and a positive outlook. Nothing is more frustrating to an initially motivated employee than a "dead-end job," that is, a position without such access.

Researchers report that the job ladder picture differs markedly among organizations.[10] Large organizations tend to have longer job ladders than small ones.[11]

Several factors promote career ladders within government agencies. Typically, the law requires public agencies to post promotion opportunities. Often, examinations are scheduled and open to everyone in appropriate job classifications. Many public agencies have strong internal labor markets in part because their work requires knowledge of regulations, protocols, and internal workings that can be learned only on the job. For this reason, it may be impractical to recruit from outside for higher-level positions.

Organizations that specialize in technical work, such as research and development, have fewer and shorter career ladders. Scientists and engineers working for such organizations tend to remain in technical slots. A "flat" hierarchy means relatively few upper-level positions to move into. Science and technology, moreover, require general rather than firm-specific skills. This undermines both the employee's promotion opportunities and his or her job security. Engineers with MBAs are available for hire into management positions. Management often sees new science and engineering graduates, with their fresh skills and relatively low salary demands, as attractive replacements for experienced workers.

Job Ladders and the "Glass Ceiling"

Women typically earn less money and have lower-status jobs than men. Women seldom rise into top management positions. Few, if any, companies have official policies barring women from upper-level slots. An invisible barrier, though, seems to block the mobility of women in many organizations. This barrier is often referred to as "the glass ceiling."

Women's movement activists have looked to organizational structure as a factor in maintaining both the glass ceiling and patterns of inferior compensation. In the 1970s, commentator Rosebeth Moss Kanter theorized that the positions into which women were placed tended to be dead-end jobs. The jobs for which women were hired, she suggested, were either short- or non-ladder. She concluded that the structural position of women's roles limited their access to desirable jobs throughout their careers.[12]

A group of researchers tested this hypothesis in the mid-1980s.[13] They asked 897 employees and supervisors in six federal agency offices about individual chances for promotion and the number of positions to which employees might eventually have access. The researchers also asked employees how satisfied they felt about their promotion prospects.

As have other investigators,[14] these researchers found that men and women occupied different positions. But they detected no differences in how men and women felt about their chances for promotion. Interviews indicated that men and women perceived that they had about the same likelihood of being promoted. Objective data (records of promotions) confirmed the employees' opinions. Job ladders on which women found themselves had no fewer "rungs" than those typical of men. Men and women, moreover, expressed the same level of satisfaction with their perceived mobility prospects.

At least in the federal agencies studied, structural features did not seem to create disadvantages for women.

The above discussion has focused on job ladders in work organizations. But opportunity ladders exist in other organizations as well. Members of political parties seek to move up the ranks to positions such as precinct captain, district chair, and national committeeman. Volunteers in charitable societies such as the Red Cross aspire to officer status. People accept difficult assignments such as volunteer recruitment and fiscal management as "springboards" to prestigious, publicly visible positions.

Why Structures Differ Among Organizations

It is clear that a broad range of structures prevails among organizations. This observation raises two questions. First, people interested in organizations ask, what explains why an organization has the structure it is found to have? Second, and more important, is the structure found in an organization the most appropriate one in view of its objectives?

Explanations for the structure of an organization can be sought through several perspectives. These include the organization's size, age, technology, environment, and leadership.

Size

An organization's size has a clear effect on structure. Larger organizations seem to require more formalization, hierarchy, and top-down locus of initiation. The relationship of size to structure is understandable in terms of basic human capacities. An *entrepreneur* (an individual who is starting up a new business) managing a small group of workers doesn't need formal rules or hierarchy. He or she can communicate directly with everyone.

In a larger organization, the top executive cannot supervise every activity. He or she cannot stay in contact with every employee. At the early stage of an organization's growth, the executive might develop written procedures to govern specific operations such as assembly and inspection of products. As the business grows, the entrepreneur must hire additional management personnel to supervise groups of workers and undertake supporting functions such as accounting and marketing. Hierarchy is the result.

Small organizations permit lots of back-and-forth communication. A worker with a good idea can get management's attention simply by stopping an executive in the hallway. This process permits bottom-up as well as top-down initiation of ideas and procedures. Bottom-up initiative is less feasible in large organizations. In large organizations, managers and workers have more clearly separate workplaces. As size increases, upper-level managers typically work in other buildings and perhaps in other cities. Hierarchy itself makes it difficult for subordinates to initiate ideas upward.

The industrial societies of modern Europe and America furnish many illustrations of large organizations that are highly formal and hierarchical. These organizations permit little bottom-up initiative. Automobile firms, which employ hundreds of thousands of workers, are said to have up to 25 levels of management, from assembly line foreman to chief executive officer (CEO).

The ancient world also offers examples. The societies of ancient Mesopotamia and Egypt drew irrigation water from the rivers that flowed through their territories. Projects of this kind were necessary to support significant populations in desert countries. Construction and maintenance of dikes, canals, and aqueducts required coordinating the work of thousands. In the ancient world, such coordination was often made possible by the institution of slavery. The importance of slavery in Mesopotamia and Egypt is well known. It is difficult to imagine an organization with clearer hierarchy and more top-down management than one using slaves as its labor force.

Age

For generations, observers have pointed out that older organizations operate differently from newer ones. Older organizations tend to be less flexible, less accessible, and less open to bottom-up initiation of thinking and action. In part, this is a consequence of increasing size. Successful organizations tend to increase in size as time goes by.

Apart from size, though, organizations tend to become less flexible and less accessible as time goes by. Political parties and religious organizations seem to exemplify this process. Early Christianity consisted of bands of devotees following Jesus Christ and the apostles. These acolytes maintained direct communication with the master. Christianity was practiced in secret in ancient Rome, presumably among tight-knit groups of coreligionists. Today, the deliberations of established churches are often closed to ordinary communicants.

One needn't go back to the ancient world to witness this phenomenon. Cults in modern America often start as small groupings of people surrounding a guru. As time goes by, rituals are developed and officers appointed. New members see the guru only in pictures or at great distance in public gatherings.

The Development of Oligarchy: An Inevitable Process?

Micheles,[15] a famous observer of political parties, developed a widely cited theory of organizational maturation. He called his theory the "Iron Law of Oligarchy." Over time, he wrote, all organizations develop into oligarchies.

Oligarchies are "corrupt" groups of people who exercise governing functions in each other's interests rather than in the interests of the organization as a whole. They isolate themselves from the interests and needs of the membership. They allocate the most important roles to each other. They develop policies guided largely by their own concerns. They allocate resources for their personal comfort.

Micheles studied the Social Democratic Party in Germany at a time when it was open to new ideas. The party's official "line" emphasized responsiveness to the working class. Over time, however, it fell under the domination of a restricted group of insiders.

Micheles concluded that formation of oligarchies occurred in all organizations as they matured: hence, his "iron law."

The maturation process of an organization is similar to aging in individuals. As they get older, many people become less interested in new ideas and more protective of the resources they control. This process has been observed in business organizations, political parties, religious movements, and government agencies throughout the world. A study of the American civil rights movement produced evidence that movement organizations, as they matured, tended to try to work within the established political system. This maturation necessitated changes in their organizational structures.[16]

Technology

Observers of organizations have written a great deal about the effect of technology on social relations. Technology affects most aspects of human thinking and behavior. Today, transportation, communication, and computers provide instant linkages between people on opposite sides of the globe. It is not surprising to find people from entirely different civilizations today all drinking Coke, playing golf, and wearing dark suits to work.

Formulations regarding the relationship between technology and organizational structure became well known through the Tavistock Institute of London in the 1950s. The Tavistock Institute is famous for developing the *sociotechnical model* of organization. This model focuses attention on the manner in which technical requirements of tasks determine interpersonal and intergroup relationships at work. The structure of formal organizations must be compatible with these interpersonal and intergroup relationships.

Studies of coal mining in Britain provide clear examples of the relationship of technology to organizational structure.[17] In the 1940s, the British coal mining industry underwent rapid mechanization. Before that time, miners worked at the rock face with hand tools. Laborers hauled the coal away in carts. Familiar firsthand with the mines, George Orwell[18] and D. H. Lawrence[19] described the strenuous pick-and-shovel work of this era. Small groups of miners worked "stalls" a few feet wide. Each work group included a lead miner, or "hewer," the hewer's "mate," and one or two men who hauled the coal away. Paid according to their production, these small work groups had strong motivation to maximize their output. They also carried out their tasks with a high level of independence and solidarity. Great variability prevailed in coal availability and safety conditions at the rock face, which limited management's ability to direct the work.

Mechanization involved introducing large drilling machines capable of breaking rock along surfaces the length of many of the old stalls. Thus, the new mining procedure was known as the "longwall" method. This method no longer permitted small, intimate groups of miners to work together as autonomous teams. Machine operations transformed the mine's staffing patterns into those of a factory. Fifty to sixty workers per shift were required to operate the machinery, all working under the supervision of a shift foreman.

Much has been written about the effects of the technical transformation in British coal mining. Some observers report high levels of dissatisfaction and absenteeism among miners. This seemed particularly true of miners who had worked under the old system for a long time. Others have reported that the transformation created a stronger sense of solidarity among shift groups as a whole. This, they say, replaced feelings of intimacy and mutual dependence in the small work groups of old. But there can be no doubt that formalization increased substantially, at least at the operative level of the mine organization. Flexibility decreased.

The story of British coal mining illustrates a pattern typical of modern industry. Long-standing traditions of cooperation and workmanship are replaced by rationally planned organization. Scientific management as discussed above cannot be blamed on Frederick Winslow Taylor alone. Scientifically formulated and delimited work roles function well in connection with machine-paced labor and are usually adopted. Formalism, hierarchy, and top-down locus of initiative prevail.

Differences observed by Burns and Stalker also illustrate the effects of technology on organizational structure. The rayon factory they described was organized as a system of highly defined roles. Issues were resolved by reference to operating manuals, a highly formalistic process. This pattern is generally true of "continuous process" industries, such as those that produce oil and chemicals. Human tasks are built into the process, which demands that certain raw materials be combined with others at specific intervals and temperatures.

Less formalization was visible in the electronics plant described by these authors. Here, the product was relatively new. No process of production had been defined that was clearly the best way to operate. Hence, the structure permitted much bottom-up initiative.

High-level research and development tends to minimize hierarchy and maximize bottom-up thinking. One of the most famous historical instances illustrating this principle was the Manhattan Project, a super-secret effort in World War II to develop the atom bomb.[20] Working hours at the research facility in Los Alamos, New Mexico, were flexible. Hierarchy was minimal. Solutions to technical problems often came from the bottom up. Encouragement of scientific creativity depended on a structure that promoted independent thinking and free communication among the scientists.

Continuous process technology, mass production, and workflow integration (the extent to which flow of work is automated, interdependent, and measurable) generally require formalization, integration, and hierarchy. The opposite is true of work that resembles the craft occupations of yesteryear. Large corporations usually allow artists in their marketing units freedom to develop creative ideas. Manufacturing firms that maintain research and development (R&D) operations often locate scientists and engineers in separate units free from the day-to-day presence of visible hierarchy.

Technology has its most visible influence on organizational structure in craft-like work activity. Developments much more immediate than the midcentury transformation of British coal mining illustrate this point. Medicine in the United States provides an important example.

As late as the 1980s, most medicine in the United States was practiced by solo doctors working in their own offices or in loosely integrated organizations. Late-century medicine saw the development of "managed care." Under this system, large numbers of doctors sold their practices to corporations. Physicians then cared for patients who had entered into contracts with the corporations. Under these arrangements, physicians faced restrictions on the drugs they could prescribe and treatments they could carry out. They were required to check with outside personnel to see whether a particular treatment was acceptable. Many other physicians kept their own practices but signed contracts with insurance companies involving significant restriction and oversight of their professional work. In return, the insurance companies funneled patients to the offices of these doctors.

A doctor's office today may look much as it did in the 1980s. But the organizational structure under which most physicians practice has changed significantly. Although doctors today work in private-seeming offices, most are tied to large, formal organizations. These ties represent much higher levels of formalization, centralization, and integration, as well as "top-down" initiation of decision making, than earlier generations of physicians could have imagined. Formalization has produced rules for practice and billing. Centralization has taken the form of payment from one or a few sources rather than from numerous individual patients. Integration has involved memos and circulars regarding treatment activities—doctors, for example, receive reports comparing their own work with that of other physicians in the plan. The organization of medicine under managed care looks more like assembly-line work than traditional craftsmanship.

Many observers have interpreted this organizational transformation as a consequence of technological change. The late 20th century saw development of extremely expensive medical technology. Coronary artery bypass graft (CABG) for heart disease and joint replacement for arthritis are two familiar examples. Patients demanded access to the new technology, greatly increasing costs to the insurance companies and employers that paid most of the bills. These payers sought methods to reduce the volume of high-technology, high-cost treatment. The organizational system represented by managed care offered a mechanism for the desired cost control.

Environment

An organization's social, economic, and physical surroundings constitute its environment. Several means through which an organization's environment exerts influence have already been described. Environment helps determine an organization's structure itself. A few examples include

- Legal environment
- Political economy
- Labor market

Legal Environment

Formal organizations in modern society function within a vast matrix of laws. Laws regarding incorporation allow organizations to become legally separate from their memberships. Resulting charters specify the manner in which the organization is to be governed. The concept of an organization as a distinct structure is made concrete through application of the law.

Laws govern the nature of work agreements in organizations. The law, for example, prohibits slavery. Expectations associated with all roles include the option of the incumbent's departure after the term of a contract or period of enlistment, or simply at will. Antidiscrimination laws increase access to job ladders within organizations.

Political Economy

An earlier chapter has described "political economy" as a society's beliefs regarding ownership of property, political power, and the rights of citizens. The term *political culture* is also frequently used regarding these beliefs. The earlier discussion characterized America's political economy as "democratic welfare capitalism." Its provisions give Americans the feeling that they must be self-sufficient but at the same time deserve fair treatment from their employers and government.

Political economy helps determine the prevailing structure of organizations in every society. Beliefs about proper patterns of thinking and behavior help determine the organizational roles people are willing to accept. These beliefs also "legitimize" or "delegitimize" the structural features of organizations.

The history of France furnishes a widely cited example.[21] Before the French revolution (1789), kings of the Bourbon family ruled with absolute power. Louis XIV is said to have invited every important noble in France to reside at his huge palace for much of the year. This forestalled temptation by France's noble class to challenge the king's absolutism. All major roads led to Paris.

A belief in centralization is an important part of France's political culture. Fostered under royal administration, this habit of mind survives today. It is little wonder that modern government agencies in France delegate little or no policy-making authority to provincial officials. Officials in French departments merely implement policy made in Paris.

Historians and political scientists have made similar observations about pre-revolutionary Russia and the later Soviet empire. Before the revolution (1917), Russia was governed by the dynasty of Romanov Czars. These rulers centralized decision making and power in Moscow. The Czars were even more powerful than the kings of France, heading the Russian Orthodox Church as well as the country's civil government.

V. I. Lenin's Communists triumphed in the 1917 revolution. They did so as a secret, highly centralized political and military organization. Most Russians might have rejected communism if they had had the choice. But members of Lenin's party still believed they had the duty to force the country in the "right" direction.

It seems natural, then, that organizations in the postrevolutionary Soviet Union were structured in a highly centralized, hierarchical, top-down manner. This was true in the government, state-run factories, and the ruling Communist Party. People, it seemed, believed that centralization and top-down decision making were necessary for order, justice, and economic well-being. Russians expressed such sentiments even after the fall of the Soviet police state.

Contrast this picture with America's political economy. The U.S. was founded by a voluntary confederation of a group of sovereign states. Independent decision making at the level of local government always enjoyed legitimacy. America was also founded by people seeking individual liberty and the opportunity to "make good" on their own. These principles make Americans suspicious of relationships involving too much top-down decision making, hierarchy, and integration. The result is that structure in American government agencies, businesses, and voluntary organizations is generally "flatter" and more open than in comparable organizations in other countries.

Labor Market

External labor markets govern availability and "price" of potential members of an organization. Work organizations must deal continuously with labor markets. Large numbers of workers relative to available jobs reduce the compensation a firm must offer. In times of abundant labor supply, firms need not spend much on recruitment. People study the classified ads carefully when jobs are scarce. Compensation and recruitment costs rise when jobs are abundant and workers relatively scarce.

In a tight labor market, firms seek ways to make themselves more attractive to workers. Direct supervision may be relaxed, amounting to reduced formalization. Job ladders may be developed and promoted as an incentive for people already recruited to remain on the job. Firms concerned with labor supply also provide workers with amenities such as pleasant surroundings and relaxation of dress codes. Few software manufactures in the booming 1990s, for example, objected to the orange hair, tattoos, and body piercings of highly sought-after programmers. Organizations can be expected to adopt more rigid structures in markets where labor is plentiful.

Environmental phenomena akin to labor markets affect organizations other than business firms. Political and charitable organizations compete for volunteers. Armies compete with civilian organizations (and against disinclination of potential recruits to accept military discipline and personal risk). A scarce supply of people for any reason predisposes organizations to appropriate structural modifications.

Leadership

It seems logical that leaders should influence the structures of their organizations. Leaders vary as much as do organizations themselves. Leaders have ample opportunity to influence structure. Over time, their preferences regarding recruitment, retention, advancement, and reward affect role expectations and hence structure.

Leadership in organizations emerges from many different quarters. People work themselves up the ranks to become leaders in both business firms and government agencies. Leaders in business may attain their positions through family ties. Executives in government often receive their posts as political appointments.

Styles of leadership differ as well. Some leaders practice an aggressive style, directly initiating strategies for attaining objectives and doing a great deal of direct supervision. Other leaders prefer to delegate. They allow subordinates to act independently in pursuit of organizational objectives.

The personality and style of the leader seem likely to affect structure. It may be speculated that leaders with a thirst for power promote centralization. Those who are suspicious of others may build highly integrated organizations, characterized by elaborate communication networks.

Researchers studying 74 business firms in Montreal have provided evidence that the leader's personality and style have marked influence on structure.[22] The investigators interviewed the CEO of each firm to determine his or her "need for achievement," a personality trait described in Chapter 2, and abbreviated as n-achievement. Measures of n-achievement reflect a person's degree of striving to meet standards of excellence, to accomplish difficult tasks, and to achieve success. People with high n-achievement are "high achievers."

The investigators found that firms headed by leaders with high n-achievement had the highest levels of formalization, integration, and centralization. Relationships between this aspect of the CEO's personality and organizational structure were strongest in smaller, newer firms. In such firms, structure had not had a chance to solidify before the interviewed CEO had assumed leadership.

Other evidence for the influence of leadership and structure emerges from Chandler's study of decentralization among multinational firms.[8] Firms in which families retained management control tended to delay adopting the new structure. It may be surmised that family members have strong attachments to tradition and thus reinforce rather than change existing structure.

Suboptimization: A Form of Structural Failure

The importance of organizational structure is best illustrated by what happens when structure is inappropriate, weak, or absent.

This chapter began with descriptions of people who carried out their roles in a manner insufficiently coordinated with the priorities and needs of the organization as a whole. Examples included soldiers breaking from the chain of command and religious people operating outside the church discipline.

But the importance of structure is revealed in the behavior of organizational subunits as well. The term *subunit* denotes a part of an organization with a specialized function, intended to support a department or the organization as a whole.

Suboptimization takes place when a subunit operates in a manner that maximizes its own rewards but is detrimental to the organization as a whole.

For example, a marketing department may be very effective at making sales. Its aggressive promotion and sales campaign greatly increase orders. This success brings bonuses for the marketing department's employees and an increase in the department's budget. The successful campaign optimizes outcomes for the marketing department.

But the marketing department's success may harm the firm as a whole. Units involved in production may be unable to fulfill the volume of orders placed. Aggressive salespeople may have made exaggerated claims about the product. Funds allocated as rewards to marketing people may be better spent elsewhere. More resources for research and development may, for example, result in an improved product. Funds allocated to updating production plants may increase volume and lower unit costs.

Suboptimization is likely to occur when an organization's structure is too weakly integrated or too complex.

Function Versus Dysfunction in Organizational Structure

An important practical issue concerns the appropriateness of an organization's structure in view of its objectives and goals. This question is crucial for an organization competing against other organizations, as in business, politics, or war. Due to error in design, accident of evolution, or change in the environment, it is likely that no organizational structure is ideal. But it is often difficult to determine whether development of a more appropriate structure is desirable or feasible.

It is safe to assume that any existing structure has some practical value. Why, one might ask, would an organization maintain a particular structure if benefits did not accrue from it? Wouldn't the membership, the congregation, the management always be on the lookout for ways to promote effectiveness and efficiency? Typically, it can be assumed that the structure observed in an organization indeed serves one or more discernible functions. The relationship between technology and organizational structure described above provides some clear examples.

Paradoxically, it can be assumed that the structure of any organization may be dysfunctional as well. A stably functioning organization, for example, may lack career ladders, ensuring periodic turnover of valued employees. Formalization may contribute to management control, yet such a feature may stand in the way of service delivery tailored to the needs of individual clients. Hierarchy may promote coordination yet discourage initiative in the lower ranks.

It is not unusual to observe organizations whose structures foster dysfunction. Inefficiency, faulty decisions, and ineffective recruitment may result. A number of factors may be identified that promote and maintain structures known to be inappropriate in view of an organization's purpose. These include

- Politics: dominance of the organization's leadership by people intent on monopolizing power
- Historical survival: maintenance of a structure that was once highly functional (such as centralization in a large corporation) but that has been rendered obsolete by the organization's scope of business
- Technical dominance: design of organizations by industrial engineering techniques resulting in sufficient dissatisfaction and conflict among employees to adversely affect attainment of objectives
- Organizational "slack": presence of resources sufficient to hide the consequences of inappropriate structure or other sources of inefficiency

It is important to remember that structure, like other features of an organization, may be functional for only a restricted number of people with interest in the organization. It is undeniable that many organizations operate less effectively than possible. Meyer and Zucker even characterize organizations in a variety of fields as surviving yet "permanently failing."[23] Yet even such dysfunctional organizations produce value for some stakeholders, such as well-paid directors or unionized workers. It is not always clear to an organization's leadership whether structural change is worth the resources and risks required to bring it about.

Issues and Applications

Structure affects both the lives of individuals in an organization and the ability of the organization itself to achieve its purposes. The structure of an organization helps determine the opportunities available to individuals and the desirability of membership. Change in structure can produce both favorable and unfavorable effects on organizational effectiveness.

- A civil engineer receives offers from two companies. One is a major international construction firm known for large-scale projects using industry-standard technology. The other is a small company renowned for applying state-of-the-art expertise to special, one-of-a-kind projects. The engineer faces a likely trade-off due to the structure expectable in each organization. The large construction firm is more likely to offer multiple and long career ladders, facilitating entry into senior management. The small company may help the engineer attain professional growth, but it is less likely to offer upward mobility opportunities.

- During her employment in a law firm, a period of 30 years, a secretary has seen favorable changes in her place in the organization. Improvement first came when the firm adopted personal computers. Members of the secretarial pool were the first to be sent for training. These women became the company "experts" in word processing. People of high status in the firm, including senior partners, asked them for advice on computer-related matters. Secretarial pool members, in turn, felt comfortable initiating communication with a broader range of the firm's employees. The trend continued as new software products were adopted. Salaries in the secretarial pool rose. For formerly low-status secretaries, technology had brought favorable change in the firm's structure.

- The leadership of an environmental action organization decides that its attempts to influence the government must be better coordinated and more sharply focused. Gradually, it replaces volunteers with paid professionals in top positions. A closed-door policy is instituted, making it difficult for volunteers to communicate with the leadership. The organization scores a few victories through expert legal maneuvering and negotiation. But membership rolls and financial contributions diminish. An initially enthusiastic corps of volunteers feels shut out by the new hierarchical structure and looks for other organizations in which to carry out its activism.

Chapter Review and Major Themes

Within organizations, structure comprises the enduring framework that guides the behavior of individuals toward each other. Organizational structure links roles in a manner that, ideally, promotes coordination of effort to achieve the organization's objectives.

Among formal organizations, important differences in structural characteristics prevail. The most readily apparent differences occur along the dimensions of formalization, centralization, hierarchy, complexity, and integration. The internal labor market constitutes a structural facet of particular interest. Some organizations have numerous and long career ladders, others short or nonexistent ones. Career ladders are chains of successively higher level positions that allow members to move from entry-level to senior status.

Organizational structure may be determined by deliberate design of roles and their reporting relationships, or by evolution over time. Researchers have documented that entrepreneurial leaders leave a lasting imprint on the structures of the organizations they found. Technology has been demonstrated as a prime determinant of organizational structure. This seems particularly true of work organizations: when production technology changes, so must relationships among individuals and subunits.

The analytical perspectives introduced in Chapter 3 provide a rich background for understanding organizational structure. Figure 5.2 outlines relationships between organizational structure and environment, function, and conflict. Again, the broad arrows in the diagram represent visible and generally expectable effects. The slender arrows represent less usually observed but potentially important effects. Signs (+ or −) associated with each arrow indicate a positive or negative effect.

All three analytical perspectives are relevant to organizational structure. Environmental features such as technology and market help determine structure, as classical work of the Tavistock Institute and A. D. Chandler attest. Less visible may be the impact of organizational structure on the environment. On the level of entire countries, material presented in this chapter has suggested that the structure of a governing elite organization mirrors public expectations. It should be recognized also that the elite organization may strongly influence the structure of society as a whole. This subject will receive significant attention in Chapter 15.

Organizational structure, it would appear, contributes to the organization's functional capabilities. Taylorism and modern industrial engineering embrace organizational design as an optimal means for accomplishing objectives. An explanation of structure in terms of its contributions to concrete objectives is a hallmark of rational systems theory.

In many organizations, though, structure has dysfunctional effects. The structural separation of units in an organization fosters suboptimization. In work organizations, an absence of widely accessible career ladders promotes frustration, dampens productivity, and encourages desirable employees to migrate. The existence of hierarchy makes it difficult for high-level personnel to benefit from the talent and experience of individuals on the organization's lower rungs.

Organizational structure can be viewed as a safeguard against conflict. In systems where everyone knows his or her place in a hierarchy, for example, conflict would seem easy to resolve. Supervisory personnel are empowered to decide issues over which their subordinates might disagree. Under hierarchical structure, however, competition and associated interpersonal conflict may become intense as

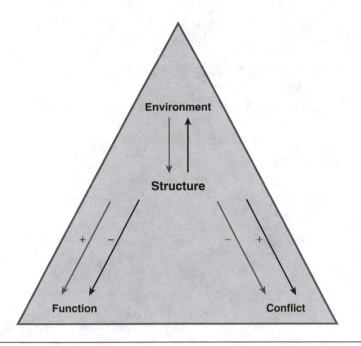

Figure 5.2   Analytical Perspectives Applied to Structure

rivals fight their way up. Complex structures, as illustrated by the modern hospital, can give rise to conflict as hierarchies compete for dominance.

If the familiarity of the organizational chart is a valid indication, structure is the most widely recognizable feature of the formal organization. Yet the actual "rule" of structure is less complete than organizational charts imply. Even the best-established structure cannot prevent the development of informal networks that share information, exchange resources, and exercise initiative according to channels of their own making. It is important to remember that organizational structure is nonphysical, ultimately residing only in the minds of an organization's members. Thus, its features are continually subject to alteration and evasion by innovators, entrepreneurs, and rogues.

Structure, moreover, cannot be said to exercise undisputed rule at the highest organizational levels. The multidivisional business organizations described by Chandler allow much liberty to regional management. Network theory, which places emphasis on relationships among organizations that in many respects are independent of each other, may be more suitable to such organizations than rational systems theory. In the 21st century, even more divisionalized arrangements have become characteristic of multinational firms. The limitations placed by such arrangements on control by central management are detailed in Chapter 15.

Discussion Questions

1. What steps can an observer take to determine the structure of an organization?

2. Identify an organization with which you are familiar. How centralized is this organization? Is this degree of centralization favorable to the organization's objectives?

3. In view of possible changes in the social, economic, and physical surroundings of today's organizations, how likely is it that fundamental changes in organizational structure will take place in the coming decades? What, if any, changes would you expect to occur?

4. Does structure affect the mobility prospects of women and minorities in organizations today? How widespread is this phenomenon? Are there important differences among organizations in this respect?

5. The concluding paragraph of Chapter 5 asserts that the "rule" of structure is incomplete. Do you think this is true in most organizations? If structure does not determine actual relationships among units or individuals, does this help or hurt the organization?

References

1. Alvarez, R., & Robin, L. (2000). Organizational structure. In E. F. Borgatta & R. Montgomery (Eds.), *Encyclopedia of sociology* (pp. 2002–2017). New York: John Wiley & Sons.
2. Taylor, F. (1947). *Scientific management*. New York: Harper and Row.
3. Scholl, A. (1999). *Balancing and sequencing of assembly lines*. Heidelberg, NY: Springer.
4. Barley, S. R. (1990). Alignment of technology and structure through roles and networks. *Administrative Science Quarterly, 35*, 61–103.
5. Salazar, A. J. (1996). An analysis of the development and evolution of roles in a small group. *Small Group Research, 27*, 475–503.
6. Burns, T., & Stalker, G. M. (1961). *The management of innovation*. London: Tavistock.
7. Taine, H. A. (1894). *The modern regime* (J. Durand, Trans.). London: Sampson, Low, Marston.
8. Chandler, A. D. (1962). *Strategy and structure*. Cambridge: MIT Press.
9. Zuckerman, L. (1999, July 22). Employee-owners' windfall: UPS hears market's song. *New York Times*, p. A1.
10. Baron, V. N., Davis-Blake, A., & Bielby, W. T. (1986). The structure of opportunity: How promotion ladders vary within and among organizations. *Administrative Science Quarterly, 31*, 248–274.
11. Kalleberg, A. L., & Van Buren, M. E. (1996). Is bigger better? Explaining the relationship between organization size and job rewards. *American Sociological Review, 61*, 47–66.
12. Kanter, R. M. (1977). *Men and women of the corporation*. New York: Basic Books.
13. Markham, W. T., Scott, S. J., Bonjean, C. M., & Corder, J. (1986). Gender and opportunity in the federal bureaucracy. *American Journal of Sociology, 91*, 129–150.

14. Huffman, M. L. (1995). Organizations, internal labor market policies, and gender inequality in workplace supervisory authority. *Sociological Perspectives, 38,* 381–397.

15. Micheles, R. (1949). *Political parties.* Glencoe, IL: Free Press.

16. Andrews, K. T. (2001). Social movements and policy implementation: The Mississippi civil rights movement and the war on poverty, 1965–1971. *American Sociological Review, 66,* 71–95.

17. Trist, E. L., & Bamforth, K. W. (1951). Some social and psychological consequences of the longwall method of coal-getting. *Human Relations, 4,* 3–38.

18. Orwell, G. (1958). *The road to Wigan Pier.* New York: Harcourt Brace & World.

19. Lawrence, D. H. (1991). *Sons and lovers.* New York: Knopf.

20. Davis, N. P. (1968). *Lawrence and Oppenheimer.* New York: Simon and Schuster.

21. De Tocqueville, A. (1955). *The old regime and the French Revolution.* Garden City, NY: Doubleday Anchor.

22. Miller, D., & Droge, C. (1986). Psychological and traditional determinants of structure. *Administrative Science Quarterly, 31,* 539–557.

23. Meyer, M. W., & Zucker, L. G. (1989). *Permanently failing organizations.* Newbury Park, CA: Sage.

CHAPTER 6

Reward and Punishment

Learning Objective

To understand how reward and punishment promote compliance with role expectations, accommodation to structure, and achievement of organizational goals.

Principles

○ Organizations must motivate people to obey provisions of their roles and ensure that roles are carried out in a manner consistent with the organization's structure.

○ Rewards in organizations include two major types:
  • Intrinsic: associated directly with the content of the role or goals of the organization
  • Extrinsic: focused on sources of gratification outside the organizational role and dissociated from the organization's activities or objectives

○ Pay is the most obvious reward in work organizations. But even in such organizations, rewards of other kinds are important. These include
  • Companionship: opportunities to socialize with other people
  • Status enhancement: prestige associated with job titles and mobility
  • Task satisfaction: gratification associated with success at tasks and challenges

○ Punishment techniques in formal organizations include pay freezes or reductions, assignment to undesirable (or hazardous) duty, career immobility, ostracism, demotion, corporal punishment, and termination.

○ Neither reward nor punishment automatically results in the outcomes sought. Greater rewards sometimes reduce productivity. Excessive punishment alienates members of an organization.

Carrots and Sticks

Every day and in every walk of life, hundreds of millions of human beings carry out organizational roles smoothly and predictably. Performance often requires the individual to undergo inconvenience. At the extreme, performance of a role may require the individual to put aside his or her most strongly felt needs and values. What makes this possible?

The question of why people comply with the demands of their organizations is at the heart of explaining organizational behavior. Only part of an individual's consciousness—the ideas, expectations, personal goals, and conceptions by which people live—is determined by his or her organization. Most people are not a perfect fit for the organizational roles they occupy. Organizational role expectations limit expression of inclinations derived from personal mental life and broader social forces. Still, most individuals comply with their role expectations and do not challenge the structure in which their roles reside.

At first, compliance with the roles, procedures, and routines of an organization seems to require little explanation. People in work organizations receive salaries. They carry out their responsibilities because they want to be paid. There is nothing mysterious about a person's compliance with the organization's needs in such instances. Employees need to earn a living. If they are unable or unwilling to perform in the required manner they simply resign.

But many organizations, perhaps most, are not of a work-oriented kind. Armies and navies, for example, have purposes other than producing goods, making profits for stockholders, or providing routine public services. Most members of the armed services cannot leave at will, particularly during wartime. But most soldiers and sailors nevertheless carry out their duties within acceptable norms.

By their very nature, voluntary organizations do not require people to join. Most offer only small-scale material benefits to their members: perhaps refreshments at meetings, maybe a few consumer discounts. Yet large numbers of people affiliate with recreational clubs, fraternal orders, churches, charitable societies, civic associations, and political parties. Members of these organizations typically obey the rules and accept the assignments they are asked to complete. Normally, members respect officers and accept their direction.

Even in work organizations, forces promoting compliance with rules, performance of responsibilities, and "fitting in" are far from simple. People of course work for pay. But many employees who show up year after year for a paycheck do their jobs with little enthusiasm. They may exercise low levels of concentration in learning or performing their jobs. In a favorable labor market, they may expend minimal effort, expecting that other positions will be available should they be terminated. In the most conventional "work-for-pay" situations, managers still face dilemmas over how much to pay, what to pay for, and how to allocate pay.

Forces favoring compliance and performance are usually referred to as *motivations*. People who study organizations often refer to motivational devices as "carrots" and "sticks." These metaphorical labels hark back to the days when farmers used mules to plough fields and pull wagons. The farmer would tempt a balking animal to exert the required effort by holding a carrot in front of its face. If the carrot proved ineffective (or if the farmer were punitively inclined), he would whack the animal with a stick to get it moving again.

In motivating people, "carrots" signify rewards. "Sticks" denote punishments, or "negative rewards." Management of people requires a sophisticated mix of positive and negative rewards. Magnitude, frequency, and type of both rewards and punishments have significant impacts on role performance.

The Nature of Rewards and Punishments

Rewards and *punishments* (also called *sanctions*) are measures that motivate individuals by enhancing or reducing their personal level of fulfillment or comfort. Rewards and sanctions can affect the individual in a biological, social, or psychological fashion. They can be physical or nonphysical, and direct or indirect. Rewards can be administered by adding material or human assets to the focal person's environment. Sanctions can be implemented by the withdrawal of resources.

Definitions of Rewards and Punishments in Organizations

Rewards comprise an organization's allocation of resources intended to increase an individual's level of gratification: biological, social, or psychological.

Punishments comprise an organization's allocation (or withdrawal) of resources, with the intention of decreasing an individual's level of gratification—biological, social, or psychological—or inflicting discomfort in any of these areas.

Types of Rewards

People reward others for carrying out desired behavior in a wide variety of ways. Classification of major types of rewards illustrates this variety. Each organization offers a different mix of rewards based on its resources and the preferences of leaders, managers, and members. Each individual receiving a reward may react somewhat differently from every other individual.

Extrinsic and Intrinsic Rewards

Extrinsic rewards are the most familiar and visible of those provided by organizations. Rewards of this kind enhance the individual's ability to obtain increased gratification from sources outside the organization, removed from his or her organizational role, and dissociated from the organization's activities or objectives.

Examples of extrinsic rewards are easy to find. The employee receives a bonus and buys a new car. The soldier receives a medal and shows it off to his civilian friends. The junior executive receives a high-visibility assignment requiring extensive travel and takes advantage of the associated amenities.

Intrinsic rewards are less frequently discussed but still familiar to most human beings. Rewards of this kind are linked directly with the content of the individual's organizational role or goals of the organization. They tend to be less readily visible than extrinsic rewards but often constitute powerful forces in people's lives.

There are many kinds of intrinsic rewards in formal organizations. The most important is personal gratification associated with success at tasks and challenges on the job. People everywhere feel good about a "job well done." Intrinsic reward is also found in fulfillment of a service ethic or mission made possible by the organization.

Examples of intrinsic rewards occur in a wide variety of organizational roles. The engineer feels personally gratified when he or she solves a technical puzzle. The positive emotions associated with this success often occur in the absence of enhanced monetary compensation. The social worker feels happy that he or she has helped a wayward youth return to family and school. Social workers choose their profession with the aim of "helping society," and this achievement validates the career choice. A construction worker finishes a difficult task on time and leaves the job site feeling that the people who use the building will benefit from his or her effort for years to come.

Intrinsic Reward in Siberia

Even under conditions of extreme material deprivation, intrinsic rewards exert a powerful hold on people.

In his book *One Day in the Life of Ivan Denisovich*, Russian author Alexander Solzhenitsyn[1] recalls this phenomenon in a Gulag prison camp.

A gang of inmates, sentenced to long terms at hard labor, had been ordered to construct a building on the frozen tundra. Although the gang leader announced quitting time, a pair named Shukhov and Senka kept working:

. . . as [the leader] strode down the ramp he called after him, jokingly: "Why do those bastards make the work day so short? We were just getting into our stride when they call it off."

Shukhov was now alone with Senka. . . .

Slap on the mortar. Down with the block. Press it home. See it's straight. Mortar. Block. Mortar. Block. . . .

Wasn't it enough that [the leader] had told them himself not to bother about the mortar? Just throw it over the wall and [****] off. But Shukhov wasn't made that way—eight years in a camp couldn't change his nature. He worried about anything he could make use of. About every scrap of work he could do—nothing must be wasted without good reason. . . .

"Finish, [****] you," shouted Senka. "Let's get out of here. . . ."

He picked up a barrow and ran down the ramp.

But Shukhov—and if the guards had put the dogs on him it would have made no difference—ran to the back and looked about. Not bad. Then he ran and gave the wall a good look over, to the left, to the right. His eye was as accurate as a carpenter's level. Straight and even. . . .

He dashed down the ramp.

Instrumental Versus Socioemotional Rewards

The concepts of *instrumental* and *socioemotional* rewards also distinguish different types of rewards. Instrumental rewards are those that members (actual or potential) of an organization value for the purpose of getting something done. These rewards can be used as "instruments" for pursuing objectives inside or outside the organizational role. Socioemotional rewards have less definite utility. They consist of good feelings about the organization or its members.

Pay is the most familiar of instrumental rewards. Cash is the most visible component of pay. Clearly, cash has value outside organizational roles, enabling the focal individual to meet his or her consumer needs. Most work organizations, and organizations with many other purposes, attract and retain human effort largely in return for cash or its equivalents.

Benefits constitute a second component of pay. These are nonmonetary items of economic value to the organization's participants. Benefits primarily include health, life, and disability insurance. In past decades, these forms of compensation were known as "fringe benefits," reflecting their unimportance relative to salary. Today, benefits occupy an important part of the employee's total compensation package. The high cost of health insurance impels many employees to seek out firms that offer this benefit and decline opportunities at firms that do not.

Organizations offer instrumental rewards other than salary and benefits. The possibility of making personal acquaintances in an organization constitutes an increasingly important kind of reward. A job in which an individual is able to make contacts yields business relationships, opportunities for employment elsewhere, friendships, and romantic liaisons. Instrumental rewards of a nonmonetary nature dominate the motivational picture in most voluntary organizations. Opportunities for contact making draw people to chambers of commerce, fraternal societies, and political clubs, where they often contribute long hours of otherwise uncompensated service.

People have multiple needs, some of which are instrumental, others socioemotional. Intrinsic and extrinsic rewards can be either instrumental or socioemotional. Several examples of the diverse rewards offered by organizations appear in Table 6.1. The most successful organizations meet multiple needs of the individuals whose participation they require.

People often seek and utilize rewards in an idiosyncratic manner. Table 6.1 designates rewards as they are normally defined. But people often place particular value on a concrete reward due to its symbolic significance. And what seems insubstantial on its face may for some have instrumental value.

What may be an instrumental reward for some may be a socioemotional reward for others. Some top Wall Street deal makers in the late 1990s, for example, earned several hundred million dollars in a single year. Yet year after year, these financiers attempted to amass yet more millions. The super-rich pursue ever-greater wealth not because they need money in the conventional sense, but because wealth serves as a "score card" tracking their achievements in life.

A person's "job" in a work organization corresponds more closely to his or her role than in organizations of other types. For over a century, industrial engineers, psychologists, and sociologists have tried to explain why people accept employment in a

Table 6.1   Types of Rewards in Organizations

	Extrinsic	**Intrinsic**
Instrumental	• money • benefits • promotion opportunities • career contacts	• improvement in skill • creative achievement • social/political mission
Socioemotional	• companionship • social status • recreation	• personal validation • professional distinction

Definitions

Work Organizations, Workers, Managers, and Related Terms

The terms *work organizations* and *workers* appear throughout this text.

Work organization denotes a formally organized collectivity of which the principal objectives are the production and delivery of goods and services. Participants in these organizations are paid. Work organizations include government agencies and organizations that are publicly or privately owned. Organizations may be nonprofit or profit seeking. Nonprofit organizations are governed by trustees, legal caretakers of assets owned by the public. For-profit firms are governed by boards of directors and owned by stockholders. Increasing the value of stockholders' investments and distributing dividends to stockholders constitute major objectives of for-profit organizations.

All business corporations are work organizations. Voluntary organizations and clubs are work organizations for paid staff but not for volunteers and members. Government agencies providing routine services are work organizations. Armies and navies are work organizations in peacetime but something quite different in war, when service for pay takes a backseat and voluntary severance becomes unusual.

The term *workers* denotes members of work organizations who (a) occupy roles within a work organization and carry out associated responsibilities on a day-to-day basis and (b) exercise no major supervisory, policy-making, or ownership-related functions. Workers are often "operatives," people who perform routine work and exercise no supervision of others. Clerical, technical, and professional employees are also workers, so long as they spend little or none of their time supervising others or making decisions on behalf of the organization or its subunits.

The term *manager* as used in this text designates an individual who spends a significant proportion of his or her time planning, supervising, and evaluating the work of others. Managers may also administer budgets for their operating units and be held responsible for productivity, revenue, and sales.

The term *executive* designates members of upper-level management. Executives include division managers, vice presidents, presidents, and their aides.

Professionals include a class of workers who have in-depth knowledge of a specialized technical field by virtue of lengthy formal education. Professionals perform tasks that are too complicated and variable to be represented by formulas or standard operating procedures. These workers often belong to independent organizations whose members set the standards through which they are deemed qualified in their fields.

given firm and why they remain there or depart. These management scientists have made special efforts to determine the conditions under which people are most productive. Studies of employment, job satisfaction, and performance provide information on the mechanisms that attract and attach individuals to organizational roles.

Among factors capable of affecting the individual's acceptance and performance of a work role, pay has received predominant attention. Other extrinsic rewards are, of course, important. But the concrete and universally meaningful nature of pay has placed it at the forefront of both management and worker concerns.

Pay

Pay, comprising cash salary plus benefits, is a very widespread method for motivating people to accept organizational roles and carry out associated responsibilities. It is the principal motivational tool of most work organizations. Pay plays an important though less visible role in organizations with social, political, charitable, and patriotic purposes. Organizations such as the Red Cross, United Way, and American Cancer Society, for example, utilize thousands of volunteers, but carry out core functions through the work of paid staff.

People usually accept employment to meet basic needs, such as those formulated by Maslow (see Chapter 2). Pay provides the resources required to meet physiological and safety needs. Pay also enables people to meet higher order needs such as companionship and love. Material resources facilitate and strengthen friendship, courtship, marriage, and the loyalty of children. Unemployment and poverty are principal causes of marital conflict and divorce.[2]

People occasionally take jobs that pay too little to meet their biological and safety needs. Actors and actresses, for example, often receive small or uncertain compensation from the theater companies in which they exercise their talent. But many supplement their income with jobs outside the theater. Political activists whose organizations pay little or nothing subsist on outside work, savings, or family resources. Employees (and principals) in start-up companies eke out a living in hopes of later riches. Whatever their commitments and hopes, however, most ultimately migrate to work organizations that pay enough to meet life's normal obligations.

Those who manage work organizations should never underestimate the importance of pay in attracting, retaining, and motivating participants. Like many organizational processes, though, payment only partially explains the individual's acceptance or performance of his or her role. Managers need to understand the limits of pay as a means of promoting desired behavior. The manner in which employers allocate pay, moreover, can be as important as how much they pay.

Pay and Satisfaction

The Importance of Pay

Research presents consistent evidence for a general truth regarding participants in work organizations: *if people are not satisfied with their pay, they will not be satisfied with their jobs.* An organization may offer interesting work and pleasant surroundings. But satisfaction with pay is usually necessary to ensure satisfaction with the job as a whole.

Despite its importance, people seldom identify pay as the most important reward associated with their work. A researcher reviewed 49 separate studies that asked workers to rate the relative importance of pay and other job characteristics such as security, chances for advancement, the nature of the work, and management. Pay received the top rating in several of these studies. But generally, pay ranked third from the top.[3] Other studies indicate that pay contributes only partially to overall satisfaction.[4] More pay, furthermore, does not seem to produce satisfaction among workers who perceive deficits in other facets of their jobs.[5]

There is reason to believe that workers interviewed in these studies understated the importance of pay. People do not want to be seen as "money-grubbers." Different wording in questions about pay have produced differences in study results.

Observing the behavior of workers provides the best indication of how important pay actually is. One famous study[6] asked workers about their level of satisfaction with pay and monitored turnover during the subsequent year. Of the workers who said their pay was adequate, 83% were still in their jobs at year's end. Of those who said their pay was too low, only 67% were still with the company. Another study found that most workers who were satisfied with their pay had good attendance records at their company, while a majority of those who felt underpaid were regularly absent.[7]

While workers may not say that pay is the most important reason they accept a job and perform the required duties, they "vote with their feet" when they consider their pay unsatisfactory. Adequacy of pay is a necessary, though not always sufficient, condition for job satisfaction.

Causes of Satisfaction Versus Dissatisfaction With Pay

Several factors determine the worker's level of satisfaction with his or her pay. The major factors include

- Level of pay
- Expectations
- Material needs

It should come as no surprise that people who receive higher levels of pay are more likely to be satisfied with their pay. But it is also true, all things being equal, that people do not raise the level at which they think they should be paid as their incomes rise.[8] People appear to have a pay target in mind that is constant. What people think they should earn does not change as their incomes rise.

People's expectations regarding pay help determine their level of satisfaction. Human beings constantly compare themselves with others. People become dissatisfied with their pay if they learn that someone else in a similar position earns more. Similarly, people who move into jobs with additional responsibilities become dissatisfied if their pay is not increased.

Labor disputes have been known to arise because workers believe that others doing similar work are paid more. Those with whom a worker compares his or her pay may have a somewhat different title or job description. Labor-management disputes arise when the workers and managers in a firm identify different "comparison groups" whose pay they believe should serve as the standard.

Finally, workers' actual needs help determine their satisfaction with pay. People who have stable expectations regarding their standard of living will generally feel satisfied as long as their level of pay supports that standard. Dissatisfaction arises with the advent of unexpected expenses, as may result from illness or similar misfortune.

In short, pay (salary plus benefits) induces people to accept roles in organizations, particularly those concerned with making products and providing routine services. People tend to remain in these roles and carry out associated responsibilities if they perceive their pay as (a) high, (b) fair, and (c) sufficient to support their customary standard of living.

Complex Relationships Between Pay and Human Behavior

Pay constitutes a leading factor in attracting people to organizations and keeping them there. Beyond this basic truth, the relationship between pay and human behavior is complex. People who work for an organization may not migrate to better-paying jobs elsewhere even if such jobs are available. Higher pay, moreover, does not necessarily induce people to work longer hours or expend more effort carrying out their roles.

Two important concepts reflect the uncertain efficacy of pay as a means by which organizations procure the human participation they require: (1) the phenomenon of *satisficing;* and (2) the *backward-bending labor supply curve.*

Satisficing behavior. Economists draw a distinction between two forms of behavior exhibited by human beings. Some people, it is said, are "maximizers."[9] Individuals of this description seek the highest rewards available. Other people are "satisficers." They are satisfied with limited rewards, as long as their needs are met.

The proportion of Americans who are "maximizers" or "satisficers" is an unresolved question. People often seem to maximize in some parts of their lives (such as sports performance) and satisfice in others (such as work for pay). At any given time, a very high proportion of modern American employees are undoubtedly satisficers.

The tendency of people to behave in a satisficing rather than a maximizing manner limits the ability of organizations to recruit members via pay. Maximization involves costs to the individual. The maximizing worker must expend effort to find out about higher-paying opportunities. When the worker finds such opportunities, he or she incurs costs in taking advantage of them. Costs include emotional challenges in becoming used to a new group of colleagues, a new commuting routine, or a long-distance move. Unless people in work organizations feel a clear dissatisfaction with pay, then, they tend to stay put.

The backward-bending labor supply curve. It seems logical that higher pay will induce people to work more hours per day or more days per year, at least if they are paid by the hour or day. This is not necessarily true. Economists have shown that workers paid by the hour increase the number of hours they work only up to a specific limit. At some point, most people feel they no longer need to substitute paid hours for hours of leisure.[10] This point comes when people feel that they gain greater "utility" from an hour of leisure than an hour's pay.

Economists describe this phenomenon by plotting a line on a graph whose dimensions are (a) wages (e.g., dollars per hour) and (b) number of hours worked per day. As wages increase, people work more hours until their additional income makes it possible for them to substitute leisure for work. The plot of income versus hours worked bends backward, indicating that, after a critical point, people work fewer hours the more they are paid.

As a reward for participation in work organizations, then, pay has limited utility. Many people have a *target income,* the amount needed to attain or maintain their desired standard of living. Once this target is achieved, more pay results in less effort.

Historians have observed evidence of the backward-bending labor supply curve among European peasants. These individuals, who farmed land owned by others, adhered to traditional lifestyles and living standards. Additional compensation, it was noted, resulted in less work. The phenomenon has also been observed among modern American physicians. When their pay exceeds their target incomes, many of these professionals cut back on working hours to spend more time with spouses, children, and golfing companions.

Incentive Pay

Description of Incentives

Incentives are defined as offers of special extrinsic rewards in return for behavior desired by management. Most pay procedures designed as incentives provide higher rewards to people who contribute more to the organization's objectives. In the work organization, these objectives usually include production and sale of goods and services.

Work organizations have traditionally employed two types of incentives: (1) fixed pay for performance and (2) bonuses. Fixed-pay-for-performance systems comprise specific dollar rewards for each unit of goods or services produced or sold. Bonuses are amounts determined by management discretion, periodically allocated to productive workers (traditionally at year's end).

Application and Consequences

Management scientists have carried out many studies of fixed-pay-for-performance systems. Traditionally, pay for performance has involved "piecework," a system under which workers were paid for each piece of work completed. Some workers in the Hawthorne study, for example, were paid according to the number of transformers they wired.

Both experimental and observational studies linking productivity to pay for performance have been conducted since the early 20th century. These have found increases in productivity associated with pay for performance in at least the 10% to

20% range.[11] In addition, incentive pay for regular attendance at work seems to produce the hoped-for results. A study[12] followed workers for 28 weeks to determine whether a cash bonus for regular attendance reduced absenteeism. Higher rates of attendance were observed when the bonus plan was in effect.

Cash Versus Noncash Compensation

As the term is used in this chapter, "pay" includes salary, cash premiums for superior performance, and benefits. Increasingly, profit-seeking firms have offered ownership shares (stock or stock options) to both managers and workers as elements of their compensation packages.

Typically, work organizations compute the cash value of compensation packages and use the total as the basis of management decisions. "Costing out" of elements is the primary step taken by management in response to union offers and demands.

But each component of the pay package has different implications for worker motivation. Benefits, for example, are less firmly tied to acceptable role performance than are salaries. Chronically late or absent workers often lose pay but retain benefits at the "standard" level. Economists counsel that increasing benefits as a proportion of the compensation package may fail to encourage job performance.[13]

On the contrary, stock distribution may act as a special motivator. The value of stock rises or falls according to the firm's level of success. Stock ownership gives the worker a personal interest in the company's fortunes. This is even truer of stock options, certificates that enable the receiver to purchase stock later at a fixed price. When stock prices rise, the values of options rise even faster. Distribution of options to employees of a new and struggling Microsoft in the 1980s made thousands of its workers into millionaires in the 1990s.

Researchers have, however, reported significant costs associated with pay-for-performance plans. Pay for performance may increase a worker's individual productivity without advancing organizational objectives. Pay arrangements intended to advance the organization's objectives may actually undermine them. Undesirable consequences of pay-for-performance schemes include

- Interpersonal conflict
- Perverse individual incentives
- Suboptimization
- Conflicts with institutions and culture

Interpersonal conflict. Interpersonal conflict has been known to occur in groups that include people intent on maximizing income and also people intent on avoiding overexertion. Studies of industrial workers have reported hostility and mistrust between high- and normal-level performers. A well-known study of workers in the 1940s contrasted those who welcomed the incentives ("rate-busters") to those who considered the incentives a threat and responded by restricting production despite the availability of rewards. For the "rate-busters," additional money seemed a mark of virtue. According to the "restricters," those who responded to the incentives were "Republican hogs."[14]

Hostility associated with pay-for-performance systems may also be directed against management. Traditionally, workers have suspected that managers institute pay-for-performance systems merely to determine how fast an employee is physically able to do his or her job. Incentive pay does motivate at least some workers to perform as fast as possible. Upon learning the worker's maximum speed, is it said, managers raise the minimum level of production required of everyone. A classic study[15] recorded a worker's advice to a newcomer on how to outwit management in this regard:

> You got to use your noodle while you're working, and think your work out ahead as you go along! You got to add in movements you know you ain't going to make when you're running the job! Remember, if you don't screw them, they're going to screw you!

Perverse Individual Incentives. Observers of incentive systems have occasionally reported perverse results. Most pay-for-performance systems reward individuals for outstanding performance. Payment based on rewards to individuals does not necessarily advance objectives of the organization as a whole.

Inappropriate measures of productivity contribute to the development of perverse individual incentives. Take, for example, a traditional measure of a placement official's productivity in a state employment office. The official is held responsible for placing applicants in jobs and is rewarded for attaining a high "placement rate."[16] An official may meet or exceed his or her quota with greatest ease by placing individuals in short-term, low-paying jobs. Concentration on such placements results in high volume. Each placement is relatively easy to make, and many of those placed will return soon for another placement.

Incentives based on placement rates do not motivate officials to advance the agency's core objectives. Short-term, low-paying jobs do not promote real self-sufficiency among the unemployed. The system leads to neglect of clients with major problems (such as need for a flexible schedule due to family responsibilities). The reward system encourages officials to concentrate on the job applicants who are easiest to place, a practice known as "creaming."

Accurate measurement of productivity is crucial for an effective system of pay for performance. This presents particular challenges to an economy in which manufacturing is becoming increasingly less important. Successful performance of technical and professional work usually demands efficacy on several dimensions, not all of which are reflected in a formal evaluation measure.

Pay for performance in elementary and high school teaching illustrates the practical difficulties of such schemes. The late 20th century saw growing support for such interventions to improve the performance of public schools. Some programs have promised bonuses to teachers based on the percentages of their pupils who attained adequate scores on standardized tests.

Teachers have objected that each classroom has a different mix of easy- and difficult-to-educate kids. Under such conditions, they argue, it would be unfair to hold all teachers to the same standard. They also raise questions regarding the standardized tests, arguing that the examinations assess only some of the capabilities the schools aim at developing. Human resources experts have raised similar questions.

Studies have suggested that test-based accountability inflates test scores without necessarily producing kids who are better educated overall.[17]

Suboptimization

Individuals seeking to maximize their personal income may act in a manner that reduces the total productivity of the work group. In order to produce the maximum number of objects, for example, an industrial worker may procure an excess of needed material and hide a portion of it. This ensures that he or she can count on an adequate supply, but deprives other workers of a critical resource. Production for the group as a whole declines. Similarly, an organizational subunit may appropriate resources for its own use, maximizing the subunit's productivity. This process, known as *suboptimization,* makes the subunit's managers look good, but reduces the productivity of the organization as a whole.

Conflicts With Institutions and Culture

Despite favorable research results, pay-for-performance plans are difficult to introduce into many workplaces. These schemes receive support from tenets of American culture such as hard work and just rewards, but Americans also value fairness, and this value has proven a barrier to implementation. Most managers realize the difficulties of making a pay-for-performance system completely fair. Difficulties in measuring job performance and job challenges unique to each worker make uniform application of abstract standards seem unjust. In response, many managers allocate pay premiums evenly among those they supervise.

Privileged classes of employees often escape the pay-for-performance system. Tenured university faculty in state institutions normally receive uniform salaries within a given grade. The professor who writes many books and teaches excellent classes often earns no more than a colleague whose performance is barely adequate.

The pay-for-performance system has bypassed many of America's corporate boardrooms. A large-scale study of American corporate CEOs in the 1970s and 1980s revealed that pay corresponded very weakly to performance.[18] Regarding a CEO who reduced his company's value by $10 million by mis-investing, the authors note:

> The total wealth of the CEO, if he is representative of our sample, will decline by only $25,900 as a result of this misguided investment—not much of a disincentive for someone who earns on average $20,000 per week.

The authors cite a "culture of politeness" among corporate directors, which contributes to protection of CEOs from dismissal or reduction in pay due to poor performance. In addition, the authors note that few corporate CEOs maintain major stock holdings in the firms they manage. These executives may receive much of their compensation in stock (or rights to buy stock at a discount), but most CEOs promptly sell these shares, reducing their personal stake in the firm's success.

Bonuses

Bonuses constitute an important part of the compensation package in many occupations. Payments of this kind constitute a form of pay for performance. Bonuses differ from the fixed-pay-for-performance incentive plans. Under these plans, firms use an explicit formula to determine payment. In the case of bonuses, a manager independently decides whether to give a bonus and how much the bonus should be worth.

A bonus system has several advantages over fixed rewards. Although workers in some firms expect bonuses each year, they never really know whether one will be forthcoming. Associated tension may translate into extra effort on the job.

Under a bonus system, the manager need not be held to the same standard of "fairness" as under a system of fixed pay. This degree of discretion allows the manager to operate at least partially on "gut feel." A general sense of the employee's productivity may guide the decision rather than a formal system of performance measurement. Discretion of this kind precludes hazards associated with formal performance measurement systems, such as inappropriate standards, limited scope, and faulty reporting.

In the absence of a formula, the worker never really knows the rationale behind the bonus he or she has received. This allows the worker to suspect that the manager has shown him or her special favor. Such thoughts promote personal loyalty to the manager. Often, the norm of reciprocity induces the worker to feel he or she should "give something back" to the manager, a feeling which may translate into extra time, effort, and production.

Performance Plus: An Employee Incentive Plan

Group Health Cooperative of Puget Sound, a nonprofit operator of health plans and hospitals, instituted "Performance Plus" in 1999. Under the plan, employees would receive cash awards if the organization achieved $3 million in net earnings for the fiscal year and met targets in two other areas:

- Clinical quality performance
- Service quality performance

"Clinical quality" was measured according to a "Clinical Quality Target Index," reflecting delivery of services such as immunization for children and cervical cancer screening for women. The target would be met if a rating of "90" was achieved.

"Service quality" was to be measured by a survey of plan members. The target would be met if 35% of the members rated their overall satisfaction as excellent.

Employees would receive larger cash rewards if the financial, clinical, and service quality targets were exceeded rather than merely met. If the organization netted at least $3 million, achieved a score of 90 on the clinical quality index, and determined that 35% of members rated their satisfaction as excellent, each employee would receive a .75% cash award, the minimum increment. This would amount to $225 for a $30,000-per-year worker. If the organization netted $9 million or more and achieved maximum levels on the clinical and service quality scales, the award would climb to 3%, or $900 for the $30,000-per-year worker.

Other Extrinsic Rewards

Pay is the most visible reward offered by work organizations. For many workers, pay is the most important reward. Many other extrinsic rewards attract people to organizations and encourage them to carry out received roles. Security, advancement, and honor are important extrinsic rewards other than pay. We will address only these three here.

Job Security

Job security is of obvious importance to many people in work organizations. Generally, protection against termination ranks approximately even with pay in importance to workers. The importance of security varies according to individual needs and values. Some people place sufficient value on security to accept relatively low-paying jobs from which they are unlikely to be terminated. Others accept risk of periodic unemployment in return for high income.

The importance of security also varies according to the state of the economy. When the unemployment rate is low, people are more willing to take insecure jobs. But in bad times, secure jobs become more attractive. In the Great Depression of the 1930s, for example, competition was keen for "security jobs" such as positions in state and federal government.

Career Advancement

Moving up a hierarchy has great value for many people. In work organizations, such movement usually brings with it higher pay. In voluntary organizations, election or appointment to a leadership positions confers prestige. Promotions validate the individual's self-worth. Organizations that offer the possibility of promotion have a special attraction for potential members.

As a reward, career advancement is particularly important for retaining members and ensuring that they carry out their received roles. The talented and ambitious often leave an organization in search of opportunities to move up elsewhere. Organizations frequently promote such people into management in order to prevent their departure. This strategy may backfire, however, as an individual skilled in machine operations or engineering R&D may make a poor supervisor of other people.

A study of schoolteachers illustrates the consequences of poor promotion prospects in an organization. According to this study,[19] schoolteachers have very limited chances for climbing a hierarchy. Teaching may be characterized as an *unstaged career*. From their first day on the job until retirement, most teachers have the same job description and the same title. The flat nature of a teaching career dampens enthusiasm of many for the teaching role.

Not all members of an organization equally value promotion. Many are content simply as line workers or members. Some organizations reinforce the value of promotion with an "up or out" policy. In others, promotion appears to be a relatively unimportant concern. The previous chapter, for example, summarized results of a study of six federal agency offices in which promotion opportunities were limited. The study found infrequent and inconsistent dissatisfaction with promotion prospects in these organizations.

Recognition and Honor

All organizations distribute rewards of recognition and honor. Kindergarten teachers give out gold stars to kids who behave. Organizations representing the professional interests of scientists award medals to their most distinguished members. Government agencies award lapel pins to people who have rendered decades of service. Corporations give star performers choice parking spaces emblazoned with their names, ensuring recognition as well as convenience. Armies and navies everywhere give stripes, ribbons, and medals to personnel who have performed heroically in battle or passed other tests of skill and valor.

Some of the most powerful rewards related to recognition and honor are never represented in concrete form. People often weigh a decision on the basis of whether others will speak well or ill of them for the action they eventually take. People may have excellent practical reasons for departing from a failing organization, for example, yet remain in the ranks for fear of what others may say. "You're a rat for deserting a sinking ship," the expression goes.

Recognition and honor are particularly relevant in nonwork organizations or in organizations without the power to pay people according to their performance. Voluntary organizations give rewards ranging from rounds of applause for the people who ran the bake sale to bronze plaques for long-term board members. Factory managers in the Communist regimes of yesteryear gave symbolic titles to high-performing workers.

Researchers have spent less time documenting the efficacy of recognition and honor than they have spent studying other extrinsic rewards. But the power of peer recognition—actual or potential, positive or negative—can be greater than pay, security, or career advancement. Countless soldiers have died in pursuit of medals and reputation.

Socioemotional Rewards

The extrinsic rewards discussed thus far are largely instrumental in nature. At least in part, they have value because they can be used to obtain other things. Pay exemplifies instrumental reward. Fetishists and misers may love money for its own sake, but most people value pay in order to purchase consumer goods. Promotions and honors have emotional components but also have instrumental features: power over others, esteem in the community, and self-affirmation.

Socioemotional rewards, though, have direct and immediate utility. They are the "goodies" of collective life. Socioemotional rewards include stimulation, companionship, entertainment, and emotional support. Like pay, security, and honor, socioemotional rewards are extrinsic to the organizational role itself. Millions hang on to jobs they do not especially like because of the socioemotional benefits they deliver. The giving of such rewards is a process common to both formal organizations and informal collectivities such as families.

Socioemotional rewards have clear importance in nonwork organizations. Recreational clubs, political organizations, and churches have objectives such as developing sports skills, lobbying elected officials, and offering thanksgiving to the Lord. But the opportunities they offer for company, conversation, and "fun and games" do much to attract people to meetings and functions and to induce them to accept work and leadership roles.

Socioemotional rewards have always played a part in work organizations and continue to do so today. Some observers believe they are becoming even more important in the modern workplace. Sociologist Arlie Hochschild[20] writes that work has developed into a form of "home" and home has become "work." Modern family life, she comments, is an uncomfortable mixture of housework, child rearing, spousal tension, and tending to elderly parents. The comments of a woman interviewed in Hochschild's research make the workplace seem considerably more rewarding:

> I usually come to work early, just to get away from the house. When I arrive, people are there waiting. We sit, we talk, we joke. . . . We sit and chitchat for 5 or 10 minutes. There's laughing, joking, fun.

Hochschild comments that stable families and strong neighborhoods are becoming less common. In contrast, the "corporate world" has created a sense of "neighborhood . . . of family at work." Work time, she writes, has become "more hospitable to sociability—periods of talking with friends on e-mail, patching up quarrels, gossiping".

An Incentive System for Physicians

Managers have developed incentive practices for a wide variety of workers. These practices can increase production of goods and services, even among workers famed for their high level of independence.

A group of researchers from the Harvard School of Public Health studied the impact of an incentive system aimed at physicians.[21] These physicians worked for a chain of for-profit, convenience health centers known as Health Stop.

Traditionally, Health Stop had paid its physicians a flat, hourly wage. The new incentive system paid physicians a percentage of the gross monthly charges they generated if the resulting figure was above the hourly wage. Physicians generated charges for the organizations in which they worked by billing for patient visits and ordering x-rays and other medical tests.

In the period following institution of the incentive, charges by Health Stop physicians increased by 28% per month, the result of a heavier volume of patient visits and increased ordering of x-rays and other tests. The majority of physicians increased the charges they generated.

Forty percent of the physicians made more money under the incentive system than they would have in its absence. These doctors increased their monthly income by 19%.

Clearly, Health Stop increased its revenues through the incentive procedure. But consumers might ask whether increased testing and additional visits helped the patients. No one knows whether the additional visits and tests made them healthier.

Intrinsic Rewards

Gratification obtained directly from carrying out a role constitutes an intrinsic reward. Such gratification may derive from two sources:

- Personal identification with the role, responsibilities associated with the role, or objectives of the organization within which the role is situated
- Affirmation, enjoyment, or stimulation from task performance within the role

Personal Identification

Strong identification with the content of a role is a familiar phenomenon in human life. As explained in Chapter 1, identification is a process by which people develop a feeling that the collectivity represents them as individuals. Identification is the conscious belief among members that the collectivity reflects their most valued qualities and operates in their interests.

When sufficiently strong, identification with an organization's mission and objectives translates into attachment to role-related tasks. If identification is powerful enough, the needs of the organization supplant the individual's choices regarding his or her preferred role or associated responsibilities.

Examples abound. Religious devotees working with the poor and sick are not deterred by the rigors of their daily occupation due to the strength of their mission. A "service ethic" transcends the nature of the actual work. Many young people who follow their parents and grandparents into a profession—law, medicine, or military command, for example—cannot imagine doing anything different or better than the roles they come to occupy.

Task Performance

Direct enjoyment, stimulation, and personal affirmation from tasks associated with roles in an organization represent another type of intrinsic reward. Intense devotion to actual work activities differs from intrinsic reward based on identification. In extreme cases, receiving payment, promotion, or honor is only incidental to the work itself.

Artists and musicians have reputations for obtaining high intrinsic gratification from their work. Many of these individuals feel that art constitutes the only occupation they could conceivably pursue. Forgoing opportunities for higher paying work, these individuals can lose track of time in an ecstasy of creation.

People who obtain intrinsic rewards from task performance may or may not also identify with the organization's values or goals. A musician with little taste for military service may find fulfillment playing in a military band. During the Cold War, scientists with pacifist leanings enjoyed satisfying careers in defense laboratories whose resources enabled them to do cutting-edge research. These scientists put aside concerns about the uses to which their discoveries might be put.

Managers have sought to augment intrinsic rewards through a technique known as *job enrichment*. Job enrichment plans add variety and decision-making latitude to tasks associated with the work role. A later chapter will explore the concept of job enrichment further.

Scientists and other professionals often take action to enrich their own jobs in a procedure known as *bootlegging*. Bootlegging is a time-honored practice by which workers use company time and resources to conduct projects of their own interest, from exploring principles of theoretical science to inventing new technical devices. As the term *bootlegging* implies, such use of company resources is ordinarily done in secret. A wise manager with sufficient resources, however, will permit the practice, realizing that bootlegging opportunities enhance intrinsic satisfaction.[22] This enhancement enables an organization to reduce turnover among technical professionals, potentially very important in a tight labor market.

It is not surprising that people in the highest-status and most-skilled work roles report the greatest satisfaction. A national study of worker satisfaction found 42% of professionals and technicians to be "very satisfied" with their jobs, and only 13% of unskilled workers to be very satisfied.[23] Much of the difference was explained by the interesting and challenging nature of the work performed by professionals and technicians. Still, the importance of intrinsic reward from successful task performance has been reported among blue-collar as well as white-collar workers.[24]

Satisfaction, Participation, and Role Performance

This chapter set out to address a key question in organizational behavior: Why do people accept organizational roles and perform these roles, usually, as they are directed?

Many rewards contribute to a person's satisfaction with his or her organization or role. But does satisfaction, in turn, actually encourage people to accept organizational roles and perform their responsibilities well?

As noted earlier, satisfaction with pay contributes to reduced absenteeism and turnover in work organizations. A review of 16 studies of work organizations produced consistent evidence that general satisfaction correlated with low absenteeism.[25]

Clearly, satisfaction contributes to "being there." But does it also contribute to effective role performance?

Maybe not.

Studies have found a positive but very weak relationship between satisfaction and productivity.[26] Industrial psychologists suggest, moreover, that satisfaction may be a consequence rather than a cause of good performance. People who perform well, they say, obtain intrinsic rewards from work itself; the organization responds to good performance by raising pay, making the worker yet more satisfied.

Clearly, satisfaction is important, particularly in nonwork organizations, where "showing up" may be as significant as carrying out specific tasks. But satisfaction alone is insufficient to ensure acceptable role performance.

Punishment

Punishment (imposition of sanctions) receives significantly less attention from people who study organizations than does reward. This is due, in part, to a conviction among psychologists that reward is better than punishment as a means of promoting desired human behavior. Wishing to appear upbeat and progressive, management scientists are reluctant to talk about negative things that take place in organizations. Still, organizations of all kinds mete out punishment. Most organizations have formal procedures for punishing people who perform below standards or break rules. Procedures not formally recognized as punishment often have punitive effects, sometimes intended and sometimes not.

Organizations in premodern societies applied punishment in ways that would be unacceptable in most places today. Owners of large country estates in the ancient Roman Empire commissioned slaves to manage their fiscal affairs and tortured them in the event of irregularities. Supervisors of administrative agencies in China resorted to *corporal punishment* (application of physical damage or discomfort) via caning to correct the behavior of their subordinates. Social historian Max Weber describes this procedure as "prodigious use of the bamboo as a disciplinary instrument."[27]

Corporal punishment survives in some modern organizations. Organized crime provides striking examples. International drug cartels kill members who exhibit behavior unacceptable to the leadership. Yakuza, known as the Japanese Mafia, may cut off the fingers of disobedient operatives. Beatings of those who don't "shape up" are said to take place in modern armies, typically carried out in secret or by peers. Instances of physical abuse are occasionally reported in child care centers and schools.

Modern organizations, though, ordinarily punish their members via ostracism, assignment to undesirable duty, salary reduction, demotion, suspension, or dismissal. Work organizations apply subtle means of punishment to members who have not performed as desired. These include not paying workers expected bonuses and passing them over for a sought-after promotion. Dismissal is the ultimate punishment in both work and voluntary organizations. Paradoxically, retention is the ultimate sanction in elementary schools (where unruly or underperforming students are "kept in" or "held back"), prisons, and facilities for the mentally ill.

Imposition of punishment may seem simple and straightforward. If a person in an organization fails to perform his or her role adequately, why not simply dismiss him or her? Cultural and legal considerations, though, restrict the options of managers and colleagues alike.

Antidiscrimination laws serve as resources for workers wishing to protest management decisions. Union contracts constitute other constraints to management. Managers who fire workers risk costly lawsuits for wrongful termination. People ejected or excluded from nonwork organizations such as professional societies and social clubs have similar legal recourse.

Organizations respond by imposing punitive measures via informal or indirect means or through highly detailed, formal procedures.

Informal and Indirect Punitive Measures

Modern organizations have many informal ways of inflicting punishment. Frequently used procedures include making undesirable assignments. People whose behavior needs to be corrected may receive dull, low-visibility, or physically uncomfortable tasks. Managers may penalize workers by giving them travel assignments to Duluth in January or Houston in July.

A related penalty is assignment of undesirable workspace. Those seen as not carrying out their role properly may be assigned to smaller offices or cubicles. They may be given locations in noisy places or adjacent to facilities that generate obtrusive sounds and traffic such as loading docks or lavatories.

Increasingly, penalties in work organizations take the form of instructional sessions in areas such as sexual harassment and cultural sensitivity. These "trainings" include lecturing and exercises requiring the trainee to respond to materials presented and to interact with unfamiliar people. There is no doubt that such sensitivity training can play a positive role in the employee's development. But it is often viewed by employees as a punitive measure. Some managers assign people to sensitivity training with punitive intent.

Punitive measures in an organization are not always taken for remedial purposes. Managers who apply punishment as a remedial intervention assume that the person can be transformed into a productive team member. Organizations, though, give up on people with long histories of underperformance or objectionable behavior. Organizations may determine that a person's skills are inadequate for present business conditions or that his or her personal qualities are incompatible with the organization's climate or culture. Sometimes a worker is penalized simply because her or she is disliked.

When remediation is not the goal, managers utilize informal and indirect punitive measures in the hope that the target employee will voluntarily depart. It is hoped that those passed over and made to feel uncomfortable will eventually "get it," resigning from the agency or dropping out of the club.

Formal Measures

For reasons stated above, organizations today often exercise punitive measures according to strict procedures consisting of several deliberate steps. This is consistent with a tendency of modern formal organizations to conduct their business according to clear and consistent rules. Formal procedure also protects the organization and its executives from legal action by the person who is penalized. A punitive action carried out according to standard procedure is unlikely to be viewed in court as discriminatory, arbitrary, or capricious.

Formal procedures utilized by organizations to penalize workers often take place according to a sequence known as *progressive discipline*. Steps utilized by a major state agency in California illustrate the principle:

1. *Initial counseling.* The supervisor identifies a problem with conduct or performance and conducts a private discussion with the employee. Options for remediation are proposed.

2. *Corrective interview.* If the initial counseling session fails to achieve resolution, the manager calls the employee for a second conference. Again, options for remediation are discussed. As a consequence of this procedure, the manager places a memo in the employee's personnel file that he or she has conducted the corrective interview and the earlier initial counseling session. The employee receives a copy of the memo and may respond if he or she chooses.

3. *Letter of reprimand.* If faulty performance or other workplace problems continue, the supervisor writes a letter of reprimand to the employee. This is the first application of formal, punitive action. A copy of the letter is placed in the employee's personnel file. The action can be appealed.

4. *Suspension or pay reduction.* The employee may be suspended from his or her job or pay may be temporarily or permanently reduced. Action of this kind may be formulated and transmitted by the agency's counsel or legal department. This action, too, may be appealed.

5. *Termination.* Ordinarily, dismissal may take place only after the preceding four steps have been taken and documented. The agency's legal counsel may be directly involved and will in any case be kept informed. The employee may appeal to an outside state agency.

This sequence of steps, and similar procedures in other public agencies and private firms, may be applied to role performance problems ranging from trivial to grave. A public agency executive reported conducting counseling sessions with one employee who wore inappropriate attire to work, with another who bathed or changed his clothes so seldom as to cause complaints from coworkers, and with a third who displayed pornographic screen savers on his computer. An executive at another agency applied the steps outlined above to a male supervisor who showed favoritism toward a female subordinate in exchange for her sexual favors.

In many instances, the full sequence of steps is unnecessary. The conscientious employee will be quite sensitive to initial counseling and do whatever her or she can to improve performance or remedy other problems that may have been identified. In the case of emotional disturbance or substance abuse, the supervisor may refer the subordinate to the organization's *employee assistance program,* or EAP, rather than write a letter of reprimand. The EAP is an organizational unit that helps the employee remedy personal problems through in-house counseling or referral. In instances where laws appear to have been broken, the agency may terminate the employee without initial counseling and institute criminal proceedings.

Generally, employees may appeal placement of memos in their personnel files, letters of reprimand, and suspension or termination actions. Appeal is made to internal officials, outside agencies, or union representatives. Documents in the employee's file reduce chances for promotion and favorable letters of recommendation for other jobs.

Punishment in the Executive Suite

Punishment applied to executives or professionals tends to be a mix of formal and informal procedures. Most executives and professionals are *exempt* employees, not under protection of union contracts or state laws specifying required overtime or benefits. Pay, promotion, and sanctions in the upper levels of organizations, then, tend to be handled less formally than among nonexempt employees. Punitive measures against managers and professionals include the same ones applied to lower-level workers, such as dead-end assignments, undesirable workspace, and low or no salary increments. Other punitive procedures include exclusion from meetings and networks, removal from contact with upper-level managers, and scapegoating.

Exclusion From Meetings and Networks

One way to punish an executive or professional is to exclude him or her from vital communications networks or places where decisions are made. An upper-level employee not copied on important memos, invited to important meetings, or appointed to working groups and task forces feels deprived and anxious due to the exclusion. He or she is likely to command less respect from colleagues and face added difficulties in obtaining resources.

Removal From Contact With Upper-Level Managers

A professional or executive accomplishes things and advances his or her career through higher-level executives. Removal from contact with higher-level executives interferes with this process. Visible demotion can bring about such removal. But so can creation of one or more new management levels above the employee's position, placing a barrier between him or her and the organization's top executives.

Scapegoating

Organizations can punish executives and professionals by blaming them for things that go wrong. They can be singled out as examples of how things ought not to be done. Eventually, scapegoating provides justification for terminating the executive when the opportunity arises.

Like workers, executives may be punished with the intent of making them feel uncomfortable and unwelcome in the organization. Eventually, it is hoped, the penalized executive will resign. Corporate mergers, government agency consolidations, and relocation of facilities from one city to another all present opportunities to terminate workers at all levels who have been found wanting.

Organizations punish executives who do not earn as much revenue for the company as promised, fail to complete contracts on time, and overspend their budgets. In this, higher-level employees face risks similar to those in the lower echelons. But executives incur additional risks associated with the political process present in all organizations. A junior executive's role, for example, may prescribe neutrality in power struggles among his or her superiors. Ambitious individuals, though, often feel tempted to take sides in hopes of accelerating their rise in the hierarchy. The person who backs the wrong side in a power struggle is likely to find himself or herself banished to a rural worksite, disqualified

A Police Officer's Punishment

It is difficult to terminate an employee in most government agencies and many corporations. Termination requires activation of tedious, time-consuming procedures. When firing an employee today, an agency and its executives face the possibility of legal action against them. Similar hassles and risks accompany disciplinary actions such as demotion and reduction in pay.

More convenient punitive procedures involve informal sanctions. In this instance, the executive uses his or her discretion to make life unpleasant for the miscreant. A Southern California police officer shared some of the techniques with which he was familiar.

One technique was known among the officers as "freeway therapy." This procedure involved assigning the officer to an area distant from his or her home. Such an assignment obliged the officer to drive many miles each day to and from the area he or she was ordered to patrol. Freeway therapy can be particularly painful in law enforcement jurisdictions such as Los Angeles County. Such jurisdictions cover thousands of square miles, stretching from the Pacific Ocean to the Mojave Desert.

Alternatively, supervisors can assign officers to "graveyard patrol," running from midnight to 8:00 a.m. This schedule disrupts normal patterns of family life, socialization, and sleep.

Graveyard patrol also exposes the officer to risk as well as discomfort. On a quiet night, he or she suffers boredom. But monotony is punctuated with periods of intense activity, as serious crimes and accidents tend to occur at night.

from future promotion opportunities, ostracized, and progressively pressured to resign.

Intense demands place officers at risk of error. Crashed police cars and incidents resulting in charges of excessive use of force occur principally during the graveyard hours. Awareness of these risks compounds the discomfort of graveyard patrol, for involvement in an accident and excessive use of force exposes the officer to still further sanctions.

Rewards, Sanctions, and Organizational Roles

Organizations must persuade human beings to forgo immediate attention to their purely individual needs, values, and inclinations. This basic accomplishment enables organizations to coordinate the actions of numerous individuals in pursuit of one or more distinct objectives. Organizations accomplish this task by assigning each individual a role, which prescribes concrete tasks and relationships with incumbents of other roles. In well-functioning organizations, each role is integrated into an overarching structure that ensures that actions within each role reinforce each other in attaining objectives.

Organizations induce people to accept roles and carry out associated responsibilities through systems of rewards ("carrots") and sanctions ("sticks"). Numerous types of rewards may be found in organizations. These include visible and simple considerations such as pay and complex intangibles such as honor, reputation, and self-affirmation. The most successful organizations meet multiple needs of the individuals whose participation they require.

Most research on organizational rewards has been conducted on work organizations and has focused on the impact of pay on participation and productivity. Pay (salary plus benefits) clearly induces people to accept roles in organizations. People tend to remain in these roles and carry out associated responsibilities if they perceive their pay as high, fair, and sufficient to support their customary standard of living.

But pay has limited utility as a reward for participation and role performance in organizations. Offers of additional pay in exchange for higher levels of performance do not always produce the desired result. Studies have found the relationship between satisfaction (to which pay contributes significantly) and productivity to be a weak one. All told, pay-for-performance systems may actually reduce productivity.

Many organizations are required to use rewards other than pay. These organizations may not have sufficient resources to give participants monetary compensation for their time and effort. In some organizations, monetary compensation of members would contradict the organization's values and undermine its objectives.

Millions of people in the United States alone contribute time and effort to organizations that reward them by providing companionship, entertainment, recreation, and opportunities to work in the interest of personal values. Work organizations offering low pay often attract the human resources they need because they offer significant nonmonetary rewards.

"Carrots" receive much more attention from management experts than "sticks." But punishment remains an important process in modern organizations. Sanctions reinforce rewards as means of tying the individual to his or her role and ensuring appropriate performance. Most formal organizations in the modern world have abandoned physical punishment. Dismissal is seldom an immediate response to problems in role performance. Short of dismissal, modern organizations utilize punitive techniques such as remedial counseling, reprimand, demotion (or barring from promotion), salary reduction, and suspension. Informal measures of a punitive nature include ostracism and removal from participation in decision making.

The range of problems to which punitive procedures are applied illustrates the fact that role expectations extend beyond performance of concrete job tasks. In work organizations, role expectations include the incumbent's appearance, manner of interaction with others, rectitude in office politics, personal hygiene, and office decor.

It is important to remember that sanctions advance organizational goals not merely to correct the behavior of participants. People are also penalized to encourage their departure from the organization's ranks. Departure of those deemed unworthy of membership reinforces awareness of the organization's role requirements, as those who remain note the personal qualities and capabilities (or absence thereof) of those ejected.

Few things happen in an organization for only one reason. This principle applies to the forces that cause people to join organizations, accept roles, and perform them more or less according to expectations. Reward and punishment induce people to suspend their individual needs in service of organizational objectives. But the opportunity to obtain a reward and the threat of incurring a sanction are processed in the individual mind via rational weighing and decision making.

Organizations cannot always depend on the individual's acceptance and performance of the roles they offer, due to the individual's immediate free will. Additional mechanisms are required for reliably binding people to organizational roles and causing them to carry out associated tasks and responsibilities. *Imperative force*, covered in the following chapter, is one such mechanism.

Issues and Applications

Rewards and punishments are as diverse as individual needs and motivations themselves. Proper balance in this area can contribute significantly to an organization's stability and effectiveness. It is not always possible to anticipate the effects of different kinds of rewards.

- Although traditionally all-volunteer, a community improvement society decides to pay its president a part-time salary. As the club has grown, the president's responsibilities have increased, as have the number of hours required to do the job. However, negative consequences ensue. As the years go by, successive club presidents spend fewer and fewer hours carrying out their duties. Adding extrinsic rewards to the president's traditionally intrinsic ones has had a negative consequence. Presidents now budget their time according to a "dollars per hour" logic rather than devotion to the organization's mission. In addition, other officers, such as the vice president, secretary, and treasurer, have begun to argue that they, too, should receive stipends. Adding extrinsic to already-existing intrinsic rewards can prove destructive. As a solution, the organization might eliminate the president's stipend and hire a half-time, nonmember assistant to all the club officers. This move would reduce the hours required for the officers' duties and restore the purely intrinsic motivation associated with office holding.

- Seeking to achieve excellence, the board of trustees of a university decides to concentrate resources on three outstanding departments: Physics, English, and Economics. Faculty in these units receive special pay raises; additional personnel are hired in these fields; a new building is constructed for each department. Other departments, however, receive no such benefits. In the ensuing years, faculty from these departments become jealous and dispirited. The quality of their research and teaching declines; turnover climbs; talented individuals ignore resulting vacancies. The favored departments flourish; however, the standing of the university itself sinks. Rewarding individuals or units may make logical sense. But the tendency of people to compare their rewards with those of others cannot be ignored. Nor can the necessity of maintaining the motivation, loyalty, and spirit of individuals throughout the organization. The board of trustees might have acted more wisely by distributing moderate rewards across a larger number of units.

- In an effort to become more profitable, a large medical practice offers bonuses to its member physicians who least often hospitalize their patients or refer them to outside specialists. The costs of hospitalization and referral to specialists are high, cutting into the practice's net income and making it more difficult to attract customers. The incentive works: referrals and hospital admissions drop. But patients incur complications that treatment by specialists might have avoided. Some require longer and more expensive hospital stays because they were not immediately hospitalized. The bonus has proven a perverse incentive, resulting in poorer patient care. More favorable incentives might focus on the actual health of individual patients or growth in the plan's membership.

Chapter Review and Major Themes

In organizations, reward and punishment promote adherence to roles and structure; ideally, they help focus individual effort on collective objectives and goals.

Organizations provide a variety of rewards. Extrinsic rewards, such as pay and fringe benefits, enable members to achieve objectives distinct from those of the organization. Intrinsic rewards involve gratification with the tasks to which the member is assigned, contributing to the organization's mission. The rewards provided by an organization can also be classified as instrumental or socioemotional. Instrumental rewards enable a person to pursue a broader personal objective, such as career advancement. Socioemotional rewards provide immediate gratification of a psychological kind, such as companionship.

Of rewards in work organizations, pay is the most easily recognized. It is doubtful whether many people can feel satisfied with their role in a work organization if they feel unfairly paid. But this type of reward has limited benefit for the organization. Pay for performance may foster feelings of unfairness and lead to social discord. Additional payment may motivate individuals to reduce their working hours. The extraordinarily high pay of today's business executives ensures neither security nor growth for the companies they manage.

Although history provides examples of physical punishment in organizations, such measures are seldom applied in modern organizations. Typically, modern organizations punish individuals by freezing their pay, declining to promote them, assigning them undesirable duty or workspace, or subjecting them to ostracism. Most public and many private organizations conduct graded procedures known as progressive discipline, beginning with verbal warnings and ending with formal dismissal.

As Figure 6.1 indicates, the methods used by organizations to reward or punish their members are strongly influenced by the environment. The surrounding culture helps determine the value placed by organizational participants on specific rewards. Thus, the social prestige of some jobs may compensate for limited pay. The law prevents most organizations from direct use of physical punishment.

It would seem that most successful organizations provide the greatest rewards to members who contribute the most to achievement of objectives. In this fashion, rewards (positive and negative) would contribute positively to function. But large rewards do not necessarily promote such contributions. Individuals at all levels of an organization tend to concentrate on objectives that are visible to supervisors, and hence are associated with pay increments. But these same individuals may neglect objectives that are equally important though less readily observable. Excessive executive pay, while weakly tied to concrete accomplishments, may also reduce resources available for other purposes.

As Figure 6.1 implies, reward and punishment procedures have significant potential to increase conflict. Unless clearly justified, vast differences in payment create envy and hostility. Pay for performance can give rise to unproductive competition among workers. Even nonmonetary rewards can foster interpersonal conflict, as titles and awards become objects of jealousy.

Examination of reward and punishment reveals some of the clearest evidence of the inability of organizations to truly control members. Involuntary servitude is prohibited in perhaps all economically advanced countries. Thus, organizations need to offer rewards desired by potential members. Individuals value different types of rewards, and organizations cannot always provide the rewards an individual desires. If a member sees the rewards offered by an organization as inadequate, he or she is free to depart.

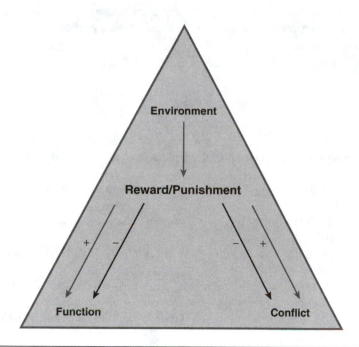

Figure 6.1   Analytical Perspectives Applied to Reward and Punishment

Discussion Questions

1. Although rewards receive much attention in management research, punishment is seldom mentioned. Can you identify punitive procedures in organizations with which you are familiar? Do they appear to be effective in reducing undesired behavior or advancing organizational objectives?

2. It seems likely, though not certain, that organizations with different objectives will offer different rewards to their members. Would a church (or other religious organization) offer rewards essentially different from an army? Would a political party offer different rewards from a retail clothing outlet?

3. To what extent do you think American workers today are willing to trade intrinsic rewards for salary and benefits?

4. Recalling the basic human needs included in Maslow's formulation (see Chapter 1), can any single organization fulfill all or most of them?

5. Can organizations in which membership is involuntary, such as prisons and mental institutions, help achieve their objectives by offering rewards to inmates and patients?

References

1. Solzhenitsyn, A. (1963). *One day in the life of Ivan Denisovich.* (pp. 105–106). New York: E. P. Dutton.

2. Sander, W. (1992). Unemployment and marital status in Great Britain. *Social Biology, 39,* 299–305.

3. Lawler, E. E. (1971). *Pay and organizational effectiveness: A psychological view.* New York: McGraw-Hill.

4. Campbell, A., Converse, P. E., & Rogers, W. L. (1976). *The quality of American life.* New York: Russell Sage.

5. Gupta, N., & Quinn, R. P. (1973). The mirage of trade-offs in job facets. In R. P. Quinn & T. W. Mangione (Eds.), *The 1969–1970 survey of working conditions: Chronicles of an unfinished enterprise* (pp. 321–334). Ann Arbor: Institute for Social Research, University of Michigan.

6. Weitz, J., & Nucklos, R. C. (1953). The validity of direct and indirect questions in measuring job satisfaction. *Personnel Psychology, 6,* 487–492.

7. Metzner, H., & Mann, F. (1953). Employee attitudes and absences. *Personnel Psychology, 6,* 467–485.

8. Lawler, E. E., & Porter, L. W. (1963). Perceptions regarding management compensation. *Industrial Relations, 3,* 41–49.

9. March, J. G., & Simon, H. A. (1958). *Organizations.* New York: John Wiley & Sons.

10. Pindyck, R. S., & Rubinfeld, D. L. (1998). *Microeconomics.* Upper Saddle River, NJ: Prentice Hall.

11. Lawler, E. E. (1973). *Motivation in work organizations.* Monterey, CA: Brooks/Cole.

12. Lawler, E. E., & Hackman, J. R. (1969). The impact of employee participation in the development of pay incentive plans: A field experiment. *Journal of Applied Psychology, 53,* 467–471.

13. Ehrenberg, R. G., & Smith, R. S. (1991). *Modern labor economics.* New York: HarperCollins.

14. Dalton, M. (1948). The industrial "rate-buster": A characterization. *Applied Anthropology, 7,* 5–18.

15. Whyte, W. F. (1955). *Money and motivation* (p. 135). New York: Harper & Row.

16. Johnson, M. (1973). *Counter point.* Salt Lake City, UT: Olympus.

17. Koretz, D. M. (2002). Limitations in the use of achievement tests as measures of educators' productivity. *Journal of Human Resources, 37*(4), 752–777.

18. Jensen, M. C., & Murphy, K. J. (1990). CEO incentives—It's not how much you pay, but how. *Harvard Business Review,* May–June, 138–153.

19. Lortie, D. (1975). *Schoolteacher: A sociological study.* Chicago: University of Chicago Press.

20. Hochschild, A. R. (1997, April 20). There's no place like work. *New York Times Magazine* (pp. 53–55).

21. Hemenway, D., Killen, A., & Cashman, S. B. (1990). Physicians' responses to financial incentives. *New England Journal of Medicine, 322,* 1059–1063.

22. Judge, W. Q., Fryxell, G. E., & Dooley, R. S. (1997). The new task of R&D management: Creating goal directed communities for innovation. *California Management Review, 39,* 72–90.

23. Gurin, G., Veroff, J., & Feld, S. (1960). *Americans view their mental health.* New York: Basic Books.

24. Young, B. S., Worchel, S., & Woehr, D. J. (1998). Organizational commitment among public service workers. *Public Personnel Management, 27,* 339–348.

25. Porter, L. W., & Steers, R. M. (1973). Organizational, work, and personal factors in employee turnover and absenteeism. *Psychological Bulletin, 80,* 151–176.

26. Vroom, V. H. (1964). *Work and motivation.* New York: John Wiley & Sons.

27. Weber, M. (1958). Bureaucracy. In H. H. Gerth & C. W. Mills (Eds.), *From Max Weber: Essays in sociology.* New York: Oxford University Press.

CHAPTER 7

Imperative Forces

Learning Objective

To recognize and understand forces that compel people to comply with the organization's mandates.

Principles

○ Organizations cannot depend merely on the individual's choosing to avoid punishment and seeking rewards. Such dependence risks instability and fragmentation. People are insufficiently consistent in their needs, and organizations may possess insufficient resources to continuously reward and punish.

○ Organizations, then, must be able to compel members to suspend independent judgment and simply accept direction. Mechanisms that make this possible may be labeled *imperative forces*. Imperative forces present in most organizations include discipline, power, and authority.

○ In some organizations, discipline is a highly visible imperative force, inducing the subordinate's immediate, automatic obedience. Power is more subtle, permitting those subject to it to consider alternatives. But power can ultimately make people act in ways that are inconsistent with their own will.

○ Authority is a system of ideas, perceptions, and beliefs that impel people to voluntarily suspend judgment and control over their own thoughts and actions. Under authority, the process of submission takes place independent of reward and punishment.

○ Power, authority, punishment, and reward work together to bind individuals to received roles and organizational structure.

The Limits of Economic Man

Reward and punishment are crucial factors in motivating adherence to organizational roles and the demands of structure. But these mechanisms alone cannot ensure stability and effectiveness. No organization can exercise rewards and punishments with sufficient precision and regularity. No individual responds exactly as expected to each positive or negative sanction. Organizations require additional mechanisms to establish and maintain adherence to roles and structure.

Although they are extremely important, rewards and punishments are often inefficient as methods for achieving coordination among individuals. The preceding chapter demonstrated that reward systems often have undesired results. For example, people frequently behave in a manner that maximizes their individual benefit but hurts the organization. Punishment repels people. In a free society, organizations that depend on punishment face major problems in recruitment and turnover.

Frequent use of reward and punishment is expensive for an organization. These mechanisms require reporting and monitoring the actions of individuals. Exercise of rewards often entails financial resources. Imposition of punishment requires staff time and may lower, at least temporarily, the productivity of the penalized individuals.

Some important theories support the predominance of reward, if not punishment, as the basic determinant of human behavior. Thinking of this kind is often labeled "the theory of economic man." This theory maintains that people continually weigh costs and benefits of alternative actions. Human beings are "driven by self interest and influenced only by carrots and sticks."[1] An individual's choice among alternatives is a conscious process, making use of intelligence, capacity for deliberate reasoning, and understanding of personal needs.

But the theory of economic man leaves much human behavior unexplained. People have many needs, and these are not always mutually compatible. People's needs and desires are subject to rapid and continuous change. Not everyone is good at weighing alternatives and making choices. Emotions often interfere with reasoned decision making.

Most important, the theory of economic man cannot fully explain why people stick together—in families, organizations, or society as a whole. Individual needs change rapidly, and new opportunities and alternatives arise every day. A reward considered meaningful yesterday might appear insignificant the next day. Individuals with common interests today may be competitors tomorrow. If people's behavior were determined only by rewards and punishments, all collectivities, in time, would fall apart.

Organizations, then, require mechanisms of cohesion other than rewards and punishments. One such mechanism is *imperative force*. Most organizations depend at least partially on imperative force to promote compliance with role expectations and adherence to structure. Imperative force impels individuals to set aside personal preferences and judgment about how to think and behave in a given situation. Imperative forces have the power to compel.

The Nature of Imperative Force

The word *imperative* means command. Command, in fact, is a visible manifestation of imperative forces. The soldier hears the word *Attention!* and snaps into the required posture without reflecting on associated physical discomfort. The political party operative or "hack" rings doorbells and posts yard signs for the candidate designated by his or her superior. The junior-level hoodlum in an organized crime syndicate carries out the instructions of his boss without a moment's reflection.

Imperative forces are subtler in other settings yet just as powerful. Formal organizations routinely coordinate the thinking and behavior of people whose roles emphasize independent reasoning and decision making. Consider a council of prelates in the Episcopal or Catholic Church debating an issue of religious doctrine. Ultimately, resolution is attained. This may take place through a vote or the decision of the individual designated as leader—the Pope, for example. Although individual prelates may disagree, they conform in speech and action.

A group of scientists and engineers responsible for deciding whether or not to launch a space vehicle constitutes another example. Each man and woman in the group has had training in a different field. Each has his or her own perspective on hazards associated with the launch. Having heard reports and listened to discussion, the team leader makes a decision to launch. This pleases some members but not others. Nevertheless, everyone on the team carries out the launch-related tasks he or she has been assigned.

Soldier, hoodlum, cardinal, and scientist all belong to formal organizations. All receive rewards for conformity and punishment for nonconformity. But most day-to-day thinking and behavior takes place in the absence of direct consequences (favorable or unfavorable). Imperative forces ensure adherence to role expectations and thus make possible routine organizational operations. Imperative forces include discipline, power, authority, and, to a lesser extent, interpersonal influence.

Discipline

Discipline constitutes the most obvious imperative force used by organizations. The soldier, party operative, and mafia trainee suspend personal judgment regarding the merit of the commanded action. Their response has the manner of a physical reflex.

Discipline may depend ultimately on fear of punishment (negative sanction) for noncompliance. But the well-disciplined individual does not take time to deliberate. His or her actions are determined not by weighing alternatives but by habituation to obedience.

Discipline comes about through strong socialization of a particular kind: forceful repetition of simple principles of whom to obey. This form of socialization can be intense, as in military boot camp. Or it can be diffuse, reinforced continually from early childhood to maturity. Socialization of this nature de-emphasizes the individual's capacity for independent reasoning.

Discipline illustrates an ingredient found in all imperative forces: suspension of independent judgment and personal needs in response to the organization's instructions. It predominates as the coordinating mechanism in the enlisted ranks of armies and repetitive work such as the assembly line. It seems well fitted to prison life and slave labor.

But discipline itself is insufficient for the needs of most modern organizations. Robotic compliance due to discipline is only one way to synchronize individual behavior to role expectations. Most roles require behavior more complex than sequences of automatic responses to commands. Role expectations in most of today's organizations require at least some independent decision making.

Power

Like discipline, power is an imperative force that results in suspension of independent judgment and personal will. But the response of an individual to another's exercise of power is not automatic. People in all settings—organizations, communities, families—recognize others who have power over them. Individuals engage in conscious calculation regarding power. They weigh options regarding what may satisfy a person who has power over them. Typically, more than one person has power over a given individual. A person often makes conscious decisions about whom to obey and how much obedience is owed to a given individual.

Power may be defined as an individual's ability to force others to act in a manner inconsistent with or contrary to their own judgment, inclination, or will. Social scientists have outlined several alternative bases and mechanisms of power. Perhaps the best known formulation is that of social psychologists French and Raven. This formulation comprises six sources of power. These include the holding of a supervisory position, the ability to punish, the ability to reward, superior skill or knowledge, possession of desirable personal traits, and possession of persuasive information.[2]

More simply, the ability to exercise power can be explained as utilization of resources of various kinds. These include resources that are

- Material: the ability to allocate rewards or inflict punishment involving money, prestige, physical comfort, or advancement of personal goals
- Emotional: the ability to control others through emotional attachments and dynamics
- Intellectual: dominance over information or expertise

The individual who finds himself subject to another's power does not obey merely because he believes the other has a right to his obedience. Power is experienced as an externally imposed force.

Individuals who perceive that someone else has power over them do not obey because they consider that the directive or command has substantive merit. They obey whether or not they agree. Obedience is externally motivated, by fear of punishment or expectation of rewards; by emotional feelings; by a belief (true or false) that the other knows more.

Power is one of the most pervasive of social forces. It is found in all settings of collective life. It is applied in a multitude of ways, sometimes direct and intrusive, sometimes indirect and barely visible.

Coercion: An Extreme Form of Power

Extreme instances of the exercise of power vividly illustrate its importance. Coercion, for example, is a form of power. Coercion occurs when one person demands involuntary submission from another and threatens to inflict extraordinary punishment (often including violence) in the event of noncompliance.

Coercion is usually associated with criminal and corrupt practices. The armed robber threatens to shoot his victim if he does not hand over his wallet. The corrupt police officer threatens to have a citizen jailed if he fails to make a payoff.

Dictatorships, both ancient and modern, often use coercion as their principal instrument of imperative force. In the Soviet Union's early years, farmers who did not give up their property to the government were shot. Later, people who spoke up against the regime were sent to Arctic prison camps. Chinese Communist dictator Mao Tse-Tung is famed for having declared, "Power comes from the barrel of a gun!"

The limitations on coercion as an instrument of control have been demonstrated time and again. Coercion promotes behavior desired by the person in command through the mechanism of extreme fear. The resulting anxiety discourages those subject to coercion from taking initiative. Much effort is expended hiding the shortcomings and errors that are natural in productive processes. Those who rule through coercion preside over populations of sullen and secretive subjects.

Coercion illustrates power in its "naked" form. Mainstream organizations in modern democratic society do not openly use coercion on their members. But coercion does occur in formal organizations. Underground, political splinter, and religious sects have been known to threaten dissidents with violence. Synanon, an organization of recovering addicts, put rattlesnakes in the mailboxes of dissidents to warn against criticism of the organization.[3]

Sexual harassment on the job is an instance of coercion, in which the perpetrator threatens the victim with termination or withholding of promotions if she withholds sexual favors.

Restraint over the use of imperative force is necessary to ensure orderly functioning over time. Power as normally used in organizations creates an atmosphere of respect and obedience to supervisors. It fosters a general sense that the incumbent of a role should pay careful attention to the provisions of roles sent to him or her by others, particularly when the role senders are superiors in an organizational hierarchy.

The normal exercise of power is much less intrusive and intimidating than either discipline or coercion. These features make power a better tool for promoting coordination of human activity than either discipline or coercion. Restrained exercise of power is the preferred imperative force in organizations because

- People will not remain voluntarily in an organization in which highly intrusive methods of supervision (such as intimidation or coercion) are used.

- People working under the power of others retain the ability to weigh alternative responses. This latitude encourages members of an organization to exercise creativity and initiative.
- Outside social forces limit the use of naked power in organizations, even in "total institutions" such as prisons and armies. Instrumentally, power is most effective when people are free from explicit reminders of its presence.

Power is exercised in organizations in a manner compatible with smooth everyday functioning. Systems of power must allow people in organizations sufficient discretion to perform complex functions and to retain feelings of self-worth. Discipline and coercion cannot produce these outcomes with any degree of consistency.

Power via Rewards and Punishments

"Reward power" constitutes control over others via allocation of positive rewards or negative rewards (punishments). This is the most familiar and visible form of power in organizations. It is important to note that the power an individual obtains from the ability to distribute rewards does not require explicit delivery or promise of reward for each instance of obedience. Rather, individuals capable of distributing rewards or imposing punishments induce the feeling in others that they should be obeyed.

Reward power in politics. Traditional American politics illustrates the use of rewards and punishments for the purpose of obtaining obedience. Throughout the 20th century, crucial areas of public life in many American cities were controlled by political "bosses." Some bosses were elected officials. These included colorful figures such as Boston's Mayor John Fitzgerald, grandfather of President John F. Kennedy, and Chicago's Mayor Richard J. Daley. Other bosses shunned the public eye, holding official positions only within the Democratic or Republican party. Sometimes, they held no formal position of any kind.

The story of Chicago's Mayor Daley, who held office for some 20 years, could serve as a textbook for the exercise of power.[4] Mayor Daley controlled city government through the distribution of favors. For ordinary citizens, the Democratic Party machine controlled by Mayor Daley constituted a vast employment agency. Men and women approached party officials at the neighborhood level when they wanted jobs, often receiving positions in city government or in firms doing significant business with the city. For the city's business leaders, sought-after favors included permits for high-rise developments downtown and award of lucrative city contracts.

Distribution of favors enabled Mayor Daley and his lieutenants to mold the behavior of Chicagoans for a generation. Holders of city jobs walked precincts and rang doorbells at election time. Big businessmen made large contributions to both the mayor and the candidates he favored. In the city council, the mayor controlled the voting behavior of most members.

Mayor Daley could also mete out punishment to the disobedient. Businessmen who failed to contribute would be cut out of city contracting. City council members who failed to vote his way would find that their districts received low levels of service from the city. The streets of one chronic dissident's district were famous for unrepaired potholes and unremoved snow in the winter.

The wishes of Mayor Daley and his cronies determined the way thousands of Chicago residents exercised their role as citizens. City workers, members of a large formal organization, spent their time in ways most favorable to the Democratic Party machine. Voters took the mayor's desires into consideration at election time. Councilmen made decisions consistent with the mayor's instructions.

Reward power in organizations. The ability to allocate rewards and inflict punishment is important not only in political parties but also in other organizations. Earlier chapters have addressed opportunities for promotion. These are important motivations for adherence to role expectations and instructions. Monetary compensation is also an important motivator and will receive special attention later in this chapter. The prospect of punishments such as demotion and dismissal encourage adherence to role expectations and support for organizational structure.

People who make decisions over allocation of material rewards have power in organizations. There are many illustrations of this obvious truth. Tales of the Middle Ages tell of heroic chivalry by lance-bearing knights. But documented histories indicate that these fighters swore allegiance and fought under the banner of the prince or duke who could offer money or opportunities for profitable plunder.[5]

In this respect, modern organizations staffed with highly educated professionals are similar. Consider the law firm. Such organizations employ highly accomplished specialists in various areas of the law, such as contracts and personal injury. But firm members known as "rainmakers" hold power. These attorneys may not possess learning and expertise on a par with their specialized colleagues. But, drawing on personal, business, and family contacts, rainmakers bring clients into the firm. Rainmakers distribute the accompanying revenue to other attorneys, who do the actual legal work.

People capable of bringing in business also hold power in the rarefied world of the "think tank." These organizations—with names like Rand, Brookings, and Battelle—do advanced research in areas ranging from engineering to the design of health and welfare systems. Project funds come largely from grants and contracts fought over intensely by competing think tanks. The scientists who obtain the most money in this competitive struggle enjoy the power to distribute it to others. A high level of funding enables the scientist to tell others what to work on, how to approach technical tasks, and, often, with whom they may communicate. Scientists in this position may even exercise power over those who officially outrank them in the hierarchy.

As indicated in the preceding chapter, punishment may be viewed as a negative reward. Totalitarian states offer the best examples of power through negative rewards. In these states, secret police officials wield considerable power. Examples in the formal organizations of democratic countries include internal auditing personnel and school officials responsible for student discipline.

Emotional Power

Material rewards—including such negative rewards as physical punishment—underlie a great deal of the power that is exercised in organizations. But power has other sources as well. Emotions help shape human behavior in every setting. Feelings having nothing to do with material rewards often determine the manner in which people carry out their roles.

As noted in Chapter 2, emotions are conscious feelings. They include love, hate, jealousy, elation, depression, frustration, and anxiety. Emotions influence the way people interact and are affected by social interaction.

Emotions are powerful and can be used as an instrument of power by one person over another. People observing an intimate relationship may remark about how much power one partner wields over the other. Such comments often reflect literal truth. A romantically involved person frequently changes his or her thinking and behavior at the partner's behest.

In organizations, giving or withdrawing positive affect may function in the manner of positive and negative rewards. People in organizations realize they will not be well liked unless they adhere to their role as sent to them by others. A "team player" receives social esteem from his or her peers at the workplace. A noncomplier is less likely to be popular among his or her colleagues. In extreme cases, people who do not carry out their roles as expected will be reprimanded by their supervisors and ignored by peers. The dissident receives fewer social contacts, invitations to outside events, greetings, and condolences in the event of misfortune.

Mentoring relationships in organizations involve emotional power. In such relationships, a junior person receives instruction, introductions, and often material assistance from an established member of the organization. The emotional tie that develops between mentor and protégé affects the junior's approach to his or her role and fidelity to the structure. No one wants to disappoint a parent.

The term *emotional* suggests spontaneous thinking and action. But emotions can also be used deliberately and are an important component in the tool kit of managers. Positive emotional gestures create feelings of obligations among others that are often sufficiently powerful to change thinking and behavior. The boss who recognizes a secretary's birthday with flowers creates positive feelings. This feeling makes the boss's request for the secretary to work late on another occasion more likely to be positively received.

Erotic impulses among people in the workplace are frowned upon in official circles. But such feelings (acknowledged or repressed) doubtlessly enhance the ability of the love object to instruct and direct the person or people who love him or her. The importance of erotic impulses as contributors to imperative force deserves more research.

Emotional forces often have the character of informal social processes. But the informal process may reinforce role expectations and underscore structure. Most people want their peers and supervisors to feel good about them. Emotion, though, is changeable, and it seems unreliable as a basis for imperative force.

Emotion can also serve as the basis of power directed in a manner unfavorable to organizational objectives. Workers at the Hawthorne plant described in Chapter 1 developed their own system of control over each other. The workers exercised power over each other in order to limit the amount of effort required of each, a practice that reduced productivity.

It seems likely that emotional and material factors often combine as underpinnings of power in organizations. Recall once again the Hawthorne workers. Each man undoubtedly limited his productive effort due to feelings of solidarity with his buddies. But a man who worked too fast also risked a sharp blow to the arm from his neighbor on the assembly line.

The Norm of Reciprocity: A Basic Organizational Principle

Norms are behavioral standards expected of everyone in society. The greater society's norms usually permeate formal organizations. One of the most important norms in almost all societies (including our own) is that of reciprocity. This norm helps make possible the exercise of power through both material rewards and emotions.

The norm of reciprocity states that people should "reciprocate" acts of kindness and largess by others. For example, people who receive a gift feel they should give a gift in return. This norm results from humankind's basic need to achieve cognitive consistency. Most people feel uncomfortable about having ill feelings toward someone who is nice to them.

The norm of reciprocity makes people feel they should "give something back." Its operation makes possible motivation through expression of positive feelings, through gestures, gifts, and minimization of social distance (the boss says, "Oh, you can call me Bill"). These emotional expressions create feelings of obligation that are the hallmark of imperative force.

The norm of reciprocity is illustrated in the mix of emotional and material factors often involved in the exercise of power through material rewards as well as emotions. In a practice initiated by IBM, some firms hiring highly talented and motivated workers elect to pay well above the market rate. In exchange for such favor, employees feel obligated to contribute an extra measure of effort, cooperation, and loyalty. Manufacturing firms have achieved similar results by overlooking minor acts of theft by employees.

Organized crime provides an extreme example of the norm of reciprocity. If Mario Puzo's *Godfather*[6] is an accurate portrayal, the Don's giving of favors extends his power well beyond that wrought by violence. Recipients of favors feel obliged to reciprocate when asked.

Of course, response to receiving a favor or gift is motivated by factors other than the need to feel good emotionally. This is particularly true when the gift giver is a Mafia boss. As noted above, reward power depends on conscious calculation. But human thinking and acts are seldom attributable to a single cause. Emotions can either reinforce or undermine a rational decision.

Knowledge Power

The term *knowledge power* recalls an old proverb. Frequently in organizations knowledge is power. People in organizations exercise control over others through

- Dominance over information: restricting access to information by keeping it secret or sharing it on a restricted basis
- Dominance over expertise: monopolizing information and know-how regarding functions and processes crucial to the organization

Information Monopoly

The flow of information in an organization is always crucial to its functioning. Chapter 10 will provide details about the manner in which information is transmitted and processed. Organizational structure determines the manner in which information is transmitted among roles.

Firms in financial distress provide illustrations of how power over information affects performance of roles. High-level managers know more about the firm's finances and prospects than do even the most careful readers of publicly available financial statements. Managers on the lower rungs as well as the rank and file may know very little about the firm's troubles.[7]

Behavior at all levels of the organization would change if the information were widely known. Some employees would seek other jobs. Others would reduce their level of effort, knowing that outstanding performance had limited potential of being rewarded. Productivity would drop as employees updated résumés, slipped out for job interviews, took long lunch breaks, or simply goofed off. The organization would have difficulty recruiting new employees.

Knowledge is power in organizations with favorable as well as unfavorable prospects. Management does not willingly share information about profits or executive salaries with the workers. Controlling information of this kind promotes the impression among workers that the "system" is fair. A feeling of fairness reinforces material rewards as an incentive to perform roles as prescribed and to support the organization's structure.

Potential recruits, new members, and people new to their positions are subject to information deficit. The informational advantage of role senders, who are more experienced in their own jobs, is great. This information advantage enables the role sender to exercise unchallenged power over the manner in which the newcomer carries out his or her role.

Consequences of information imbalance may include strict adherence by the newcomer to the role's formal requirements. Later, he or she may learn how previous occupants of the role cut corners, delegated responsibilities, and exerted less effort.

Recruiters are notorious for selectively transmitting information to prospective employees. They represent personal growth and promotion opportunities in a more positive light than the facts may warrant. They play down potential career barriers. Few, if any, recruiters are likely to tell a San Jose State graduate that all the company's CEOs went to college at Berkeley or Stanford. Thinking that they had unlimited opportunities for advancement, ignorant employees have worked many extra hours.

Restriction of information is an instrument of power available to lower-level managers and operatives. Workers and line managers do not always share complete information with their superiors. The line manager may not provide complete data on his or her productivity or costs. The operative may not tell the manager how much he could really accomplish if he "felt like it." Managers without means for ensuring high-quality information "from the bottom up" are potentially subject to the power of their subordinates.

Expert Power

Expertise denotes an unusual command over esoteric or technical knowledge. *Esoteric* knowledge constitutes understanding of rules and operating procedures of an individual organization, a particular group of people, a specific community, or a specialized market. It is often organization-specific. *Technical* knowledge comprises general principles, practices, and problem-solving techniques applicable in many different organizations. Technical experts include specialists in engineering, medicine, law, and finance.

Expertise requires extensive training or experience. People acquire esoteric knowledge through experience in a single organization or industry. Talented people who remain with one organization or industry for many years become familiar with the rules, operating routines, and ways of getting things done on an informal basis.

Esoteric experts are the virtuosos of organizational routine. Often, they also attain familiarity with people outside the organization whose collaboration is required or helpful. For the business firm, important outsiders include customers, suppliers, and perhaps regulators. For the public agency, such outsiders include officials at other agencies and elected officeholders. For voluntary organizations, they include financial contributors and people willing to donate services.

Technical experts attain their basic capability through formal education, usually in colleges and universities. Their capabilities can generally be applied in many different organizations. People of average intelligence can attain command of any area of technical knowledge if given access to training and sufficient time.

Expert power is based on the dependency of nonexperts. People in organizations use expertise—either demonstrated or merely claimed—as an instrument of power. They use this power as a means of affecting the role performance of others or to maintain the liberty to carry out their roles in the manner they choose.

Professional Power

Professionals are a class of experts who often exercise significant power in organizations. *Professionalism* requires command of a body of technical knowledge. But professional knowledge is also partly esoteric. Lawyers say that no two cases are exactly the same and doctors comment that every patient and manifestation of disease is different. A professional's judgment requires not just "book learning" but years of experience in problem solving. A doctor or teacher cannot always express a patient's or pupil's problem in explicit language. Years of experience enable these professionals to develop a "feel" for each unique case and formulate a solution.

Professionals draw basic values and norms from sources outside the organizations that employ them. All professions have organizations that hold meetings, publish journals, and lobby elected officials. Traditionally, professionals have not looked to organizational superiors for resolving technical issues or establishing standards. Instead, professionals have relied on other members of the profession for information and guidance.[8]

Medicine, the most distinguished of the professions, illustrates the power that professional status makes possible. The preceding chapter described the peculiar organizational structure of American hospitals. This structure comprises several hierarchies. The administrative hierarchy does not exercise supervision over physicians. The physician's professional independence has given rise to this type of structure. The law prohibits nonphysicians from overriding physicians' diagnoses or dictating the therapies they must provide. It is rare, moreover, for one physician to tell another physician what to do.

Physicians, then, are in a position to resist attempts of others to exercise power over them in the organizations where they work, such as hospitals and clinics. But physicians exercise power over others in these organizations. For a large part of the 20th century, physicians held major decision-making power in hospitals. Only a small percentage of Americans requiring health care come directly to hospitals. Typically, physicians admit patients from their private practices to the hospital.

The hospital, then, was dependent on the physician for its revenue. Physicians could dictate organizational decisions such as purchase of equipment. Facilities were staffed and equipped according to the desires of the medical staff even when administrators considered the actions bad business decisions.

Today, the expert knowledge of the medical profession has become more widely shared. Computerized decision-making tools known as "expert systems" have been developed that can make clinical decisions similar to those of an experienced doctor. Today, these systems are used merely to assist the physician in making difficult decisions. But it seems likely that physicians' power will diminish as their knowledge base becomes more widely disseminated and accessible to nonphysicians.

Workers' Power

People with high levels of education and prestige are not the only ones who exercise power due to command of esoteric or technical knowledge. Many executives depend on the "lower orders" of the organizational hierarchy. Secretaries, for example, may hold considerable power due to their knowledge of the boss's files and schedule. Executives may depend on their secretaries for functions ranging from copying documents to finding out which other executive might be able to provide a required resource. Many executives do not learn to use office equipment and are thus helpless after the secretary goes home for the night.

The secretary, on the other hand, is not particularly dependent on the boss. Theoretically, the boss can fire the secretary. But replacing an employee often requires considerable effort. Memos must be written, potential lawsuits regarding discrimination or unlawful termination considered, an announcement of the open position prepared, and candidates screened, interviewed, and selected.

Even if terminated, nonexecutive and subprofessional workers lose less than the higher-order employees because they have less "investment" in the organization. They are less likely to assess their personal self-worth according to their success in the organization than are the higher-ups.

When terminated, workers in relatively low positions often find reemployment more readily than would their superiors. Low-level workers usually have less "firm-specific" skills than executives. Workers accept considerably lower levels of compensation. In good economic times, a secretary or assistant can a new find job without excessive difficulty.

In many situations, then, workers have power over their superiors. The boss depends on the secretary or office assistant for help in meeting a pressing deadline, and thus must exercise skilled diplomacy in requesting these personnel to work late. The boss may need to negotiate extra rewards. On a larger scale, employers face strikes by organized workers when diplomacy and negotiation fail. Organized workers are most likely to win a strike when their skills are in short supply—that is, when the employer is most dependent on them.

Power in a French Factory

Sociologist Michele Crozier studied a system of government-owned industrial plants in the early 1960s.[9] The plants operated on the basis of rules made by a central ministry in Paris. Unexplained patterns of social relationships resulted in accumulations of power where it was least expected.

Employees at each factory included foremen, maintenance workers, and machine operators. A director, an assistant director, a comptroller, and a technical engineer made up the management team.

Crozier interviewed all personnel to assess job stresses and levels of satisfaction. Directors and assistant directors appeared least satisfied. They made few important decisions because most plant operations were dictated by rules beyond their control.

Maintenance workers and the technical engineers complained about low status and pay. In contrast to directors, assistant directors, and machine operators, though, they expressed high levels of job satisfaction.

Crozier traced the engineers' and maintenance workers' satisfaction to the power they wielded in the plant. Unlike other employees, people in these job categories prevented others, including upper-level managers, from supervising or criticizing their work. Maintenance workers could keep inadequate performance a secret. Under certain conditions, engineers and maintenance workers controlled the amount of work done at the plant.

In the factories studied by Crozier, maintenance workers and technical engineers were the only ones who exercised true power. Due to their power, machine operators, foremen, and directors acted in ways contrary to their own judgments and inclinations.

Dependence by everyone on the ability and willingness of the engineers and maintenance workers to keep the machines running explains the power of these employees. No one outside these job categories had the skills necessary to fix malfunctioning equipment.

Engineers and maintenance workers took steps to keep others from acquiring knowledge and skills that would diminish their power. Crozier details the maintenance workers' strategy for keeping power as follows:

> They prevent both production workers and supervisors from dealing in any way with machine maintenance. . . . The one "unforgivable sin" of a machine operator is to "fool around" with her machine. Maintenance workers keep their skill itself as a rule-of-thumb skill. They completely disregard all blueprints and maintenance directions, and have been able to make them disappear from the plants.

Crozier remarks that he could never find on plant premises "any written instructions about the . . . maintenance of the different kinds of machines" although these instructions were "easily available" in the offices of the central ministry.

Crozier's study illustrates a major principle regarding sources of power in organizations. Power, he writes, derives from the ability to resolve uncertain situations. The maintenance workers, for example, knew how to fix the factory's machines. This capability enabled these workers to keep others from criticizing them, although the director, assistant director, foremen, and other workers all had complaints. Everyone in the factory wanted to maintain a level of production recognized as acceptable. The presence of an unrepaired machine introduced an element of uncertainty and risk.

As illustrated here, workers' power over management resembles that of physicians over hospital administrators. The physicians maintain independence and control over decision making through their ability to reduce uncertainty in the hospital's revenue stream. When a physician admits a patient, the doctor bills for the medical services provided. When a physician examines, medicates, or operates on a patient, the hospital bills for use of its facilities, equipment, personnel, and supplies.

The Limits of Power

Power is unquestionably important in organizations. But it has several limitations as a means of ensuring adherence to received roles. Politicians, officials, executives, experts, and employees all may exercise power, as illustrated above. But well-functioning organizations require stable exercise of imperative force. Organizations benefit most from imperative force that is conducive to performing roles in a manner that effectively contributes to organizational objectives.

Principal limitations on power as an instrument of imperative force include

- Potential lack of legitimacy
- Limitations on resources
- Diffusion through the ranks

Lack of Legitimacy

People who exercise power do not necessarily have the allegiance of their subjects. Employees of business organizations and members of political parties obey the boss's instructions. But they may not consider his or her ability to command as *legitimate,* that is, consistent with principles governing the right of some people to have power over others. Principles of recognition may arise from laws, traditions, and the values of society as a whole or a particular subgroup.

Ultimately, power without legitimacy is unstable, ineffective, or both. Illegitimately empowered people face constant threat from rivals. Personnel in organizations function poorly under a regime of commanders whom they consider illegitimate and commands with which they fundamentally disagree. Top-down command aggravates disagreements with superiors who depend on power for controlling their subordinates' behavior.

People often use the term "naked power" to describe power without legitimacy.

For many centuries, the limitations of *naked power* have served as subject matter for writers and thinkers. In the early 20th century, pioneering management scientist Mary Follett[10] observed that power alone was insufficient for effective management. She commented that people comply most faithfully with orders when these orders make sense and fit the needs of the situation at hand.

"The Sword of Damocles," an ancient tale, illustrates the instability and risk inherent in rule through power. Damocles was the underling of a tyrant king. Upon hearing Damocles' confession of envy regarding his power and luxury, the king placed Damocles on the throne. A sumptuous banquet was set. In the midst of the festivities, Damocles glanced above his head to see a heavy sword suspended by a single hair. To the terrified Damocles, the king remarked that this was how he had felt every day of his reign.

Exhaustion of Resources

The exercise of power often requires expenditure of resources. Material rewards in the form of money, employment, or promotion definitely promote obedience. Jesse Unruh, an important California politician in the 20th century, is reputed to have underscored this point by saying, "money is the mother's milk of politics."

But people who exercise power via rewards must have rewards to give. A politician who runs out of favors can no longer discipline members of his or her organization. The same is true of punishments. A person in command will exhaust the goodwill of subordinates whom he or she regularly punishes. Subordinates will try to evade instructions or carry them out with minimum commitment. Excessive punishment results in alienation rather than allegiance.

Diffusion of Power

Power itself can be exercised without regard to the organization's objectives. As documented by Crozier, people outside the executive ranks can possess considerable power. The existence of power in roles low as well as high on the chain of command may seem democratic. But nonexecutives who exercise power in pursuit of their own prosperity and comfort do not necessarily advance the organization's objectives.

The "democratic" distribution of power in the plants studied by Crozier does not focus effort on manufacturing the product. Rather, the distribution focuses on a stable equilibrium of power. Plant directors do not take action when poor performance by the maintenance workers is brought to their attention. They are afraid to risk alienating these employees and possibly bringing on a strike. A condition of stalemate prevails at the plants. Occupants of specific roles respect each other's power and privilege. The resulting equilibrium brings about stagnation and low productivity, as managers are unable to exercise discipline and initiate reform.

* * *

Power is a natural ingredient in human relationships in organizations. Much power derives from reward and punishment. People in power employ "carrots" and "sticks" to obtain the behavior they desire from others. People experience the exercise of power as an imperative force in much the same way that domestic animals receive rewards and punishments from their masters.

Power invariably helps determine adherence to roles and the way in which they are carried out. But it does not necessarily do so in a manner that advances organizational objectives. Power is often used to enhance the independence and privilege of individuals without regard to needs of the organization as a whole. Power tends to be unstable. Its excessive use risks widespread alienation of the organization's participants.

Another imperative force is ultimately more effective in molding role performance and maintaining organizational structure. This force is known as *authority*.

Authority Versus Power

Like discipline and power, authority is a force that impels people to set aside personal preferences and judgment regarding thought and action. Authority differs from other imperative forces in its willing acceptance by those subject to it. When one individual accepts the authority of another, he or she concedes that the other has a "right" to exercise judgment, make decisions, and issue instructions or commands.

Power is usually sufficient to make people take on a role or carry it out in a certain fashion. Under normal conditions, only the foolhardy, delusional, or heroic refuse direction by those in power. But power typically affects only visible behavior. Among people under the power of others, disagreement and hostility often seethe below the surface.

Under authority, though, people voluntarily allow others to decide how they should think or behave. Authority does not exist without a minimum degree of voluntary submission. Below-the-surface conflicts between subordinates and superiors are restrained in an atmosphere of authority. Authority is characterized by voluntary suspension of conflicting views or alternatives. As one commentator has written, a person accepts authority "whenever he permits his behavior to be guided by the decision of a superior . . . without independently examining the merits of that decision."[11]

Authority has its roots in both individuals' mental lives and their social world. Basic psychological processes and personal values contribute to authority. So do social institutions and the broader culture surrounding individuals and organizations.

On the psychological level, the process of identification lays the groundwork for authority. Identification is the process by which people develop a feeling that another individual or a group represents them as individuals, reflects their aspirations, and benefits them spiritually or materially. Psychologists have used the term *ego ideal* to designate the object of an individual's identification. An individual's ego ideal is the person the individual would like to become.

Values, another element of mental life, also help make authority possible. Values, it will be recalled, denote preferences held by individuals about what is desirable.

For individuals, values distinguish what is good and desirable in an object or a person. People who express or reflect the values of others often command authority.

Fundamentally, authority stems from social institutions. Institutions are generally approved and stable patterns of behavior governing key aspects of collective life. The family, the school, the political party, and the business firm are all American institutions. Each institution comprises a complex of ideas and prescriptions for behavior associated with some specialized function. Institutions identify roles whose occupants have legitimate rights to make decisions and command obedience in specific situations.

A social scientist's classic comment summarizes the connection between institutions and authority, defining authority as "the complex of institutional rights to control the activities of members of a society, with reference to their bearing on the attainment of collective goals."[12]

Personal values motivate people to accept the authority of others. Most Americans value honesty, hard work, and innovation. People are more likely to suspend independent judgment of individuals who demonstrate such qualities than of people known to be tricky and unoriginal. But generally the appeal of these qualities is disseminated and maintained by institutions.

Authority in Kindergarten

Everyday events in kindergartens throughout the world illustrate the nature and importance of authority.

The teacher steps out of the room. Instantly a fracas ensues. Some of the kids begin to quarrel over a desired toy. Others leave their seats to play with some of the toys. Soon everyone is talking, laughing, or shouting. Children begin chasing each other around the room.

Then the teacher returns. Employing a standard procedure for restoring order, she claps her hands loudly. Instantly, the kids scramble back into their chairs.

As in most organizations, the children come to order for a variety of reasons. They may fear they will lose a promised treat, an instance of the teacher's reward power. Or, they may desire to please the teacher, for whom they feel affection.

But they also feel that the teacher represents what it is like to be "big." Everyone wants to be big like the teacher. The kids identify with her. They accept her direction because they feel they will become more like her if they do.

Less directly, the "institutional" nature of the school motivates obedience. School is America's primary institution for educating children. An individual school is a formal organization. "School," however, is an institution, an enduring model of behavior required for carrying out social functions. Obedience to teachers is one of the institution's mandates.

Children in kindergarten don't read books or receive memorandums. But they are well aware of the institutional underpinnings of the teacher's commands. Older brothers and sisters have given them pointers about what is expected. Mothers and fathers have told them stories about classrooms long ago.

In the small child's perspective, teachers have the "right" to be obeyed. Everyone obeys the teacher. It would be unthinkable not to.

To summarize, authority is characterized by

- The subordinate's suspension of independent judgment regarding the superior's decisions and directives
- The subordinate's voluntary compliance with the superior's directives
- The subordinate's belief that the superior has the "right" to make decisions and issue orders because he or she represents a social institution or advances important values

As an imperative force, authority is at the same time stronger and more limited than power. Voluntary submission and compliance promote reliable conformity with the superior's decisions. But authority always operates in an atmosphere of limits. Authority depends on social institutions and values. A person in authority cannot exercise imperative force outside the areas "authorized" by the pertinent social institutions. The superior cannot expect compliance from subordinates if he or she deviates from their values.

Religious organizations provide good examples. A clergyman usually commands authority as a biblical interpreter or spiritual counselor. But he risks rebellion among his parishioners if he uses the pulpit to support a candidate for public office. The institution defines the clergyman's "place." Values also affect the clergyman's range of behavior. Religious leaders are bound in their personal lives to follow the moral code they preach to their following. Those who transgress lose authority even if they keep their jobs.

Informal and Formal Authority

Human collectivities exercise authority in a wide variety of ways. Like human collectivities themselves, authority can have either a formal or informal character. Formal authority is a central feature of the formal organization. But informal authority exists in the formal organization as well. Normally, informal authority in an organization reinforces the formal authority system.

Studies referred to in Chapter 1 of this book described the Karimojong, a cattle-herding tribe in East Africa. Authority was a key asset in the organization of this tribe, as well in a neighboring tribe known as the Nuer. Comparison of the two tribes illustrates the differences between formal and informal authority and the function of each.

Families played an important part in both Nuer and Karimojong society. The family served as the basic unit in the cattle-herding economy. Within the family, coordination was achieved through informal structure. The family's informal structure in both tribes assigned roles to family members in farming and herding operations and helped them resolve disputes. Informal structure was important and powerful. In Nuer society at large, for example, disputes were frequent and often led to violence. But within the Nuer family, disputes were resolved by the senior male relative, known as the "bull."

Informal authority is compatible with the structure of families and other primary groups. Informal structure is "particularistic," including (and open to) only members of a single, identifiable group. Informal structure involves many spontaneously formulated procedures, rules, and decisions about who occupies the position of superior versus subordinate.

Face-to-face contact characterizes the collectivities in which informal structure prevails. Such contact allows direct exchange of instruction, criticism, and factual information among all members. These exchanges are likely to be verbal rather than written. Exchanges in such settings are often affective as well as instrumental.

Informal authority operates through multiple, often mundane-seeming mechanisms rather than standardized rules and procedures. Face-to-face relationships enable people exercising authority in primary groups to use such mechanisms to motivate conformity to role expectations. Personal and emotional ties among individuals make a general feeling of disapproval by peers into a powerful tool for shaping the atmosphere in which an individual member carries out his or her role. Mechanisms available under informal authority include ostracism, denial of access to the group's resources, and withdrawal of assistance by peers.

Examples of informal authority can be found in much more immediate settings than aboriginal Nuerland. The father of a suburban family may use informal authority to encourage his teenage son to improve in school. He may begin by lecturing the young man. The boy's mother may join in, issuing daily reminders of the father's displeasure. Siblings may take up the cudgel, making fun of their brother for his academic shortcomings. Words may be enforced with concrete actions, such as withdrawal of access to the family car.

Informal authority in the suburban family utilizes no standardized rules and procedures. The young man has not been demoted in rank or haled into court. But he receives a powerful message backed up by concrete sanctions. Few sons, moreover, would contest a father's right to act in the manner described above, however much they might resent it.

Studies of work groups provide many examples of informal authority. Workers in the Hawthorne plant described in Chapter 1 consistently controlled their level of production through an informal authority system. A man whose work speed exceeded group norms would be treated with hostility. Men on the assembly line would inflict light physical punishment to get "rate-busters" to work at a less demanding pace. Norms of the group gave men the "right" to inflict such reminders.

Informal authority systems depend on the unique relationships group members have with each other. The suburban father and the Nuer "bull" exercise authority only over people who are related to them. The Hawthorne workers could impose restrictive practices only on people they knew personally. But informal authority ultimately depends on social institutions. Authority exercised by heads of families depends on long-established patterns of dominance and subordination approved and supported by the society at large. Authority among peers in the workplace is regulated by public law, union contracts, and social practice of long standing.

Formal authority is much more readily visible and focused in its intent and operations. This is consistent with the deliberate design of formal organizations to achieve specific ends. Also, the size of modern corporations, agencies, or other agglomerations of people limit face-to-face contact, making formal authority necessary.

Formal authority is exercised through specific rules and procedures. These are almost always codified and preserved in written form. Charters, bylaws, charts depicting who reports to whom, job descriptions, and standard operating procedures are the hallmarks of formal organizations. The right of the occupant of one role to direct the occupant of another role is specified in the organization's documents.

Formal authority is highly compatible with formal structure. Superiors in formal organizations issue commands and apply punishments through mechanisms recognized and duplicated throughout the organization. Long-term, affective, or face-to-face relationships are not required for such procedures. Within a formal structure, instruction, rewards, and punishments given by people in authority tend to be highly specific: a civil servant is directed by official circular to revise an auditing routine; a worker is docked a day's pay (no more, no less) for not wearing his safety goggles. In formal organizations, authority is often recognized and reinforced by ritualistic behavior, as when the people in a courtroom rise at the judge's entrance.

Formal and Informal Authority Work Together

Formal and informal authority differ as abstract principles. But actual human interaction often mixes the two. Formal and informal authority usually reinforce each other.

People who possess formal authority frequently avoid using it, knowing that they may attain more control by saving formal procedures for extreme circumstances.

A small-town policeman provides a useful example. The officer stops a teenager for speeding down Main Street. Instead of reaching for his ticket book, the cop lectures the young man: "I'm going to let you off with a warning this time, but I'll be real unhappy if I catch you speeding again."

The officer is doing more than playing "Mr. Nice Guy." He knows that the youth will remember his lecture longer than he would a traffic fine. And he has learned that the sense of obligation people develop when they are "let off" has a greater impact than simply paying a fine.

Authority as exercised by the policeman in this example is informal in nature. He uses affective language, expressing his feelings about the matter. Rather than threaten a specific consequence for future infractions, he evokes diffuse possibilities.

The norm of reciprocity operates in this illustration. In exchange for the policeman's favor, the youth will pay extra attention to his driving. The certainty of future face-to-face contact between the two men facilitates the officer's exercise of informal authority.

The officer, of course, must possess formal authority to make his informal authority effective. His ability to write a ticket, have a license suspended, or worse, gives weight to his threat of becoming "real unhappy" if the youth speeds again.

Some officials and supervisors indeed exercise only formal authority, due to personal choice or organizational requirements. But these supervisors lose a measure of control by never deviating from "the book." By never giving a "suspended sentence" for infractions and errors, they lose opportunities for developing personal loyalty among their subordinates. They come to be known as rigid and cold, and in extreme cases, as cranks.

Sources of Authority

Voluntary submission to another person's direction is the hallmark of response to authority. Submission of this kind occurs because people "believe in" the values, ideas, and institutions that stand behind the person in authority. Rarely, people attribute authority to an individual human being because they believe he or she personally embodies their values and aspirations or speaks on behalf of a deity.

Akin to their explanations of power, researchers have classified authority into several distinct types, according to its source. Among the most widely cited types of authority are

- Traditional
- Rational-legal
- Charismatic

Traditional Authority

Under traditional authority, people obey a superior because others in the past have done so. Practices carried out by previous generations have power over the generations that follow. Nearly every society has customs and practices that pass from generation to generation. These are rooted in the society's basic culture and fundamental beliefs about the ordering of the physical and social universe. Traditional authority is most visible in premodern or aboriginal societies.

Medieval Europe offers many examples of traditional authority. In the Middle Ages, people typically accepted the direction of other individuals according to lineage. Entire countries gave automatic allegiance to the new king because he was the eldest son of the prior monarch. Peasants took orders from their lord and asked him to resolve their private disputes because such respect had always been accorded. People in the Middle Ages believed in a natural ordering of humankind. Under this natural order, commoners were obliged to obey nobles. Nobles themselves fell into a hierarchy, the baron owing allegiance to the marquis, the marquis owing allegiance to the duke, and so forth.

Alternatively, holders of authority under traditional systems receive their designation due to time-honored rules of recognition. The famous Dalai Lama, the god-king of Tibet who fled his country in the 1950s, did not receive his crown because his father had been a dalai lama. Rather, Tibetan holy men searched for a child born just after the old Dalai Lama's death who seemed to have qualities that are divine according to traditional criteria. Tradition dictated that Tibetans accept the authority of a king selected in this fashion.

Aboriginal societies like the Karimojong and Nuer seem to live under systems of traditional authority. Both respect the authority of people who are heads of households. Tribesmen bring family disputes to the eldest member of the family, who has authority over family disputes.

Of all types of authority, the traditional form is the most stable and the least readily subject to revision.

Rational-Legal Authority

Rational-legal authority is the most important imperative force in modern organizations. People who hold rational-legal authority base their ability to exercise control over others on rules and laws. Within organizations, much authority stands on public law—that is, laws governing employment, business practice, and administration of public agencies. Apart from public law, organizations develop their own systems of rules and procedures that specify the characteristics of roles, both their content and interrelationships.

As discussed in Chapter 3, laws typically represent values held by large numbers of people in a society. Ideally, laws reflect widely held values regarding how people should behave toward each other in a given situation. Laws specify the duties and rights of both individuals and organizations. Of the hundreds of thousands of items in modern legal codes, the majority govern control by individuals and organizations over physical property and human services.

The government's powers of enforcement promote adherence to laws. But most laws are obeyed not simply because there are police officers standing by. People believe in the laws. This is particularly true in democratic countries, where citizens elect the men and women who make the laws.

Governance via laws formulated by popularly elected representatives is a unique feature of modern, democratic society. Ancient Athens and Rome had legislatures whose members were elected by citizens. But women, slaves, and sometimes people without property were barred from voting. Law played an important part in medieval society. But laws emerged from the king's or duke's throne room and from parliaments elected by privileged segments of the population.

Enactment via democratic procedures strongly promotes adherence to laws. People feel like participants in the process. The statement that "the majority rules" reflects one of the most important values in modern America and in many other modern democracies.

Some laws in modern society are in fact traditional, dating back to medieval Europe or even earlier. But all law in modern society is subject to deliberate change.

The history of the United States has seen modification and rescinding of some of its most far-reaching laws. A 1920 amendment to the United States Constitution prohibited the sale of alcohol, a commodity in widespread use since the dawn of civilization. The amendment was rescinded 12 years later. The state of Hawaii has recognized the legality of marriage between same-sex couples. This measure has radically transformed a principle of collective life unchanged since ancient times.

What Makes Law "Rational"

The term *rational-legal* reflects several qualities of modern legal systems. A "rational" system contains laws that are mutually consistent. In past eras, laws were an "irrational" collection of idiosyncratic formulations and decisions by legislators, judges, and kings accumulated over generations. Legal systems in many parts of Europe had this character before 1800. Napoleon, then the master of the European continent, decreed a "rationalization" of law in the countries under his jurisdiction. The resulting "Napoleonic Code" is still law in France and the state of Louisiana.

The term *rational* also reflects the belief among modern people that the legal system has a definite purpose: the promotion of social well-being. Each law, it is believed, advances a specific objective associated with the security and quality of life. Laws governing contracts, for example, reduce conflict; laws governing family life protect dependent wives and children. Everyone recognizes that there are some "bad laws." But most view the law as a set of devices that work in a coordinated manner to advance social goals.

Belief in the validity of the law is an exceedingly powerful social force. In modern democracies, citizens believe that the law is "by the people" and "for the people." This belief underlies rational-legal authority in modern society. Its strength is sufficient to ensure compliance even among people who contest the wisdom of an individual measure.

Rational-legal authority motivates people to accept social roles and perform them in a particular fashion in authoritarian regimes as well as democracies. Even in countries with unpopular dictators, most citizens comply with the law and do so with some measure of free will. It is said, for example, that Hitler accomplished many of his evil works not only because he commanded widespread devotion. Even Germans who disliked Hitler carried out their assigned tasks because they felt compelled to remain "law-abiding" citizens.

The principles of rational-legal authority translate easily into formal organizations. Many organizations, and almost all large ones, have internal legal codes. Public agencies have regulations, operating procedures, and formal chains of command. Business organizations have charters specifying authority in areas such as ownership and governance. Nonprofit and voluntary organizations have bylaws governing the obligations of members, duties of officers, and appointment of executives.

The predominance of rational-legal authority in the broader society fosters respect for an organization's rules. People expect organizations to have rules. This is as true for a community improvement organization as it is for a multinational corporation. Most people believe that the rules of the organizations to which they belong serve necessary functions. This belief binds people in organizations to their received roles.

Rational-legal authority in society at large strengthens the structure of organizations. People who accept employment make a contract (a legal agreement) with their employer. These contracts make explicit the expectations of each party. Union contracts provide a good example of such agreements, recognizing specific rights and obligations of workers and managers. Legislation regarding military service obliges men to accept the warrior role during national emergencies. Each military service has an elaborate code of laws, rules, and regulations governing the smallest instances of behavior and human relationships.

Charisma

On rare occasions, *charisma* serves as the principle that establishes authority. People who exercise charismatic authority are believed by their followers to represent powers far beyond the capabilities of human beings. The power the charismatic individual represents may be that of a deity, or an individual's charisma may reflect a political ideal or social creed. Charismatic individuals are thought of as personal embodiments of divine will, revolutionary political agendas, or humankind's ultimate potential. Through such qualities, charismatic figures exercise a magical hold on others.

Some of history's most striking figures have exercised their authority though charisma. Religious figures provide many examples. The prophet Ezekiel roamed the desert in torn garments exhorting the ancient Hebrews to abandon their sinful ways. Joan of Arc exercised similar powers in another millennium. Both were thought by their followers to communicate the words of God directly to humankind. Modern charismatic figures, such as civil rights activist Martin Luther King and Nation of Islam leader Elijah Muhammad, mingled spiritual and social messages.

Extraordinary personal presence distinguishes charismatic figures from other people. These features ordinarily include physical appearance and powers of speech. Charisma may also be established through gestures and written communication. Meher Baba, a mystic from India, exercised authority over a far-flung organization of devotees. Yet he uttered not a single word during his last 40 years of life.[13] His very silence demonstrated spiritual distinction to the faithful.

Charismatic authority depends on neither laws nor traditions, but on the qualities of the charismatic figure. Charismatic figures often disrupt customary ties and standing relationships. Holders of traditional and rational-legal authority nearly always look negatively on charisma due to its potential for undercutting their dominance. The traditional and rational-legal forms of authority are "conservative." Charismatic authority causes change, potentially to a revolutionary degree.

The word *charisma* is overused and often applied inappropriately in contemporary writing and speech. Actors and candidates for public office are said to be charismatic. "Charisma" has served as the brand name for several commercial products, including a perfume. In popular speech, charisma is taken to mean physical attractiveness, personable manners, and enthusiasm.

The test of true charisma is whether the reputedly charismatic figure represents something beyond himself or herself. Gandhi, who spoke for Indian nationalism, and Hitler, who agitated for German world dominance, could hardly be called conventionally physically attractive. Yet Gandhi well represented his people's desires for dignity and cultural independence, and Hitler forcefully embodied Germany's dreams of grandeur. Both "looked the part," Gandhi in his robes and Hitler in his military uniform. For their followers, both Gandhi and Hitler embodied values and aspirations of the highest importance.

Charismatic authority seldom develops through normal organizational channels. But charismatic figures often establish their own organizations or cause organizations to form around them. Gandhi founded the India Congress Party, and Martin Luther King, the Southern Christian Leadership Conference. The image of each dominated his respective organization. The charismatic figure's personal appeal, a combination of individual gifts and representation of values and goals, induces people to join the organization and adhere to its directions. Rarely, a charismatic person may take over an existing organization.

Charisma, however, can profoundly affect interpersonal relationships in organizations. The extraordinary atmosphere of the Los Alamos laboratory, cited in Chapter 5, for example, owed its existence to the outstanding physicist who managed the installation, J. Robert Oppenheimer. Oppenheimer is said to have personally embodied the organizational structure that eventually developed: collegial, egalitarian, and highly conducive to interpersonal communication. Oppenheimer's charisma enabled him to articulate and vouch for the organizational order.[14]

Though perhaps the most exciting of the forms described here, charismatic authority is the least stable. Some who have identified charisma as an important underpinning of imperative force have characterized it as "quicksilver" in quality.[15] Authority of this kind is vested in an individual and is thus dependent on his or her unique gifts. The resulting right to their obedience cannot automatically be delegated or bequeathed. Like everyone, charismatic individuals eventually die. Charismatic figures often die early, their flamboyance and antagonism to established power marking them for assassination.

The Importance of Influence

A brief look at "influence" is valuable before concluding discussion of imperative force. Influence amounts to persuasion of individuals who have not surrendered decision making and control to others. Such force is not truly imperative.

People who are good communicators, enjoy prestige, or have significant achievements to their credit often exercise influence over others. A surgeon known to have an outstanding record of success influences others to copy his or her techniques. A brilliant scientist may shape the thinking of generations due to the strength and originality of his or her theories. A personally popular worker may persuade many of his or her peers to vote for union representation.

Influential people of this kind do not exercise authority. They lack the magical hold charismatic figures have over others. They possess neither legal means nor traditional powers for compelling others to comply with their desires. An individual who submits to the influence of another does so because he or she decides the recommended course of action is desirable on its merits.

Influence, though, promotes coordination of human acts and is potentially important in organizations. A person possessing authority is often more effective when he or she avoids using it. Influence allows the subordinate to maintain a feeling of autonomy, ultimately leading to stronger commitment.

Issues and Applications

Imperative forces such as power and authority are crucial resources for promoting adherence to roles and structure. But the best way to apply these resources is not always obvious. Even individuals with significant formal power and authority cannot always ensure that their decisions are carried out.

- The director of research at a financial services firm encounters difficulties in meeting the deadline for an important report. His technical staff tells him that they cannot finish required programming in time and are unable to work over the intervening weekend. The director has become subject to expert power, since he is unfamiliar with the statistical software the staff is using. Several alternatives may be open to him, however. If he has sufficient technical background, he can study the manuals and complete the programming (or some of it) on his own. Or, if he has sufficient resources, he can hire an outside consultant to do the programming, enabling him to meet the deadline.

- Historically, coercion has provided the underpinnings of order in prisons throughout the world. Under this system, infractions are promptly followed by penalties, extending from confinement in disciplinary cells to application of lethal force. Modern prisons, though, make extensive use of rewards to promote order: good behavior can bring the prisoner commissary privileges, television in his or her cell, placement in the "honor block," or transfer to a lower-security facility. Reward power of this kind is more stable than coercion and likely requires less intense and vigilant supervision by guards. Yet it is difficult to imagine operating a prison in which coercion was not available to back up the reward and privilege system.

Chapter Review and Major Themes

Reward and punishment cannot alone ensure the consistency and coordination of behavior required in a formal organization. The theory of "economic man" holds that people's conscious decisions about what is best for them determine their actions. Emotion, however, often reduces a person's ability to make reasoned decisions among alternatives. The needs of individuals change over time, making reward systems less effective. Pursuit of individual gain risks fragmentation in an organization, as people and subgroups look out primarily for their own self-interest.

Imperative forces are an essential ingredient in the human collectivity. These forces cause individuals to suspend independent judgment regarding their own actions or thoughts. Imperative forces include discipline, power, and authority. Imperative forces allow a superior to direct the actions of a subordinate without appeal to his or her immediate self-interest.

Power is the most visible form of imperative force common to a broad range of organizations. Individuals often establish power through their ability to distribute rewards and apply punishment. But control of information, expertise, mentorship, and even interpersonal affection can also serve as the basis of power.

Of all imperative forces, authority is the most stable and pervasive. This is particularly true of authority that stems from traditional or rational-legal sources. Superiors may exercise authority in a formal or informal manner. The most effective managers often use informal methods of coordinating their subordinates' actions on a day-to-day basis, saving formal mechanisms for instances of special need.

As illustrated by Figure 7.1, the organization's environment plays an important part in the types of imperative forces that are available for use in an organization. Law and the broader culture, for example, are likely to prohibit the use of coercion. The educational experience of professionals often includes expectations of autonomy, which limits the applicability of imperative force. The Uniform Code of Military Justice gives the soldier the right to disobey an illegal order. On the other hand, institutional support for supervision in work organizations leads to acceptance of power and authority. Discipline is considered a natural component of life in military organizations.

Imperative force can be highly functional when applied in a manner consistent with the organization's objectives. But it has a strong potential for becoming dysfunctional if misapplied. This is particularly true of coercion. Although the direct exercise of coercion may yield temporary obedience, its dysfunctional consequences include fear, resentment, and evasion. The same is also true, though less acutely, of power.

As this chapter has noted, the most effective leaders exercise authority or persuasion in preference to power. Due to the stability of its effects, authority is more effective than power (and certainly more effective than coercion) as a routine measure. Authority, though, requires acceptance by the membership. For this reason, authority has important limits as a resource for control. In ordinary transactions, rational-legal or traditional authority is more frequently encountered than the charismatic type. Rational-legal and traditional authority are subject to strong limitations from the legal and cultural environment.

Figure 7.1 indicates that imperative forces can both reduce and increase conflict in an organization. The presence of individuals (or roles) with the power or authority to settle disputes can reduce active conflict. However, the constraint and repression often experienced by people over whom power and authority is exercised can breed adverse consequences ranging from resentment to rebellion.

Despite their importance, rewards, punishments, and imperative forces still provide an incomplete picture of the organization's resources for coordination and cohesion. In addition, effective and long-lasting organizations often possess a comprehensive set of shared values and beliefs about the organization's purpose and methods of operation. These systems of ideas and conceptions are known as organizational cultures, which are the subject of the next chapter.

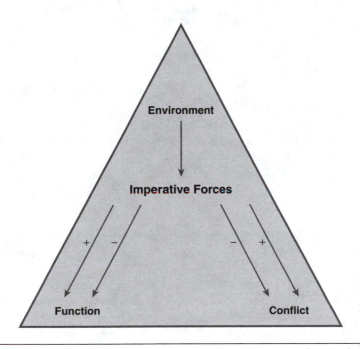

Figure 7.1   Analytical Perspectives Applied to Imperative Forces

Discussion Questions

1. To what extent can any organization achieve its objectives without resorting to the imperative forces described in this chapter? Can you identify any specific organizations that use imperative force only minimally, if at all?

2. Some organizations have relied heavily on a combination of discipline, power, and authority. The army of a totalitarian country or a modern terrorist organizations may exemplify such organizations. To what extent can such organizations control their members solely through these means?

3. To what extent can a technical expert, who lacks formal power or authority, affect the actions of his or her organization? What factors might enhance such an individual's influence?

4. What interpretations of imperative force in modern organizations might critical theory or postmodernism offer?

5. Is the distinction between power and authority broadly meaningful to Americans today? To what extent might appreciation of this distinction affect their behavior in organizations?

References

1. Stewart, J. (1993). Rational choice theory, public policy, and the liberal state. *Policy Sciences, 26*, 317–330.

2. French, J. P., & Raven, B. (1959). The bases of social power. In D. Cartwright (Ed.), *Studies in social power.* Ann Arbor: Research Center for Group Dynamics, Institute for Social Research, University of Michigan.

3. Michelle, D., Michelle, C., & Ofshe, R. (1980). *The light on Synanon.* New York: Sound View Press.

4. Royko, M. (1971). *Boss: Richard J. Daley of Chicago.* New York: Dutton.

5. Tuchman, B. W. (1978). *A distant mirror: The calamitous 14th century.* New York: Knopf.

6. Puzo, M. (1969). *The godfather.* New York: Putnam.

7. Lipman, J. (1986, December 15). In time of trouble, candor is often the first casualty. *Wall Street Journal.*

8. Wilensky, H. L. (1964). Professionalization of everyone? *American Journal of Sociology, 70*, 137–158.

9. Crozier, M. (1964). *The bureaucratic phenomenon* (p. 174). Chicago: University of Chicago Press.

10. Follett, M. P. (1926). *Scientific foundations of business administration.* Baltimore: Williams & Wilkins.

11. Simon, H. (1964). Quoted in Scott, W. R., Theory of organizations, in R. E. L. Faris (Ed.), *Handbook of modern sociology* (485–529). Chicago: Rand McNally.

12. Parsons, T. (1958). Authority, legitimation, and political action. In C. J. Friedrich (Ed.), *Authority* (pp. 197–221). Cambridge, MA: Harvard University Press.

13. Hopkinson, T. (1981). *Much silence: Meher Baba, his life and work.* Bombay: Meher House.

14. Thorpe, C., & Shapin, S. (2000). Who was J. Robert Oppenheimer? Charisma and complex organizations. *Social Studies of Science, 30*, 545–590.

15. Smith, D. N. (1998). Faith, reason, and charisma: Rudolf Sohm, Max Weber, and the theology of grace. *Sociological Inquiry, 68*, 32–60.

CHAPTER 8

Organizational Culture

Learning Objective

To understand how systems of values and beliefs help shape behavior in organizations.

Principles

○ Cultures are systems of values and beliefs that members of a collectivity hold in common. Art, literature, music, writing, and religion express and mold the beliefs and values of society at large. Organizations have cultures of their own that promote common values and views of the world among their members. The culture of a successful organization justifies its operating practices, helps its members accept their roles, reduces conflict, and promotes achievement of the organization's goals.

○ Culture sets the tone of life in an organization. Differences among organizations in method of communication, style of leadership, and pattern of rewards reflect differences in organizational culture.

○ Organizations express their cultures through written and spoken communications, such as mission statements and speeches by executives. But the organization's history, the perceptions of workers, and "artifacts" such as office decor, workplace attire, and corporate logos also provide clues to culture.

○ Culture affects an organization's operations in concrete ways. These include
  • Justifying reward systems
  • Legitimizing imperative force
  • Validating structure
  • Fostering personal identification with the organization and its goals

○ Organizations may have multiple cultures. Executives often embrace one culture while workers embrace another.

○ Shared values and beliefs often contribute to an organization's success. Some organizational cultures, though, may endure for many generations without benefiting the organization's cohesion or productivity.

What Are Organizational Cultures

Three features of organizations enable them to maintain the coordination and cohesion necessary to attain their objectives. Chapters 6 and 7 have described two of these: first, rewards and sanctions; and second, imperative forces. Both these features of organizations may be thought of as systems of interaction among people and of allocation of material resources. A third feature that promotes cohesion and coordination in an organization is *organizational culture*.

Like rewards, sanctions, and imperative forces, organizational culture constitutes a system. Successful organizations reward their members by systematically allocating rewards for the same kind of actions in every division and unit. Imperative forces are systems as well, with managers of the same rank exercising about the same range of control in each part of the organization. Higher-level managers support the manner in which supervisors below them exercise power and authority and allocate rewards.

Organizational culture is a system of ideas and perceptions about

- The meaning of life in an organization
- Desirable versus undesirable features of individuals and their behavior
- The characteristics of social relationships to be encouraged or discouraged

Organizational culture is made up of ideas and their verbal and physical representations. For this reason, organizational culture may seem less significant than reward, power, and authority. But organizational culture is just as powerful a force for promoting coordination, cohesion, and attainment of objectives. Neither rewards nor power are consistently effective without a supporting culture.

Organizational culture owes its significance to the fact that the organization's most important features reside entirely in the minds of its members. Roles, for example, may be specified in an organization's book of job descriptions. But individuals' actual behavior reflects their personal understanding of their roles. Organization charts depict the organization's official structure. But the patterns of communication, supervision, and exchange that make up organizational structure operate only according to individuals' interpretation of such charts and acceptance of the relationships they mandate. Values and beliefs, then, play an indispensable part in promoting adherence to the roles and structures that constitute organizational machinery.

Social scientists have long appreciated the relationships between culture, individual thinking, and behavior. Culture is an important social force. According to a classical definition, culture is "the complex whole which includes knowledge, belief, art, morals, law, custom, and any other capabilities and habits acquired by . . . members of a society."[1] Culture accounts for a large part of human *consciousness*: the ideas, expectations, personal goals, and conceptions of right and wrong by which individuals live their lives.

In a manner of speaking, organizations are little societies operating within the larger society. It is expectable that they have their own cultures. Business leaders in the 1970s began to realize that history and tradition had important impacts on the functioning and achievements of their organizations. The term *corporate culture* began to be heard in executive suites and boardrooms. It was not long before members of organizations involved in pursuits other than business began to find the concept useful. Today the terms *organizational culture* and *corporate culture* are used interchangeably.

Edgar Schein helped familiarize both social scientists and managers with the concept of organizational culture. He defined organizational culture in terms of the fundamental beliefs held by members, or, as he called them, "basic assumptions." According to Schein, organizational culture comprises

> the pattern of basic assumptions that a given group has invented, discovered, or developed in learning to cope with the problems of external adaptation and internal integration, and that have worked well enough to be considered valid, and . . . to be taught to new members as the correct way to perceive, think, and feel.

Schein cites beliefs about human motivation, nature, and actions as the most important ideas in an organizational culture.[2] Bowditch and Buono characterize organizational culture simply as "the repository of what members agree about."[3]

Beliefs about what constitute acceptable human relationships are elements of culture that differ among organizations. In some organizations, for example, it is expected that people will encourage each other, help each other solve problems, and assist others in carrying out their tasks. In other organizations, people believe in open criticism and in leaving individuals to "sink or swim" in response to the challenges they encounter.

Members of some organizations assume that cooperation and mutual encouragement are the best ways to get work done. People in other organizations are just as likely to believe that the most important individual accomplishments are those attained through personal effort, intelligence, creativity, or other gifts.

Prevailing values also distinguish the cultures of different organizations. Some organizations may have a culture that encourages cooperation for its own sake, not just because it is believed to help get things done. The culture of other organizations may value individual intellectual prowess and thus encourage widespread, mutual criticism. Some organizations will value mutual honesty. In others, so much emphasis will be placed on individual achievement that deception of coworkers and even backstabbing (intentionally harming a colleague's interests) are condoned.

Organizational culture has been characterized as an "interpretive system,"[4] that is, a method of allowing members to see meaning and purpose to their roles. The cultures of research labs, hospitals, and schools foster a belief that actions prescribed by roles help promote human well being now and in the future. Banks and financial trading houses foster a belief in taking risks that, if successful, result in material rewards for both the worker and the firm. Organizations without a shared sense of meaning and purpose risk seeing roles carried out as sequences of acts that have significance for their incumbents only as ways of obtaining an income and avoiding trouble with the supervisor.

Beliefs and values exist only in human minds but require tangible methods to keep them there. All cultures are transmitted and reinforced by physical objects and ritualistic procedures that promote relevant beliefs and values and carry them forward over successive generations. This is as true in organizational cultures as in the culture shared by an entire society. Traditional American values—honesty, patriotism, and self-reliance, for example—are spread and maintained by salutes to the flag, summers in scout camp, and pilgrimages to Disneyland. Long-standing values of organizations are perpetuated via trips to corporate resort facilities, officer investiture ceremonies at social clubs, and boot camp in the military services.

Music is a basic instrument of culture on every level. Just as the United States has a national anthem, many large companies have corporate anthems. High schools and colleges have school songs. Every military branch has a hymn to celebrate heroism, service, and fellowship.

Corporate Art

Representations of organizational culture often take the form of pictures and "graven images." Corporate art has the power to express values and, closely associated with these, the organization's purpose. Examples abound:

The seal of New York City (originally a corporation in the legal sense) contains a windmill, a beaver, and a pair of barrels. The windmill and beaver recall the city's original Dutch population and initial reliance on the fur trade. For the modern onlooker, though, the windmill and beaver symbolize values: the ability to harness nature; industry; entrepreneurialism; and initiative. The barrels symbolize productivity and wealth.

Stock certificates of the United Technologies Corporation feature a man holding a slide rule (a calculating device used by engineers before the invention of personal computers) and a woman surrounded by chemical laboratory apparatus. A factory with smokestacks forms the backdrop. Belief in science's contributions to industry and profit making are thus celebrated.

The emblem of the Shriners' hospital system comprises a man in a fez holding a small child in one hand and a pair of crutches in the other. This image celebrates the system's principal value (charity) and its mission (help to crippled children).

Some of modern humankind's most familiar visual images have been designed to express the values organizations wish to project to the outside world: the Pillsbury doughboy's symbolism of wholesome nutrition; Mr. Peanut's promise of fun times; the Rolls Royce hood ornament's expression of expensive quality; the Red Cross's juxtaposition of white for impartiality and red for willingness to assist in the most challenging (bloody) of human misfortunes.

An organization's culture may be discovered through techniques anthropologists use to piece together the cultures of present-day "primitive" societies and civilizations that have vanished from the earth. Living individuals (sometimes called *informants*) may be interviewed to learn what they value and how they believe their organization works. Corporate myths—stories whose truth is uncertain yet widely shared—may be collected and analyzed. Charters, mission statements, and press releases yield similar clues. Watershed events may be identified, making possible assessment of the beliefs and values that guide the organization in times of crisis. Pictures and physical products tell much about any collectivity's beliefs and values.

As national culture is the soul of France or Japan, corporate culture is the spirit that animates and sustains Exxon, Clorox, and the Federal Bureau of Investigation. Like societies themselves, formal organizations mold and sustain values and beliefs as means to promote cohesion and coordination.

The "Lower Your Trousers!" Tale: An Organizational Myth

Myths are stories of important events that, though told and retold over the generations, cannot be authenticated. Whether true or not, myths often transmit important lessons from elders to newcomers. Myths provide clues to the beliefs and concerns of the tellers and hearers. Well-worn stories in the office or clubhouse are pieces of organizational culture that help the observer become aware of prevailing beliefs, concerns, and values.

Yiannis Gabriel recounts a story he heard from recruits at a British naval training station on the eve of their first liberty.[5] Prior to being granted leave, the recruits were required to pass an inspection to ensure that their appearance represented the service favorably after they left the base. Anxious about the possibility of failing and seeing their leaves delayed, the men described what a particularly feared officer had once done:

> He had asked recruits to lower their trousers while standing to be inspected. He then proceeded to cancel everyone's leave. The motherland, he explained, had gone to great trouble and incurred substantial cost in providing each recruit with three full sets of underwear as part of the military uniform. But, he observed, the recruits had discarded the regulation white boxer shorts stamped with their serial number in favor of a motley assembly of underwear. This he regarded as a violation of the military code with disciplinary consequences. The recruits needed a reminder that a soldier was to be a soldier through and through—a reminder reinforced by spending more time in the barracks.

The absurdity of this event makes plain some of the basic assumptions among members of military organizations. First, many rules are absurd. Second, servicepersons are individuals despite the uniformity achieved by training: just look at the diversity of underwear they choose! Third, many of the organization's rules are easily, regularly, and justifiably evaded. And finally, enlisted personnel have the right to make fun, at least among themselves, of their superiors.

The "Lower Your Trousers!" myth and the beliefs and values it reflects help underdogs in the organization maintain their self-esteem and tolerate their subservient roles.

In summary, organizational culture is a system of values and beliefs deliberately promoted and widely shared within an organization. Specific values and beliefs concern both the organization's operations and interpersonal relationships within the organization. Ideally, the values and beliefs prevailing in an organization coalesce into a "vision" shared by all members. Such a vision gives legitimacy and meaning to each small, workaday act that occurs in an organization, to the organization's objectives, and to the periodic transformations that organizations undergo.

The Components of Organizational Culture

Values and beliefs, the fundamental elements of culture, are ideas that reside in individual minds. Some writers refer to these core elements as *subjective culture.* To determine these elements, an observer would have to gain access to people's thoughts. He or she would need to "go behind the scenes" by interviewing members of the organization or sitting in on their conversations. The observer might compile records of the actions people took at critical times. How, for example, would people treat a new manager hired from outside the ranks? Would they be welcoming and helpful or would they distance themselves? The observer might carry out experiments: for example, he or she might cause an unusual situation in order to assess people's reactions.

More tangible elements of organizational culture may be seen, touched, or heard without asking deliberate questions or keeping records. These elements include flags, insignias, logos, mission statements, award ceremonies, and artwork. Readily observable objects and procedures of this kind are sometimes called *objective culture.*

Objective culture serves to promote adoption of subjective culture: that is, shared beliefs about what makes things happen in the world and what values are accorded to different things, people, and types of behavior. To promote such sharing, organizations manufacture physical objects, formulate verbal statements, carry out rituals, and make up stories. Anthropologists and cultural historians refer to such objects, formulations, and procedures as *cultural items,* Table 8.1 illustrates the manner in which four classes of cultural items, manifestos, symbols, narratives, and rituals, affect beliefs and values.

Items of objective culture often directly affirm the organization's values and beliefs. The Boy Scout Motto, for example, exhorts the organization's youthful members to be honest, reverent, clean, and, most important, "prepared." Items of objective culture can also be negative, criticizing or poking fun at thinking or actions that contradict central elements of the culture. The "Lower Your Trousers!" tale has a negative flavor, yet sends the following indirect message regarding naval culture: the most junior seamen still deserve to be treated with dignity. Many values and beliefs are similarly "honored in the breach," that is, exhibited and affirmed only on those occasions when they are violated.

The distinction between objective and subjective culture illustrates the fact that an organization's culture is often distinct from what its mission statements and physical symbols assert. Like roles, core cultural elements ultimately reside only in the human mind. Manifestos, symbols, narratives, and rituals are sometimes manifestations of underlying ideas and beliefs, but exaggerated, as illustrations often are. These elements of objective culture are also instruments by which managers attempt to promote a subjective culture that, though appropriate to the organization's needs, does not yet exist.

Modern organizations are clearly appropriate for study by anthropologists. Familiar cultural items are readily observable in most, if not all, organizations. Terms that anthropologists have applied to *aboriginal* people, whose beliefs and practices have not been influenced by modern society, apply equally well in the modern formal organization.

Table 8.1   Organizational Culture: Cultural Items and Their Functions

Item	Definition	Examples	Function
Manifestos	Verbal (written or spoken) communications regarding the organization	Mission statements Speeches by executives Circulars and memos Authorized histories, biographies	Explicitly state "official" goals, values, and objectives
Symbols	Visual representations (e.g., pictures, statues) of beliefs and values	Corporate art Architecture and decor Letterheads and logos Insignias Clothing	Create in the physical environment reminders of major beliefs and values
Narratives	Recollected events and episodes	Histories Unofficial commentaries Mythical events	Expose beliefs and values of importance on the organization's operational level
Rituals	Regularly or occasionally repeated ceremonies and procedures	Officer investitures Membership, stockholder, and board meetings Christmas parties and picnics Conventions and rallies Examinations and graduations Demotions and executions	Provide social reinforcement for both official and operational values and beliefs

Anthropologists, for example, have always displayed and written about *artifacts*. Artifacts (physical products of a society), including art, architecture, and attire (both contemporary and historical) help promote understanding of organizational culture. Artifacts that bear recognizable images are of particular interest due to their symbolic value. It is intriguing to ask what the pinched face of John D. Rockefeller might tell us about corporate culture at the bank today operated by his descendants (Chase Manhattan) or what the obtrusive nose of J. P. Morgan might symbolize for the financial institution that today bears his name. For what reason, one might inquire, does an Australian brewery or a Russian vodka distiller print the picture of its industrial plant on the label of its bottles?

Rites of passage are among the cultural elements most regularly documented by anthropologists. Rites of passage are rituals that mark the movement of individuals from one status to another in a society. Often, they signify the evolution of "candidates" into full members. Aboriginal peoples have marked the advent of male puberty with circumcision and scarification procedures. The Nuer provide an example. Among the youths of this tribe, only those who have received gar (a ritual slashing of the forehead) are permitted to dine among the men and carry spears.

Modern formal organizations conduct rites of passage, too, often involving discomfort. Fraternity initiations occasionally involve pain, but more often humiliation. "Making partner" at a law firm is accompanied by required investment of a large sum of money, often perceived as painful to the promoted attorney. Ironically, Nuer scarification, fraternity initiation, and law partnership assessment are all accompanied by parties, complete with music, dancing, and consumption of intoxicants.

Totems constitute another cultural item identifiable in both aboriginal societies and formal organizations. Totems are objects found in nature (usually animal species) that human beings identify as being of special personal significance. So-called primitive societies all over the world have adopted totems, although the practice is particularly famous among Native Americans. People believe that by adopting an animal as their totem, they receive its protection and its strength, cunning, speed, or grace. In return for the totemic animal's protection, believers decline to kill or eat members of the species.

Sports and educational organizations today seem highly charged with totemic belief. Players, fans, students, faculty, and alumni refer to themselves as Tigers, Bears, Cougars, Wolverines, Huskies, and a Noah's Ark of other beasts. They wear images of these creatures on their clothing and, among fanatics (the word from which "fan" is derived), tattoo them on their skin.

The *taboo* is among the most famous of concepts employed by cultural anthropologists. Taboos are rules that prohibit specific forms of behavior, such as transgressing physical boundaries, eating certain foods, or having sex with certain people. Adherents to modern religions practice taboos, as do Jews and Muslims regarding consumption of pork. Modern business organizations also observe taboos, such as may regard handling certain product lines or selling in certain markets.

It can be fun to play cultural anthropologist in today's formal organization. Like the anthropologists who studied the Karimojong and Nuer tribes, people today can observe the symbols and practices that preserve and promote core values in the organizations to which they belong. Everyone should do at least an informal study of the culture of his or her work, social, or professional organization. Over the years, bits of conversation, scraps of paper, and records of everyday events can be assembled to bring basic beliefs and values into distinct focus.

Few people are likely to construct a formal ethnography of their firm, political party, or sports club. But everyone should develop informal habits of observation akin to the ethnographers' techniques.

Strength of Organizational Culture

Although most organizations have cultures of some kind, not all are equally strong. Strong organizational cultures have three distinct characteristics. In organizations with strong cultures, first, people share an extensive set of values and beliefs. Second, strong cultures are widely shared in an organization; weak ones have relatively few adherents, or adherents in only a few organizational units. Finally, a

Toolbox for the Amateur Organizational Anthropologist

(With Instructions for Use)

Famed anthropologists such as E. E. Evans-Pritchard lived among tribal peoples for years, collecting artifacts, observing rituals, and interviewing informants. From such research emerged detailed descriptions of the objective and subjective culture, as well as associated behavior patterns, of peoples in the world's most remote places. These descriptions are known as "ethnographies." The anthropologists of old have left ethnographies that inform modern men and women of the practices, symbols, and ultimately the fundamental beliefs of now-extinct tribes and nations.

People in formal organizations today may have reason to construct their own ethnographies. Interest in doing so need not be academic. Understanding an organization's culture provides clues to the individual's future prospects. Most people cannot feel comfortable or succeed in an organization unless they fit in with the culture.

Classical anthropologists used simple instruments and techniques. All are available to everyone today at little or no cost. They include the following:

- Diary: for recording celebrations, rituals, and key events. Use to identify which events are marked by special episodes of standardized human interaction. Note what values are reinforced.
- Photo album: to develop a detailed description of attire worn by people in different positions. Use to recognize patterns of dress that distinguish members of one organization from like-ranked members of another, and to distinguish people in different units. Assess the manner in which dress expresses people's beliefs about themselves and their functions.
- Lexicon: a list of words and phrases used (or having special meaning) only within the organization. This tool is very useful in assessing values. Note the actions, personal qualities, or physical objects designated by positive or attractive words and phrases: these are closely tied to the organization's core values.
- Tape recorder: to record interviews with informants. Tales of old-timers may be particularly valuable. Note which acts or events have brought positive or negative reactions from the organization's members and leadership, and which elements of past history have come to be viewed in a positive or negative light. These tales indicate both positive and negative values.
- Scrapbook: to preserve logos from stationery and clippings from the organization's newspaper. Images of this kind express both values and core beliefs. Interpretations of these visual images by others may be of significant value.

strong culture specifies which beliefs and values are most important and which are peripheral to the life of the organization. Strong cultures are sometimes characterized as "thick" and weak ones as "thin."

The Variety of Organizational Cultures

The culture of an organization can be immediately and strikingly visible to observers. No anthropological tools are needed to detect its presence. The values and beliefs that underlie some organizational cultures may often be readily discerned. A few examples illustrate the presence of organizational culture in a wide variety of settings.

College Life

A college undergraduate attends a party given by a fraternity to which he is considering applying for admission. The walls of the fraternity house are plastered with framed photographs of stars from the college's football team from years past. Several shelves and a glass case in the common room display athletic trophies. Another shelf is lined with a collection of vessels for consumption of beer: stoneware steins from Germany, pewter tankards from England, glass mugs with the college insignia. Many of the party's hosts wear sweaters or blazers with crests and letters signifying varsity team membership. The center of attention is a large keg from which drinks are liberally tapped. Loud rock and roll blares from an elaborate sound system. Talk focuses on upcoming athletic face-offs and sorority coeds.

It is not hard to guess the dominant values of the organization holding the event: sports and parties. The decor of the rooms, the objects on display, and the attire of the members all suggest these values. The content of conversation confirms visual impressions.

One-on-one discussions with current members would likely follow if the visitor retained his interest in joining. Such conversation might reveal some basic beliefs about the world held by the fraternity members. Most might believe, for example, that academic achievement counted for very little in the world outside the classroom. Conversation might reveal a "present" rather than a "future" orientation, the belief that the pleasures of the life made possible by the college setting are more important than preparation for the future. Alternatively, the fraternity men may believe that competitive ability and support among friends are more valuable in achieving success after graduation than A's in English or calculus. The observed emphasis on sports and camaraderie may well express this belief.

Cultural differences between organizations are even more apparent than the culture of one organization. Some fraternities, for example, are quite different from the one just described. Many seek a balance between academic achievement and youthful pleasures and a few focus specifically on academics or community service.

Colleges themselves have distinct cultures. Compare two American universities in the last half of the 20th century, the University of Southern California (USC) and the University of Chicago. Both were well-established, private, coeducational organizations concerned with higher education and research. Both got their start in the late 1800s and have served as the jumping-off place for generations of professionals, businesspeople, and politicians in their respective regions. Classical building styles dominated the architecture of both campuses.

Organizational cultures at each campus were quite different, though. The importance of football provided an immediate clue. The stadium used by the USC Trojans was located within a few blocks of the campus's main facility. Autumn Saturdays saw traffic jams on the freeways and throngs of pedestrians streaming from campus to the stadium.

Though located at the center of campus, the University of Chicago's stadium was a complex of crumbling concrete, all but abandoned since the university disbanded its football team in the 1950s. Saturdays in autumn were quiet, dreary times.

This is not to say that the Chicago campus was deserted on autumn Saturdays. The libraries were full of students cracking books on Greek philosophy and biophysics. In offices and laboratories, graduate students and faculty worked on research projects. By the late 1970s, the football stadium had been razed to make way for a new undergraduate library. There were times when the university community turned out in large numbers for campus events. Such events took the form of concerts and plays, as well as readings and lectures by well-known authors, theologians, and social critics. As much alcohol was consumed at Chicago students' parties as at USC. But the tipsy talk was much more likely to concern science or politics than sports.

Sports-related triumphs provided opportunities to celebrate and reinforce beliefs and values underlying USC's culture. The university enjoyed over 20 Rose Bowl victories in the latter half of the 20th century. These victories sparked pride throughout the university community. With sports in the driver's seat, USC's culture reflected the belief that preparation for professional life could take place in an enjoyable setting, where friendly ties useful in later life could be cultivated.

Celebration of the University of Chicago's culture focused on distinguished scientific and academic achievements. During the 20th century, University of Chicago faculty captured over 20 Nobel Prizes, awards that seemed to shine on everyone, from the university president to the youngest undergraduate. In the latter half of the century, the football field became less renowned for athletic contests than for a scientific event that occurred below its surface. In an underground laboratory, scientists in the 1940s achieved the world's first self-sustaining nuclear chain reaction, paving the way for development of the atomic bomb.

An abstract sculpture reminiscent of a nuclear mushroom cloud today marks the location of the famed laboratory. This cultural artifact does not project orientation toward normal, upper-middle-class life, as do cultural items observable at USC. Rather, the monument reflects a drive toward extraordinary achievement and reconciliation to the discomfort and disruption such achievement may involve.

Corporate America

A blue chip corporation. The corporate culture of International Business Machines Corporation, or IBM, is perhaps the most visible and talked about in American industry. IBM exercised undisputed worldwide leadership in the computer field prior to the personal computer's appearance. In the 1950s and 1960s, people used the term *IBM machine* to mean "computer" just as they used the words *Xerox* and *Kleenex* to mean "copying machine" and "tissue." As late as the mid-1980s, IBM booked 40% of the computer industry's worldwide sales and received 70% of all profits.[6] IBM achieved its dominance through manufacture and sale of massive "mainframe" equipment that occupied entire floors of buildings. Machinery was typically leased rather than sold to users.

People talked of IBM executives and sales personnel as a particular "type." IBM types were said to dress in a uniform manner, featuring gray suits, white shirts, and black, wing-tip shoes. They projected a well-groomed, confident appearance to outsiders. The physical appearance of IBM personnel seemed to match the well-engineered, conventionally packaged products with which IBM dominated the market. Departments had mundane-sounding yet durable-seeming names, such as "Information Systems and Storage." A "no-alcohol" policy was in force at IBM gatherings.

Strong feelings of loyalty, teamwork, and concern for product quality prevailed inside the company. IBM workers never unionized and had a turnover rate of less than 3% per year. People stayed with the company despite the heavy demands it placed on them, such as relocating executives to new cities every few years. IBM employees used to quip that the company initials really stood for the phrase, "I've been moved." Generous pay and benefits encouraged this level of devotion, as did a "no layoff" policy that was in force for 70 years.

Clear ideas and values stood at the core of IBM's corporate culture. Famed CEO Thomas J. Watson, Jr., son of IBM's founder, actively preached three "basic beliefs" as fundamental to the company:

- Pursue excellence
- Provide the best customer service
- Treat employees with "respect for the individual"

Watson once said that to succeed, IBM must be willing to change everything "except these basic beliefs."

These basic beliefs were clearly compatible with IBM's needs in its era of its market dominance. The firm built and maintained its reputation by clearly being the best in the computer industry. A near monopoly on computer technology, which eventually resulted in federal charges of monopoly practices, helped it retain predominance in the market. To retain the best scientific, engineering, and management personnel, though, IBM cultivated a sense that these individuals would not be mere "cogs in the machine." Particularly in the 1950s and early 1960s, the educated and talented feared employment in large firms due to the atmosphere of conformity such organizations were believed to impose.

IBM stands out as a corporation that has tried to make its corporate culture clear to employees and a force in their lives. Management at other companies pays less attention to fostering a distinct set of beliefs and values. Corporate culture in such firms plays an important role even if it is not readily visible. In these firms, corporate culture has an implicit rather than explicit quality.

A Regulated Utility

Like the culture of IBM, that of Pacific Gas and Electric (PG&E) was stable and pervasive during much of the late 20th century. The firm was an investor-owned utility serving much of northern California. It operated hydroelectric, fossil fuel, nuclear, and geothermal generating plants. In addition, the firm owned vast tracts of California coastal and forest land. Wall Street regarded PG&E, like IBM, as a blue chip, to be depended upon for steady corporate earnings.

Ever Onward IBM

The verses below have been taken from an IBM rally song written in the 1930s. These words were sung into the 1960s, when IBM exercised undisputed domination of the computer industry and had few women in professional or management jobs. The song confirms the often-noted centrality of loyalty and pride in IBM's corporate culture:

> Ever Onward,
> Ever Onward,
> We're bound for the top to never fail.
> Right here and now we thankfully pledge
> sincerest loyalty
> to the corporation that's the best of all.
> Our leaders we revere and while we're here
> let's show the world just what we think of them!
> So let us sing, men, sing, men,
> once or twice then sing again for the
> Ever onward IBM.

PG&E's culture attempted to promote a familylike sense of belonging among both workers and managers. Like many family businesses, the firm tended to hire relatives of those already employed in its ranks. This particularism extended to executives, who usually came from upper-middle-class San Francisco Bay area families and who attended Berkeley or Stanford, the region's leading universities.

PG&E expended significant resources on building stable, often affective, ties among its employees and personal identification with the firm. The company operated resort facilities on its forest and coastal lands for employees and their families. It held events such as seaside crab feasts that were attended by hundreds. It helped maintain social and sports clubs for employees.

Employees in this era expressed appreciation of the company atmosphere, positive feelings reinforced by satisfaction with pay. Employment security added to the sense of comfort. Workers were seldom fired or laid off, a practice reinforced by the presence of a strong union. Even managers, who could not look to the union for help, seldom left the company involuntarily. People got to know each other. It was not uncommon for a worker transferred to a new locality to find himself among people he or she had worked with decades earlier.

Despite their level of comfort, some employees expressed a feeling that the stable, familylike atmosphere had a negative side. Expectations, some felt, emphasized steady performance of standardized functions rather than outstanding work. The union promoted standards of this nature for the workers. But management personnel expressed similar impressions. Stability and steady performance, then, appear to have been the principal values that the culture embodied.

A third value was apparent as well: people believed in the importance of mutual tolerance and protection. Open criticism among peers was unusual, particularly in the management ranks. One observer cites the case of an alcoholic station manager, whose subordinates covered for him during periods of incapacitation and helped keep his problem secret from upper management. Workers ignored each other's petty thievery and corner cutting.

PG&E's culture suggested a view of the world as a reasonable, predictable place. The culture encouraged the belief that reasonable effort at nonchallenging tasks was sufficient to get the job done. Individual problems could be overlooked or compensated for by redundancy. Employees, both workers and managers, of course had complaints. But most stuck with the system because it allowed them to live the good life in northern California.

For many years, the outlook promoted by PG&E's corporate culture was realistic. Delivery of gas and electricity were essential pubic services. No electrical utility had gone bankrupt since the Depression. Electrical power was produced and distributed by legal monopolies nearly everywhere. Profits did not depend on successful competition with business rivals. Cordial relationships with state agencies that regulated the utility industry, favorable public opinion, and labor peace, though, were essential to the bottom line. PG&E placed primary value on reduction of conflict at all levels.

A World Class Bank

Comparison among units of large organizations provides some of the best views of culture. Often, different cultures prevail in different parts of the same organization. Artifacts, dress, and ways of thinking differ among units of a single organization in a manner compatible with the functions each performs.

The modern commercial bank serves as an example. Commercial banks deal with businesses rather than individual consumers. Major commercial banks such as Chase Manhattan, Citibank, and Banker's Trust today conduct business on a worldwide basis. These organizations have multiple divisions, each mandated to generate profits through specialized work. Activities such as investment banking, merchant banking, and trading constitute only three specialized functions of subunits within a modern financial organization.

The trading units of major banks deserve special attention due to their distinctive practices and culture. Major banks accumulate large amounts of cash. While local banks may invest their funds in mortgages, multinational banks hold an endless variety of financial instruments such as stocks, bonds, and futures (contracts to purchase or deliver certain assets at a specified date). Banks doing international business have vast holdings in the currencies of all nations: dollars, euros, and yen, as well as South American and mainland Asian monies. More money can be made by continuously trading these assets than by holding them as long-term investments. Thus, large multinational banks operate trading departments housing hundreds of employees.

Financial trading pits participants against each other on the floors of institutions such as the New York Stock Exchange and the Chicago Board of Trade. Bank-based traders typically work on computer terminals linked to exchange facilities or other traders throughout the world. Pressure is high. Assets may be held for only a few moments. Billions of dollars worth of "paper" changes hands every minute. Huge rewards are reaped by those capable of making rapid successions of high-quality judgments. Much, if not all, of a trader's compensation is based on the volume of his or her trading profits.

Not surprisingly, values such as risk taking and financial success are emphasized in trading units. A famed ritual in some firms reflects and reinforces these values. Every Friday afternoon, trading unit supervisors summon the week's three worst-performing traders into their offices. The traders are summarily fired. They will be replaced by new personnel on Monday and the ritual will be repeated at the end of the week. The ritual serves to remind traders of the consequences of poor performance.

This ritual may seem brutal to outsiders. But professional traders accept it as part of their working life. The culture of the firm emphasizes making money and justifies risk of human failure in its pursuit. The culture of trading organizations, in short, is one of gambling. Physical artifacts reinforce this impression. One need only observe newsstands in the lobbies of buildings that house institutions such as the Chicago Board of Trade, festooned with racing forms and gambling-related magazines.

Organizational units other than trading have cultures that are quite different. Merchant banking, for example, involves services to businesses, such as lines of credit and international funds transferal. Values in merchant banking divisions emphasize relationships with clients. Personal behavior associated with these values includes the ability to converse, entertain, and dress tastefully yet fashionably. The personal attractiveness of merchant bankers helps maintain client faith in the bankers and the services they provide, and thus promotes future sales.

Investment banking concerns itself with raising capital for large corporations. Corporations require funds to purchase new equipment, expand operations, or tide themselves over during difficult periods. They raise funds by issuing stock (shares in the business) and bonds (interest-bearing certificates) to be sold to investors. Companies issuing these securities sell them to investment bankers. In a process known as underwriting, an investment banker raises money, sometimes billions of dollars, to purchase the newly issued stocks or bonds. Then, the investment banker sells portions of the issue to other people (sometimes smaller-scale investment bankers), who in turn arrange to have small portions sold to mutual funds and individuals. An investment banker can earn hundreds of millions of dollars from a single deal.

Values of investment bankers emphasize maintaining ties with the nation's financial elite. To raise the funds for underwriting, investment bankers need to sustain the confidence of people capable of lending them money or becoming partners in purchasing the new issue. A compatible worldview assumes the stability of the system and one's position as a member of its leadership.

Culture and Clothing: What to Wear?

Body coverings and markings have played an important part in culture since the earliest days of humankind. As sociologist Emil Durkheim[7] pointed out, tribesmen of yesteryear painted their faces, tattooed each other, and even knocked out some of their teeth in order to create a common appearance with their comrades. According to the famed manual "Dress for Success," the color of a man's or woman's attire today indicates his or her place in the organizational hierarchy.[8] In the Middle Ages, the law required peasants to wear only black or brown clothing, reserving for nobles alone the right to bright colors, as well as frills, ruffles, and jewels.[9]

Attire is an important cultural item in the modern formal organization. Military personnel, of course, wear uniforms that both mark them as members of the organization and designate their place in the organization's hierarchy. The manner in which an enlisted person wears his or her uniform has significance itself. Naval recruits are told to wear their sailor hats directly on top of their heads. Wearing the hat forward on the head is reserved for those who are more "salty," that is, who have already spent years in the service.

Banking personnel are famed for distinguished attire. As recently as the late 20th century, men in striped pants and bowler hats could be seen in London's financial district dashing to and from their jobs. On Wall Street, veterans of the great commercial banks can still identify the unit to which an employee reports simply by observing what he or she wears. Watching the throngs riding a bank of escalators at Citibank in the 1980s, an observer commented:

"See that one? He's an investment banker. Note the blue pinstripe suit, white shirt, black Churchill shoes, and Hermes tie. Perfectly correct.

"And that one? Merchant banking. Blue pinstripe suit also, but it's double-breasted. High fashion! And that pink shirt! You'd never see someone dressed that way underwriting a bond issue.

"Now that one's on his way to the trading room. He's wearing a blue pinstripe suit, too, but if you look closely you can see it's a lot more expensive than the one the merchant banker has on. That suit costs at least $2,000. The merchant banker's was $350, tops. Now look: blue striped shirt, suspenders, bow tie. Definitely a trader. And those shoes! Loafers with tassels! A dead giveaway!"

Clothing favored by the bankers in each specialty reflects the beliefs and values prevailing in each one's organizational unit. Investment bankers see themselves as members of the elite and pillars of society. Merchant bankers identify their mission as one of partnership building. Traders believe that people of skill and daring deserve the immense rewards they can earn on a good day. Like gamblers everywhere, they wear obviously expensive, flashy clothing—flashy by the standards of the banking world, of course.

"If someone in the investment banking department dressed like a trader he'd be fired," commented the observer at Citibank. "And if the merchant banker wore Churchills, he'd be laughed out of the bank!"

Why Organizations Need Cultures

The fact that culture is so frequently observed in formal organizations suggests that it contributes something of importance. A phenomenon as widespread as organizational culture, a functionalist would say, must add to the organization's capabilities.

Establishment and maintenance of culture requires the organization to expend resources. Holding rituals, drafting manifestos and logos, and delivering speeches all require personnel time, often drawing on the scarce hours of top executives.

What does the organization obtain in return? To appreciate the contribution of culture, it is useful to recall the basic problems organizations must solve. Organizational roles and structures represent constraints upon individual inclinations and needs. Human beings naturally resist such constraints. Organizations must cause individuals to put personal inclinations and broader social influences aside, at least for limited periods of time.

As detailed in Chapters 6 and 7, organizations accomplish this task through rewards and imperative forces. Rewards (both positive and negative) motivate individuals to fulfill the requirements of their roles by offering (or withholding) means for meeting personal needs. Imperative forces impel individuals to put aside their own needs in recognition of the rights or power of others.

Organizational culture may constitute a third resource used by organizations to promote adherence to roles and submission to structure. Beliefs and values promoted and maintained by culture in a well-functioning organization help strengthen the organization's mechanisms of coordination (rewards and imperative force) by

- Justifying reward systems
- Legitimizing imperative force
- Enhancing structure

Organizational culture may do more than promote acceptable role behavior and submission to structure. Culture helps the individual identify with the organization. This process reduces the discrepancy individuals experience between their own needs and those of the organization. Organizational culture also transmits a cognitive understanding of the organization's most important objectives to its members. Culture helps focus individual effort directly on achieving the organization's objectives. In this manner, culture acts as a "failsafe" mechanism, capable of compensating for shortcomings and defects in role expectations and structure.

Justification of Organizational Machinery

Reward Systems

Nearly every organization rewards its members in an unequal fashion. Distributing unequal rewards raises the risk of dissatisfaction. Most workers have a sense of what their services are worth on the open market. They know that a doctor earns more than a nurse, an engineer more than a technician, a chef more than a kitchen helper. But even so, there is much to dispute regarding rewards, both monetary and otherwise. People occupying one position often argue that they should earn as much as higher paid people in a comparable one. Those who acknowledge that others have a right to earn more than they do may still consider the salary differential too large.

Organizational culture helps reconcile participants to reward differentials. Through its culture, the organization may inform members that it favors people with particular skills, experience, or personal characteristics. The United States Air Force, for example, has traditionally favored pilots over other types of officers. Officers with different qualifications may complain that they have comparable years of training and commitment to the service. They know, however, that the core values of the Air Force include the actual flight function. This understanding blunts the edge of dissatisfaction. Who, some nonfliers might ask, can fight this strong a tradition?

Imperative Force

Imperative forces employed by organizations include both power and authority. Authority, the most stable and perhaps most important imperative force in an organization, requires the subordinate to believe that the superior has a right to his or her assent and obedience. Acceptance of another's authority requires the subordinate to justify the other's dominance. Social institutions (such as the employment contract) provide substantial justification. But organizational culture makes an additional contribution.

People feel better about submitting to the authority of others if their superiors are deserving of that deference. Such a quality can be imparted by organizational culture. Washington legal and public relations firms, for example, traditionally hire executives from past presidential administrations. The broader cultures of these organizations stress kinship with the elite "inside the Beltway." Executives who have had experience in the White House have enhanced authority in the firm. Who, a subordinate might reason, can presume to feel he or she knows more about how Washington works than the former official?

Structure

Structure also receives support from organizational culture. Culture helps justify organizational structure in the minds of the organization's members. An organization's objective culture, moreover, provides physical representation of structure, making it clearer and more meaningful in the minds of individuals.

The elements of culture are reflected in the career paths of organizations, identified in Chapter 5 as an important feature of organizational structure. The blue-collar career path at PG&E provides an example. Most workers in the late 20th century started off as electric-meter readers. These positions, at the bottom of the hierarchy, were dirty, relatively low paid, and occasionally hazardous—meter readers occasionally encountered poison oak and vicious dogs. To attain more desirable jobs, meter readers were required to spend two years on gas crews—a period designated as "going on the street." Gas was outdoor work, exposing personnel to heavy physical labor, bad weather, and occasional explosions.

For the PG&E blue-collar labor force, being on the gas crew was an extended rite of passage from entry level to the upper ranks. Everyone accepted the peculiar structuring of career mobility. The rite can be interpreted as a means of justifying individual mobility up the ranks: everyone pays the same dues.

Artifacts in the form of office arrangement and architecture reflect the structural features of an organization. Physical representation, in turn, strengthens structure. It is no accident that top-level managers are housed in special suites on the highest floors of corporate office buildings. This pattern of office allocation (and the high-rise building itself) mirrors social hierarchy. The physical arrangement minimizes the likelihood that people far removed from each other on the organizational chart ever meet by chance.

By contrast, organizations with nonhierarchical structure often house themselves in low-rise buildings and multiunit campuses. The open spaces of these settings provide opportunities for people of unequal status or in different specialties to meet and chat. In a move reflecting a desire to change the traditional structure of government, an agency as traditional as the New Jersey Mortgage and Finance Corporation has built a facility with an open-office floor plan and space for use by outside, nonprofit groups.

Other Functions of Culture

Organizational culture can provide more diffuse contributions to an organization. Culture, first, promotes individual identification with the organization. As noted in Chapter 1, personal identification is a process by which people develop a feeling that the group represents them as individuals. People who identify with their group feel happy that others see them as members of the group and believe that the group's actions benefit them personally. People identify with formal organizations just as they identify with groups.

A strong, appealing organizational culture helps members identify with the organization. Imagine Red Army soldiers marching past a statue of Lenin or MGM employees filing onto the company's premises under the picture of a roaring lion. Observable symbols put extra spring in the step of both Russian soldiers and MGM employees. If someone feels uplifted by the organization, he or she is less likely to feel diminished when placed under the authority of that organization's agent. Identification, in turn, enhances the member's commitment to helping achieve the organization's objectives.

In a well-functioning organization, finally, organizational culture helps maintain its members' consciousness of the organization's objectives. Along with personal identification, such consciousness can help workers solve problems in the absence of supervision. Thus, organizational culture may partially compensate for inappropriate assignment to roles, faulty structure, or inadequate management.

Where Do Organizational Cultures Come From?

Organizational culture can be emotionally moving, physically imposing, and aesthetically pleasing. It is sometimes colorful and droll. But what causes an organization—or a society for that matter—to develop its distinct culture? At least four sources of organizational culture can be identified. They are (a) survival of obsolete practices; (b) legacies of prominent leaders; (c) historical accidents; and (d) responses to structure.

Instances of survival of obsolete practices are evident within many organizations. Examples abound. Seamen in today's US Navy wear flaps of cloth that hang over their shoulders. Once, this protected the sailor's clothing from the tar carried by many in hair queues to work the ropes. The practice died out 150 years ago but the distinct clothing remains. During the selection of a new Pope, the College of Cardinals is sealed in the Sistine Chapel by a specially constructed brick wall. Once, this wall may have actually isolated the decision makers from distraction during their sacred deliberations. Today, cardinals can contact the outside world (and presumably receive its input) via cellular telephone.

Like societies themselves, organizations are shot through with vestigial practices that were once practical but are now obsolete. The wearing of wigs by English lawyers and judges, a practice dating from the 17th century, is widely ridiculed but has proven impossible to abandon. Cultural items have a way of perpetuating themselves.

The preferences and practices of founding figures and prominent leaders affect culture. Admiral Rickover, the "father of the atomic submarine," ordered that all personnel train on live reactors rather than simulators. This practice long survived the Admiral's command. The influence of high-achievement-oriented founders on a firm's structure has already been noted.[10] These individuals doubtlessly influence the organization's culture as well.

Culture is often shaped by accident. In the 1990s, Allstate Insurance Company hired a training consultant with ties to the Church of Scientology. Within a few years, Scientologist management techniques and terminology had become noticeable among Allstate personnel. Scientology practice dictated "managing by statistics." It preached that managers should reward employees with "up statistics" and hold them immune from criticism for any reason (including ethical issues). The rulebook demanded applying ruthless pressure to those with "down statistics." Allstate executives ceased to use the consultant and banned Scientology-inspired training literature when employees complained. But the practices had taken secure root in some sections of the company.[11]

Finally, aspects of an organization's culture may result from human responses to organizational structure. People need to make sense of the structures in which they find themselves. To do so, they develop beliefs and values regarding the structure. Cultural responses to structure help people live with the constraints structure necessarily imposes. Employees of agencies that exercise high levels of control over individual actions, for example, may develop cultures extolling the virtues of tight discipline. Alternatively (or in parallel), such structural surroundings may spawn cultural ideas that ridicule the authority figures, and thus enable individuals to feel that they are still free. The "Lower Your Trousers!" anecdote earlier in this chapter illustrates such a cultural reaction.

The Complexities of Organizational Culture

Organizational culture is more complicated than it appears at first. This should not be surprising. Culture in society as a whole is complex. What, for example, is

American culture? Is it the "high" culture encountered in libraries and concert halls? Is it the "pop" culture that flows out of radios and television sets? Does it include the "subcultures" of street gangs or the "countercultures" of yesterday's beatniks, hippies, and punks? All these cultural segments are part of American life and all must be included to achieve a comprehensive understanding of American culture. The same is true of organizational cultures.

Excepting organizations with unusually "thick" cultures, observers should assume that organizations may contain multiple cultures encompassing divergent sets of ideas, rituals, and myths. Cultures vary in content across levels and among subunits of the organization. Achieving a comprehensive understanding of an organizational culture can require significant time and attention, particularly when the organization is large.

An organization with a complex structure may be expected to have a complex culture. As stated above, organizational structure helps determine culture. An individual's place in the structure determines whom he talks to and works with on a day-to-day basis. Communication about problems and issues (both technical and social) gives rise to common conceptions of how the organization works and where individuals should concentrate their efforts. Development of full-blown cultures, complete with artifacts and rituals, may follow close behind.

Managerial Versus Rank-and-File Cultures

Managers and workers often develop distinctly different cultures.[12] These two classes of employees clearly occupy different positions in the structure, or, stated simply, different rungs on the ladder. They communicate with different people, face different challenges in performing their tasks, and develop different beliefs, values, rituals, and myths.

Beliefs regarding customer service provide an example. Modern managerial thinking places the customer first. Management personnel spend significant time in seminars designed to teach sensitivity to customer needs. Like ritual procedures in aboriginal tribes, these "trainings" reinforce beliefs regarding dependence of the company's success on customer service.

Customers, though, are actually served by workers. Service frequently takes place in stressful and fatiguing settings, such as retail store counters, airport luggage carousels, and hospital emergency rooms. Customers are on edge and readily blame the worker for malfunctions and delays. Normally, workers formulate explanations of and remedies to these challenges not with managers in seminars but with peers in employee lunchrooms.

Resulting worker cultures often involve an "us versus them" system of beliefs regarding managers, customers, and work itself. Workers often suspect managers' motives and look for negative implications in new management projects. Workers may develop hostility toward consumers, particularly demanding and impatient ones. Work itself poses challenges, especially if it is dirty, physically demanding, or stressful.

Workers' cultures often emphasize the following: (a) skepticism toward managers; (b) emotional distance from customers; and (c) alleviation of physical demands and boredom. Workers invent ritualistic games to pass the time on boring jobs. Anecdotes from the 1950s tell of workers welding Coke bottles into the mufflers of expensive cars, hoping that the noise would prove vexing to their upscale purchasers. In a story of his days as an ill-paid waiter, George Orwell recounts a ritual among his colleagues of spitting on the dishes before bringing them to the tables.[13]

The attempt to divine an organization's culture from the testimony of its managers, particularly those at the very top, is likely to result in oversimplification. To interview only the boss makes no more sense than for an anthropologist to interview a tribe's chief and none of his followers. Similarly, focusing only on a single department or profession within an organization may be misleading, as such units and individuals may develop their own cultures.[14]

Subculture, Counterculture, and Microculture

Subcultures

The term *subcultures* is widely used today in a variety of contexts. Teenagers, sports enthusiasts, jazz fanciers, and drug addicts are all said to belong to subcultures. *Subculture* may be defined as a set of beliefs and values that share some but not all features with the dominant culture. Members of subcultures hold beliefs and values that are distinct from the dominant culture. But subculture members accept the dominant culture's basic elements and presuppositions.[15]

Divisions across function and level of seniority in an organization foster development of subcultures. Examples are found among graduate students, medical interns and residents, junior military officers, and technical professionals (scientists, engineers, software specialists, etc.) at all career stages. The differences in bankers' attire described above reflect the subcultures of various banking departments.

Organizational subcultures are of particular interest when they occur among technical professionals, an increasingly important classification of workers in modern economies. Values of technical professionals are likely to emphasize technical achievements—inventing things, solving mathematical puzzles—more than serving clients. Technical professionals often believe that their own contributions are more important than those of management. They hold their own gatherings and exchange their own in-jokes. They seek ways to distinguish themselves from others in the organization. "This is a jeans and T-shirt operation," a programmer might assert, distinguishing members of his or her subculture from the "suits" elsewhere in the organization.

Subcultures diverge from the organization's principal culture. But they share the principal culture's basic elements. As much as members of the subculture distinguish their own thinking, they still believe in the company, school, or service branch. Ultimately, many subcultures affirm the basic beliefs of the principal culture.

Countercultures

Countercultures differ from subcultures in their antagonism to mainstream beliefs and values. The Bohemians of Greenwich Village and the hippies of Haight-Ashbury are among history's most famous counterculturists. Groups such as these explicitly rejected beliefs of mainstream America such as beliefs in the value of hard work, marriage, and organized religion.

In organizations, countercultures develop among people who are alienated from the mainstream. *Alienation* refers to an emotional separation from other people and their values. A person may become alienated because he or she feels that the organization's objectives are meaningless or antagonistic to his or her personal values or beliefs. Members may experience alienation due to feelings of powerlessness regarding the organization's methods and objectives or regarding their personal prospects. Alienation may result simply from social isolation from other organization members. Alienated people find each other, identify with each other as underdogs, and reinforce each other's deviant beliefs and values.

One of the most striking examples of organizational counterculture emerged in the United States Army in Vietnam. Many soldiers, themselves conscripted for service, realized they were fighting a war unpopular at home. A counterculture developed that was at the same time pacifist and self-protective. Soldiers in this counterculture adhered neither to the service's dominant beliefs, that the war was just and winnable, nor to its values, that soldiers should fight with bravery and conviction.

Organizational countercultures are typically more benign, often recognizable as cabals of disgruntled employees habitually complaining to each other.

Microcultures

Finally, multiple systems of beliefs and values known as *microcultures* may occasionally be found in organizations. Microcultures resemble countercultures in that the principal elements of both oppose those of the organization's main culture. But adherents to countercultures distance themselves from and avoid the organization's mainstream culture when possible. Adherents to a microculture confront the mainstream, claiming that their beliefs and values have greater validity. Participants in microcultures believe their values and objectives should replace those of the mainstream.

Microcultures can exist only in organizations that lack a strong mainstream culture backed up by a well-functioning authority system and well-integrated structure. Organizations of this kind tend to harbor multiple microcultures. They have no clear, single, principal culture. Each microculture competes with the others for domination of the organization's thinking. Competition among microcultures may require considerable resource expenditure on the part of the organization's participants.

The numerous hierarchical levels and technical specialties of modern formal organizations predispose them to developing multiple cultures. Differences in personal values and influences of outside institutions also play a role. The length of an individual's career ladder and the speed with which he or she ascends may make him or her more strongly attracted to subcultures and countercultures than to the principal organizational culture. Corporate mergers result in organizations with multiple cultures, as personnel from the merged parts cling to the values and beliefs nurtured in their original settings.

Culture Wars: Microcultures in a Community Action Project

A community action project conducted in Seattle during the 1990s illustrates the phenomenon of microculture. The project aimed at finding ways to reduce isolation among community members and decrease their dependence on social welfare agencies.

Disputes arose over approach, objectives, and methods.

Two distinct cultures emerged. The first was developed and maintained by a group of "project professionals," employees of a large formal organization that had obtained foundation funding for the work. Adherents to this culture believed in centralized decision making, accountability to the funding agency, and systematic, outside evaluation.

The second culture, evolving among personnel with a "community activist" background, held that the community should control the project. Adherents believed that ground level, operational personnel should have the liberty to set their own direction and that only self-evaluation by project personnel should take place.

Members of each group fell into patterns of thought and communication recognizable as culture. Within each group, concepts and language evolved to express shared convictions; favorite stories were told and retold to endorse the group's perspective; heroes and villains were identified and praised or criticized.

Neither the "project professional" nor the "community activist" culture achieved dominance during the project's years of operation. Relationships between adherents to each culture were tense and occasionally rancorous. Practical decisions of even limited scope acceptable to both sides required extended negotiation, drawing resources away from actual project tasks.

How Functional Is Organizational Culture?

Organizational culture, particularly in private-sector corporations, has received major attention from both observers and managers of organizations. Articles on corporate culture grace the pages of the *Wall Street Journal* and the bookshelves of executives. Culture has been identified as the key to efficiency and profitability.

It is tempting to attribute cultural survivals and even some bizarre items as functional for organizational needs. This is undoubtedly true some of the time. The bricking-in of Catholic cardinals serves a symbolic function in modern times, demonstrating the importance and solemnity of papal selection. Admiral Rickover's training dictum made sense in indoctrinating young sailors to the need for extreme caution at all times in the use of nuclear technology. Scientology's aggressive techniques made sense in an industry newly exposed to competitive market forces.

Organizational culture, though, does not always yield benefits to corporate stability, worker satisfaction, or the bottom line. Various characteristics of organizational or society-wide culture may create dysfunction in the form of various costs to the collectivity or its individual members. Cultures are not strictly determined by structure, and they do not always serve an identifiable organizational need.

Tail End of the Human Race:
Dysfunctional Elements of Culture

Anthropologist Allen A. Holmberg[15] lived with the Siriono, a Bolivian jungle tribe, during the early 1940s. Members of the tribe suffered from constant hunger and fatigue. Life expectancy hovered between 35 and 40 years.

Holmberg attributed the tribe's fortunes—considerably poorer than those of neighboring aboriginal peoples—in part to their culture.

Nine-foot bows were the tribe's principal hunting weapon. The size of these artifacts made them manifestly impractical for use in dense jungle, particularly as tribesmen were required to climb trees to shoot small game. Yet, the tribesmen rejected smaller bows, claiming that they were "no good."

A Siriono taboo prohibited eating snakes, although these abounded in the environment. The meat of all such creatures was believed to be poisonous. Hungry Siriono gathered around Holmberg as he roasted and devoured a thick bushmaster steak but refused his invitation to share his meal. Instead, they killed and ate the vultures that scavenged the leftover snake meat.

Beliefs in modern organizations have been characterized as similarly dysfunctional. Railroad companies in the mid-20th century conceived of themselves as simply involved in rail travel. Had these companies conceived of themselves as freight transportation concerns, they might have diversified into trucking, preventing the bankruptcies that ensued. Like the Siriono, the railroad executives ignored rich resources due to entrenched beliefs.

Limiting an organization's perspective and options is a potential drawback of any organizational culture. This drawback is particularly serious in view of the fact that cultures, both in organizations and in society at large, are very difficult to change. Massive attempts to change culture by revolutionary regimes have seldom been completely successful, as the resurgence of religion in post-Communist Russia demonstrates. The same is true of corporations.

Culture may be functional for some parts of an organization but not for others. Sociologist Sonia Ospina described a large municipal agency employing three classes of workers: clericals, operators, and analysts.[16] According to her study, the operators received much encouragement from two elements of the organization's culture. The first was a belief in the necessary and commendable nature of the operators' work despite the fact that it was often difficult and dirty. The second was a widespread belief that operators could move up the career ladder if they had the desire and ability. Availability of training resources and opportunities for communication with management reinforced these beliefs. Clerical personnel and analysts received no such encouragement. The agency's culture enriched the working lives of operators but discouraged and alienated occupants of other roles.

Finally, conflicts related to culture may drain an organization's resources. The fact that organizations tend to form multiple rather than single cultures creates this potential. Associated conflict may outweigh the benefits created by culture.

Organizational Culture: A Solution and a Challenge

Organizational culture constitutes a major force linking the individual with his or her role in a formal organization. Culture joins rewards and imperative force in accomplishing this bonding function. Culture provides individuals with a rationale for the organization's system of reward and imperative force. Organizational structure helps mold culture, as individuals receive and develop beliefs and values in the process of interacting with colleagues. Culture helps maintain structure, the organization's central beliefs and values reinforcing required patterns of social relations within the organization's boundaries. Culture both influences and reflects many other facets of the formal organization.

Organizational culture, though, can give rise to serious challenges. Well-functioning organizations have cohesive cultures that promote beliefs and values capable of fostering positive identification by most, if not all, participants. Some organizations, though, have cultures that are inappropriate to their structures or tasks. Under these conditions, culture can foster perspectives damaging to the organization's prosperity and cohesion. The presence of multiple cultures may foster creative interchanges among people with different ideas and concerns. But adversarial relationships among subcultures can lead to conflict. Development and maintenance of organizational culture, finally, requires expenditure of scarce resources.

Organizational culture, along with its benefits and costs, is often beyond the control of management. Corporate leaders, particularly when new, have blitzed their organizations with manifestos, speeches, posters, lapel pins, and other paraphernalia. These campaigns, however, typically change vocabulary rather than basic beliefs and values—organizational "climate"[17] rather than culture. Organizational culture has a life of its own.

Issues and Applications

Organizational culture often represents a powerful force favoring coordination and cohesion. But organizational culture is not always matched well with the purposes of the organization. Culture is difficult to create deliberately. More often, it develops slowly and spontaneously. Members of organizations with strong cultures must find means of personal accommodation to feel comfortable within them.

- A state agency analyzes proposed laws for their fiscal impact. The agency's culture emphasizes extremely high professional standards. Graduates of top policy schools are recruited. Highly detailed and lengthy reports are produced. Supervisors carefully review details. Outside observers have questioned the minuteness of the unit's work. Lawmakers and their staff, they say, would find short write-ups of fiscal impact more useful. An "academic" culture may be responsible for the unit's overly rigorous practices, appropriate for advanced economics or political science classes but not for practical decision makers. A change in task emphasis would require a change in culture.

- The executives of a small manufacturing firm decide to develop a corporate culture as a means of improving productivity. An outside agency is retained to create a corporate identity, complete with a new logo and mission statement. A special assembly is called to announce the new culture. Posters are put up with appropriate symbols and messages. After a time, the posters are gone and no one seems to remember the mission statement. Better results are likely to have been achieved by identifying traditional values and past successes that are widely shared in the organization and highlighting the relevance of these for the organization's objectives and goals.

- As the monthly meeting of a sport fishing club in Oregon begins, a latecomer tries to sneak in unnoticed. Having rushed from work, he's still in suit and tie. Someone notices and soon everyone is laughing. The others are dressed in slacks, dungarees, checked flannel shirts, and in the case of many, suspenders. Attire reflects the club's belief in informality and the down-to-earth values of loggers and fishermen in times past. The latecomer removes his jacket, loosens his tie, rolls up his sleeves, and relaxes into the meeting.

Chapter Review and Major Themes

Like society as a whole, in which culture constitutes an important property, organizations develop their own internal cultures. Organizational culture may be understood as a pattern of basic beliefs and values to be celebrated and taught to new members. These beliefs and values help promote shared perceptions, thoughts, and feelings in an organization. Organizational cultures help members interpret their surroundings within the organization. Components of organizational culture are given physical representation: the logos and mascots organizations often adopt, the arrangement of chairs during meetings, the architecture of buildings owned by the organization.

Like imperative force and rewards, organizational culture generally helps advance coordination and cohesion by promoting adherence to roles and structure. Organizational culture explains the acceptance of structure that might otherwise be experienced as oppressive. Organizational culture justifies reward systems that might, according to other perspectives, seem unfair. Organizational culture helps legitimize the application of imperative force by officials who, viewed outside the cultural lens, might be seen as arbitrary or domineering.

An organization's culture can be better discerned through direct observation than from official statements. Observation of members' dress furnishes clues about the feelings of role incumbents about their duties and relationships. Stories told by longtime members illustrate the values and beliefs that are most consistently honored.

Commentators on management have prescribed a strengthening of organizational culture to treat a variety of problems. The dominance of business firms such as IBM has been attributed to their organizational cultures. However, organizational culture can also become divisive and undercut objectives and goals. As does society at large, organizations experience the development of subcultures and countercultures whose values and beliefs may contradict those of the broader collectivity.

As suggested in Figure 8.1, the relationship between organizational culture and the organizational environment is richer than is the case in other mechanisms of cohesion and coordination. An organizational culture can reflect the culture prevailing in the broader society. But it can also oppose elements of the main culture. Some organizations pride themselves on having distinct values. Organizational cultures themselves may influence the main culture.

This chapter has emphasized positive functional consequences of organizational culture. An organization's culture may be a powerful force promoting cohesion and coordination. However, negative effects on function can occur as well. Not all cultures are functional. A culture of conservatism can reduce initiative. A culture of individual achievement and reward can undermine cohesion. Subcultures and microcultures can promote conflict to a highly dysfunctional and disruptive degree.

Like other features of organizations, culture ultimately exists only in the thinking of individuals. Organizations may expend much effort to promote a widely shared culture. Physical representations of culture, such as symbols and architecture, may promote organizational culture. Yet, the individual remains at liberty to accept or reject this culture. Alternatively, individuals may reject the mainstream organizational culture and embrace a subculture or counterculture. It seems likely that many people adopt attitudes of detachment or skepticism to all variants of the organizational culture.

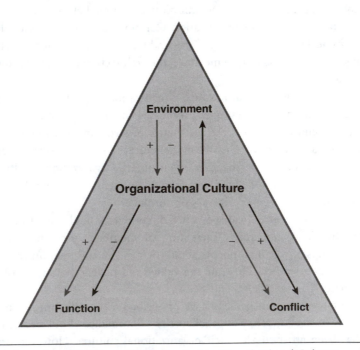

Figure 8.1   Analytical Perspectives Applied to Organizational Culture

Discussion Questions

1. What can modern managers learn from the study of aboriginal cultures?

2. Can the presence of multiple organizational cultures contribute to achievement of an organization's objectives? How might this happen? In what types of organizations would this be most likely?

3. Do any organizations with which you are acquainted have particularly strong cultures? How did you become aware of these cultures? How widely are they shared in the organization?

4. To what degree can an organization's leadership depend on changes in organizational culture to improve achievement of its objectives?

5. How might critical theory interpret organizational culture, and how might this interpretation differ from that of institutional theory?

References

1. Tylor, E. B. (1871). *Primitive culture: Researches into the development of mythology, philosophy, religion, language, art, and custom* (Vol. 1). New York: Henry Holt.

2. Schein, E. H. (1984). Coming to a new awareness of organizational culture. *Sloan Management Review, 25,* 3–16.

3. Bowditch, J. L., & Buono, A. F. (1994). *A primer on organizational behavior.* New York: John Wiley & Sons.

4. Van Maanen, J., & Barley, S. R. (1985). Cultural organization: Fragments of a theory. In P. J. Frost et al. (Eds.), *Organizational culture* (pp. 31–53). Beverly Hills, CA: Sage.

5. Gabriel, Y. (1991). Organizations and their discontents: A psychoanalytic contribution to the study of organizational culture. *Journal of Applied Behavioral Science, 27,* 318–336.

6. Hays, L. (1994, May 13). Gerstner is struggling as he tries to change ingrained IBM culture. *Wall Street Journal,* pp. A1–A4.

7. Durkheim, E. (1965). *Elementary forms of religious life.* New York: Free Press.

8. Molloy, J. T. (1975). *Dress for success.* New York: P. H. Wyden.

9. Tuchman, B. W. (1978). *A distant mirror: The calamitous 14th century.* New York: Knopf.

10. Miller, D., & Droge, C. (1986). Psychological and traditional determinants of structure. *Administrative Science Quarterly, 31,* 539–560.

11. Sharpe, R. (1995, March 22). How Allstate applied Scientology methods to train its managers. *Wall Street Journal.*

12. Davis, T. R. V. (1985). Managing culture at the bottom. In R. H. Kilmann, M. R. Saxton, & R. Serpa (Eds.), *Gaining control of the corporate culture* (pp. 163–183). San Francisco: Jossey-Bass.

13. Orwell, G. (1961). *Down and out in Paris and London.* New York: Harcourt Brace Jovanovich.

14. Schein, E. H. (1996). Culture: The missing concept in organizational studies. *Administrative Science Quarterly, 41,* 229–240.

15. Holmberg, A. A. (1950). *Nomads of the long bow: The Siriono of eastern Bolivia.* Publication No. 10, Smithsonian Institution, Institute of Social Anthropology. Washington, DC: U.S. Government Printing Office.

16. Ospina, S. (1996). *Illusions of opportunity.* Ithaca, NY: Cornell University Press.

17. Denison, D. R. (1996). What is the difference between organizational culture and organizational climate? A native's point of view in a decade of paradigm wars. *Academy of Management Review, 21,* 619–654.

PART III

Organizational Dynamics

Parts I and II of this book have described the basic requirements of organizations. All organizations promote cohesion among individuals and coordinate action in support of organizational objectives. Every organization is a system of roles linked by an invisible yet powerful structure. Reward systems, imperative forces, and organizational culture maintain structure and reinforce role expectations.

Upon becoming familiar with these features of organizations, some may view them as mechanical operations. But moment to moment, the manner in which actual organizations operate depends on the desires and decisions of their members. Every successive generation brings with it new ideas and objectives. Outside conditions change. Even the best-designed organizational machinery is subjected to the actions of many different "drivers" and to alterations in both its external and internal environment.

Organizations do not replace natural patterns of human thinking and interaction. They merely modify and channel them. Within organizations, people retain the capacity for independent judgment even if they cannot always speak their minds. Individuals continuously seek ways to obtain personal advantage in the form of raises, promotions, self-improvement, and freedom from direct supervision. People independently develop ideas about how to improve the organization's performance, and they act to implement their ideas.

The fact that people in organizations occupy relatively standardized roles does not eliminate uncertainty in organizational functioning. Even individuals with identical roles see their responsibilities and opportunities differently. People innovate. They challenge authority. They look for ways to protect themselves and their allies. They carry ideas, values, and conflicts from the broader society with them into the organization. Interrelations among people, and between people and organizational structure, give rise to organizational processes such as politics and conflict. Organizational structures have unanticipated consequences for communication and decision making, as people respond to the patterns of interaction their roles prescribe.

The roles, structure, imperative force, reward systems, and culture discussed in Part II capture organizational "statics." These features establish an organization's basic stability. Part III addresses organizational "dynamics," or processes that reflect and resolve challenges natural to all organizations.

Leadership is often the most visible feature distinguishing one organization from another. This element of organization is the most easily identifiable as human and dynamic. Simply put, people manage organizations. But leadership encompasses much more than the commanding presence of an individual exercising power or authority. Modern observers portray leadership as a process through which leaders and followers continuously engage each other, molding each other's thinking and negotiating over resources.

Communication and decision making constitute interrelated, dynamic features of organizations. An organization's structure strongly affects the patterns of communication within it. But members of organizations seek and utilize opportunities presented by the structure for unanticipated reasons. Decision making draws on the processes of both communication and leadership.

Politics, conflict, and change are essential features of the human community. These processes occur in every organization. Politics, despite the connotations of the word, represents a potentially healthy organizational process. Well-conducted politics reconciles desires with possibilities, leads to constructive exchange of resources, and builds cohesion among diverse units. Understanding and skill in politics are crucial assets in individual success seeking.

Conflict is found in all human relationships and perhaps all organizations. In organizations, a strong dynamic occurs between the basic mechanisms of cohesion and coordination and the level of conflict. These mechanisms can promote as well as reduce conflict. Conflict is included among the analytical perspectives emphasized in this book because of the continuous back-and-forth between basic organizational mechanisms and levels of conflict. Successful management of conflict is essential for achieving objectives.

Change contradicts the formal organization's rationale: stable functioning in pursuit of objectives. But organizations are continually faced with both internal and external change. The most successful organizations are those that acknowledge the need for change and bring it about in an orderly manner.

The dynamics of organizations covered in Part III constitute challenges to members at all levels. Understanding these dynamics and developing solutions to the issues they pose is an important asset in improving the organization's performance and ability to meet the needs of its members. The key tasks facing an organization's management involve understanding and working with these dynamics.

CHAPTER 9

Leadership and Followership

Learning Objective

To recognize the importance of leadership, its basic functions, qualifications for leadership, the forms that leadership takes, and relationships between leaders and followers.

Principles

Leaders are people who make decisions within organizations and cause others to support and implement these decisions. Leaders utilize rewards, imperative force, and interpretations of culture to obtain the collaboration of others. Leadership in its highest form develops a common understanding with followers and changes their basic ways of thinking. Leaders engage in distinct forms of behavior, such as

- ◯ Taking initiative
- ◯ Evaluating followers' needs, aspirations, and capabilities
- ◯ Maintaining relationships within the organization
- ◯ Founding relationships with other organizations
- ◯ Collecting and disseminating information
- ◯ Providing the resources needed to achieve success
- ◯ Representing members' aspirations and values

P eople recognized as leaders often have traits suggesting ability to command. These traits include drive, desire to lead, self-confidence, intelligence, and outstanding capabilities in technical areas valued by the organization. But leadership also requires being a good team member and maintaining the trust of others.

An individual's natural gifts do not alone enable him or her to become a leader. Individual capabilities must match the organization's specific needs and mesh well with its history and culture. There are many different kinds of leaders, some performing routine organizational functions, others guiding organizations through great transformations.

The outlook and behavior of followers help determine whether a leader can function effectively. Subordinates make their best contributions by being neither habitually critical nor always supportive of the leader's outlook, methods, and objectives.

The Importance of Leadership

Modern observers of organizations are often dismissive of leadership. They argue, for example, that factors such as structure and culture determine much, if not most, individual action. Structure, rules, and regulations, it is contended, tie the hands of people in leadership positions as securely as they govern the lowest operative. Chapter 1 of this book characterized leaders in formal organizations as "impersonal," promoted to their positions due to standard qualifications and closely constrained by structure. Many investigations have highlighted the limits of leadership. In a classic case study, for example, Guest attributes the success of a plant manager not to his leadership capabilities but to favorable treatment by the parent company.[1]

This belittling of leadership represents, in part, a reaction to overemphasis on leadership in the past. Historians and the public have often attributed humankind's great achievements to great individuals. Emperor Napoleon Bonaparte of France (1769–1821), vividly depicted astride a rearing horse, personifies the "great man" of history. His genius alone, some have maintained, enabled Europe to throw off the last vestiges of the Middle Ages and enter the modern era. Every schoolchild has learned that George Washington is the "father of his country." Names like Albert Einstein, Martin Luther King, and Bill Gates are household words. In the opinion of many, these and similar giants have magically transformed the world by virtue of personal gifts.

Several factors have led to downgrading leadership as a force in organizations as well as in society as a whole. Some of the most visible leaders of the 20th century were dictatorial rulers. Men like Hitler and Stalin wreaked death and terror throughout the world. Lesser tyrants such as Fidel Castro and Saddam Hussein terrorized only their own countrymen and -women. The excesses of these individuals have bred mistrust of leaders. Americans, due to their egalitarian political culture, tend to be suspicious even of leaders who have won election by legitimate means.

As if in response to the hero worship of yesteryear, writers today often "deconstruct" the famous of past generations. *Deconstruction* in this context means critically reanalyzing the lives and achievements of history's leaders and other important figures. Famous writers and scientists are known to have stolen the ideas, creations, and inventions of subordinates, friends, colleagues, and lovers. Political leaders have fared especially poorly in the light of such reanalysis. President Lyndon Johnson (1908–1973), for example, is alleged to have shirked military service in World War II, wronged his wife, and won a key election by smearing his opponent and stealing votes.[2]

Despite the distaste of some, leadership remains one of the most important subjects in the study of organizations. Books about leadership jam the management sections of bookstores and line the shelves of executive offices. The word itself creates a sense of excitement. An understanding of leadership and the criteria by which leaders should be judged is important for everyone involved in an organization: the leaders themselves, members of the organization who are not leaders, and outsiders who depend on the organization's performance, such as government agency clients and corporate stockholders.

Leadership is clearly important to organizations. People in leadership roles carry out functions that are indispensable. Organizations may deal with routine matters most of the time, but unexpected events demand leadership. Organizations comprise integrated systems of roles, backed up by rewards, imperative force, and culture—but actual human beings determine when and how to utilize the specific resources available under these systems. Leaders evaluate how well the organization and its components are working. They take initiative in exercising oversight and developing remedies. Leaders express the organization's purpose and often the values and aspirations of its members. Leadership gives a human voice to abstract statements of mandate, mission, and vision. The memos that issue from the leader's office, the thoughts he or she exchanges with members of every rank, and the speeches he or she makes on important occasions enliven the organization, promoting achievement of its objectives.

Leadership is and will always remain a topic of importance for a separate reason. Many people want to become leaders. Something fundamental in human nature makes people desire to be the boss. Often, extrinsic factors impel people to seek leadership positions. In modern formal organizations, leaders typically earn more money and enjoy better surroundings at work. They receive more social contacts than followers and are more likely to have their telephone calls and e-mails returned. Leadership brings with it visibility, which increases the likelihood of promotions and competing offers from other organizations. Leaders receive the respect of others. Finally, people in leadership positions have better opportunities and more resources to carry out personal projects and move the organization in the directions they desire.

People also desire to become leaders for purely intrinsic reasons. Becoming a leader and functioning effectively in this role raises the individual's self-esteem. Many people simply desire to be "out front." Others feel frustrated working under the plans and agendas of others.

Leadership is important for organizations, finally, because of the conflicts and issues it may raise. Leadership struggles take place in every type of organization. Losers in corporate conflicts over leadership often lose their jobs; losers in struggles over leadership in some governments, political parties, and organized crime entities may forfeit their lives. Palace revolutions, coups, corporate takeovers, and street shoot-outs often are really contests over leadership. In more restrained settings, the succession of new leaders after a key executive's death or retirement can constitute a major challenge. The process of allocating leadership slots can be quite costly to an organization if mishandled.

An understanding of the functions and characteristics of leaders can be valuable to people who aspire to leadership positions. Perhaps more important, such an understanding allows people to recognize good leadership. Those promoted into leadership positions do not always have accurate ideas about what such roles involve. Heroes created by mass media, whether fictional or real, provide a very limited view of leadership. People in leadership positions require a more balanced picture.

People in the position of follower can also benefit from a comprehensive understanding of leadership. Those responsible for carrying out the directives of others deserve good leadership. Consistently effective leadership requires partnership between leaders and followers in a fashion that meets the needs and advances the objectives of both.

An understanding of leadership has practical importance for subordinates. In modern organizations, subordinates constantly ask questions about the competence and style of their superiors. An understanding of leadership enables followers to ask the appropriate questions and act accordingly. Pertinent issues may involve how much loyalty a follower owes his or her leaders and what level of performance the leader is entitled to request. Dilemmas of this kind are not new. A New Testament parable states, "Render unto Caesar what is Caesar's; render unto God what is God's." As emperor of Rome, Caesar was all-powerful. But people still questioned what they legitimately owed him and what they were entitled to withhold.

Leadership in a free society presents a paradox. People value liberty, yet realize that collective activity requires leadership. Constraint experienced by people in organizations becomes physically visible in conflicts with superiors. An important feature of modern organizations makes the paradox yet more vexing. Few roles in organizations today involve only leadership. Most leaders have superiors up the line. Large numbers of people today must deal simultaneously with the dilemmas of both leadership and followership.

Who Leaders Are

Most people can recognize leadership without reading a textbook. Every human being has experienced the leadership of others. In any group, however, people's discussion about their leaders would reveal some surprises. Leadership occurs in unexpected places and is exercised by people who do not immediately look like leaders.

People with titles and uniforms suggestive of leadership, moreover, do not always function as leaders.

Observers of leadership often focus on hierarchy and power. A definition consistent with this view casts leadership as "a relationship between people in which influence and power are unevenly distributed on a legitimate basis."[3] Legitimacy refers to the individual consenting to submit by signing a contract, recognizing a relevant tradition, or accepting a principle acknowledging the leader's superiority.

The hierarchical view of leadership is certainly applicable to organizations. Formal organizations designate places in their structures that provide resources and opportunities for leadership. Organization charts indicate roles whose responsibilities, wholly or in part, include leadership functions. People who plan, direct, oversee, evaluate, and reward the activities of others occupy positions in which leadership may be exercised.

Other conceptions of leadership, though, de-emphasize hierarchy and control. James MacGregor Burns sees leadership in terms of awakening convictions within a collectivity and giving common direction to the desires and aspirations of individual members. A political scientist, Burns thinks of the organization as a *polity,* that is, a body whose members share resources, needs, and communal feelings. According to Burns, leadership is exercised when "persons with certain motives and purposes mobilize, in competition or conflict with others, institutional, political, psychological and other resources so as to arouse, engage, and satisfy the motives of followers."[4] This view of leadership downplays command structure. Instead, it emphasizes a sharing of common cause between leaders and followers.

Burns makes a strong distinction between leadership and the exercise of "naked power." Influence, though not a true imperative force, can play an important part in the exercise of leadership. As described in Chapter 7, influence results in voluntary compliance or agreement. People of influence may persuade others but may, alternatively, find themselves looked to as references to validate decisions or endorse strategies. Influential people can change many minds in an organization.

Still, imperative force is a major asset in the exercise of leadership. So is reward. Many leaders depend on their control over the organization's resources for cohesion and coordination.

Leadership occurs in many forms, but ultimately boils down to two capabilities: (1) selecting among alternative courses of action and (2) bringing and keeping other people on board.

Leaders accomplish these functions by

- Deciding upon objectives and means for attaining them
- Capturing the attention, energy, and commitment of others
- Expressing and representing the needs, values, and aspirations of others
- Impelling others to think and act in a desired manner through rewards and punishment

Whether conceived as exercise of power or mobilization through persuasion or through exchange of valuable things, leadership involves decision. Alone or in collaboration with others, leaders select among alternative perspectives and directions open to the organization. Then, leaders utilize their personal resources or those of the organization to involve and motivate others to implement their decisions.

This essential function of leadership can be accomplished within a wide variety of roles and through many different forms of action. People in many different positions in organizations function as leaders. Some slots offer their occupants more opportunity for leadership than others. The places where leadership occurs illustrate the multiplicity of forms this function may take. Many forms of leadership may be observed in a single organization. Within most organizations, for example, leadership of both a formal and informal nature may be recognized.

Formal Leadership

People in positions of formal leadership have authority over others. Their leadership status is designated by formal titles such as foreman, lieutenant, director, chief executive officer, and president. In modern organizations, basic duties of people in these positions are specified in articles of incorporation, bylaws, and job descriptions. An earlier chapter distinguished formal from informal structure. Formal authority, which characterizes modern organizations, provides a framework for leadership in its most visible form.

Generally, people in formal leadership positions are referred to as administrators, managers, and executives. These words are often used interchangeably. Actually, they indicate positions in which different kinds and levels of leadership are possible. Administrators, managers, and executives are distinguished from each other by two properties of their positions: *scope* and *discretion*. Scope refers to the range of people and operations over which they exercise potential leadership. Discretion refers to the amount of choice they have in making their decisions and doing their work.

Administrators

Administrators oversee operations whose objectives and methods are determined by others. Their scope of work is restricted to a specific area of organizational functioning, perhaps a single unit or subunit. Typically, administrators have little discretion over the instructions given to workers or the rewards they may distribute.

Administrators may have formal authority over workers, including operatives and professional staff. But they make few, if any, decisions about the operation as a whole. The administrator of a state prison, for example, may review the performance of guards and take action in the event of irregularities. But he or she usually operates "by the book." Civil service laws mandate personnel practices. Separate agencies determine expansion and capital improvement plans. In the event of serious problems (such as a prison riot), higher authorities may give instruction or take over the operation entirely. George Nolan, the assistant principal at Hamilton Middle School described in Chapter 4, communicates policy to teachers and enforces rules regarding pupils but does not establish direction.

Administrators often work under the direct authority of others. Physicians in a professional partnership, for example, may hire an administrator to handle routine business matters. The administrator hires and supervises office staff such as secretaries and bookkeepers. He or she deals with issues that may arise with insurance companies and may be involved in the purchase of equipment and pharmaceuticals. But the administrator merely implements the principles established by the partners.

Administrative positions give their occupants some opportunities for leadership. Speaking for the organization, they transmit policy and express purpose. They do not, however, set direction or determine nonroutine use of resources. Administrators lack sufficient discretion to exercise much leadership.

Managers

Like administrators, managers spend a significant proportion of their time supervising and evaluating the work of others and monitoring income and expenditures. Managers, though, hold responsibility for the achievements, prosperity, and ultimately, the survival of their units.

Unlike the responsibilities of administrators, those of managers include decision making, direction setting, and ensuring acceptable outcomes. Managers have at least partial responsibility for setting the objectives of their units. Managers engage in strategic planning. They negotiate with their superiors regarding criteria for acceptable or outstanding performance.

Managers, moreover, are heavily involved in procuring the wherewithal required to meet their objectives. Unlike administrators, they do not simply receive allocations of money and personnel. Managers negotiate with higher authorities for such resources. In the private sector and in some public agencies, managers have major responsibility for obtaining revenue. Managers meet this requirement through processes such as developing new products, influencing legislators, applying for grants, soliciting gifts, and a thousand other procedures of both ancient and recent vintage.

Executives

The term *executive* connotes membership in upper-level management. Executives are usually thought to include division managers, vice presidents, presidents, and their aides. In day-to-day conversation, the term *executive* is synonymous with prestige and high rank.

As early as the 1930s, Chester Barnard formulated a conception of the executive that is still widely used today. Barnard was himself a high-ranking executive in the telephone industry. He defined the executive as a person whose contribution was

The Manager of a Research and Development Department

The holder of a management position in an organization resembles that of an independent businessperson. As an example, consider the manager of a corporate research and development (R&D) unit. This unit's responsibilities include developing products for the parent company as well as carrying out advanced scientific research. The unit's dual functions are interrelated. Advanced research serves as the basis for development of future products. The parent company may manufacture these products itself or offer the technologies to other companies in exchange for financial compensation.

The R&D manager's primary responsibilities include setting objectives and procuring resources. These processes are carried out through negotiation with parent company officials. Company officials may demand that the laboratory produce a new computer component in no more than a year. Knowing that such a task will take considerably longer, the manager must persuade his superiors to accept this larger limit. Corporate officials may ask the manager to commit to obtaining significant outside funds through contracts to perform basic research for the government or develop products for other companies. The R&D manager needs to negotiate achievable objectives in this area, too.

The R&D manager must negotiate for resources appropriate to the objectives for which he or she accepts responsibility. Upper management may desire to cut personnel while adding to the unit's performance requirements. Here, too, the R&D manager must enter into hard negotiation.

Managers may achieve short-term peace by acquiescing to their superiors' initial requests. But in such acquiescence, the manager incurs substantial risk. Failure may mean loss of face, diminution of promotion chances, or termination.

Apart from negotiation with superiors, the R&D manager must direct, motivate, and inspire staff. This process requires utilization of resources provided by the organization for the achievement of cohesion and coordination in support of specific objectives. The manager allocates rewards, exercises imperative force, and appeals to organizational culture. He or she transmits the directives of the broader organization and interprets policy for local application.

It is obvious that people in management positions have more opportunity for leadership than those in administrative slots. True managers have decision-making power over objectives and exercise discretion over use of organizational resources. Even administrators whose scope of work extends over several organizational units have fewer opportunities to act as leaders.

"maintaining the organization in operation" rather than performing its production-related tasks.[5]

According to Barnard, the executive does not directly manage other individuals. Rather, he or she maintains the cooperative effort required to keep the organization functioning as a unified whole. The executive's key function is formulating the organization's purpose. Such formulation is a continuous process, carried out in communication with colleagues and subordinates. The executive, according to Barnard, promotes constant reevaluation of purpose and its reformulation when necessitated by changing conditions. The executive carries out these functions by hiring appropriate individuals, ensuring the continuous flow of intelligence, and making sure that managers and other executives maintain required contact with each other.

More recently developed conceptions of the executive are consistent with Barnard's. According to James MacGregor Burns, the job of the executive is to promote the unity, cohesion, order, and performance of the collectivity as a whole. In a formal organization, this includes establishing required processes, seeing that key functions are carried out, and understanding the perspectives and needs of subordinates and other executives.

To summarize, executive functions emphasize identification of purpose and maintenance of cohesion. These functions lend themselves to exercise of leadership. Identification of direction, particularly when several alternatives are available, is a key outcome of leadership. Building teamwork among management personnel and other executives is itself an important form of leadership. The executive's hierarchical position contributes to his or her leadership potential. Executives stand above the heads of multiple operating units and can command significant organizational resources.

It is important to note that people who occupy upper-level slots in an organization's hierarchy do not always exercise leadership. Administrative positions typically have little discretion over decision making and thus offer little opportunity for leadership. People in management and executive slots generally have more discretion and often greater scope. These factors present opportunities for leadership. But not everyone takes advantage of these opportunities. Not every executive and manager decides upon a specific direction in which he or she prefers to see the organization progress. Not every executive or manager captures the energies of others or uses them to advance objectives he or she supports.

Constraints in the form of organizational structure, politics, and culture inhibit managers and executives from taking leadership. Structure in some organizations leaves even top officers little discretion. Politics and culture create risks of punishment for failure, discouraging executives and managers from taking initiative. Finally, not every manager or executive desires to assume a leadership role.

Informal Leadership

Just as leadership may be absent where it is expected, leadership often appears in unexpected places. Occupying a high-level position does not make an individual a leader. In fact, people who do not occupy high-level positions in the formal hierarchy sometime emerge as leaders.

Organizations, it should be remembered, encompass more than formal structure. Over and above the mandates of formal relationships, organizations host networks of informal ties. These networks add richness and complexity to organizational functioning. Informal ties give rise to primary groups, whose members share information, encouragement, and support.

As detailed earlier, primary groups develop their own leadership structure. According to ethnographies, heads of families function as leaders among the Nuer. Classical sociology records how young men willing to make sacrifices for their buddies became leaders of Boston gangs. Spontaneous social process and formation of groups among people in direct communication with each other occur within formal organizations. Primary social ties exist alongside formal ones.

It is natural for people linked by informal ties to select their own leaders. Observers of organizations have noted many types of informal leaders. A few examples illustrate the phenomenon of informal leadership within formal organizations.

Task Leaders

Even organizational units that operate under strict rules rely on informal social ties to accomplish tasks. Generally, leaders emerge in primary groups composed of individuals connected by informal social ties. Even though they lack official position, leaders of these groups help assign tasks, set production goals, and determine the pace of work.

Some of the most cohesive informal groups in formal organizations develop among individuals occupying the same workspace and performing a common task. The Hawthorne studies cited earlier illustrate the importance of primary groups in task performance. In the Hawthorne assembly operation, groups influenced productivity within the limits acceptable to most members. Other task groups increased productivity, though, as members divided up elements of the task, faster individuals helped slower ones, and an atmosphere of mutual encouragement developed.

In the informal task group, leadership may be given to the individual with the greatest seniority, best technical skill, or most personal assertiveness. Sometimes, an individual becomes leader of a task group merely because others habitually look to him or her to initiate activity or solve problems.

Socioemotional Leaders

Previous chapters have referred to two basic functions of human collectivities: *instrumental* and *socioemotional*. Instrumental functions refer to accomplishment of concrete tasks, carried out for creation of concrete products and services. Socioemotional functions refer to nonmaterial, though personally gratifying, communications and activities that are part of nearly every human group: personal validation, companionship, recreation, and expressions of esteem.

The task leaders described above may also be characterized as *instrumental* leaders. Similarly, people who take initiative and engage others on a social or emotional level are known as *socioemotional leaders*.

In most primary groups, individuals emerge who are especially skilled and forthcoming in personal and emotional matters. These people are socioemotional leaders—those people approached in a crisis for sympathy. They arrange birthday celebrations and department outings. They raise questions about how members of the group feel regarding speedups, cutbacks, and layoffs. They make people feel at ease about expressing themselves, drawing them out for detail. Socioemotional leaders are the first to praise others in their group in recognition of distinctions and achievements.

Though less material than that of the task or instrumental leader, the socioemotional leader's function is often crucial. Socioemotional rewards such as good feelings and personal affirmation promote adherence to role expectations and stability of structure. Socioemotional leaders help make socioemotional rewards available in an otherwise cold-seeming, formal organization.

Network Leaders

Networks are usually thought of as systems of personal ties maintained along-side formal structure. People use networks principally to obtain information. Networks provide intelligence regarding jobs, business opportunities, and hazards such as management changes, audits, and layoffs.

People who occupy key positions in networks are often regarded as leaders. Located at the intersection points of multiple channels of communication, these individuals are sometimes known as *sociometric stars*. The term *sociometric* refers to the type and frequency of communications in which individuals engage and the partners with whom they communicate. A sociometric star stands at the center of many communication pathways. Lines of communication radiate outward in all directions from a sociometric star, hence the name.

Professional communities both inside and outside organizations furnish good examples of network leaders. A famous study of introducing a new technology illustrates the principle of network leadership.[6] In this study, the researchers sought to determine which doctors first prescribed a new drug that was clearly superior to formerly used medications. The earliest utilizers tended to be those who attended national conferences and maintained contact with national leaders. These physicians were sociometric stars in their local communities. A second tier of early utilizers included physicians who maintained frequent contact with the sociometric stars. These stars exercised professional leadership by serving as conduits for disseminating technical advances. Within organizations employing physicians and other professionals, similar networks operate alongside official structure.

Network leadership operates outside professional and other high-status circles, too. An executive secretary often stands at the center of a communications network. He or she screens calls, takes notes, and regulates access to the boss. Secretaries and assistants to executives are important sources of information for people outside the executive suite. They influence their superiors either by providing direct input or by helping determine which people the boss sees, the information he or she receives, and the matters to which he or she pays attention.

Gurus and Rabbis

Technical specialists outside formal leadership positions often exercise informal leadership. Most organizations reward their successful participants by promoting them into management. Many organizations discourage people who are not promoted from remaining in the organization. An "up-or-out" policy mandates termination of those who are not promoted. Even in the absence of up-or-out policies, those not promoted often leave, realizing that they are unlikely to receive significant increases in pay or prestige. They also know that they will soon be surrounded by younger, more recently educated personnel, some of whom will become their new bosses. Law, accounting, and engineering firms typically function in this manner.

A few people who are not promoted, however, find viable niches in the organization. They may achieve recognition as experts in a technical area of law or a highly specialized field of engineering. These individuals do not rise in the hierarchy but retain long-term employment. Due to the advanced learning and gray hair of these survivors, colleagues often refer to them via religious titles such as "gurus" and "rabbis."

Gurus and rabbis occupy positions ideally suited to informal leadership. Their specialized knowledge guarantees them regular contact with at least a few others. They have opportunities to influence decisions of those in formal leadership positions. They may even gather around them a "flock" of people who look to them for perspective, history, and advice.

How Formal Organizations Capture Informal Leaders: The Phenomenon of Co-optation

The formal leaders of an organization often realize that their informal counterparts exercise significant influence. Rather than ignore or oppose this informal leadership structure, formal leaders often attempt to make use of it. Formal leaders do this by working out cooperative relationships with those who have attained leadership outside the formal hierarchy. This process is known as co-optation.

In co-optation, members of the formal leadership structure invite the informal leader to collaborate with them. The formal leader may offer resources or threaten punishment to establish collaboration. Co-optation may take the form of merely convincing the informal leader of management's perspective.

Prisons in the mid-20th century American South furnish an often-cited example of co-optation. Guards and wardens identified inmates whose strength, aggressiveness, or other capabilities enabled them to exercise influence or power over other inmates. These inmates were invited to become prison "trustees." As trustees, they received extra privileges and resources from the administration, not the least of which included official approval of their rule. In exchange, trustees helped enforce prison regulations and helped maintain order.

Co-optation occurs in many other settings. Unions co-opt task group leaders in industry. City governments co-opt neighborhood leaders. Some organizations co-opt the leadership of others in order to achieve influence over these organizations.[7]

For a time, the term *co-optation* acquired a negative connotation. Informal and community-based leaders co-opted into larger, more powerful structures were said to have "sold out." But co-optation often requires the formal leadership to make concessions to the informal leader who has been co-opted. In this light, co-optation appears as a method by which informal leaders make the needs and aspirations of their followers known to the formal leadership structure.

It is noteworthy that the capabilities that allow people to become leaders in informal settings also serve as leadership resources within the formal structure of an organization. An individual in a management position, for example, uses his or her networking skill to exchange resources and garner support for his or her projects. This informal capacity enables the manager to act as a true leader. Executives utilize socioemotional talents to determine the needs and aspirations of management personnel, thus promoting collaboration. As in many aspects of organizational functioning, formal and informal processes are not entirely segregated. They are often intermingled, mutually supporting each other.

The "Work" of Leadership

Leaders perform two closely tied functions: (1) they decide among alternative courses of action open to the organization or one of its subunits; and (2) they obtain support from other people and organizations for implementing the decision. Leaders in actual organizations contribute to these functions through many concrete actions. Some leadership actions, such as firefighting and maintaining lines of communication, are routine. Others, such as meeting major crises and redirecting the organization's mission, are extraordinary. The actual work of leaders, whether routine or extraordinary, comprises a variety of day-to-day tasks. The following examples illustrate leadership operation "on the ground."

Taking Initiative

Taking initiative constitutes the most fundamental task of leadership. Leaders take action in situations where action is required. They spot opportunities and convince others of their importance. They are the first to detect problems on the horizon and mobilize the organization's resources to remedy them.

Initiative constitutes the clearest indication of leadership in an informal setting or small subunit of a formal organization. "Doc," the street corner gang leader described in Chapter 1, often determined how the boys should spend their time. Most social groups seem to have a member who regularly suggests things to do and activities to initiate. In a more serious context, observers of military operations have commented that battles are won by the initiative of individuals on the ground who perceive opportunities to advance and urge their comrades to follow their leadership.

Initiators of action in organizations have become some of history's most important leaders. Consider the example of Martin Luther, the 16th-century founder of Protestantism. In Luther's time and still today the Catholic Church was an extremely large and powerful formal organization. Luther charged that the Church was malfunctioning in pursuit of its major objective, the salvation of Christian souls. He alerted large segments of the organization's membership to the necessity of reform.

Taking initiative in detecting and remediating problems distinguishes leaders in many modern organizations. Union politics provides an example. Corruption, often in the form of mishandling of funds, has constituted a perennial problem in American unions. Reform has often been initiated by a handful of members especially aggrieved by the corrupt practices. These individuals initiate action by running as reform candidates in union elections or banding together to support a new leadership.

Taking initiative can be much more mundane, however. Leaders detect routine problems and take steps to solve them. Leaders in business organizations detect revenue shortfalls and order economies to ensure that there are sufficient funds to meet payroll. Managers in manufacturing plants are the first to hear when a supplier fails to deliver key materials; they take action to find alternative sources. Factory floor leaders, whether formal or informal, note hazards and order their removal or cleanup.

Evaluating Followers' Needs, Aspirations, and Capabilities

Leaders also achieve their objectives by assessing followers' needs and aspirations. Such action lays the groundwork for motivating members to contribute to the leader's objectives. People like to be listened to. Knowing their needs and aspirations enables the leader to develop appropriate rewards and to present his or her agenda in language reflecting the members' needs and aspirations.

Joseph Stalin, dictator of the Soviet Union for several decades during the mid-20th century, is known to history as a ruthless tyrant. But he was in fact a very good "listener." Observers of the early years of his reign tell of Stalin patiently lingering in the company of rank-and-file Communist Party members, smoking his pipe and listening patiently to their concerns and complaints. It is doubtless that in-depth understanding of his people helped Stalin maintain and exercise power as long as he did.

Understanding needs and aspirations is even more characteristic of leaders in democracies. Franklin D. Roosevelt, president of the United States during the Depression and most of World War II, was famed for broadcasting "fireside chats," which acknowledged the public's concerns and provided reassurance. Today, candidates for office spend huge sums conducting opinion polls, assessing the public mood as a tool for attaining and exercising leadership.

Understanding an organization's members also involves knowledge of their capabilities, including energy and commitment. Leaders continually assess these properties of the membership and adjust their objectives accordingly. A military officer adjusts his objectives based on the readiness of his troops. A research manager formulates objectives based on the staff's mix of technical background. While assessment of membership capacities in some instances leads to adjustment of objectives, in other instances it leads to adjustments of the membership's capabilities, by means such as targeted hiring and dismissal.

Fostering and Maintaining Relationships

Promoting stable and productive relationships within the organization constitutes one of the most important leadership activities today. This is especially true in large organizations pursuing multiple objectives. Large size, complexity of structure, and diversity of task counteract the factors leading to cohesiveness. Divergent responsibilities and objectives lower members' visibility and importance to each other. Physical distance makes face-to-face relationships almost impossible to maintain. These conditions hamper coordination between individual and subunits. The sense of common purpose upon which formal organization depends is undermined. In extreme cases, the organization may disintegrate into subunits and primary groups working at cross-purposes and characterized by mutual antagonism.

Experienced executives have said that the hardest part of their work is "getting the management team together." Modern, global business makes it especially difficult to assemble team members in a single physical place. Personnel reside in different cities and carry on operations across the world. Even when team members work in the same city or building, though, the press of meeting individual deadlines and "fighting fires" keeps people out of touch. The tendency of organizational units to maximize their own resources—referenced earlier as *suboptimization*—reduces the willingness of managers to exchange ideas.

The day-to-day actions of effective leaders include efforts to prevent such fragmentation. Some of the more visible techniques involve getting people together at social events, such as luncheons, retreats, and afternoons at the country club. Though many poke fun at "businessmen's lunches" and rounds of golf, such activities foster informal ties among managers. Many observers, among them the famous Chester Barnard, have identified establishment and nurturing of informal relationships among executives as a key leadership concern.

Less visible relationship-building activities include introducing new employees of work organizations or new members of a club. Introductions to people the new member may never directly work with are of particular importance, because they give the new member a sense of the organization's range of activities and broader mission. Simple introductions lay the groundwork for good interpersonal relationships.

Fostering and maintaining relationships constitute key leadership activities in most formal and informal settings. Leaders initiate instrumental relationships when they assign people to work in teams and task forces. They foster informal ties when they host parties at their homes.

Some of the most important actions that leaders take are intended to promote relationships across organizational boundaries. The leader's role as representative of his or her organization in many settings provides opportunities for collaboration. Conversations between leaders may have special value for thawing relationships between traditionally competing and hostile organizations. Highly visible and publicized handshakes between top executives help initiate working relationships. Joint press conferences in the White House Rose Garden between formerly warring heads of state, for example, help inform their followers that normalization is at hand. Career diplomats are then assigned the technical work of negotiating agreements. Closer to home, high profile meetings between cinema executives conclude with the request, "have your people talk with my people."

Organizational Entropy

The term *entropy* refers to a tendency in nature for things to move from a state of organization to one of chaos. A similar process can happen in organizations.[8] Unless countervailing forces of sufficient power prevail, individual inclinations and needs will impel members to act in their personal interest rather than in the interests of the collectivity. Similarly, subunits of the organization will seek ways to maximize their own security and resource levels, unless centralizing forces prevail.

Rewards, imperative force, and organizational culture counteract organizational entropy. But leadership is often the most immediate force that keeps the organization's members and subunits together and concentrates their resources on achievement of the organization's objectives.

Providing Resources

Command of resources, both material and nonmaterial, promotes the exercise of leadership. The entrepreneur who provides capital to a start-up company attains influence over its operations. The scientist achieves leadership by obtaining research funds, enabling him or her to assemble teams of colleagues and assistants and exercise leadership over them. Material resources allow people who already occupy leadership roles to function more effectively. President Thomas Jefferson, as well as "Doc," the gang leader in William F. Whyte's *Street Corner Society*, both impoverished themselves (at least temporarily) making loans and paying for good times with their friends and associates. Followers come to depend on such resources, reinforcing their loyalty.

That those who control resources also exercise power is a basic principle in organizational life. Chapter 7 demonstrated this connection by reviewing the history of hospitals in the United States. In an era when hospitals looked to private donors for key support, private donors made the most important decisions. Later, when hospital revenue came mostly from paying patients, the doctors who admitted these patients moved into the lead. Still later, solvency depended on skillful handling of government regulations and negotiation with health plans. In this era, professional managers moved into leadership positions.

It is not surprising, then, that leaders devote much effort to obtaining resources. Leading partners in law firms, for example, spend much of their time procuring business for the organization. These "rainmakers" may do no actual legal work, distributing technical responsibilities to other attorneys in exchange for a percentage of their billing. Business executives meet often with bankers to ensure the availability of capital through loans and stock offerings. The presidents of charitable organizations, universities, and other nonprofits seek out and cultivate potential donors.

Members look to leaders for resources other than material ones. Strategic plans formulated by executives also constitute resources, providing direction to the management teams that work under them. In war, strategy itself becomes a crucial resource. Napoleon commanded leadership not only because he cut a striking figure.

He also developed strategies that won battles. More routine human endeavors also illustrate the importance of nonmaterial resources. W. Edwards Deming, inventor of Total Quality Management (TQM), emphasized managers' responsibility for developing systems of technology and work organization that ensure productivity.[9] As directly as military strategies, such systems ensure the success of industrial enterprises and work organizations of all kinds. Leaders may procure resources of this kind by developing their own strategies and plans or hiring consultants or staff to do so.

Collecting and Disseminating Information

The need for leaders to collect and disseminate information is similar in importance to their resource-related tasks. Information is itself a resource. Leaders often see themselves as repositories of information regarding the organization and its environment. A top executive stands out from others in his or her grasp of the total picture. People known as reliable sources of information often become leaders, as people turn to them for direction. Information about the organizational environment helps people develop other resources. Knowledge of the environment forms the basis for successful strategic plans, product development, marketing, and sales. Knowledge of the capabilities and needs of other organizations helps determine the desirability of these organizations as partners.

Leaders spend significant time reading and hearing reports from others. They meet with consultants and study marketing survey results. They attend management seminars and peruse *Fortune* and the *Wall Street Journal*.

But most also collect their own information. Executives have breakfast and lunch with managers who share information about the operation of their units. Sales managers shop at the stores of their competitors. People whose success depends on reliable delivery of materials from outside their own organizations tour the facilities of their suppliers to assess their capabilities and efficiency. Managers of manufacturing operations leave the office now and then to tour the factory floors and loading docks. They chat with foremen and operatives. This activity has been labeled "management by walking around."

Good information promotes good decision making, a core function of leadership in organizations. Historians credit Napoleon Bonaparte with mastery of huge amounts of information regarding geography, economics, and politics throughout the Europe of his time. The French emperor left colossal volumes of letters to and from his appointees and officers in the countries that he ruled and beyond. The range of subject matter and extent of Napoleon's writings are astounding in view of his era's primitive information technology. The capacity to grasp and integrate this volume of intelligence doubtlessly contributed to Napoleon's ability to formulate strategy and maintain the confidence of subordinates.

Representing Members' Aspirations and Values

Among the day-to-day acts of leaders, one of the most consistently noted has been the expression and symbolization of their followers' aspirations and values. Pericles, statesman of ancient Athens, was characterized as the city's "first citizen" because he held no formal power. By expressing widely shared convictions of his peers, though, the statesman guided them through the greatest war of the age. People in informal settings may attain leadership by speaking for the group. It is no accident that candidates for office in modern democracies expend vast sums on public opinion polls. They hope to garner public support by expressing sentiments they know are felt by the public.

Formal organizations of all kinds assign leadership roles to people believed to reflect the values and aspirations of members. Church and evangelical organizations provide the most visible examples. Clergy are expected to be visibly devout, as indeed the title "reverend" suggests. Parishioners look to their spiritual leaders as symbols after whom to model their own thinking and behavior. In day-to-day life, ecclesiastical leaders take pains to look and act upstanding. Religious leaders, of course, are occasionally caught in sinful acts, as was evangelist Jimmy Swaggart in the 1980s. But such misfortune often strengthens their ability to lead. As wayward clergy confess and undergo rehabilitation, they demonstrate that they share everyone's need to now and then repent and reattain divine grace.

Leaders of professional organizations also exemplify the values and aspirations of those in the ranks. At midcareer, many physicians become managers of hospitals and health plans. Significant management responsibilities make it impossible for these doctors to continue caring for patients. Still, many physician-managers do everything possible to look and act like doctors. It is not uncommon to see a high-level hospital manager striding the halls in a white coat with a stethoscope protruding from his pocket and attending grand rounds. Often, these doctors have not treated patients in years. But physician-managers feel they must demonstrate their continuing concern with the practice of medicine to exercise effective leadership.

Symbolizing values and aspirations promotes leadership functions in less elevated pursuits as well. Executives of brokerage firms go to great efforts to look prosperous, as if to symbolize the wealth their organizations specialize in pursuing. At the Mary Kay cosmetics firm, those who have risen to the top of the pyramid drive pink Cadillacs provided them by the company. The flashy opulence of these vehicles symbolizes the glamorous success striven for in the ranks. These often self-made women demonstrate to all the rewards of success.

George Washington as Symbolic Leader

Every schoolchild knows that George Washington, first president of the United States, was the "father of his country." He is famed for military exploits such as crossing the ice-filled Delaware River to surprise the Hessians at Trenton. But analysts today consider Washington's military achievements to have been exaggerated. Washington, they say, attained the presidency and achieved mythic fame primarily because he exemplified the values and aspirations of his fellow citizens in the new republic.

Washington's popularity seems to have arisen from the public's trust in him. In rebellion against a tyrannical English king, the colonists hoped to found a country in which the high-ranking saw themselves as servants of the public. Along with their suspicion of power, the American revolutionaries venerated simple virtues such as self-sacrifice, justice, sobriety, and modesty. Washington, an unassuming Virginia planter who repeatedly turned down opportunities to exercise political power, was viewed as exemplifying the new republic's aspirations.

Barry Schwartz, a modern analyst of Washington's life, observed that the first president's contemporaries praised his personal virtue rather than his military genius. People of Washington's time contrasted him with Caesar and Napoleon because Washington achieved his victories through means other than "the agonies of the human heart" and knew how to "lead without dazzling mankind." Schwartz writes that the colonists searched for a leader who they assumed had disinterested motives and respected the role of the citizen-soldier. Washington became an "absolutely credible symbol of the nation's political morality" and a "visible symbol of the values and tendencies of his society."[10]

A more modern example of such a leader was Robert Oppenheimer, who managed the project that produced the first atomic bomb. To other scientists, Oppenheimer seemed to symbolize scientific expertise and open colleagueship.[11]

Who Becomes a Leader?

Ambitious people in modern society usually want to be leaders. For whom is leadership a reasonable goal? Most organizations are hierarchical, with many people occupying lower-ranked slots and relatively few on top. This would suggest that leadership is a privilege reserved for just a few. Perhaps only a limited number of human beings have the talent to exercise leadership. Alternatively, modern organizational structure may simply not provide enough opportunities for everyone to utilize his or her leadership capabilities. There is truth to the saying that not every member of a tribe can be the chief.

Many people believe that the "natural" leadership talents of some set them apart from other human beings. Throughout the ages, people have looked for external signs by which to recognize natural leaders. An Old Testament tale tells of the search for Israel's first king. A prophecy declared that the king should stand "head and shoulders" above any man in the land. Thus King Saul of biblical fame was found. Modern organizations have sometimes sought leadership talent through informal means. A famous writer serving in World War I chronicled such a procedure. He and his fellow officers organized football games among the recruits and observed the action. Men who took charge and called plays were singled out as candidates for promotion to corporal and sergeant.[12] Organizations today employ formal tests and questionnaires developed by psychologists to screen for potential leaders.

Much human experience suggests that attainment of leadership is far more complex than spontaneous elevation of the naturally talented. Many people, though not officially recognized, seem to have functioned as effective leaders "behind the scenes." Writers of fiction have spun tales of humble servants who have assumed leadership in times of uncertainty and crisis. Sir James Matthew Barrie's play *The Admirable Crichton* is a well-known example. In the play, the servant Crichton assumes practical leadership when his master, an English aristocrat, is shipwrecked on a desert island. The aristocrat serves as a handyman. As soon as the party is rescued, though, Crichton again becomes a mere butler and the aristocrat resumes his customary supremacy.

Real life furnishes many examples of nonleaders who have clear leadership talent. As in fiction, the talent of these people becomes visible in times of crisis. During battles, enlisted men have often exercised leadership when their commanders have been absent, incapacitated, or killed. Usually, these men return to their ordinary positions after official command has been reestablished.

Many people whose social position, appearance, race, or gender prevent them from attaining formal leadership titles possess considerable leadership talent. The wife of President Woodrow Wilson (1856–1924), for example, is said to have exercised actual executive power in the final years of her husband's life, during which time he was incapacitated by a stroke. Thus a woman functioned as president during an era when election of a woman to the post would have been unthinkable.

Traits

Those who believe in "natural" leadership often attribute the required capabilities to *traits*. Traits are long-lasting features of an individual's emotional makeup, such as optimism and extroversion. Traits are thought to emerge early in an individual's life, perhaps from his or her genetic background. Traits give rise to enduring patterns of thinking and behavior. An individual's traits offer an explanation of his or her vocational selection, socialization patterns, and level of success.

Characteristics traditionally known as "leadership traits" include

- Intelligence
- Dominance
- Self-confidence
- Energy or action orientation
- Task-relevant knowledge

Although a "self over others" orientation is suggested by these traits, some authors add community-building capabilities to the mix, such as truthfulness (with special attention to keeping promises and commitments) and good judgment. Peters and Waterman, authors of the famed treatise *In Search of Excellence,* suggest that leadership traits also include the ability to develop a shared mission and a sense of common values.[13]

People who believe in traits tend to explain the fortunes of humankind on the basis of individual contributions and acts. In this perspective, work history has developed as it did due to the actions of "great men." The "great man" theory is frequently used to explain the success or failure of organizations as well. In many cases, a single trait allegedly possessed by the "great man" is said to account for the success of his organization. The rise of Standard Oil as a great American conglomerate is attributed to the acquisitiveness of John D. Rockefeller. The Allied victory in World War II is laid to the organizational talents of General Dwight D. Eisenhower. The dominance of Microsoft at the close of the 20th century is credited to the genius of Bill Gates.

Research has sometimes found an actual relationship between traits and effective leadership. A series of studies has shown that intelligence, dominance, self-confidence, energy or action orientation, and task-relevant knowledge coincide with effective leadership.[14] However, these studies suggest a generally weak relationship of these traits to leadership. Studies of individual traits such as dominance and self-confidence have sometimes shown them as unrelated to or potentially undermining effective leadership. Dominance and self-confidence, especially if excessive, seem likely to raise followers' suspicions. More recent research suggests that traits such as honesty, integrity, and ability to arouse confidence, in addition to the traits referenced above, are particularly valuable to leaders.

According to some observers, favorable traits help people become effective leaders. They help people achieve leadership positions and acquire leadership skills. But they do not guarantee success as a leader.

Napoleon and Kutuzoff: Leaders With Different Traits

The name Napoleon has appeared repeatedly in this chapter. One of history's best-known leaders, Napoleon clearly possessed the traits of dominance, self-confidence, and action orientation. Napoleon dressed elegantly and cut a dashing figure on a horse. The painter David portrayed him as commanding and majestic.

Drawing on historical chronicles, the writer Tolstoy provides a detailed picture of Napoleon's character in his epic novel *War and Peace*. According to Tolstoy, Napoleon was a fierce egotist. He enjoyed watching men perform needlessly hazardous feats in his honor. Napoleon rewarded the survivors with medals but did nothing to stop senseless self-sacrifice.

Tolstoy also provides a detailed description of General Kutuzoff, Napoleon's principal adversary in his attempt to conquer Russia. Kutuzoff is portrayed as short and pudgy. He rode not a heroic steed but a homely, sagging mount. According to Tolstoy, Kutuzoff preferred the post from which he had been recalled, governing a provincial city, to military command. A film portrayal of the Russian campaign shows Kutuzoff as a folksy, approachable officer, prone to scratching under his wig.

Kutuzoff's command style contrasted with that of Napoleon. Tolstoy describes an important battle in which Kutuzoff had no apparent strategy. He allowed junior officers to suggest tactical moves. Kutuzoff accepted some of these suggestions, complimenting the men who had made them. He declined other suggestions, politely thanking the officers responsible and noting that their advice might be applied later. Gradually, the accepted moves coalesced into a strategy appropriately geared to the changing situation on the battlefield.

Napoleon and Kutuzoff probably shared the traits of extreme intelligence and skill at strategic thinking. But beyond these they differed. Napoleon's most apparent traits included self-confidence, ambition, and desire to dominate. Kutuzoff's traits included flexibility, a willingness to listen, and the ability to cultivate the support (indeed the affection) of subordinates.

Despite the differences in their traits, Napoleon and Kutuzoff were both highly effective military leaders.

Kutuzoff, it should be remembered, ultimately triumphed. The French suffered disastrous defeat in Russia. French losses were stupendous for the early 19th century, numbering 350,000 dead or captured. Defeat in Russia cost Napoleon his throne and landed him in exile.

Situational Leadership

People who possess at least some of the traits described above seem more likely to become leaders than those who do not. But traits do not tell the whole story. As demonstrated earlier, organizations mold much human behavior and thought. Structure presents opportunities to some and denies them to others. Culture helps determine the capabilities that are most valued and the traits that are considered most desirable. People come to organizations with definite traits, dispositions, and personalities. But the same personal qualities that help people advance in some organizations inhibit their advancement in others. Some organizations encourage certain human characteristics while others discourage them.

It is not surprising, then, that the same person may attain leadership in some organizations but not in others. Within the same organization, people with different traits and capabilities may be more suited to leadership roles in each subunit. Organizations in different stages of development, utilizing different technologies and facing different challenges, require different kinds of leaders.

Some researchers have developed a conception of leadership that places primary importance on the tasks and challenges facing the organization itself rather than the personal characteristics of leaders. This concept is known as *situational leadership.*[15] Situational leadership calls for people whose capabilities match the organization's immediate needs, that is, its changing situation. As the organization's situation changes, individuals with different capacities become leaders.

The organization's age has a crucial impact on its needs regarding leadership. As Chapter 5 indicated, organizations age just as do people. A "young" organization is usually small and has relatively few procedures and rules. Fighting to establish stability, a start-up business hustles to obtain product orders, a new public agency strives for political support, a new nonprofit aims for public visibility. Leaders appropriate to these tasks are youthful, energetic, and inclined to take risks.

In contrast, a "mature" organization may concern itself primarily with protecting its established position. People who attain leadership in such organizations are likely to be conventional and conservative. They have little to gain by taking risks and do not take many.

A well-known example of situational leadership was observed in the early days of the Silicon Valley boom of the 1980s. Steve Jobs, a young entrepreneur, founded Apple, the first large-scale manufacturer of personal computers. Apple's user-friendly devices became wildly popular and helped make the personal computer a fixture in American offices and homes.

Once established as a major American firm, however, Apple needed to maintain stable relationships with suppliers, bankers, and retailers. Technical and market innovation began to take a backseat. Steve Jobs lost his leadership position and left the management team. Still an extremely wealthy man, Jobs departed to found yet another start-up company.

In one of the ironies of business history, Jobs reassumed leadership of Apple a few years later. The invention of Windows software enabled competing computer manufacturers to offer products as user-friendly as those of Apple. Apple's sales faltered and bankruptcy seemed possible. Again, innovative product design became essential for attracting customers. Jobs was brought back to revitalize the company.

The state of the economy itself can affect situational leadership. In prosperous times, firms emphasize expansion. With money to be made by moving product out the door, people with sales expertise are invited to occupy leadership positions. When business slows, firms become more cautious, emphasizing conservation of resources. In these situations, personnel with fiscal backgrounds (accountants and comptrollers) become key leaders.

Organizations, then, require leaders with traits and skills that match their immediate needs. In addition, organizations require leaders with different leadership styles as situations change. Leaders sometimes have styles that emphasize giving explicit instructions and setting specific criteria for adequate performance. The style of such leaders may be characterized as *proscriptive*. Other leaders delegate decision making to subordinates, presenting them with objectives and allowing them to select their own means. The style of these leaders may be labeled *collaborative*. There are many additional ways in which differences in personal leadership style may be characterized.

The appropriateness of each leadership style differs according to the organization's situation. Labor force characteristics, for example, help determine whether proscriptive or collaborative leadership styles may be most effective. The proscriptive style works best in supervising inexperienced and unskilled workers. These workers have little preparation for making decisions and may be unfamiliar with the practical features of their jobs. The proscriptive style, though, would work poorly if applied to highly trained, independent-thinking professionals or managers. Accustomed to setting their own direction, such personnel would feel uncomfortable if given direct instruction. Orders might be obeyed with little enthusiasm or even, if workers have sufficient job security, be completely ignored. The desire to dominate, a trait often associated with leadership, becomes a drawback in situations that require a collaborative style.

Changing external situations can necessitate changes in leadership style. Organizations facing immediate hazards often require proscriptive-style leadership. The chief executive officer of a business with a cash-flow crisis may have to simply order his or her subordinates to cut expenditures by a fixed percentage. The director of a government agency facing special scrutiny by the president or Congress may tighten his or her control over bureau administrators, requiring explicit milestones and frequent reports.

In general, the situational approach suggests that many different people may achieve leadership and function effectively in such slots. Specific traits may help people become leaders in some organizations but not in others. Training in a given technical specialty helps qualify people as leaders in some phases of the business cycle but not in others. A given style of leadership may work well in some settings but may provoke resistance and hamper productivity in others.

Leadership Behavior

People respond in diverse ways when their positions offer them the opportunity to lead. Some seize leadership with energy and enthusiasm. Others carry out leadership responsibilities cautiously, avoiding major decisions and trying not to interfere with subordinates' normal routines. Those who actually exercise leadership do so through a variety of methods. Leaders select their methods according to both personal and organizational objectives. The leader's individual inclinations and tastes help determine his or her approach to leadership. Organizational structure and history help determine the degree of leadership that individuals exercise and the methods they use as leaders.

Avoidance of Leadership

As indicated earlier, true leaders make decisions and cause others to support and implement these decisions. People with titles such as "executive" and "manager" seem most likely to act in this fashion. People in these positions typically control rewards, imperative forces, and expression of culture. These resources enable executives and managers to promote acceptance and implementation of their decisions.

Executives, managers, and other people in formal leadership positions, though, may not in fact lead. Executives and managers decline to exercise leadership by avoiding responsibility for key decisions, such as choosing a future direction for the organization or resolving a crisis. Unwillingness by upper-level personnel to make key decisions is a frequent cause of complaint among subordinates.

Students of organizations have documented many instances where expected leadership has failed to take place. According to research, managers avoid making decisions by excessive use of the rulebook. A manager may avoid leadership by resolving all questions through direct application of organizational policies, rules, and standard operating procedure. This approach is sometimes called *managerialism.*

Managers operating in this fashion cannot make decisions regarding new or complex challenges. They may refer such issues to higher authorities. Or they may delegate decision making to a committee of subordinates or experts. True leaders, of course, utilize such panels. But they draw on them for information and advice, or utilize them as a means of learning the needs, aspirations, and opinions of members. Leaders interpret and synthesize committee findings and take responsibility for ensuing action.

Committees and panels are frequently established in government agencies. It is no accident that little or no action usually results from the committee's work. By the time the committee has completed its deliberations, the crisis that preceded its formation has blown over.

Tense or hostile organizational settings discourage managers and executives from exercising leadership. As in a case of a "failed" plant manager described by Perrow,[16] close surveillance by higher-ups causes managers to avoid potentially risky decision making and to allow their subordinates sufficient latitude for effective implementation. Organizational settings in which subordinates may readily dispute or ignore executive decisions discourage leadership. Universities, many of whose employees cannot be fired, are infamous for establishing committees for issues both significant and routine.

Noting the disinclination of managers to exercise leadership under certain conditions, some observers have drawn a sharp distinction between managers and leaders. John P. Kotter, a noted business writer, characterizes managers as people skilled simply at coping with day-to-day problems and maintaining established direction. According to Kotter, the manager's job is to maintain orderly progress toward established goals through techniques such as staffing, budgeting, establishing schedules, and seeing that scheduled tasks are completed on time. Leaders, Kotter writes, distinguish themselves by creating strategies, identifying potential, and motivating and inspiring others. Kotter believes leaders are people who initiate change, while managers merely cope with changes put in motion by others or resulting from forces outside the organization.[17]

Other observers of organizations disagree. These observers argue that no one can effectively exercise leadership unless he or she has mastered at least some of the routine management functions. People who develop strategies need, at the very least, to appoint others to see that grand strategies are implemented. Leaders everywhere are famed for delivering speeches to the troops, employees, or stockholders. But leaders in organizations have direct subordinates, whom they supervise by communicating expectations regarding assets, objectives, schedules, and milestones.

Even the most mundane management functions may constitute tools of leadership. Budgeting, for example, may appear to be a routine practice. The process of negotiating a budget, though, can alter the staffing and reporting relationships within an organization. A budget agreement can reflect retention of some objectives and abandonment of others. A manager skilled at negotiation can sometimes invisibly ensure that his or her preferences regarding the organization's direction are accomplished.

Transactional Versus Transformational Leadership

True leadership in fact includes several different forms of behavior. Not all resemble the heroic acts of famous figures from history. Among people who genuinely exercise leadership, two separate approaches can be distinguished: (1) transactional and (2) transformational. Both transactional and transformational leaders make decisions and motivate others, but they do so in different ways.

Transactional leadership is marked, first, by the leader's relative separation from his or her followers. Leaders of the transactional type often set objectives without discussing them with subordinates. The objectives set by these leaders may simply reflect their personal views of the organization's needs, or the transactional leader may simply pursue private objectives utilizing the organization as a tool.

More important, the transactional leader motivates others to implement his or her decisions through reward, punishment, and application of imperative force. The transactional leader achieves implementation of his or her decisions through pay, perquisites (such as coveted office and parking space), and promotion. Motivation of personnel takes place through exchange of valued things. Of course, rewards can be negative; transactional leaders punish insubordination via techniques ranging from withholding of bonuses to murder.

Transactional leaders constitute the workaday world's supervisors and figures of authority. Transactional leadership occurs in numerous forms, many quite familiar both inside and outside organizations. Transactional leaders include small town business owners, big city political bosses, and "banana republic" dictators. Dependent on their ability to allocate valued objects (or to withhold sanctions), transactional leaders face limits to the range and efficacy of their actions. Transactional leaders take people as they are, motivating through their existing needs and aspirations.

Transformational leadership integrates the leader more fully with his or her followers and reaches further into the follower's internal motivation. Transformational leaders develop strategies if not by direct contact with followers, at least with their ideas in mind. Transformational leaders derive inspiration from the perceived needs and outlook of the people they lead. In turn, these leaders inspire their following. Transformational leaders go further than allocating valued rewards to their followers. They cause their followers to reconsider and alter what they consider valuable. At best, transformational leaders uplift their followers with new vision, a sense of shared purpose, and enhanced moral commitment.

C. Everett Koop: A Transformational Leader

Surgeon General C. Everett Koop was one of the most visible members of President Ronald Reagan's administration (1981–1989).

A pediatric surgeon from Philadelphia, Koop was known for his conservative views on controversial issues such as abortion. The president's right-wing advisers expected that Koop would fit right in. His was an important appointment. As head of the U.S. Public Health Service, the surgeon general takes lead responsibility for the actions of federal physicians and public health workers nationwide. His office issues statements and reports that make news.

Koop surprised the administration by taking an unexpected stand. Alone among major Reagan appointees, Koop declared AIDS a significant public threat. He directed personnel and agencies under his jurisdiction to vigorously promote awareness of AIDS and take steps initially opposed by the White House to halt its spread.

Several features of Koop's leadership distinguish it as transformational. He challenged business as usual at his agency. He gave voice to the convictions of thousands of public health professionals, having almost certainly conferred with many of them while formulating his position. Perhaps most important, Koop gave Public Health Service employees a renewed sense of mission, placing them in the forefront of a powerful social movement. Bearded and imposing in his dress uniform, Koop was clearly not just another bureaucrat or political hack.

Lower and Higher Leadership

Many different types of behavior are in fact compatible with the concept of leadership. Transformational leaders are clearly more exciting than transactional ones. Managers who exercise leadership through backroom processes such as budgeting and agenda setting attract little attention. But reserving the distinction of leadership only to those who are transformational ignores leadership that is much more common and often of great consequence.

It makes more sense to recognize the diversity of leadership behavior than to celebrate some of its forms and ignore others. The types of behavior discussed here may be conveniently categorized as "higher" and "lower" leadership. Higher versus lower leadership is not distinguished by the hierarchical level at which leadership is exercised, but rather by how directly and extensively people use leadership opportunities.

People who exercise lower leadership maintain the status quo. Often, they rule invisibly. They offer conventional rewards, often extrinsic in nature, to their subordinates. They are often motivated by a genuine desire to promote organizational objectives rather than their own personal ones. Lower leadership tends to direct action from the top down.

People who exercise higher leadership look for new ways of doing things. They do not merely reward or punish their subordinates, but capture their imagination and mobilize their energy. They process information from below into a working consensus. They help organizations and individuals progress toward new objectives and levels of achievement.

Transactional leaders and managers who use routine techniques to set direction almost always exercise lower leadership. Higher leadership is visible and requires involving a broad range of followers. Leadership of the highest form transforms not just organizations but entire civilizations.

In real life, it is not unusual to find successful leaders who employ both "higher" and "lower" techniques. A leader may stir the consciousness of his or her followers in personal communications and public speeches. But he or she may make deals and offer rewards behind the scenes to those for whom ideological persuasion is insufficient motive.

Charismatic Leadership

Occasionally, leaders distinguishable as *charismatic* arise in human society. Charismatic leadership has driven human history at crucial junctures. As detailed in Chapter 7, people with true charisma are believed by their followers to have powers far beyond those of individual human beings. According to their followers, the power of charismatic leaders originates from forces outside themselves. This power may reflect a political ideal, social creed, or divine presence. Famous charismatic leaders of the past have included such diverse figures as Christ, Gandhi, and Hitler.

The sociologist Max Weber, active in the early 20th century, helped introduce the concept of charisma into discussions of leadership. According to Weber,[18] charismatic leaders appear to have supernatural qualities derived from powers outside themselves. Followers feel duty-bound to obey these leaders because of the higher forces (such as God or the Fatherland) from which their powers derive. Weber wrote that several other features characterize charismatic leaders, including the following:

- Self-appointment: charismatic leaders feel "called" by invisible powers to a social mission.
- Independence: charismatic leaders rise to prominence outside conventional rules, structures, and institutions.
- Miraculous power: charismatic leaders demonstrate their extraordinary status by performing miraculous or at least extremely unusual feats.
- Radicalism: charismatic leaders seek fundamental change in society, necessitating destruction of conventionally accepted practice.
- Personal rule: charismatic leaders communicate directly with supporters and dispense favors on a personal basis, unrestricted by conventions and structures.

The concept of charisma used by social scientists differs strongly from the term's popular usage. People now apply the term very broadly, to describe anyone who has great personal magnetism. One often hears the term applied to actors.

Charismatic leadership must still be acknowledged as an important if rarely encountered force. Religious organizations and political parties—particularly organizations that are radical or cultlike—may be expected to spawn charismatic leaders from time to time. Charismatic leadership is almost unthinkable in formal organizations except at the very top. Formal structure contradicts charismatic individuality. Members who act inconsistently with existing role expectations are disciplined or ejected.

Even outstanding leaders are seldom charismatic in the traditional sense. Transformational and other "higher" leaders are usually not charismatic. Figures like C. Everett Koop receive their offices through conventional political processes. According to Schwartz's deconstruction, George Washington was nothing but a conventional Virginia gentleman who was selected by duly appointed officials to serve as a symbolic leader.

A realistic examination of the lives of charismatic leaders makes them seem less mysterious than they might at first. The rise to charismatic leadership takes place through planning, organization, and staging. Months before a march or rally, Martin Luther King sent "advance men" (trained organizers and publicists) to whip up enthusiasm and ensure a proper backdrop for his appearances. Hitler went all out. He organized youth groups and paramilitary organizations to trumpet his support. He is said to have practiced for hours in front of a mirror to perfect the proper poses. Planned dramatics have been used since ancient times to transform ordinary men into charismatic leaders. Aristotle tells the tale of how Pisistratus, a politician intent on seizing power in Athens, reemerged from exile imposed as punishment for an earlier putsch:

(A supporter) first spread abroad the rumor that Athena was bringing back Pisistratus, and then, having found a woman of great stature and beauty (actually a flower-seller from the countryside), he dressed her in a garb resembling that of the goddess and brought her into the city with Pisistratus. The latter drove in on a chariot with the woman beside him, and the inhabitants of the city, struck with awe, received him with adoration.[19]

Leader-Follower Relationships

Because all leaders exercise some measure of control over followers, it is easy to forget that leaders and followers are joined in relationships of mutual dependence. Leaders can accomplish nothing unless they can induce others to implement their decisions. Modern work organizations require conscientious compliance with a leader's wishes in the absence of direct supervision. In past eras, surveillance over workers on a farm or assembly line may have sufficed to ensure productivity. Today, workers' tasks are more complex, more dependent on the worker's independent judgment, and less accessible to direct management oversight. The inclinations and behavior of subordinates toward their leaders, then, are as important as the plans and strategies that leaders develop to motivate and coordinate the actions of subordinates.

As noted at the beginning of this chapter, leadership poses a paradox for members of a free society. On one hand, most people realize that leadership is necessary for organizing any collectivity of significant size. On the other, individuals do not like to subordinate themselves to others any more than necessary. This paradox lurks in the background of many leader-follower relationships as a potential cause of dissatisfaction and mistrust.

Followers need to remember that their attitudes and behavior affect the quality of their leaders' performance. Leadership is visible and prestigious. "Followership," though, can require as much—if not more—skill, wisdom, patience, and initiative. Appropriate action by followers sometimes increases the leader's ability to impel others to carry out his or her decisions. Sometimes, though, followers must find ways to reduce the leader's power for the good of the organization. Deciding on the proper course of action may be both difficult and risky for the follower.

Leader-Follower Relationships as Exchange

Some observers of organizations describe leader-follower relationships as sequences of exchanges. Everyone is familiar with the process by which material rewards are exchanged for services. The norm of reciprocity governs many leader-follower exchanges. Leaders allocate extraordinary rewards such as bonuses or relief from burdensome office regulations on the expectation that followers will perform better service. The *quid pro quo,* or exchange of favors, is an essential feature of social relations and tool of leadership.

Some of the most important exchanges involve nonmaterial benefits. Leaders, for example, offer subordinates entry into their networks. Access to the leader's network opens valuable opportunities for the subordinate. In business, access to the leader's network may generate sales opportunities; in science, advance information on grants; in public administration, advantageous relations with elected officials. The leader's network is likely to be more valuable to the subordinate than the subordinate's own. It may prove a key resource in the subordinate's career advancement.

In return for access to his or her network, the leader expects the subordinate's loyalty and discretion. Followers must reflect well on the leader. They must do good work. They must not disseminate sensitive or negative information. They must not make side deals or otherwise deprive the leader of future opportunities.

For their part, followers need to view leaders objectively. Does the leader provide extraordinary rewards when they put themselves out? Does he or she open opportunities and networks? Do the leader's capabilities and achievements reflect well on subordinates? A failing leader makes even a well-performing subordinate look bad to outsiders.

Successful sequences of reciprocal exchanges create a community of interest between leaders and followers. Confidence is built on both sides of the exchange relationship. Leaders give followers assignments with more responsibility. Followers take risks with leaders, such as making suggestions and offering criticism.

Leader-Follower Dysfunctions

A follower's action can make or break the leader. Unfavorable attitudes or behavior by subordinates who are weakly tied to the organization or who perform unimportant roles may be of little consequence. At other times, poor followership can severely damage the organization and harm those who depend on its protection or service.

Too much attention by subordinates to immediate rewards damages the leader-follower relationship. Such expectations create an atmosphere in which all parties ask "What's in it for me?" A generalized feeling that everyone will eventually benefit from contributions to the organization creates a more stable system. Repeated failure by the leader or follower to act in the expected reciprocal manner, though, damages or destroys the exchange relationship.

At the extreme, exchanges become negative.[20] In this situation, both follower and leader watch for each other's transgressions or mistakes and apply whatever punishments or retaliative moves may be available to them.

Higher leadership fosters a partnership between leaders and followers. Transactional leaders coexist in stable equilibrium with followers. Leader-follower relationships become dysfunctional when followers are either habitually critical or uncritically compliant.

Chronic and extreme criticism of leaders ultimately reduces the quality of leadership, causing the organization itself to become ineffective. A fictional example in novelist Herman Wouk's *The Caine Mutiny* illustrates leadership deficits that are aggravated by poor followership.

The Caine Mutiny illustrates the effect an atmosphere of severe criticism may have on a leader. Even a normal person becomes defensive under ostracism and ridicule. Queeg indeed had emotional problems, aggravated by severe combat experience. But an atmosphere of constructive loyalty would have allowed him to function as an effective officer.

Uncritical compliance, the opposite of events on the *Caine*, represents another form of leader-follower dysfunction. Leaders surrounded by "yes-men" lack a resource essential for becoming aware of factual error or bad policy. Habitually uncritical subordinates can permit their leader to develop delusions of grandeur and set impossible objectives for the organization.

Leadership and Followership in Crisis

Wouk's story takes place on the Navy minesweeper *Caine* in World War II. As was typical during that period, most of the ship's officers had been rapidly trained and pressed into service.

Trouble begins when a new captain, Francis P. Queeg, assumes command. Captain Queeg exercises tighter discipline than his predecessor, displeasing both the crew and the junior officers.

As time goes by, it becomes apparent that Captain Queeg, a veteran of several years' combat at sea, suffers from emotional problems. He enforces regulations to an unprecedented degree, ordering time-consuming and seemingly absurd procedures to detect and punish minor infractions. He never admits a mistake. He has migraines. He keeps a pair of small steel balls in his pocket and fidgets nervously with them.

Many of the *Caine*'s officers poke fun at Queeg behind his back. They make up derogatory names and songs about him. One ensign, a writer, introduces the notion that the captain is insane. He familiarizes his fellow officers with a Navy regulation permitting removal of a captain who has become incapacitated.

The crux of the tale takes place as the ship rolls and pitches in a severe typhoon. With huge waves crashing over the vessel, the second-in-command pleads with the captain to make a defensive maneuver. Captain Queeg refuses. Pressure mounts as the ship is tossed violently by the storm.

Suddenly, the captain falls into a stupor. The second-in-command orders the ship onto a safer heading. Regaining himself, Captain Queeg rescinds the order. The second-in-command declares that he is taking over and that Queeg is relieved under the Navy regulation regarding a captain's incapacitation. Although the ship rides out the storm, the junior officers are charged with mutiny.

At court marshal, the officers are acquitted, thanks to a skilled Navy lawyer. But in private, the lawyer castigates the men. If they had given their captain the "constructive loyalty" he deserved instead of ridiculing him, conflict would never have developed to the point it did. The argument during the typhoon would never have occurred and Queeg would not have cracked. Despite Queeg's shortcomings, an atmosphere of mutual respect and collaboration could and should have been established.

Developing shared perspectives and interests is a mark of favorable leader-follower relationships. But subordinates who are entirely uncritical can create a partnership that is dysfunctional for all concerned. At the extreme, such leader-follower relationships can develop into a psychiatric condition know as *folie à deux*, in which two or more afflicted individuals reinforce each other's delusions.

A famous example of folie à deux is said to have occurred in Hitler's bunker during the final days of World War II.[21] Hitler's forces had been reduced to a few battalions fighting desperately in the streets of Berlin. But believing that his vast armies remained intact, the Nazi leader ordered the nonexistent units into action. High-ranking officials in the bunker were unwilling to contradict Hitler and instead reinforced his delusions. On the eve of final defeat, these officials came to believe the lies themselves. In the end, all lived in a world of complete and mutually reinforced fantasy.

The two foregoing examples indicate some of the principal challenges of followership. Followers walk a fine line between excessive criticism and compliance. As indicated earlier, the best leaders develop partnerships of trust and mutual assistance with their subordinates. The best followers do their part in helping build such partnerships.

The Complexities of Leadership

The essence of leadership, again, is twofold. To exercise leadership, people must decide among available options and obtain the collaboration of others. Every day, leaders in most organizations attain the required cooperation largely by allocating rewards and applying power, authority, and discipline. In its highest form, though, leadership creates commitment throughout the organization to commonly held values and objectives.

The study of organizations suggests that nearly every member can become a leader under the proper conditions. The situation prevailing in an organization determines the capabilities and traits it will emphasize in selection of leaders.

The preceding overview of leadership illustrates the dynamic nature of organizations. The fact that organizations depend heavily on structure suggests a mechanical quality. Yet, it is clear that leadership is much more complex than giving commands, allocating rewards, and exercising authority. Leaders' need to periodically negotiate new bases for collaboration and maintain favorable relations with followers indicates the fluid nature of relationships and processes within formal organizations.

It is important to note that many of the forms of leadership described in this chapter overlap. People holding administrative or management positions may not exercise leadership in a manner similar to Washington or Napoleon, yet, in restricted areas of organizational functioning, they may initiate action and motivate personnel in an effective manner. The same individual may carry out both transactional and transformational leadership. Franklin D. Roosevelt, for example, may have had charisma and become famous for articulating a new vision of America. But it is beyond doubt that he also distributed favors to his friends and patronage to his supporters. In any actual organization, individuals combine qualities that may be abstractly distinct.

Concentrating on communication and decision making, the next chapter will address subjects of particular importance to effective leadership. Communication and decision making are essential organizational processes. Like leadership, they illustrate the variable and fluid nature of human relations even within formal organizational structure.

Issues and Applications

This chapter has covered the numerous forms that leadership can take. It has emphasized the diversity of qualities that enable a person to assume leadership. Participants in organizations can apply these principles to promote collective goals and their personal effectiveness. Some examples are the following:

- The manager of a production unit has been repeatedly passed over for promotion. Eager for executive rank, he feels his ability to control production costs is unappreciated. He should consider moving to a firm where production management is seen as a serious problem, a situation in which his leadership would be sought.

- A woman is appointed director of a state-level department of finance. Eager to carry out the program of the state's new administration, she assigns tasks to a key department head. Months later, little has been done. She should assess the department head's actual leadership capabilities. In addition, she should determine whether he has truly accepted her leadership.

- The leader of a community agency has missed the deadline for a grant-in-aid from a foundation. He telephones the foundation's program officer to ask for an extension. The program officer replies that he does not have the power to grant such a request. The applicant should try to contact a higher-level official who might have sufficient discretion to grant the extension.

Chapter Review and Major Themes

Leadership is a key component of an organization's functioning. The essence of leadership is selecting a course of action and getting others on board. Some individuals attain leadership by virtue of the organization's formal structure, others through informal groups and networks.

Essential tasks of leadership include taking initiative, assessing followers' needs and capabilities, fostering and maintaining relationships, providing resources, obtaining and distributing information, and reflecting members' aspirations. People with quite different capabilities may become leaders. Leadership is *contingent:* the situation in which the organization finds itself determines the capabilities necessary for leadership. Leadership styles differ, as in the transactional versus the transformational leader.

Figure 9.1, which represents relations of leadership with function, conflict, and environment, is highly similar to Figure 7.1, which focuses on imperative force (see Chapter 7). This reflects the fact that leaders often have access to imperative force. Leadership can have a positive or negative effect on both function and conflict. The conditions under which a leader may have adverse effects on function and conflict include instances when the leader resorts too readily to imperative force; the leader lacks skills required by the organization; or the leader acts not according to the needs of the organization but according to personal agendas or the interests of outsiders. The organization's environment affects its leadership in a number of ways. It helps determine, for example, the style of leadership acceptable to the organization's members.

Characteristics of individual leaders and the situations in which they work affect the level of conflict within the organization. A leader who enjoys the confidence of his or her subordinates can settle disputes, reducing conflict. But competition among individuals seeking leadership status can be a major source of conflict. Rivalry between a formal and an informal leader, whether open or covert, can result in significant conflict.

A positive outlook among followers regarding their leaders generally promotes the organization's ability to achieve its goals. Negative feelings can have a variety of adverse effects, mutiny being the most extreme. Ultimately, the individual decision of the follower determines the leader's effectiveness. The individual decides whether he or she respects the leader, carries out instructions, and helps build the leader's prestige. In situations far less acute than a ship at risk of sinking, individuals periodically experience conflict over whether to accept their leaders' judgment or question their decisions.

Both today and in the past, leaders have faced the challenge of exercising their function without an ability to control subordinates' thinking and behavior. Examples furnished by history include both Napoleon and Kutuzoff, described earlier in this chapter. Despite their differences, both commanders were able to "harness the egos" of the men under them by providing opportunities to achieve the glory or (at least as the subordinates perceived) to influence the conduct of historic battles. Modern examples might include figures as different as Presidents Ronald Reagan and Franklin D. Roosevelt, who retained enthusiastic staff support in part by symbolizing the American spirit in the face of hard times. Microsoft's prestige and ability to offer monetary rewards enabled CEO Bill Gates to exercise leadership over talented and often unconventional individuals.

Reducing perceived differences between their concerns and those of their subordinates is the mark of an outstanding leader. Such an individual exercises leadership without emphasizing control over subordinates. The most effective leader achieves the appearance of membership in the same community of purpose as his or her subordinates. As a classic comment by Follett reads, "One *person* should not give orders to another *person*, but both should agree to take their orders from the situation (facing the organization)."[22]

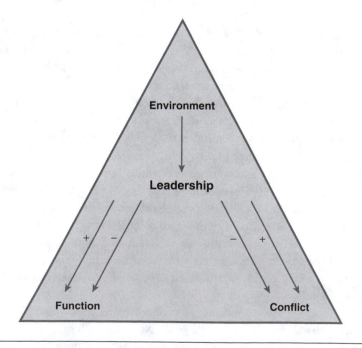

Figure 9.1   Analytical Perspectives Applied to Leadership

Discussion Questions

1. To what extent can the leadership role be exercised without the use of imperative force?

2. Among leaders in American organizations today, can you identify any who are truly charismatic? What characteristics give them this quality? Has their charisma enabled them to be productive in their positions?

3. In what instances do you believe opposition to an organizational leader by his or her subordinates is justified? Can an employee oppose the leader without endangering his or her own position? What type of opposing actions may be most effective?

4. Think of leaders you have known or whose careers have been widely reported. What enabled these individuals to attain their leadership positions? What lessons do these careers teach to those who want to lead?

5. Imagine yourself as the CEO of a large, formal organization. What steps can you take to avoid hazards of leadership such as losing the leadership position or performing ineffectively?

6. In a large, formal organization, how important are these personal qualities in attaining a leadership position: extroversion; industriousness; being a source of new ideas? Can any of these traits make it more difficult to become a leader?

References

1. Guest, R. (1962). *Organizational change*. Homewood, IL: Dorsey.

2. Caro, R. A. (1990). *Means of ascent*. New York: Knopf.

3. Bowditch, J. L., & Buono, A. F. (1994). *A primer on organizational behavior* (3rd ed.). New York: John Wiley & Sons.

4. Burns, J. M. (1978). *Leadership*, p. 18. New York: Harper and Row.

5. Barnard, C. I. (1938). *The functions of the executive*. Cambridge, MA: Harvard University Press.

6. Coleman, J. S., Katz, E., & Menzel, H. (1966). *Medical innovation: A diffusion study*. Indianapolis, IN: Bobbs-Merrill.

7. Selznick, P. (1949). *TVA and the grass roots*. Berkeley: University of California Press.

8. Buckley, W. (1967). *Sociology and modern systems theory*. Englewood Cliffs, NJ: Prentice Hall.

9. Deming, W. E. (1991). *Out of the crisis*. Cambridge: MIT Press.

10. Schwartz, B. (1982). George Washington and the Whig conception of heroic leadership. *American Sociological Review, 48*, 18–33.

11. Thorpe, C., & Shapin, S. (2000). Who was J. Robert Oppenheimer? *Social Studies of Science, 30*(4), 545–590.

12. Graves, R. (1957). *Good-bye to all that*. Garden City, NY: Doubleday.

13. Peters, T., & Waterman, R. H. (1982). *In search of excellence*. New York: Random House.

14. Stogdill, R. M. (1974). *Handbook of leadership*. New York: Free Press.

15. Fiedler, F. E. (1967). *A theory of leadership effectiveness.* New York: McGraw-Hill.

16. Perrow, C. (1970). *Organizational analysis: A sociological view.* Belmont, CA: Wadsworth.

17. Kotter, J. (1990). What leaders really do. *Harvard Business Review, 63,* 103–111.

18. Weber, M. (1968). *Economy and society* (Vol. 1). Berkeley: University of California Press.

19. Godolphin, R. B. (1942). *The Greek historians.* New York: Random House.

20. Sparrow, R. T., & Linden, R. C. (1997). Process and structure in leader-member exchange. *Academy of Management Journal, 22,* 522–552.

21. Kets de Vries, M. F. R. (1978). Folie a deux: Acting out your superior's fantasies. *Human Relations, 10,* 905–924.

22. Metcalf, H. C. (1926). *Scientific foundations of business administration.* Baltimore, MD: Williams & Wilkins.

CHAPTER 10

Communication and Decision Making

Learning Objective

To understand the individual, interpersonal, and organizational factors that promote or inhibit high-quality communication and decision making.

Principles

○ Communication and decision making are dynamic processes essential for an organization's functioning. Communication involves transmission of information among individuals and subunits. Decision making uses information to set direction and solve problems.

○ Structure and the informal dynamics of interpersonal relationships influence communication in organizations. Structure determines the basic direction, volume, and content of information flow. Informal pathways of communication, under the influence of organizational structure, operate in all organizations.

○ Information is transmitted through diverse modes such as speech, writing, symbols, and body language. Negotiation represents a specialized form of communication.

○ Communication circuits or loops reflect organizational structure. Like structure itself, specific types of communication circuits match the tasks in which the organization engages.

○ Even decision makers who receive complete and high-quality information may not use this resource well. Many decide issues without factually evaluating the alternatives open to them. Domination of a decision maker's thinking by fixed ideas in the form of ideologies or slogans prevents him or her from appropriately using facts.

Communication and Decision Making: Significance and Issues

Receiving and transmitting information and making good decisions based on information constitute core challenges for organizations. It is no accident that outstanding political leaders throughout history have been talented orators. Though lacking power in a formal sense, Pericles of ancient Athens shaped key decisions about war and peace through his speeches. More recently, President Ronald Reagan displayed an uncanny ability to assess the public's mood and reassuringly convince Americans that his policies were appropriate. Reagan became known as the "great communicator."

Ultimately, though, the characteristics of the organization itself are more important than the gifts of individuals as communicators. A favorable configuration of roles and structure promotes high-quality communication and decision making. The relationship of organizational features to quality of communication and decision making, though, is complex. A structure that allows the focal person to initiate contact with occupants of all other roles relevant to his or her job promotes information exchange. For some purposes, such access may be favorable to the organization's needs. For other purposes, restriction of access to information channels may make more sense. Decision makers who receive too much information risk falling into confusion and inaction due to the flood of facts, figures, analyses, and opinions.

The manner in which information is exchanged in an organization is not always obvious. Organization charts certainly do not tell the whole story. Such charts depict subordination of each management level to the next higher. As systems of communication, though, organizations support information flows that are not just hierarchical, but lateral and sometimes seemingly idiosyncratic. Some parts of organizational communication systems carry large volumes of information; some, tiny quantities. Some parts of the system deliver information to all or nearly all personnel. Others are "plugged into" highly specific sets of receivers.

Likewise, everyday logic does not provide a complete understanding of the manner in which organizations make decisions. Decision makers, it would appear, should dispassionately develop a list of options, obtain all pertinent information, and objectively weigh evidence for and against each option. Such behavior should not be taken for granted. The social interplay among people on a decision-making team has profound effects on the options they consider and choose.

The Sociotechnical Process of Communication

Communication should be viewed as a sociotechnical process. This is so because each method of communication offers technical capacity to the user. However, people select and use communication methods according to their objectives. Individual objectives may be to communicate accurately, but also to withhold all or parts of a message, to slant information, or to communicate only through hints. Familiar methods of communication include verbal, nonverbal, and symbolic. Each of these is sometimes referred to as a communication mode.

Verbal Communication

Verbal communication is the most easily recognizable mode of information exchange. This communication mode is characterized by use of words and numbers. Verbal communication has clear advantages over other modes for the exchange of deliberate messages. The value of written communication for explicit, factual information is obvious. Transmission of data is always a verbal process. Although numbers and words are different from each other, both are explicit "packages" of information. Numbers are merely more explicit and exact than most words.

Words also allow people to transmit specific emotional messages to others. Anyone who has received a love letter or cried over the ending of a novel can attest to the emotional power of words. A skilled novelist or playwright can transmit an emotional message not only by telling his or her readers how the characters feel but also by describing their interaction or conversation. The mental process through which the reader or theatergoer infers the character's feelings strengthens the story's impact.

Both written and oral communications belong to the verbal communication category. Each variety of verbal communication has advantages and disadvantages in human collectivities. Sometimes written and oral communication can be used interchangeably. At other times, only one variety of verbal communication is truly functional.

Written communication. The availability of written language enables the communicator to carefully compose his or her transmission to make its meaning explicit and unambiguous. Written words allow agreements to be cited and enforced. The famous "Statute of Frauds," inherited from medieval England as a cornerstone of American property law, mandates that agreements of significance be preserved as written contracts. The special dignity of written language is expressed every time someone seeking to seal an agreement insists on "getting it in writing."

Written communication is the form of information exchange most compatible with formal organization. When it is written, information exchanged may become part of a durable record of communication. Such records make possible standardized procedures to which all members of an organization can be held accountable. Written language allows the formulation and preservation of job descriptions with highly specific and detailed elements. Job descriptions constitute an important part of the organization's role-sending process. Formal organizations, of course, are marked by roles characterized by highly explicit sets of expectations.

Oral communication. Oral communication is clearly less formal. It is a more basic form of information exchange than writing. Interaction in most informal collectivities takes place on the basis of oral communication. Still, oral communication is crucial to formal organization.

Oral communication provides the flexibility and elasticity necessary in all human relationships. Information can be exchanged via spoken words that people would be reluctant to communicate in writing. People have more liberty to experiment and negotiate in oral than in written language.

The process by which an individual in a formal organization seeks to expand his or her role provides an example of the function of oral communication. An individual seeking to expand the scope of his or her role often feels more comfortable initiating change through oral exchanges. People may informally ask permission or carry out the required actions in the absence of writing. An experienced nurse, for example, may seek to expand her professional role by asking a doctor to give a patient a particular drug. Although the nurse would never think of putting an order in writing, she attains effective control over the patient's medication by verbally communicating her preferences. The doctor may write the order but the nurse has made the treatment decision.

The fact that oral communication provides participants with greater freedom and flexibility does not imply that oral communication is trivial. Billion-dollar deals are concluded over drinks and sealed with handshakes. Among preliterate peoples such as the Karimojong, oral communication suffices to initiate and enact complex patterns of behavior required for redress of grievances. Ritualistic repetition substitutes for written manuals of procedure in societies without a written language. In modern formal organizations, ritual use of spoken language allows factual material to be exchanged in a more forceful and acceptable manner than can be achieved in writing.

Ritual in Oral Communication

Sociologist Erving Goffman became famous for identifying rituals in the exchange of oral messages and determining their functions.[1] Goffman's analysis indicates that much communication among people takes place under rules and procedures governing what can be said and how messages may be delivered.

In everyday contact, communication rituals enable the exchange of information that is potentially disturbing to transmitters, receivers, or both. Rituals governing exchange of information allow people to receive potentially disturbing messages in a manner that does not expose them to feelings of denigration, dismissal, or danger.

In any formal organization, for example, most people work under the direct or indirect supervision of others on higher rungs of the hierarchy. Reminders of inferior status are often necessary. A skilled supervisor, though, engages in rituals intended to cushion the impact of such reminders. He or she may, for example, remind the subordinate of his status through a joke. Similarly, a skilled supervisor assigns a disagreeable job in self-deprecating language such as, "Well, the supervisors always palm off the really hard work on the analysts, right?"

A widely read essay by Goffman focuses on efforts made by individuals to "save face." In this essay, Goffman characterizes "face" as the socially valued image of oneself that an individual wishes to have recognized by others. Much interpersonal exchange is governed by rituals or gestures that enable participants to maintain face. People find ways to avoid or withdraw from communication with others who they fear may say things that will make them lose face.

Enabling a demoted or dismissed employee to save face is a mark of good management. Communication of disagreeable information can still be done with courtesy.

Rituals intended to allow individuals to save face take place every day in routine business, professional, and official life. Executives, for example, receive invitations to resign rather than be terminated. Or they may be "kicked upstairs," given fancy titles and desirable office space yet essentially removed from management. On the lower end of the hierarchy, workers facing involuntary severance may be offered retirement or disability options. These transitions are often accompanied by congratulations and parties.

A striking incident from the Cuban revolution (1960) illustrates the dynamics of face-saving. In the months following his seizure of power, dictator Fidel Castro executed many officials from the government he had overthrown. Castro allowed Havana's deposed police chief to give the order for his own execution. The privilege of shouting "Ready! Aim! Fire!" to the soldiers before him, rifles raised, enabled the fallen potentate to preserve his self-image as a tough guy in command.

Oral communication may seem spontaneous and disordered. In most collectivities, though, oral communication follows a structured order. Structure indicates which parties may exchange information, what information may be exchanged, and how the information exchange process should take place. Lines of communication are more explicit and stable in formal organizations than in informal collectivities. Ritual helps safeguard the stability of the structured order by making it easier for individuals to follow and live with it. Culture prevailing in the broader society and in the organization itself helps shape interaction rituals. The cultures of some organizations, for example, will protect the feelings of individuals. Other organizational cultures encourage bluntness, reflecting valuation of abstract information and personal toughness.

Most organizations occasionally engage in ritualistic relaxation of structure. Company parties constitute an important example. These may occur around holidays in celebration of company achievements, as did a ritual at the biotech firm Genentech known as the "Ho-Ho." Relaxation of ceremony and exaggeration of familiarity on such occasions give oral communication a special quality, characterized by Goffman as "a happy babble of disorganized sound." Substantive information is nevertheless exchanged on these occasions, namely affective expression of group solidarity.

Functions of written and oral communication. Written and oral exchange of information, both forms of verbal communication, have specific functions in organizations. The function of written communication is to transmit explicit information. No form of communication works better for exact communication of factual material. High-volume data transmission cannot take place other than by media that are readable by people or machines. Detailed scientific, financial, and legal information, which must be studied to be understood, requires transmission via writing. Long-term storage and recognition of information requires writing. Oral traditions, both inside and outside organizations, tend to introduce flux into the information flow.

Oral communication is more appropriate for exchange of information that the sender wishes to make ambiguous or to encompass multiple meanings: hence, the suitability of oral communication to the rituals illustrated above. Oral communication allows participants in the exchange process to mix emotion with fact. It would be unthinkable for a physician to inform a patient that he or she had a fatal disease via memorandum. Oral communication enables exchangers of information to engage in intimacy and secrecy. It is easier to carry out informal interaction rituals through the oral than the written medium. Generally, oral communication provides opportunities for personal and spontaneous elements to mingle with the often mechanical-seeming processes of formal organizations.

Nonverbal Communication

Communication that takes place through expressions and gestures rather than words is known as *nonverbal communication*. Nonverbal communication may predate development of language. Animals express feelings for each other through expressions and gestures. Apes express affection by grooming each other. Wolves bare their teeth to express hostility. From a very early age, human infants express feelings through facial expressions such as smiles and frowns. It may be speculated that early human beings exchanged information largely through expressions and gestures.

Nonverbal communication retains a critical function in modern collectivities. Some information is most efficiently expressed trough nonverbal means. A hand-wave greeting saves many words. The smile or frown of a supervisor about to discuss a subordinate's work provides a succinct summary of his or her reception of the subordinate's efforts. People express disinterest in the comments of others by faking a yawn, closing their eyes, or letting their heads droop. One person nonverbally tells another to hurry up by repeatedly looking at his or her wristwatch.

Like other modes of information exchange, nonverbal communication has a particular function in formal organizations. Efficiency in some contexts has already been mentioned. Nonverbal communication has special value in exchanges of affective information. People often feel unwilling or unable to express feelings explicitly. Thus, many a college or office romance has begun with flirtatious expressions such as smiles and giggles. Natural inhibitions as well as the task-oriented and public setting of the office or schoolroom make nonverbal communication easier than verbal for many people.

Nonverbal communication is also well-suited for exchange of information that people have difficulty organizing into explicit thoughts. Half-formed thoughts may be impossible to express in words yet readily annunciated through gestures. These thoughts become the subject of nonverbal communication, as people express ideas and emotions to others of which they themselves are not entirely aware.

Body Language as Nonverbal Communication

A skilled observer can detect messages exchanged among people in both formal and informal collectivities through body movement and positioning. A popular book published in the 1970s by Julius Fast characterized this mode of information exchange as body language.

Body language is particularly well-suited for communicating emotional information. People feel more comfortable transmitting their feelings with nonverbal gestures than with words. The unconscious mind seems to play an important part in body language. People transmit information about feelings they are not aware they have. Others receive this information not as explicit information about the mental state of others, but as "intuition" about their feelings.

Fast gives several examples that illustrate the ways people in formal organizations use body language: [2]

- The listener leans back in his chair, arms and legs crossed, as he listens to the speaker's ideas. When the listener reaches a point where he disagrees with the speaker, he shifts his position in preparation for delivering his protest. He may lean forward and uncross his arms and legs. Perhaps he will raise one hand with the forefinger pointed as he begins to launch a rebuttal. When he is finished he will again lean back into his first position, arms and legs crossed—or perhaps into a third, more receptive position where his arms and legs are uncrossed as he leans back, signaling that he is open to suggestion.

- People group tightly together to keep others out. They turn away when they don't want to listen. People [sit] parallel to each other to symbolize an alliance against a third who may sit facing them. Also playing with a finger ring is a sign of nervousness, and swallowing while casting eyes down is a sign of guilt. Taking off glasses is sign of not wanting to see or be seen.

- The "big boss" will have a desk large enough to put him at [a] distance from his employees. He can also remain seated at this distance and look up at an employee without a loss of status. The entire man is presented for his view.

- A young man I know, well over six feet tall, was extremely successful in business because of his ability to show empathy for his associates. Observing him in action in some successful business transactions I became aware that whenever possible he stooped, sloped his body, or sat, in order to allow his associates to achieve dominance and feel superior.

According to Fast, modes of communication resemble "wavelengths" on radio and television bands. All modes of communication blend together in the delivery or receipt of messages. The communication spectrum includes "spoken language," "whatever else is transmitted on the vocal wavelength," "visual language including body language and self-imagery," and "tactile . . . which sometimes overlaps the visual but is really a more primitive and basic form of communication."

Symbolic Communication

Symbolic communication uses neither words nor gestures to transmit information. Rather, a person utilizing symbolic communication employs sequences of actions to tell others of his or her thoughts or desires. What economists refer to as "revealed preferences" illustrate the operation of symbolic communication. People give evidence of their preferences and desires through choices in the marketplace. The keeper of a grocery store across the street from a high school does not need to ask his teenage customers whether they prefer candy bars to carrots. Their buying behavior reveals this information. If asked, a few teenagers might say they prefer carrots, an instance of "expressed" preference. Such testimony would seem to provide less reliable information than preferences revealed at the cash register.

Organizations, too, evidence revealed preferences. In a work organization, employees obtain critical information through symbolic communication. An organization's leadership informs workers of what they value through symbolic means. A risk taker—the worker who spends time cultivating an unlikely client or a speculative invention, for example—receives praise and bonuses for success in some organizations. In other organizations, the risk-taking worker is criticized for wasting resources when he or she fails and receives no special rewards in the event of success.

Symbolic communication allows workers to assess their position and prospects in an organization. A junior executive who receives a series of high-visibility assignments and pay raises may safely infer that upper-level managers appreciate his or her capabilities. Another employee may notice that he or she receives no opportunities to represent the firm to outsiders and only modest pay raises. Senior managers do not consider the employee for higher-level openings and do not invite him or her to important meetings. "What are they trying to *tell* me?" the employee might ask.

Pay and promotion systems may be viewed as systems of symbolic communication. Observation of which personal characteristics and actions tend to be rewarded reveals information about the organization's values and goals. Employees are generally intense observers of each other's compensation and advancement. Many adjust their own actions accordingly.

Blockages to Interpersonal Communication

As noted at the beginning of this chapter, the configuration of roles and structure in an organization fundamentally determines the quality of communication and decision making. However, actual communication ultimately involves two people: a transmitter and a receiver. Quite apart from structure and roles, malfunctions at the level of *interpersonal* communication can cause problems in organizations. Interpersonal communication takes place when two individuals are communicating directly with each other: face-to-face, in writing, or via telephone. Edgar Schein[3] has identified the following blockages to interpersonal communication as among the most frequent:

- Lack of intersubjectivity (disconnection of affect)
- Ignorance about what other people think and value
- Lack of self-knowledge
- Culturally conditioned stereotyping

Lack of Intersubjectivity

Intersubjectivity denotes common affective feelings or factual perceptions by two or more individuals regarding a person, physical phenomenon, or social situation. As summarized in Chapter 2, people's basic patterns of emotional response tend to become established in early childhood. Throughout life, many people automatically respond positively to one type of person and negatively to another. Two individuals with different response patterns toward a third individual will have trouble communicating with each other about that individual.

Communication difficulties resulting from lack of intersubjectivity go beyond simple disagreements. People in an organization often disagree about whom to hire and whether to praise or criticize another's actions. Under normal conditions, people who disagree can express objective reasons for their differences. Such an exchange makes eventual agreement possible. People with fundamentally different response patterns toward types of individuals, though, are often unable to identify the source of their disagreement. They ignore each other's positions because their basic thinking has been determined by events and experiences that occurred long ago.

Lack of intersubjectivity can also arise from fundamental cognitive differences. Two scientists trained in different fields, for example, are likely to view proposed solutions to a problem differently. They may work under principles and assumptions so different that they have trouble giving each other's positions a fair hearing.

Ignorance About Others' Thoughts and Objectives

People often mistakenly assume that others have thoughts and objectives inimical to their own. False assumptions of this nature allow people to assume the worst about others. A scientist may find himself or herself omitted from a team performing research that would help him or her publish an important paper. He or she may assume that the personnel assigned to the team want to be the first to publish the work. In fact, the team members have no interest in publishing in this area, and would be quite willing to share their findings with him or her. Instead, the scientist breaks off communication with the team.

People who suffer disappointments in organizations—a pay raise or promotion not received, an office not granted—may assume that others desire to harm them. Backstabbing certainly occurs in modern organizations, but it is a rare event in most of them. People who assume that others desire to do them harm will be reluctant to transmit true and complete information to these others. People who assume others' ill will distort the messages they receive from them.

Lack of Self-Knowledge

People must know themselves and define their own goals before they can hope to be good communicators. This potential communication barrier has both an objective and a subjective dimension. Objectively, people cannot communicate well unless they have thought out their positions on an issue. According to Schein,[3] this principle applies particularly well to people in leadership positions of all kinds. He remarks:

> Leaders and managers especially must know where they are going and they must be able to articulate their own goals. Parents and spouses must make a valiant effort to lift to the surface what often is left implicit—their own life goals and targets—so that there can be genuine negotiation among family members in the different life stages.

On the subjective dimension, an individual's personality, communication style, or appearance may inhibit others from effectively exchanging information with him or her. A person with an authoritative tone of voice, for example, may give others the impression that he or she is judgmental or a poor listener. People need to build an understanding of how they are seen by others to understand and remedy such problems.

Stereotyping

Stereotyping—based on gender, ethnicity, or race—is one of the most widely discussed blockages to interpersonal communication today. Its visibility stems from liberation movements of the late 20th century that led the labor force to become significantly more diverse along gender, ethnic, and racial lines. Today, people encounter as peers many more individuals different from themselves than they did in earlier generations.

Still, many people today adhere to the gender, racial, and ethnic stereotypes held by their grandparents and great-grandparents. This may mean that people discount the value of information obtained from people of different gender or race and consider these individuals difficult to communicate with. People who discount the value of ethnic groups other than their own may not make sufficient effort to transmit information to them or to understand what they write or say.

Solutions to Interpersonal Communication Problems

Skilled managers are sensitive to the development of blockages to communication in their organizations or subunits. Several standard procedures are often used as remedies. In addition to these, everyone in an organization can benefit from developing personal skills to restart the flow of information where it has been blocked.

Retreats. Retreats are a classic method for promoting exchange of information among individuals experiencing blockages. Retreats may last half a day to several days. They almost always take place away from the organization's customary place of business. Ordinarily, issues to be confronted at a retreat are broken down into separate sessions. The individual's removal from immediate operational concerns and intense exposure to a restricted group of peers promotes communication.

Specialists known as *facilitators* are often brought in from outside the organization to aid focus on important issues and establishment of communication.

Training, encounter, or sensitivity groups. In another time-honored procedure, managers assemble small numbers of people in groups to help develop mutual understanding. Originally called "t-groups" ("t" for training), these procedures were in use as early as the 1950s. It is thought that the small group setting and the assurance that proceedings will be confidential lowers participants' inhibitions. According to the theory, these conditions allow group members to exchange honest impressions of each other. Participants in t-groups may learn about each other's technical capabilities, which may increase their motivation to initiate and receive communication. Participants may learn how others see them: perhaps as threatening or personally distant or cold. People who learn that they strike others as threatening or distant may take steps to reduce resulting barriers to communication.

Diversity training. A near-universal presence in today's large formal organizations, diversity training aims at familiarizing people with each other's backgrounds and cultures. People of different genders, cultures, and races often have quite different life experiences. Individuals of different backgrounds often use different vocabularies. They may interpret the same event or behavior in an entirely different manner. Diversity training aims at fostering *cultural competence,* that is, an understanding of the life experiences, challenges, and beliefs common among different genders, ethnicities, and races. Diversity training reduces barriers to communication that arise from stereotyping. Accurate knowledge about others makes it difficult to see them as stereotypes.

Reformulation of roles. In response to communication problems, managers may choose to revise role relationships rather than train or reorient individuals. Under this strategy, managers identify individuals in a team who are skilled at communication, enjoy good working relationships with others, or both. These individuals are then assigned to central communication roles. As neutral third parties, these individuals facilitate the flow of information between peers who have difficulty establishing intersubjectivity. Individuals in these "communicator" roles may communicate back and forth with their peers or compile information for supervisors. Alternatively, communicators may become decision makers themselves.

Personal Repair Strategies

Retreats, encounter groups, and trainings represent management-initiated procedures for overcoming barriers to interpersonal communication. There is no substitute, of course, for individual initiatives in this area. Communication blockages can reduce an individual's productivity and damage his or her career prospects. Many remedial procedures are available to individuals. Some examples include the following:

Take the role of the other. Taking the role of the other means to imagine oneself facing another person's responsibilities, challenges, and role set. Achieving empathy in this way promotes an understanding of the other person's concerns and priorities. Information couched in terms of a person's priorities and concerns will attract his or her attention more readily than abstract issues of policy or productivity.

Identify intermediaries. Not all individuals are capable of establishing or maintaining communication with each other. People often have emotional reactions to each other that make smooth communication impossible. The sources of these reactions may be too deep to be readily addressed by training or counseling. On a more operational level, the person with whom one needs to communicate may simply be too busy to answer his or her calls or e-mails. In such instances, people should locate other personnel in the communication target's unit who can provide required information or talk directly with him or her when necessary.

Designate others as communicators. Many people lack skill as communicators to a degree that training cannot completely remedy. Many others are simply disinclined to communicate as a matter of personality or personal taste. These individuals may still be valuable members of an organizational team. People whose best skills do not include communication should identify others who can supplement their own capabilities in this area. An executive with skills in financial or technical areas, for example, may prefer to spend his or her time on such matters, delegating communication tasks to an assistant.

Negotiation: A Special Type of Communication

Much interpersonal communication takes place in a manner determined by the unique characteristics of the communicators. But interpersonal communication also occurs in definite patterns reproduced in all collectivities and organizations. One such pattern is known as *negotiation*. Negotiation merits special attention. This communication process performs a necessary function in defining the received roles of individuals. Negotiation has a broader function as well, affecting the strategies, prospects, and accomplishments of formal organizations.

What Is Negotiation?

The subject of negotiation appears in Chapter 4 in reference to the content of individual roles, describing this process as bargaining. This is the term's most common usage. Chapter 4 also characterizes negotiation as a process in which two individuals communicate to each other about what each is willing to do to help achieve a mutual objective. Negotiation in a broader sense serves as a means by which two individuals (or collectivities) communicate about their desires, expectations, and beliefs.

Most people think of negotiation as dickering over price. Nearly everyone who has purchased houses, cars, or goods in Mexican open-air markets has engaged in such haggling. Both parties to such negotiation share the objective of seeing the transaction take place. Negotiations cease if either party lacks sufficient motivation to reach this objective. The seller refuses to budge from his initial price and the potential buyer walks away.

Negotiation over nonmonetary matters involves the same back-and-forth communication process. The worker verbally states (or symbolically signals) a desire for a greater or reduced scope of responsibility to his or her supervisor. The parents of a teenager stipulate the he or she must return home by 10:00 p.m. The youth proposes a later hour. Each individual states what he or she wants or is willing to give. Successful negotiations end when the two parties conceive an exchange or state of affairs acceptable to both.

The process of negotiation may be restrained and sophisticated as it often is among art dealers, noisy and demonstrative as it is among floor traders on commodity exchanges, or loud and emotional as it frequently becomes between parents and children. Many societies have developed rules and rituals to ensure that negotiation takes place in an orderly, peaceable manner. Traders on the New York Stock Exchange do not negotiate directly with each other but through intermediaries known as "specialists." Members of traditional societies accompanied negotiation with days of feasting and drinking before allowing a final bargain to be struck. The resulting camaraderie blunts potential ill feelings associated with regret by one or both partners over the final deal. The modern United Nations (UN) functions as a vast stage for ritual negotiation. The pomp and prestige of the UN allow representatives of world powers to more easily exchange offers without losing face.

Functions of Negotiation

Negotiation has both manifest and latent functions. As explained in Chapter 4, manifest functions are visible and explicitly recognized. On the level of manifest functions, negotiation constitutes a means by which two parties successively approximate a position on which both might agree.

Negotiation has several functions that are latent—invisible, ignored, or not fully acknowledged or understood by participants. Other than the manifest, stepwise process of reaching agreement, negotiation allows one or both partners to express affect. The teenager described above may not succeed in convincing his or her parents to relax their 10:00 p.m. stipulation. But the teenager obtains affective satisfaction by asserting his or her maturity and right to independence. Negotiation serves a latent function for the worker attempting to extend his or her scope of responsibility. The process enables the worker to assert his or her desires and claim his or her worth. Agreement may result from neither the teenager's nor the worker's effort at negotiation. But the transmission of affective information that takes place in the negotiation process allows conflicts to be aired and tension to be reduced.

Negotiation also enables two parties to obtain information initially unknown to either. Labor disputes provide examples. Often, neither union officials nor managers possess full information about important matters in the beginning phases of contract negotiation. Neither labor nor management, for example, may know how long workers are willing to strike. This can be learned only through experience as negotiations continue without resolution. Many extended strikes could doubtlessly have been avoided if managers had had advance information about the workers' resolve. Many strikes could be avoided if workers initially knew what their time was truly worth to management. Often, workers and managers must discover this information in the course of negotiation.

The objective of negotiation can be thought of as achieving a state of equilibrium between the two sides involved. Negotiated equilibrium is reached when both sides have achieved their minimum objectives and neither has further incentive to change its position. Further gains by either side would risk reducing the value placed by the other on the deal and hence its likelihood of acceptance or durability. When both sides place equal value on a given issue—for example, salary—equilibrium requires "splitting the difference" between the minimally acceptable demands of each.

Mathematical principles have been derived to predict possible points of agreement along individual and multiple dimensions in a dispute.[4] In reality, resolution requires a process of repeated offers and responses. This process allows both sides to determine the value the other places on a given dimension (e.g., salary or benefits) and what the other side's minimal terms may be. This process requires skilled listening and development of alternative offers. Effective labor negotiators may offer "sweeteners," benefits of limited concrete value (such as free health club memberships), to promote acceptability of a marginal deal.

Negotiation Pathologies

Clearly, negotiation is part of the natural process of communication both within and between organizations. Skillful, efficient negotiation benefits both individuals and the collectivity. But pathologies often occur in the process. These glitches may arise from lack of skill by negotiators or unfavorable conditions in the organization or environment. Negotiation experts Roger Fisher and William Ury[5] have described several of these.

Positional bargaining obstructs the negotiation process. Under positional bargaining, each side places strong emphasis on a particular position, such as price. Negotiation focuses on arguing for or against the position. Like other modes of negotiation, positional bargaining occurs in step-by-step fashion. People abandon one position and adopt another. In traditional price negotiation, for example, the seller demands $5,000 for a used car and justifies the demand on the basis of the vehicle's blue book value. The purchaser offers $3,000, arguing that the car has several dents. The seller counters with an offer of $4,000, and the process continues until agreement is reached or one or both parties withdraw.

This process often produces agreement. Positional bargaining, though, involves risk and anxiety. Even if the process begins in a collegial atmosphere it tends to take on the characteristics of a competitive game. Agreement often comes after each side has grudgingly conceded a succession of positions. A hostile atmosphere may develop lasting far beyond the day when agreement is reached.

Positional bargaining may be appropriate for arriving at a single agreement, such as a onetime salary increase. It may be sufficient for negotiation between strangers, whose continued relationship is not important. But its potential for failure makes it inappropriate for negotiations among people who are required to work together. The ability of positional bargaining to damage vital, working relationships also suggests the limited usefulness of this technique.

Positional bargaining cannot be relied upon in situations where ultimate agreement is mandatory. Consider two countries on the brink of war. One issues an ultimatum. Predictably, the other refuses. Negotiations cease; armies march; both nations are devastated and impoverished.

Soft bargaining may also be viewed as negotiation pathology. The soft bargainer values human relationships over positions. He or she does as much as possible to meet the opposite side's demands. Soft bargaining may feel more comfortable. But it can ultimately lead to harm. The soft bargainer may make agreements that prove too expensive in monetary or nonmonetary terms. Despite such concessions, soft bargaining may damage continuing relationships. Conditioned to expect favors, the recipient of concessions may become demanding and exploitative. Disappointment and frustration appear in all quarters, and relationships collapse.

Factual and Affective Negotiation

As the preceding paragraphs suggest, objective and factual negotiation results in an agreement more often than emotional display. Professional negotiators operate under this principle. But occasionally, affective communication is desirable or necessary.

Projecting a feeling of confidence across a negotiation table can make one's opponent think twice about making excessive demands. Negotiators have been known to use aggressive language or even adopt threatening postures, distracting opponents with a transient fear that they may be beaten up. Occasionally, affective communication of this kind can lead to a successful strategy of "winning through intimidation."

Professional negotiators, though, most often employ affective communication to satisfy the needs of their clients. A professional employed by a teacher's union told how he would bang his fist on the table, deliver long lists of demands, and engage in flowery elocution at the opening of contract negotiation. This behavior, he explained, was intended to make the union officials in attendance feel well-championed. As the day wore on and the union reps departed, the negotiator abandoned his rhetoric and concentrated on objective comparison of positions.

A professional negotiator can usually recognize when his or her counterpart across the table is grandstanding. Professionals recognize that this is sometimes necessary to please clients. A labor negotiator told of using coded language to allow management representatives to distinguish which of the positions he was stating should be taken seriously.

Organizational Structure and Communication

Structure determines the form and content of most information exchange in organizations. A skilled individual can negotiate his or her role expectations and occasionally affect structure. Such impact, though, is rare. Typically, negotiation over a role affects only the focal person, his or her immediate supervisor, subordinates, and peers. Informal and spontaneous, face-to-face communication occurs in formal organizations as it does in all collectivities. But structure itself determines the individual's opportunity to engage in communication of this kind.

The provisions of each organizational role include instructions regarding whom a person may communicate with, the conditions under which communication may take place, and the type of information that he or she may exchange. A preceding section has described the effects of hierarchy—only one dimension of structure—on communication patterns. Structure creates and reinforces the flow of information according to prescribed patterns. Information transactions of course take place outside these patterns. But like sparking and errant magnetic fields in electrical circuitry, these are unintentional and potentially destructive to the system's purpose.

Three features of organizations promote the flow of information according to stable, predictable patterns. These include

- Defined information pathways
- Information coding
- Specialized communication roles

Defined Information Pathways

Defined information pathways refer to *channels* and *circuits* that guide the flow of information in an organization. Flow of information may take place in a single direction, as when a senior officer issues a command to a subordinate who, in turn, issues a command to a soldier. Information may be exchanged in a *recursive* (back-and-forth) fashion, as it is among physicians in different specialties deciding what to do about a case. A single individual may transmit information to numerous others through written memos and circulars, electronic listservs, and broadcasts via intercom, radio, television, Web site, podcast, or bullhorn. A single person receives information from numerous others. All organizations develop mechanisms that encourage selective exchange of information.

Communication channels and circuits in an organization reflect its structure. The organization uses core resources—imperative force, culture, rewards and punishment—to encourage role incumbents to communicate according to defined patterns. Few organizations of significant size allow communication to take place via spontaneously created chains.

Deliberate patterning of information flow is an essential feature of formal organization. Selective channeling is necessary for ensuring that all members have the volume and type of information they need to fulfill their role expectations. Restricting information exchange is also essential. Excess information for any role incumbent may prove confusing or distracting. Providing unnecessary information to any role incumbent raises the likelihood that someone will leak important facts to a business competitor, dishonest outsider, or political or military opponent. Organizations develop restrictive information pathways to reduce risk of internal chaos and external challenge.

Information Channels

Information channels are linkages that enable individuals or subunits within an organization to exchange information with other individuals or subunits. Concretely, these linkages have two components: (1) media and (2) social access.

Media are the physical resources and mechanisms required to transmit and receive information. Use of media begins with the transmitter (an individual or subunit) transforming thoughts or observations into a signal. The process concludes with a receiver (also an individual or subunit) transforming the signal back into recognizable words, numbers, feelings, and sensations. Spoken communication constitutes the most elementary of media, requiring only the capabilities of speech and hearing. Media include degrees of technical development ranging from paper-and-pencil notes through microwave signal transmission via satellite.

In an organization, the "terminals" associated with media linkages are their most important feature. Only individuals or subunits connectable by shared media have a channel through which information can flow. Two operatives in an industrial plant cannot be said to have a channel of communication if they cannot understand each other's words over the din of machinery. Every civil servant may have the liberty to write to the chief executive of the governmental unit for which he or she works. But the medium used by the official does not constitute a communication channel if his or her letters never physically reach the executive's desk.

Social access to channels refers to the individual's right to utilize existing media resources. This form of access is ultimately more important than the physical presence of a medium. It is not an accident that dictatorships take pains to prevent ordinary citizens from using the press, radio, and television to express their ideas. These resources have physical capacity to transmit messages among vast numbers of people. However, the entrenched leadership mandates that print and broadcast media be used only for its benefit.

Restriction of social access to media necessarily occurs in formal organizations. The leadership controls access to *house organs,* company newsletters and newspapers. Workers seldom come close enough to top managers to transmit verbal messages. A middle manager whose telephone calls never get through to his or her department head (due perhaps to screening by an assistant) cannot be said to have a channel to this individual.

Communication channels differ according to directions in which they allow information to flow. An important feature of communication channels is the degree of *symmetry* they create between the roles at either end of the linkage. Symmetrical communication takes place when roles at each end of the channel receive and transmit the same volume of information. Asymmetrical communication channels permit most messages to originate at only one end of the linkage.

The most familiar of asymmetrical channels are found in strictly hierarchical organizations. Here, channels are not only asymmetrical but *vertical.* Vertical channels link two individuals who are clearly in a superior-subordinate relationship. Asymmetrical communication channels that are lateral exist as well, as in the relationship between the workers at the counter and the grill in a fast-food joint.

The counter-person transmits orders from customers —"double cheeseburger!" "order of fries!"—and the grill worker simply hands the product up front. The counter-person and the grill worker occupy approximately the same level in the organizational hierarchy.

Information Circuits

If information channels constitute links in a communication chain, an information circuit (or loop) is the chain itself. Communication circuits connect multiple individuals or subunits. The configuration of an information circuit expresses which individuals are linked by direct channels and which are not. Communication takes place among all individuals in a circuit. Anyone truly isolated from the information flow cannot be considered to be within the circuit, and, as a widely used expression goes, is "out of the loop." People not linked by direct channels exchange information only through others.

Observers of organizations have described information circuits of distinct sizes and shapes (see Figure 10.1). These circuits reproduce the basic structure of the organization or specific subunits. The simplest circuits comprise direct lines of vertical, often asymmetric communication. In these, an operative can communicate only with his or her superior, a middle manager only with incumbents of roles directly below or above his, and so on. Vertical, asymmetrical channels make up circuits of this kind. Such circuits reflect the hierarchical structures shown in most organizational charts.

Three other examples of information circuits are illustrated in Figure 10.1: the "Y," the "wheel," and the "open channel." In the "Y" information circuit, most channels are vertical and asymmetric. At the very top, however, there are two roles (or subunits) that are at the same organizational level. Each may initiate communication with the same subordinate role, which then transmits information down the line. The Y circuit can be seen in a "two-headed" hierarchy, characteristic of organizations with two bosses or governing bodies.

The "wheel" information circuit transmits information from the roles at the ends of its "spokes" to a central role at the "hub." Individuals at the ends of the spokes do not communicate directly with each other. All channels flow to the center. Circuits of this kind may characterize a small business or specialized subunit in a large organization. Roles at the spokes may take care of specialized, technical operations necessary for achievement of the organization's objectives. Only the boss or department head may have the technical capability to understand what each role incumbent is doing. Alternatively, several subunits with specialized product lines or territories may report to a central office. Information flow in this configuration characterized the "division" structure adopted by large corporations in the mid-20th century.

The "open-channel" circuit consists of a set of symmetrical communication channels. It links all roles with each other. The open-channel circuit allows everyone to communicate with everyone else. This type of circuit is most often found in professional working groups and organizations with only a few levels of supervision. It also characterizes relatively young organizations, in which structure is still flexible and open to change.

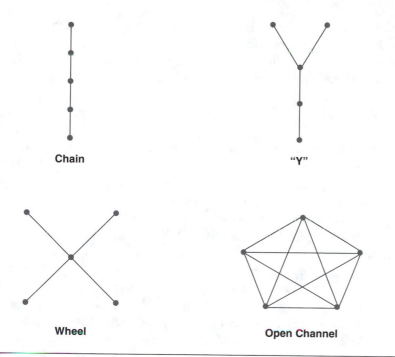

Figure 10.1   Illustration of Communication Channels

Throughout the 20th century, psychologists conducted experiments to determine which type of information circuit works best. To study information circuits,
these scientists arranged desks in their laboratories separated by movable barriers.
They recruited experimental subjects, often college undergraduates, placed them
at the desks, and assigned them simple tasks. Barriers between the desks were
arranged differently for successive groups of subjects, re-creating circuits of different forms by allowing communication between some individuals and preventing
it between others. Late in the century, computer terminals linked to each other in a
selective manner were substituted for the movable barriers.

The efficiency with which subjects completed assigned tasks was monitored.
Comparisons were made between levels of efficiency for each type of circuit.
Generally, the psychologists found that circuits containing few linkages produced
more efficiency of communication than circuits with many linkages. Facts were
transmitted more rapidly and with fewer errors in hierarchical chains and wheel
circuits than in open-channel arrangements. But the efficiency of task completion
presented a more complicated picture. Circuits with few linkages (amounting to
many restrictions in communication) tended to work better for simple tasks.[6]
Circuits with many linkages worked better when the assigned tasks were complex.[7,8]

Factors other than the simplicity versus complexity of a task bear on the appropriateness of information pathways. The research of Nasralla focused on the types
of individuals involved in task performance, their workload, and the speed required
for task completion. Levitt and Glynn assessed the value of imposing structural
limitations on communication among individuals in various work situations. They

found that such structure was beneficial to efficiency when any of these conditions existed: people with many different skill types were present; some individuals had high levels of skill and some low; people with different skills needed to collaborate; the workload was high; or work needed to be done rapidly.[9]

Defined Information Pathways and Informal Processes

Strictly speaking, defined information pathways exist not only in formal organizations. They are observable in most human collectivities. In many informal groups, at least some people lack a direct channel of communication to one or more people with whom they wish to communicate. People may need to borrow a cell phone, work through an intermediary, or sweet-talk a secretary to establish contact with the communication target. Most groups have informal communication specialists, distinguished by curiosity, sociability, and articulateness. The discussion in Chapter 9 of "network leadership" in a medical community illustrates this phenomenon. All informal groups have some vocabulary recognizable only to members.

In formal organizations, though, information channels are explicitly designated to exist between specific roles rather than people. Communication specialists have definite job descriptions. Specialized language and nomenclature are defined and codified in circulars, manuals, and officially recognized texts. Through these mechanisms, defined information pathways in organizations attain the explicitness and stability that characterizes the organizational structures that they reflect. As with structure itself in a well-functioning organization, defined information pathways promote cohesion and coordination in support of shared objectives. All things being equal, organizations discourage communication outside established channels.

Information Coding

Transforming messages into forms appropriate for different subunits and roles is known as *encoding*. This process helps maintain the defined patterns of information exchange described above. Encoding has an instrumental function, helping make information understandable and useful to people in different parts of the organization. Encoding also has an affective function, promoting favorable emotional reception of messages. Like defined patterns of communication based on channels and circuits, encoding reflects organizational structure. Encoding contributes to the organization's effectiveness and stability by fitting messages to the needs of the organization's diverse units and individuals.

Encoding takes place in three ways:

1. Reducing information scope

2. Specifying technical focus

3. Managing conflict and affect

1. Reducing information scope. Encoding, first, involves revising the scope of messages as they pass among levels of an organization or across subunits.

Communication upward or downward along a hierarchy, for example, requires revision in the scope of messages. An executive with organization-wide responsibilities must develop messages specifying actions required of his or her subordinates. The executive has the responsibility for developing a broad, balanced view. The department head requires only a piece of this picture to grasp the nature of his or her objectives. The salesman or -woman may benefit from general understanding about the firm's challenges but requires specific information only about the products to emphasize and the territory to cover.

Reducing the scope of information concentrates the attention of role incumbents on their required functions. Excessive information requires additional time for processing and comprehension. Too much information leads to confusion, as channels become overloaded and essential items ignored.

2. *Specifying technical focus.* Language or other images in the information channels must be made consistent with the recipient's technical training, background, and expectations. Individuals and subunits in modern organizations are often highly specialized. People in different parts of the organization communicate and size up problems according to technical training received inside or outside the organization. Encoding for technical purposes requires either translation of ordinary speech into technical language or translation of the language of one specialty into that of another.

Examples are easiest to observe in familiar technical specialties such as law, engineering, and medicine. Members of a manufacturing firm's legal department cannot always see the board of directors' concerns from a broad business perspective. Legal training predisposes them to think in terms of contract modifications, liability, torts, and other applications of the law. Employees in an engineering unit see the firm's challenges in terms of tolerances, strength of materials, and machine design. Top executives need to have their objectives and concerns coded into messages compatible with the training and language used by these technical specialists.

Organizations in the health service industry face multiple coding requirements. In a hospital, for example, a physician sees an acutely ill patient in an emergency room. The doctor records the patient's complaints in a medical record and admits him or her to the wards. The information so recorded is not clearly meaningful to managers without medical training. For these managers, medical information is often recoded into categories and symbols meaningful in financial terms. In the late 20th century, a system known as Diagnostic Related Groups (DRGs) was developed in part for this purpose. The DRG system automatically translates information meaningful to physicians into messages regarding the hospital's financial receivables.

Encoding can be observed literally in some subunits and organizations. Police officers use codes in radio communications as references to law used for apprehension and booking. Agencies doing classified work often communicate, literally, in codes.

Encoding reflects not only technical specialization but also the cultures of technical specialties and subunits. Nontechnical encoding is visible in the jargon and in-jokes observable in work groups everywhere. Private detectives, journalists, and soldiers at war are said to converse in language laced with obscenities, reflective of the isolation and danger inherent in their occupations.

3. *Managing context and affect.* As noted earlier, information is contextual and affective as well as factual. Organizational units do not always circulate purely factual information. Along with factual information, leaders often provide context. They may wish subordinates to view the facts in the light of broader tasks and issues. The general may seek to inspire his troops by pointing out the pivotal importance of an upcoming battle. The principal researcher may encourage his or her subordinates by announcing that the recipient of the Nobel Prize will be determined in the next six months.

Organizations often encode information to soften the affective impact of unfavorable facts. Instances of fiscal distress and plans for dismissing personnel provide familiar examples. Management announces such moves not as firings, dismissals, or layoffs but as "reductions in force, downsizing, and reengineering." Those retained are assured that the company will be "leaner, meaner, and more competitive." Skeptics may interpret such language as an encoded message that those not laid off will need to cover not only their former responsibilities but those of the individuals who were let go.

Generally, encoding of information promotes stable, reliable patterns of communication that reflect and reinforce organizational structure. Reduction in the scope of messages as they pass down a hierarchy decreases the risk that subordinates will second-guess managers regarding strategies and objectives. Encoding into specialized language promotes comprehension within subunits and discourages the development of informal networks across departmental lines. Presentation of information in euphemisms and favorable contexts promotes feelings of comfort with the organization, belief in the legitimacy of management, and acceptance of management decisions. Encoding for affective purposes reduces cross-talk in the ranks, a potentially disruptive process as information channels become overburdened.

Coding Corporate Crises

Encoding takes place not only within organizations but also across organizational boundaries. The *Wall Street Journal* has documented ways in which business organizations tailor messages to soften the impact of unfavorable developments.[10] "Faced with announcing downbeat news," the *Journal* reports, "companies . . . retreat behind a screen of euphemisms rather than bluntly admit that they've fouled up."

Examples included the following:

- *Nutrition-supplement company Herbalife International, Inc.* The firm paid $850,000 to settle charges that it made false claims in promoting its nutritional and weight-loss products. Herbalife also agreed to rescind claims made for several of these products. Triumphantly, though, the company proclaimed:

Today represents a milestone for Herbalife—a solid foundation that is built on the confidence given to us today by statements issued by state and federal regulatory agencies . . . [The agencies] have independently determined that Herbalife products have been and are safe for the American public. Furthermore, all of our product claims, labeling, and marketing materials are now in conformance with the spirit and letter of both federal and state law.

- *The First National Bank of Boston.* The bank pleaded guilty to a criminal charge of "knowingly and willfully" failing to report cash transfers as legally required. The transfers involved over a thousand transactions and totaled $1.22 billion. The bank paid a $500,000 fine. Company officials brushed off the violation, explaining their malfeasance as "systems failure" and an "internal glitch."

Specialized Communication Roles

Every role includes expectations regarding whom the incumbent can communicate with and under what conditions communication may take place. Organizations, though, also develop roles specifically designed to regulate and facilitate information exchange among other roles. Occupants of some of these specialized communication roles act as informational traffic cops, ensuring that communication takes place through the defined pathways established by the organization. Other communication specialists have the function of promoting rather than restricting information exchange. Incumbents of still other roles mediate information exchange across the organization's boundaries: with outside individuals, other organizations, or the general public.

Internal communications specialists. Internal communications specialists include individuals whose roles focus on regulating the flow of information within organizations. These roles include two opposite types: *gatekeepers* and *boundary-spanners.* Gatekeepers enforce official restrictions on communication. Boundary-spanners either encourage others to communicate outside customary channels and networks or transmit information between individuals and between subunits not normally in direct contact.

Gatekeepers. Gatekeepers do what their name implies: regulate the flow of communication to executives and other key decision makers. The most visible gatekeeper role is that of the executive secretary. Occupants of this role screen telephone calls, e-mails, and visitors. They may answer the boss's mail and keep his or her calendar. Though not necessarily a member of management, the executive secretary exercises significant power over information flow in an organization. He or she often has significant discretion over whom the boss sees.

Other gatekeepers are themselves executives empowered to regulate access to the top decision makers. Some of the best examples of executive gatekeepers were observable in the administrations of U.S. presidents Nixon, Reagan, and Clinton. In the Nixon and Reagan administrations (1969–1974 and 1981–1989, respectively), individuals with the title "chief of staff" played important gatekeeper roles. T. R. Haldeman, a key official in the Nixon administration, was reputed to wield enormous power due to his "absolute control over both the people and the paper that reached the President's inner office."[11] Donald T. Regan played a similar role in the Reagan White House.[12] Haldeman and Regan enjoyed significant public visibility in their day, due to scandals in which they may have been involved.

The Clinton administration had no figure of similar public notoriety. In the mid-1990s, though, gatekeepers became visible in the administration's attempt to develop a plan to reform health care in the United States. The administration assembled hundreds of technical experts in Washington, DC, and assigned teams responsibilities in specific policy areas. A hierarchy of gatekeepers was developed to filter passage of reports and ideas to the key administration officials charged with developing legislation.[13]

Large organizations depend heavily on gatekeepers to ensure that information normally flows along predetermined pathways. Gatekeepers exercise the function of reducing traffic in information channels to decision makers. They reduce criss-crossing communication between operatives in some units and managers of other units. An absence of gatekeepers would result in chaos in a complex organization.

Boundary-spanners. In contrast to gatekeepers, boundary-spanners facilitate communication, principally among parties not normally in contact. Boundary-spanners include facilitators of group training sessions, liaison personnel, and managers required to draw their teams from among members of several different departments (which is sometimes called *matrix management*). Many people with titles such as affirmative action officer or race-relations manager are boundary-spanners, facilitating communication among people of different races.

Boundary-spanning roles are often created to ensure that important subgroups have a voice in high-level decision making. Hospitals in the United States provide an important example. Most hospitals in the United States are nonprofit organizations governed by trustees who are not medical doctors. Physicians who admit patients to these hospitals are usually independent practitioners rather than employees. Hospitals, though, owe most of their income to these physicians, who admit patients to the wards. Thus, physicians represent an important and independent interest group within the hospital. Traditionally, they have elected a person holding the title "president of the medical staff" to represent them on the board.

Development of corporate medicine and large-scale health care systems has given rise to significant changes in U.S. health care. More physicians today have strong contractual ties with their hospitals and health plans, reducing their independence. Still, nonmedical management staff cannot exercise authority over physicians or employ their technical vocabulary. New boundary-spanners have evolved to carry out required communication between management and the medical staff. Occupants of these roles often have the title "vice president for medical affairs." Unlike the traditional medical staff president, the vice president for medical affairs speaks for management. He or she does not represent the medical staff to the board; rather, the vice president for medical affairs transmits the board's concerns and directives to the doctors.

Boundary-spanners may specialize in transmitting information throughout the organization rather than to individual role incumbents or subunits. These boundary-spanning roles include editors of a company newspaper or club newsletter. Boundary-spanners also collect information from the lower ranks and conduct it upward. Many such roles are visible across the spectrum of formal organizations, including troubleshooters in businesses, precinct captains in political parties, ombudsmen in hospitals and universities, and trustees in prisons.

Boundary-spanners are as important as gatekeepers in maintaining a reliable flow of information along predetermined pathways. Boundary-spanners provide a limited number of open doors in a social system where most channels are closed. An organization without boundary-spanners would fall prey to error or paralysis as people not connected by direct channels failed to obtain information from each other at crucial times. Absence of boundary-spanners would also lead to tension and discontent. Occasionally, people need someone outside their normal communication loop to whom to complain or from whom to seek redress. Without identifiable boundary-spanners, people would seek to establish new channels, threatening the organization's structural integrity.

External communication specialists. External communication specialists transmit information across an organization's boundaries. They formulate and deliver messages to outsiders. They solicit and receive messages from the outside, in turn relaying them to peers and superiors. Organizations that are highly dependent on their environment for resources or fear adverse actions from outside require significant work by contact people.

People in these roles have job titles such as general counsel (the head of an organization's legal department), legislative representative (better known as "lobbyist"), public relations specialist, and press or public relations representative. Holders of these positions attempt to create a pubic image for the organization. They work with legislators to enact laws favorable to the organization and block measures detrimental to its interests. They negotiate with legal authorities and potential opponents in court to terminate disputes.

Among the most important of an organization's contact people are its salesmen and -women. Sales roles include positions as diverse as director of marketing, broker on a trading floor, door-to-door salesperson, and telemarketer. Salespeople try to project a favorable image of the organization's products. They assess market conditions. They play a liaison role with customers by managing their relationships with the organization, fielding complaints and offering special deals. Equivalent personnel in public agencies are classroom teachers and social workers, who express their parent agency's desired image and report on the attitudes and concerns of clients.

Less visible among contact people are covert operations personnel in government agencies and private firms. These include undercover police officers and spies employed by the Federal Bureau of Investigation (FBI) and Central Intelligence Agency (CIA). In a process known as industrial espionage, private firms assign personnel to find out about a competitor's costs, suppliers, forthcoming products, and trade secrets.

Structure, Communication, and Organizational Challenges

Organizational structure determines dominant communication patterns in formal organizations. Structure, in turn, can be recognized by observing communication patterns. Defined information pathways reflect patterns of social relationships. Structural features of organizations are maintained and reinforced by authority, rewards, and culture. Defined information pathways are maintained and reinforced by the process of information encoding and specialized communication roles.

As noted in Chapter 5, an organization's history and tasks help shape its structure. The need to survive in its environment and make required technology work represent key challenges to organizations. Consequences are visible in the communication circuits that predominate in different organizations. Organizations engaged in straightforward, simple tasks function well with circuits routing information to (and receiving it from) a centrally placed individual. Organizations engaged in complex or creative tasks work best with circuits linking each individual to all others.

Environment influences the predominance of specific information-related roles. Organizations whose fortunes depend on the perceptions of the public and the availability of outside resources make extensive use of external communication specialists. Examples include electrical utilities. Prices charged by these firms have traditionally depended on actions by government regulators. Consequently, utilities have employed staffs of government representatives. It is to be expected that utilities will expend fewer resources on these functions as regulation becomes less important to them.

It is important not to overemphasize the significance of formal structure in organizational communication. Formal structure may be the key determinant of organization-wide communication pathways. But a good deal of local communication takes place through more spontaneous means. Executives over martinis or on the golf course, as well as workers across cubicle partitions and around water coolers, participate in communication pathways outside the control of formal structure.,The primary groups and networks of informal ties that form in all organizations constitute communication pathways alternative to official channels. The presence of informal communication pathways explains the frequency with which privileged information becomes common knowledge within organizations and top secret information is "leaked" to outsiders.

A great many leadership functions involve dimensions of communication not determined by organizational structure. Network leadership, described in Chapter 9, provides one illustration. The "leadership" exercised by executive secretaries and other personnel at communication nexuses stems from accident of position rather than formal authority. Individuals with formal leadership authority enhance their ability to lead by sharing privileged information with subordinates. When skillfully done, such sharing promotes interpersonal bonding and, via the norm of reciprocity, extra motivation in the subordinate. Key executive functions, such as maintaining internal lines of communication and making connections across subunit and organizational boundaries, reflect the degree to which communications may be less standardized and more fragile than an organizational chart might suggest.

Information and Decision Making

In organizations, information and the system governing its transmission support many routine functions. But information achieves special significance when managers and executives use it to make decisions. Decisions involve *selection among available courses of action.* Often, the quality of decision making depends on the executive's use of information or the quality of information available to him or her. Poor decision making signals possible problems with the organization's communication system: the pathways, practices, and personnel involved in information exchange.

Two factors tend to determine the amount and kind of information decision makers seek and utilize. These are

1. The criteria that serve as bases for decision making

2. The processes by which alternatives are selected

High-quality information helps managers make good decisions but does not determine how well decisions are made. Some highly important roles require their occupants to make good decisions in an information-poor environment. Decision makers such as doctors, airline pilots, and traders on the floors of securities exchanges cannot count on immediate availability of complete, high-quality information. The ability to make good decisions in the absence of complete, high-quality information is a test of managerial and professional skill.

Skilled executives, in turn, recognize the importance of high-quality information and the factors that promote the availability of this resource. Decision makers need to sift through the messages they receive, assessing accuracy and relevance. A manager who emphasizes factual information in his or her decision making pays close attention to the quality of the organization's communication system.

Organizational decision makers, on the other hand, do not always make the best use of the information available to them. Executives utilize different criteria and processes to make decisions. It is not unusual for decision makers to ignore glaring facts.

Criteria for Decision Making

Researchers have devoted considerable attention to the criteria that managers and executives use to make decisions. It would seem natural for decision makers simply to systematically apply factual information from their subordinates as the basis for selecting alternatives. Researchers have documented that "rational" processes of this kind predominate in some organizations. But other observers argue that systematic analysis of facts seldom forms the basis for decision making in actual organizations.

Decisions as rational choice. As Chapter 7 notes, rational behavior denotes the deliberate arrangement of human and material resources in a manner likely to achieve a specific objective. Industrial engineering and the construction of legal codes are rational processes. People working in a rational manner objectively evaluate components of a broader whole, such as single parts in a machine or individual laws in a legal code. Then, they build systems in which these components fit together reliably and efficiently. The rational process requires focus on concrete objectives and employs logic, scientific theories, and objective information.

Rationally oriented decision makers evaluate alternatives on the basis of how well their choices will advance their organization's objectives. The executive's personal objectives, it is assumed, promote those of the organization. Ideally, business executives strive to achieve profits because their compensation increases when they are successful. Members of Congress strive to meet their constituents' needs because they want to be reelected.

Decision making on a rational basis places great emphasis on high-quality information. Business executives scrutinize production costs and profit margins. Elected officials commission polls. Tools of rational decision making in the modern world increasingly include mathematical processing of information.

Some researchers believe that rational decision making is most likely to take place when mistakes can be costly. The employment of statisticians and applied mathematicians by Wall Street firms illustrates this interpretation. Even slight miscalculations of stock values and interest rates may cause banks and brokerage houses to lose billions of dollars.

Nonrational decision making. Despite the value of rationality and logic, many decision makers clearly carry out their tasks under a different orientation. Observers of human decision making have commented that people often decide among options without convincing themselves that they will obtain personal benefits. Although millions of people in the United States vote every year, few believe that the candidate they select will help them personally. Fewer believe that their individual vote will swing the election. Emotions play a role in all human deliberations.

Within organizations, many decisions are made in the absence of rational choice. Many more are made in which rational choice plays a strictly limited role. Pioneer organization observers Cyert and March documented processes that executives use instead of deliberate weighting of facts and figures.[14] Managers, they write, impose their personal views in discussions with others. Alternatives are evaluated according to the clout of their proponents rather than expected utility. The most visible and clearly grasped of alternatives may be favored over more serviceable choices. This process of decision making is sometimes likened to a person's rummaging in a garbage can for something he can use. Unable to see the contents or get to the bottom, he or she simply selects the most visible or talked-about object.

In the real world, decisions take place as a mixture of rational and nonrational processes. The concept of *bounded rationality* has been used to describe decision making.[15] Executives and decision-making groups almost always carry out some rational thinking. But they do so only within the boundaries of established values, norms, and habitual practices. Basic values, norms, and practices are questioned only at times of extreme crisis. With some irony, the work of Nobel Prize laureate Herbert Simon indicates that the more important a decision, the less its amenability to purely logical, factual, and rational solution.[16] Logically, the most important decisions should require consideration of a very broad range of current facts and potential consequences. Few, if any, executives can actually command so broad a range of considerations.

Decision-Making Processes

Criteria for making decisions are part of the decision maker's mental life. Decision making also involves social processes. These processes involve communication among multiple individuals who either provide information to a decision maker or themselves share in decision making.

The basic process of decision making requires four steps: (1) becoming aware of a problem; (2) formulating a set of alternative solutions; (3) gathering the information required to assess the alternatives; and (4) deliberating over the information obtained to identify the preferred alternative. Actual processes, though, differ over time and among different organizations. Processes in actual use do not necessarily include all these elements. Some decision makers omit one or more of these steps, and the steps may occur in a sequence other that the one specified above.

The research of Paul C. Nutt illustrates the variety of decision-making processes used in different organizations and at different times.[17] Nutt describes the process of decision making as comprising five essential "stages." These include

- *Formulation*: defining problems, needs, and opportunities
- *Concept development*: formulating alternative ways of meeting the need or attaining the objective
- *Detailing*: identifying concrete alternatives
- *Evaluation*: determining the objective merits and costs of each alternative
- *Implementation*: installing the alternative selected

Reviewing a large number of decisions by organizations, Nutt detected five different decision-making processes. The most widely used processes omitted the stage of concept development. Decision makers typically skipped the concept-development stage, sticking with preexisting ideas about how the problem should be solved. Only 48% of the decision processes observed included an evaluation stage. Thus, nearly half the time, decision makers in organizations carried out no objective analysis of information regarding alternatives under consideration. Instead, they copied the methods and products of other organizations with which they were familiar, adopted pet ideas of top managers, or engaged in extended searches for appealing options without a distinct, advance notion of the object of their search.

Information exchange takes place in every decision-making process. Exchange of factual information seems likely to predominate in processes that include significant conceptual development and evaluation. In others, where decision makers jump directly from formalization to implementation, information of an affective type may predominate, as when positive feelings about a proposed alternative spread through the group via gestures, smiles, and laughter.

Dysfunction in Decision Making

Bad decisions in organizations have adverse consequences for the organization itself, for individual members, and for society as a whole. Selection of the wrong alternative by managers can bring dangerous products to market, cause workers to lose their jobs, and drive businesses into bankruptcy. Disastrous wars, ranging from the blunders of Roman emperors to the late 20th century's Vietnam conflict, may be said to have resulted from faulty organizational decision making.

Bad decisions often result from the characteristics of individuals. Some decision makers lack sufficient talent or skill to react appropriately in the absence of complete information or under pressure. As noted earlier, interpersonal factors—ignorance of others' values and cultural stereotyping, for example—can block transmission of information required for good decisions.

Human error, of course, takes place occasionally even among the most competent and best informed.

In the long run, though, structure and process determine the organization's tendency to make good versus faulty decisions. Two often-observed problems regarding transmission and use of information are particularly important:

1. Structural and historical blockages to communication

2. Ignoring of information by decision makers

Structural and Historical Blockages to Communication

Organizational structure essentially determines the way communication takes place. Several of the structural dimensions described in Chapter 5 may cause communication blockages. "Historical" factors comprise features of organizational culture and practice that also affect communication. Examples presented below are hierarchy, internal rivalry, and secrecy.

Hierarchy. Hierarchy is a structural feature found in most formal organizations of significant size. The strict subordination of some individuals to others in hierarchical organizations reduces opportunities for direct interpersonal communication. In many hierarchical organizations, people are prohibited from communicating directly with anyone above their supervisors and below their immediate subordinates.

The habits bred by hierarchy can reduce the quality of communication even between people connected by direct information channels. Unambiguously aware of their inferior status, subordinates have little motivation to approach their direct superiors with information that may be disturbing or controversial. Viewing their subordinates as not just organizationally but personally "beneath them," superiors tend to discount the accuracy or value of the information they provide.

The World War II disaster at Pearl Harbor is often cited as a consequence of communication blockage due to hierarchy. Subordinate intelligence officers attempted to communicate warnings of the impending attack to superior personnel. But the information they provided was ignored due to their inferior status.

Interdepartmental rivalry. The combination of high organizational complexity and weak integration tends to inhibit communication. The modern firm, for example, is divided into departments specializing in strategic planning, accounting, production, personnel, and marketing. Each unit has a specific jurisdiction and its own budget. Typically, unit managers seek to protect their jurisdictions and increase their budgets. The degree to which separate units engage in rivalry results in part from an organization's unique history. At the extreme, rivalry results in suboptimization (see Chapter 5), in which individual units maximize their resources at the expense of the organization's overall objectives.

Managers of rival units have little direct incentive to share information. These managers may not wish to assist competitors for the organization's resources. Some individuals provide others with incomplete or even erroneous information in the hope that the other will perform poorly, look bad, and eventually face dismissal. Each individual unit possesses a pool of vital information. But due to self-protective orientations, units keep this knowledge to themselves. Information from all units is never appropriately synthesized and presented to decision makers.

Secret operations. Deliberate restriction of information is deeply imbedded in the history and practice of many organizations. Government units such as the FBI and CIA are famed for employing secret agents in domestic and foreign settings. Business firms are known to spy on each other to obtain trade secrets. Managers have covertly observed behavior of employees for generations and conducted secret intelligence-gathering activities regarding pro-union sentiments. Many organizations purposely distribute information on a "need-to-know" basis, providing personnel with information only when it is necessary for them to carry out orders.

Sociologist Harold L. Wilensky[18] has studied the effects of secrecy on the quality of information available to decision makers and observed several unanticipated consequences. An atmosphere of secrecy, he writes, encourages personnel to withhold rather than share information. Dependence on secured internal channels, moreover, tends to insulate executives from alternative perspectives available through public sources.

Organizations dependent on secret information sources, Wilensky writes, tend to attract either untalented or unreliable personnel. Police departments, for example, have historically depended on criminals to inform them of crimes committed by others. Motivated by the desire to avoid long prison terms, these informants often exaggerate facts or lie outright to impress police officers with the value of their information. Similar behavior patterns prevail among espionage agents working for pay.

Wilensky comments that blockages to information flow are most severe when secrecy is combined with interagency rivalry. He illustrates with an example from the operation of municipal police departments:

> Information supplied by informers to the burglary detail about robbery is typically withheld from the robbery detail; not only are the [officers] of the two sections rivals for promotion and budget money, but the standard payoff for the thief-informer is the dropping of charges for his own crimes, a payoff that can be guaranteed only by the police to whom he reports.

Ignoring of Information

Even when communications function well, executives do not always apply the information available to them in making decisions. Under such executives, information gathering is undertaken for ritualistic purposes, perhaps to please stockholders or congressional watchdogs. The actual decision process omits an objective evaluation phase. Strong, preconceived notions by an organization's leaders help bring this problem into being. An organizational climate featuring strict adherence to an ideology or doctrine makes it difficult for executives to reach decisions based on objective facts. Under these conditions, information is ignored if it contradicts current policies.

Several well-known events in business and politics illustrate the doctrinaire thinking that can lead to incorrect and costly decisions. These include the following:

The notion of a "Sino-Soviet Bloc." From the 1950s to the 1970s, the U.S. State Department characterized America's adversary in the Cold War as the Sino-Soviet Bloc. Under this concept, officials believed that a powerful and enduring alliance existed between the People's Republic of China and the Soviet Union. Consequently, American officials passed up opportunities to befriend China, which would have greatly eased international tensions. In the later years of this period, however, the international press regularly reported a split between China and the Soviet Union, going as far one time as an armed skirmish on the border between the two countries.

Marketing the Edsel. In the late 1950s, Ford marketed a large, luxurious-looking car called the Edsel. The make was designed to appeal to the working class, which Ford executives believed to desire big cars. At the same time, market researchers were reporting that American workers were turning to more modest and economical vehicles. The Volkswagen "Beetle" was first beginning to achieve significant sales figures at that time.

Escalation of the war in Vietnam. In the early to mid-1960s, a close circle of American officials promoted sending U.S. forces to South Vietnam to ensure victory of its sitting government. This group, including Presidents Kennedy and Johnson and their secretaries of state and defense, believed that the Vietnamese public supported the existing government. Under the famed "domino theory," this group also believed that all Southeast Asia would become Communist if the South

Vietnamese government fell. Frequent reports in the international press and by scholars and diplomats contradicted these beliefs. Nevertheless, the United States sent massive forces to Vietnam, only to suffer defeat in a costly war. Even in an information-rich environment, some have argued, a tight-knit group of White House and Pentagon decision makers mutually reinforced each other's erroneous beliefs.[19]

Communication—the exchange of information via symbols, words, gestures, and a variety of other modes—is a visible and dynamic force within organizations. The patterns by which communication takes place reflect and affirm organizational structure. Even so, people in every organization develop informal communication networks. These may strengthen or weaken organizations. Both interpersonal and structural factors affect the quality and completeness of information exchange. Decision making represents one of the most important applications of communication. Executives make poor decisions, however, even in the presence of high-quality information.

It may be observed that some fundamental properties of formal organizations result in information system dysfunctions. Hierarchy, for example, often inhibits information flow. People concerned with organizational effectiveness have developed options for resolving this problem, some of which are presented in chapters to come.

Many observers regard communication as an organizational resource capable of solving key problems such as conflict. The next chapter, though, indicates that conflict may thrive even in organizations that have excellent communication systems. Communication may help resolve conflict. But organizations exercise other functions to deal with conflict. Politics constitutes one of the principal means that organizations use for this purpose.

Issues and Applications

Communication and decision making are among the most vital and complex of functions within an organization. Fine-tuning of both interpersonal communication and structure can have important effects. This is true at the most everyday and the most crucial levels of organizational functioning.

- A worker asks his boss for a raise. She smiles, shrugs, and walks away. Nonverbal communication of this kind avoids ill feelings and potential conflict. The boss is relieved of the need to justify her refusal. The worker is given a chance to save face in what may have been a communication initiated with some anxiety.

- In an effort to increase efficiency, the manager of a team of technical experts takes steps to discourage lateral communication. He has found that considerable time is spent in conversation among the personnel, reducing the time available for actual task performance. He requires that all communication must take place through him. This procedure appears inappropriate during normal times, when accomplishment of tasks is likely to benefit from unrestricted colleague communication.

However, it may be appropriate under conditions of high workload and short deadlines.

- After the United States invasion of Iraq in 2003, the presence of weapons of mass destruction (WMDs) in that country became a matter of public controversy. As a reason for the invasion, officials of the Bush administration had claimed that Iraq possessed WMDs. But inspectors found no such weapons after the war. Some analysis suggested that the CIA, under pressure from a war-eager President Bush, had exaggerated reports of WMDs. Critics commented that such pressure was easy to apply because the CIA chief reported only to the president, who could fire him. Perhaps people whose reporting of accurate information is vital should be protected in some way.

Chapter Review and Major Themes

The quality with which information is transmitted and utilized in an organization is affected by both interpersonal and structural factors. Factors such as stereotyping, emotional distance, and ignorance of the language or values of others can obstruct interpersonal communication. Obstruction of interpersonal communication has implications beyond face-to-face interactions. Organization-wide communication channels are composed of individuals, each of whom has some degree of control over the accuracy of the information he or she handles.

Structural factors govern much communication by allowing some people but not others to communicate with specific role incumbents. Highly structured communication appears beneficial when tasks are simple and urgent. Open systems of communication are more appropriate when tasks are complex and workload is low or moderate. Hierarchy tends to reduce and distort information as it passes through multiple levels of an organization.

To promote communication in vital areas, organizations employ specialized personnel charged with both internal and external communication tasks. Organizations appoint internal communication specialists such as gatekeepers to restrict and channel the flow of information. However, neither internal communication specialists nor structure itself absolutely determine how information flows and who receives it. Informal networks of communication compensate for structural blockages to communication. An individual performing low-status work in the office of a top executive can short-circuit a carefully managed communication pathway.

Good information does not ensure good decision making. Decision makers often discount the value of information provided by low-status individuals. Doctrine can override facts and logic. There is a tendency among decision makers to rely on solutions that have worked in the past, or to accept the suggestions of strong advocates.

Like mechanisms of coordination and cohesion, the processes of communication and decision making both affect and reflect the organizational environment. Communication and decision making also affect the organization's level of function and conflict. Focusing on communication, Figure 10.2 illustrates these relationships.

In Figure 10.2, the arrows linking communication with environment emphasize the importance of two-way information flows. External communication specialists such as public relations personnel and lobbyists transmit messages from the organization to the environment, while market researchers, sales personnel, and sometimes covert agents send information in. Good communication yields valuable benefits to the organization, supporting favorable decision making and strategy. Bad communication, conversely, can lead to disaster. Communication can reduce or increase conflict in a number of ways. Inclusion in a communication loop, for example, reassures the individual of his or her importance, while exclusion often breeds alienation and hostility.

Clearly, information channels in organizations are not under the full control of management. Managers can, however, compensate for possible contamination of intelligence by self-interested communication specialists. Obtaining information from multiple, independent channels can acquaint the decision maker with varying perspectives and allow him or her to cross-validate the content received. This process, as well as consultation with experts outside the organization's boundaries, can loosen the hold of fixed ideas, doctrines, and other factors that reduce the quality of decision making.

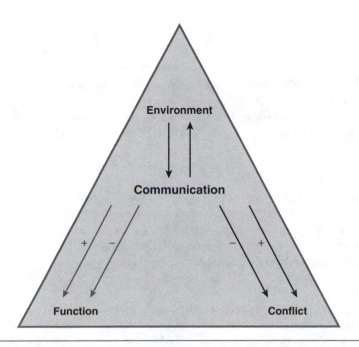

Figure 10.2   Analytical Perspectives Applied to Communication

Discussion Questions

1. Communication via e-mail predominates in many formal organizations. Does this mode of communication have any function for the organization other than convenience? Is its use ever dysfunctional?

2. What part can affective elements play in the process of negotiation? Are such elements necessarily favorable or detrimental to achieving an outcome acceptable to both sides?

3. Information technology (including computers, the Internet, GPS) has become ubiquitous in the 21st century. How might this technology affect organizational structure in organizations that are traditionally hierarchical, such as military services and police forces? How might this technology affect activities that have traditionally taken place within flat structures, such as R&D and medicine?

4. Think of an organization in which you have been involved. Was any type of information encoding used in organizational communication? Did this help or hinder achievement of the organization's objectives?

5. A high percentage of organizational decisions are made without explicit considerations of alternatives or evaluation of outcomes. What explanations can be offered for this phenomenon? Is decision making conducted in this fashion necessarily bad for the organization?

References

1. Goffman, E. (1967). *Interaction ritual: Essays on face-to-face behavior.* Garden City, NY: Doubleday.
2. Fast, J. (1970). *Body language* (p. 115). New York: J. B. Lippincott.
3. Schein, E. H. (1981). Improving face-to-face relationships. *Sloane Management Review, 22*(Winter), 43–61.
4. Morrow, J. D. (1995). *Game theory for political scientists.* Princeton, NJ: Princeton University Press.
5. Fisher, R., & Ury, W. (1991). *Getting to yes.* New York: Penguin.
6. Guetzkow, H. (1965). Communications in organizations. In J. G. March (Ed.), *Handbook of organizations* (pp. 534–573). Chicago: Rand McNally.
7. Shaw, M. E. (1964). Communication networks. In L. Berkowitz (Ed.), *Advances in experimental social psychology* (pp. 111–147). New York: Academic Press.
8. Blau, P., & Scott, R. W. (1962). *Formal organizations.* San Francisco: Chandler Publishing.
9. Nasralla, W., Levitt, R., & Glynn, P. (2003). Interaction value analysis: When structured communication benefits organizations. *Organization Studies, 15*(5), 541–577.
10. Lipman, J. (1986, December 15). In times of trouble, candor is often the first casualty. *Wall Street Journal.*

11. Walsh, E. (1973, May 1). Haldeman, intensely loyal, key to access to Nixon. *Washington Post*.

12. Severo, R. (2003, June 11). Donald Regan, 84, financier and top Reagan aide, dies. *New York Times*, p. C17.

13. Johnson, H., & Broder, D. (1997). *The system: The death of health care reform in 1993–1994*. Boston: Little, Brown.

14. Cyert, R. M., & March, J. G. (1963). *Behavioral theory of the firm*. Englewood Cliffs, NJ: Prentice Hall.

15. March, J. G. (1981). Decisions in organizations and theories of choice. In A. H. Van de Ven & W. F. Joyce (Eds.), *Perspectives on organizational design and behavior* (pp. 205–244). New York: John Wiley & Sons.

16. Simon, H. (1957). *Administrative behavior*. New York: Free Press.

17. Nutt, P. C. (1984). Types of organizational decision processes. *Administrative Science Quarterly, 29*, 414–450.

18. Wilensky, H. L. (1967). *Organizational intelligence*. New York: Basic Books.

19. Kaiser, D. (1999). *American tragedy: Kennedy, Johnson, and the origins of the Vietnam War*. Cambridge, MA: Harvard University Press.

CHAPTER 11

Conflict, Politics, and Change

Learning Objective

To comprehend the causes and consequences of conflict among an organization's members and subunits, and between members and the organization itself; to analyze and appreciate the political process in organizations; to understand the causes and process of organizational change.

Principles

- Within organizations, *conflict*—a term that signifies enduring, emotionally charged disagreement—occurs among individuals, groups, and subunits; conflict may also be directed at the organization itself.

- Conflict among individuals may arise from substantive disputes, incompatibility of individual personalities, factual misunderstanding, or diversity among participants in the organization. Conflict with the organization itself is more likely traceable to perceived unfairness, injustice, or lack of voice in the organization's affairs.

- Procedures effective in controlling interpersonal and intergroup conflict include direct intervention and mediation. Conflict involving individuals and groups versus the organization may require structural change for resolution.

- Politics constitutes a process for reconciling actual or potential disputes over resources, strategies, and objectives. The political process can determine an organization's direction and secure the commitment of its members.

- Change in an organization may result from internal causes, such as poor performance, decisions by leaders, and major conflict. Change also results from new developments in the organization's environment, including technology, market conditions, demography, political climate, and actions by other organizations.

Conflict, Politics, and Change: Challenges to Organizations

Conflict, politics, and change are processes that challenge the stable elements of formal organizations. Roles and formal structure, the core features of organizations, encourage human behavior to follow predictable patterns. But conflict, politics, and change place established practices and relationships in question.

Although they interrupt an organization's routine functioning, conflict, politics, and change are natural parts of life in formal organizations. They can invigorate the lives of people in the organization, enhance the organization's capacity for achieving its ends, and extend the organization's life. They can also be dysfunctional. They can distract people from contributing to the organization's objectives. They can degrade rather than improve structure.

While each is different, the processes of conflict, politics, and change are often interconnected. Each of these processes can aggravate or moderate one or both of the others. Politics can cause conflict, as people choose sides in organizations and develop opposing viewpoints and programs. But politics can help defuse conflict, as when opponents compete in a fashion that does not damage the organization. Change often creates conflict, as advocates for change clash with people who prefer the existing order.

In moderate amounts, conflict, politics, and change represent healthy challenges to organizations. Competition among supporters of differing objectives makes members and decision makers aware of alternatives. Conflict can strengthen an organization's internal solidarity and decision-making functions. Politics allows conflicts to be worked out in an orderly fashion. Organizations must accept change in order to exploit new technology and adapt to new developments in their environments.

Organizational Conflict

Conflict between separate organizations is clearly normal. A competitive economy promotes and celebrates competition among business firms. Government agencies competing for limited tax funds publicly disparage each other. Some organizations, such as sports teams and armies, identify defeat of other organizations as their central purpose. Conflict inside organizational boundaries may seem less natural, but it is very common.

Conflict internal to an organization is sometimes visible and sometimes covert. Conflict between two individuals readily becomes apparent to others. Even those not directly involved are affected. Noncombatants may be prevented from working with one or both of the conflicting parties. Innocent bystanders may find their quality of life diminished by the atmosphere of antagonism. Conflict between workers and managers, though, may be less apparent, as individuals with relatively little power develop covert responses to perceived wrongs.

Interpersonal conflict in organizations arises from properties essential to all formal organizations. Organizations assign roles. People experimentally expand or diminish responsibilities associated with their roles, displeasing members of their role set. Organizations distribute rewards, causing people who feel insufficiently rewarded to develop vendettas against management. Organizational structure defines career ladders. Antagonism among rivals for promotion is legendary. Some of the most damaging conflict occurs in cases where the conflicting individuals or units are interdependent, relying on each other for resources or other support.

Conflict among units of an organization can have more serious effects than conflict between individuals. More often than outsiders suspect, managers hide opportunities and divert resources from other managers. Their motive may not be personal hostility but rather a desire to prevent another unit from outstripping theirs in size, resources, and influence in the executive suite. The manager does not necessarily enhance the standing of his or her unit. But his or her behavior potentially diminishes the ability of the organization as a whole to attain its objectives.

Another variety of conflict occurring in organizational contexts is of an intrapersonal variety. Such conflict, occurring within an individual's mind, recalls material in preceding chapters. Contradictions between personal needs and social conventions are said to produce much emotional disturbance. Role conflict (see Chapter 4) occurs when expectations of an individual role are incompatible or contradict the incumbent's personal values. Role conflict also occurs when the incumbent occupies multiple roles, each of which has expectations incompatible with another.

Conflict also occurs between members (or groups of members) and the organization itself. Conflict of this kind may be least amenable to management solutions. This is because conflict between individuals and the organization, though focused on the organization's routines, structure, and reward system, may raise or reflect issues of broad social importance. Challenges and decisions required by individuals who find themselves at odds with their organizations are addressed in detail in Chapter 14. The present chapter, though, introduces this basic concern and illustrates ways in which it may appear.

Conflict of this kind has similarities to protest behavior and movements in the broader society, for example, when workers seek redress of grievances. Perhaps more often, conflict between individuals and the organization occurs in covert forms. Instances of this kind include deliberate withdrawal of productivity, vandalism, and sabotage.[1] Industrial psychologists have typically classified such behavior as "deviant." In this sense, the adversely behaving worker is seen as a "misfit" or "malcontent." As in the broader society, though, so-called deviant behavior can be viewed as legitimate protest by individuals who have no other means of protest.

Generally, conflict may be defined as a state in which the parties involved experience *a sense of opposition or incompatibility of goals or other concerns.*[2] Unpleasant feelings and expression mark all varieties of conflict. People on opposite sides attack their opponent's technical capability, management skill, and moral character. *Stereotyping* and *scapegoating* often accompany conflict. Conflicting parties *stereotype* each other by exaggerating their flaws. *Scapegoating* occurs when parties on opposite sides blame all the organization's problems on their opponents. Stress also marks many conflicts, as parties sense danger to their interests and fear reprisals.

Workplace Violence: Conflict at the Extreme

Workplace violence regularly makes headlines.

The most famous instance involved a dismissed post office employee. He shot up the post office where he had worked, murdering 12 former coworkers. "Going postal" has come to signify a workplace killing spree.

In reality, extreme violence among coworkers is rare. But its occurrences make visible the daily conflict that occurs within organizations. This incident provides an illustration.[3]

On June 28, 2000, Dr. Jian Chen shot Dr. Rodger Haggitt dead in his office. Chen, a pathology resident at the University of Washington Medical Center, had been fired from his position. Haggitt was his supervisor.

A medical student from Taiwan, Chen had looked highly qualified on paper. But he encountered difficulty early in the residency program. Chen had trouble speaking English, relating to other people, and following instructions.

An acquaintance recalled: "The faculty basically didn't allow him to practice after . . . about two months into [the job]. Even so, Haggitt was" trying to help Chen find another position. Chen was upset with both the program and Haggitt."

After shooting Haggitt, Chen killed himself.

"It's a tragedy," a police officer commented. "Two highly educated men, now gone."

The incident described above illustrates conflict in a supervisor-subordinate relationship at its most extreme. It may be explained in part as a consequence of life in the pressure-cooker setting of a top medical center. Independent-minded, ego-driven people are often concentrated in such venues. Less sensational manifestations of conflict, both interpersonal and between individuals and their organizations, are not unusual. Reporting data from a survey conducted in 2003 and 2004, Table 11.1 covers only instances severe enough to become visible to management.

Table 11.1   Manifestations of Conflict in U.S. Business Organizations

Incident	Percentage of Business Organizations Reporting in the Past Year
Shooting or stabbing	1.6
Sabotage	7.5
Physical assault, fistfights, pushing, kicking	12.6
Sexual harassment	22.1
Bullying, social isolation, intimidation	24.5
Written or verbal threats	33.3
Incivility	60.6

SOURCE: National Organizations Survey.[4]

Social scientists have reported that conflict occurs according to cycles. Conflicts begin, reach a climax, and get resolved. Later, new conflicts arise. The manner in which conflicts take place and reach resolution depends on the history, culture, and conflict-resolution capabilities of the organization. An understanding of expectable stages in the conflict cycle can promote a great deal of understanding. By knowing the likely stages, individuals in organizations become alert to potential outbreaks of conflict and what to expect as actual conflict develops.

According to one observer, the conflict cycle takes place as follows:[5]

1. *Latent conflict.* Underlying causes of conflict exist, such as competition for scarce resources, desire for autonomy, and differences in objectives among subunits. Members have no sense of conflict, but signs of its potential development are evident.

2. *Perceived conflict.* Individuals and subunits develop awareness that areas of incompatibility exist between them. Perceived conflict may or may not be accompanied by hostility or stress, as parties in conflict situations ignore what they consider to be unimportant or irreconcilable differences.

3. *Felt conflict.* This stage occurs when conflict becomes personal and emotional. Antagonistic feelings and stress as described above arise in this stage. Perceived issues regarding resources and opportunity become linked with actual human beings, who then become objects of negative emotion.

4. *Manifest conflict.* In this stage, conflict involves exchange of words and actions. Open aggression, the most obvious form of manifest conflict, includes extremes such as verbal abuse and physical violence. More common manifestations include political maneuvering (described below) and withdrawal from activities that potentially benefit the opponent. Lower-ranking individuals in an organization may rigidly enforce rules in an effort to hinder actions of their superiors.

5. *Conflict aftermath.* Conflict aftermath denotes conditions resulting from resolution of manifest conflict. The quality of resolution affects how future conflicts develop and resolve. Resolution of a conflict in a manner perceived as fair by both sides will predispose parties in future disputes to seek collaborative solutions. But parties who feel their grievances have been settled unfairly or ignored may use more aggressive techniques in the future.

Each stage prior to the aftermath represents more visible and intense conflict. Conflict may escalate to a point where its original causes are forgotten. New focuses of antagonism are identified and further inflame the situation. But a cycle of intensification is not inevitable. Latent conflict does not necessarily result in perceived conflict, as potential parties never focus on their differences. Perceived conflicts may be ignored or just written off as the way things are. Conflict with and without objective cause can often be managed through widely available intervention techniques.

Sources of Conflict

Fundamental Causes

Several factors have already been cited that give rise to conflict within organizations. A wide variety of additional forces raise the risk of conflict within organizations. These include the following:

Personality conflicts. Researchers have produced evidence that people with different personality types have a tendency to conflict with each other. The familiar distinction between "Type A" and "Type B" personalities provides an example. People with Type A personalities are said to be energetic, assertive, ambitious, and anxious. They tend to impose their agendas on others. Type B personalities are thought of as passive and calm. They seek ways of accommodating the needs of others and are predisposed to accepting compromises. Conflict develops as Type Bs feel pushed by Type As, and Type As become impatient with Type Bs.

Conflicts in values. The importance that people place on values makes values a frequent source of conflict as well as cohesion. Values emerge from the outside culture as well as organizational culture itself. Values constitute components of professional culture. Differences on important values held by distinct individuals or subunits constitute a good example of latent conflict.

Differences in values among individuals involved in an engineering project provide an illustration. Researchers have often reported that technical professionals subscribe to alternative sets of values: (a) professional discipline orientation or (b) client orientation.[6] Professional discipline orientation emphasizes values such as rigorous adherence to scientific methods, contributions to science, and obtaining favorable reception from technically qualified colleagues. Client orientation rests on values such as pleasing clients and organizational superiors, advancing in the organizational hierarchy, and obtaining a large income. Engineers with a professional discipline orientation may view client-oriented engineers as panderers, bean counters, and money-grubbers. Engineers with a client orientation may view professional discipline-oriented engineers as "academic" or "nerdy."

Differences in objective. Individuals and subunits in organizations often pursue different objectives. Management scientists frequently cite differences in the objectives of manufacturing and marketing units. Manufacturing unit managers aim at producing the largest volume of goods at the highest quality and lowest cost. They enjoy only a limited degree of flexibility due to plant capacity, supply delivery schedules, and union contracts. Managers in the marketing unit aim at maximizing sales and pleasing customers of special importance. Sales personnel are rewarded for keeping customers happy and raising corporate income.

Manufacturing and marketing objectives occasionally conflict. A salesperson, for example, may promise a client delivery of more product than can be manufactured with current resources by the agreed-upon delivery date. The plant manager faces the constraints cited above. He or she may be able to increase delivery speed by using inexpensive components and paying for additional personnel with the money saved. More product may be shipped but of a lower quality. The plant manager's solution eventually weakens the ability of marketing to achieve its objective.

Task orientation differences. Even individuals performing highly similar tasks may approach their work differently. The memoir of a physician-in-training provides an example of different task orientations.[7] He describes the operating routines of two surgeons in the same hospital. One liked his operating room cold, claiming that it minimized the patient's bleeding. The other liked the room warm, insisting that a higher temperature improved his and his assistants' manual dexterity. The two surgeons insisted on using different size needles. One ordered that needles be thrown on the operating room floor after use to ensure that they would not be reused after they had become dull. The other prohibited disposal of needles in this fashion, observing that needles discarded on the floor endangered staff and punctured tires on mobile equipment. Each surgeon looked down on the other's technique. Personally, the two were antagonistic toward each other.

Workforce diversity. Participation of a wider variety of people in organizations today than in earlier eras is often reported to cause conflict. People usually think of diversity as racial. But demographic change in America has brought formerly marginalized people of many descriptions into the mainstream. Formal organizations today include members not only of different races but also of different genders and age-groups. Differences in the length of time individuals have been in the organization (job tenure) are also a measure of diversity.

A study of conflict in 45 work groups at three business firms has reported that some forms of diversity increase conflict while others reduce it.[8] Greater racial diversity tends to increase conflict, as does greater diversity in job tenure.

Perceived injustice. Conflict between individuals and the organization itself is often attributed to perceptions of declining control. Studies of the causes of antagonism against organizations have identified specific causes such as dissatisfaction with compensation, pace of work, and breaks, or perceived deterioration of the organization's mission or effectiveness.[9,10] A classical formulation in sociology helps illuminate conditions that are either more or less conducive to conflict due to causes such as these. Hirschman formulated the dichotomy of "voice" versus "exit."[11] Possession of "voice"—means for articulating and obtaining redress of grievances—seems capable of reducing conflict directed against the organization. In the absence of voice, people exit the organization. Most visibly, exit would take the form of leaving the organization. But when people do not have this option, conflict seems likely to result. Exit often takes a passive form, such as withdrawal of productivity, theft, or sabotage.

Organizational structure. The ability of organizational structure to promote conflict has already been referenced. A "peaked" organization, one whose hierarchy includes very few high-level positions relative to total membership, may breed conflict among ambitious members for positions on narrow career ladders. Hierarchy itself, though, can promote antagonism toward the organization. Peaked organizations discourage communication upward, as members in the lower ranks find it impossible to communicate with higher-level supervisors. This structural feature reduces the member's sense of voice.

External politics. The environment of the organization affects the degree to which members may experience conflict with the organization or its managers. A general social atmosphere of conflict can penetrate organizational boundaries. Societies, for example, differ in the degree to which workers identify organizations as tools of oppression operated by managers and property owners. The feminist movement in the United States has helped women identify issues within male-dominated organizations. If external movements promote conflict between individuals and the organizations to which they belong, these movements may encourage vocal expression and provide focus and vocabulary for what began as internal conflict.[12]

Conflict Catalysts

None of the factors listed above necessarily results in manifest conflict with its accompanying confrontation, hostility, and stress. Several characteristics of organizations tend to act as *catalysts,* factors that cause higher-stage conflict to develop. These catalysts include the following:

Nonroutine work. Organizations whose functions are carried out according to a stable set of routines tend to be relatively conflict-free. It appears that tasks of a routine nature present an organization's members with little to argue about. The opposite is true of organizations that must innovate regularly.

Short-term memberships. Organizations with a high percentage of new members appear at high risk of conflict. People who have not had the opportunity to become familiar with each other are less likely to share values and task orientation than are long-term colleagues.

Interdependence. Organizations whose members depend directly on each other for performing their roles have greater likelihood of conflict than the ones in which people work independently. Relative isolation of individuals creates a buffer against personalization of latent conflicts. People who interact intensely have plenty of opportunity to pick fights.

Conflict stemming from interdependence seems particularly likely in small organizations and organizations physically isolated from society at large. Prisons provide a vivid example. These organizations deliberately isolate their members from the outside world. Prisoners are highly interdependent for stimulation and mutual security. Serious conflict in the form of prison riots is a constant danger. Enterprises such as ocean cargo handling and mining are similar. A high likelihood of strikes has been documented among workers in these industries,[13] whose dissatisfaction over wages and working conditions seems to be intensified by isolation.

Dysfunction and Function of Conflict

Most observers of organizations emphasize the dysfunction of conflict. Conflict-related dysfunction is in fact evident. Stress associated with conflict reduces the quality of life in most organizations. Workplaces beset by arguments or below-the-surface hostility are unattractive. Elevated levels of turnover seem likely to result. The practice of short-circuiting the work of others acts as an impediment to productivity. Withdrawal of effort or commitment by people seeking to avoid conflict inhibits achievement of objectives. Losers in conflict-related struggles feel personally diminished.

Conflict, though, has positive functions in at least some organizations. Organizations and organizational subunits involved in creative work cannot avoid conflict. Members of research and development (R&D) teams, for example, regularly encounter entirely new design problems. Individual team members typically propose several competing solutions, each of which is enthusiastically supported by its advocates. This process allows the manager to select the option for which the best argument can be made. Controversy can be similarly functional in the development of a marketing plan or the design of a new government program.

Deliberate use of conflict to generate options has been documented at the highest executive levels. Policy makers in business and government often pit experts with different perspectives against each other. Exposure to the arguments of each expert enables the policy maker to make the best-informed decision. Franklin D. Roosevelt, U.S. president during the turbulent Depression and World War II years, was famous for recruiting competing experts to the White House.

Conflict acts as an antidote to several of the decision-making pathologies considered in Chapter 10. The presence of opposing positions makes it unlikely that decision makers will be blindsided by information from a single source or have their judgment dominated by untested doctrines. *Lobbying,* or the attempt to influence votes in Congress or a state legislature, may sound sleazy. But today's lobbyists, often quite well armed with facts in their specialty areas, can contribute to the quality of legislative decision making.

Second, conflict can contribute to the solidarity of individual subunits. Solidarity, or the feeling among individuals that they belong together, is an essential component of all collectivities. Interunit conflict promotes solidarity within the competing units as members pull together in the face of a perceived challenge from outside. It is no accident that organizations whose members live at close quarters regularly sponsor intramural sports events and other controlled, solidarity-building competitions.

Finally, allowing limited conflict to take place helps keep conflict from escalating. As noted above, many organizations harbor latent or perceived conflicts. Most of the time, these do not mature into an active state, such as manifest conflict. By suppressing recognition of latent conflict, though, organizations risk allowing more serious and acrimonious conflicts to develop over time, as unresolved though genuine grievances become personalized, manifest, and disruptive.

An organization's culture helps determine the degree of conflict it permits. The cultures of innovative organizations tolerate and even promote conflict.

The cultures of organizations involved in stable business or government operations do the opposite.

Managing Conflict

In well-functioning organizations, conflict eventually gets resolved or is reduced to a tolerable level. Two distinct sets of mechanisms for management of conflict can be observed in organizations. The first set utilizes formal procedures and is typically initiated by management. The second set takes place through informal practices that evolve over time. Although informal practices receive no official support, they are often recognized as valuable by management.

For generations, organizational process specialists have tried to develop improved conflict-resolution methods. Conflict-resolution consulting is today a distinct industry. People concerned with resolving conflicts in actual organizations should consult the many specialized texts in this area. The mechanisms of conflict resolution specified below constitute only illustrative examples.

Formal mechanisms. Formal methods of conflict resolution are deliberately constructed processes that guarantee a hearing to opposed positions. Actual procedures are diverse in staffing, resource intensity, and responsibility for the ultimate outcome.

Direct intervention. Tales of direct management intervention to resolve disputes have been told since ancient times. Doubtlessly the most famous is King Solomon's proposal to cut a baby in half to resolve a dispute between two women claiming parenthood. Managers today still settle conflicts between subordinates through unilateral judgment. This conflict-resolution procedure differs little from Solomon's in the Old Testament. A modern manager's most agreeable option may be to "split the difference" between warring parties.

Many managers, though, use procedures that prevent their decisions from appearing to reflect personal preference. They may seek judgment via application of a rule or regulation. They may order disputing parties to settle differences on their own, mandating only a specific date by which resolution will be required. Managers may initiate a process for resolving all such disputes, such as a formal budgeting procedure. They may look for ways to reduce direct interaction between conflicting units.

Communication-based techniques. Mechanisms under which conflicting parties provide each other with information about their needs, objectives, and grievances constitute another widely used approach. Several of the communication-stimulating procedures referenced in Chapter 10 are frequently applied for conflict resolution purposes. Communication-based intervention seeks to promote conflict resolution through mutual understanding.

Widely used communication-based techniques include t-groups, trainings, workshops, and retreats. Interventions of this kind appear most effective for discovering and defusing perceived and felt conflicts. In such instances, where conflict often results from misunderstanding, exchange of information can reduce tension and fear on both sides. A workshop-type, communication-based technique might contain the following sequence of steps:[14]

1. *Image exchanges:* members of conflicting groups determine how they see themselves, how they see the other group, and how they think the other group sees them.

2. *Problem identification:* the groups work together to identify a list of problems.

3. *Organizing for problem solving:* lists of problems are arranged in priority order, and teams of individuals are formed from the membership of both groups to work on them.

4. *Problem solving:* work groups develop proposed solutions, present their findings to the workshop as a whole, and modify their solutions on the basis of full group discussion.

Principled negotiation, another communication technique useful for conflict resolution, has been discussed in Chapter 10. This procedure is valuable for identifying the needs and objectives of conflicting parties. Aiming to develop a set of procedures or package of resources capable of meeting everyone's needs, its mechanism is more concrete than the workshop or t-group approach.

Communication-based procedures are often inappropriate for resolving conflicts stemming from deep-seated differences or objective grievances. In these cases, communication may actually increase conflict, as the parties involved become better informed of each other's incompatible interests.

Mediation. In mediation, a neutral third party helps conflicting individuals or groups reach agreement. Mediation differs from direct management intervention because the conflicting parties formulate their own resolution. The presence of an active third party distinguishes mediation from communication-based conflict resolution methods.

The facilitator in a t-group or workshop may encourage parties to share their perceptions and opinions. A mediator, though, plays an active part in developing an agreement. Mediators are typically outside consultants brought into an organization to resolve conflicts. They are best known for their work in heading off strikes. But they also help resolve disputes between high-level managers and executive teams seeking consensus on major corporate decisions.

Mediation has been characterized as a five-step process.[15] These steps include

1. *First contact:* the mediator ensures that the conflicting parties know how mediation works and are committed to the process; he or she learns as much as possible about the conflict.

2. *Opening meeting:* the mediator brings the conflicting parties together, physically or by telephone; the mediator states the conflict as he or she sees it; each conflicting side states the problem from its own vantage point.

3. *Caucuses:* the mediator conducts separate meetings with representatives of each side, learning each side's needs and interests as well as facts about the

disputed item or issue; he or she develops and suggests solutions consistent with the party's interests, needs, and constraints.

4. *Joint/shuttle meetings:* the mediator holds successive caucuses with each side, going back and forth in search of an agreement acceptable to all; meetings including both parties may help move the process forward.

5. *Closing:* the mediator reviews the agreement for possible flaws, requests that the parties make a final review, and puts it in writing.

Mediators differ according to personal style. Some aggressively push the conflicting parties toward a solution the mediator has devised. Others permit the process to move at its own pace. The technique of back-and-forth caucuses mirrors the "shuttle diplomacy" of international relations.

Except when a high-level executive directly intervenes and acts as judge, all formal conflict-resolution methods require commitment by participants. Conflicting parties must willingly adhere to the procedure and agree to abide by the solution reached. Bad faith in the process or violation of a resulting deal raises the level of conflict and makes future formal resolution efforts less promising. Visible backing of the process by higher executives is a distinct asset. Some argue that communication-based processes work only when they are ordered by high-level managers.

Informal mechanisms. Informal methods of conflict resolution prevail in many organizations. Often, these resemble the communication-based techniques described above. Informal mechanisms, though, are not deliberately formulated. They evolve spontaneously.

Organizational culture specialist John Van Maanen describes informal conflict resolution among detectives in the London Metropolitan Police Department.[16] These detectives have a reputation for drinking and brawling. Attending many of the officers' drinking bouts, Van Maanen discovered that these raucous sessions helped resolve conflict in a high-stress work environment. Van Maanen observed that detectives talked freely about assignments they considered impossible to fulfill. Officers of different ranks exchanged points of view on cases in heated and sometimes vulgar language. Sometimes, appropriate revision of work assignments would occur in the days and weeks to follow.

Large amounts of beer and liquor made possible high-volume information exchange. Trading of factual and affective information took place with drunkenness as an excuse. In sober day-to-day interaction, hierarchical structure and officer machismo usually short-circuited the communication required for conflict resolution. Drunken parties, though, provided an organizational "time-out" in which exchange was permitted. According to Van Maanen's notes, officers did not experience embarrassment afterward. Drinking bouts were well-accepted elements of their organizational culture. During the parties, officers seemed to exaggerate their degree of intoxication, shouting, stumbling, and falling. These gestures may be viewed as symbolic claims of immunity from punishment for things said.

Other Resolution Processes

Absence or failure of openly conducted methods does not mean conflict remains unresolved. Resolution may take the form of withdrawal by one or both conflicting parties. Not wishing to stand out as problem employees or non-team players, people at all levels often decide to merely withdraw. For some people, withdrawal takes the form of ignoring perceived conflicts or suppressing associated feelings after a bout of manifest conflict. Cessation of open conflict is not necessarily favorable to the organization. Still-aggrieved parties often resort to passive-aggressive behavior, withdrawing commitment to organizational objectives or employing obscure regulations to delay or derail an opponent's projects. Observers should assume that there is more conflict in a formal organization than appears on the surface.

Individual parties often act on their own to resolve conflict in a manner of their choosing. Individuals and subunits exercise power and influence, use instrumental and socioemotional resources, and appeal to organizational culture (see Chapters 6–8) to ensure resolution favorable to them. Unlike procedures explicitly intended to resolve conflict, such efforts are not neutral with respect to conflicting positions. They are, on the contrary, competitive. Competitive efforts to resolve conflicts—latent or manifest, actual or potential—constitute a major part of organizational politics.

It is important to note that most of the conflict resolution processes described above were developed for use with interpersonal or intergroup conflict. Their applicability in cases of conflict directed against the organization itself is less clear. It would appear that most interpersonal conflicts could be resolved without changing routines or broader patterns of social relations in the organization. But for conflicts involving individuals or groups versus the organization, which directly address standard operating procedures or structure, political solutions may be required.

Politics in Organizations

Politics is a process by which a person or group attempts to influence collective thinking or action. Like other dynamics described in this chapter, politics represents a continuing internal challenge for the organization. Unlike conflict, politics is used to accomplish a deliberate purpose. Some employ politics as a means of challenging stable expectations and accepted practice. Others use politics as an instrument for resisting such challenges. Some people in organizations use politics to engage core values and beliefs in hopes of moving the organization in a new direction. Others use politics to mobilize collective resources to their benefit or that of their allies.

Politics is a competitive process. In politics, people promote the thinking or action they desire over the preferences of others. The process of politics is informal. It is typically carried out through persuasion, image management, and exchange of favors. This is true even in settings where, like the United States Congress, highly specific rules govern proceedings.

People resort to politics when standard operating procedures appear unlikely to produce the results they want. Politics sometimes takes place in full public view, as when dissident stockholders take the microphone at a corporate annual meeting. At other times, politics is practiced in secretive settings: across a desk, over dinner, on the golf course.

Politics occurs in all human collectivities that are of sufficient development for the articulation of objectives and the maintenance of collective resources. The connection of politics with resources in which members have collective interest is reflected in words such as *commonwealth* and *republic,* whose original meanings reference that which is owned by the citizens. Politics in formal organizations operates much as it does in collectivities as diverse as tribal bands and nation-states.

People ignorant of an organization's politics often find its actions mysterious. Learning of an abrupt project cancellation, an engineer asks, "Why was the project stopped? We were making steady progress." A junior executive wonders, "Why did *she* get the promotion? I've been here five years and she was just hired." A union member says to his buddy, "Why was the strike vote postponed? We've all made up our minds." Many answers can be found behind the scenes, recognizable in such tabloid terms as *influence peddling, favor trading, power wielding, jaw boning,* and *string pulling.*

People generally expect their organizations to focus on achievement of official objectives. Members at all levels sense that something is wrong when evidence surfaces that individual persons, subunits, or cliques have redirected the organization's energies to their own interests. Such actions constitute what the man or woman in the street recognizes as "politics."

The Functions of Politics

Politics often seems wasteful, frivolous, or unfair. But politics performs an important function for the organization itself and the people in it. No organization can run entirely on the basis of rational planning and explicit rules. People initiate political action when technical formulas or standard management procedures do not provide answers to important questions or produce desired results.

Functions for the collectivity. Organizations cannot rely on standard formulas or established management principles to deal with unexpected developments. Developments of this kind may take the form of changes in the organization's environment. They may stem from obsolescence in the organization's production technology. They may originate from the initiative of leaders who want the organization to significantly improve its performance or pursue new objectives.

Many situations arise to which an organization has no standard response. In these instances, top managers seek new solutions. As discussed in the preceding chapter, solutions are usually developed through a political process, several executives and their staffs advocating for the courses they favor. Once a strategy is determined, political techniques such as persuasion, deal making, and exercise of power must be employed to motivate members to support the new program.

Functions for individuals. Politics proves an attractive option for people and subunits that perceive that their aspirations are blocked. In order to expand his or her role, an ambitious person can not only negotiate with his or her supervisor but seek support from other employees for doing so. An individual who feels he or she is in conflict with another can take steps to get others on his or her side. Such steps can include offering (or hinting at) rewards: "If our side wins this committee vote, you'll have an opportunity to move up along with us." "If the man I'm recommending gets hired, you can ask me for a favor when you need one." The members of a volunteer organization use the same techniques. These individuals may use politics to focus the organization's attention on new concerns or to obtain an appointment as the local chapter's state or national representative.

The Game of Politics

Thus far, politics has been described as a mysterious process involving secretive maneuvers. In practice, politics is more open and diverse. It is useful to think of politics as a game in which players strive to accumulate more support than their opponents. In an election, experienced campaigners formulate systematic steps to obtain one more than 50% of the votes to be cast. Leading members of the United States Senate craft strategies designed to garner the votes of 51 senators. Observing measures by government agencies to secure appropriations from Congress, political scientist Aaron Wildavsky indicates the steps an organizational unit needs to take to win in political competition:[17]

Working with clientele. The manager of a subunit needs to identify individuals both inside and outside the organization who benefit from the subunit's work. Individuals who rely on the subunit's services or products have a natural interest in seeing it operate effectively. Client individuals and organizations know that effectiveness depends at least in part on adequate resource levels. Effective political strategy focuses not on the organization as a whole but on managers and other subunits who, first are beneficiaries and, second, occupy positions of influence. The subunit should serve these clients as well as possible and ensure that they communicate their satisfaction to higher officials.

Building confidence. Politically successful individuals and subunits benefit greatly from establishing a favorable reputation. Keeping in regular contact with other people builds confidence. People naturally trust those they see frequently more than those they only encounter occasionally. *Schmoozing,* or casual yet intimate-seeming conversation, is an important item in the tool kit of most organizational politicians.

Successful completion of highly visible projects contributes to organization-wide confidence of an individual or subunit. This principle captures several other practices of the politically successful. One is to avoid all projects that are unlikely to succeed. Another is to expend as little effort as possible on projects whose success will be attributed to someone else, such as one's supervisor or parent unit.

Exploiting opportunities. Conflict and imperfect communication in an organization present clever members with ample opportunity to build support for themselves, their subunits, and their projects. At all levels, individuals may be found who are engaged in latent or manifest conflict. These individuals seek allies wherever they may be. A deal involving exchange of support or resources, known in international diplomacy as the *quid pro quo,* is nearly always waiting to be made.

Incomplete communication networks enable the clever to pass blame for their shortcomings onto others: superiors, subordinates, or peers. A more positive version of this strategy is to share credit for a visible accomplishment. People with sufficient confidence can publicly thank others, even if their part in the achievement has been small.

Playing to Win

According to many, women were woefully naive about the game of politics when they first began to occupy executive positions in the late 20th century. Writer Betty Lehan Harragan felt that most men learned the game through traditionally male sports. She translated sports jargon into lessons she felt women needed in order to be effective as organizational players:[18]

Sports talk: Master the skills you need to earn a place on the team.

Corporate politics: Know your job duties and perform them well.

Sports talk: Never lose your head in practice or in the game.

Corporate politics: Don't let anger or fear drive you to impulsive actions that you may regret.

Sports talk: Never disagree with the coach on the field, but express your views in pregame or postgame strategy sessions.

Corporate politics: Never criticize or challenge your boss at meetings where others are present.

Sports talk: Don't get angry when a substitute takes your place.

Corporate politics: Don't try to do everything or be all things to all people.

Sports talk: Do not become discouraged or depressed when a play fails to score. Find the weaknesses and strive to correct them.

Corporate politics: Learn from mistakes and put-downs. Figure out better tactics for the next try.

Sports talk: Take advantage of the psychological moment. If you recover a fumble or complete a long pass, capitalize on your opportunity.

Corporate politics: Don't disparage any success you achieve. Publicize and promote yourself at every opportunity.

Higher and Lower Politics

Most day-to-day politics resembles the gamesmanship described above. Ultimately, though, another form of politics is often more important. These politics compete not for jobs and payoffs but for hearts and minds. It should be recalled that leadership takes place in a "higher" and "lower" form (see Chapter 9). So does politics.

Higher politics corresponds to higher leadership. Higher leadership is characterized as developing (or facilitating development of) innovative directions, engaging others, and bringing them into a cohesive group intent on achieving the new objectives. Higher politics emphasizes inspiration. Great oratory such as Lincoln's Gettysburg Address represented a famous exercise of higher politics, raising the audience above their immediate concerns and defining American ideals for an entire generation. Those who engage in higher politics focus their attention more on shaping the thinking of the collectivity than on the distribution of its resources. The famous theorist Max Weber characterized these people as "living for politics."[19]

Lower politics is the kind carried out under lower leadership. It emphasizes skillful game playing. Utilizing exchanges of resources and favors, the practice of lower politics in organizations is reminiscent of the big-city bosses of yesteryear and Tammany Hall, New York's old-time bastion of graft, corruption, and political horse-trading. Lower politics aims not at transforming convictions but at promoting allies into positions of higher authority and pay. Max Weber characterized practitioners of such activity as "living *off* politics."

Higher and lower politics coexist within most settings. Just as transformational leaders use transactional methods at times, practitioners of higher politics build alliances and offer quid pro quos. Leaders who live for great ideals still need to act like old-time politicians. Leaders as different as Franklin D. Roosevelt and Adolf Hitler were both big-idea men. Yet both shook hands, kissed babies, and distributed patronage.

Dirty Politics

Both higher and lower politics as discussed above rely on mainstream techniques for obtaining resources in an organization and affecting its direction. Less legitimate means include character assassination, sabotage, and backstabbing. Though frowned upon, these techniques are widely used. These furtive procedures represent the "dirty politics" of organizations, as do vote fraud, slander, and bribery in the broader political arena.

Character assassination is a series of actions intended to destroy an opponent's technical credibility, management credentials, or ethical reputation. Secret communications with decision makers or persons of influence represent key tools of character assassination. Whispered conversations over drinks or on the golf course have caused many a career to founder. Leakage to the press about long-past missteps or outright hoaxes are also effective.

Sabotage involves purposeful disruption or destruction of another person's work. In its grossest form, sabotage may include breaking another department's equipment, making sure critical communications are lost, or causing products to disappear. These steps prevent units from meeting expectations. Managers heading these units are made to look bad, losing power, influence, and potentially their jobs.

Backstabbing refers to adverse action by a trusted colleague. Shakespeare's play *Othello* provides a classic example. Othello, an army general, is cultivated by a subordinate, Iago, who envies his position. Concerned about the loyalty of his wife, Othello confides his suspicions to Iago. Eventually, Iago brings Othello down by fanning the flames of his jealousy. Similar phenomena take place every day in modern America's officers' quarters, party caucuses, and boardrooms.

Politics in an AIDS Laboratory

Distinguished organizations involved in world-class science are not immune from politics. The *Wall Street Journal* illustrated this fact in a story about a federal laboratory on the cutting edge of AIDS research.[20]

Political Conflict in a Scientific Laboratory

As intense public concern with the AIDS epidemic became acute, a nongovernmental biologist urged the Federal Centers for Disease Control (CDC) to determine whether nonoxynol-9, a widely used spermicide, could kill the AIDS virus. It was argued that nonoxynol-9, available at any drugstore in America, might allow thousands to avoid contracting AIDS.

James Curran, a key CDC official, refused to provide the sample of AIDS virus required for the study. Curran's subordinates, though, allowed the experiment to take place, and nonoxynol-9 was found indeed to kill the AIDS virus, if only in a laboratory dish.

Normally, scientific findings are made known worldwide through publication in specialized journals. Curran, though, forced a delay in publishing the spermicide test results and caused them to appear in a less-visible form. A colleague explained that Curran, appointed by the conservative Reagan administration, wished to downplay prevention methods compatible with gay sex practices.

Politics internal to the lab were observed as well. A prominent scientist wanted experiments to be conducted using a strain of AIDS virus he had isolated. While other scientists were absent from the lab, he ordered a technician to dismantle all experiments using other AIDS strains. At least one top scientist whose experiments had been discarded quit a few months later.

Organizational Change

Change represents a fundamental challenge to the formal organization. As stable systems of roles, organizations are designed *not* to change. Eventual change, though, is inevitable. Change does not always represent progress. It may symbolize an organization's decline. Organizations that are unable to change when necessary decline and ultimately disband.

Many different processes of change are found in organizations. Change may be *natural* or *intentional*. Natural change in an organization results from forces outside the control of managers, directors, or owners. Intentional change occurs, or is at least initiated, at their behest. Both natural and intentional change may originate from forces or persons external or internal to the organization.

Significant organizational change is frequently accompanied by conflict and politics. Change has varying consequences for each individual and subunit. Relations between those who benefit from change and those who lose by it are often characterized by conflict. Politics can serve as an instrument to promote change or a barrier to the process.

Change potentially affects everyone in an organization and everything the organization does. It is perhaps more vital, then, for people managing or working in formal organizations to understand change than any other organizational process. Research on organizational change suggests four questions as particularly important:

1. What factors cause organizations to change?

2. By what process does change take place?

3. What techniques can managers apply to control the change process and ensure positive outcomes?

4. How do people in organizations adapt to change?

Change is never easy in a formal organization. Managers sometimes initiate change and sometimes have it imposed upon them. Whether change is desired or imposed, natural or intentional, particularly difficult challenges may be expected in the areas listed above.

Why Organizations Resist Change

As stable systems of roles—enforced by rewards, imperative force, and culture—organizations naturally resist change. Normally, roles and their occupants constitute a system in social equilibrium. Under equilibrium, most individuals accept each other's role expectations and performance standards. As in the French factory described by Crozier (see Chapter 7), occupants of specific roles come to accept each other's power and privilege. In Crozier's example, equilibrium brings about stagnation and low productivity, due in part to the disinclination of managers to exercise discipline and initiate reform. Equilibrium states need not be unproductive ones, though. Features of organizations such as roles and values typically represent adaptations to production needs and environmental conditions. Organizations become skilled by sticking to stable objectives and methods.

The capacities that enable organizations to coordinate the efforts of individuals in a long-term, stable fashion themselves constitute barriers to change. Organizational reward systems illustrate this principle. People who have developed technical skills, social practices, and networks that enable them to obtain rewards under an existing system are reluctant to see that system change.

Justifiably, individuals fear that new norms, expectations, and relationships will not work as well for them as have the existing ones. Operatives fear challenges associated with new work and systems of supervision. Executives are concerned with loss of privilege and potential replacement by personnel with different skills and networks.

Examples of organizations that are models of stability, then, are easier to find than models of change. Even organizations whose objectives focus specifically on change are often remarkably stable. The Communist Party of the old Soviet Union was a classic instance. As the Soviet Union's only legally functioning political organization, the Communist Party purportedly strove to build a new kind of society. But the structure of the party—extremely hierarchical and centralized—persisted virtually unchanged for the Soviet state's 70-year existence.

Organizational change represents a paradox. Change is unlikely in a well-functioning organization, as structure and the properties that enforce it promote loyalty to the status quo. But organizational change occurs regularly in modern economies. Organizations that are unable to change often face decline and eventual dissolution.

Recognizing Change

An organization truly changes only when its basic structure and the means it uses to enforce role expectations undergo alteration. Changes in structure signal genuine organizational change. An organization genuinely changes when it becomes significantly more (or less) hierarchical, flexible, or centralized. Genuine change occurs when organizations revise the methods they use to assess personnel for recruitment, advancement, punishment, and reward. Revision of core beliefs and values also signals true change. For change to be recognized as genuine, the fundamental manner in which an organization coordinates human action for the purposes of attaining objectives and sustaining itself over time must be altered.

Some social scientists apply the term *deep structure* to describe both basic patterns of role relationships and core elements in members' thinking. These observers say that genuine change takes place only when one or more parts of the organization's deep structure are transformed. Organizational structure as defined in Chapter 5 is only one dimension of deep structure. Other elements include[21]

- Core beliefs and values regarding the organization, its employees, and its environment
- Distribution of power within the organization
- The nature, type, and pervasiveness of control systems (including reward, punishment, and imperative force)

Superficial or cosmetic alterations do not amount to real change. Firms often pursue new corporate images by redesigning employee uniforms, repainting equipment, or mounting advertising campaigns with new songs and slogans. Organizations regularly alter objectives and change leaders. But genuine change is unusual. Slogans, leaders, hiring campaigns, and reductions in force (RIFs) come and go without involving the organization's basic structure or mode of operation.

The Causes of Change

A multitude of forces impose change on organizations from time to time. Every organization owes its structural features to forces that are subject to change. As indicated in Chapter 5, an organization's structure may be traced to factors such as its size, age, technology, environment, and leadership. Changes in any of these factors result in pressures in the direction of organizational change. Organizations often change as they grow, age, or adopt new technology. Environmental developments impel organizations to change, whether these involve changes in the organization's legal, political, demographic, or physical surroundings. Powerful leaders can change organizations, particularly when organizations are young and their structures are still flexible.

Both external and internal factors cause organizations to change. The constant flux of modern society continuously challenges organizations. Ultimately, organizations are composed of people, and few individual human beings are completely satisfied with their surroundings or tools. Individual dissatisfaction facilitates change.

External causes of change. Changes originating outside organizations are easiest to see. Chapter 3 highlighted liberation, immigration, and economic change as key challenges to American organizations in the late 20th century. All have necessitated organizational change.

Changes in social environment. New developments in the beliefs of the surrounding population have reduced the feasibility of existing organizational structure and practices. Liberation movements involving minorities, women, and people of diverse sexual orientation challenged the deep structures of many organizations. Changed expectations regarding these groups forced organizations to reduce traditional restrictions on hiring and promotion. Female executives have sued employers for excluding them from traditionally male-only sporting and social events held for important clients.

Liberation movements have also reduced the ability of formal organizations to expect conformity from their members. Many people no longer keep their sexual orientations secret, conceal nonmainstream religious beliefs, or automatically consent to long overtime hours and transfer to distant cities.

Changes in the economic environment. Increased competitiveness has forced work organizations to modify structure and core practices. Global competition and deregulation have required industrial firms to continuously upgrade quality and reduce costs. Such necessity has made it impossible for many work organizations to offer long-term employment as a reward for appropriate behavior. As product cycles have shortened, organizations need to regularly recruit personnel with new skills. Investor expectations of high financial returns may shorten executive tenure. Increased turnover at all levels challenges organizational culture and the authority of supervisors.

Competition and deregulation in the late 20th century promoted another form of organizational change among private-sector organizations: acquisitions and mergers. Corporate takeovers resulted in personnel reassignment, RIFs, and cultural disruption.

Demographic change. Changes in the distribution of personal characteristics among Americans have required revision in organizational structure and related properties. Americans have become more diverse. In some parts of the United States, the share of the population composed of non-Hispanic Whites has declined sharply. Minority and female members of the labor force often have different expectations about organizations than traditionally dominant White men. Demographic change often signals changes in the public's taste for consumer goods, raising issues for organizational objectives and hence modes of functioning.

Political change. Political economy is a social force that profoundly affects organizations. Historic changes from capitalism to communism (and vice versa) necessitated major revision in the structure and function of Eastern European economic enterprises. On a more immediate level, changes in government policy affect a broad range of organizations, particularly those in the public sector.

Internal causes of change. Phenomena taking place primarily inside an organization's boundaries also result in change. A few of many possible examples include the following:

Failure to achieve objectives. Failure to achieve objectives is an impetus for change as both managers and workers lose faith in doing business as usual. Even without visible failure, people in organizations come to desire change to help accommodate their changing needs. In a start-up situation, for example, employees may value flexibility. Once established in their careers, the same individuals choose regularity over spontaneity. Changing values among organizational member constitute pressure to change.

Ambition of leaders. The desire of organizational leaders to achieve unusual levels of success acts as an impetus for change. Often, leaders take such action in the latter half of their careers, seeing their remaining active time as limited. People in charge of organizations may develop ambitions to create a revolutionary product, achieve market dominance, make scientific breakthroughs, or win election to high office. Aspirations of this kind often require higher productivity standards, changes in technology, or hiring of new staff and executives. All these actions create pressure for organizational change.

Decline of family management. Many formal organizations, usually business firms, begin under the leadership of members of a single family. Successive generations of top leaders are appointed on the basis of kinship. Eventually, family members lose interest in the enterprise or produce no offspring qualified for executive responsibilities. This phenomenon occurred in Germany's famed Krupp Industries after centuries of family rule. Following the demise of family management, routes to leadership positions may be expected to be significantly more universalistic.

The organizational life cycle. Several references have already been made to the effect of age on an organization. Hierarchy and openness to new ideas are said to decrease as an organization ages. Focusing on government agencies, commentator Anthony Downs writes that government bureaus experience cycles of growth and decline.[22] During the growth period, young people with fresh ideas flock to the new agency.

Promotion opportunities are abundant. New ideas are proposed and accepted. As growth levels off, promotion opportunities decline. Younger people are not hired, average age of the staff increases, and emphasis shifts from creativity to control.

Organizational Decline at NASA

Howard McCurdy[23] illustrates the principle of organizational life cycles in a study of the National Aeronautics and Space Administration (NASA) in the 1970s and 1980s.

Created in the 1950s to beat the Soviet Union in the space race, NASA enjoyed generous funding. Staff expanded rapidly, rocketing from 10,000 in 1960 to 36,000 in 1967. NASA attracted top engineering talent away from other industries. During its growth phase, NASA offered promotion opportunities to one in five staff members. Technical professionals did direct, hands-on science. NASA's heyday climaxed in 1969 with the landing of American astronauts on the moon.

Rapid decline followed this triumph. Budget cutbacks, competing government priorities (including Vietnam War spending), and declining public support led to decreased funding. Staff levels dropped to 22,000 by 1982. Promotion opportunities declined proportionally. Average age of remaining staff rose from 38 in 1966 to 44 in 1978. Reduced staffing forced NASA to contract out much scientific work. A majority of NASA technical professionals became administrators of the resulting contracts.

Conservatism, stagnation, and inability to attract enough top talent are blamed by many for the agency's failures in the 1980s and 1990s. These included spectacular events such as the loss of the space shuttle *Challenger*, faulty manufacture of the Hubble Space Telescope, and the failure of two advanced Mars probes.

It should be noted that the cycle described by McCurdy resulted not only from internal organizational dynamics but also from external factors such as reduction of federal funding. NASA's decline cannot be thought of as intentional change, though federal funding decision makers must have known that reduced support would have adverse consequences for the agency.

Origins of Intentional Change

Intentional change can originate either outside or inside an organization. External factors initiate intentional change, as when stockholders demand improved performance from a corporation or Congress mandates change in a public agency. Internal factors can lead to intentional change, as when an organization experiences multiple failures to achieve objectives. Leadership is a crucial factor in intentional change. Appropriate modification of structure, culture, and objectives in response to changing external conditions may be necessary to an organization's survival. Such modification cannot occur without initiation and direction by effective leaders.

Environmental Change Confounds an Organization

Major environmental shifts require organizations to change, but not all organizations can do so. Inability to change when change is necessary leads to decline and dissolution.

An Orthodox synagogue that closed in 1999 illustrates this principle.

Changing Demographics

The synagogue had served New York City's borough of the Bronx for 72 years. According to a long-time member, the synagogue had been "the social hub of the neighborhood," holding four different services on Sabbaths and holidays, "each one . . . filled, with people out around the block."[24]

But most Jewish residents left the Bronx in late decades of the 20th century, their numbers declining from 600,000 in the 1940s to fewer than 100,000 by the century's end. Congregation membership collapsed, skidding from 3,500 to under 100.

The synagogue struggled to continue operations, its rabbi raising funds from outside the neighborhood and urging his board not to give up. Ultimately, however, everyone realized that the organization's "consumer base" had disappeared.

Might intentional change have saved the synagogue? Distinguished houses of worship elsewhere have prospered as multidenominational institutions, allowing multiple faiths to share physical facilities.

The organization's core beliefs and values made such transformation impossible. Steeped in centuries of tradition, Orthodox synagogues are prohibited from even selling their building to other faiths. Dissolution seemed the only alternative.

The Process of Change

Observers of organizations have described two different processes of change: slow (evolutionary) and rapid (revolutionary). Some researchers have followed organizations for considerable periods of time. They have described minute revisions in procedures and communication patterns that, over a period of years, result in fundamental change. But according to others, genuine change occurs only during short periods of opportunity. In this view, the change process is rapid and intense.

Evolutionary change: The California Industrial Accident Commission. Sociologist Philippe Nonet chronicled evolutionary change in a California state agency known as the Industrial Accident Commission.[25] The agency's mission was to determine whether workers who claimed to have been injured on the job were entitled to compensation under state programs. In its early days, the Commission functioned as a government agency ordinarily does. Applicants whose claims were contested by their employers or insurance companies would request the agency to determine whether compensation should be granted.

Over the years, the Commission took on the appearance not of a government bureau but of a courtroom. Rather than unilaterally decide cases on the basis of state law, officials of the Commission encouraged employees and employers to present oral arguments before them. Claimants were encouraged to hire lawyers. The Commission officials took on the trappings of judges. Office furniture was arranged to mimic a court setting, with the official sitting at a table placed on a raised platform with a large American flag as a backdrop.

This process of change was clearly evolutionary. It took place little by little, over a period of decades. No emphatic dictums were issued by higher officials or the state legislature. Rather, periodic memorandums circulated among Commission officials about how they should conduct business. Successive memos addressed small details but over time changed the way the Commission worked. The outcome of this slow process was significant. At its origin, the Commission had been dedicated to helping people too poor or ignorant to help themselves. Afterward, only parties represented by strong organizations (such as unions) or good lawyers could effectively press their claims.

Nonet attributes this change to a desire by the Commissioners to avoid outside criticism. Organized labor and business interests seemed always ready to find fault with the agency. By appearing neutral, the Commission avoided criticism and the possibility that it might be dismantled by legislation. A desire for prestige by Commission officials may also have played a part. By appearing more like judges than desk-bound officials, Commission functionaries may have felt they raised their standing in the minds of the public.

The public did not appear to benefit from the agency's evolutionary change. Originally, the Commission had been established to aid workers who were otherwise at the mercy of powerful employers. At the conclusion of its change cycle, the agency provided little help to workers who lacked strong union representation or were unable to hire attorneys on their own. The Commission, moreover, never functioned as a court actually does. In a court, judges deal with cases that are open to debate and decide them on the basis of often-original arguments. Despite the courtroom trappings, the Commission confined its work to application of standard regulations. Truly difficult questions, factual disputes, and problems with the regulations themselves were referred to real courts.

Processes similar to the one described here occur in many organizations. There is evidence that change is a natural and routine feature of organizational functioning. Even within the most stable structure, individuals constantly negotiate their role expectations. Both workers and managers continually seek ways to increase the benefits they draw from membership. Subunits, too, promote their power and prestige and seek means for limiting effort and risk. Over time, this jockeying results in revisions of basic organizational features such as reward systems, culture, and structure itself.

Revolutionary change in organizations. According to some observers, genuine change never takes place in organizations without sharp disruption of routine. A formulation by pioneering researcher Kurt Lewin asserts that organizational change takes place in three stages: freezing, moving, and refreezing.[26] These words imply that at most times an organization's structure and methods of function are strong, stable, and not subject to change. Rarely, it is said, traumatic events and pressures make the organization's core features fluid, allowing change to take place.

Connie Gersick, a more recent observer, writes that organizations change only through a process of *punctuated equilibrium.*[27] Equilibrium, again, signifies a state in which rewards, culture, and imperative forces effectively discourage challenges to the status quo. Both workers and managers feel that more can be gained by living with the existing system than by attempting to change it.

According to Gersick, equilibrium must be disrupted for change to take place. Equilibrium fails when people in an organization perceive that the organization can no longer solve important problems. Markets have dried up. Products have failed. Executive talent cannot be recruited. People in the organization lose respect for authority and commitment to the organization's values. Gersick describes periods of punctuated equilibrium as times of "wholesale upheaval." These periods may be characterized by strong emotional discharge, as people feel a sense of distortion and loss, but also optimism and stimulation.

Field observation suggests that major disruptions are required for genuine change to take place. Repeated failure to produce successful products can be interpreted as the result of routine engineering problems if basic ideas and social relationships remain intact. Executives must come to the conclusion that the system is "just not working" before fundamental restructuring can be considered. Catastrophe must threaten for people to put aside personal goals and private agendas in order to seek long-term solutions.

Techniques for Changing Organizations

Managers employ a wide variety of techniques for causing organizations to change. Two types of techniques may be distinguished. The first emphasizes collaboration between members for the purpose of improving the organization. The second emphasizes managers' direct confrontation of individuals and coalitions (both formal and informal) that oppose the changes the managers desire.

Collaborative Change: Organizational Development

Managers seeking to improve the capabilities of their organizations often utilize techniques known as *organizational development,* or OD. Initiation of an OD project typically results from management's desire to improve the organization's functioning. OD usually involves intensive communication among groups of employees on subjects not normally discussed or at an unusual level of intensity. The purpose of conducting OD projects is to promote favorable changes through better utilization of members' capabilities. Through OD, organizations may rediscover and reemphasize valuable elements of existing culture. Organizations may also deliberately modify their structure to promote better communication or appropriate response to environmental conditions.

Management researchers and consultants continually developed new OD procedures throughout the 20th century. Three principal features characterize most OD efforts. First, most OD efforts include convening of discussion groups charged with identifying problems and formulating solutions. Second, the majority of OD projects employ a "change agent." Change agents are individuals assigned to promote discussion, build consensus, and promote required action. Finally, many OD procedures include "action research," that is, collection and analysis of facts to support discussion and decision making in pursuit of change.

Group Problem Solving

Group problem solving and consensus building constitute the core of many OD efforts. Under such procedures, managers draw on the experience and ideas of personnel to identify problems and create solutions. Often, these groups include people who do not normally communicate with each other. In a business firm, middle managers from sales may be placed alongside people of equal rank from manufacturing. In a government agency, personnel with direct client contact responsibilities may be placed alongside program planners. Individuals in different specialties and in different ranks attain a balanced view of the organization's challenges and opportunities.

Group problem solving and consensus building can serve as a model for change. As Chapter 10 demonstrated, organizations often lack sufficient communication channels and circuits. Consequently, individuals may lack the information required to do their best for the organization. Lessons learned from group consensus building may be absorbed into the organization as changes in structure, allowing better exchange of information to take place.

Change Agents

OD efforts resulting in organizational change require more than meetings of diverse individuals and arrival at consensus. An individual or group of individuals specifically empowered to promote change is necessary. Individuals fitting this description include people from within the organization who are assigned to assemble and conduct problem-solving groups. These individuals may be assigned to report the results of group discussions to upper management, or they may themselves be high-level executives who desire to see change take place or who have received a mandate for change from the organization's governing body. Increasingly, the individuals and groups assigned to identify problems, formulate solutions, and push for implementation are consultants hired from outside the organization. Individuals and groups with mandates of this kind are known as *change agents*.

The operation of an external consulting group as a change agent provides an example of change through organizational development. Large consulting firms such as McKinsey deploy teams of experts to the firm in several areas. These teams may spend months holding group problem-solving meetings. They may also interview individuals or conduct surveys. Often, the team will review technical features of operations and finance. The consulting job ends with a report to management.

Actual change requires action by an internal change agent. The executive in charge of the consulting contract often plays this role. His or her success depends on the willingness of the governing body—the board of directors in a firm and the board of trustees in a nonprofit—to accept the recommendations and implement them. Plans based on broad input have the best chance of success. Personnel who have been consulted are most likely to feel that the plan reflects their opinions and interests.

Action Research

Action research refers to collection and analysis of data pertinent to the process of change in an organization. Change agents inside an organization may contract with outside consultants to carry out this research or have it done in-house. Action research aims at providing information that is important in successive stages of the change process and feeding this information back to the change agent. An action researcher begins by helping define a problem. Once a problem is defined, he or she gathers and analyzes data associated with proposed alternatives for solution. Finally, the action researcher evaluates the impact of interventions designed to bring about change. Action research may utilize surveys, direct observation of operations, or focus groups (structured discussion situations to provide ranges of opinions on selected issues). Action research differs from more traditional forms of inquiry because it regularly provides successive waves of feedback to decision makers at each point in a cycle of activities intended to produce change.

Grassroots organizations representing community residents in American cities, sometimes known as community-based organizations (CBOs), have begun using action research in their attempts to bring about change. CBOs typically use the term *empowerment evaluation* to describe what is called action research in the corporate setting. CBOs, for example, often wish to build their membership in a manner that reflects the characteristics of the surrounding community. They often seek to develop a structure that results in decision making that is beneficial to the community. Research personnel develop descriptions of the surrounding community to help guide recruitment strategy. After this step, the research team surveys informants in the community to determine whether the CBO is perceived as being truly representative.

Organizational Development

The widely used term *organizational development* (OD) denotes an array of procedures used by managers to promote an organization's well-being. These techniques may address effectiveness, efficiency, creativity, sustainability, or quality of life within the organization. Organizational development often focuses on improving interpersonal relationships within an organization.

Techniques associated with organizational development include

- Group problem solving and consensus building
- Employment of a change agent
- Action research

Whether it takes place in corporate, government, or community settings, OD-type change involves development of mutually acceptable steps by multiple individuals and groups. Most often, this process is initiated and guided by existing management. Collaborative change techniques fit well with evolutionary change.

Confrontational Change: The Process of "Creative Destruction"

Some organizational change techniques of great importance differ strongly from those associated with OD. Nearly always initiated by existing management, OD utilizes channels and networks already in place and strives for consensus. Confrontational techniques differ in that they are often imposed from outside. They set aside existing communication channels and networks. They impose new objectives, methods, and values not necessarily endorsed by the organization's members.

Sociologist Nicole Woolsey Biggart's study of the United States postal system in the early 1970s[28] provides a detailed example of a confrontational change intervention. During this era, the old Post Office Department was transformed into the present-day United States Postal Service. The United States Post Office Department had delivered the mail for over 100 years. It functioned as a large government agency. The *Postal Manual,* an official volume weighing nine pounds, prescribed details of operation. Executive positions were allocated by successive presidential administrations as rewards to their political allies. Pay and promotion for the mass of workers, employed under Civil Service regulations, were based on how long they had worked for the agency. Managers feared surprise visits by postal inspectors and were neither encouraged nor inclined to make decisions.

The organization operated by the Post Office Department was clearly obsolete by the 1960s. Huge volumes of mail clogged postal depots, and deliveries sometimes took weeks. In 1971, Congress passed legislation mandating the Post Office Department to modernize. The agency, to be renamed the United States Postal Service, was ordered to select its leadership on the basis of nonpolitical criteria, enable the most capable (rather than the longest-lived) personnel to attain promotion, sell bonds to raise capital, and most important, make a profit.

Despite the congressional mandate, plans for change faced powerful opposition. Change required supervisors to make decisions, innovate, and encourage workers to think of themselves as personnel in a for-profit firm. Many post office managers and workers had been satisfied with the old system's drab but predictable and often-undemanding ways. A "service at all costs" ethic prevailed, undermining efficiency. Unless their outlook and actions changed, the United States Postal Service would function much like the old Post Office Department, albeit under a different name. Unless both managers and operatives genuinely accepted the new system, moreover, they had sufficient power to rescind the innovation. Representing hundreds of thousands of employees, postal unions and management associations maintained powerful lobbying operations.

Winton Blount, the new agency's first postmaster general, realized this and took steps to ensure that actual change occurred. His actions serve as a procedure manual for changing an organization. This change agent's actions included

- Changing ideology
- Replacing leaders
- Forging power bases and alliances

Changing ideology. Ideology denotes a set of beliefs and values about human relations, particularly regarding who should be in charge and what collective action should aim for. Ideology is part of organizational culture. Blount knew he would have to change basic employee thinking about what the organization was and how it should work. He used four techniques to bring about this transformation:

- *Symbolic reorientation.* As in any cultural transformation, ideological change required replacement of old symbols with new. The Postal Service underwent a visual makeover. Traditional olive drab equipment was repainted red, white, and blue. The time-honored logo featuring a galloping rider was replaced with a poised eagle. Unveiling of new decor was marked by celebrations and public tours at every post office. The agency's new name itself suggested transformation and independence.

- *Internal communication.* Blount used the organization's internal communication resources as a key mechanism of organizational change. Articles were placed in house organs to present the new management position on efficiency and instill a sense of urgency among employees. A special house organ was begun for supervisory personnel, highlighting high-performing post offices and publicizing newly open promotion opportunities. Executives traveled the country to brief supervisors. The agency brought large numbers of supervisors to Washington for intensive training sessions.

- *External communication.* Reducing the possibility that interest groups within the U.S. Postal Service would forge alliances with outside opponents of change required an outside sales effort. For the first time, the agency purchased advertising to publicize its new image. Visits by the mass media to newly redecorated post offices were arranged.

- *Training and indoctrination.* The agency instituted a vigorous effort to change the thinking of management personnel. Over 20,000 supervisors were brought to the Postal Service Management Institute in Washington for intensive classes. High-level managers received training at the Harvard Business School in decision making and competitive management practices.

- *Replacing leaders.* Persons achieving leadership in an organization are usually committed to the organization's culture and methods of operation. Such commitment is valuable in normal times. But it can obstruct change, as managers cling to old values and methods of supervision. Many of Blount's efforts focused on replacing old leaders with people unburdened by traditional thinking and practice. Means of replacing leaders included the following:
    - *Encouraging retirement.* Older, senior postal officials were offered bonuses equivalent to six months pay if they retired immediately. Of 6,000 eligible personnel, 4,000 accepted the offer.
    - *Opening promotion opportunities.* The reorganization effort included several measures to encourage new personnel to move into leadership positions. These measures included reducing the importance of seniority in qualifications for promotion, allowing employees to apply for positions outside their own localities, and removing a requirement that postmasters reside in the towns where they work.

- o *Recruiting new leaders.* The Postal Service actively recruited new managers from outside, particularly newly graduated holders of management degrees.
- *Securing power bases and alliances.* The new organization needed to assure and assuage outside forces that possessed sufficient authority or power to reverse the change process. Two examples are the U.S. Congress and the American Federation of Labor and Congress of Industrial Organizations (AFL-CIO), with which the American Postal Workers Union is and was affiliated. Congress, of course, could rescind the legislation that mandated the change. The AFL-CIO could exercise significant political might in safeguarding or undermining the new agency. Steps intended to forge alliances with these forces included the following:
  - o *Establishing a clear voice.* Blount issued a gag order that declared that all communication with Congress would go through his office, ensuring that only information supportive of the organization's transformation was transmitted to this important body.
  - o *Economic accommodation of the union.* In return for their support of the legislation establishing the United States Postal Service, the AFL-CIO received a 14% pay increase for postal workers and the exclusive right to bargain on behalf of these workers.

Biggart characterizes the process resulting from these techniques as "creative destruction." This term is borrowed from the famous economist Joseph Schumpeter,[29] who used it to described competitive economies. Competition results in destruction, as formerly successful firms and industries fall prey to more efficient competitors and advanced technology. But competition is also creative because it makes better and cheaper goods available to the consumer. In the same way, forceful confrontation of existing practices and management results in personal discomfort and removal of long-term employees. But the process ultimately results in a more effective organization.

Reaction of Members to Change

People in high positions, usually directors or executives, initiate change. But change cannot take place unless it is understood and implemented by subordinates. Workers must be informed about coming changes, instructed in their implementation, and motivated to provide willing assistance. The post office case study illustrates means by which change agents try to bring this about.

Members of organizations below the top slots, though, accept change neither passively nor automatically. People at all levels are alert to the slightest hints of change. They piece together impressions on the basis of small pieces of information. They seek ways to channel forces of change in directions favorable to them.

Managers require an understanding of the processes by which an organization's members react to change. The ability of an executive to obtain the results he or she seeks from change may depend on the perceptions and countermoves of lower-level managers and workers.

Perceptions of change. Research on change in organizations suggests that workers react to change in stages. Management personnel outside executive ranks go through similar stages. The process of perception runs parallel to the amount of information available and the immediacy of change in the individual's immediate surroundings.

Stages of perception. A study of 42 managers by Lynn Isabella identified four stages in responses to developing change.[30]

1. *Anticipation.* People receive early indications that something may be happening. Available information arrives via leakage from the executive suite. Speculation spreads through gossip networks. The anticipation stage may also be characterized as the *rumor phase.*

2. *Confirmation.* Active discussion of possible change begins among lower-level managers and workers. Colleagues compare tidbits of information. People recall events they have witnessed at other times or in other organizations. Marked by informal gatherings to pool fragmentary material, this time period may be called the *water-cooler phase.*

3. *Culmination.* Personnel now receive official information about the change and how it will affect them. Individuals get new work assignments, new supervisors, and new physical surroundings, sometimes including long-distance moves. Some receive dismissal notices. Workers and other nonexecutives discuss with each other how they have been affected. They piece together a comprehensive view of what has happened in the organization as a whole. People may be seen packing up their desks. This period may be called the *moving phase.*

4. *Aftermath.* Personnel try to figure out whether they have benefited or lost out due to the change. They reflect upon who else has won or lost. They assess the future. The aftermath period might be called the *recovery phase*, as employees move beyond the "surgical shock" that change often causes.

Management of perceptions. The stages of change described above underscore the importance of reaction by an organization's membership. Communication leaks from top management are inevitable, and rumors begin early on. People at all levels talk with peers and formulate personal opinions and strategies.

The communication patterns and perceptual dynamics taking place in each stage suggest interventions available to managers to limit misunderstanding, anxiety, and antagonism. At the anticipation stage, executives and change agents may initiate internal communications to disseminate information about the options actually under consideration. During the confirmation stage, managers may conduct group meetings and bull sessions focused on upcoming changes. These group sessions give management an opportunity to participate in the formation of worker perceptions. At the culmination stage, management might address the employees' feelings of anxiety and loss by making the "moving" process as

pleasant as possible, considering gratuities such as assistance with physical relocation, training, bonuses, or time off.

Politics of Change

Management encounters difficulty in controlling the process of change when
workers have resources and will to resist. Workers with knowledge power constitute
one example. Unionized labor represents another.

Well-functioning organizations employ political processes to control conflict. As
described earlier in this chapter, politics is an advocacy-oriented procedure that
enables conflicting parties to achieve resolution. Through the political process,
individuals and subunits press competing claims on the organization's resources.
Individuals and subunits struggle to determine the organization's operating procedures, objectives and culture. Disputants negotiate with each other and seek allies.
The outcome of successful politics is a state of equilibrium. Under equilibrium,
most members feel most of the time that acting consistently with role expectations
is preferable to changing or leaving the organization.

Researchers Bacharach, Bamberger, and Sonnenstuhl illustrate the politics of
change in a study of the airline industry in the 1980s.[31] Prior to that period, airlines
had functioned under federal regulation. Regulators set prices and determined
airline routes. Individual airlines had no incentives to cut costs as they would in a
competitive market. Deregulation in the 1980s suddenly threw airline companies
into a sea of unrestricted competition.

Competition rapidly reduced quality of working life for airline flight attendants.
Pressure for operating efficiency forced airlines to reduce flight attendant crew
sizes. Other efficiency measures included more time in the air and less on the
ground when on duty, relocation to distant air hubs, and assignment to teams of
unfamiliar coworkers.

Labor-management relations within the airline companies underwent a basic
change, moving from one state of equilibrium to another. Initially, equilibrium
characterized by "communalism" prevailed. Communalism constituted a sense of
personal commitment by both flight attendants and managers to common values,
mutual interdependence, and quality service. The change period concluded with
establishment of a new equilibrium dominated by formal work rules.

Top executives were the first to abandon communalism. They instituted strict
economies to keep from having to raise fares. For the flight attendants, emphasis on
economical operations meant loss of communal ties with both employers and
colleagues as well as fatigue and work-home conflicts. Drug and alcohol abuse
became a worrisome problem.

The flight attendants' union at first attempted to restore communal ties with
management by asking for a new benefit: an employee assistance program (EAP) to
provide counseling to affected workers. Fearing associated costs, top management
refused. Union representatives forged a temporary alliance with middle managers
and first-line supervisors. These managerial personnel helped stricken employees

obtain sick leave and referral to a union-operated EAP. But this alliance soon collapsed, as middle managers realized that their personal advancement required support of corporate policies. For middle managers and first-line supervisors, this meant keeping flight attendants in the air, not in counseling or on disability. Left on its own, the union focused its attention on work rules, negotiating for favorable contract provisions and strict enforcement of contracts.

Change, then, took place as a series of shifting alliances between different groups of stakeholders. First approaching top management, workers appealed to the industry's traditional communalism. Rebuffed, they turned to supervisors and middle managers, forming a temporary alliance. Eventually, middle management abandoned the alliance due to the reward power of the top management echelon. Isolated, the flight attendants resorted to protection of rules negotiated by their union. Antagonism prevailed in labor-management relations. By the mid-1980s a new equilibrium had been established. This equilibrium provided stable role expectations and working relationships within the airline companies, albeit in an atmosphere of suspicion and gloom.

Issues and Applications

Conflict, politics, and change are important processes within organizations. However, they are poorly understood by both outsiders and participants. Often, these processes operate out of sight and have unexpected outcomes.

- Significant interpersonal conflict is said to have occurred within the administration of President Franklin D. Roosevelt (1933–1945), yet this administration helped create institutions that remain important parts of American life. Because this conflict was task-related rather than interpersonal, however, its impact was constructive. According to some, Roosevelt encouraged conflict over ideas, believing that this process would produce the best thinking.

- A group of students has been campaigning to convince their university to pull its investments in countries with poor records of protecting human rights. They have organized well-attended demonstrations and met with the dean of students, who has expressed personal sympathy with their cause. In view of their successes, the students are surprised when the board of trustees, the university's governing body, takes no action. Influences unknown to the students have motivated the board to keep the investments where they are.

- The management team in a supermarket announces that it is planning to make changes. Dress codes are altered. A staggered work schedule is developed. Posters are displayed in the employee area for a "zero defects" campaign. But it is erroneous to characterize these steps as genuine change. They neither involve relationships among roles nor elements of "deep structure," such as beliefs, values, and rewards.

Chapter Review and Major Themes

Conflict, politics, and change are interrelated phenomena. Each can involve competition for loyalty and resources. Each may disturb existing equilibrium either between individuals or within the organization as a whole. Differences in values and objectives or the diversity in a group are potential sources of conflict. Conflict can benefit an organization if it involves tasks rather than personal feelings. Organizations have both formal and informal processes available to them to manage conflict.

Politics may be thought of as a controlled form of conflict, in which individuals or subunits compete for resources or for control over the organization's direction. Politics can take the "high road," addressing people's values and aspirations, follow the "low road," promising favors in exchange for loyalty, or even resort to character assassination and backstabbing.

While not coming naturally to most organizations, change is ultimately necessary in many. Outside factors, such as economics or demographics, induce change in an organization, or inside forces, such as management ambition or chronic failure, may induce change. Change may be deliberately planned through an organizational development process or result from an unexpected crisis.

Figure 11.1 captures some of the dynamics of the organizational change process. This diagram emphasizes the importance of environmental factors in initiating change. Organizational change, whether initiated by internal or external factors, has a potential impact on the environment. The organization's peers or clients may experience difficulties or benefits due to the changes the organization has undergone. Other organizations may imitate changes viewed as beneficial.

Clearly, a favorable organizational change can improve function. But organizational change is not necessarily favorable. Intentional change in structure or culture may give rise to less- rather than more-effective operations. Changes such as those carried out by Al Dunlap (see Chapter 2), while seemingly forward-looking and bold, weakened the companies he managed.

In some instances, organizational change may reduce conflict, as in cases where communication is made easier, structures are simplified, or new career paths are established. But the degree to which change may increase conflict should not be underestimated. People are likely to protest or obstruct change if their interests are threatened. Discomfort and ill will often result when management reconfigures individual roles or dismisses personnel. To a greater or lesser degree, change involves struggle.

Similarly, politics can either promote or reduce both function and conflict. Civilly conducted politics can mitigate conflict, substituting principled discussion for competition. Openly competitive politics, on the other hand, easily becomes conflict. Either way, politics can have a positive or negative impact on function. Losers in a struggle for power often harbor resentment, undercut the victors, or leave the organization. As suggested above, however, competitive, conflict-laden politics may be a precondition for meaningful change.

Conflict, politics and change all involve disturbances, intentional or accidental, of an organization's existing equilibrium. All involve control by management that is imperfect at best. The organization's leadership can initiate change and conduct politics, but both processes also arise spontaneously. Members of organizations at all levels can receive training and exercise options to control interpersonal conflict, but conflict between individuals and the organization itself may involve less tractable social issues.

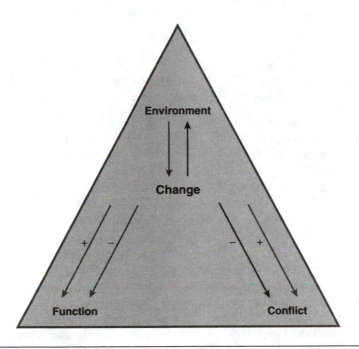

Figure 11.1   Analytical Perspectives Applied to Change

Discussion Questions

1. Although extreme interpersonal violence is unusual in most organizations, instances of severe "everyday" conflict (such as verbal and physical assaults) are not unusual. Are there causes of such violence in formal organizations that are absent in informal settings such as groups and families? To what extent can such violence be eliminated in formal organizations?

2. How well have organizations in the United States responded to the issue of sexual harassment? Provide examples from actual organizations.

3. To what extent can politics as described in this chapter be considered a constructive process?

4. If a member of an organization becomes the object of character assassination or other forms of "lower politics," how can he or she respond?

5. Episodes of organizational change can be traumatic in nature, as members are propagandized, reassigned, or terminated. Can true changes in "deep structure" be achieved without such trauma? What procedures can be employed?

References

1. Morill, C., Zald, M. N., & Rao, H. (2003). Covert political conflict in organizations: Challenges from below. *Annual Review of Sociology, 29,* 391–416.
2. Thomas, K. W. (1992). Conflict and negotiation process in organizations. In M. D. Dunnette & L. M. Hough (Eds.), *Handbook of industrial and organizational psychology* (2nd ed., pp. 651–717). Palo Alto, CA: Consulting Psychologists Press.
3. Jamieson, R. L., & Schubert, R. (2000, June 29). Two die in UW medical school shooting. *Seattle Post-Intelligencer.*
4. Smith, T. W., Kallberg, A. L., & Marsden, P. V. (2002). *National organizations survey* (computer file). ICPSR04074-v1. Chicago: National Opinion Research Center (producer), 2003. Ann Arbor, MI: Inter-university Consortium for Political and Social Research (distributor), 2004.
5. Pondy, L. R. (1967). Organizational conflict: Concepts and models. *Administrative Science Quarterly, 12,* 296–320.
6. Wilensky, H. L. (1968). The professionalization of everyone? *American Journal of Sociology, 70*(2), 137–158.
7. Doctor X [pseud.]. (1979). *Intern.* New York: HarperCollins.
8. Peled, L. H., Eisenhardt, K. M., & Xin, K. R. (1999). Exploring the black box: An analysis of work group diversity, conflict, and performance. *Administrative Science Quarterly, 44,* 1–28.
9. Edwards, P. K., & Scullian, H. (1982). *The social organization of industrial conflict: Control and resistance in the workplace.* Oxford, UK: Basil Blackwell.
10. Watson, B. (1971). Counter-planning on the shop floor. *Radical America, 5,* 77–85.

11. Hirschman, A. O. (1970). *Exit, voice, and loyalty.* Cambridge, MA: Harvard University Press.

12. McAdam, D., McCarthy, J. D., & Zald, M. N. (1996). Introduction. In D. McAdam, J. D. McCarthy, & M. N. Zald (Eds.), *Comparative perspectives on social movements: Political opportunities, modernizing structures, and cultural framings* (pp. 1–29) Cambridge, UK: Cambridge University Press.

13. Kerr, C. C., & Siegel, A. (1954). The interindustry propensity to strike: An international comparison. In A. Kornhauser, R. Dubin, & A. Ross (Eds.), *Industrial conflict.* New York: McGraw-Hill.

14. Burke, W. W. (1974). Managing conflict between groups. In J. D. Adams (Ed.), *Theory and method in organizational development: An evolutionary process.* Arlington, VA: NTL Institute for Applied Behavioral Sciences.

15. Slaikeu, K. A. (1996). *When push comes to shove.* San Francisco: Jossey-Bass.

16. Van Maanen, J. (1992). Drinking our troubles away: Managing conflict in a British police agency. In D. M. Kalb & J. M. Bartunek (Eds.), *Hidden conflict in organizations: Uncovering behind-the-scenes disputes* (pp. 32–62). Newbury Park, CA: Sage.

17. Wildavsky, A. (1988). *The new politics of the budgetary process.* Glenview, IL: Scott, Foresman.

18. Harragan, B. L. (1978). *Games mother never taught you.* New York: Warner Books.

19. Weber, M. (1958). Politics as a vocation. In C. W. Mills & H. H. Gerth (Eds.), *From Max Weber: Essays in sociology.* New York: Oxford University Press.

20. Kwitny, J. (1986, December 18). Science follies at CDC's AIDS lab: Egos, power, politics and lost experiments. *Wall Street Journal*, p. 1.

21. Tushman, M., & Romanelli, E. (1985). Organizational evolution: A metamorphosis model of convergence and reorientation. In L. L. Cummings & B. M. Shaw (Eds.), *Research in organizational behavior* (Vol. 7, pp. 171–222). Greenwich, CT: JAI Press.

22. Downs, A. (1966). *Inside bureaucracy.* Boston: Little, Brown.

23. McCurdy, H. E. (1991). Organizational decline: NASA and the life cycle of bureaus. *Public Administration Review, 51,* 308–315.

24. Stewart, B. (1999, November 22). Jewish bulwark from an earlier Bronx fades away. *New York Times.*

25. Nonet, P. (1969). *Administrative justice: Advocacy and change in government agencies.* New York: Russell Sage Foundation.

26. Lewin, K. (1951). *Field theory in social sciences.* New York: Harper and Row.

27. Gersick, C. J. G. (1991). Revolutionary change theories: A multilevel exploration of the punctuated equilibrium paradigm. *Academy of Management Review, 16,* 10–36.

28. Biggart, N. W. (1977). The creative destructive process of organizational change: The case of the post office. *Administrative Science Quarterly, 22,* 410–426.

29. Schumpeter, J. A. (1950). *Capitalism, socialism, and democracy.* New York: Harper.

30. Isabella, L. A. (1990). Evolving interpretations as a change unfolds: How managers construe key organizational events. *Academy of Management Journal, 33,* 7–41.

31. Bacharach, S. B., Bamberger, P., & Sonnenstuhl, W. J. (1996). The organizational transformational process: The micropolitics of dissonance reduction and the alignment of logics of action. *Administrative Science Quarterly, 41,* 447–506.

PART IV

The Future Organization

This textbook has described the organization as a set of stable human relationships focused on achieving objectives. Organizations described in this way sound impersonal and mechanical. As Chapters 9, 10, and 11 indicate, though, organizations are not machines fueled by human effort. Organizations are driven by people, either as individuals or in leadership groups. Whether inside or outside leadership positions, people establish their own information pathways and seek to affect decision making. In even the most stable organizations, periodic conflict challenges established structure and forces of change impose themselves. Nevertheless, most organizations reestablish stability in due course. Conflicts are mediated. People reach accommodation. Defined structure and stable role expectations again predominate. It is noteworthy that an observer cited in Chapter 11 described organizational change as a process of "punctuated equilibrium."

Formal organizations have demonstrated themselves to be a resilient and durable framework for collective action. The modern world could not function without this resource for coordinating the behavior of large numbers of people. But the term *organization* is quite general. It was defined in Chapter 1 as *a body of individuals working under a stable system of rules, assignments, procedures, and relationships designed to achieve specific goals.* Many different arrangements fit under this broad definition. As demonstrated earlier, organizations may be hierarchical or egalitarian, centralized or decentralized, flat or tall. They vary in degree of actual formality.

It is certain that formal organizations will dominate many areas of life in industrialized countries in the coming century. Their dominance in the 21st century will likely be even greater than in the 20th century. But the way the formal organization will look and the characteristics of organizational life in the century to come can only be guessed at.

One type of formal organization seems very likely to dominate the 21st century: *bureaucracy*. The word *bureaucracy* suggests something disagreeable to modern Americans. It connotes burdensome procedures and functional inefficiency.

To scientists who study organizations, though, bureaucracy means something less objectionable. Bureaucracy is formal organization with some very specific features. First, bureaucracies prescribe highly specific behaviors for all members and set the most fundamental in written form. Second, bureaucracies recruit and promote workers on the basis of their ability to do the required work. Third, bureaucracies insist that workers separate their personal concerns from the exercise of duties on behalf of the organization. Fourth, bureaucracies pay workers in money and offer steady employment. Several additional characteristics also distinguish bureaucracies from other organizations.

In contrast to popular thinking, moreover, many organizational specialists consider bureaucracies more efficient than other types of organizations. People in bureaucracies carry out their duties in routine fashion over long periods of time. They can be counted upon to act in a manner consistent with the direction set by leadership. These features make bureaucracy a highly reliable tool for administration. Some claim that bureaucracy is ideally suited to the needs of both capitalism and democracy.

Most analysts acknowledge drawbacks in bureaucracy. Alienation of workers due to highly specialized tasks, loss of creativity, and impersonal service are most often cited as deficits. Critics of bureaucracy claim that these drawbacks both lower worker satisfaction and reduce productivity. As a consequence, people concerned with organizations have searched for ways to moderate the undesirable features of bureaucracy or find workable, alternative forms of organization. This search began in the early 20th century and continues up to the present.

The search for alternatives has spawned a wide variety of interventions capable of being inserted into existing organizations. These have names familiar to most managers. *Pay for performance* contradicts a fundamental principle of bureaucracy, which provides workers with fixed rewards for achieving a minimum standard of productivity. *Team management*, which involves workers in decision making and quality control, attacks the bureaucratic principles of specialization and hierarchy. *Flextime, alternative career ladders,* and *telecommuting* chip away at the lockstep features of the bureaucratic career and the strict separation of work and private life.

People searching for alternatives to bureaucracy have also formed entirely new organizations dedicated to conducting business differently. Perhaps the most famous is the Israeli *kibbutz*, or collective farm. Inspired by socialistic ideals, these organizations doggedly pursued equality. Not even the top leaders were free from the requirement of manual labor. People regularly switched jobs.

In the United States, a group of politically committed women founded *Ms. Magazine* under antibureaucratic principles. Hierarchy was de-emphasized. Informal communication was substituted for formal communication channels such as regularly scheduled meetings.

Little evidence has surfaced to support the likelihood that nonbureaucratic organizations will triumph in generations to come. The kibbutz movement attracted international attention but never drew more than a small minority of Israelis to its ranks. *Ms. Magazine* foundered in its second decade. Few management-initiated interventions such as participatory management have been shown through data to have borne fruit. Popular interventions such as *Total Quality Management (TQM)* and *reengineering* fit nearly into the traditional bureaucratic framework, not really challenging the principles of hierarchy, specialization, and routine.

Still, is would be unwise to cease the search for alternatives to bureaucracy and other traditional forms of organization. As noted in Chapter 5, economic conditions and technology play a major role in determining the structure of organizations. Twenty-first century technology may indeed make new organizational forms possible or even predominant.

Bureaucracy

Learning Objective

To understand the principles of bureaucracy; to distinguish bureaucracies from other types of formal organizations; to appreciate the positive and negative features of bureaucracies; to comprehend the reasons for the predominance of bureaucracy in modern industrialized countries.

Principles

○ Bureaucracy is a particular kind of formal organization. It is distinguished from other organizations by its degree of formalization, that is, the extent to which it defines activities required and permitted by members. Bureaucracies are the most "formal" of formal organizations.

○ Disinterested application of rules helps distinguish bureaucracies from other organizations. By encouraging rule-governed performance of duty, bureaucracies reduce the likelihood of insubordination toward superiors and bias toward clients. Viewing their jobs as steps in a career, workers in bureaucracies become skilled at what they do.

○ Critics of bureaucracy claim that this form of organization has serious drawbacks. They cite resistance to change and inability to innovate. Also noted is the tendency of standardized, repetitive work to reduce employee motivation and opportunity for personal fulfillment. Critics have also observed that bureaucratic employees relate to the public and each other in a cold, mechanical fashion.

○ But bureaucracy serves modern society well. It allows government to administer laws in the fair, neutral manner that citizens of democracies expect. It reduces operating costs in private business. It provides employees with secure jobs and enables them to live independent lives when away from the workplace. It provides managers with effective administrative tools.

Bureaucracy: The Ultimate Formal Organization

Formal organizations have existed since ancient times and in all countries of significant cultural and economic development. Many formal organizations, for example, were found in medieval Europe. These included guilds, universities, and monasteries. Modern organizations such as labor unions and universities often resemble their historical ancestors. Modern industrial society, though, seems dominated by a type of organization much less familiar in earlier eras: *bureaucracy.*

In everyday conversation, "bureaucracy" suggests something distasteful. To most people, bureaucracy connotes an inefficient, burdensome process. Typically, government agencies are considered bastions of bureaucracy. Most galling to the man or woman in the street is a sense that bureaucracy imposes unnecessary barriers to getting things done. Citizens doing business with the government often encounter chains of requirements, including forms, appearances, inspections, hearings, certification, and appeals. Each step in this gauntlet may require waiting in lines and paying fees. Insufficient attention to a minute detail may stop the process and require return to the first step. Applicants for building permits and liquor licenses, clients of public welfare organizations, students in state universities, and sailors and in nearly all countries are examples of those familiar with bureaucracy on a day-to-day basis. For many, the most vexing feature of bureaucracy is that it seems unnecessary.

To citizens thus aggrieved it is surprising to learn that most specialists in organizations believe bureaucracy to be a necessary feature of modern society. These experts consider bureaucracy the most efficient way to organize people to accomplish certain objectives. The list of functions thought by experts to be best carried out by bureaucracies is increasing. Commentators on public affairs have also identified bureaucracy as desirable, since it helps achieve key goals of modern democracy.

To many, it is also surprising to learn that bureaucracy frequently occurs outside government. Bureaucracy is apparent in many large corporations. Hospitals and health maintenance organizations (HMOs), often both private (nongovernmental) and nonprofit, became increasingly bureaucratic in the last decades of the 20th century. Students at private universities often encounter as much bureaucracy as their counterparts in state institutions.

Consumers, citizens, and experts tend to emphasize bureaucracy's drawbacks. People working for bureaucracies are said to lack incentives for creativity and excellence. Many specialists in the quality of life believe that working in a bureaucracy makes people overcautious and reduces tolerance for change. People in bureaucracies are said to feel detached from their work and are forced to seek satisfaction in family and recreation. Communication specialists have expressed concern that executives become blindsided due to loss of information transmitted from lower to higher rungs in bureaucratic hierarchies. Historians and political scientists believe that bureaucracies have repeatedly short-circuited the will of top executives, sabotaging government reform and social change.

Still, there is much evidence that bureaucracy is the organization of the future. No observer—consumer, citizen, or management scientist—would deny that bureaucracy has undesirable features. But at least for the large-scale operations upon which modern society depends, bureaucracy may well be superior to any type of organization feasible now or in the future.

A Consumer Experiences Bureaucracy

Bureaucracy in modern American society is nowhere more striking than in the health care system. Until the 1980s, most Americans saw private doctors in small offices. A smiling receptionist or nurse, seemingly on familiar terms with everyone, scheduled appointments. By the century's end, most care was delivered by businesses and nonprofit firms known as health maintenance organizations (HMOs). This fictional account illustrates the experience of many:

Velma Wills has had a cough for two weeks and decides to see a doctor.

She phones her HMO.

Her call is answered by a recorded voice: "If this is an emergency, please hang up and dial 911. If you are calling to renew a prescription, hang up and call the pharmacy. If you are calling for directions to the clinic, press 1. If you are calling to cancel an appointment, press 2. If you are calling to schedule a new appointment, press 3."

Ms. Wills makes an appointment and sees her physician the following Thursday. He gives her a referral to a lung specialist. Later, she calls for the required appointment. Over the phone comes a recorded voice, saying, "If this is an emergency, please hang up and dial . . . "

The lung specialist gives Ms. Wills a handful of papers ordering laboratory tests. She proceeds to the lab. She takes a number and sits in the waiting area. A technician draws blood but tells her that she will have to make an appointment at the Special Diagnostics Unit for one of the tests.

Ms. Wills goes down the hall to the Special Diagnostics Unit. She waits in line for the receptionist. The receptionist informs her that she needs to make an appointment for her test, and that this must be done by telephone. The receptionist hands her a card with a phone number.

The next day, a Friday, Ms. Wills calls the number and requests an appointment. The person who answers says, "Oh, Gladys makes those appointments. She works Tuesdays through Thursdays, 8:00 to 6:00. You'll have to call back then."

Ms. Wills says, "I'll be out of town next week. Can't anybody help me now?"

The receptionist says, "Gladys schedules those appointments."

"Well, thanks," says Ms. Wills.

"Oh, no problem!" says the receptionist.

This story captures the vexing nature of many consumer encounters with large administrative structures: waiting in lines (or on hold), going from office to office, sensing that no one can, or cares to, take simple steps to solve a problem. "Damn bureaucracy!"

In fairness to Ms. Wills's HMO, it must be acknowledged that specialty services and advanced tests would have been unavailable a generation earlier. Better care requires more doctors, nurses, technicians, and support personnel under one roof. The sentimental, horse-and-buggy days of old-time medicine have emotional appeal—but delivery of 21st-century care may require bureaucratic organization.

What Is Bureaucracy?

Basic Principles

To most people, the word *bureaucracy* suggests large numbers of functionaries seated at desks arranged in close-order ranks. The word also suggests suppression of emotion in favor of rules and regulations. The term *bureaucracy* connotes impersonal service and inflexibility. Human beings make decisions and carry out functions in bureaucracies, as in all organizations. But the individuals behind the desks of bureaucracies are frequently said to be—and often characterize themselves as—"cogs in a machine," officials automatically applying rules and carrying out preset procedures. Bureaucrats, it would appear, have little more decision-making latitude, creative opportunity, or emotional involvement than the desks they sit at. The actions and thinking of people in a bureaucracy often seem as much the creation of an external power as files, desks, cubicle partitions, and other inanimate furnishings.

The phenomenon of bureaucracy has proven fascinating to observers of the modern world. Social scientists have devoted much attention to distinguishing bureaucracies from other types of formal organizations. Conclusions reached by social scientists often restate and extend popular impressions. Social scientists have characterized bureaucracies as organizations dominated by strict role expectations. Social scientists also distinguish bureaucracies from other organizations on the basis of *rationalization,* a word that addresses both an organization's roles and structure.

Roles, expectations, and orientations. Organizations can be distinguished from one another by the characteristics of the roles found in them. Expectations associated with roles differ from organization to organization. In addition, the orientations of members to their roles differ among organizations. In describing the nature of roles, Chapter 4 noted several contrasting patterns of role expectations and orientations. These included

- *Affective versus affectively neutral.* In some organizations, role expectations and orientations are predominantly affective (emotional); in others, they are affectively neutral (emotionally detached).
- *Universalism versus particularism.* In some organizations, role expectations and orientations are predominantly universalistic, mandating equal treatment to all; in others, they are particularistic, mandating special treatment to personal friends, relatives, and acquaintances.
- *Achievement versus ascription.* Some organizations emphasize achievement, recruiting and promoting on the basis of demonstrated competence; others emphasize ascription, allocating positions according to social status and ancestry.
- *Specificity versus diffuseness.* Roles in some organizations are usually specific, giving each member clear and limited jobs; in others, roles are diffuse, ill-specified, and broad-ranging.

Roles in bureaucracies are characterized by affective neutrality, universalism, achievement, and specificity. Typically, the individual in a bureaucracy thinks of his or her role in an unemotional fashion. He or she feels obliged to treat all clients or customers alike. People in bureaucracies expect to be paid and promoted according to testable competence. They are assigned highly specific job descriptions with responsibilities clearly distinguished from those of others.

Rationalization. Bureaucracies are recognizable as highly rationalized organizations. Rationalization in this sense refers to fitting resources and activities together into a consistent whole for the purpose of achieving objectives. Concrete elements of rationalization include

- Division of required operations into routine tasks
- Arrangement of these tasks into an appropriate system

Rationalization, first, involves dividing the operations required for attaining objectives into sets of routine tasks. Routine tasks are necessarily limited in scope, allowing individuals charged with them to operate according to formula. In a highly rationalized organization, each task covers a limited area of responsibility and requires limited expertise. Second, rationalization involves arrangement of tasks and positions into a consistent whole. Based on objective observation and comparison of alternative arrangements, every task is deliberately designed to complement every other task. Rationalized organizations pursue their objectives by assigning tasks to individuals and supervising them in a manner that keeps task performance consistent with organizational objectives.

Rationalization of task performance closely resembles Taylorism as applied to industrial operations (see Chapter 5). Taylorism called for deliberate design of each tool and specification of how the operative was to use it. This approach to industrial labor specified not only the content of each operative's tasks but the time and physical motions required. Bureaucracy applies major principles of Taylorism in administrative and service-oriented settings.

In bureaucracies, supervision takes place according to systems of departmentalization and hierarchy. Departments are usually organized along functional lines: a research and development organization, for example, may have units specializing in basic science, design, engineering, contract services, sales, and personnel. If truly bureaucratic, each unit will have several levels of personnel, with titles such as Scientist I, Scientist II, Senior Scientist, Associate Director, and Director. Managers of each unit report to upper-level managers, who, in turn, may report to executives of a parent corporation. It is expected that communication channels will extend from subordinates to superiors in the same unit. Direct communication with superiors above one's immediate supervisor or with other functional units is discouraged.

All formal organizations share some characteristics with bureaucracy. Roles in all organizations, for example, are specific to some degree. Division of labor has existed in human collectivities since earliest times, but bands of Neolithic hunter-gatherers were hardly bureaucracies. Team positions in a recreational football league reflect specific tasks and expectations, but the players are in no way bureaucrats. All organizations are rationalized to some extent, coalescing around recognizable objectives and deliberately allocating human and material resources in their pursuit.

Bureaucracy, though, represents an extreme. It is the most highly rationalized and formalized of organizations. Bureaucracy defines the activities required of and permitted to members in an unusually minute fashion. The formalization characteristic of bureaucracy requires a high degree of role specificity. This can be observed in the numerous and detailed job descriptions that characterize bureaucracies. Universalism, affective neutrality, and achievement orientation contribute to the bureaucracy's ability to allocate resources in a technically objective manner— a hallmark of rationalization.

A Definition of Bureaucracy

Bureaucracy defies a simple definition. Organizations of this kind have existed for thousands of years and in many countries. Bureaucracies assume different qualities under the influence of the social forces and cultures that surround them, but a core definition of bureaucracy applicable everywhere can be specified. This definition conjures up the routinized, regimented, and emotionally cold colossi familiar across national boundaries and generations: Bureaucracies are organizations characterized by rules binding on the actions of all members; hierarchical supervision; specialization by personnel; prohibition of personal gain other than fixed salaries; and continuous operation over time.

Operating Characteristics

Modern management science owes much of its understanding of bureaucracy to a German thinker of the early 20th century named Max Weber. A scholar of tremendous depth, Weber made a study of organizational structures throughout the history of the civilized world.[1] Weber found evidence for the existence of bureaucracies in the Middle Ages and as long ago as ancient Egypt, China, and Rome. According to Weber, though, bureaucracy as we know it today became possible only in modern times. This "fully developed" bureaucracy contains several key elements in addition to those in the definition stated above.

Weber and others have developed a list of definite characteristics to distinguish bureaucracies from other kinds of organizations. These characteristics tend to be interrelated. They reflect the formalism of bureaucratic organizations and contribute to rationalization of their operations. The characteristics of bureaucracy include the following:

Rules binding on the actions of all members. All bureaucracies function under rules. These rules, which are typically highly specific and written, govern the actions of all members. Modern government agencies operate under rules proposed by agencies of the executive branch (the federal Department of Labor or the California

Department of Corporations, for example), commented upon in public hearings, and then adopted into public law. Rules dictating operations are systematically presented in codes of regulations, technical assistance guides, and loose-leaf binders of official memorandums and circulars. Medieval monasteries also functioned under rulebooks, such as one written by St. Benedict to govern operations in Benedictine houses.[2] Even top officials in a federal or monastic bureaucracy do not have the liberty to set the rules aside in formulating actions, directing subordinates, or carrying out discipline.

Hierarchical supervision. Supervision of lower-level personnel by more highly placed individuals is a hallmark of bureaucracy. It is generally acknowledged that higher-ranked individuals can set aside decisions made by the lower-ranked, at least in their own unit. Today, similar hierarchies are found in government, business, religious, and political organizations. Supervision and decision making are "top-down." Weber characterized the army of the late Roman empire as increasingly bureaucratic; the strictness of hierarchy in that organization is legendary.

Specialization of personnel and subunits. Division of the organization's functions into highly defined tasks is a key characteristic of bureaucracies. Tasks associated with each job description tend to be routine. Most decisions are made within a restricted set of options, if not entirely by formula. Boundaries between individual roles tend to be quite sharp. In modern factories, for example, machine operators are usually not required (and resist requests) to perform machine maintenance. Subunits in bureaucratically organized research and development organizations also perform highly specialized functions. Turf battles over areas of responsibility are major causes of conflict among both individuals and subunits in bureaucracies.

Prohibition of personal gain from operations. Modern bureaucrats receive fixed salaries based on the positions they hold. Salaries are tied to the job classification rather than the amount or quality of work done. Unlike employees of nonbureaucratic business organizations, personnel in bureaucracies traditionally receive no commissions or bonuses. Higher pay may be attained only through promotion or increments tied to number of years in the position. Fixed rewards by virtue of position were given in ancient and medieval bureaucracies. Before the development of stable money systems, payment was made in kind. In medieval Europe, priests and other church officials received fixed salaries or their equivalent. Mandarin bureaucrats in ancient China received fixed allotments of rice.

Continuous operation over time. Every bureaucracy has a built-in mechanism for continuing in operation generation after generation. Bureaucracies have proven remarkably capable of maintaining business as usual despite upheaval in the surrounding society. The greatest social transformations of the 20th century, including the Russian Revolution (1917) and the Nazi takeover in Germany (1933), left preexisting bureaucracies largely intact. Foreign conquerors (such as Germany over France in World War II) typically do not abolish the indigenous bureaucracy. Rather, they issue it new orders. Today, public-sector bureaucracies almost always outlast elected leaders, and bureaucrats in business firms outlast CEOs. At least in the public sector, new leaders who threaten to shake things up seldom cause consternation. Rank-and-file employees know that they will still be at their desks when the new boss is long gone.

Maintenance of documents and records. The presence of documents, filing cabinets, and banks of computer terminals is one of the clearest visual symbols of bureaucracy. Operation under rules would be difficult, if not impossible, without written documents. Bureaucracies maintain personnel files to promote orderly oversight by staff. Public agencies maintain files of client information to determine eligibility for public programs and the level of benefits to which a client is entitled. Increasingly, public agencies maintain databases for the purpose of reporting their activities to executives and legislative bodies. Businesses assemble and maintain records on customers, and nonprofit organizations use records to track contributions and contributors.

Separation of organizational and personal resources. Bureaucracies typically require strict separation of the organization's resources from those of individual members. With few exceptions, employees of bureaucracies work on the organization's physical premises. To do so, they leave home, where most of their personal property resides. Likewise, individuals are officially prohibited from making personal use of the organization's resources. Often, these rules are relaxed or overlooked, as when employees bring home pencils and stationery or make personal calls on office telephones. But management has the well-established right to withdraw such privileges at any time, even though such withdrawal has been known to cause dissatisfaction among workers.[3] Management expects workers to acknowledge that their salaries, fixed according to their job classification, are payment in full for their effort.

Recruitment according to objective qualifications. Basing recruitment and often advancement on objective tests reflects the universalism and achievement-orientation characteristic of bureaucracies. This feature makes bureaucracy remarkable in a world where most jobs are still obtained via informal contacts, most often family. Well-functioning bureaucracies seldom hire employees' or executives' friends and family members on the basis of kinship alone. To be considered for a job in most public agencies, applicants must pass examinations given by an appropriate unit of government or present credentials that document adequate testing elsewhere—a public accounting certificate (CPA) or engineering degree from an accredited university, for example. Agency executives may hire according to scores on the examination or select among people who have scored above a designated cutoff (the "Civil Service List"). Similar practices were carried out as long ago as ancient China, in which hopefuls for administrative positions took examinations in subjects such as calligraphy and knowledge of Confucian odes.

Career employment. Few bureaucracies explicitly guarantee permanent employment. But people take jobs in many of them with the presumption that they will not be fired as long as they perform adequately. Positions are seen as steps in an orderly career rather than jobs that will eventually be completed or eliminated. Operation under rules promotes this presumption. Individuals in bureaucracies seldom fear that they will be terminated due to arbitrariness or favoritism of their supervisors. Rewards in bureaucracy favor long-term if not actually permanent employment. Salaries generally rise in proportion to years of service, and almost all bureaucracies give pensions to retirees. The tendency of bureaucracies to survive through good economic times and bad, despite wars and revolutions, promotes employment for life among individuals.

Advancement through seniority. Although objective qualifications serve as criteria for promotion, seniority also plays a part. In promotion examinations, bureaucracies often award extra points to candidates based on years of service or require only individuals with fewer than a stipulated number of years of service to take the exam. Among individuals who have passed the exam, many bureaucracies select the individual not with the highest score but with the most years of service. The United States Post Office Department serves as a prime example of this phenomenon, described by Nicole Biggart (see Chapter 11) as awarding promotions entirely on the basis of how many years the employee had served. Large government agencies and business organizations tend to have ladders that offer advancement opportunities to people familiar with the specifics of the organization's operations (see Chapter 5). Knowledge of this kind reflects direct experience in the agency or firm rather than technical expertise, which might be hired from outside.

Disinterested treatment of clients. "Disinterest" on the part of members is a major characteristic of modern bureaucracies. Disinterest in this sense means that the employee or official separates his or her personal preferences from performance of his or her job. Operation according to rules applies to people outside the bureaucracy as well as to its own members. For this reason, all citizens, customers, and clients may expect to receive the same treatment. Police officers are expected to address all drivers whom they stop with the same degree of courtesy. The president of the United States pays the same price for a first class postage stamp as an ordinary citizen.

Perception of jobs as honorable. Individuals in a well-run, modern bureaucracy experience a sense of honor in performance of their duties. This fact may seem surprising to modern Americans, who often think of bureaucracies as low-status venues. But examples of individuals who take pride in bureaucratic careers and the agencies for which they work abound. Many people in bureaucratic agencies consider the work they do to be a lifelong, personal mission. These individuals include social workers in welfare agencies; teachers in public schools; nurses and physicians in public health departments; police officers and firefighters; and soldiers and sailors. The Internal Revenue agent, America's antihero, often believes his or her duty is to outwit tax cheats and defend fairness in support of democratic government. Not very long ago, European civil servants of all stripes wore insignia-adorned uniforms, and wore the uniforms proudly.

Bureaucracy Past and Present

Premodern history furnished important examples of bureaucracies. Continuously operating, hierarchical organizations that run according to rules, with specialized personnel receiving fixed salaries, have existed for thousands of years. Max Weber cites their importance as far back as ancient Rome and China. In its fully developed form, though, bureaucracy seems to have only appeared in modern times. Equal treatment of all clients, lifetime employment, and complete separation of organizational and individual property seems characteristic of the industrialized world. The character of qualifications for office seems to have changed as well since early times. Today's employment and promotion examinations test technical capabilities required for performance of concrete tasks. Examinations of administrators in ancient China assessed the individual's spiritual rectitude, considered vital at the time for proper exercise of governmental functions. This procedure was rational from the Confucian point of view, which associated war, civil discord, and other public misfortune with spiritual flaws among a country's rulers.

What Organizations Are NOT Bureaucracies

Understanding what is not a bureaucracy makes it easier to understand what a bureaucracy is. Certain role expectations and orientations are clearly outside the bureaucratic mold. These include particularism (giving special treatment to others on the basis of personal preference), affective orientation (mixing personal emotion with role performance), and diffuseness (mixing tasks and roles). There are also organizations that are clearly nonbureaucratic, including those that are

- *Collegial.* The term *collegial* signifies discussion and decision making among individuals who neither give nor take orders from each other. Organizations without hierarchies or in which hierarchies play only a minor part in operations are known as collegial. All members of a collegial organization need not be of identically equal standing. But in such organizations everyone has a right to be heard in the process of making decisions.
- *Patrimonial.* Like bureaucracies, patrimonial organizations are hierarchical. Unlike bureaucracies, though, superiors justify their authority over subordinates through claims on personal loyalty. Claims of personal loyalty may be based on cultural, religious, or historical grounds. A highly successful conqueror in the past exercised control over subordinates by distributing favors (such as titles to estates) to them. Today, many successful business owners function in a similar manner.
- *Internally competitive.* Organizations that are hierarchical may lack the bureaucratic element of fixed salaries associated with position and orderly promotion through a career. People in these organizations receive rewards based on performance. These include commissions for sales or deal making among such personnel as brokers, lawyers, and investment bankers. Retention

and promotion are attained through a combination of performance and successful politics. "Up-or-out" organizations fall in this category of nonbureaucracies.

- *Family-dominated.* An increasingly rare but still important phenomenon in advanced economies is the family-dominated organization. Such an organization is too particularistic to be a bureaucracy. Children and spouses receive top management positions and retain control over key decisions. Family firms with thousands of workers and billions of dollars in assets still operated in the United States at the turn of the 20th century.

Most actual organizations are neither pure bureaucracies nor purely collegial, patrimonial, internally competitive, or family-dominated. Large government agencies, for example, are typically bureaucratic. But they are not entirely so.

Most personnel in government agencies perform routine functions. Many obtain their jobs through competitive examinations and rise in the ranks on the basis of seniority. Top leaders in these agencies, though, receive their positions through appointment by elected officials such as mayors, governors, and presidents. Elected officials use political criteria in making these appointments, seeking to ensure visible representation of a voter group (such as women, Southerners, or Asian Americans) in government or to reward an individual for support in a campaign. These appointees do not perform routine functions. They network with elected officials and other appointees, represent the agency in public, and grapple with strategic questions and emergencies not solvable through standard operating procedures.

The fundamental form, then, under which public agencies are organized is bureaucratic. But organization at the top is both patrimonial and collegial. The appointment process is patrimonial because the appointee serves at the elected official's pleasure. Elected officials often request their appointees to resign when they do not serve an intended political function, such as pleasing an important interest group. On a day-to-day basis, public executives operate in a collegial fashion, communicating with their counterparts in other agencies, testifying in hearings, and making decisions in collaboration with personal staff.

Conversely, some formal organizations are fundamentally nonbureaucratic but have units that are bureaucratically organized. These organizations include professional corporations, such as law and architecture firms and medical partnerships. Professionals in such corporations often interact in a collegial fashion, attempting to improve practice and solve problems as peers. They frequently receive payment proportional to the value of business they bring into the firm, whereas compensation in a bureaucracy is determined by a specific job classification. But professional firms also require performance of routine administrative and technical functions. In firms of significant size, these functions are performed by specialized departments that are bureaucratically organized. Both medical corporations and law firms have record-keeping and financial services departments. It is noteworthy that law firms and medical corporations at the beginning of the 21st century often attained significant size, requiring extensively organized support service departments.

The law firm Pillsbury, Madison, and Sutro employed thousands of attorneys, and the Permanente Medical Group, thousands of physicians.

There is considerable variation in the degree to which organizations in different areas of specialization were bureaucratized at the beginning of the 21st century:

- *Government.* Government agencies are predominantly bureaucratic, for reasons specified above.
- *Religion.* The organizational pattern of several major religions is also bureaucratic. Many classify Catholicism as bureaucratic, due to the hierarchical organization and lifelong tenure of clergy. Top leadership of Catholicism and other hierarchical churches is collegial, as are the structures of less hierarchical faiths.
- *Health care.* Health care may be thought of as partially bureaucratic. Most hospitals and health plans in the late 20th century had bureaucratic administrative structures supporting collegial groups of health professionals.
- *Education.* Public elementary education in the United States is highly bureaucratic. Teachers are generally hired for life and follow strict curricular guidelines. Supervision is hierarchical. Colleges and universities tend to be partially bureaucratized. Hiring for faculty positions is often idiosyncratic, and job descriptions are vague. Promotion is more often based on performance than length of service. "Publish or perish" is the academic version of "up-or-out." Determination of eligibility for promotion is a collegial and political process. Like health care organizations, colleges and universities have bureaucratic administrative structures.
- *Nonprofits.* Charitable, service, and advocacy organizations are partial bureaucracies. As elsewhere, top leadership is collegial and patrimonial. Mid-level employees are bureaucratic. Large nonprofits such as the American Red Cross, the American Cancer Society, and the United Way require periodic effort by large numbers of volunteers for fundraising, advocacy, and emergency action. Volunteers, who receive no salary and typically participate on a short-term basis, constitute a nonbureaucratized labor force.
- *Business.* Business firms of significant size today are partially bureaucratized. In firms such as AT&T and Chevron, workers typically function under hierarchical supervision, perform highly refined, routine tasks, and receive promotions based on length of service. Top leadership is collegial, patrimonial, and sometimes family-dominated. R&D units may be collegial with bureaucratic support systems.
- *Politics.* Political organizations (parties and political advocacy groups) in the contemporary United States tend to be only slightly bureaucratized. On the entry level, the criterion for participation is largely willingness to contribute time or money. Upper levels tend to be patrimonial. The staffs of elected officials, like the agency heads they appoint, serve at the officials' pleasure.
- *Law.* As discussed above, law firms are collegial and patrimonial, although the large ones rely on bureaucratic administrative structures.

Table 12.1   Degrees of Bureaucratization in Different Organizations

Area of Function	Degree of Bureaucratization	Explanation
Government	Dominant	Agencies function under rules and regulations made by public representatives.
Religion	Dominant	Schools operated by several major religions train clergy who are hierarchically supervised.
Health	Partial	Hospitals, HMOs, and insurance companies are increasingly bureaucratic; professional functions remain collegial.
Education	Partial	K–12 education is highly bureaucratic; universities remain in part collegial.
Nonprofit	Partial	Permanent staff is bureaucratic; volunteers are heroic.
Business	Partial	Routine functions are bureaucratic; family, patrimonial, and collegial organizations survive.
Politics	Slight	Most organizations are patrimonial or collegial.
Law	Slight	Most organizations are patrimonial or collegial.

The Growth of Bureaucracy

Bureaucracy's Predominance

Most of the organizations in Table 12.1 are bureaucratic. Even those characterized as slightly bureaucratic have specialized units in which bureaucracy dominates. The predominance of bureaucracy represents the final stage of a transformation that occurred over hundreds of years. Bureaucracies may have existed in ancient Rome and China, but they did not achieve predominance until well after the industrial revolution. Bureaucratic government developed in Europe in the 19th century and took firm root in the United States in the early 20th century. Bureaucracy is as prevalent worldwide as it is in the United States. Year in and year out, workers sit at banks of desks performing highly defined tasks under explicit rules in organizations as diverse as Mexican banks, Japanese insurance firms, and the Communist Party of mainland China.

Signs visible in everyday life illustrate the growth of bureaucracy in the United States. The neighborhood hardware store constitutes a familiar example. Small businesses of this kind employed only a few people. Each of them did a wide range of jobs. They often acted in a particularistic manner toward customers, extending credit, for example, to people they knew.

Large retailers such as the familiar "big box" stores have replaced small hardware businesses in many locations. Built on a warehouse model, one store may employ hundreds of people. Personnel tend to specialize in one area. It is unusual for an employee to be on familiar terms with a customer. Credit is not extended on the basis of personal familiarity, but through explicit formulas applied in-house or by credit card companies.

According to many, health care rapidly became bureaucratic in the last two decades of the 20th century. Hospitals have always employed administrative personnel as well as medical professionals. Chapter 5 describes a dual hierarchy traditional in American hospitals. Much of the administrative work has probably been organized in bureaucratic fashion for the past few generations. Medical work itself, the diagnosis and treatment of illness, was organized collegially. Patients did not often encounter the bureaucratic, administrative structure.

The administrative structure of health care is much more apparent to consumers today. The vignette above describing a patient's experience with her health plan illustrates this change. Physicians may not yet have jobs that are truly bureaucratic, but bureaucratically organized employees exercise significant power over doctors' actions. Most hospitals specify the drugs physicians may prescribe for inpatients. Increasingly, health plans specify protocols, or sequences of steps physicians should take in response to the patient's symptoms. Health plans often specify the amount of time a physician should spend with a patient. Developed by outside medical experts working with plan managers, protocols and time constraints are designed to promote both effective care and profitability. Physicians who consistently deviate from the rules may be fired.

The beginnings of this phenomenon were described as early as the 1970s.[4] Modern doctors are not yet bureaucrats. They do not have lifetime jobs and seldom work under an actual hierarchy. But an increasing number of them practice according to bureaucratic rules. Physicians today are much more likely to tell a patient that he or she cannot do something because of a rule or regulation than in earlier generations. Under today's time constraints, physicians often relate to patients in an emotionally cold, rushed fashion. The patient experiences the care he or she receives as a bureaucratic product.

Utilization Review:
Bureaucratic Supervision of Professional Work

Bureaucracy brings to mind close-order ranks of tightly supervised employees performing standardized tasks. Doctors' offices do not have this appearance. But according to many, the organization of health care providers is rapidly evolving in this direction. A process known as "utilization review," crucial in deciding medical treatment, looks and feels like bureaucracy. The mechanism by which decisions are made is a better clue to the structure of health care organizations than the patient's-eye view of doctors, nurses, and waiting rooms.

Under utilization review, outside personnel scrutinize doctors' decisions to determine whether they are medically appropriate and cost-effective. Increasingly, doctors or their office staffs must obtain prior approval from utilization review personnel for tests, medications, operating room procedures, and referrals to specialists. Utilization review personnel are hired or contracted by the health insurance companies that pay the physician. Without approval, the physician will not be paid.

Utilization review workers are often registered nurses. They sit behind computer terminals that provide rapid access to lists of drugs and procedures, detailing which are covered by health insurance for a given condition and which are excluded. Each worker wears a headset to take phone calls from physicians and medical office staff. Located sometimes thousands of miles from the actual doctor and patient, utilization review workers make decisions without emotional involvement. Day and night, a hubbub rises from their cubicles as workers receive calls and respond according to computerized rulebooks.

In the boom period of the late 20th century, interactions in business and the professions seemed to become increasingly standardized, rushed, and cold. Bureaucracy replaced many traditional structures. As individuals, people often seemed unhappy with the change. But decision makers in organizations found bureaucratization advantageous and often necessary.

Reasons for Bureaucracy

Three principal factors seem to account for the predominance of bureaucracy in the modern world. These include

- Superiority of bureaucracy in efficiency and reliability of performance over other forms of organization
- Compatibility of bureaucracy with the political economy and culture of prosperous, democratic countries
- Calculability and security in matters affecting everyday life

Efficiency and Reliability

Most analysts believe that bureaucracy, though drab-seeming, works better than other forms of organization for most purposes. The division of labor among factory workers makes sense. A similar case can be made for the organization of nonmanual workers. Tradition may have fallen by the wayside when the craftsmen of old found themselves (or their offspring) on assembly lines. But industrial division of labor, necessary for working with machines, caused output to increase and consumer prices to drop. There is nearly universal agreement that bureaucracy can carry out large, continuous, and repetitive jobs (such as writing and sending Social Security checks) extremely well. The spread of bureaucracy from government to sales, education, and medicine may boost productivity, lower costs, and enhance the quality of life. As Max Weber wrote,

> The decisive reason for the advance of bureaucratic organization has always been its purely technical superiority over any other form of organization. The fully developed bureaucratic mechanism compares with other organizations exactly as does the machine with nonmechanical modes of production.[1]

Each individual feature of bureaucracy contributes to its efficiency, reliability, or both. An organization's efficiency refers to its ability to produce units of output at relatively low cost. Reliability signifies the ability of an organization to perform consistently and pursue the objectives set by top management without deviation. Table 12.2 summarizes advantages that result from each feature of bureaucracy.

Table 12.2   Contributions of Bureaucratic Features to Efficiency and Reliability

Bureaucratic Principle	Contribution to Efficiency
Rules binding the actions of all members	Contributes to integration of roles and coordination of members' activity; focuses effort on objectives.
Hierarchical supervision	Ensures reliability by promoting top management's control of members' activity and quality of their performance.
Specialization of personnel and subunits	Enhances skills with which functions are performed through experience and repetition.
Prohibition of personal gain from operations	Focuses attention of members on activities within their job descriptions; protects against alienation of outside individuals and organizations.
Continuous operation over time	Safeguards functioning of organization in the event of death or removal of leadership or disruption due to unexpected developments in the social, economic, or natural environment.
Separation of organizational and personal resources	Conserves the organization's resources; enhances control of resource deployment by top management.
Recruitment according to objective qualifications	Enhances skills with which functions are performed through prior training and natural capabilities of members.
Disinterested treatment of clients	Protects against alienation of clients; enhances top management's control over members' actions.
Career employment	Focuses individual on performance of tasks and pursuit of organizational objectives.
Advancement through seniority	Focuses individual on performance of tasks and pursuit of organizational objectives.
Perception of jobs as honorable	Focuses individual on performance of tasks and pursuit of organizational objectives.

- *Rules binding the actions of all.* Rules in bureaucracies reduce or eliminate individual variation in performance of duties. They make role expectations explicit. Standardization of individual actions under rules makes the organization more reliable. Rules also reduce capriciousness by members of the bureaucracy. Absence of capriciousness translates into more reliable services for clients and expectation of fair treatment among members by colleagues and supervisors. Workers who expect impartial treatment are more likely to stay with the bureaucracy for their entire career, providing the organization with ever-increasing experience and expertise.

- *Hierarchical supervision.* Subordination of the individual member's predisposition and objectives to those of the leadership promotes reliability and coordination in any organization. Hierarchical supervision helps maintain focus on the tasks with which each member is charged. Hierarchy helps maintain attention and adherence to the organization's rules.

- *Specialization of personnel and subunits.* The payoffs in productivity attributable to specialization have already been described. Individual specialists naturally perform their tasks with more speed, greater precision, and less error than amateurs or people with talent but without training or experience. The same is true for subunits of an organization, which, in bureaucracies, are made up of personnel with training and skills supportive of the subunit's function.

- *Continuous operation over time.* All bureaucracies have provisions for continuing operations over time. Most formal organizations have rules of succession, indicating who is empowered to make decisions if the top executive is absent or disabled. Bureaucracies today take elaborate precautions for the safeguarding of databases, securing copies in bank vaults and underground caverns capable of withstanding nuclear explosions. Demonstrated ability to continue operation over time augments the organization's reliability and therefore its ability to attain business, governmental, or political objectives.

- *Separation of organizational and personal resources.* Rules separating the organization's property from that of individual members ensure that members do not use the organization's resources for private objectives. Such action would make these resources less likely to be unavailable for pursuing the organization's objectives. If teachers took pencils and chalk home (as many do), shortages in the classroom might result. Thus, the practice is discouraged.

Similarly, requiring members of an organization to make personal resources available for the organization's use reduces efficiency. Even after a member has "delivered the goods," he or she hopes to be able to take them home at the end of the day. This interest reduces the likelihood that the resources will be placed at the full disposal of top management. The contributor does not want them damaged or exhausted, and he or she acts toward them in a protective fashion.

"Ownership" of Military Assets:
The Advantages of Bureaucratic Organization in War

In premodern organizations, the distinction between personal and organizational resources was often indistinct. Warfare furnishes striking examples. Under the patrimonial systems of medieval Europe, a king had a recognized right to summon the nobles of his realm (dukes, marquises, earls, and barons) to appear on a given day, bringing with them a quota of men and horses, armed and ready to fight. The required quota typically included a number of knights—well-trained, armored horsemen—who lived on the noble's estate and received a livelihood from him in peacetime. These knights represented an important personal resource for the noble. They allowed him, for example, to exercise power in his neighborhood and protect his property rights.

In medieval war, nobles enjoyed and often exercised a "right of independent withdrawal." Under this convention, a noble could withdraw his knights from a battle at will. Nobles often did so when a battle went badly. Loss of his knights would cost the noble power and prestige back home. Major battles in the Middle Ages were lost as nobles withdrew their forces when the tide went against them.[5] No such ownership of military assets exists in modern armies, where generals have purposely sacrificed units to attain overall strategic objectives.

Some modern armies have required or allowed personal and organizational assets to become mixed, and have suffered as a consequence. The Kazakhs, a semiautonomous and warlike people of Czarist Russia, were pressed into service in World War I (1914–1918). Serving as cavalry, these fighters were required to furnish their own horses for battle. Though the Kazakhs fought fiercely, Russian troops were slaughtered by the bureaucratically organized German and Austrian armies.[6]

The 1950s and 1960s saw Israel as a consistent victor over far more numerous Arab forces. Though many factors allowed tiny Israel to defeat Egypt, Syria, Jordan, and Iraq, blurring of distinctions between organizational and personal property apparently played a role. In the latter half of the 20th century, many Arab countries were governed by juntas, coalitions of officers in personal command of important military units. Individual officers would be forced out of the junta (and perhaps executed) if the units they controlled were heavily damaged or destroyed. These officers depended on their military units to protect their position and thus considered them an important personal asset. According to an Iraqi observer, officers in that era kept their units out of the fighting when hazards loomed, ensuring victory for the bureaucratically organized Israelis.

- *Recruitment according to objective qualifications.* Stipulating appropriate skills as a requirement for employment has obvious advantages for performing the tasks required to attain organizational objectives. The opportunity to be hired into a secure job has motivated many to take courses and degrees that provide the required qualifications. Self-preparation saves the organization the cost of training the already hired. Advancement through competitive examinations motivates staff to improve their skills.

  Recruitment according to objective qualifications is by no means universal in the modern world. Family firms often practice nepotism in hiring, showing favor to kin. Stories of business failures due to incompetent family members in key positions are widespread. Some government hiring takes place through patronage, or payback for personal favors, as in political campaigns. In the United States, establishment of the Civil Service and the Progressive Movement led most government units to become largely bureaucratized by the 1920s. Government inefficiency often results from patronage, a "particularistic" practice that contradicts the principles of bureaucracy. It is ironic that the public still blames bureaucracy for inefficient public service.

- *Disinterested treatment of clients.* Disinterest in clients refers to removal of personal feelings, other than commitment to organizational objectives, from transactions. Disinterest of this kind contributes to the reliability of members' actions, promoting adherence to the rules even when they contradict personal feelings. Top managers could not have confidence that their directives would be consistently implemented if they felt that employees made allowances for personal characteristics of clients. Disinterested treatment of clients also helps build public confidence, reducing the likelihood that outsiders will charge the agency or business with favoritism.

- *Career employment.* Like several other features of bureaucracy, the expectation that each job is a step in a secure career reduces turnover in the organization. Reduced turnover contributes to efficiency by helping create a labor force that is skilled in performance of standardized duties. Reliable employment with the chance for promotion attracts high-quality workers and maintains their loyalty. A norm of reciprocity prevails, with workers adhering to the rules that govern their jobs in the expectation that their superiors will reward them with steady employment and occasional promotion. Thus, career employment contributes to both effectiveness and reliability.

- *Advancement through seniority.* Like career employment, advancement through seniority promotes loyalty and conformity among employees. People are more likely to obey an agency's rules if they feel continued employment there is of value. The desire to hold a higher position and earn more money is widespread in the modern world.

  It should be noted that few bureaucracies promote personnel entirely due to seniority. Competitive promotion examinations or less formal but still objective criteria are often important. The United States military services greatly reduced seniority as a criterion for promotion as the 20th century progressed.[7] But organizations with strong internal labor markets (see Chapter 5) tend to benefit from the presence of workers who are familiar with their unique rules, procedures, and issues. In these organizations, promotion according to seniority promotes efficiency.

- *Perception of jobs as honorable.* The perception among bureaucrats that they do work worthy of honor contributes to loyalty and conformity. Just as people who perceive their jobs to be steady and expect periodic promotion tend to stick to their positions, so do people who derive satisfaction from feeling that they carry out honorable functions. The perception of honor is particularly important in organizations that are run according to rules and in which management is hierarchical. In a free society like the United States, most people do not like to feel dominated by others. If a person feels that his or her position is a source of honor, he or she is more willing to play the required, subordinate role.

Career employment, advancement due to seniority, and a sense of honor combine to encourage workers to accept their positions in the hierarchy and obey the rules. Favorable employment prospects and a feeling of honor are organizational properties that maintain structure much more efficiently than fear or coercion. Max Weber writes that administrators in ancient Rome were kept in line by torture and in China by "the prodigial use of the bamboo as a disciplinary instrument." But, he continues,

> The chances for such direct means of coercion to function with *steadiness* are extremely unfavorable. . . . Strict discipline and control, which at the same time has consideration for the official's sense of honor . . . work in the direction of strict mechanization. . . . [A sense of high status] among officials . . . agrees with the official's readiness to subordinate himself to the chief without any will of his own.[1]

Few, if any, organizations include all the features of bureaucracy outlined above, yet each of these characteristics should seem familiar to 21st-century Americans. The total picture suggested by these elements is one of a highly formal, rational organization, staffed by technically trained people, year after year carrying out standardized tasks according to rules. Business, government, and other concerns throughout the world have embraced this type of organization due to its superior efficiency and reliability. Again, to quote Max Weber,

> Precision, speed, unambiguity, knowledge of the files, continuity, discretion, unity, strict subordination, reduction of friction and of material and personal costs—these are raised to the optimum point in the strictly bureaucratic administration. . . . As compared with all (collegial, volunteer, and amateur) forms of administration, trained bureaucracy is superior on all these points. And as far as complicated tasks are concerned, paid bureaucratic work is not only more precise but, in the last analysis, it is often cheaper than even formally unremunerated (volunteer) service.[1]

The economics of the modern world require collective effort to be organized in a highly efficient and reliable fashion. Governments in the early 21st century employ millions of people. The public expects government to deliver products and services in a reliable, cost-effective fashion: social security payments, public school education, police protection, and countless other benefits. Businesses employ hundreds of thousands of workers, often dispersed throughout the world. The public depends on these workers to provide an endless array of goods and services, instantly and of assured quality. The scale of economic operations alone appears to make bureaucracy inevitable.

Political Culture

The material payoff of bureaucracy—efficiency and reliability in performance of large-scale, complex operations—does not completely explain why bureaucracy is so widespread today. Fundamental features of political culture in the prosperous democratic countries in Europe and North America also contribute to bureaucracy's predominance. Political culture embodies the values and beliefs associated with a society's political economy. Both political culture and political economy are macrosocial forces, practices and patterns of belief that exert powerful influence over all members of society.

As explained in Chapter 3, America's political economy may be described as "democratic welfare capitalism." Its provisions give Americans the feeling that they must be self-sufficient but at the same time deserve fair treatment from their employers and government. Fairness is a principal value in American culture. Representative government and respect for law are also major values in the United States and other democracies. Belief in both fairness and law contributes to the prevalence of bureaucracy.

Demand for Fairness

The operation of democratic welfare capitalism requires bureaucracy. This principle is most readily visible in government. Governments everywhere take money from the people in the form of taxes. Then, government returns money to the people as payment for services to the government or as public benefits. Services to the government include everything from work on the construction of roads and bridges to research on the causes of cancer. Units of government offer contracts to the private sector when they need work done by outside personnel.

Public benefits include conventional services such as park maintenance and garbage disposal. Increasingly, government has provided individuals with cash. Governments allocate financial aid to the poor and disabled, scholarships and low-cost loans to students, pensions to the elderly, and subsidies to farmers. Cash payments of this kind are often referred to as *government largess*.

Competition for both government payments for service and largess, amounting to hundreds of billions of dollars by the end of the 20th century, is often intense. Bureaucracy provides a means of distributing these billions in a manner considered fair by most citizens.

Competition for public money occurs whenever the government requires work to be done outside its own agencies. In the early 1990s, for example, the Department of Defense requested aircraft manufacturers to develop a new fighter airplane, capable of meeting the requirements of the new century. The state of California requested nonprofit organizations to provide services designed to prevent schoolchildren from using tobacco products. In both these instances, government issued a request for proposals (RFP), to which several competing companies responded. The government read each of the competitors' applications and awarded a contract to the bidder it considered best and least expensive.

Competition for government largess takes place in a different manner. Individual clients do not compete with each other over who is approved for Temporary Assistance to Needy Families (TANF), the largest public assistance program for the poor, or a college loan. But advocacy organizations representing TANF recipients or college scholarship seekers compete with advocates supporting other forms of welfare, such as farm subsidies and medical care for rare diseases.

The competitive atmosphere surrounding public largess creates bureaucracy. Citizens feel they should be getting all benefits to which they are entitled. Most people, moreover, feel that no one should receive greater benefits than the law allows. For this reason, the public and its representatives demand an elaborate system of regulations associated with the administration of programs distributing largess. Other parties in a democratic system seek to influence the manner in which largess is distributed. These include legislators, professionals, and public employees. The demands of pressure groups result in additional rules and regulations.

In a democratic society, all public agencies are required to act in a manner consistent with the desires of the public and its representatives. This principle is called accountability. Legislators, public agency executives, and judges develop rules, regulations, and standardized procedures to ensure accountability.

Public policy commentator Lawrence E. Lynn describes a strong connection between demands for accountability and the growth of bureaucracy:

> Bureaucracy grows because of pressure to have every [government] transaction, and the steps leading up to it, conform to someone's expectations of how they should be performed: with legislative intent, with the public interest as defined by interest groups, with the values and norms of bureau professionals and service workers, or with concepts of equity and fairness as defined by the courts. An effective way to ensure that expectations are fulfilled is to specify the procedures to be followed in designating and conducting the transactions.[8]

Rules, regulations, and standardized procedures are key principles of bureaucracy. The public demand for fairness also necessitates disinterested treatment of clients. Agencies charged with distributing largess require specialized workers sufficiently familiar with the required procedures. These agencies encourage career employment to retain such workers. Disinterest, specialization, and career employment add up to bureaucracy.

The procedures used by government to obtain services from private individuals or firms involves rules and regulations, too. Government RFPs require numerous and detailed pledges and assurances by bidders that they will obey laws regarding nondiscrimination, a drug-free workplace, restrictions on political lobbying, and a dozen other areas of public concern. Requirements that bidders include appropriate declarations and signatures and submit their proposals by the official deadline are stringently enforced. Contractors desiring to work for the government must submit massive volumes of paperwork. This is bureaucracy, indeed. But every provision, declaration, signature, and deadline reflects the public's desire to ensure that bidders compete on a level playing field.

Belief in rules. Respect for law is a central tenet of democratic welfare capitalism. People in the prosperous democracies of Europe and North America live under constitutions that have broad public support. As discussed in Chapter 7, most modern societies are held together by rational-legal authority. Although citizens often consider some laws bad or ill-advised, civil disobedience is unusual. People believe in governance by rules. They have faith that bad or ill-advised measures will eventually be repealed through the democratic process.

A belief in the rationality of the law strengthens public adherence. Laws in modern society are rational in that, ideally, each law is consistent with every other law. Laws are also considered rational because they aim at making society better. People in modern society believe that laws make sense and have emerged from the wisdom of goodwilled legislators and jurists functioning in the public interest. It is no accident that today's political leaders are usually lawyers by training, their legal skills fitting neatly into the fundamental political culture.

The principles of rational-legal authority translate easily into formal organizations. People expect organizations to have rules. Bureaucracies merely take the principle of rational-legal authority further than other formal organizations. Bureaucracies have more rules. Rules in bureaucracies cover minute details of inside operations and transactions with the outside. Modern men and women are accustomed to rules and often feel more comfortable doing business with (or working for) an organization run by rules than through alternative methods of coordination. Premodern people followed leaders empowered to lead by tradition or possessing charismatic gifts. Most moderns prefer systems explicitly designed by human beings for understandable purposes, in both their government and the organizations they join. Thus, while people as individuals vilify "bureaucracy," the political culture supports it.

Calculability and security. Technical advantages of bureaucracy over other formal organizations include its reliability as an instrument for attaining the objectives of top management. The dimension of reliability also provides day-to-day benefits to people served by the bureaucracy, individuals within the bureaucracy, and middle- to lower-level managers. In his classic essay, Weber comments that "the increasing demand of a society . . . for order and protection . . . in all fields exerts an especially persevering influence in the direction of bureaucratization." The consequences of this demand are visible in many quarters.

The public. Citizens in modern countries, including the United States, make strong demands on government for assured performance. Numerical standards for both performance and safety have widespread public support. In the first years of the 21st century, for example, public concern arose for the performance of public schools. In response, many school systems instituted standardized testing of elementary and high school students. Teachers in many places objected. They pointed out that every child is an individual and each should be given a different learning objective. Teachers further objected that the new system would force them to "teach for the test," drilling kids on exam questions rather than promoting comprehensive understanding of subject matter. Nevertheless, standardized testing began in many places.

The teachers had a point. Standardized, numerical objectives breed standardized education. Under a testing-based education system, principals will direct teachers to follow standard instructional routines to raise test scores. The result is greater bureaucratization of public education.

A striking example occurred in connection with a serious accident at a nuclear power plant in the 1980s. In this event, water intended to cool the reactor core boiled away. This allowed fuel rods to melt, damaging the reactor and releasing radiation. Placing most of the blame on human error in reading instruments and following emergency procedures,[9] investigators recommended making examinations for operators more exacting, augmenting monitoring of operators, and strengthening emergency procedures. Steps of this nature move an organization closer to bureaucracy.

The worker. It has already been noted that several features of bureaucracy protect workers from arbitrary or capricious actions by their supervisors. Promotion procedures emphasizing testable qualifications and seniority inhibit nepotism and favoritism. Rules in bureaucracies also address more day-to-day matters, such as working hours, protecting workers from adverse phenomena such as uncompensated overtime.

Deliberate attempts to improve the lives of workers have also spurred bureaucratization. Organized labor is frequently cited as a culprit. Union negotiations result in contracts with management that dictate highly specific provisions regarding wages, hours, and working conditions. On the operational level, these provisions result in detailed work rules. Often-cited examples include rules regarding job descriptions, prohibiting workers in one job category from performing functions specified in another. Formal specialization of this kind is a key element of bureaucracy. Union contracts also encourage bureaucratization by tying pay to the worker's job classification. The payment of fixed salaries thus established is a hallmark of bureaucracy.

The manager. Finally, bureaucratic rules often make the lives of managers easier. In an organization where rules play a minimal role, managers face the constant challenge of making decisions from scratch. Making a separate decision for every new set of events requires significant time and effort. Applying a rule to decide an operational question or respond to an employee's request, though, can be a "no-brainer."

Bureaucratic features also protect managers from criticism and the bad feelings of others. Outside a bureaucracy, the manager risks incurring hostility from subordinates when his or her decisions displease them. A manager who enjoys broad discretion in decision making becomes the object of personal animosity. Such hostility is much less likely in bureaucracy. The manager can explain to workers that his or her hands are tied by the organization's rules and regulations. Restrictions on individual action in a bureaucracy also protect the manager from criticism by his or her superior. The manager who is required to decide an issue because of a rule cannot be personally blamed if the decision has a bad outcome.

The Shortcomings of Bureaucracy

Max Weber viewed bureaucracy as inevitable. According to his thinking, bureaucracy represented social technology superior to other forms of organization.

Superior technology rapidly replaces more primitive methods of getting things done. Weber did not seem happy about this. His writings suggest a drab future, dominated by standardization and bureaucracy. He characterizes the era to come as an "iron cage of rationality" and a "long polar night."

Not everyone agreed with Weber's prognosis. Throughout much of the 20th century, social critics and management scientists strove to develop a new understanding of bureaucracy. Weber's formulations, after all, were based on world history and culture. Taylor's scientific management, which advocated "bureaucratic" principles in the factory, was based on engineering theory. Conducting experiments and spending time in actual organizations and workplaces, psychologists and sociologists formulated powerful arguments against either the value or the inevitability of bureaucracy. They argued that bureaucracy had three major shortcomings:

1. High human cost: although bureaucracy may be highly efficient, it serves humankind poorly.

2. Technical inefficiency: bureaucracy is much less efficient than early theorists believed.

3. Infeasibility: bureaucracy as described by theorists, in corporate organization charts, and in government operating manuals is impossible in the real world.

Just as every principle of bureaucratic operation can be viewed as contributing to efficiency and reliability, most can be connected with an adverse outcome. Table 12.3 summarizes several possibilities.

A basic feature of bureaucracies, for example, is their operation according to highly specific rules. Operation according to rules contributes to integration of roles, helps coordinate members' activity, and focuses effort on the organization's objectives. But an environment that emphasizes rules may be expected to foster inflexibility among employees. An employee who is punished for breaking a rule will think twice before doing so again. After 20 to 30 years on the job, such an individual may be relied upon to obey rules but to do little else. Bureaucrats who operate strictly by the book perform poorly when faced with unexpected developments or the need to innovate.

Some social scientists believe that there is, in fact, a "bureaucratic personality." People thus described, it is said, feel comfortable in a highly structured environment. A need for security leads these individuals to accept the authority of others in exchange for regular employment and occasional, small steps up. A belief in hierarchy and conformity makes the system of supervision and subordination seem right. Some believe that long years in a bureaucracy can actually turn someone into a bureaucratic personality. Others say that people already having bureaucratic personalities seek out employment in bureaucracies. The bureaucratic personality is often contrasted with the "entrepreneurial" personality, which emphasizes innovation, autonomy, and risk.

The specter of human beings becoming automatons driven by rules may seem distasteful. Still, such a development may be justified if it produces better and cheaper goods and services for humankind. The employees, it may be argued, need

Table 12.3   Threats by Bureaucratic Features to Productivity and Satisfaction

Bureaucratic Principle	Potential Problem
Rules binding the actions of all members	Inflexibility of personnel; "bureaucratic personality"
Hierarchical supervision	Timidity; overconformity; information pathologies
Specialization of personnel and subunits	Trained incapacity; loss of consciousness of objectives of organization
Prohibition of personal gain from operations	Reduced motivation
Continuous operation over time	Resistance to dissolution
Recruitment according to objective qualifications	Overemphasis on technical skills
Disinterested treatment of clients	Emotional distance from clients; discourtesy; amorality
Career employment	Complacency among personnel
Advancement through seniority	Underemphasis on technical qualifications
Perception of jobs as honorable	Excessive esprit de corps; secrecy; defensiveness

be robots only eight hours per day. Bureaucratic organizations, though, do not always produce real value for society.

Social relations in all bureaucracies are rational, in that they coordinate human behavior in a consistent manner focused on an objective. Not all bureaucracies, though, are substantively rational. Substantive rationality prevails when rules, hierarchies, promotion systems, and other structural features are actually configured in a manner likely to produce desirable social outcomes (such as high-quality and inexpensive goods and services). Some bureaucracies, though, are only formally rational. In them, rules, job descriptions, supervisory relationships, promotion procedures, and other structural features are mutually consistent and reinforcing, but do not produce outcomes of social value. Formally but not substantively rational bureaucracies may be inefficiently organized. They may produce marginally useful or useless output. They may have strong survival capacity but be unable to justify their costs of operation, either material or human.

The Human Cost of Bureaucracy

Critics of bureaucracy have placed emphasis on the cost such organizations exact from their employees and society as a whole. These observers argue that bureaucracies exact an unacceptable cost from individuals even though they may produce useful outcomes for humankind. In the opinion of these critics, bureaucratic surroundings have a negative emotional impact on the individual, reduce his or her level of skill, and damage his or her capacity to make moral judgments. These critics, in short, think of bureaucracy as "dehumanizing."

Alienation

Alienation, as defined in Chapter 8, refers to emotional separation of people from other human beings. It can also refer to a sense of loss among individuals of the things they consider most important. Social scientists have presented evidence that bureaucracies produce significant alienation among workers. In a study of several industries, sociologist Robert Blauner identified several distinct features of alienation. These include feelings of powerlessness, meaninglessness, social isolation, and self-estrangement.[10]

All these forms of alienation seem likely to occur in bureaucracies. Working under strict rules and the authority of others seems conducive to feelings of powerlessness. Performing highly defined tasks with little variation and only remote connection to concrete objectives appears likely to induce a sense of meaninglessness. Restriction of internal communication to official channels and prohibition of affective exchanges with clients doubtlessly produces a feeling of social isolation among some. *Self-estrangement* refers to a feeling among individuals that they are not fulfilling their mission in life or spending time in a manner consistent with how they would like to view themselves. As seen by another, the self-estranged person appears detached from what he or she is doing, is regularly bored, and is often absent from his or her position in the organization.

Diminution of Capacity

Industrial relations specialists have coined the term *trained incapacity* to describe a consequence of specialization in bureaucracies and other highly formal organizations. In bureaucracies, people become experts by repeating the same tasks over and over again. At the same time, they lose the capacity to do other things. Loss of capacity to do anything other than a constantly repeated assignment, it is argued, constricts the human experience and lowers the individual's quality of life.

Amorality

Two key features of bureaucracy make it difficult for members to assess the outcomes of the organization's actions according to moral criteria. Performance of specialized tasks blinds the bureaucrat to the organization's overall objectives. The emotional detachment that members of bureaucracies are encouraged to maintain from clients and other outsiders makes a critical perspective on how they are treated unlikely if not impossible. Detached as most are from final outcomes, bureaucrats often feel little or no responsibility for what their organizations actually do. Solving technical problems, pleasing one's superior, or positioning oneself for promotion have much more day-to-day visibility in a bureaucracy than holding the organization's objectives up to moral scrutiny. Bureaucracies, then, function as amoral instruments for the concentration of vast human efforts on objectives. History provides striking examples of bureaucracies whose objectives seem repugnant to most human beings—including many within the bureaucracy itself.

The most striking use of bureaucracy for morally repulsive purposes occurred in connection with genocide in Nazi Germany during World War II. It is often said that few Germans actually knew about the deportation of Jews, Gypsies, and other minorities to the death camps. Within Germany, some officials compiled lists of the future victims. Some scheduled train traffic. Some performed design work on execution equipment and crematoriums. Thousands of bureaucrats in occupied Poland and France also carried out minute details of the extermination effort. At postwar trials, few, if any, admitted knowledge of the atrocities that they helped make happen. Even highly placed officials such as the notorious Adolf Eichmann claimed that they had only functioned as "cogs in the machine."

Bureaucratic amorality occurs in democratic countries as well. During the decades of the Cold War (1946–1989), thousands of American scientists labored to produce more powerful and deadly nuclear weapons. Few of these scientists thought of themselves as bomb makers, though. Many specialized in design of details as tiny as a bolt. Others performed abstract tasks in theoretical chemistry or physics. Often, a scientist contended that he was concerned only with doing "good science." It is in the interest of bureaucracies doing work that is socially frowned upon to keep operatives' attention focused on small details rather than the big picture.

A Parable: When a Bad Bureaucrat Becomes a Blessing

Normally, employees in a bureaucracy carry out their tasks in an atmosphere of moral neutrality. They function as reliable servants to top management. Adherence to the rules, making decisions according to regulations and formulas, obeying supervisors, and maintaining separation of personal interest from task performance are the marks of a good bureaucrat. Like the hardworking clerks at city hall, honest bureaucrats are valued and honored almost everywhere.

Imagine the comment by German playwright Bertolt Brecht, famous for works such as *The Threepenny Opera*, that the happiest day of his life was when he met a corrupt official.

Brecht had been a hunted man in Nazi Germany, on a list of artists and writers the regime sought to arrest. He went from port to port seeking to slip out of the country, only to be refused the required exit visa. Officials consulted the government's "wanted list" and refused to stamp his passport.

Finally, Brecht entered an office in a small seaside town. Immediately, he is said to have recalled, he sensed that the official behind the desk would be willing to take a bribe. Payment was made and the required certification issued.

Every "honest" official had blocked Brecht's escape. Only a functionary who violated principles such as obedience to rules and prohibition of personal gain from exercise of duty enabled the playwright to avoid imprisonment and likely execution.

Acknowledging the amoral nature of bureaucracy, it seems reasonable to say, at least occasionally, "Hurray for corruption!"

Barriers to Productivity

Apart from the allegedly dehumanizing effects of bureaucracy, management scientists have questioned the actual efficiency of this form of organization. On paper, bureaucracy seems like an optimally performing machine. Questions about efficiency arise when actual human beings are observed in bureaucratic jobs.

Questions about effectiveness arise as well, regarding certain objectives that many believe bureaucracies are incapable of attaining, even with generous resources.

Goal displacement. Social scientists use the term *goal displacement* to describe the forsaking of an initially identified goal in favor of another one. Goal displacement is not a deliberate replacement of one aim for another, but a gradual, unconscious process. In bureaucracies, goal displacement takes place as the member focuses more and more minutely on his or her immediate tasks and less and less on the organization's overall objectives. Ultimately, one researcher has concluded, "adherence to rules, originally conceived as a means, becomes transformed into an end in itself."[11]

Goal displacement and trained incapacity are distinct but mutually reinforcing phenomena. Consider the example of a lawyer employed by a manufacturing firm as a risk manager. Risk management is a process by which organizations assess risk to earnings and assets due to accidents, malpractice, bad debt, and other potential liabilities. Faithfully carrying out his function, he assesses a new product and files a form with top management recommending that it not be manufactured due to potential lawsuits. As time goes by, it is observed that the lawyer reaches the same conclusion regarding every new product. Were his recommendations to be followed, the firm would forgo opportunities for significant earnings. But this concern is outside the lawyer's immediate consciousness. He identifies his job as identifying risk, displacing the company's overall objective of manufacturing products and making sales. Reinforced by his place in the bureaucracy, the attorney's legal background can be interpreted as trained incapacity: he is sensitive to legal but not business matters. This trained incapacity contributes to his setting aside the firm's ultimate objectives, a process of goal displacement.

Resistance to creativity. Strong arguments have been made supporting the benefits of bureaucracy for administrative tasks. The argument that bureaucracies can efficiently accomplish creative or innovative work is less powerful. People assigned to small, repetitive tasks do not seem likely to come up with great ideas. Hierarchical supervision is not conducive to development of new perspectives that challenge prevailing thought.

Ideas and inventions that transformed the 20th century did not emerge from bureaucracies. Einstein developed the theory of relativity while an employee of the Swiss government patent office. But Einstein performed this creative labor at home, in his spare time.

Chapter 5 described the Manhattan Project, in which the United States developed the atomic bomb during World War II, as distinctly outside the bureaucratic mold. Scientists who worked at the Los Alamos laboratory, where critical activity took place, describe it as a highly collegial setting. The nonbureaucratic nature of the laboratory stood in marked contrast to the bureaucratically organized United States Army, which administered the installation. Bureaucratic regulations required scientists to turn in time cards and military police to lock the laboratory doors at 5:00 p.m. Scientists sawed locks off the doors, continued working until dawn, and submitted time cards on which the number of hours worked seemed outrageous to the bureaucrats who read them.

It would be an error to assume that creativity takes place only within groups of equal and inspired colleagues. Nobel Prize-winning research often occurs in laboratories headed by authoritarian big shots, who issue orders to immediate subordinates, who, in turn, direct scientists and technicians under them. Such organizations have bureaucratic features in that people sometimes move up the hierarchy. Still, they are more accurately described as patrimonial systems, dependent on the resources and preferences of the top scientist. It is noteworthy that Manhattan Project research units other than Los Alamos were more hierarchical. A scientist who had worked under bossy Ernest Lawrence at the University of California, for example, recalled, "You did whatever task they assigned you and learned not to ask why."[12]

Reduced motivation and complacency. Several features of bureaucracy appear to depress worker motivation, resulting in a labor force that expends just enough effort to stay out of trouble. Consider the provision that employees not receive personal gain (other than salary) from operations. Rather than commissions and bonuses, employees in bureaucracies receive fixed salaries tied to their job classifications. On a day-to-day basis, extra effort or extraordinary skill yields no extrinsic reward. It has been widely observed that people who work for fixed rewards reduce their level of effort to the acceptable minimum. The presumption of career-long employment, it is argued, reinforces the depressive effect of fixed salary upon level of motivation.

Encouragement of disinterested treatment of clients also helps explain the bleary-eyed look on the face of many an operative performing routine tasks in a bureaucracy. Bureaucratic procedures encourage affective detachment as a safeguard against corruption. But transactions devoid of emotion often produce discomfort among customers and clients.

Information pathologies. As detailed in Chapter 10, hierarchy presents a risk of information pathology. Messages get distorted and sometimes lost as they travel between levels of organizational structure. Managers and operatives in separate functional units often consider it advantageous to restrict the transmission of information to all parties who may benefit from it. Information pathology leads to bad decision making. Bureaucracies, characterized by hierarchy as well as strict division of labor among subunits, should be considered at constant risk of information pathology.

Inappropriate promotion. Promotion in bureaucracies takes place according to technical qualifications, seniority, or both. Organizational psychologists have observed that this principle may be effective in ensuring fairness to employees and technical competence in each position. But neither seniority nor technical competence ensures adequate performance in many jobs. Particularly in management, personal qualities such as ability to communicate and to form collaborative relationships are crucial. Bureaucratic promotion rules may eclipse or even prohibit consideration of such qualifications. Personal qualities such as communication skill and ability to get along with peers are difficult to assess via standard measures. They tend to be bypassed in bureaucratic promotion decisions for this reason.

Self-perpetuation. Continuous operation is a valuable property of bureaucracy. This capacity ensures uninterrupted service to the public even after highly disruptive natural or political events. But the ability of bureaucracies to perpetuate themselves indefinitely must be viewed with suspicion. A newly elected Republican Congress in 1994 attempted to disband nearly 150 federal departments and agencies. Most, if not all, of these agencies remained in operation. Despite the public stereotype of the uninspired bureaucrat, bureaucratic agencies have significant motivation and skill at survival. Bureaucrats are barred from personal interest in individual transactions. But many of them passionately support the mission of their agency as a whole. In addition, members of bureaucracies at all ranks have a vested interest in the organization's continuation, since time in the service usually brings higher pay and increased opportunity for promotion.

Bureaucracies have many tools at their disposal to help ensure survival. Career officials alone know the regulations and procedures required for accomplishing their agency's mission. Unless top management—an elected official or top corporate executive—considers the bureaucracy's function expendable, he or she must work with the existing bureaucracy.

Bureaucracies also use political tools to stay in business. They build friendships with powerful allies, in part by configuring service capacity to benefit supporters. When they are attacked, bureaucracies seek protection from the recipients of these services. A classic study of a public bureaucracy, the Tennessee Valley Authority (TVA), illustrates how bureaucracies build ties with outside powers. Officials of the TVA made sure that large farming interests, industry, and state college systems received top priority for flood control and cheap electricity.[13]

Organizations do not willingly cease working even after their missions have been accomplished. After the conquest of polio, for example, the March of Dimes found a new mission: combating birth defects. The number of organizations in the modern world that year after year hire, train, promote, perfect bylaws or regulations, hold meetings, and issue reports, yet do not accomplish anything of true social worth, is undoubtedly large. Given their tight internal organization and sometimes monopoly over crucial information, bureaucracies both inside and outside government seem better adapted than most other collectivities to continue operation in the absence of apparent need.

Seen from one perspective, continuous operation of a bureaucracy is desirable. Continuous operation must be seen as negative when it amounts to entrenchment. Entrenchment develops within bureaucracies even when the organization's existence is not at issue. Bureaucracies are structurally designed for status quo operations and naturally maintain existing routines.

Infeasibility of Pure Bureaucracy, or, "It Doesn't Really Work That Way"

A final challenge to the belief in, if not endorsement of, bureaucracy involves its actual feasibility. Thinking consistent with Weber's regards individual human beings as parts in a vast machine. According to this thinking, human will is completely subordinated to organizational structure. The theory implies that people will uncritically submit to bureaucratic rules and supervision if they receive steady salaries, protection from arbitrary treatment by superiors, and honor in their roles. These features should ensure automatic and continuous operation of the bureaucratic machine.

Informal structures and processes often coexist with formal ones in organizations. These informal phenomena may either reinforce or undermine the organization's formal features. As individuals, human beings are seldom as passive as implied by a set of rules or organizational chart. They engage in negotiation, politics, and other forms of self-assertion designed to improve their lives in the organization.

An understanding of how bureaucracy really works has significance well beyond theory. Managers often assume that it is sufficient to understand the formal features of an organization to ensure effective operations. Deviation in the real world from bureaucratic norms illustrates the error in this assumption.

Universality of Informal Structure

In several places, this book has identified processes by which spontaneously evolved patterns of behavior affect activity within formal organizations. Leadership patterns may emerge alongside the official hierarchy, as technically or socially skilled persons help determine their colleagues' patterns of action or thought. Communication never seems to take place entirely within official channels. It seems unlikely that an organization exists anywhere without a system of private information networks or a rumor mill. Patterns of informal social interaction, the give-and-take of normal life in any human collectivity, are often given the label *group dynamics*. These informal yet often powerful sets of interactions modify actual (if not official) role expectations and bend structure according to the needs of those who live within it. Workers observed in the famous Hawthorne experiments illustrate the significance of group dynamics. Even within a strict system of rules, the Hawthorne workers developed their own expectations regarding pace of work, norms of production, and practice of discipline.

It is important to remember (see Chapter 7) that imperative force and structure itself can be informal as well as formal. Informal authority is compatible with the structure of primary groups such as families, work groups, and stable groups of friends. Informal authority and structure are particularistic, in force only among members of a single, identifiable group. Informal structure involves many spontaneously formulated procedures, rules, and decisions about division of labor, leadership, and subordination.

Sociologist Peter Blau pioneered in researching informal relationships within bureaucracies. Studying several public agencies, he detected numerous instances in which business was conducted according to procedures inconsistent with the rules.[14] Examples include the following:

- *A naval unit.* In isolation from nonnaval personnel, formal rules were relaxed. Protocols for formal recognition of higher ranks fell into disuse. The commanding officer, normally isolated from other ranks, became a frequent social participant. Natural leaders emerged in day-to-day tasks and received recognition.
- *A federal law enforcement agency.* Agents investigated firms for possible violations by auditing books, reviewing records, and interviewing employees. Each agent was assigned responsibility for an individual case, determining whether a violation had occurred and recommending action. Agents were required to

report their findings and recommendations to their supervisors, and prohibited from discussing their cases with anyone else, including colleagues. Reluctant in many cases to reach conclusions on difficult cases, though, the agents found ways to discuss cases directly with their peers. They did so in an informal manner, chatting about interesting aspects of the case or talking about abstract issues connected with it. In this manner, they did not formally violate agency rules, but effectively conducted consultations outside approved channels.

Informal authority and structure appear likely to be present in all bureaucracies. They represent departures from the norms of bureaucratic behavior. On close inspection, bureaucracies often seem to operate quite differently from the way they appear on paper.

According to Blau, departure from the norms of bureaucracy makes a functional contribution to the organization's operation. Regarding the remotely stationed navy unit, he remarks that the men accomplished their "day-to-day and long-run tasks with efficiency, zeal, and spontaneous initiative not characteristic of official bureaucratic machinery." Analyzing the federal law enforcement agency, Blau concludes that informal communication among agents increased the expertise of the group as a whole. The discussion sessions he describes improved each agent's capabilities through a process of mutual education. Informal communication about cases helped control the agents' tension as well. Agents experienced anxiety about having to admit to the supervisor that they had not resolved a case. They feared that the supervisor might detect an error in their work. A display of inability to resolve a case, they feared, might jeopardize their promotion prospects.

Bureaucracy run entirely by the book appears likely to be inefficient. It may even be completely infeasible in the real world. No one can design rules and standard operating procedures to meet every possibility. Members of bureaucracies such as those described by Blau form relationships and devise procedures that enable them to perform their duties.

Informal relationships also enable bureaucracies to carry out the nontask functions essential in all human collectivities. Most organizations may expend the bulk of their resources on attainment of objectives. But all organizations expend some resources on maintenance of the organization itself. Organizations must carry out *maintenance processes* such as distribution of informal rewards, promotion of positive feelings among members toward the organization and each other, and growth of *esprit de corps*. Reliable performance and loyalty to the organization, central to bureaucracy, are unthinkable without informal networks for mutual assistance, banter to let off steam, and parties to recognize the importance of personal life events such as marriages, births, and promotions.

Resistance to Bureaucratic Authority

Departure from bureaucratic norms is not always functional for the organization as a whole. Members of a bureaucracy, as in any organization, look for ways to make their participation as personally satisfying as possible. Personal and group objectives may focus on reduction of effort, protection from job insecurity, or reduction of stress. Organizational objectives may suffer as a consequence.

Crozier's study of a French industrial plant (see Chapter 7) illustrates procedures used by subgroups in a bureaucracy to make their lives more secure, rewarding, and interesting. The industrial monopoly studied by Crozier comes as close as possible to a pure bureaucracy. Rules made elsewhere govern the responsibilities of all personnel; supervision, at least on paper, is hierarchical. Employment is long-term, salaries are fixed, and many employees seem to derive a sense of pride in working for a government-owned industry. Informal social relations and group dynamics play an important role in the operation of plants. Bound by the rulebook, plant directors have limited power. But engineers and maintenance workers have power far beyond what might be suggested by the organization chart.

The engineers and maintenance workers derive their power from specialized knowledge, a hallmark of bureaucratic roles. They alone know how to keep the plant's obsolescent machinery operating. They guard this knowledge jealously. Crozier's study documents the manner in which engineers and maintenance workers reduced the plant's productivity to secure concessions from management. The power of these classes of workers enabled them to successfully challenge the authority of the official boss.

All bureaucracies appear at risk of the phenomenon reported by Crozier. Specialized knowledge allows workers to challenge the authority of management, middle managers to challenge the authority top executives, and career executives to challenge the authority of elected officials. Challenges of this nature potentially inhibit the organization from achieving its objectives.

Bureaucracy and the New Economy

As the 21st century approached, observers of industrialized countries began to speak of a "new economy." The new economy was said to encompass primarily advanced technology industries. The lead industries in the new economy included computers, telecommunications (primarily Internet-based), and enterprises made possible by computers and telecommunication, such as information retrieval and online sales. Biotechnology and specialty fields in engineering and finance (such as automated international funds transfer) were also considered part of the new economy. By contrast, "old economy" concerns encompassed mining, manufacturing, transportation, and other fields reminiscent of the noise and smoke of the Industrial Revolution. Government, an age-old function, seemed to fall into the old economy category.

According to several observers, the new economy was incompatible with bureaucracy. Bureaucracy, it was argued, made sense only for performance of tasks that changed little over the decades. In the new economy, it was asserted, technology was developing too rapidly for stable task performance to make sense. The sectors in which the new economy predominated, moreover, were highly competitive, necessitating rapid strategic shifts and adaptation to new challenges. Such an atmosphere contradicted fundamental principles of bureaucracy such as high role specificity, fixed rewards, and career employment.

Financial writers made much of the effects of the new economy on work organizations. One widely cited report predicted that the "job" itself, familiar to every generation since the early 1800s, would cease to exist. Writing in *Fortune*, William Bridges argued that the jobholders of yesteryear would be increasingly replaced by contractors and temporary workers.[15] In support of these assertions, the *New York Times* reported[16] that the annual payroll for temporary workers in the United States grew between 1981 and 1991 from $3.5 billion to $14 billion. Growth in the number of contract and temporary workers doubtlessly accelerated as the 1990s went by. Contract and temporary workers included a broad range of classifications, from clerks and secretaries to accountants, engineers, and doctors. Some estimates of the segment of the American labor force occupied by contract and temporary workers ranged as high as 33%.

A strong, continuous trend toward temporary and contract workers would certainly spell a decline in the importance of bureaucracy. Bureaucracy relies on individual workers' becoming adept at a highly specific function within an organization. The temps and contractors to which the business reporters of the 1990s referred moved readily between organizations, revising and renewing their skills with every step. An assessment whether bureaucracy will continue to occupy a predominant place among organizations in industrialized countries must take account of the new economy. It is certain that many people who occupied stable bureaucratic positions in the past are now nomads, moving from job to job as itinerant preachers and peddlers did in past generations. The age of bureaucracy may not be over, but bureaucracy seems likely to play a smaller role in the economies of industrialized countries than it once did. Greatly increased frequency of temporary employment has been reported not only in the United States but also in Europe and Japan, as traditions of lifetime employment and legal protection of workers in traditional jobs have weakened.[17,18]

The Balance Sheet on Bureaucracy

The material presented in this chapter raises two key question areas regarding bureaucracy. First, is bureaucracy fundamentally desirable or undesirable? Should it be tolerated or perhaps even encouraged, or should new organizational forms be sought to replace it? A strong case can be made that bureaucracy, despite its shortcomings, represents the best alternative for organizing most large-scale efforts today.

Second, people concerned with organization of work and other key activities may ask whether changing social and economic conditions are likely to reduce the importance of bureaucracy in the years to come. Insufficient evidence exists at this time to suggest that the preeminence of bureaucracy will soon decline. It is true that fewer people in the early 21st century held traditional jobs than in earlier generations. But future scenarios can be theorized involving long-term survival and perhaps even resurgence of bureaucracy.

Why Bureaucracy Is Desirable

Attainment of objectives. After considering the drawbacks of bureaucracy, this form of organization still has distinctly positive features as a means of coordinating human effort for attainment of specific objectives. Bureaucracy demands only what is reasonably expectable from each of its members: average ability, moderate effort, and simple honesty. Bureaucracy does not demand heroic effort or extraordinary talent. Bureaucracies coordinate, focus, and sustain expectable levels of effort by average human beings. By assigning roles of small scope to individuals and linking these roles according to a rational structure, bureaucracies attain large-scale objectives as diverse as building battleships, conducting mass inoculation campaigns, and policing metropolises.

It is true that bureaucracies are seldom engines of creativity and change. Neither, though, are many other types of formal organization. The dominance of traditional patrimonial leaders such as medieval dukes or modern political party bosses inhibits creativity as much as does bureaucracy. Collegial bodies, such as university faculties, are notorious for dithering.

It is unwise to look to bureaucracy for innovation. But large organizations often establish specialized units for innovation, invention, research, and development. For generations, for example, mammoth American Telephone and Telegraph (AT&T) operated the highly innovative Bell Laboratories. Units such as these may be partially bureaucratic but have important collegial features.

Bureaucracies are naturally conducive to continuity rather than change. But like the United States Post Office Department described in Chapter 11, they change in response to decisions by top management (assuming that top managers are sufficiently skilled and forceful at prosecuting change). Top management and leadership ranks are patrimonial and collegial rather than bureaucratic.

Well-being of members. Much has been written about the stifling of human beings and the alienation of workers in bureaucracies. But bureaucracy makes positive contributions to members' personal lives as well. Freedom from caprice of supervisors and career employment have already been mentioned. These characteristics have delivered generations of workers from anxiety over unfair treatment and unemployment. And while the clear separation that bureaucracy maintained between the world inside the organization and the world outside it has been called a cause of alienation, the separation has a positive feature as well. Members of most bureaucratic work organizations enjoy complete choice of lifestyle when away from work, a freedom not forthcoming in the patrimonial organizations of the past, such as family businesses. What critics of bureaucracy have characterized as compartmentalization—splitting of organizational from private life—might actually be understood as liberty.

Theories that blame overcautious behavior and ritualism on bureaucracy may err in their assessment of cause and effect. People gravitate to the organizations in which they feel most comfortable. Most personality features arise from a combination of heredity and early childhood experiences. To the individual with a previously formed "bureaucratic personality," bureaucracy may provide a comfortable home.

Why Bureaucracy Will Prevail

Much evidence can be cited to suggest that bureaucracy will remain the predominant form of organization in the developed world far into the future. Powerful forces such as political culture emphasizing equality and rational-legal authority promote bureaucratization. The effects of the new economy on the structure of formal organization are unknown. Today's collegial or patrimonial start-up companies may become the bureaucracies of tomorrow. Maturation of an organization generally corresponds to formalization. People may become less willing to work as contractors or temporary employees as they get older and take on family responsibilities. Organizations may prefer to hire contractors and temps; but, at least in times of high labor demand, they may be unable to hire sufficient numbers of workers on these terms. Even an organization composed largely of contractors and temps, moreover, needs a stable, bureaucratically organized core to maintain direction, ensure continuous quality standards, and perform central support functions.

A strong case can be made that nonbureaucratic features of organization may increase in importance yet not weaken the hold of bureaucracy. Informal social relationships within bureaucracies strengthen such organizations and, it may be argued, are essential to their ability to function. Widespread application of organizational development principles may prompt managers in bureaucracies to recognize the importance of informal relationships and take steps to strengthen them. Yet, the basic structure of bureaucracy will continue to prevail.

The presence of nonbureaucratic organizations strengthens rather than undermines the predominance of bureaucracy. Work not performed well by bureaucracies can be outsourced by them or carried out within specialized departments. R&D units, think tanks, art departments, and securities trading rooms are typically nonbureaucratic but are often lodged within large, stable bureaucracies. Bureaucracies tolerate the eccentricities of employees in such units while profiting from their creativity and risk taking.

Personal heroism, typically unpaid, is often touted by the mass media, enthusiastic managers, and tradition-minded politicians. But it is no substitute for bureaucracy. Voluntarism requires bureaucratic backup to be sustained over time. Material resources normally available only through bureaucracies are required for voluntarism to be effective.

Personal Heroism: An Alternative to Bureaucracy?

New York City writer and former schoolteacher Sara Mosle wanted to help humanity.

She "adopted" a group of disadvantaged children, staying in contact with them from their early childhood through their teens.

Mosle served as a "mentor" for these children—an activity many believe can reduce school drop-out rates and drug use. She took the kids to bowling alleys and skating rinks, parks, and concerts. She helped with personal and family crises.

Reflecting on the experience, though, Mosle recognized the limitations of personal effort.[19]

"I'm not a very good volunteer," she concluded. "To work, mentoring has to be performed constantly, over a sustained period of time and preferably one-on-one. For the first couple of years, I saw my kids as often as twice a week. But now I'm lucky if I see them once a month and I almost never see them individually."

(Continued)

(Continued)

 Mosle's observations on the importance of specialized formal organizations in initiating and sustaining the work she attempted are instructive:

"Although I was never a better volunteer than I was that first year, my success owed far more to the financial and institutional support I was receiving than to my idealism. My apartment in New York was far too small for me to have all my kids over at once. Because the school was the ostensible sponsor of my program, it let me borrow a classroom after hours for my group. This meant desks! And access to scissors, crayons and glue. There was a chalkboard for writing out assignments, a tape player for playing music, an easel for displaying charts, a class library and so on."

 A commentator responded: "You can't have a volunteer in a school without a schoolhouse. Government institution-building increases volunteering."

 Mosle interpreted her experience to mean that government-type organization—that is, bureaucracy—was essential to support the natural helping networks essential to effective mentoring.

Bureaucracy was already well established in most industrialized countries by the early 20th century. Predominance of this organizational form sparked negative emotional responses from many observers, those of Max Weber being the most famous. People concerned with the effectiveness of organizations and human well-being did more than describe and decry bureaucracy They began to systematically seek alternatives, not only to bureaucracy but to all formal organizations featuring the hierarchy and specialization that are most apparent in bureaucracy. Bureaucracy seems likely to survive far into the future—but few would deny that most formal organizations, even when well run, suffer from inefficiency, have difficulty adapting to new conditions, and fail to engender their members' best efforts. The next chapter surveys some of the better-known experiments and innovations intended to improve the functioning of formal organizations and the quality of life of their members.

Issues and Applications

Standardization, rationalization, and disconnection from human emotion are essential features, at least in theory, of bureaucracy. Bureaucracy represents a paradox. It juxtaposes efficiency and neutrality, features valued by the public, against a cold detachment that the public fears.

- The trustees of a highly regarded public university decide to eliminate personal interviews and letters of recommendation from the admission process. Henceforth, standardized tests – SAT, GRE, GMAT, and so forth—will serve as the primary criteria for evaluation of applicants. The trustees feel that the admission process must be conducted in the most objective and dispassionate fashion possible. Yet, potential applicants worry that such standardized procedures ignore unique personal features that would make them successful students and assets to the university community.

- President Woodrow Wilson (1856–1924) and Max Weber (1864–1920) were historical contemporaries. Both recognized that bureaucracy could make government more efficient. Yet, both seemed to fear that bureaucracy could diminish human well-being. Wilson's concern focused on the possibility that bureaucratic officials would too easily forsake responsibility to the public. In his famed essay "The Study of Administration," Wilson raised a question that remains unanswered today:

> The bureaucrat is everywhere busy. His efficiency springs out of *esprit de corps*, out of care to make ingratiating obeisance to the authority of a superior, or at best, out of the soil of a sensitive conscience. He serves, not the public, but an irresponsible minister. The question for us is, how shall our series of governments within governments be so administered that it shall always be to the interest of the public officer to serve, not his superior alone but the community also, with the best efforts of his talents and the soberest service of his conscience?[20]

Chapter Review and Major Themes

Bureaucracy is best distinguished from other forms of organization by its degree of formalization. Actions of bureaucracies take place under rules. Reporting relationships are clear. At least ideally, transactions within bureaucracies take place without emotion, as officials serve clients without regard to personal familiarity or social standing. Bureaucratic organizations encourage long-term employment, which promotes individual skill in highly specialized areas.

In a testimony to the essential independence of individuals, bureaucracies seldom operate in the purely mechanical fashion suggested in the preceding paragraph. Primary relationships develop within working groups. Informal networks arise to exchange information. Supervisors circumvent formal procedure to accommodate needs of their subordinates and increase efficiency.

Although actual bureaucracies depart from the ideal portrayed by Max Weber, they yield many of the efficiencies that he attributed to them. Bureaucratic organization is well adapted to performance of large, standardized tasks involving production of goods or administration of government programs. Growth of bureaucracy has been encouraged by public demand for equal treatment and reliability.

Figure 12.1 uses the analytical perspectives emphasized in this book to illustrate issues and outcomes associated with bureaucracy. The figure depicts bureaucracy as a form of organization that develops and functions under the strong influence of the environment. The predominant theme in the U.S. political economy, that of democratic welfare capitalism (see Chapter 2), promotes both large government programs and the expectation of equality. Bureaucracy fits well with this mandate. Technical development in modern society also meshes well with bureaucracy, as factory workers conduct standardized industrial processes and soldiers fight with standardized weapons.

Bureaucracy, in turn, influences the social environment. According to at least one influential author, the bureaucratic model of government can set the tone for society as a whole.[21] Bureaucratic practices become attractive to nonbureaucratic organizations under the pressure of public demands for accountability.

If Weber's interpretation is to be accepted, bureaucracy greatly increases an organization's functional capacity. However, subsequent research has found organizational pathologies to occur in bureaucracies, such as failures of information transmission and lack of lateral communication. To these may be added the costs to individual human beings of impersonal and overspecialized work. However, these same factors appear capable of reducing conflict. The clarity of lines of authority and the minuteness of roles may leave little room for disputes.

Ironically, managers may be said to exercise less control in bureaucracies than in any other type of organization. This is true because the rules under which bureaucracies function are typically made outside the bureaucracy. In agencies of state government, for example, rules that cover hiring and discipline are made by state personnel boards or civil service commissions. Similarly, budgets are determined by legislatures rather than by market forces.

The recollections of a man who served as director of a U.S. government science agency illustrate the phenomenon of management without control. The official, a prominent statistician in private life, had accepted the position with enthusiasm. He had hoped to exert a major influence on the direction of government-funded research. On the job, however, he discovered that he controlled almost none of the dollars in the agency's budget. Nearly all these monies had been earmarked by Congress for programs and projects already under way.

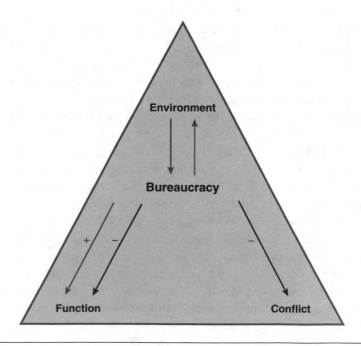

Figure 12.1 Analytical Perspectives Applied to Bureaucracy

Discussion Questions

1. Support or dispute the following statement by Max Weber: "As far as complicated tasks are concerned, paid bureaucratic work is not only more precise but, in the last analysis, it is often cheaper than even formally unremunerated [volunteer] service."

2. The preceding chapter asserts that the organization of work will become more and more bureaucratic in the years to come. Do you agree or disagree? Explain.

3. The inability to differentially pay for performance within bureaucratic job categories is often cited as a source of frustration to managers and of poor performance by bureaucratic agencies. What strategies may managers in bureaucracies employ to motivate subordinates and improve performance?

4. What forms of "de-bureaucratization" might be possible in U.S. government agencies today? Would the public respond positively to such measures?

5. Although union membership has declined severely in the United States in recent decades, it has grown rapidly in bureaucratically organized, public employment settings. Why has this been the case?

References

1. Gerth, H. H., & Mills, C. W. (1972). *From Max Weber: Essays in sociology* (pp. 208–214). New York: Oxford University Press.
2. St. Benedict. (1948). *Rules for monks.* Collegeville, MN: Liturgical Press.
3. Gouldner, A. (1954). *Patterns of industrial bureaucracy.* New York: Free Press.
4. Mechanic, D. (1976). *The growth of bureaucratic medicine: An inquiry into the dynamics of patient behavior and the organization of medical care.* New York: John Wiley & Sons.
5. Tuchman, B. W. (1978). *A distant mirror: The calamitous 14th century.* New York: Knopf.
6. Olcott, M. B. (1995). *The Kazakhs.* Stanford, CA: Hoover Institute.
7. Janowitz, M. (1971). *The professional soldier.* New York: Free Press.
8. Lynn, L. E. (1981). *Managing the public's business* (pp. 36–37). New York: Basic Books.
9. Omang, J., & Reid, R. R. (1979, May 18). Nuclear plant operators misread data in accident. *Washington Post,* p. A8.
10. Blauner, R. (1964). *Alienation and freedom.* Chicago: University of Chicago Press.
11. Merton, R. K. (1985). *Social theory and social structure.* New York: Free Press.
12. Davis, N. P. (1968). *Lawrence and Oppenheimer.* New York: Simon and Schuster.
13. Selznick, P. (1949). *TVA and the grass roots.* Berkeley: University of California Press.
14. Blau, P. M. (1964). *Bureaucracy in modern society.* New York: Random House.
15. Bridges, W. (1994, September 19). The end of the job. *Fortune,* pp. 63–72.
16. Diesenhouse, S. (1993, May 16). In a shaky economy, even professionals are "temps." *New York Times.*

17. Cooper, C., & Kamm, T. (1998, June 4). Much of Europe eases its rigid labor laws, and temps proliferate. *Wall Street Journal,* p. A1.

18. Strom, S. (1998, June 17). Japan's new "temp" workers. *New York Times.*

19. Mosle, S. (2000, July 2). The vanity of volunteerism. *New York Times Magazine,* pp. 22–55.

20. Wilson, W. (1941). The study of administration. *Political Science Quarterly, 56*(4), 481–506.

21. Crozier, M. (1964). *The bureaucratic phenomenon.* Chicago: University of Chicago Press.

CHAPTER 13

Experiments and Innovations

Learning Objective

To learn how people have tried to redefine organizations and how successful have been attempts to increase productivity, attain social objectives, and serve the personal needs of members.

Principles

○ Formal organizations are clearly necessary in the modern world. But executives, participants, and management scientists continually ask whether new organizational processes might be devised or new organizational forms invented that would work better than those in existence today. Many are concerned with the need to produce goods and services more efficiently. Others seek ways to make life within organizations more humane and uplifting. Still others believe that organizations should develop processes and structures capable of serving as models for broader social change. Bureaucracy is often identified as the organizational form most in need of revision.

○ Hundreds of experiments and innovations are currently being carried out in organizations of all types. Attempts to make organizations work better and more adequately fulfill human needs include some with familiar names, such as quality circles, flextime, Total Quality Management (TQM), reengineering, and reinventing government.

○ Many innovations have clear value. But some of these interventions have excited enthusiasm only to fade from visibility after a few years. Some of today's most popular innovations have never undergone objective evaluation. Managers wishing to innovate must select carefully among available options. Models that work well in some settings may perform poorly in others.

Reforming Formal Organizations

No one would maintain that today's formal organizations represent ideal settings for human productivity and fulfillment. Management experts, social scientists, and critics often argue that organizations could do better both in meeting their members' needs and in attaining their concrete objectives. For over 100 years, forward-looking people have sought remedies to the shortcomings of formal organizations. Measures suggested and tried by these visionaries have ranged from reform of existing practice to complete redesign of organizations as they are ordinarily recognized.

Work organizations are venues for much human unhappiness. Each day, millions of people return from work fatigued and irritable, due not to physical demands but to boredom, frustration, and stress. A growing number of workers experience cross-pressures between work and nonwork responsibilities. Personal dissatisfaction undermines the basic rationale of formal organizations: creation of cohesion and coordination for pursuit of shared objectives.

Bureaucracy may solve these problems for some individuals. Bureaucratic organizations require only limited time, effort, and attention from their members. People are free to do as they like when they are away from the office. For many, the exchange of constraint at work for freedom elsewhere works well on a personal level.

But bureaucracies cannot be said to capture the best possible efforts of most employees, as people reduce their efforts to an acceptable minimum. Bureaucracy has proven itself effective for many ordinary tasks but cannot claim to optimize human satisfaction or effort. Most nonbureaucratic formal organizations also represent departures from what, theoretically, might be obtained from and by the labor force.

Formal organizations outside the work setting have similar drawbacks. People involved in political parties and movements often feel that their voices are not heard by the leadership. Volunteers for charitable organizations feel that their talents are underutilized. It would be wrong to blame these problems entirely on bureaucracy. Participants in collegial organizations—these are as diverse as firms of doctors or lawyers, boards of hospitals or foundations, and amateur sports teams— often feel they take a backseat to those with the most prestige, loudest voices, or best political skills.

While most critics have faulted organizations for their imperfect performance in attaining goals and personally fulfilling members, some have developed more basic critiques. Formal organizations have incurred criticism for being mirrors of the surrounding society, reflecting and perhaps magnifying its less praiseworthy features. The United States Army practiced segregation as late as the 1950s. Social relationships within most business firms reflect the hierarchies of class, race, and gender outside. As Micheles has shown (see Chapter 5), even organizations that espouse equality tend to lock up decision making within a restricted elite.

Experiments and innovations have been both reformist and revolutionary. By far more common, reformist innovations typically address the pressure points within organizations. They aim at making organizational role expectations easier to accept and fulfill. They attempt to more effectively harness and reward the creativity and industry of members. Radical experiments have striven for human equality and flexibility of roles and structure.

Reformist concepts have come and gone over the decades. Revolutionary experiments are typically confined to enterprises that are small, short-lived, or both. Most innovations have worked best in organizations with special needs or facing special challenges peculiar to particular industries or historical times. But all experiments and innovations have value to managers because they demonstrate what may be possible with sufficient planning, thought, and insight. Even the most radical and shortest-lived experiments deserve continuing attention as sources of ideas and inspiration.

A Break With Tradition: The Human Relations and Quality of Work Life Movements

Innovations designed to improve the fit between the needs of individuals and those of organizations receive much attention today. Yet interest in such innovation did not become widespread among managers until recently. A major change in traditional ideas about how to organize human effort was needed. The required break, the *human relations movement* referenced earlier in this text, occurred in the middle third of the 20th century (see Chapter 3 for discussion of associated theory). The movement helped to inspire generations of managers, scientists, and consultants to devise innovations in the design and operation of organizations.

Prior to this movement, managers usually thought of organizations as machines. Consistent with the principles of Taylorism, individual jobs were ideally conceived as constant repetition of a single operation. Managers and most social scientists had never heard of Max Weber. His work was not translated into English until the 1940s. But industrial organizations and government agencies in the United States definitely followed the trend Weber had detected in Europe. Though not often pure bureaucracies, organizations in the United States became increasingly formalized and hierarchical. The principles of scientific management had helped bring about major economic growth between 1880 and 1920. But they did so at a cost. People were seen by managers as (and often considered themselves to be) small parts in vast, impersonal operations, without individual uniqueness or will, and replaceable if they malfunctioned or wore out.

By midcentury, commentators on organizations had spun several new theories of people in organizations. These theories emphasized meeting the individual's needs and supporting his or her potential as a contributor to the organization. Two of the best-known theories were Douglas McGregor's *Theory X and Theory Y* and Frederick Herzberg's *motivation-hygiene theory.*

Theory X and Theory Y. McGregor's formulation of two alternative theories of human behavior, called Theory X and Theory Y, became famous.[1] Managers of old were assumed to have worked under Theory X, which saw people as selfish, lazy, and often dishonest. Under Theory X, only material reward and strict supervision made sense as means of ensuring desired behavior. Theory Y, on the contrary, taught that people were naturally goodwilled and cooperative. Under Theory Y, managers could profit by establishing collaborative relationships with their employees.

The motivation-hygiene theory. A related formulation by Herzberg asserted that the goodwilled, cooperative nature of human beings becomes evident when their biological needs have been met. Herzberg identified factors such as salary and security as dimensions of "hygiene." Like biological hygiene required to prevent illness, hygiene in an organization promotes the worker's physical well-being. Only under conditions where hygiene prevails, the theory argues, can "motivators" such as advancement, recognition, and work itself contribute to performance. By ensuring the sustenance and security of its members, then, an organization can liberate their basic willingness to cooperate and intrinsic interest in their work,[2] both of which contribute to output. Maslow's thinking on the hierarchy of human needs (see Chapter 2) is consistent with that of Herzberg.

Many decades have passed since the establishment of the human relations school. Other lines of thinking have developed and flourished that focus on the thinking, needs, and personal goals of people in organizations. The Quality of Work Life (QWL) movement, for example, appeared in the 1970s. People involved in this movement initially focused on the personal difficulties and dissatisfaction of workers. Later, managers and worker representatives became convinced that a higher quality of work life could boost productivity.

Significant inventiveness has gone into developing practical interventions to allow members of organizations to better meet their personal needs. Key intervention techniques have included

- Incentive innovation
- Participative management
- Worker accommodation
- Family-friendly arrangements

Interest in developing better systems of incentives long predates the human relations movement. Fixed salary systems today predominate in the United States. These are consistent with bureaucratic principles of organization. The fixed salary system has received much blame for limiting work motivation. Critics of bureaucracy have observed that under a system of fixed incentives workers tend to gravitate toward a minimally acceptable standard. On the individual level, people who feel they do more than average are likely to become dissatisfied if they do not receive proportional rewards.

Attractive alternatives to fixed rewards have not been obvious. Pay-for-performance plans are logically appealing. Why not simply pay productive workers more? Recurring problems with pay for performance, though, were listed in Chapter 6. Human relations research has contributed much in this area. Pay for performance tends to produce interpersonal conflict, with workers becoming jealous of each other and taking steps to limit each other's productivity. Perhaps more important, pay for performance can reduce an organization's total productivity. Workers hoard resources, as employment agency personnel were known to do with job opportunities. Organizational units engage in competition for favorable treatment by top management, alleging that they are more productive than their counterparts. Such competition reduces the likelihood of future cooperation.

Organizations have experimented with methods for rewarding performance, but at the same time limiting the damage this can do to cohesion and collaboration. Perhaps the best-known of these innovations is the Scanlon Plan.[3] This innovation originated in the 1950s as the brainchild of a union official named Scanlon. Under the plan, workers receive bonuses not for individual performance but for the profitability of the firm as a whole. The Scanlon Plan aims at focusing the worker's attention, not on his or her individual performance, but on outcomes shared by everyone. Rather than encouraging individuals to compete with each other, this plan aims at promoting collaboration and mutual assistance.

Another classic experiment exemplifies the features of innovative incentive giving. In the 1940s, the Lincoln Electric Company initiated a plan that provided rewards based on both organization-wide and individual performance. Only if the firm had a successful year could employees earn bonuses. But individual employees received bonuses only if they received favorable performance ratings.

Organization-wide incentive plans are still in widespread use. Group Health Cooperative's Performance Plus (see Chapter 5) represents an example of a present-day Scanlon Plan. Performance Plus calls for every worker to receive an additional percentage of his or her salary if certain corporate goals are reached, such as customer satisfaction and completion of procedures deemed necessary for good patient care. A minimum percentage is given if the organization reaches a minimum target. Greater percentages are given if the target is exceeded.

Related incentive innovations tie rewards more closely to personal performance. Some plans reward performance associated with the individual's work group or unit. Hybrid plans provide some reward for individual performance and some for performance of the work group or organization as a whole. Modern group incentive plans seldom dictate an employee's total salary. Generally, these plans cover only what amount to bonus payments.

Participative Management

Participative management falls more squarely than incentive innovation into the human relations and QWL movements. As the label implies, participative management allows personnel not traditionally involved in organizational decision making to take part in it. Several distinct lines of thinking support participative management interventions. First, people often contend that workers have a greater right to participate in the decisions that shape their lives than they have traditionally enjoyed. Second, proponents of participative management believe that participation will raise worker satisfaction. Finally, supporters of participative decision making believe such innovation will increase productivity. Workers, they think, will have more favorable attitudes toward their jobs if they feel less socially and emotionally distant from their managers. In this sense, workers are expected to buy into decisions in which they have played a part. In addition, supporters of participative management believe that pooling information among individuals from different levels of the organizational hierarchy will promote higher quality decision making.

Three applications of the principle of participative management illustrate the many approaches that have been tried: (1) collaborative goal setting; (2) formal peer collaboration, or self-managing work teams and quality circles; and (3) worker participation in corporate decision making.

Collaborative Goal Setting

Under collaborative decision making, subordinates and superiors work together to formulate objectives that both meet the superior's needs and lie within the subordinate's capabilities. In the negotiation process, the superior presents the needs of the organization as a whole or of the unit he or she manages. The subordinate focuses on the limits imposed by the resources at his or her disposal. These resources include the number of hours the subordinate is willing and able to work per week, the personnel at his or her disposal, and the capacity of machinery in an industrial operation. Where a sales objective is concerned, the subordinate must also consider market demand for the product or service he or she handles.

Successful collaborative goal setting adjusts the superior's expectations to the constraints imposed by resources. The process may raise the level at which the subordinate aims. Under appropriate incentive plans, the subordinate who achieves his or her objective receives a merit raise or bonus.

The principles of human behavior suggest that collaborative goal setting can increase motivation. Participation in the negotiation process allows the subordinate to have a voice in the level of performance to which he or she will be held. This, in turn, increases the subordinate's emotional commitment to the objective. The norm of reciprocity (see Chapter 6) may increase commitment and motivation as well. If the superior has backed off from a demanding initial proposal, the subordinate is likely to feel he or she has received a favor. This results in a special motivation to achieve the reduced objective.

Collaborative goal setting supersedes the traditional practice of simply giving orders. Instead, superiors and subordinates negotiate objectives for a given quarter, year, or other period of time. Superiors become better informed about the capacity of the units they supervise. Identification of concrete objectives gives the subordinate something specific to shoot for and a factual basis on which to expect reward.

Management by Objectives

The best-known form of collective goal setting is *management by objectives* (MBO). MBO usually involves only management personnel. Under a comprehensive MBO plan, each manager negotiates with his or her superior and subordinates. To meet the objectives to which they have agreed in negotiations with *their* bosses, managers must obtain the necessary level of performance from their subordinates. For this reason, managers are often forced to take tough positions in MBO procedures.

MBO typically leaves individuals free to achieve their objectives by the means they think best. This feature of MBO allows both managers and workers to use their ingenuity and specialized knowledge to best advantage. MBO is the opposite of *micromanagement,* the practice by which superiors make operating decisions for their subordinates. Micromanagement, in which a superior takes over his or her subordinate's role, is frowned upon in modern management science. No manager, it is argued, can command the range of skill and factual knowledge of large numbers of subordinates. Micromanagement discourages the subordinate's creativity and willingness to take risks. MBO is an antidote to this practice.

Successful MBO requires the manager to be a skilled negotiator and a good listener. Success is most likely when the superior exercises true leadership, inspiring the subordinate and demonstrating to him or her the importance of his or her performance to the organization's well-being. MBO is least likely to succeed when the manager inflexibly demands performance that is impossible given the subordinate's resource limitations.

Formal Peer Collaboration

Workers have always influenced the manner in which they carry out their activities and their level of output. The Hawthorne studies illustrate this fact, as do many later investigations. Often, workers distribute tasks and set production norms for the purpose of reducing effort and protecting comfortable features of their work lives. "Formal" peer collaboration constitutes a recognition of this principle and an attempt to apply it for the entire organization's benefit.

Peer collaboration differs from MBO in two important respects. First, peer collaboration signifies collaboration among people of equal status, that is, peers. Peers typically include people who do the same kind of work and receive approximately equal pay. In contrast to peer collaboration, MBO takes place through negotiation between individuals at different levels in the organization's hierarchy. For example, the two parties to an MBO negotiation may include an executive and an operating manager.

Second, peer collaboration, as a deliberate organizational innovation, usually involves groups of workers. These workers handle day-to-day manufacturing or customer service functions. Their knowledge base focuses on "nuts and bolts" rather than the broader challenges of the organization. Typically, individuals involved in peer collaboration projects do not supervise others.

Among the most widely used procedures of peer collaboration are *self-managing teams* (SMTs) and *quality circles.* In both these settings, workers promote organizational objectives by improving coordination of individual activities and sharing information. Groups assembled for these purposes are given the explicit assignment to contribute to the organization's objectives. They receive resources required for their task, including information (such as marketing and financial data) on the organization's status and challenges. Members of these groups may receive incentives for achieving results, such as bonuses for increasing production.

Peer collaboration is believed to promote worker morale. Critics of modern organizations comment upon the "compartmentalization" of workers' lives. This is particularly true of bureaucratic organizations (see Chapter 12). It is believed that the extremely specific roles that characterize such organizations limit personal growth and produce a dispirited workforce. Peer collaboration is cited as a remedy for this condition, promoting communication among coworkers, expanding horizons, and enhancing feelings of self-worth. Many management scientists share the impression of Hackman and Oldham that "work high in task variety, autonomy, identity, significance, and feedback fosters internal work motivation, which in turn leads to high performance and satisfaction."[4] Peer collaboration, it is believed, enables these conditions to prevail.

SMTs are defined as *groups of workers assigned the responsibility for making decisions over the manner in which work will be carried out, setting schedules, assigning individuals to perform specific functions, and evaluating members' performance.* SMTs are accountable to management, which reviews their performance in comparison with hoped-for levels of success. Still, SMTs enjoy a measure of autonomy. The term *empowerment* is often applied to SMTs, signifying the independence and power that these groups receive in helping meet organizational objectives.

Management scientists typically cite several famous examples of SMTs. The best known cases include the following:

The Volvo Udevakka plant. Beginning in the mid-20th century, organization of work in this plant departed strongly from the classic procedure for automobile assembly. In contrast to specialized functions on an assembly line, Volvo workers were assigned responsibility for assembling entire automobiles as a team. Each individual could do several different jobs, rotating among them as needed. Inspection functions were delegated to the assembly team. The team determined the pace of its work and scheduling of breaks. The team as a whole was accountable to management for a high-quality assembly job.

The Topeka General Foods plant. In the same era, management at General Foods experimented with self-management at a Topeka plant involved in the manufacture of pet food. Workers in this plant were divided into teams of about seven individuals. Each team was responsible for a specific functional area, such as finishing or packaging. Within each team, distinctions among individual jobs were reduced or eliminated. A leader with foreman-level experience was appointed to each team.

Each team was responsible for developing strategies for accomplishing its assigned tasks. The team had the power to select new members when a member left. Each team selected an individual to represent it before plant management. Team members were given the function of correcting those who lagged behind standards.

While also applying the principle of peer collaboration, quality circles differ from SMTs. Quality circles are discussion groups rather than production units. Workers usually volunteer to participate in quality circles, or they are asked to participate on a volunteer basis. These units often meet after working hours. They receive production and financial data (often via user-friendly graphics) and may have the services of a management-appointed facilitator. Quality circles aim at making recommendations to management for improvement of the functioning within the unit or facility from which the members are drawn.

Quality circles achieved fame through their use in Japan during that country's economic boom of the 1970s and 1980s. They were typically found in manufacturing concerns. Many observers attributed Japan's prosperity during this period to quality circles or to the spirit of collaboration between workers and managers that quality circles reflected.

In the United States, quality circles have been instituted in a wide variety of organizations. Some of the most interesting applications have been observed in the health care industry. In the late 20th century, managers of health care delivery organizations became intensely concerned about controlling costs as costs in their industry skyrocketed and patients and insurance companies showed increasing reluctance to pay. Quality circles seem particularly well suited for hospitals. Hospitals serve as the workplace for a wide variety of professionals. Though functionally interdependent, many of these professionals have little direct contact with each other. Within a quality circle, though, a floor nurse may inform a pharmacy technician about the challenges she faces in timely medication of patients. This information enables the pharmacy technician to modify his schedule for sending drugs to the service area. Peer communication contributes to better patient care. But it does not take place in sufficient volume without deliberate mechanisms such as quality circles.

Worker Participation in Top Decision Making

More visionary forms of participative management have involved actual participation by workers in the governing boards of major corporations. Arrangements of this kind are known as *codetermination*. Most experiments with codetermination have taken place in the industrialized countries of Europe, notably Sweden, Germany, and Yugoslavia prior to that country's dissolution in the 1990s.

Germany in the late 20th century provides some of the best examples of codetermination. Following World War II, the non-Communist German state (then the Federal Republic of Germany) established laws requiring that worker representatives be given seats on the boards of directors of major firms. In the crucial coal and iron industries, half these seats were allocated to representatives of the workers. In other industries, one-third of board membership was reserved for worker representatives, with the remaining seats going to investors. Worker representatives were often union officials but were sometimes elected independently by employees.[5]

Despite movements aimed at enabling European business concerns to operate more like those in the United States, codetermination has survived into the 20th century in Germany, Sweden, and several other countries of the European Union (EU). Worker representatives have taken special interest in management issues that affect labor. These include investment decisions, mergers and acquisitions, and downsizing. Their influence on boards of directors has been substantial. Worker representatives, for example, opposed plans by the English firm Vodaphone to acquire the German telecommunications concern Mannesmann. Workers feared that German employees would be laid off following the merger. Although the acquisition eventually took place, the German worker representatives insisted upon provisions for preserving jobs.

Codetermination is not a one-sided arrangement in favor of an organization's workers. Rather, it has a function similar to other forms of participative management. By sharing concerns from several differing perspectives, potentially opposing parties are impelled to seek mutually agreeable strategies. Executives are compelled to forgo actions detrimental to workers. Workers are made to understand that their rates of compensation cannot undermine the viability of a profit-seeking firm. The community of interest fostered by codetermination leads to feelings of mutual concern and respect. Workers are committed to the success of the firms that employ them. Extended, costly strikes are avoided. Sweden and Germany, two of the world's most productive economies in the decades following World War II, knew almost no major strikes in the latter half of the 20th century.

As observed in Europe, codetermination must be understood in the context of the organizational environment. Two important features of an organization's environment are the culture and the political economy that prevail in the surrounding society (see Chapter 3). Europe's culture places greater emphasis on cooperation among diverse segments of society than does the culture of the United States. In the United States, individuals and groups often think of each other as adversaries in a struggle for social and economic advantage. America's political economy accords different rights to labor and management. Labor law in the United States protects the rights of unions to bargain for wages, hours, and working conditions, but reserves operational decision making to the firms' owners and their representatives. American political culture places labor and management in a tug-of-war, in which the most important disputes are settled in court or on the picket line. Codetermination has clear advantages over such a system. But such mechanisms would require changes in the organizational environment to be feasible.

Employee Stock Ownership Programs and Buyouts

Much more familiar in the United States than codetermination, employee stock ownership programs combine aspects of both participative management and incentive innovation. Many corporations enable workers to purchase their stock at a discounted price through payroll deductions. Such arrangements are known as employee stock ownership plans, or ESOPs. Encouragement of employee stock ownership presumably gives the employees an incentive to contribute to the company's success.

Transfer of controlling interest via stock sales to employees, known as employee buyouts, enables workers' representatives to participate directly in management. Such a transaction took place at United Airlines in 1994. Management transferred 55% of the firm's stock to the airline workers' unions in exchange for wage and benefit concessions. As a result of stock transfer, workers' representatives occupied three seats on the firm's board of directors.

Participative Management in a Performance Organization

The Orpheus Ensemble, a New York chamber orchestra, serves as a model of self-directed work.

Many organizations have embraced participative management as a means of reducing dependence on formal leadership. It is widely thought that such empowerment promotes individual responsibility and unleashes energy and creativity.

Founded in the 1970s, the Orpheus Ensemble began with rejection of the conductor's leadership role. Since its inception, the orchestra has performed without a conductor.

Musicians in most orchestras have relatively little say in either artistic or business matters.

The Orpheus Ensemble, though, operates under consensus-based self-management, a process essentially unchanged throughout its history.

According to a *New York Times* report,[6] rehearsals in the ensemble's early days were free-for-alls. "We'd argue for an hour about one measure and then take a vote on how to play it," a musician recalled.

The consensus process became streamlined as the organization matured. A three-member artistic committee selected the music. Principal players from each section, who changed from piece to piece, were responsible for the interpretation of each work.

Full, direct democracy prevailed when the orchestra came together for full rehearsal. Interpretation of the music was hotly disputed, and sessions were at times so tempestuous that chairs were thrown.

The orchestra has encountered many challenges typical in the lives of organizations. Musicians acquired families and had less time for travel. Conflicts occurred between the musicians and a professional administrator.

Still, the orchestra achieves "remarkably polished" performances and takes on highly challenging compositions. Multinational corporations and a major business school have hired the ensemble to provide instruction on negotiating decisions and resolving conflict.

Member Accommodation

Member accommodation involves helping meet individual needs that are less quantifiable than money but still concrete. Modern employees require personal time and must fulfill family responsibilities. Many active individuals in today's labor force must overcome physical challenges. Successful and socially conscious organizations have expended significant effort formulating ways to meet related personal needs. The person-friendly organizational strategies described below represent only a few examples of the many that have been tried.

Flextime

Flextime denotes an arrangement that permits individuals in an organization to adjust their working hours according to personal preference and convenience. Under flextime, people work the same number of hours as they would conventionally. But they work according to a schedule different from the traditional 9:00 a.m. to 5:00 p.m., Monday-through-Friday arrangement.

Several flextime arrangements are in widespread use. Some take the form of fixed though unconventional schedules. Such plans, for example, permit employees to work four 10-hour days per week, yielding a total of 40 hours. Other plans allow employees to exercise maximum latitude in selecting their hours. A plan of this kind might require employees to be present only during specific "core" hours—say, 9:30 to 11:00 a.m. and 2:00 to 3:30 p.m. Additional hours required to complete a 40-hour workweek might be logged any time from 6:00 a.m. to 6:00 p.m.

Potential personal benefits are obvious. Fixed flextime arrangements allow individuals to extend weekends, an opportunity highly valued by people with a recreation-oriented lifestyle. Open-ended schemes enable people to take care of personal needs such as banking and medical appointments, to slip into the office before the morning rush hour, and to wait out the traffic before leaving for home at day's end.

Flextime would appear highly functional for the organization as well. Management experts have argued that such arrangements promote worker satisfaction, increasing productivity and reducing absenteeism and turnover. Fixed flextime arrangements may enable organizations to accommodate additional workers in existing physical space. All flextime systems reduce road traffic at peak hours. Plans for reducing automobile commuting by employees are now legally required in cities such as Los Angeles, where smog and traffic mitigation are important public concerns.

Flextime is one of the most widely adopted innovations in American business. As Table 13.1 (on page 395) indicates, the majority of U.S. business establishments offered flextime to their employees in 2002. More appeared likely to follow in later years.

Telecommuting

Telecommuting refers to the practice of performing salaried work for an organization while at home. People have always performed paid work at home. In the modern world, home has long served as the workplace for professionals such as doctors and dentists and freelancers such as artists and authors. The late 20th century saw increasing interest among people holding regular jobs in formal organizations performing at least some of their duties at home. While at home, these individuals stay in touch with supervisors and subordinates via telephone and computer linkages.

As in previous eras (see Chapter 5), technology creates opportunities for organizations to operate in new ways. Individuals in far-flung locations can be linked to central offices reliably and cheaply via telephone and e-mail. Managerial and professional personnel can receive and transmit large arrays of financial and technical data for immediate review and response.

Benefits that can be expected from telecommuting resemble those of flextime. Telecommuting provides flexibility for the worker, since he or she need not physically report to a work site. Telecommuting holds significant promise of reducing the burden of physical commuting: time consumed in travel to and from the office, as well as air pollution and energy consumption from motor traffic. Individuals who telecommute, it has been said, avoid the tension that prevails in some office environments. They do better work because they operate in a setting with fewer physical and social distractions. Telecommuting is a boon for workers who wish to live beyond normal commuting distances from their offices.

In the late 20th century, relatively few Americans were classifiable as telecommuters. Surveys conducted in the late 1980s suggested that less than 1% of people in the U.S. labor force could have been so classified. But many expected this percentage to increase as communication technology improved and associated costs declined.

Innovative Task Scheduling

Innovative task scheduling refers to the timing of individual day-to-day performance requirements. Measures of this kind differ from flextime. Under innovative task scheduling, people ordinarily work traditional eight-hour days. But their activity on the job varies in a manner designed to promote employee productivity, satisfaction, and retention. Two examples illustrate this type of innovation.

Time segment restriction. High-tech firms have begun experimenting with breaking the workday up into restricted blocks of time. Some time segments, for example, are to be spent performing individual tasks, while other time segments are freed up for one-on-one conferences, group work, or formal meetings. Such segmentation, it is believed, promotes improved personal time management and reduces worker anxiety.

Sociologist Leslie Perlow has provided a useful illustration of time segment restriction in an engineering firm.[7] Management instituted the system to ease a "time famine" among the engineers. These professionals were highly trained and highly motivated. But many complained that they were unable to complete their required tasks. This was true even among the many who worked extra night, weekend, and early-morning hours.

To address this problem, management instituted blocks of uninterrupted time. Several hours were specified during the workday for this purpose. During these periods, personnel were advised not to call meetings or hold group or one-on-one conferences.

Time discretion. Time discretion refers to control by an employee over the volume and pace of his or her work. Employees in industries that characterized most of the 20th century enjoyed little time discretion. Workers in industrial assembly plants had next to none. In automobile manufacturing plants, for example, worker behavior was synchronized with the speed of the assembly line. Consistent with Taylorism, this was believed essential for optimal efficiency. Independent businesspeople and professionals have traditionally occupied the opposite end of the spectrum, independently deciding upon the number of hours they work and the speed at which they complete tasks.

It is now known, though, that discretion over time can be valuable to members of all organizations. This is particularly true of people with chronic health problems. Many active individuals today have histories of chronic illnesses such as arthritis or diabetes. Normally, these conditions are nuisances rather than serious threats to comfort or function. But these illnesses are subject to periodic flare-ups. At such times, people may require a few moments to take special medication, an hour to rest and let the flare-up subside, or a half-day to visit the doctor. People with chronic conditions may need to take leaves of absence for medical care.

Research has shown that people with chronic disease are more likely to remain in the labor force if time discretion is allowed. This is true even of people with histories of cancer, a fear-engendering and often life-threatening disease. Time discretion promotes an individual's ability to hold a job, even if he or she earns a relatively low income and has severe pain or other physical symptoms.[8]

Employee Assistance Programs

Employee assistance programs (EAPs) have become familiar in most organizations employing large numbers of people. EAPs provide employees with services intended to address personal problems that may affect their productivity. The modern EAP's rationale dates back to the human relations movement, which looked to the employee's personal life to explain friction between the employee and his or her role within the organization.

EAPs today provide employees with a broad range of services. Most, if not all, provide psychological counseling. Many offer marriage counseling or classes in anger management. EAPs provide diversity training, antismoking interventions, and substance-abuse interventions. Often, EAPs provide less-traditional services such as credit and debt counseling.

Management may provide an EAP for reasons other than providing direct help to employees. These programs serve as a safeguard against legal liability stemming from violence and harassment on the job. The presence of an EAP can also help an organization faced with a wrongful dismissal lawsuit. The fact that a dismissed employee was offered or received EAP services can constitute evidence that the employer made a good faith effort to keep the employee before firing him or her.

EAPs are often specialized subunits in an organization's human resources department. Occasionally, an organization may purchase EAP services from an outside vendor. Organizations may save money by contracting with an outside EAP service supplier. In addition, an organization may wish to have EAP services delivered outside its boundaries to protect the confidentiality of employees in need.

Worker Accommodation and the Law

Federal legislation in the late 20th century heightened the importance of worker accommodation. Signed into law in 1990, the Americans With Disabilities Act (ADA) has had continuing impact. The law defines a person with disabilities as anyone with "a physical or mental impairment that substantially limits one or more of his/her major life activities."

ADA Title I states that businesses "must provide reasonable accommodations to protect the rights of individuals with disabilities in all aspects of employment." "Reasonable accommodations" may include "restructuring jobs, altering layout of work stations, or modifying equipment." All organizations with 15 or more employees are legally required to comply with the ADA.

Several of the worker-friendly modifications of the traditional workplace covered in this chapter fall under the heading of "reasonable accommodation." These may include reasonable time discretion or performing part of a job at home. It is likely that many employers have made these and other accommodations due to legal measures such as the ADA.

Family-Friendly Arrangements

Of all changes in the modern workplace, the business pages devote the most attention to family-friendly arrangements. Family-friendly arrangements resemble and overlap with worker accommodations, as described in the preceding section. Worker accommodations are designed to meet the needs of a wide variety of personnel, many of whom may have no dependents or family responsibilities. Family-friendly programs are intended specifically to promote satisfaction, productivity, and loyalty among workers facing demands from children, spouses, and elderly parents.

Family-friendly arrangements in the United States are driven by economic and demographic changes that became impossible to ignore in the late 20th century. These included, notably, the importance of working women. In 1950, only about 10% of women who were mothers of children under six were in the labor force. By 1990, the proportion approximated 60%.[9]

Three family-friendly arrangements are most prominent in the United States today: (1) child and elder care, (2) release time, and (3) alternative career tracks.

Child and Elder Care

Child care has received perhaps more attention in discussion of the family-friendly workplace than any other arrangement. In order to work, people with children must have either a family member to take care of them or a paid, outside person or organization to perform the service. Most parents today rely on the latter.

Table 13.1 indicates the ways in which business establishments in the United States helped employees reconcile family needs with work requirements in 2002. Child care was directly provided by about 10% of firms and subsidized by another 10%. Paid leave for parents of newborns was provided by just under 30% of the firms, and unpaid parental leave was permitted by nearly 85%. Elder-care assistance was provided by over 12%.

Release Time

Flexible hours, an option made available in nearly two-thirds of U.S. firms, are important to workers with and without family responsibilities. Their special value to people with children or dependent elders is obvious. Organizations enable people with such away-from-work responsibilities to fulfill them through other mechanisms as well.

One such arrangement is release time. Release time contributes to flexibility in working hours. Release time means occasional time off from work for taking care of family or other personal responsibilities. A parent needing to care for a sick child

Table 13.1   Family-Friendly Arrangements in U.S. Business Organizations

Family-Friendly Arrangement	Percentage of Business Organizations Providing
Child care on-site or elsewhere	10.7
Subsidy for off-site child care	10.1
Paid leave to parents of newborns	29.7
Unpaid parental leave	84.8
Elder-care assistance	12.8
Option of flexible hours	64.4

SOURCE: National Organizations Survey.[10]

or deal with a problem at school may request time off from his or her supervisor or work coverage from colleagues. A parent needing to pick up his or her children at the end of the day may avoid overtime or beg off working on a rush job that needs to be completed after hours.

Release time may be formal, under personal leave policies that allow a specified number of absent hours for any reason. Alternatively, release time may be obtained through informal negotiation among peers and between workers and their supervisors. The category of "flexible hours" in Table 13.1 reflects release time (both formal and informal) and formal flextime.

Informal social processes and organizational culture often play a part in release time. Peers without family responsibilities may consider a parent's duties more important than their need for rest and recreation. A supervisor may feel that employee-parents will pay back flexibility with better work in the future. Expectations around the *norm of reciprocity* contribute to the willingness of supervisors and peers to permit work release time. Better or more work in the future is expected in exchange for the favor. An organizational culture emphasizing family friendliness also contributes.

Alternative Career Tracks

People with responsibilities at home have resorted to part-time employment for generations. Most often, women who were also homemakers sought such positions. Expectations of part-timers were typically low. Salary, benefits, and job security were typically limited. Part-time jobs were viewed as filler positions, offering little or no prospect of advancement.

With the increasing number of women in management and professional jobs came a need for more desirable alternatives to traditional, full-time employment. Two widely encountered arrangements are (1) job sharing and (2) temporary part-time status.

1. *Job sharing.* Under job sharing, two individuals fill a job that was formerly held by one worker. This arrangement is typically sought by individuals initially in full-time jobs. Two previously full-time employees may fill the job formerly performed by one. Alternatively, the experienced employee may train a newcomer to do part of his or her job. Job sharing enables the organization to retain expertise that might otherwise be lost. It may also help an employer accomplish needed downsizing.

   Job sharing avoids several undesirable features of part-time work. People who share jobs continue to exercise important roles in the organization rather than serving as mere fillers. Job sharers retain their former salary levels (in proportion to their percentage of full-time hours). They typically receive full benefits, although they may make greater personal contributions. It is expected that they will have permanent careers with the organization.

2. *Temporary part-time status.* In the past, many women committed to careers have taken maternity leave to have babies and care for them for a few months. Today, more and more arrange to return as part-time workers for several years, changing back into full-time employees when their children are old enough. As men take a greater role in child rearing, the words *family leave* and *paternity leave* have been added to America's corporate vocabulary. On principle, the sequence of family leave and part-time status continues an individual's career in the organization. Job sharing may provide a means for a part-time employment phase that follows family leave.

Mother-Friendliness in the New Age

In 1993, the *Wall Street Journal* reported that forward-looking organizations were beginning to install "lactation stations" for working mothers.

Many mothers today believe that their own milk is better for their infants than formula. Among other benefits to the infant, research suggests that mothers' milk promotes resistance to contagious disease.

While at work, many mothers today use breast pumps to extract their milk, storing it for actual feeding at a later time.

To help employees carry out this procedure in comfort and privacy, Amoco Corporation has installed a "lactation station" in its Chicago headquarters office building. According to the report, Amoco spends $12,000 per year to operate the facility, which includes private cubicles, armchairs, magazines, and a "lactation consultant." The Department of Health of Jefferson County, Missouri, opened a similar facility for its employees.

Amoco provided its lactation station at the instigation of a physician employee who, as a new mother, had resorted to pumping breast milk for her infant daughter in a supply room.[11]

Management Movements

Many widely publicized innovations in the modern organization focus on the members' needs. Incentive innovation, participative management, worker accommodation, and family-friendly arrangements all strive to make life in the organization easier or more personally rewarding to the member. These innovations are consistent with the human relations movement, whose central tenet may be summarized as, "Be nice to your workers and they will perform better." Other lines of innovation in modern organizations focus less on the needs of the worker and more on the needs of the organization itself.

Innovations of this kind do not forsake the workers' interests. Everyone should benefit from involvement with a more efficient and stable organization. But these innovations are less dependent on worker commitment for success and more dependent on the plans and actions of managers and executives. Thus, they are designated here as *management movements*.

Many management movements have bloomed and faded over the past generation. Only three will be discussed here as illustrations:

- Reengineering
- Total Quality Management (TQM)
- Reinventing Government

Reengineering

The concept of reengineering became famous in the early 1990s through a book by Michael Hammer and James Champy, *Reengineering the Corporation*.[12] This concept directly opposes the bureaucratic form of organization. Essential features of bureaucracy, it will be recalled, include role specialization and hierarchy. According to Hammer and Champy, these structural characteristics create significant inefficiency and waste.

Waste is created in hierarchical organizations, they argue, because people at each level require continual supervision and control by superiors. At the same time, they contend, everyone loses sight of the organization's objectives. Executives are too far from the customer or the production process to make high-quality decisions. High levels of specialization, they contend, were crucial in the days when hardware and heavy industry dominated the economy. But they argue that specialization contributes to fragmentation in an organization. It is potentially dysfunctional in today's competitive, service-oriented industries.

As an initial remedy, Hammer and Champy recommend clear, forceful vision statements by executives. Vision statements must be specific, sharp, and future-oriented. A good vision statement should remind all members of the organization's primary objective. Hammer and Champy illustrate desirable features of a vision statement with the terse dictum of Federal Express: "We will deliver packages by 10:30 tomorrow morning." Hammer and Champy assert that executives must emphasize the need for rapid, forceful change, resorting to alarm if necessary to shock the organization into action.

Reengineering takes place through concrete procedures aimed at reallocating and readjusting work flows, job responsibilities, and production design. As a result of reengineering, for example, operating units may create highly efficient subunits to replace dependence on outside, specialized departments. Cross-training is often instituted to enable one worker to carry out functions exercised by several under the preexisting system. New procedures may be specified for producing and delivering goods and services.

The feature of reengineering most clearly recognizable by workers and managers alike, though, is quite specific: systematic reduction of middle-level staff. It is contended that middle management staff can be reduced if higher-level personnel spend more time observing production processes and assisting in customer-contact functions such as service and sales. Under reengineering, workers themselves are "empowered" to take on greater responsibility and exercise functions once reserved for management. Hammer and Champy illustrate successful reengineering with examples from large firms such as IBM.

Technical innovation in the late 20th century contributed to the popularity of the reengineering concept. Efficient, inexpensive telecommunications and e-mail facilitated contact between lower- and higher-level people. Miniaturization of computers and peripherals created access to production, service, and sales-related databases for personnel at all levels. The use of handheld devices by waiters and rental car attendants illustrates such access. Hammer and Champy argue that such innovation makes hierarchy in organizations considerably less necessary and creates opportunities for reengineering.

Reengineering has often been adopted as the philosophy of executives seeking to create a "lean and mean" organization. The concept of reengineering fits nicely with major layoffs carried out by firms such as Xerox and Aetna in the 1990s. *Rightsizing*, a term that evolved from the more-familiar downsizing, is often associated with the reengineering concept. Rightsizing results from adjustment of staff levels to those appropriate in view of reduced need for hierarchy and specialization in modern organizations.

Total Quality Management

Total Quality Management (TQM) is perhaps the best-known of the management movements of the late 20th century. It is strongly linked with the work of W. Edwards Deming.[13] The operational system of TQM draws inspiration from industrial engineering. According to Deming, all work takes place within an organization's social and technical system. The social facet of the system involves the pattern of social relations that prevails within it, including the expectations people have of each other, the mutual assessment process, and the rewards and punishment used to promote desired behavior. The technical side of the system encompasses design and quality of machinery and equipment. Existing systems make a specific level of production possible, and at the same time place a cap on the organization's level of achievement.

The manager's first task is to make sure that the existing system operates as effectively as possible. This takes place through a process of *continuous quality improvement* (CQI). From the perspective of an industrial engineer, Deming illustrates CQI as a chart tracking deviations from a statistical ideal. In the manufacture of precision machine parts, for example, deviations beyond a narrow range of tolerance constitute defective product. Management's job is to successfully reduce deviations from the sought-after length or diameter as time goes by. This principle, as Deming has said, applies equally well to open-heart operations and the manufacture of automobiles. It is the manager's responsibility to find ways to reduce the magnitude of deviation to the point at which no further reduction can be accomplished.

Deming provides, and recommends that others construct, graphic illustrations of this process in the form of *run charts*. Each chart illustrates the number of deviations from the norm over time. Good management results in a steady decrease in over- or undersized product, instances of excess or below-normal production. Graphically, the "control limit," or range of deviation, becomes smaller and smaller. The end point of this process occurs when the range of deviation becomes constant, that is, achieves *statistical control*.

Deming, who spent many years in Japan advising industrialists in that country, attributes Japan's post-World War II success to continuous quality improvement and bringing industrial systems into statistical control. Toyota and Honda conquered the American market, he commented, because each automobile deviated so little from the manufacturer's high standards. The manufacture of virtually identical autos ensured that each consumer would receive a highly reliable vehicle.

A system in statistical control represents a successful end point of one era's management. But a system in statistical control can achieve no further improvement. Management responsibility changes at that point. When the initial system has stabilized, it must be transformed into a new system of social relations and equipment, which then must itself be brought into statistical control. Continuous improvement of existing systems and transformation into new systems lowers production costs, improves quality, increases profits, and creates jobs.

Unlike Hammer and Champy's system, which involves radical change, urgent response to developing conditions, and often extensive dismissal of middle and lower-level managers, Deming's movement emphasizes measured progress and cooperation. Deming argues that America must abandon adversary relationships among individuals and firms. Productive relationships must be cultivated, between firms and their suppliers and between managers and workers. In the Japanese tradition, for example, Deming recommends that firms should identify one or two suppliers of raw materials, work with them to improve their products, and stick with them as they improve. Likewise, Deming emphasizes the value of loyalty and mutual support in the employment relationship. "Drive out fear!" is one of 14 points that summarize TQM.

Concrete procedures associated with TQM include much fact gathering and internal discussion. TQM places great emphasis on communication with customers as well as monitoring them to assess their requirements and perceptions of the firm's products. As noted earlier, much effort goes into observing the work process and product characteristics and presenting findings in understandable graphics. Creation of cross-functional teams to identify and solve quality problems is a TQM hallmark. Firms with serious TQM programs are marked by frequent, intense discussion in settings that resemble quality circles. Through such groups, it is believed, management makes use of the workers' understanding of the day-to-day problems of production and cements their commitment to making improvements. Throughout TQM there is a sense that proper management, education, and support will make an existing labor force productive.

Deming criticizes several widespread management practices. He believes slogans such as "zero defects" do more harm than good. Such slogans, he remarks, amount to impossible and hence frustrating tasks. He castigates the modern American corporation for its short-term orientation. According to Deming, the long term must be stressed: research and development, worker training, and continuous improvement rather than the firm's quarterly dividend. Deming takes a dim view of both individual and group-focused pay-for-performance schemes. He believes that such mechanisms undermine teamwork and universal commitment to improving the system.

TQM, which achieved great popularity at the end of the 20th century, has much in common with a management movement at the century's beginning: Taylorism (see Chapter 5). Taylor saw the human element in the process of production as capable of improvement through appropriate design of schedules and equipment. This early industrial scientist placed primary responsibility not on worker motivation but on system design. TQM makes use of worker input to help improve quality. But it places primary responsibility on the manager for developing systems, bringing them into statistical control, and transforming them when further improvement cannot be made.

Reinventing Government

The *reinventing government* movement is distinguished from TQM and other management movements in its focus on the public sector. Reinventing government resembles the other movements described above in that it urges revision of traditional organizational practices. Reinventing government mandates reduction of formal procedures, such as approval and inspection by superiors. It shares these priorities with reengineering and TQM.

As its core, reinventing government opposes bureaucratic principles. Historically, bureaucracy has been more apparent in government agencies than in private organizations. Though often maligned, bureaucracy in government serves important public values. A clear separation of the organization's resources from those of its members constitutes a key example. As Chapter 12 indicates, this enables the organization to deploy resources in pursuit of its objectives more effectively. Bureaucratic operation according to strict rules also serves the public. The practice prevents employees from treating friends with special favor, a practice that occurred frequently in the 19th century, before American government became highly bureaucratized.

Advocates of reinventing government highlight negative consequences of bureaucratic operation in public agencies. These critics claim that governance by strict rules inhibits commitment to objectives, courteous treatment of the public, and adaptation to changing conditions. The critics argue that bureaucratic administration is no longer necessary in the 21st century. One reason is that information is readily available to a large number of people, enabling a larger segment of an organization's members to make high-quality decisions.

Proponents of reinventing government argue that government agencies should adopt practices traditionally associated with business. These include rewarding individuals and subunits for superior performance; promoting competition between private providers and public agencies; and allowing lower-level personnel to make decisions and take initiative. Agencies that have undergone reinvention, they say, become "leaner," capable of carrying out their responsibilities with smaller staffs. As do reengineering and TQM adherents, supporters of reinventing government believe in "empowering" subordinate individuals. Reinventing government extends empowerment beyond the organization's boundaries, advocating closer participation of the general public in the decision making of public agencies.

According to David Osborn and Ted Gaebler, two pioneers in the movement, reinvention of government has been widespread. Emphasizing entrepreneurship, they report diverse examples with a common thread:[14]

> Most entrepreneurial governments promote *competition* between service providers. They *empower* citizens by pushing control out of the bureaucracy, into the community. They measure the performance of their agencies, focusing not on inputs but on outcomes. They are driven by their goals—their *missions*—not by their rules and regulations. They redefine their clients as *customers,* and offer them choices—between schools, between training programs, between housing options. They *prevent* problems before they emerge, rather than simply offering services afterward. They put their energies into *earning* money, not simply spending it. They decentralize authority, embracing participatory management. They prefer *market* mechanisms to bureaucratic mechanisms. And they focus not simply on providing public services, but on *catalyzing* all sectors—public, private, and voluntary—into action to solve their community's problems.

Osborn and Gaebler cite the example of a public swimming pool in Visalia, California, which would never have been built if city government there had not been "reinvented." A city official noticed a pool for sale at a rock-bottom price. To beat other potential purchasers, the official went lickety-split to the seller with a $60,000 deposit check. Such prompt action would have been impossible under traditional agency practices. But in the spirit of reinvention, Visalia had created a pool of unrestricted funds that allowed rapid response by officials to favorable purchasing opportunities. Under the usual bureaucracy, city officials would have waited weeks for approvals and clearances to be completed. By that time, the opportunity would have been lost.

Direct collaboration with people and organizations outside their boundaries is a hallmark of government agencies that have undergone reinvention. Exciting examples include *public-private partnerships* under which government agencies help initiate and support private organizations to carry out public missions. Visalia helped start and gave financial support to a private organization charged with building affordable housing. Governments everywhere have turned to *outsourcing,* or contracting traditional public services to outside, private organizations. Garbage collection, public building security, and even prisoner incarceration have become familiar examples. It is argued that city departments become more efficient when they fear that their function may be contracted out. Government agencies in many places have instituted community boards, in which agency officials meet regularly with community residents to monitor the content and quality of public service.

Organization for Equality

Of the features of formal organization that people find displeasing, inequality is perhaps the most prominent. Most formal organizations have hierarchical structures. The ambitious spend their lifetime trying to climb the ladder. A lifetime of taking orders based on the decisions of others does not seem fully human. People in superior positions also have reason to regret the existence of hierarchy. Traditional discouragement of fraternization with subordinates separates those in favored positions from the greater community.

It is little wonder that people through the ages have sought to make society more level. Some have participated in social movements aimed at bringing about a more egalitarian society. Others have attempted to establish formal organizations as small social systems whose members were to be social equals. Such organizations have been intended not just to be enclaves of egalitarianism within the broader society. They have been promoted as beacons to demonstrate the feasibility and wisdom of reducing formal ranking among human beings.

Three examples illustrate organizations in modern society founded with the intent of demonstrating the feasibility and merits of equality.

Illustrations of Egalitarian Organization

Case 1: The Israeli Kibbutz

The kibbutz is a collectively owned farming and industrial organization in Israel. Perhaps 100 kibbutzim (the Hebrew plural of *kibbutz*) existed at the beginning of the 21st century, home to a small fraction of the country's population. They are clearly formal organizations, receiving charters from the government and doing business as corporations. They own land, farming equipment, industrial facilities, and housing tracts. They operate schools, food services, and child care facilities. No one owns significant personal property. Everyone is an equal partner in the enterprise.

Kibbutzim began to appear in Palestine in the early 20th century. They were products of left-wing Zionist movements in Europe. Zionism refers to the belief that Palestine is the natural homeland of the Jewish people and that Jews can escape persecution only by establishing an independent country of their own. In Europe, many Zionists were also socialists. Groups of these individuals migrated from Poland and Russia to Palestine, a country initially part of the Turkish Empire and later under British administration. Zionist migrants established kibbutzim to lay the groundwork for a Jewish state.

The migrants had more immediate objectives as well. They desired to establish a society free of the oppressive features of the ones they had left. European society was tradition-bound, with great emphasis placed on religion and male domination. Czarism still prevailed in Russia and Poland. Sexual mores were Victorian.

The *kibbutzniks* (as kibbutz members were called) established small, semi-independent societies where all this was abolished. Religion and family domination were immediate targets. Children were reared communally, living apart from their parents in children's houses. Meals were taken not at home but in a communal dining hall. Sexual relations outside of marriage were tolerated.

(Continued)

(Continued)

Although there were a few religious kibbutzim, most were atheistic, allied economically with networks of farming and marketing cooperatives and left-wing political parties.

Most important, fierce egalitarianism ruled. No one received a salary. All were equally entitled to housing, clothes, food, medical care, and a little pocket money. Top decisions were made in communal meetings. Although the kibbutzniks elected officers, these positions rotated among the membership. People in supervisory positions continued to do the menial work required of all kibbutzniks. The kibbutz president could be seen washing dishes at the dining hall, an image rich in symbolism.

Throughout most of its history, the kibbutz movement adhered to the doctrine of self-labor. This meant that kibbutzniks themselves would be required to perform all tasks needed to make the community function. Hiring of workers for some jobs, they reasoned, would undermine the ideal of equality, since the hired workers would undoubtedly perform work the kibbutzniks considered undesirable. Hiring employees from outside would create an "underclass" within the kibbutz of farm hands and factory operatives.

Case 2: Cooperatives and Collectives

Cooperatives and collectives are organizations among whose principal objectives is equality among members. Cooperatives are a well-established type of organization in American life. Their principal objective is usually marketing or purchasing on behalf of members who are producers or consumers. Farmers have formed cooperatives to sell their products, obtaining greater efficiency by accumulating individual production into significant pools. Consumer cooperatives such as Recreation Equipment Incorporated (REI) make large-scale purchases and pass discounts on to the membership. Cooperatives also have the feature of vesting governance equally in all members. Each member has one share in the cooperative and one vote.

The term *collective* is often used to describe a type of organization that strives to allow all members to have equal control over resources and to participate in decision making. "Collectives" may be formally organized but sometimes are not. Collectives became widespread as part of the social movements of the 1960s and 1970s. It was not unusual to see small businesses such as restaurants or groups of craftspersons organized as collectives. Principles governing collectives de-emphasize formal decision-making procedures, hierarchy, and leadership.

Though most collectives and kindred organizations are small-scale operations, in a few instances they have been large and nationally visible. An outstanding example was *Ms. Magazine,* as it existed between 1972 and 1989. With prominent figures from the women's movement at its core, *Ms.* as an organization strove to maintain a structure markedly different from other publishing enterprises. The people who worked at *Ms.* felt that bureaucracy and hierarchy were "patriarchal" practices that the women's movement needed to overcome.

The organization operated in a manifestly egalitarian manner. Everyone, including clerical staff, was invited to attend meetings where editorial policy was determined, and to speak up. At meetings, the organization's leaders sat not at the head of a table or a podium but in an ordinary spot among the others. No one had a formal title. Names on the magazine's masthead were listed in alphabetical order.[15]

Case 3: The Community-Based Organization

Community-based organizations have become important to government agencies and philanthropic organizations pursuing innovations relevant to communities and neighborhoods. Americans have recently placed increased emphasis on neighborhoods, realizing that individual quality of life depends on the individual's immediate environment. Throughout the 20th century, however, economic and demographic change threatened the stability of neighborhoods across America. Many once viable communities fell victim to urban decay.

Historically, personnel within governments and foundations formulated interventions designed to improve education, safety, and stability in American communities. By the end of the century, however, it became apparent that many of these schemes had proven ineffective. Agency and foundation personnel lacked sufficient knowledge about the communities they hoped to assist. The interventions formulated—public health and stay-in-school campaigns, for example—proved of little interest to community members.

As a solution, governments and foundations have turned to community-based organizations (CBOs). CBOs are organizations whose membership is concentrated in a defined community and is open to all residents. A general sense prevails within CBOs that community residents should determine the organization's objectives and participate in decision making. Consistent with these beliefs, CBOs typically seek people for decision-making boards whose qualifications are knowledge of the community rather than professional or social prominence. They regularly hold open meetings to encourage everyone interested to contribute. Foundations play a major role in fostering CBOs, providing grants to existing organizations or encouraging communities to start new ones.

Organizations Without Walls

As the 21st century began, much was heard about the *virtual organization* as an innovation of exceptional promise. Like the virtual machine in computer terminology, virtual organizations do not exist as concrete structures with visible boundaries. Rather, they are the contributions of separate organizations pieced together on an as-needed and often highly temporary basis. The virtual organization is an assembly of capacities from several different sources with specified interrelations that prevail for only a limited time.

Experimentation with the virtual organization has occurred extensively in the health care industry. In health care today, the integrated delivery system (IDS) has replaced the solo physician of yesteryear. The IDS combines several of the resources required for delivery of modern health services. Every IDS offers the services of physicians, hospital facilities, and an insurance product to cover costs. People (or their employers) subscribe to the IDS for a monthly fee.

Traditionally, the IDS provided all three types of service within its own organizational boundaries. Some organizations that have operated in this fashion are known as HMOs, or health maintenance organizations. Kaiser Permanente, for example, the largest HMO in the United States, owns hospitals and makes exclusive contracts with large corporations of physicians. An umbrella organization, the Kaiser Foundation, acts as an insurance carrier.

The new, virtual organization does not include all needed capacity under one roof.[16] It acts only as "general contractor," making contracts with physicians (singly or in groups), hospitals (or specific services from several different hospitals), and insurance carriers. Consumers buy health care coverage from the virtual organization, which in turn pays the contracting organizations for their services. A system of contracts makes possible the equivalent of a large, complex organization; the actual entity putting together the array of contracts is in reality very small.

The possibilities offered by virtual organizations are striking. Consider, for example, a virtual university. Comprising neither gothic campuses nor football stadiums nor beer hangouts, the virtual university would contract with universities throughout the country to allow subscribers to take selected courses. Subscribers to the service could take the courses over the Internet. They could participate in class discussions via chat rooms and bulletin boards and submit exams via e-mail. In the end, the student would receive a degree, perhaps without ever having entered a classroom or met a professor. Faculty staffing itself would often be arranged on a temporary basis, professors serving on short-term contracts and coming and going as student preferences change.

The virtual organization represents extreme flexibility and consumer choice. The core organization can look anywhere for the most appropriate capacity within other organizations. If a contractor does not meet expectations or prove economically advantageous, its contract does not have to be renewed. Theoretically, the opportunity to make contracts with any appropriate organization enables the virtual organization to offer an endless array of products and services.

Have the Experiments Worked?

This chapter has presented a dazzling array of possibilities for the future. Each of the experiments and innovations listed above has attracted much attention. Each has been the subject of extensive writing and claims many supporters. But the wise executive and intelligent critic alike must ask whether all or, in fact, any of these innovations can be counted upon to deliver the promised results. High-quality research studies have been conducted on some of the innovations. Little or no systematic evaluation has been done on others, although valuable reports by well-informed observers sometimes exist.

Complete assessment of all examples presented above is beyond the scope of this textbook. Reservations, though, may be cited for each approach to improving the quality of life in organizations, streamlining their structure, or increasing their productivity. These issues are cited in Table 13.2.

The examples that follow highlight research results and comments by objective observers.

Human Needs

Incentive Innovations

As Table 13.2 indicates, incentive innovations such as the Scanlon and Lincoln Electric plans attempt to remedy the shortcomings of traditional piecework. But a problem common to all pay-for-performance schemes is measurement of productivity. This may have been easy in an economy dominated by industrial production. At that time, managers could simply count the units an individual or department

Table 13.2   A Report Card on Organizational Innovations

Form of Innovation	Desired Outcomes	Potential Problems
Incentive Innovation		
	Individual motivation without divisive effects of piecework	Measurement of productivity Worker dissatisfaction
Participative Management I: MBO		
	Increased Motivation	Setting of unrealistic goals
Participative Management II: Peer-Based		
SMTs	Better-informed managers	Intimidation of subordinates
Quality Circles	Increased individual responsibility	Anxiety and conflict among peers
ESOPs	Improved morale	Reluctance by employees to accept expanded roles
Codetermination	Improved operational procedures	Lack of training and support
Employee buyouts	Avoidance of major labor-management conflict	Decrease in management independence
		Weakening of collective bargaining
Worker Accommodations		
Flextime	Reduced absenteeism and turnover	Complexity of management
Telecommuting	Greater employee satisfaction	Difficulty of implementation
Innovative time segmentation	Reduction in fatigue	Practicality
EAPs	Reduction of impact of personal problems on productivity	Loss of privacy
Family-Friendly Arrangements		
Child care	Reduced absenteeism and turnover	Equity issues
Release time	Improved employee commitment	Uncertainty of cost-effectiveness
Alternative career tracks	Reduction of emotional conflict (work versus family role)	Loss of career momentum ("Mommy track")

(Continued)

(continued)

Management Movements		
Reengineering	Improved productivity	Displacement of workers
Total Quality Management (TQM)	Higher quality	Anxiety among personnel
Reinventing Government	Reduced cost	Difficulty of implementation
	Improved responsiveness to customers	Uncertainty of results
		Incompatibility with political culture
Organization for Equality		
	Reduced alienation	Reduction of decision-making capacity
	Increased participation	Maturation
		Conflict
		Domination by informal elites
Organizations Without Walls/Virtual Organizations		
	Advancement of political ideals	Loss of integration
	Increased capacity	Loss of community
	Flexibility	

had produced. Today, the value produced by a worker is more likely to be units of service or contributions to group projects. Accomplishments of an organization itself are no less easily measured. Even in a profit-seeking firm, productivity may be measured alternatively by sales volume, retained earnings, or stock appreciation. Disagreements over criteria for awarding bonuses may produce antagonism among individuals or between workers and management.

Research on outcomes of innovative incentive plans have not proven encouraging. Research on companies that have implemented the Scanlon and Lincoln Electric plans indicates that increased profitability followed. But researchers demonstrated neither that profitability increased due to the plans nor that the plans could work in all firms.[17]

Participative Management

Participative management stands out among organizational innovations and experiments because of the numerous forms it has taken and the attention it has received. Management scientists have taken particular interest in self-managing teams (SMTs), as has the business press.

A study conducted within a large firm compared employees in groups that exercised significant self-management to employees under traditional supervision. Workers in the self-managing groups reported greater work satisfaction.

Knowledgeable managers reported higher levels of performance effectiveness among those in the self-managing teams. No differences were detected in absenteeism.[18]

Difficulties associated with much research in the social sciences make it difficult to draw firm conclusions from this study. The SMTs under consideration existed prior to the study. It may be argued that high-quality workers were drawn to such groups or selected for them over the years. Measures of satisfaction and productivity were subjective. Where results were measured objectively, such as absenteeism, SMTs and traditionally managed units evidenced no difference.

Less formal observation also raises questions about the SMT approach. In 1997, the *Wall Street Journal* covered self-management at the Eaton Corporation, a metals manufacturing concern. Not all workers felt comfortable in the teams. Some complained about feeling constantly watched by teammates to make sure they performed adequately. "They say there are no bosses here," the story quoted a worker, "but if you screw up you find one pretty fast. It can feel like having 100 bosses.[19]

Similar problems surfaced at Levi Strauss, a clothing manufacturer that instituted SMTs. According to the *Wall Street Journal,* the firm instituted SMTs of 10 to 35 workers in the late 1990s. Traditionally, workers did specialized tasks (such as stitching pockets or belt loops on pants) and were paid by the piece. Under the SMT plan, workers were paid according to the number of garments completed by the team.

Significant discomfort and dissatisfaction resulted for many. Anxious over the fact that reduced production would result in lower pay, team members pushed fellow workers who were slower, inexperienced, or injured to speed up. Shouting and threats became a daily occurrence. Frustrated by loss of pay due to slower colleagues, the fastest workers simply reduced the effort they expended on the job.[20] Labor costs actually rose at both Eaton and Levi Strauss.

Problems have surfaced in other forms of participative management as well.

Management by objectives. MBO has promised to bring out the best in managers, causing them to raise their estimation of what they might actually accomplish. But MBO critics point out that superiors typically dominate the process of negotiation. MBO exchanges risk, forcing subordinates into promising more than they can reasonably hope to deliver. This process produces anxiety in the subordinate, forces him or her to expend superhuman effort, and may not ultimately improve organizational performance.

Codetermination. Codetermination in the United States has been unusual, taking place largely through employee buyouts. In Europe codetermination has numerous critics. Tradition-minded executives contend that codetermination keeps them from performing their duties to stockholders. Leftist critics argue that worker representatives eventually come to share management perspectives, become co-opted, and "sell out" employee interests.

Quality circles. Decline of the once popular quality circles has already been mentioned. Research indicates that quality circles, where instituted, tended to become less effective over time. After initially identifying obvious problems, quality circles were often unable to remain productive. They often proved costly to maintain since they required facilitation and other forms of support. As costs increased and productivity became less apparent, pressure mounted for their abolition.[21]

Worker Accommodations

Person-friendly organizational modifications are appealing due to the concern they reflect for the individual. They represent clear departures from tradition. But examination of their feasibility and efficacy has surfaced numerous problems.

Flextime. Research indicates limited benefits for flextime. A large utility company instituted an experimental flextime program of one year. The organization hoped that the program would reduce absenteeism and turnover. Research personnel observed absenteeism and turnover rates during the year the flextime plan was in effect, as well as several years before and after. Absenteeism dropped in the year when the plan was in effect and rose to its former level when the plan was terminated. No effect was detected on turnover,[22] perhaps a better reflection of overall worker satisfaction.

Flextime appears to have a limited impact on an organization's members. But reports of managers suggest that it can be difficult to implement. Many operations require a critical mass of workers to be present at all times. Definite rules governing flextime seem essential. Otherwise, conflict may result as managers are perceived as unfairly allowing some employees to leave work and not others.

Telecommuting. Perhaps the best argument in favor of telecommuting is that communication in the 21st century is cheaper and more convenient than transportation. Getting on the Internet is easier than getting into a car or onto a bus. But research indicates that telecommuting is less attractive to workers than many believe. In the 1990s, for example, Pacific Bell offered a work-at-home program to 190,000 employees. Only 90 accepted.[23]

There are many drawbacks to telecommuting. Workers lose the pleasure of socializing with colleagues. Identity as a professional or breadwinner may weaken. Success in many organizations requires daily, face-to-face networking. As Arlie Hochschild (see Chapter 6) reports, many people today positively value the office environment because it frees them from the stresses and distractions of family life.

Telecommuting creates problems for managers as well. Personally, managers take pride and comfort in the physical presence of their subordinates. Physical absence of workers creates problems in coordination. Organizational culture is put at risk when many individuals are regularly absent.

Innovative time segmentation. Innovative time segmentation such as the plan researched by Leslie Perlow (see above) holds much promise. The plan she observed in an engineering firm seemed successful in the short run. Engineers estimated that their own productivity rose, and their supervisors expressed the same impression. Personnel reported working fewer evenings and weekends.

But the long-term practicability of such systems is uncertain. The system in the engineering firm failed to become permanent, withering away after the experiment ended. It appeared impractical in terms of the organization's needs and objectives. The technical nature of the work seemed to require periods of intense social inter-action as well as quiet time for technical tasks. Crises created a need for numerous interruptions of quiet time, necessitating evening and weekend work. An organiza-tional culture compatible with these conditions prevailed, awarding the status of hero to workaholics.

Employee assistance programs. EAPs are a solid item in the human resources tool kit of most large corporations and government agencies. Critics, though, have raised the possibility that EAP services pry into the employee's privacy. They ask, for example, whether a psychological counselor in the pay of the boss might not be pressured to inform on the client. Firms offering services in sensitive areas have often turned to outsourcing to reduce the likelihood that privacy will be breached.

Family-Friendly Arrangements

Family-friendly arrangements share many features with person-friendly modifi-cations. They clearly respond to changing features of personal and family life in the United States. All the examples in Table 13.2 raise issues for management, though.

Child care, release time, and similar arrangements. The key issues facing management regarding benefits such as child care and release time (as well as elder care and to some extent flextime) involve (a) equity and (b) cost-effectiveness. Equity issues arise when one group within an organization feels another group has received benefits not shared by all. A backlash regarding family-friendly arrangements appeared to be taking place as the 21st century got under way. Single people began expressing the feeling that child care and release time for people with families constituted an unfair privilege. They argued that family life represented a choice made freely by their colleagues. If an indi-vidual remained single, should not he or she be equally entitled to release time for recreational activity or courtship as was a parent for attending a parent-teacher meet-ing or school pageant? Should an individual who chose to remain single (or was unable to form a family) work extra hours so that parents might have time off?

Equity issues regarding benefits such as release time and child care have made their appearance on the political stage. Gay and lesbian workers have argued, often successfully, that family leave should be extended to them and their partners.

Workers in every walk of life benefit from family-friendly organizational modifications. But such arrangements are not cost-effective for all organizations. A survey of family-friendly programs indicates that only a minority of business establishments in the United States offer the family-friendly arrangements illus-trated in Table 13.1. As might be expected, large firms and firms that employ a high proportion of women are most likely to offer family-friendly arrangements. Firms that offer family-friendly arrangements also place high value on committed work-ers and rely on independent decisions of their workers. Family-friendly arrange-ments, then, would appear cost-effective only for organizations that benefit from long-term employment and personal identification by workers with the quality of their performance.[24]

Alternative career tracks. Alternative career tracks create challenges for both organizations and personnel. Organizations depend on full-time personnel for their most important functions. Clients may not feel comfortable working with two individuals who share the same job. Discomfort may be particularly acute when the job involves personal confidence such as financial counseling.

Few organizations, moreover, look to part-timers as candidates for executive rank. A woman who elects to spend more time with her young children transfers to what is sometimes called the "mommy track"(see Chapter 3). Many face difficult challenges regaining full executive status when their children have grown. Men who decline rush assignments and late evenings at the office fall prey to a similar phenomenon. Devotion to duty is often viewed as a requirement for the fast track. Severe trade-offs between work and family have faced workers for generations. Writing of Wall Street lawyers in the 1970s, sociologist E. O. Smigel observed that "many a partnership was lost on the Long Island Railroad."[25]

Management Movements

Reengineering, TQM, and reinventing government have several problems in common. Management movements create anxiety when they hit the workplace, as long-term employees fear disruption of comfortable routines and potential reductions in force. The sometimes complex packages of interventions represented by management movements are often difficult to implement. Most important, results such as increased productivity or profitability have almost never been conclusively demonstrated. The reengineering and reinventing government movements have been associated with termination of workers, negatively affecting the lives of many human beings. Key tenets of these movements contradict the political culture in which organizations must continue to live.

Reengineering

As indicated earlier in this chapter, reengineering has a poor public image due to its association with mass firings. Shortened hierarchies and cross-trained workers mean fewer total personnel. Changes in the market and technology may necessitate reductions in force. Still, downsizing and rightsizing shock the part of American political culture that assumes that workers should be protected. The bad press garnered by corporate downsizing artist Chainsaw Al (see Chapter 2) illustrates this principle.

It is far from certain whether reengineering has produced its desired results. Almost no outcome studies of management movements have been carried out that conform to the standards of normal science. As in assessments of management interventions, those involving reengineering usually are single case studies of firms that underwent reengineering and later prospered. Such studies often assume, without justification, that prosperity resulted from reengineering rather than from changing market conditions or mere good luck.

A survey of some 500 hospitals casts doubt on the efficacy of reengineering.[26] This study assessed whether reengineering was associated with each hospital's becoming more cost-competitive in its local market. Disappointingly, the authors concluded that reengineering exerted a negative influence, increasing hospital costs relative to those of competitors. They explain that new procedures and massive changes in an organization tend to reduce the reliability of performance.

Nationwide, reengineering seems to have missed one of its key objectives: thinning the ranks of middle managers. According to a survey of Fortune 500 companies by the *Wall Street Journal,* the number of managers per 100 employees increased by about 8% between 1990 and 1995.[27] The *Journal* characterized reengineering during this period as a "craze," accompanied by widespread layoffs of management personnel.

TQM

The most widely applied of contemporary management movements, TQM, has also attracted the most critical scrutiny. Implementation appears to have been a major difficulty. Long-term application is a major tenet of TQM advocates. Comparing TQM requirements with Japanese management practice, these advocates have asserted that the intervention might take decades to achieve full effects. Implementation of TQM requires major corporate resources. These include formation and support of cross-functional groups, development and maintenance of data systems on internal productivity and customer satisfaction, and allocation of scarce time by executives.

Implementation of TQM has seldom, in fact, taken place in "textbook" fashion. Management researchers Hackman and Wageman[28] reviewed the extensive writings on TQM and several major surveys of organizations that had adopted related interventions. This research determined that most organizations do not adopt the full TQM program. Most often adopted are efforts to build relationships with suppliers and operation of cross-functional, quality circle-like groups. Least often adopted are data systems and statistical procedures for identifying and solving production problems. Such systems, supporting continuous "management by fact," are the central components of TQM.

Hackman, Wageman, and several others have observed that corporate TQM programs actually include components contradictory to textbook TQM. While TQM in practice omits central components such as production data systems, it often includes pay-for-performance schemes. American executives tend to pick and choose parts of available systems for improving their organizations rather than buying whole packages.

The resulting mix of interventions makes it nearly impossible to determine whether TQM is effective. Management consultants Ronald Ashkenas and Robert Schaffer comment:

> Companies simultaneously launch dozens of quality activities, superimposed on each other and on the other activities of the company. The result is no observable link between cause and effect. It is like researching a cure for a disease by giving a group of patients 10 different new drugs at the same time.[29]

Based on extensive review of TQM studies, Hackman and Wageman reach a similar conclusion:

The research literature on TQM effects includes few studies whose designs permit definitive statements to be made about causes and effects. More than 80% of the published assessments of TQM describe what happened when the program was installed in one particular organization. The outcomes most frequently reported are improvements in error rates, . . . decreased time needed to complete a process, . . . [and] dollar savings from process efficiencies. . . . Such findings are consistent with the aims of TQM interventions, but the absence of appropriate research designs makes it impossible to attribute them directly to TQM.

The business press has been hard on TQM. Reporting on an Ernst and Young study, the *Wall Street Journal* characterized application of the "total quality" movement as "amorphous" and "stumbling," and its results as "shoddy." Small minorities of workers in firms subscribing to TQM seem to be involved directly in the programs. Most executives are rewarded for total profitability rather than quality improvement. Quality-boosting activities often play an occasional, marginal role in organizational operations. A critic blamed the shortcomings of quality programs on the "proliferation of consultants, each of whom preaches his own pet strategy."[30]

Reinventing Government

Many of the issues that arise in reengineering and TQM have surfaced as well in reinventing government. Assessment of the movement's effect has been indefinite. Critics of Osborn and Gaebler have pointed out that they merely cite selected cases of apparent success. No long-term follow-up studies of examples such as Visalia, California, are available.

Even more than reengineering the corporation, reinventing government confronts opposition from the political culture. Citizens believe that government should operate differently from profit-seeking firms. This belief, given substance by the Constitution, ties the hands of government officials intent on reinvention. Public expectations regarding government are different from those regarding business. People expect government to operate under strict rules. As Lynn writes (see Chapter 12), expectations of fairness and universalism promote bureaucracy. Bureaucracy in government is highly compatible with democratic principles.

Public expectations also mandate that government operate in a more benign fashion than business. Citizens may cheer government's attempts to become "lean," but would likely be put off by a government that was clearly "mean." At least some features of reinventing government may appear to many as mean. One such feature is outsourcing. Municipalities that contract work to private individuals or firms reap huge dollar savings. Personnel costs under contract to private firms or individuals are a fraction of those paid to workers on payroll. Workers on contract, though, typically earn less than those on city payrolls, have much less job security, and receive few, if any, benefits.

A downturn in the fortunes of workers needn't trouble a private business. But government is less easily separated from public requirements and sentiments.

Government has traditionally been viewed as a source of social mobility for the disadvantaged. Government incurs financial liability when former public employees land on unemployment or welfare rolls. Appeals by unions to values such as opportunity and fairness are more likely to find sympathy among voters than among corporate stockholders or directors.

Much evidence suggests that management movement interventions are costly and of uncertain effectiveness. Nevertheless, they have been extremely popular among executives. Management scientists and business journalists have characterized many as mere fads.

The popularity of management movements, though, may be best explained in terms of affective benefits and latent functions. In the opinion of management scientist Eric Abraham,[31] several social and psychological forces explain the rapid rise and often temporary popularity of management movements. High-level executives desire to appear innovative and forceful. They place their personal stamp on the package of interventions they adopt. Managers fall in line, though workers, made cynical by repeated cycles of abandoned programs, may laugh behind their backs.

John F. "Neutron Jack" Welch, the famously successful CEO of General Electric (GE) from 1981 to 2001, made the "big idea" a cornerstone of his management style. A major vehicle for Welch's big ideas (if not a big idea itself) was GE's Six Sigma program. Like TQM, Six Sigma aims to reduce manufacturing defects. Welch placed his personal stamp on GE's Six Sigma program, specifically rejecting proposals from other executives to adopt TQM.[32]

The early years of the Clinton administration (1993–2001) gave high visibility to reinventing government. In 1993, the administration issued a report with 800 suggestions about how to make government run better for less. The report called for making it easier to fire faulty government employees and changing procurement procedures from rules to "guiding principles." Old government hands doubted that much would come of the plan. At a time when confidence in government was low, however, the new administration needed to demonstrate concern. The reinventing government bandwagon provided a vehicle.[33]

Organization for Equality

Organizations whose reason for being is at least partially equality among members have regularly faced at least four challenges. Two challenges stem from weakening of roles and relationships among roles that normally promote coordination and regularity. Second, commitments to ideals and social equality itself diminish over time.

Kibbutzim. The kibbutz has been the subject of extensive research ever since its beginnings. Early in their history, many kibbutzim were marked by squabbling among members as expectations regarding work assignments and expectations regarding levels of individual effort were worked out. The kibbutz stabilized as the Israeli state was established. Still, a shrinking proportion of Israelis lived in kibbutzim as the population grew.

There is evidence that kibbutzim today have declined as communal societies. Children are less likely to live in buildings other than their parents' homes. Fewer meals are taken in the dining hall. In a development unthinkable earlier in their history, many kibbutzim permit members to have television sets in their own dwellings. Kibbutzim seem to have undergone organizational maturation, recognizable as a cooling of revolutionary fervor.

Many kibbutzim eventually hired outside labor. Key temptations to doing so included the value hired labor could generate for kibbutzim. Kibbutzim with substantial investments in factories were more likely to hire outside workers than those that were largely agricultural.[34]

Skeptics have long contended that kibbutzim were hierarchically organized even if they lacked an organization chart. Individuals who were able and willing to lead were repeatedly elected to executive positions, they say. According to this thinking, a small number of prominent or strong-willed individuals in kibbutzim determine policy through informal influence. Although they have no formal authority, runs the argument, they rule nevertheless.

Collectives. The argument that nominally egalitarian organizations actually operate according to an invisible yet real structure may be applied to collectives as well. A striking illustration is that of *Ms. Magazine,* which, between 1972 and 1989, operated as a collective. Structure and distinction among roles was not clearly visible. But according to some members, structure and differential levels of power existed nevertheless. One worker commented that "structurelessness" was a "smokescreen for the strong or lucky to [establish] unquestioned hegemony [undisputed domination] over others." People with the strongest personalities and leadership skills seem to have exercised great influence, a phenomenon also reported in kibbutzim.

The value placed on egalitarianism appeared to hamper decision making and general efficiency. Under the belief in inclusiveness, many different individuals commented on and revised written work for publication. Roles were unclear, making it difficult to determine who was responsible for getting a job done.

Egalitarianism and lack of recognized structure also caused conflict. People serving editorial functions had trouble holding writers to deadlines. Members, particularly those who could command higher salaries elsewhere, protested about their pay.

CBOs. Observations of CBOs in the late 20th century evidenced challenges to the effectiveness and stability of these organizations. As do collectives, CBOs strive for inclusiveness, which retards decision making. As an example in Chapter 8 illustrates, strong ideas and lack of clear lines of authority can cause conflict.

Organizations Without Walls

Organizations without walls (virtual organizations) existed largely as concepts in the early years of the 21st century. The health care industry's experiments in this area, though, indicate the kind of challenges future virtual organizations may face. Large numbers of the virtual managed care firms formed in the 1990s failed. Failure could often be traced to an inability to coordinate functional partners such as hospitals and medical groups and focus their effort on the objective of making profits. Coordination and focus on objectives are the basic functions of organizations as they have been traditionally known. Major bankruptcies of virtual organizations in health care left physician groups with mountains of uncollected bills and a bad taste in their mouths regarding future involvement.

Implications for the Future

The innovations and experiments described above all had a futuristic appeal when they first appeared. Many still do. It is indisputable that many—perhaps most—of these reforms have had desirable effects in some organizations. Innovations spawned by the human relations movement, from child care to EAPs, have undoubtedly helped many workers. Quality circles and TQM programs have served as sources of encouragement and involvement among workers. SMTs and peer review have raised productivity in some firms. Organizations such as kibbutzim have inspired whole generations and helped achieve major political objectives.

But one or more challenges have surfaced in connection with each innovation. Some are difficult or expensive to implement. Many prove unsustainable. Clear evidence of efficacy is absent from many, and several have produced unanticipated, negative consequences. The approaches described here are only examples of innovations with which people in organizations have experimented. Many more will doubtlessly appear in the years during which this book is used. Practitioners and observers must apply objective analysis to future approaches, despite the enthusiastic rhetoric with which they may be touted by their advocates.

Review of problems and issues with organizational innovations and experiments yields an important message: the formal organization that prevailed around the year 2000 is likely to endure indefinitely. The innovations described above may be useful for particular tasks. They may help motivate workers in particular industrial niches. They may be temporarily useful. But most key functions in modern society will continue to be carried out by people performing defined roles linked together by formal structure. Bureaucracy will remain a keystone of everyday life.

Issues and Applications

Management consultants and commentators today tout a variety of remedies to organizational problems such as low quality of working life and poor productivity. Yet, many such ideas have proven difficult to implement and disappointing with regard to outcomes. Managers have reason to hesitate before adopting any of the recently popular formulas.

- An executive with an engineering background finds TQM attractive. However, she does not adopt the program. She understands TQM may produce significant results only after years of steady application. She is unsure that her successor would continue her commitment to TQM should she be promoted to a higher rank or leave the firm. Moreover, she has observed that the firm's directors pay much closer attention to quarterly performance than to long-term prospects.

• The president of a large nonprofit firm decides to institute a number of human relations-type innovations, including an enhanced EAP program, extended family leave, and expanded flextime. He sees these interventions as consistent with the humanistic culture of the organization. Despite the comments of critics, he believes that the innovations will improve both the internal and external image of the organization. Image improvement, he believes, is valuable in itself, since it is likely to promote increased employee loyalty and donor support.

• The owner of a small chain of restaurants decides against initiating participative management in his outlets. He has always found comments from his employees to be valuable. But he fears that most of his workers would shy away from formal participative mechanisms such as quality circles. He believes that the employees, strongly identified with family and community, might find the extra time required for meetings and discussion unacceptable. In addition, he believes that many of the immigrants in his workforce would prefer to keep a "low profile."

Chapter Review and Major Themes

Visionaries have long sought alternatives to the conventional formal organization. These searches respond in part to the human costs often exacted by formal organizations. In addition, it is widely believed that organizations could better serve the needs of society if they were given a form different from what most organizations have today.

A number of innovations have addressed individual discomfort in work organizations. In a manner consistent with the human relations school, innovators have developed mechanisms for helping people reconcile their work roles with family and community responsibilities. Established methods such as flextime and family leave provide illustrations.

Others have focused on promoting feelings of participation in decision making and empowerment. Quality circles and self-management are illustrative. Methods such as ESOPs and group reward systems are intended to build employee commitment. These innovations recognize the potential benefit of framing the organization as a community of autonomous individuals rather than a centrally controlled machine.

Management objectives have spearheaded some forms of innovation. Examples include TQM and reengineering. Innovations of this type have aimed at greater productivity through reconfiguring structure and roles. Often constituting top-down measures, these innovations reconfigure rather than replace traditional structures and roles.

Innovations with broader social missions have proven exciting. Organizations in this tradition have included those that have dismantled hierarchy. Participants in such innovations have hoped that their organizations would serve as models for broader social reform. Codetermination as practiced in Europe may also be viewed as part of a broader social mission.

Environment has played an important part in spurring many of these innovations, as emphasized in Figure 13.1. Greater competition on the world stage has acted as an impetus for TQM and reengineering. Social movements throughout the

20th century inspired innovations such as the kibbutz, the collective, and codetermination. Apparently successful and well-publicized examples inspired interest and imitation in the broader universe of organizations.

Still, objective assessment of innovations such as those outlined in this chapter has been infrequent. Many of these innovations may well be constructive only in specific contexts. Methods tried in the past may be improved in the future. But, as depicted in Figure 13.1, direct contributions to the organization's function have usually been uncertain.

The practices introduced and organizations created by innovators, moreover, have not been conflict-free. Family-friendly initiatives may reduce the role conflict experienced by individuals with family responsibilities. But single individuals may resent the privileges these initiatives involve. Reduction of hierarchy may reduce the constraint individuals experience due to organizational structure. However, weak structures and poorly defined roles may deprive the organization of important mechanisms for conflict resolution. As appealing as they may sound, group-based reward systems have been observed to breed both interpersonal and intergroup conflict.

The innovations and experiments described in this chapter tacitly acknowledge that organizations do not control their members. The needs addressed by many of these interventions arise from outside the organization. Inspired by the human relations school, innovations and experiments have attempted to make organizations more compatible with features of their members that the organization cannot readily change. Strong proof has not been found that these measures improve productivity or profitability. But given the needs that have inspired such innovations and experiments, further work in this area should be encouraged.

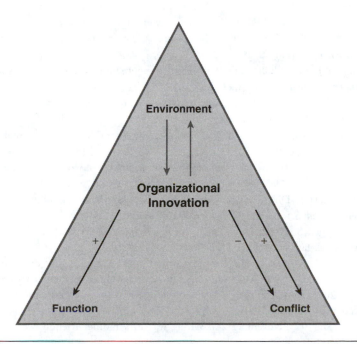

Figure 13.1   Analytical Perspectives Applied to Organizational Innovation

---

Discussion Questions

1. Would the "virtual university" as described in the preceding chapter be superior to the colleges and universities most familiar today?

2. Imagine yourself as a consultant asked by the CEO of a major charitable organization to recommend a program to increase fundraising productivity and reduce staff turnover. What intervention(s) would you recommend, and why? Would you discourage the CEO from adopting any particular intervention or interventions?

3. Would it be possible to apply the principle of pay for performance in a bureaucratically organized public agency? If so, how might it be done? Why might it be expected to yield favorable results? Consider (a) workers in public agencies and (b) members of volunteer service organizations.

4. Would codetermination as it is practiced in Europe be a good idea for firms and unions in the United States? What issues might be raised about its practicability and impact?

5. What issues might proponents of critical theory raise about the innovations and experiments described above? What innovations, if any, would this theory best support?

References

1. McGregor, D. (1960). *The human side of enterprise.* New York: McGraw-Hill.
2. Herzberg, F. (1966). *Work and the nature of man.* New York: Crowell.
3. White, J. K. (1979). The Scanlon Plan: Causes and correlates with success. *Academy of Management Journal, 22,* 292–312.
4. Hackman, J. R., & Oldham, G. R. (1975). Development of the Job Diagnostic Survey. *Journal of Applied Psychology, 60,* 159–170.
5. Hunnis, G., Garsin, G. D., & Chase, J. (1973). *Workers' control: A reader on labor and social change.* New York: Vintage.
6. Kozinn, A. (1999, October 27). Orpheus Ensemble reconsiders the way it makes music. *New York Times,* p. B1.
7. Perlow, L. A. (1998). The time famine: Toward a sociology of work time. *Administrative Science Quarterly, 44,* 57–81.
8. Greenwald, H. P., Dirks, S. J., Borgatta, E. F., et al. (1989). Work disability among cancer patients. *Social Science and Medicine, 29,* 1253–1259.
9. Shellenbarger, S. (1992, January 17). Managers navigate uncharted waters trying to resolve work-family conflicts. *Wall Street Journal,* p. B1.
10. Smith, T. W., Kallberg, A. L., & Marsden, P. V. (2002). *National organizations survey* (computer file). ICPSR04074-v1. Chicago: National Opinion Research Center (producer), 2003. Ann Arbor, MI: Inter-university Consortium for Political and Social Research (distributor), 2004.
11. Koman, K. (1993, November 24). Wrong way to a mother-friendly workplace. *Wall Street Journal.*

12. Hammer, M., & Champy, J. (1993). *Reengineering the corporation*. New York: Harper.

13. Deming, W. E. (1986). *Out of the crisis*. Cambridge: MIT Press.

14. Osborn, D., & Gaebler, T. (1992). *Reinventing government: How the entrepreneurial spirit is transforming the public sector* (pp. 19–20). Addison-Wesley.

15. Farrell, A. E. (1994). A social experiment in publishing: *Ms. Magazine*, 1972–1989. *Human Relations, 47*, 707–730.

16. Robinson, J. C., & Casalino, L. P. (1996). Vertical integration and organizational networks in health care. *Health Affairs, 15*, 7–22.

17. Lawler, E. E. (1973). *Motivation in work organizations*. Monterey, CA: Brooks/Cole.

18. Cohen, S. G., & Ledford, G. E. (1994). The effectiveness of self-managing teams. *Human Relations, 47*, 13–43.

19. Appel, T. (1997, September 8). Not all workers find the idea of empowerment as neat as it sounds. *Wall Street Journal*, p. A1.

20. King, R. T. (1998, May 20). Levi's factory workers are assigned to teams and morale takes a hit. *Wall Street Journal*, p. A1.

21. Lawler, E. E., & Mohrman, S. A. (1986). Quality circles after the fad. *Harvard Business Review*, January–February, 65–71.

22. Dalton, D. R., & Mesch, D. J. (1990). The impact of flexible scheduling on employee attendance. *Administrative Science Quarterly, 35*, 370–387.

23. Boas, S. (1995). Home: The perfect workplace? In S. Zadeck (Ed.), *Work, families, and organizations*. San Francisco: Jossey-Bass.

24. Osterman, P. (1995). Work/family programs and the employment relationship. *Administrative Science Quarterly, 40*, 681–700.

25. Smigel, E. O. (1973). *The Wall Street lawyer: professional organization man?* Bloomington: Indiana University Press.

26. Walston, S. L., Burns, L. R., & Kimberly, J. R. (2000). Does reengineering really work? An examination of the context and outcomes of hospital reengineering initiatives. *Health Services Research, 34*, 1363–1388.

27. Markels, A. (1995, September 25). Restructuring alters middle-manager role but leaves it robust. *Wall Street Journal*, p. A1.

28. Hackman, J. R., & Wageman, R. (1995). Total Quality Management: Empirical, conceptual, and practical issues. *Administrative Science Quarterly, 40*, 309–342.

29. Ashkenas, R., & Schaffer, R. (1992, May 3). The lemmings who love total quality. *New York Times*, sec. 3, p. 13.

30. Fuchsberg, G. (1992, May 14). Quality programs show shoddy results. *Wall Street Journal*, p. B1.

31. Abraham, E. (1996). Management fashion. *Academy of Management Review, 21*, 254–285.

32. Gabor, A. (2000, November 29). Anticipating Welch on Welch. *New York Times*, Part C.

33. Birnbaum, J. H. (1993, October 7). Latest plan to make government work just might work. *Wall Street Journal*.

34. Simons, T., & Ingram, P. (1997). Organization and ideology: Kibbutzim and hired labor, 1951–1965. *Administrative Science Quarterly, 43*, 784–813.

PART V

Organizations, Personal Interests, and Responsibility

The preceding chapters mark a long journey from the private worlds of individuals to the regimented structures of modern bureaucracies. Chapter 14 focuses again on individuals.

Chapter 13 dealt with steps taken by organizations to enhance their capacity to achieve organizational objectives. Chapter 14 focuses on opportunities open to members for achieving personal objectives. The theme addressed throughout this book that organizations do not fully control their members is important here. The fact that individuals in perhaps all organizations enjoy some measure of freedom underscores the individual's responsibility for his or her own well-being and ethical conduct.

Ordinarily, people in organizations seek to maximize their personal benefit. Many try to maximize rewards such as income and position in the organizational hierarchy. Some focus on redefining the organization's objectives and leaving a mark on its future. Others seek humbler returns, such as increased security and reduced effort.

A grasp of the principles by which organizations function can help members meet the challenge of achieving personal objectives. By misperceiving the fundamental characteristics and dynamics of organizations, talented people often fail to attain rewards commensurate with their qualifications. Chapter 14 suggests actions that can help avoid such misfortune.

A second challenge that many face involves avoidance of ethical or legal infractions. Most people acquire moral values through early childhood socialization and educational and religious institutions. Later, many find themselves in organizations whose expectations clash with their personal codes.

An understanding of organizations can help individuals avoid malfeasance. The 20th century saw striking instances in which individuals succumbed to the evil intent of their leaders. Everyday methods of organizing enabled the Nazis and Communists to deploy millions of operatives for tasks resulting in infamous atrocities. Most participants in these crimes are believed to have been emotionally normal human beings channeled into heinous acts through common organizational devices.

Chapter 15 extends the book's perspective to the broader social environment in which organizations operate. Earlier chapters have addressed the organizational environment, but in a limited sense. The earlier chapters have dealt with aspects of the social environment as constraints and resources for organizational operations. Chapter 15 concentrates on the impact organizations have had on the surrounding society and the world as a whole. Social commentators have made much of the possibility that large corporations threaten democracy and community. This potential is particularly alarming in the context of globalization. Chapter 15 examines the multinational corporation as an entity capable of vesting control over vast numbers of human beings in the hands of only a few international managers.

Chapters 14 and 15 represent crucial applications of this book's major theme: that organizations never fully control the thinking and behavior of their members. Through a number of mechanisms described in the preceding chapters, organizations do achieve sufficient levels of coordination and cohesion to pursue their objectives. But organizations face the ever-present possibility of compromises in the willingness of members to carry out roles, coexist with structure, adopt organizational culture, and accept the authority of managers. On the world stage, management control is challenged by a particularly large and complex environment as well as by independence-minded personnel in far-flung subunits.

CHAPTER 14

Organizations and Individual Decisions

Learning Objective

To review the factors that prevent organizations from fully controlling their members; to underscore the importance of individual responsibility; to identify features that promote personal success in organizations; to become aware of options for reducing risk of ethical and legal transgression.

Principles

Roles, structure, rewards, imperative forces, and organizational culture channel day-to-day thinking and behavior in organizations. These organizational resources promote cohesion and coordination, but do so imperfectly. The imperfections of these mechanisms leave individuals free to make choices regarding their career prospects and personal ethics.

Knowledge of formal organizations can help people protect themselves from exploitation, career immobility, involuntary termination, and involvement in unethical or illegal acts.

Guidelines for achieving personal success include

- Divining the organization's true objectives
- Selecting leaders advantageously
- Assessing internal labor markets
- Supervising in a strategic manner
- Keeping time horizons short
- Avoiding heroism

Principles for avoiding unethical and illegal behavior include

- Assessing options according to one's own values
- Maintaining contact with people and agencies outside the organization's boundaries

Organizations Versus the Individual

This chapter turns to questions of personal strategy and choice in formal organizations. Like other human technology, organizations should enable individuals to develop their gifts and achieve their personal aims. Formal organizations often do the opposite, reducing freedom, choice, and the opportunity to pursue personal objectives. No organization, though, has the power to completely substitute its ends for those of its members. Knowing the rules by which organizations operate can help individuals preserve their autonomy and achieve their aims.

Every member of an organization is in a sense its captive. Organizations channel the individual's capacity toward objectives he or she may not share. All organizations divert the individual's attention, at least for a time, away from his or her own desires. Most organizations place restrictions, ranging from momentary to lifelong, on the individual's ability to depart their confines. Even people who voluntarily join and remain in an organization are in a sense "captured." People get caught up in the organization's routines and procedures, seemingly losing independent control of their lives. Many forsake personal goals and values as the years in a firm, army, prison, or other formal organization go by.

But individuals never lose the *capacity* for independent thought and action. As noted earlier, people cannot be programmed (see Chapter 2). This is true even in authoritarian settings. Survivors of the dictatorships and concentration camps of the 20th century made much of this potential. Certainly in normal times, people can take action on their own behalf.

The Limitations of Organizational Control

The core features of organizations enable them to achieve *cohesion and coordination*. Through these means, described in Chapters 4 through 8, organizations cause individuals to relinquish personal autonomy. The degree of submission that organizations require of their members varies widely. Modern corporate and governmental bureaucracies permit employees to live as they like when away from the office. Totalitarian political parties and monastic religious orders seek to dictate every aspect of their members' lives.

A brief reexamination of resources used by organizations to achieve coordination and cohesion, though, reveals their limitations as determinants of human behavior. These resources include roles, structure, rewards and punishment, imperative force, and organizational culture. Imperfections in the organization's ability to exercise social control allow individuals to achieve at least some autonomy. When sufficiently motivated and skilled, individuals in organizations make the most of these opportunities to attain personal or group objectives.

Although social roles (Chapter 4) may be the basic building blocks of organizations, the degree to which they dominate human thinking and behavior is limited. Social psychologists Katz and Kahn[1] defined roles in organizations as "prescriptions for behavior." Roles affect behavior, though, far less automatically than this definition suggests. People in an organization often have different expectations regarding a given role. Matters are further complicated as people negotiate their roles. People are constantly reducing, expanding, and redefining their responsibilities according to personal desire.

Similarly, organizational structure exerts considerably less than absolute control. In the formal organization, structure is manifested in explicit rules regarding inter-relation among individual roles. Yet in a manner similar to roles, structure is subject to modification according to the perceptions and desires of the organization's members. Individuals and groups, low as well as high in the organizational hierar-chy, can cause structure to change. If, for example, operatives successfully negotiate the right to communicate directly with middle managers rather than their imme-diate supervisors, they change organizational structure.

In a like manner, neither reward nor punishment (Chapter 6) can ensure that members behave in a manner consistent with management's intent. Certain highly valued rewards are often beyond the control of management. Rewards of a socio-emotional nature are more likely to be provided by the member's primary group. Thus, workers are often able to establish their own norms about the speed and qual-ity of performance. Some rewards highly valued by professionals are also beyond the control of management. These include intrinsic satisfaction from work per-ceived to meet the standards of professional peers. Among professionals such as physicians in an HMO, standards are set largely by colleagues outside the organiza-tion. Individuals outside the organization may also mete out punishment such as license suspension or revocation.

Imperative force (Chapter 7)—including power, coercion, authority, and discipline—would seem to be the heavy artillery of organizations. No imperative force, though, enables supervisory personnel to dominate others indefinitely or with complete efficacy. People who seek to control others by forces such as coercion obtain compliance of a low quality, if not outright rebellion. Organizations are obliged to use imperative force with restraint. The labor of willing workers, furthermore, is more efficient and less costly than that of workers who must be constantly watched and threatened.

In many well-functioning organizations, organizational culture (Chapter 8) pro-motes common beliefs and values among members. These, in turn, help concentrate individual thinking and actions on common objectives. Even in successful organiza-tions, however, not all members share the mainstream culture. Organizations often develop multiple cultures, whose values and beliefs may be mutually antagonistic. Managers may subscribe to one culture, workers to another. In organizations where a single culture in fact prevails, some people may be strongly attached and others alienated from it. The messages of dominant organizational culture, furthermore, may not support the objectives of management. Management can exercise only lim-ited control over the cultures that prevail in their organizations. Most organizational cultures develop spontaneously over the course of decades, if not longer.

Organizations, then, are not machines whose parts move automatically in response to management instructions. An understanding of how organizations really work can help people make the most of the personal autonomy they are thus allowed. Capitalizing on this measure of autonomy can be crucial for the individual. It cannot be assumed that even a highly successful organization will ensure the individual's success or motivate him or her to stay within the bounds of ethics and legality. People in organizations are wise to develop strategies aimed at maximizing personal success and security irrespective of the organization's fortunes. Several principles are presented below as practical guidelines for formulating such strategies.

Strategies for Survival and Success

Reading Organizations

A person's ability to survive and prosper in an organization depends on his or her understanding of how organizations work. "Reading" an organization amounts to understanding its imperfections: faulty communication systems, suboptimization, reward systems that favor the unproductive, and many more. Most members of the organization believe what they are told and expect to be rewarded for conformity. But a true understanding of how organizations work opens special opportunities for the sophisticated.

Lessons derived from the preceding chapters are summarized below as sets of simple principles. One set of principles can help individuals avoid personal risks. Another can assist members of an organization in making the most of opportunities for success.

All the principles below have a single common feature: they contradict the way in which goodwilled, intelligent people usually think about human relationships. People normally assume that interpersonal relationships have clear objectives and that they will be treated fairly by their fellow human beings. They assume that they will be appropriately rewarded for hard work. These assumptions are not valid for many organizations.

Organizations Are Not Completely Rational

All formal organizations have nonrational features, which affect relationships among members. The individual's relationship with a formal organization is often colored by its nonrational rather than its rational features. Organizations are rational in as much as they arrange human and material resources in a manner deliberately calculated to achieve objectives. But not all features and actions in organizations are rational.

Chapter 5, which explores organizational structure, illustrates this principle. Taylorism suggests that organizations can be designed as rational machines. But history and environment cause organizations to develop in unexpected ways. The personalities of an organization's early leaders leave lasting effects. These can cause organizations to function in ways that are not technologically optimal.

Organizations are more like animals than machines. Well-designed machines are composed of deliberately designed subsystems and parts. Each contributes to the machine's function. Animals are products of evolution and successive accidents. Many function with just enough efficiency to survive in the competition for resources. Organizations are capable of learning and adaptation. But they retain useless appendages (as the human body does with the appendix), reject useful resources in the environment (as do people with allergies), and occasionally behave in self-destructive ways (as do neurotic and psychotic humans).

People who understand the nonrational features of organizations do well in them. Appreciation for the hidden motivations of individuals and the unwritten rules of collectivities can form the basis of an effective personal strategy.

Avoiding Pitfalls

A few points have great value for individual self-protection in organizations. Practical application of these principles can save someone in an organization from career stagnation and involuntary termination. Others are external, threatening the quality of the individual's life outside the organization's boundaries.

Generations of bureaucrats, soldiers, teachers, union members, and political activists have learned the following lessons, often too late to make best use of them.

Organizations are smart. New members of an organization are often struck by its apparent dysfunctions. The boss seems incompetent. Pockets of inefficiency and waste are evident. Manufacturing procedures, accounting practices, and customer services appear faulty. Management seems clueless.

The people running the organization may in fact lack talent and drive. But the organization itself is smart. Trial, error, and evolution have given it sufficient adaptive capacity to survive. Over time, a process of *organizational learning* has taken place.[2] In this process, lessons from both successful and unsuccessful experiments and ventures are retained, helping shape organizational structure. These principles, along with illustrative examples and myths, are absorbed into the organization's culture. They are successively refined and transmitted from generation to generation.

What look like an organization's limitations may actually constitute strength. Consider an organization that lacks enthusiastic personnel and energetic leadership. This may reflect a history over whose course the organization has attracted members with the personalities, work habits, and talents it needs. The work of the organization may not require ambitious personnel. Employment of such individuals might raise payroll costs and the risk of interpersonal conflict. Replacement of laid-back managers with more aggressive ones might overextend an organization, alienate workers, or promote more aggressive behavior by competitors.

Many people enter an organization believing that they can improve its functioning because they are smart. They believe they have better technical and management skills than the people in charge. This belief may be true but it is usually irrelevant. Organizations, except for very new ones, have made basic adaptations to their environment and attained internal equilibrium. A newcomer's presumption that he or she has better ideas is more likely to induce the hostility of others than lead to actual change.

Organizations take care of themselves. Millions of people dedicate their lives to organizations. Sometimes this makes sense. People may identify with an organization's mission, such as advancing knowledge in a university or practicing religious devotion in a church. In such instances, the organization exemplifies the member's personal concerns.

Most work organizations are not set up to advance their members' ideals. Workers join simply to make a living. As years pass, however, some begin identifying themselves primarily as members of the organization. They wear the company logo. They work extra hours; professional and managerial personnel do so without extra compensation. Workers, even the lowest placed, lose sight of their own desires and objectives.

People in organizations without a mission (other than earning money and staying afloat) invent missions for their organizations. Examples of imagined pseudo-missions occur in every industry. A high school teacher maintains the belief that his school system aims at improving education for humankind; the organization's actual objective may simply be preparing pupils for standardized tests. A brokerage employee believes that his firm aims at ensuring fair valuation of the public's assets. A cannery worker fantasizes that his company aims to place the world's best tuna on the grocer's shelf.

Overidentification with an organization represents a kind of psychopathology. People subject to this condition can forsake personal needs and goals. They tolerate inadequate pay and unpleasant working conditions. In extreme cases, they neglect family and personal life for the sake of the agency or firm.

The organization's mechanisms of cohesiveness and coordination encourage such behavior. Promotion, pay increases, and expressions of gratitude by managers encourage individuals to produce. Rewards provided by the organization can compensate members for perceived inadequacies in personal areas such as marriage and family.

Thus passes many a human lifetime. Ironically, the organization survives. It continues to function according to a steady routine even after the dedicated individual is buried and forgotten. The overcommitted member fails to realize that the organization commands the resources it needs to keep going, irrespective of his or her contribution. People need to strike a balance between dedication to an organization and the other things life has to offer. They need to assess whether the organization actually has a sufficiently compelling mission to merit personal devotion.

The bottom line rules. Although organizations may have difficulty specifying their goals, all have recognizable objectives. In businesses, the most visible objective is monetary earnings. This objective can be measured in a clear, quantitative manner. Other quantitative criteria for objective achievement include scores on standardized tests for public school systems or units of finished goods shipped by a manufacturing operation. A borrowing from the language of bookkeeping and accounting, the term *bottom line* refers to quantitative achievement by an organization in a given unit of time.

"No Margin, No Mission": A Charitable Organization's Dilemma

It is often difficult to assess the importance of mission in an organization.

Catholic hospitals in the early 21st century constitute an example of this dilemma.

Orders of Catholic nuns have provided health care to the poor for over a thousand years. They have served in this capacity on every continent. The orders comprise formal organizations including both ordained clergy and lay employees in their ranks.

In the 19th and 20th centuries, Catholic orders established modern hospitals throughout the United States. By the mid-1900s, they owned and operated hundreds of facilities. The hospitals served both paying patients and people dependent on charity. Most hospitals in the United States, with or without religious ties, provided charity care. But charity constituted a central mission of the orders.

The politics and economics of health care changed radically in the late 20th century, reducing resources available for charity care. Hospitals faced the need to increase income and reduce costs in order to survive.

"No margin, no mission" became the watchword of several orders. The term *margin,* which means surplus of revenue over expenses, is used to signify profit in nonprofit organizations.

According to some observers, emphasis on margin began to replace mission. One order, the Sisters of Charity, accumulated so much wealth that investment professionals referred to it as the "Sisters of Currency."[3] Economy moves at one hospital greatly reduced benefits and job security for large numbers of dedicated nurses.

Replacement of mission by margin recalls the process of organizational goal displacement described in Chapter 12. Social scientists use the term *goal displacement* to describe the forsaking of an initially identified goal in favor of activities originally intended as only instrumental. The means become the ends.

The degree to which margin may be ultimately substituted for mission among the Catholic orders is uncertain. Individuals committed to the mission, though, should periodically reevaluate whether these orders continue to merit their personal devotion.

Everyone in an organization should determine his or her supervisor's bottom line and concentrate on contributing to it. In a well-functioning organization, every supervisor evaluates subordinates according to how much they contribute to his or her bottom line. Over the years, workers or managers who contribute the most to their superior's bottom line should receive the best raises. In cycles of cutbacks and layoffs, the boss's compassion or goodwill cannot be counted upon to protect a worker or subunit whose bottom line is unhealthy.

The progressive management techniques described in Chapter 13 tend to be adopted and retained in organizations with healthy bottom lines, or in those in which managers can see direct linkages between progressive management and the bottom line. Progressive and humanistic management practices are said to take place only in firms with *organizational slack*—extra money, vacant space, and personnel whose time is not fully occupied. Experiments such as participative management, family-friendly programs, and employee assistance are often terminated in downturns. It is no accident that firms that offer family-friendly arrangements tend to employ large numbers of female employees and require a low-turnover workforce. In such firms, flextime and child care assistance promote the degree of stability in the workforce that is required for doing business.

Determining the organization's actual bottom line often presents a challenge to its members. Organizations are not always honest about their true objectives. A voluntary organization may state publicly that its mission is to serve the disadvantaged. But members of top management may be most concerned with maintaining their salaries and perquisites. A think tank may recruit young scientists by stressing the importance of groundbreaking research. Yet obtaining money through grants and contracts may be the boss's chief preoccupation.

Easy targets get hit. People in organizations don't always have enemies, but everyone should assume they do. Competition for desirable positions and advancement occurs everywhere. Envy, a normal human emotion, is as strong a force in formal organizations as elsewhere. Jealous of their positions and anxious about obsolescence of their skills, senior officials often feel threatened by their juniors. Some people simply enjoy being "spoilers," disrupting the plans, ruining the projects, and frustrating the ambitions of others.

Too often, people of outstanding talent and strong ambition become targets of such hostility. They make the mistake of letting their talent and ambition show. They speak up at meetings. They obtain large contracts. They arrive early, stay late, and show up at the office on weekends. They seek and willingly accept extra assignments. Behavior of this kind makes someone an easy target. He or she is seen as "the one to beat" in the competition for resources and advancement.

Anxious peers have at their disposal many devices for harming the would-be star. They may tempt him or her with challenging assignments, hoping for failure and making much of failure when it occurs. Ironically, the supervisor may place the ambitious one not on the fast track but the end of the line for prime assignments and promotion. The supervisor may have distaste for open ambition or extraordinary talent. He or she may fear alienating other workers by treating the would-be star with special favor. Ultimately, the supervisor may fear for his or her own position.

The "easy target syndrome" described here illustrates an organizational principle introduced in Chapters 3 and 6, regarding norms of behavior and social restrictions on productivity. As the classic studies of industrial psychology have reported, workers who exceed productivity norms are viewed negatively by their peers. In the blue-collar world of decades past, these workers were known as "rate-busters," and their fellow workers hit them to remind to remind them to slow down to the prevailing pace. The same dynamics occur in the worlds of the professional employee and junior executive of the 21st century.

Critics also make easy targets. People who speak up about business strategies with which they disagree, technical decisions which they believe are flawed, or practices which they feel are morally questionable attract attention. In most organizations, critics risk negative reactions from management. They become easy targets at layoff time.

The worker who feels strongly that something is amiss faces a difficult dilemma. Inaction can prove catastrophic for the organization or the broader public. But critics place themselves at personal risk. Moral dilemmas of this nature, will be addressed later in this chapter, which constitute one of the most important challenges of living with organizations.

Subunits are selfish. All organizations of sufficient size are divided into subunits: divisions, regiments, departments, bureaus, or programs. Subunits are key elements of organizational structure. It is the executive's job to see that all subunits contribute to the objectives of the organization as a whole in an efficient and orderly manner. But for most workers and managers, the subunit's success is most important for his or her well-being.

The individual worker and manager, it should be remembered, are evaluated not by the organization's executives but by managers in their subunit. Subunit managers are most directly concerned with the well-being of the subunits. Most learn from experience that their budgets and staffing may be reduced even as the organization as a whole thrives. Conversely, favored subunits receive increased support even when the organization as a whole faces cutbacks. The budgets and staffing levels of a subunit depend as much on the manager's political and negotiation skills as on its productivity.

No manager willingly accepts cuts in the funding or staffing of his or her unit. To do so would reduce his or her standing in the organization as a whole. Even more than most people, managers have egos to defend. For them, large staffs and munificent budgets are sources of gratification.

It is not surprising, then, to find suboptimization in most formal organizations. As discussed in Chapter 5, a suboptimizing unit maximizes its own rewards but does so in a fashion detrimental to the organization as a whole. Suboptimization, though, is completely natural. Some compensation systems attempt to control suboptimization by tying bonuses to total organizational performance (see Chapter 4). But these typically are minor portions of the manager's or worker's income.

Appreciating the natural selfishness of subunits should form the basis of individual strategy. Executive memos may transmit the company-wide perspective. But individual pay and job security depend on subunit performance. The subunit is particularly important in organizations with democratic structures and cultures. If everyone in the organization can vote (as in many voluntary organizations), those within individual subunits are most effective when they vote as a bloc.

Individuals are dispensable. The first chapter of this book asserted that "organizations are mostly people." This statement describes organizations accurately. Organizations do not think or act. Only their members do.

But organizations do not depend on the presence of any particular individual—at least in normal circumstances. Organizations mold the individual's thinking and channel his or her actions. The essential properties of organizations, such as structure, culture, rewards, and punishments, promote consistent patterns of behavior among individuals in similar roles. When the organization encounters a crisis of external origin, most people respond in a manner consistent with their peers.

Organizations, then, create the behavior they require. They recruit the type of individual likely to fit in or capable of developing in the desired direction. Entrepreneurial organizations recruit entrepreneurs and encourage them to take risks. Bureaucracies recruit people with "bureaucratic personalities" and reward them for obeying the rules. Organizations unable to recruit appropriate individuals and mold their behavior as needed decline and die.

Rarely does an established organization require contributions that only a given individual in its ranks can make. In highly formal organizations such as government bureaucracies and mass production plants, most individuals can be readily replaced by outsiders of comparable talent and physical capacity.

Most people have felt on occasion that they were indispensable to their organization. Supervisors foster this impression. The feeling that he or she is making vital contributions motivates many a conscientious worker. Well-meaning people everywhere pitch in to help their primary group during busy periods, believing that the organization depends on their extra effort.

But in reality, organizations almost never depend on extra effort or creativity from a single individual to achieve their objectives. Well-functioning organizations reward people for extraordinary contributions. But a healthy organization motivates numerous individuals in the appropriate direction. Successful organizations are adept at replacing people who quit, retire, die, or are dismissed. Many a worker has wondered how the company or team could get along without him only to later observe the organization doing well in his absence.

Playing to Win

The six points stated above constitute organizational facts of life. As basic as they are, they are seldom discussed. They are not "politically correct." Often, they remain invisible except in time of crisis. Though normally hidden, these principles are genuine and enduring. They retain validity over generations, even as ideas such as those covered in Chapter 13 come and go.

Basic human autonomy, though, enables individuals to take positive action on their own behalf. People in organizations have power, whatever their position. They can develop positive strategies for achieving personal objectives. Widely shared objectives include avoiding involuntary severance, securing desirable assignments, and rising in the hierarchy. The following points can function as building blocks in strategies for success:

Determine the organization's true objectives. An organization's true objectives may differ from those that are asserted by management. Among explicitly stated objectives, moreover, those that receive the most visible emphasis may not be most important. Obvious examples include organizations that act as "fronts" for illegal operations, such as an international trading company whose real purpose is to hide the earnings of a drug cartel.

More readily observable examples are easy to cite. In an election, the leaders of a political party energize volunteers with rhetoric about good government. The organization's real purpose, though, is often to obtain elective office for its leaders and patronage jobs for campaign workers. Churches and synagogues nominally exist for the purpose of religious devotion. But providing opportunities for members to develop social and business ties is also important. Critics have charged that the true objectives of many nonprofit organizations are to provide their executives with high pay and valuable perquisites rather than to serve society.

Few members of an organization may know all the purposes the organization serves. All collectivities have latent as well as manifest functions. Organizational objectives, furthermore, are dynamic. Means can become ends through the process of goal displacement. The organization's objectives can be transformed as a consequence of more general organizational change.

Over time, the organization allocates its biggest rewards to members who advance its true, primary objectives. Members can discern the organization's objectives by observing who receives the biggest rewards—and for what actions members are punished.

City government provides an illustration. No official has ever been commended for closing down a gambling operation whose proprietor is friends with the mayor. The true objective of the police force in some towns may be to protect the mayor's cronies rather than the citizens.

Select leaders advantageously. People intent on success must exercise self-interest in their relationships with leaders. Goodwilled people everywhere are naturally inclined toward teamwork. Similarly, most people are predisposed to support the leader of their group or organizational unit, whoever he or she may be.

Pursuit of personal success, though, requires departure from habitual behavior of this kind. Not all leaders are equally capable of benefiting their followers. Assessing the leader's ability to benefit oneself is crucial.

A successful leader benefits his or her followers. Such a leader can obtain resources from upper-level management to augment the unit's operating budget and number of personnel slots. These translate into raises and promotion opportunities for subordinates.

Unsuccessful leaders drag their subordinates down. These managers see their budgets cut rather than augmented, and their personnel slots reduced. Opportunities decline rather than expand for their subordinates.

People who are successful in organizations continually reassess their supervisors. They listen to the comments of workers in other units. They note which executives receive space in the company newspaper. They become attentive to whether or not their leader goes on trips with the CEO or receives appointments to important committees.

Canny individuals make sure they are supervised by people on the fast track and avoid working for those who are going nowhere. People of ambition who find themselves in units headed by a dead-ended supervisor should request transfers. If transfer is impossible, the employee should seek work in another organization. Failure to do so risks not only career immobility but involuntary termination. When the weak supervisor is sacked, his or her subunit is likely to be diminished or dismantled.

Not every successful leader, though, brings his or her subordinates along. As they move up, some leaders retain their former assistants as managers. Others look for new seconds-in-command who can open additional networks for the leader. Old colleagues get left behind. It is important to know how the leader has treated his subordinates in the past as he or she has ascended the ladder.

Supervise strategically. It is just as important for people intent on success to deal strategically with subordinates. Subordinates may be employees (or unpaid members) of the organization. But managers should also view them as personal assets in the competition for advancement. The successful manager rewards subordinates for behavior that helps him or her advance. Every subordinate should be expected to boost the manager's reputation. Subordinates unable to follow such a program should be reprimanded or terminated.

Experience leads many to a crucial assumption regarding advancement in an organization: individuals do not automatically benefit in proportion to the organization's prosperity. Everywhere, politics strongly influences who gets what, when, and how much. A manager is as much a political boss as a supervisor of work. Successful managers play to win.

The thinking of Machiavelli (1469–1527) has great value for managers in modern formal organizations. Machiavelli is history's best-known guru of politics. Kings, dictators, and presidents have read his work for hundreds of years. Machiavelli learned the art of politics in the cutthroat world of Italian city-states, where assassination and *coups d'état* were common. He wrote that political success requires self-interested strategizing, impaired by neither emotion nor humanitarianism. Today, people use the term *Machiavellian* to denote putting one's interests ahead of those of others and using cold calculation to achieve success.

Among his many prescriptions,[4] Machiavelli wrote that leaders must take bold action to solidify their rule immediately upon taking power. According to Machiavelli, unpopular steps taken at the beginning of a reign are soon forgotten. Afterward, a manager can distribute small favors to his or her underlings over time, building popularity and feelings of obligation.

Consistent with this thinking, CEOs in modern corporations often fire the department heads they inherit from their predecessors. Then, they appoint individuals of their own choosing to these positions. Owing their jobs to the new CEO, the freshly appointed department heads are likely to have strong feelings of loyalty to him or her. New personnel hired from outside are unlikely to have ties within the organization independent of their boss. For this reason, they are unlikely to form independent and potentially hostile alliances.

Machiavellianism can also benefit a leader when applied to his or her own subordinates. A team leader can motivate subordinates to extraordinary performance by implying that they will move up along with him or her. Upon promotion, though, the leader may find it more advantageous to hire his or her lieutenants from outside.

Elected public officials often function in this manner. Campaign workers are often motivated by the expectation that they will receive government jobs if their candidate wins. But to the newly elected official, cultivating new communities and interest groups can be more advantageous than rewarding campaign workers. The official needs a steadily expanding group of supporters to continue moving up.

Assess the internal labor market. Those who succeed in organizations do so by identifying opportunities and pursuing them. Organizations differ in the amount of opportunity they offer—and to whom they offer opportunity. People increase their level of responsibility and compensation by identifying positions for which they might eventually qualify and acquiring the skill and experience these positions require.

A person's success in an organization does not depend only on the individual's personal capabilities. It depends as much, if not more, on the characteristics of the organization itself. In some organizations, people have numerous opportunities to move into new, more desirable jobs. In others, most jobs are dead ends. Most organizations are selective in the opportunities they offer. They allow advancement for people in some positions but not in others. The job ladders available in an organization affect an individual's future as much as his or her personal gifts or technical training.

An organization's internal labor market reflects its basic structure (see Chapter 5). Some organizations have long career ladders. These allow relatively unskilled people to start on the bottom rung and gradually ascend, sometimes as high as top management. Public agencies that operate under rules not readily learnable on the outside usually have long career ladders. Other organizations have career ladders that are short or nonexistent. Examples of organizations with short career ladders include those with "flat" hierarchies or those whose functions require capabilities obtainable on the outside. New technology firms typically have short job ladders, since their hierarchies have only a few levels and the skills they require are obtainable on the outside (e.g., in engineering school).

Qualifications for entry into desirable positions vary among organizations. In some organizations, people are viewed in a "universalistic" manner (see Chapter 4). Anyone demonstrating the ability to do a management job can qualify for it. In other organizations, roles have a "particularistic" quality. Only people with the right social background or family ties can advance.

People who desire advancement should familiarize themselves with the qualifications for entering the slots above their own. They should note the attributes of the individuals who receive promotions and compare these with their own characteristics. Those who determine their organization's internal labor market to be small or closed must look elsewhere for advancement opportunities.

Keep horizons short. Complacency is a hazard of organizational life. The routines present in most organizations are mesmerizing. They lull even the ambitious into a sleepy sensation of satisfaction regarding their position and future in the organization. Many are shaken from this state when the organization encounters a crisis. All too often, people experience shock at how limited their opportunities turn out to be and how vulnerable they are to termination. No one should permit himself or herself to be taken by surprise.

People should never allow themselves to feel too comfortable in an organization. Accommodation to the day-to-day routine can allow the years to pass smoothly. As they do, though, the talented individual finds that he or she has become trapped in a dead end.

Many succumb to a belief that things are bound to get better. Eventually, the employee's talents will be recognized. A new supervisor or CEO will take over and institute a fairer system of promotion and pay. Management slots will open for the employee when he or she is older.

This is sometimes true. Both human and organizational memories tend to be short. Political errors are sometimes punished by short stays in organizational "penalty boxes": temporary immobility, relocation to an unpopular site, or assignment to undesirable duties. Members of organizations must determine whether immobility is temporary or permanent.

It is vitally important for people to continuously reassess how much promise their organization really offers. A personal schedule for advancement can be valuable for this purpose. People should set advancement objectives for specific time periods. Horizons should be short. If a reasonable objective is not reached within three years of employment, the individual should look to another organization.

A sequence of short-term attachments to different organizations can take people much further than loyalty to a single one. In each three- to five-year involvement, the individual moves up another step. Personal cost may be high, requiring, for example, regular relocations to different parts of the country or even the world. But job-hoppers assume, often correctly, that no one organization will allow them to move from step to step fast enough to build a career.

Keeping a short time horizon can be valuable not only in work organizations but in organizations concerned with volunteer activity or politics. These organizations tend to fall into inaction, surviving only because they provide socioemotional rewards to their members. An individual committed to a cause must be prepared to switch his or her organizational allegiance if concrete, effective actions have not occurred in a reasonable period of time.

Avoid heroism. It is important to remember that the modern formal organization neither seeks nor benefits from heroism. Every well-functioning organization develops expectations of individual performance and applies its resources to maintaining performance at this level. Extraordinary effort by individuals to exceed these expectations doesn't necessarily help the organization. People who make such efforts do not usually help themselves.

Heroism may be thought of as *extraordinary effort and risk against long odds.* As such, it puts the individual at peril. Failure, the usual outcome of heroic effort, always looks bad. As noble as his or her intentions have been, the would-be hero is blamed for placing the organization's reputation in jeopardy and wasting its resources.

Success can also put the hero at risk. Outstanding achievements incur the jealousy of colleagues. Some may dismiss extraordinary achievement as mere luck. Others may fear that extraordinary performance demonstrated by the hero will become the norm, raising expectations for everybody. The hostility against "rate-busting" observed among industrial workers (see Chapters 1 and 6) occurs among managers and professionals as well. The hero's visibility as a competitor for advancement and bonuses can motivate colleagues to make him or her look bad.

Even if successful and appropriately rewarded, heroism has significant personal costs. Leslie Perlow's example of overwork in an engineering firm (see Chapter 13) provides an illustration. The firm she described awarded hero status to workaholics. Driven by new technology and crisis-prone, the firm required regular night and weekend work. Employees had little time to take care of personal business or establish intimate relationships on the outside.

Many organizations consider extraordinary effort to be required rather than exceptional behavior. Wall Street investment banks and high-powered law firms are examples. So are breakthrough high-tech organizations. Even after achieving world-class status, software giant Microsoft required days of 12 hours or longer from its lead technical personnel.

But high expectations should not be confused with heroism. Performance norms vary among organizations, and in some they are very high. Individuals should determine whether heroic-seeming performance is normally expected or not. A good test is to see how many people, in fact, work extra hours. If the worker finds him- or herself alone in the office after hours, his or her effort is indeed heroic. If the after-hours atmosphere is abuzz with laboring personnel, computer screens alight, coffee cups and pizza crusts piled high in the wastebaskets, what seems like extraordinary effort merely reflects the norm.

Find the right fit. Except under extraordinary conditions, organizations are unlikely to change (see Chapter 11). For this reason, it is important for the individual to assess his or her level of comfort within the organization. People should ask themselves whether their talents and skills are valued by the organization. Periodic advancement indicates that the answer is positive. Getting passed over for desirable slots indicates the negative.

Social and emotional compatibility is of equal importance. Are the conversations in the elevator or at company parties of interest to you? If the talk is always about football and golf, but your sport is scuba diving, you may be in the wrong surroundings. If you find you would rather not socialize with your colleagues on the outside, you may be in the wrong organization.

Finding the right organizational fit has both an instrumental and a socioemotional function for the individual. Much business gets done in the context of informal conversation and socialization. Only people seen as reflecting the corporate culture are tapped for top management. Simply feeling comfortable in an organization is important, too. People spend a high proportion of their waking hours in organizational settings, and the quality of the fit can shape their entire outlook on life.

People in organizations that are wrong for them often accept personal blame for lack of success. Experiments in basic social psychology highlight the importance of organizational surroundings on the individual's apparent performance capacity. The case study of a boy in summer camp is a classic example. The boy was observed to be unpopular and regularly picked on by his group. Counselors switched the child to a group of somewhat younger kids. The child immediately emerged as a leader, befriended by all, and possessed of many talents. Everyone who has felt dead-ended in his or her organization should remember this tale.

Finding the right fit is as important in nonwork organizations as it is in business firms and government agencies. People, of course, look to organizations for opportunities to have fun, meet others, and act on political and social convictions. Members should continuously ask themselves whether such organizations make use of their capabilities and contribute to their objectives. Does the sports club emphasize technical skill rather than having a good time? Does the social action group sacrifice idealism to broader public acceptance? Are members outside a ruling clique barred from leadership positions in the charity organization? Characteristics such as these make an organization a poor fit for many individuals.

Doing the Right Thing: Ethical and Legal Challenges in Organizations

In most, if not all, organizations, people can find ways to protect themselves from harm and advance their own interests. People also have the freedom to decide between right and wrong. The actions of individuals in organizations may cause harm to others or damage to the organization itself. Personal consequences can be mild: guilty feelings experienced in private or shame before others. Penalties for wrongdoing can also be severe, ranging from ostracism and termination to imprisonment. Beyond its impact on individuals, *malfeasance*—a term denoting either ethical or legal breach—has led to bankruptcies in corporations and scandals in public agencies.

Individuals in organizations, first, face *ethical* challenges. *Ethics* are obligations of individuals to act toward others in a manner consistent with socially reinforced values. For many, values supersede satisfaction of personal needs, organizational role expectations, and boss's orders. The values that determine ethics are tied to the basic moral principles by which people live their lives.

The broadest values emerge from the general culture. A traditionalist author has defined ethics as "the normative standards of conduct derived from the philosophical and religious traditions of society."[5] The organization, of course, also serves as a source of values. People in organizations, finally, obtain their values from outside groups and agencies to which they feel obligation or allegiance. Today, individuals must balance values derived from many sources as well as of their own formulation.

In addition to ethical challenges, people in organizations face *legal liability*. A person's efforts to fulfill role expectations may place him or her at risk of breaking the law. Tragically, people have done time in prison simply because they have tried to do their jobs as well as possible.

Ethics in Organizations

The Nature of Ethics

The term *ethics* implies testing one's behavior against formal or informal codes of conduct. Codes of conduct consist of moral principles that express core values. Many such codes are formally worked out by a collectivity and publicized in written form. Ethical codes are developed by work organizations. They are also put forward by professional societies, such as the American Medical Association. Today, many people develop codes of conduct that are largely personal, selecting elements from many sources.

Human beings have sought formulas for correct behavior for thousands of years. From ancient to modern times, philosophers and theologians have formulated rules of human behavior based on what they considered "right." Medieval theologians deemed human actions good or bad according to their interpretation of religious doctrine. These commentators believed, for example, that charging interest on loans was unethical. Many people today look to religion for ethical guidance.

Renaissance philosophers (1400s and 1500s) began judging the actions of individuals according to humanistic principles. They focused on the effects of human acts in the secular world. The Industrial Revolution (1700s) gave rise to *utilitarianism,* judging human behavior according to its consequences for advancing human well-being. Utilitarians consider an action good when it can be shown to promote "the greatest good for the greatest number."

In modern times, *relativism*—a sense that what is right for one individual or society may not be right for another—dominates ethical thinking. Such thinking contrasts with *absolutism,* an often religiously based belief that universally valid standards should govern human behavior. Modern authorities place great importance on individual responsibility and choice. The political culture dominant in modern society reinforces relativism, encouraging people to develop their own values rather than rely on traditional beliefs or religious doctrine. Unlike in past times, people today are faced with the challenge of formulating, and sometimes defending, their own standards.

Why Be Ethical?

A concern for ethics seems dispensable in today's competitive world.

People normally do not go to jail for ethical transgressions. Ethical codes receive little day-to-day attention in most organizations. Niceties such as ethics are seldom invoked except in connection with major scandal or financial loss.

Ethics, though, have practical consequences. Shady practices in providing goods and services repel customers even if they are not illegal. People viewed as sharp dealers or corner cutters have trouble obtaining leadership positions in organizations. Utilitarian thinking emphasizes the functional nature of ethics. Unless people have confidence in the rightness of each other's actions, social ties disintegrate, and with them the cohesion and coordination upon which economic and technical achievement depends.

Ethical behavior is a normal human quality. Few people act solely according to personal need. Psychologists and psychiatrists consider people whose values ignore the feelings or well-being of others to be abnormal, diagnosing them as sociopaths.

Ultimately, most people act in an ethical manner because they wish to feel good about themselves. They want their behavior to be emulated by the young. They wish to be remembered as good human beings rather than as egoists or crooks.

Ethical Dilemmas in Organizations

The connection between ethics and social norms—many of which are traditional and religious in origin—cannot be completely severed. Consistent with today's emphasis on freedom and choice, however, modern authorities on ethics do not exhort people to accept particular values. Rather, they encourage people to develop their own directions regarding ethical behavior.

Terry Cooper,[6] a well-known writer on ethics in organizations, highlights individual self-examination as the key to ethical behavior. Everyone, he writes, lives according to personal principles based on core values. Upon reflection, most people would identify closely held values such as self-expression, duty to children and spouses, and service to humankind.

Ethical challenges arise when an individual realizes that his or her values are in conflict. As an example, Cooper cites a city employee who observes citizens falling ill due to bacterial contamination in a popular lake. Upon receiving the information, though, his superior instructs him to take no action. The superior counters that the contamination is insignificant and an alert may necessitate installation of costly filtration equipment.

The situation places several of the employee's values in conflict. His values include loyalty. Thus, feels he must obey his superior's instructions. His values include public service. Thus, he feels compelled to make information about the contamination public. His values include caring for his family. For this reason, he feels compelled to forgo actions that may place his job at risk. An honest and informed choice among these values constitutes ethical behavior.

Crime in Organizations

Ethical transgressions invite public scorn but do not usually constitute crime. People recognized as unethical lose business. They may be criticized by peers and be called before the boards of professional organizations. But they are seldom, if ever, imprisoned. Crime itself, however, is an organizational fact of life. Organizations are capable of committing crimes just as are individuals: theft, reckless endangerment of life, and murder.

Criminal corruption. Criminal corruption in organizations (called "corporate crime" in the private sector) includes wrongdoing toward the organization's owners (typically stockholders), workers, or the general public. Visible, small-scale crime takes place in many organizations. Such acts include falsification of time cards and "shrinkage," or minor pilferage, of supplies. Less visible is minor "white-collar crime." Examples include small-time embezzlement by administrative personnel, acceptance of bribes by civil servants, and favored treatment of cronies by elected officials. Consequences of crimes on this level are usually restricted to the organization or its clients.

Illegal acts originating at the highest corporate level become major public concerns and chapters in history books. The 20th century furnished many examples. In the century's early years, oil magnates Edward L. Doheny and Harry F. Sinclair bribed the secretary of the interior of the United States to allow them to pump oil from a publicly owned reserve. In a scandal that came to be known as

Teapot Dome, the secretary of the interior went to prison and the magnates paid colossal fines.

The century ended as it began. In the late 1990s, evidence surfaced in Los Angeles that police officers in an elite antigang unit known as Community Resources Against Street Hoodlums (CRASH) had stolen drugs from evidence storage rooms, planted evidence on innocent citizens in order to make arrests, and robbed a bank.[7] The revelations became known as the "Rampart scandal," after the neighborhood in which CRASH was based. Included in the scandal were at least some supervisory personnel.

The 21st century promises to be no different. In 2001, the Securities and Exchange Commission sued onetime corporate turnaround artist Al Dunlap ("Chainsaw"), alleging that he falsified the books of the Sunbeam Corporation. Dunlap, it seemed, wished to make it appear that the mass layoffs he engineered had increased profits when in fact they had not.[8] One year later, the Enron Corporation replaced Teapot Dome as America's symbol of big-time corporate wrongdoing. Officers of Enron, a Houston-based energy-trading giant, ran the firm into immense debt while manipulating financial reports to make the company look profitable.[9] Investigative reporters made the situation public and the firm instantly collapsed. Convicted on a number of fraud-related charges, Enron's CEO Kenneth Lay faced possible life imprisonment but died before he was sentenced.

Malfeasance by corporations has caused human suffering as well as public outrage. Business ethicist John Darley describes disastrous examples, such as the Pinto automobile manufactured by Ford and the Dalkon Shield, an implanted birth control device made by the Robbins Company. Ford executives knew that the Pinto gasoline tank could rupture and explode on collision but took no action. The quality control supervisor at a Dalkon Shield manufacturing facility reported a health hazard to his supervisor but was sternly discouraged from discussing it further.[10] Technical personnel at Morton Thiokol, which built space shuttle components, warned their supervisors of a potentially faulty part but were rebuffed.[11] Drivers and passengers burned to death in Pinto autos, women died needlessly from Dalkon Shields, and the crew of the space shuttle *Challenger* perished when the vehicle exploded. The Enron debacle cost billions in investor losses, 4,000 employee jobs, and the life of at least one former executive, who committed suicide.

Crimes against humanity. Outrage against lying, stealing, and placing lives at risk as described above is justified. But such malfeasance is trivial compared with the brutality exercised by organizations with political, ideological, and nationalistic missions. In China and the Soviet Union (now dissolved into Russia and several nearby countries), Communist parties killed millions of citizens. The Communist parties in these countries took control of the government. Then Communist leaders used the army and police to protect their power and reshape society according to their philosophies. In Germany, the Nazi Party terrorized and killed not only its own citizens but millions throughout Europe. By the beginning of the 21st century, totalitarian organizations ruled in only a few scattered countries. But organizations of criminals such as the Russian Mafia and South American drug cartels threatened the well-being of millions in their countries and beyond.

Causes of Evil in Organizations

The wrongdoing so frequently encountered in organizations can sometimes be attributed to evil individuals, either in the ranks or at the top. In fact, much evil is perpetrated by emotionally normal individuals living conventional lives. The very features that allow organizations to function cause people to perform condemnable acts. The division of required functions into roles, the operation of reward systems, and the presence of organizational culture promote coordination and cohesion among individuals. However, they can also impel people to lie, cheat, and kill.

Personal justifications. One explanation of wrongful acts by normal people lies in the fact that people think differently in organizations than they do when alone or in their primary groups. The large size and abstract-seeming objectives present in organizations transform individual judgment. According to Saul Gellerman's study of business malfeasance,[12] this atmosphere allows individuals to commit acts they would never commit on the outside.

People often explain an act they know to be unethical or illegal according to the following rationalizations:

- *It isn't really illegal or unethical.* Workers and managers believe that the malfeasant act is really acceptable. This is particularly tempting when the action is widespread, making it seem routine. As an example, several observers of Wall Street have cited the practice among brokers of selling undesirable securities to the public. The brokers justify their conduct with the Roman proverb *caveat emptor:* "let the buyer beware."
- *It is in the organization's best interests.* People naturally identify with the well-being of their firm or agency. This enhances motivation, increasing the likelihood that the ethics and legality of an act will be overlooked. Examples include the covering up by companies of problems and errors. The Manville Corporation and Ford knowingly concealed the dangers, respectively, of asbestos and the Pinto automobile. In a public-sector example, the Republican administration of U.S. president Richard Nixon (1969–1974) covered up its involvement in a burglary of a Democratic Party headquarters (the "Watergate scandal"). Executives at Manville and Ford, as well as President Nixon, believed denial to be the safest means of damage control.
- *It will never be discovered.* People are willing to take chances in order to achieve desired ends. In organizations, risking discovery of a frowned-on act is encouraged by the knowledge that others have gotten away with it. In the instance of business history cited above, Al Dunlap never believed that his bookkeeping gimmicks—charging expenses to a year in which they did not occur, reporting incorrect valuation of inventory, and providing inflated estimates of sales volumes—would come to light.
- *It will be condoned because it will help the company.* People believe that transgressions will be overlooked as long as objectives are achieved. Often, executives give subordinates precisely this message. During an aggressive growth period at Continental Illinois Bank in the 1970s, a loan officer was found to have received a $565,000 kickback from a customer. The officer, who had closed an $800 million deal with the customer, received only a mild reprimand from management.

It is important to remember that people who perform unethical or illegal acts are usually normal, everyday individuals. These justifications are often compelling at the time the act in question takes place. Often, the individual appears to have been clearly in the wrong only after later events have unfolded and officials, journalists, and historians have pieced together the whole story.

Adoption of these justifications may amount to self-delusion by line managers. Without endangering themselves, though, leaders encourage subordinates in this direction. Gellerman writes:

> Top executives seldom ask subordinates to do things that both of them know are against the law or imprudent. But company leaders sometimes leave things unsaid or give the impression that there are things they don't want to know about. In other words, they can seem, whether deliberately or otherwise, to be distancing themselves from the subordinates' tactical decisions in order to keep their own hands clean if things go awry. Often they lure ambitious lower level managers by implying that rich rewards await those who can produce certain results—and that the methods for achieving them will not be examined too closely.[12]

Out of Sight, Out of Mind: Abstract Harm Versus Tangible Gains

People naturally consider immediate, personal benefits from an action as more important than the remote possibility of harm to others. This fact explains many misdeeds in organizations.

A manager knows that his or her bottom line will suffer if a product cycle is delayed. He or she may suspect that marginal corner cutting might result in poor service or injury to someone, somewhere. But it is not certain that anyone will really be ill served or injured. Any undesirable outcome will, in any case, occur far away, in someone else's jurisdiction. In contrast, the manager knows for certain that his or her bonus will be larger if the product is delivered on time.

A worker observes a shoddy or illegal practice. His or her conscience is disturbed. Yet, the worker does not wish to harm his or her relationship with management. The substandard product or legal transgression may, in any case, never be discovered. Those who are injured are unlikely to be personal acquaintances. The worker feels certain, though, that looking the other way will not endanger his or her job.

Organizational encouragement of misdeeds. The four factors described above enable people guilty of malfeasance to convince themselves that they have done no significant wrong. Self-justification can be viewed as an attempt to attain cognitive consonance. Through this process, people who do bad things can continue to believe they are good human beings.

Factors associated with the properties of organizations themselves, though, also contribute to wrongdoing by individuals. Some organizations exert particularly strong influences on their members to commit acts widely seen as evil by outsiders. Other organizations do nothing unusual, and still gradually seduce their members to commit acts of malfeasance. The essential properties of organizations can cause people to set aside the moral principles they have been socialized to accept.

Tasks, tools, and functional specialty. Sometimes, the tasks with which organizations are charged and the methods required to carry out their responsibilities create risk of evildoing among members. The organization's "subject matter" can lead to socially destructive behavior. Organizations in which significant evildoing takes place often have tasks and modes of functioning such as the following:

Objectives that require deadly force. Some of the most prominent public-sector organizations use deadly force to carry out their day-to-day work. Organizations such as armies and police forces are the best-known users of such resources in their day-to-day work. Experienced soldiers and law enforcement officials understand the consequences of deadly force better than most citizens, and most are reluctant to use it. But the presence of deadly weapons creates a potential for serious misdeeds. Newspapers and history books abound with examples.

Historians have attributed wartime atrocities to organizations with objectives as different as German armies in World War II and the U.S. forces in Vietnam. German soldiers may have acted on the orders of a genocidal command structure. But the Americans in all likelihood acted without the knowledge or approval of top commanders.

It is not clear why organizations with weapons periodically use them against unarmed opponents and peaceful citizens. The organization's need to habituate its members to using violent means and to legitimize their use appears likely to play a role.

It may also be the case that illegitimate use of deadly force may result simply from the ready availability of weapons. Criminal gangs in the United States—which, it should be remembered, sometimes have the basic properties of formal organizations—are known for their tendency to settle disputes with guns. Much of the killing seems to take place in highly inflamed emotional settings. Some gun violence occurs in controversies as concrete as those over drug deals; other instances occur as teenagers react to perceived disrespect or compete for prestige.[13] The simple availability of guns may transform the yelling match or jostling contest expectable among youths into capital crime.

Presence of vulnerable clients. Unethical and criminal acts often take place in organizations that care for incarcerated, dependent, or otherwise vulnerable people. Such people include prisoners, hospitalized patients, and children who are wards of the state. All share the inability to escape insensitive treatment or abuse.

The inability of people to leave an organization charged with their supervision or care aggravates their vulnerability. Inattentiveness of staff can be a problem at nursing homes, whose residents lack the capacity to protest or depart. Every reader of Charles Dickens knows of the mistreatment of children, represented in the character of Oliver Twist, in the orphanages of yesteryear. Rape is regularly reported in jails and prisons, directly perpetrated by staff in some instances and perpetrated by inmates with staff knowledge in others. Some of the most atrocious acts of misconduct have been reported in hospitals. Staff members have taken sexual advantage of mental patients with insufficient competence to refuse. A Sacramento anesthesiologist in the 1970s was found to have repeatedly abused unconscious women awaiting surgery.

Sociologists refer to organizations such as prisons and mental hospitals as "total institutions" (see Chapter 6). The label *total institution* refers to the fact that all aspects of inmate lives are under the control of organizational rules and staff decisions. People in total institutions often have no means to limit the power of the staff. Ironically, observers have noted a tendency for total institutions to foster the very behavior they are empowered to discourage. Mental patients become more depressed, anxious, and disruptive due to the frustration of confinement. Convicts become more confirmed as criminals due to their need to adopt unscrupulous and illegal measures to survive incarceration.

Abundance of unwatched, movable resources. Organizations that place members in contact with abundant, accessible resources create opportunities for malfeasance. Notable examples include businesses that handle large amounts of cash. Cash is easy to transfer and its trail difficult to follow. It is understandable that some personnel cannot resist the temptation to sneak money into their own pockets.

Malfeasance in the gaming industry is legion. Casino transactions are carried out via banknotes and cash equivalents such as chips. Both workers and management have been observed to engage in illegal behavior. Management invests in elaborate surveillance systems to prevent dealers and croupiers from pocketing stakes. But theft occurs. Management itself has engaged in large-scale fraud, secretly taking cash from the counting rooms. Known as "skimming," this procedure steals tax revenue from the government and fair dividends from investors.

Access to cash, weapons, drugs, and other valuables seized from felons reportedly has a corrupting effect on police officers. The Rampart scandal referenced above provides a 21st-century illustration. Working without direct supervision, police officers have been known to keep assets seized from suspects for sale or their own use.

Elected officials and their staffs provide a final example of how access to resources fosters malfeasance. Some officials control budgets that include significant funds not legally earmarked for a specific purpose. This allows the official to allocate the funds at will. Others channel lucrative contracts and provide profitable information on pending government actions to friends and allies. Family members may be hired into publicly funded jobs under which they do no actual work. It is doubtful that sufficient public scrutiny can be applied to eliminate financial malfeasance in government. Every presidential administration and governor's office seems to produce its own crop of scandals.

Time and resource pressure. Strict deadlines and limited resources can impel people in organizations to commit ethnical and criminal transgressions. In wartime, rapid production schedules have caused manufacturers of materiel to cut corners. The *Challenger* disaster provides a civilian example. Executives of the agencies involved had postponed or cancelled a series of shuttle launches and felt pressure to bring off a prompt, successful effort. Pressure for action contributed to management's rejection of a postponement urged by technical staff.

Financial pressure can lead to malfeasance. Under pressure for financial performance, executives may prefer to ignore or cover up information about a defect or risk. Firms often incur significant *sunk costs*—money and time tied up in a specific program—in developing new products. These costs can be recovered only if the product is commercially successful. Thus, its manufacturer had strong reasons for keeping the Dalkon Shield on the market.

Pressure to make money or cut expenditures tempts people in the finance and health care industries to commit unethical, illegal, and socially condemnable acts. Stockbrokers are pressured by traders to unload undesirable securities on their clients. Traders take risks by purchasing stocks and bonds they expect to increase in value. When they realize they have guessed wrong, the traders depend on their firm's brokers to sell them to unsuspecting customers.

Health maintenance organizations (HMOs) face financial pressure potentially greater than any other organization today. These organizations accept contracts to provide all the health services a group of patients will use in the coming year. They risk bankruptcy if the patients consume more resources than their contract provides. At the beginning of the 21st century, HMOs faced charges by consumers that they were denied the services they needed. Lawsuits were mounted against HMOs believed to have denied life-saving treatment to patients, and major legislation was introduced to protect patients' rights.

A Drift Toward Disaster

Events at a B. F. Goodrich Corporation unit in the 1980s show how an organization can edge toward corruption even though no individual intends to transgress.

Eager to do business with defense manufacturer LTV, Goodrich proposed to deliver an innovative four-disk brake, whose small size fit the needs of an aircraft LTV was designing.

Trouble started after the contract was won. A junior engineer, assigned by Goodrich to test brake lining material, discovered that the four-disk design was unworkable. The original engineering calculations had been wrong. The young man reported his findings to the senior engineer who had designed the brake and to the project manager.

Having already announced that initial tests had been successful, though, Goodrich management was unable to admit to LTV that redesign might be necessary. The project manager told the junior engineer to stick to his job, searching for a brake lining that worked.

Later, a test engineer noticed that someone had wrongly calibrated testing equipment to ensure a favorable outcome for the brake assembly. He brought the news to his boss and the unit's top manager. The managers responded that it wasn't the test engineer's responsibility to approve or disapprove, and that they were too busy to intervene themselves.

The brakes were delivered to LTV and installed on airplanes. Several near crashes occurred. The junior engineers talked with an attorney. A congressional investigation ensued.

No single villain can be identified in this case. Numerous people knew about the brake's defects but hid rather than confronted the problem. The engineer who made the initial discovery buried his concerns and participated in the fraudulent tests. The senior engineer and managers above him were reluctant to admit mistakes. Everyone felt pressure from higher-ups to deliver the product as promised.

Organizational machinery. Above and beyond the work in which it is involved, the means of coordination and cohesion that an organization employs can foster malfeasance. All organizations require coordination and cohesion. The choices (deliberate or evolutionary) that an organization makes about how it will achieve coordination and cohesion affect the likelihood that its members will engage in misdeeds. Four examples—leadership, structure, culture, and authority—illustrate this principle.

Charismatic leadership. Charismatic leaders (see Chapter 9) exercise power not through rules or traditions but via belief among subordinates that they personally represent divine will, the thrust of history, or some other extraordinary or supernatural force. Personal magnetism is an essential property of charismatic leaders. Among modern charismatic leaders, people are likely to think of John Kennedy and Martin Luther King.

The star quality associated with charismatic leadership has positive appeal. But people should remember that charismatic leaders have often led their followers into condemnable deeds. Hitler and Mao exemplified these tendencies in the 20th century. Both these individuals set aside historical precedents and established procedures to carry out their will. Their personal gifts motivated their followers to break with tradition. Untrammeled by rules and traditions, Hitler and Mao were able to order some of the most extensive mass slaughters of history.

Charisma, then, is an instrument of social control equally capable of being used for good or evil. The terrorism and fanaticism that have characterized the 21st century's early years in some parts of the world have been inspired by charismatic leaders. On a more immediate scale, the personal charm of an executive has seduced many into corrupt actions.

Charisma sounds exciting and attractive. But leadership via charisma has led many an organization and individual to destruction. Democracies require checks and balances on their leaders. Similarly, rules and traditions in an organization are valuable to check the inclinations of a leader whose objectives may be risky, destructive, or unwise.

Excessive hierarchy. Chapter 10 points out the downside of hierarchical structure. Although hierarchy contributes to coordination, it tends to block communication from bottom to top, and vice versa. Extreme hierarchy in an organization can also foster ethical transgression and criminal acts.

Hierarchy makes leadership invisible. In organizations with numerous layers separating leadership from the workers, those at the top acquire a mythical character. They are seldom if ever seen by subordinates a few rungs below them. It becomes hard for subordinates to realize that those above them are human beings with normal limitations in judgment, honesty, and goodwill.

Leaders who are invisible appeal to some workers. These are people with "authoritarian personalities," as described in Chapter 2, who feel most comfortable in an atmosphere of orders received from on high. All things being equal, an organization with extreme hierarchical structure will attract a membership in which the authoritarian personality predominates.

Extreme hierarchy makes socially destructive acts more likely in an organization. In such a setting, the orders of an unethical, criminal, or genocidal leadership are unlikely to be questioned. Even when the leadership is goodwilled, extreme hierarchy may foster malfeasance in the organization. Communications problems associated with hierarchical structure often prevent top executives from learning about what is happening in the ranks. Intelligence about legally or ethically questionable practices on the ground may never reach the top leadership level.

Cultural chauvinism. Some countries have *chauvinistic* cultures—beliefs and values that claim superiority over other nations. Chauvinists believe that their country, due to its cultural or moral superiority, has the right to attack its neighbors. Cultural chauvinism helps explain atrocities such as ethnic cleansing in the Balkans at the end of the 20th century.

Organizations, too, can have chauvinistic cultures. The leadership and members of such organizations may believe they are superior to the general public in intelligence. Or they may believe that people outside the organization are incapable of making good decisions, using their money wisely, or living peacefully with each other. These chauvinistic beliefs are used to justify acts toward the public ranging from petty swindles to mass violence.

Cultural chauvinism is common in organizations whose members are socially isolated from outsiders. Such isolation has been observed, for example, among police. Police officers interact intensely with the public in the course of their official duties. But according to a classic study, they socialize principally with each other when off duty.[14] Isolation from the broader society also occurs within businesses whose members perform highly specialized work or lack day-to-day, physical contact with the public.

The Rampart scandal in the Los Angeles Police Department illustrates how chauvinistic organizational culture can encourage misdeeds. The CRASH unit had a "rough justice" culture. This was symbolized by the unit's logo: a white skull with a cowboy hat, framed by playing cards arranged in the "dead man's hand"—aces and eights. The unit's street-smart officers, it is said, knew who the crooks were, but didn't trust civilian courts and juries to remove them from society. The unit's culture justified direct action.

According to reports, it was commonplace for officers to shoot a suspect and plant guns and drugs on his or her body to justify their action. The practice came to light when a young Honduran was found to have been shot and framed by CRASH officers. Having been sentenced to 23 years in state prison, the youth was later released, crippled for life by the police bullets.

Wall Street furnishes other examples of misdeeds encouraged by corporate culture. Michael Lewis's famous book, *Liar's Poker,*[15] describes the corporate culture of Salomon Brothers in the 1980s, a hugely profitable period for the firm. The game of liar's poker itself represented a ritual to legitimize the practice of outwitting one's neighbor for profit. Another ritual, gluttonous weekly food blowouts, symbolized acceptability of excessive personal gratification. Encouraged by these values, Lewis reports, brokers knowingly steered customers into bad investments that profited the firm.

Diffusion of responsible authority. Authority is the most important dimension of imperative force. As defined in Chapter 7, imperative forces are mechanisms by which the organization causes people to act according to another person's judgment or desires rather than their own. Authority, power, and discipline all play a part in the well-functioning organization. Authority is the most consistent and durable of imperative forces. An individual's authority is considered legitimate by others in the organization and is typically restricted to a limited area of the organization's functioning.

Organizations in which no one has or accepts authority over ethical issues and legal risks appear relatively likely to commit malfeasant acts. Such conditions exist in many large organizations today. The very size and complexity of modern formal organizations make it difficult for anyone to claim or accept responsibility for a single product, much less the organization as a whole. Thus, the quality control supervisor in the Dalkon Shield case had sufficient expertise to detect a hazard, but insufficient authority to demand that a remedy be found. The same was true of the technical specialist reporting on the *Challenger*'s faulty part. In neither case did managers up the line intervene.

Whistleblowers in Formal Organizations: Heroes or Fools?

Most people feel they should stop others from doing evil, either directly or by alerting higher authorities. In organizations, though, people who report wrongful acts often place themselves in peril. An immediate superior may reject or ignore a subordinate's warning of improper acts and begin thinking of him or her as a troublemaker. Reporting a supervisor's misdeeds to higher-level managers involves even greater risk. Supervisors resent workers who go over their heads. In particularly serious cases, the worker may report questionable behavior to an outside watchdog group or law-enforcement agency. Acts of this kind are known as whistle-blowing.

Federal law protects workers who expose fraud against the government and rewards people who save the government money by exposing fraud. But blowing the whistle is still very risky. It is not uncommon for employers to take action against whistle-blowers, known or suspected. Managers, for example, harass whistle-blowers. Methods of harassment include intense surveillance, on or off the job.

When a chemist at Westinghouse Hanford Company started speaking out on safety problems in nuclear waste storage, her home was repeatedly broken into, her telephone rang day and night, and a note appeared on the dashboard of her daughter's car reading, "You Are Being Watched."

Workers are also dismissed. Westinghouse employees who raised nuclear storage safety issues were let go.[16] After pressing his case to upper management, the quality control supervisor at Robbins who detected the Dalkon Shield hazard was dismissed in a corporate reorganization.

Whistle-blowing may not result in justice. In the Goodrich matter, the engineers who identified the faulty brake design eventually resigned. No legal charges were brought against the company. The managers who encouraged the cover-up were reportedly promoted.

Strategies for Avoiding Misdeeds

Avoidance of malfeasance, either ethical or criminal, is relevant on two levels. First, individuals must make personal decisions regarding action or inaction. The individual's basic self-worth may be at stake in these matters.

Second, organizations themselves benefit from discouraging ethical or legal breaches at all levels. Most organizations suffer when public confidence is lost. Criminal charges are costly to contest and settle. Undetected malfeasance cuts into profits and reduces the quality of public service. The features of an organization have a powerful impact on its members' thinking and behavior. Organization-wide strategies for discouraging malfeasance, then, have greater impact than the behavior of individuals.

Personal Decisions

Values and Action

Ultimately, members of organizations decide for themselves whether or not to commit ethical transgressions or crimes. Human beings cannot be programmed. Organizational means of coordination and cohesion may powerfully affect individual actions, but structure, culture, and imperative force leave the individual with enough, perhaps just enough, room to decide between a "right" and "wrong" action.

Ultimately, an individual's action is based upon his or her values. Traditionally and socially approved values motivate people to behave in an ethical manner. Most people obey the law not from fear of punishment but rather because they believe that government is necessary and they value the principle of lawful behavior.

It is easy to understand why *deviants* from the social mainstream act unethically or illegally. Narcissists, sociopaths, and many career criminals are psychologically abnormal, valuing only fulfillment of personal need. The severely mentally ill or developmentally disabled are often *amoral,* lacking consciousness of values.

Most people, though, act unethically or unlawfully due to contradictions among widely shared values. Situations that call forth contradictory values constitute the greatest challenges that organizations present to their members. The case at the B. F. Goodrich unit described above provides an example. Consider the junior engineer who discovered the design flaw in the aircraft brake system. Some of his values doubtlessly were based in principles of honesty and professional integrity, such as

- Good engineering work
- Objective fact-finding
- Truthful reporting of findings
- Upholding engineering ethics

These values explain his communication of concern to his immediate supervisor and higher-ups.

He seems to have had other values as well:

- Loyalty to superiors
- Commitment to on-time completion of projects
- Contributing to the company's success
- Being a good team member
- Feeling productive
- Safeguarding his job and income

Conflict among these values explains the engineer's erratic behavior regarding the aircraft brakes: first pressing his misgivings on management; then, pushing back and contributing to the cover-up; and, finally, going public with a protest. Anyone today can find himself or herself in a similar state of conflict. The ethical absolutism of yesteryear is seldom adequate to resolve today's ethical conflicts.

Analyzing Options

A systematic examination of one's values can help resolve personal conflict. Table 14.1 provides a tool for such an examination. People can list their values that apply to the issue causing conflict. One or more actions can be identified as consistent with each value. Finally, each action can be analyzed regarding its likely impact, first on the individual and then on others.

The table represents some conflicting values that the engineer in the Goodrich aircraft brake episode might identify. It systematically explores values pertinent to the decision of whether to pursue or abandon the claim that the brake design is faulty.

The table assists analysis of options by displaying and comparing multiple values, actions, and outcomes. After considering its contents, many might decide that none of the favorable outcomes—peer approval or job security for oneself and others—would justify endangering the pilots who would test the planes that would be equipped with the faulty brakes.

Others might well decide to abandon the claim that the brake design was a failure. Saving Goodrich jobs, they might reason, is more important than saving test pilot lives. Such logic may seem coldhearted. But it should be recalled that tangible gains carry more weight in human thinking than abstract harm. Loyalty to superiors produces tangible gains: job security and promotion potential. Peril to the individuals who might eventually be harmed is abstract.

Even closely reasoned analysis, then, may not provide clear direction for doing the right thing. In formal organizations, the interplay of multiple values and diverse consequences promotes ethical ambiguity. The fact that the consequences of an act cannot always be anticipated increases ambiguity. It is uncertain, for example, whether revealing or concealing the brake design flaw would help the company. Short-term gains may be traded for long-term losses. People who safeguard the organization from long-term losses, though, may not survive to enjoy the fruits of their efforts.

Resolving Conflicts

As illustrated in the preceding example, logic alone is not necessarily sufficient to resolve a personal conflict. The individual must make a final judgment. Getting outside the organization can be important at this time. Outside people and groups—friends, professional colleagues, clergy, and therapists—can provide opinions independent of organizational priorities and culture.

Table 14.1   Examination of Personal Values

Value	Action	Impact on Self	Impact on Others
Truthful reporting	Pursue claim	Personal satisfaction	Safety of test pilots; layoff of coworkers
Loyalty to superiors	Abandon claim	Job security; potential for promotion	Job security for coworkers; peril to test pilots
Being a good team member	Abandon claim	Positive feelings from colleagues	Peril to test pilots
Upholding engineering ethics	Pursue claim	Feeling ethical; pride in professionalism	Strengthen independence of engineering profession; protect test pilot safety
Contributing to the company's success	Uncertain	Unknown	Unknown

Judgment at Nuremberg

Shortly after World War II, high-ranking Nazi officials were put on trial at the German city of Nuremberg. Faced with charges of murder and genocide, many of these officials pleaded that they were acting under orders and hence should be absolved of personal guilt. Top Nazi officers claimed to have been only subordinates, soldiers doing their duty, cogs in a machine. The tribunal rejected this defense, asserting that people are responsible for their acts even when they are under the authority of others. With only a few exceptions, the defendants were sentenced to death and hanged.

In war and peace, individuals ever since have looked to the Nuremberg judgment as a touchstone of personal responsibility when under the command of others. The argument that an individual was only following orders, regardless of whether these clash with higher moral values, is known as "the Nuremberg defense."

Organizational Safeguards

Individual analysis of options is of course important. But safeguards must be built into the organization itself to reduce individual malfeasance. These safeguards must counteract the organizational factors that promote legal and ethical breaches by individual members.

Formal Codes of Conduct

Many organizations today have formal codes of conduct. Colleges and universities have *codes of honor* that forbid malfeasant acts such as cheating on examinations or purchasing term papers from Internet-based suppliers. Firms such as Xerox have issued ethical codes to sales personnel prohibiting them from selling unneeded products to their customers. Every organized profession issues ethical guidelines to its members, the most famous being medicine's *Hippocratic Oath.* The Oath obliges physicians not to harm patients and to serve all people, whatever their economic means or social station. Organizations that employ large numbers of professionals tend to endorse such professional codes.

It is doubtful whether formal codes of conduct directly affect personal conduct. College students still cheat and salespeople apply high-pressure tactics. Medicine's credo has been ridiculed for generations as more "hypocritic" than Hippocratic. Codes of conduct, though, may have merit in fostering a positive corporate culture over time. They can also be used to help decide whether a member's act can be considered malfeasant after the fact, contributing to the process of organizational learning.

Structural Remedies

Structural innovations will be required to systematically forestall malfeasance in formal organizations. The health care industry provides some good examples. These include ethics committees in hospitals. Human subjects committees—also known as institutional review boards (IRBs)—have been established in organizations doing biomedical research and other kinds of experiments on humans.

Ethics committees. Ethics committees review behavior of health care workers identified as questionable. They have the power to criticize doctors and nurses for violating codes of conduct and recommend their severance from the organization.

Institutional review boards. IRBs are mandated to protect human subjects involved in research projects. They are found in nearly every university and private firm that conducts research involving people. Scientists must submit their plans to IRBs before beginning experiments. IRBs examine these plans to determine whether the drugs or procedures can harm the people on whom they will be tested. They require scientists to develop protocols to inform subjects about risks they may face. Today, IRBs have sufficient power to hold up millions of dollars in research contracts if their requirements are not met.

Future Innovations

Along the lines already followed by hospitals, it has been suggested that organizations of all kinds institute specialized ethical review boards. Staffed by people outside the regular hierarchy, these units would report directly to the organization's top governing body: the board of directors or trustees. An arrangement of this kind would safeguard the review board from potential interference by line managers.

Sufficient independence and authority are critical. It has been argued that the disaster of the space shuttle *Challenger* resulted from weakness and lack of independence of watchdog units. Several safety committees in fact existed. But none were independent of NASA and Morton Thiokol management, which pressed for the hazardous launch. No personnel primarily responsible for safety were present at the final decision-making session. It is significant that the extensive investigation and procedural revisions that followed the *Challenger* disaster were insufficient to prevent another space shuttle failure, that of *Columbia,* 17 years later. Researchers have reported similar resistance by managers to technical information in the case of *Columbia.*[17]

Lawsuits and criminal investigations have made organizations increasingly concerned with stemming possible malfeasance by members. Many organizations today have risk management programs designed to control such liability. Ethics committees, IRBs, and independent units responsible for honesty and safety are likely to play increasingly important roles in risk management.

Issues and Applications

Issues involving personal risk taking and ethical behavior are among the most difficult ones encountered in organizations. Making choices of this kind is much more difficult in real life than on paper. The examples below reflect the difficulty of such decisions.

- Intent on a management career, an ambitious young man begins work at a government agency. After a time, he notices that all unit supervisors are at least 15 years his senior. Official policy states that competition for vacant supervisory positions is open. All, however, seem to go to applicants with seniority. He resolves to quit. But, realizing that jobs are scarce in the locality, he hesitates.
- During a dinner party, a corporate controller, long an employee of the firm, receives a whispered suggestion from the CEO to delay reporting certain liabilities. She struggles with the dilemma of whether to take the suggested action, ignore the request, confront the CEO with her legal and ethical concerns, or make the CEO's request known to the firm's directors.
- An executive for a U.S.-based multinational firm has been given the responsibility of establishing business in a developing country. To grow the business, she needs permission to import products into the country and to hire nationals as employees. She discovers that government officials will award her the necessary business licenses only in exchange for bribes, a violation of her firm's code of ethics. Colleagues at firm headquarters advise her to purchase costly, salable items for the officials and report associated expenses to the firm simply as "business gifts." She ponders her options.

Chapter Review and Major Themes

Individuals are never fully controlled by the organizations to which they belong. An examination of the methods used by organizations to achieve coordination and cohesion underscores this point. Ultimately, individuals choose whether or not to occupy the roles, submit to the structure, and accept the rewards, or buy into the culture of an organization. The clever and well-placed person can often evade imperative forces.

Figure 14.1 presents a picture of the organization emphasizing the choices of which individuals are capable. Organizations cannot be understood only as systems within which managers apply organizational resources to promote coordination and cohesion. In the figure, the means by which organizations attain coordination and cohesion are connected to the individual member by arrows pointing in both directions.

The organization utilizes mechanisms such as role expectations, structure, rewards, imperative force, and culture in a manner believed to advance its objectives.

As the arrows pointing outward from the individual suggest, however, people "push back" on these mechanisms. Members of organizations often negotiate their roles. They may evade structure. They may reject organizational culture or contribute to the development of a culture of opposition. Figure14.1 is not intended to suggest that an organization's members are free to directly or continuously act in opposition. Rather, it reflects the concept that pushes for accommodation and change occur continually. These arise from needs, aspirations, and rebellion on both the individual and group level. The broader culture, moreover, contributes to these challenges through its influence on the beliefs, values, and aspirations of the organization's membership.

The ultimate freedom of the individual underscores the importance of personal responsibility. People cannot exclusively blame the organizations to which they belong for misfortunes such as lack of personal development, career frustration, or unfavorable severance. It is important to become an informed observer of the organizations to which one belongs. An understanding of the structure, reward systems, and politics of an organization alerts the individual to current and future hazards.

The ability of individuals to make choices creates a high level of personal responsibility as regards organizational wrongdoing. Individuals must remain alert to the gradual process by which involvement in wrongdoing often takes place. Safeguards against such involvement include maintaining values, perspectives, and social ties independent of the organization.

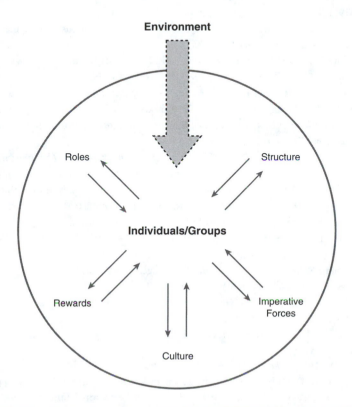

Figure 14.1   Organizational Mechanisms Challenged: Individual and Group Push-Back

Discussion Questions

1. The preceding chapter links career success with putting one's personal interests ahead of the organization's—for example, by keeping time horizons short and avoiding heroism. How comfortable would you feel taking such an approach? Explain.

2. How often do service-oriented nonprofit organizations experience conflict between their core values and the actions required for continuing operation?

3. Describe an ethical challenge that you or a colleague has encountered in an actual organization. What decisions did you or your colleague make? What led to these decisions? Were any lessons learned?

4. What may be done to prevent episodes such as the Rampart scandal from occurring within other organizations involved in law enforcement or other services potentially requiring use of deadly force?

5. Had you been a highly placed executive at Enron before the organization's fall, do you believe that you would have "blown the whistle"? Explain your answer.

References

1. Katz, D., & Kahn, R. L. (1978). *The social psychology of organizations* (2nd ed.). New York: John Wiley & Sons.

2. Levitt, B., & March, J. G. (1988). Organizational learning. *Annual Review of Sociology, 14*, 319–338.

3. Langley, M. (1998, January 7). Nuns' zeal for profits shapes hospital chain, wins Wall Street fans. *Wall Street Journal.*

4. Machiavelli, N. (1947). *The prince.* New York: F. S. Crofts & Co.

5. Means, R. (1970). *The ethical imperative.* New York: Doubleday.

6. Cooper, T. L. (1990). *The responsible administrator.* San Francisco: Jossey-Bass.

7. Boyer, P. J. (2001, May 21). Bad cops. *New Yorker.*

8. SEC accuses former chief executive of Sunbeam of huge accounting fraud. (2001, May 16). *New York Times,* p. A1.

9. McLean, B., & Elkind, P. (2004). *The smartest guys in the room: The amazing rise and scandalous fall of Enron.* New York: Portfolio Trade (Penguin Group).

10. Darley, J. M. (1996). How organizations socialize individuals into doing evil. In D. M. Messick & A. E. Tenbrunsel (Eds.), *Codes of conduct: Behavioral research into business ethics* (pp. 13–43). New York: Russell Sage Foundation.

11. Vaughan, D. (1990). Autonomy, interdependence, and social control: NASA and the space shuttle *Challenger. Administrative Science Quarterly, 35*, 225–257.

12. Gellerman, S. W. (1986). Why "good" managers make bad ethical choices. *Harvard Business Review, 64*(July–August), 85–90.

13. Tonry, M., & Moore, M. H. (Eds.). (1998). *Crime and justice: Vol. 24. Youth violence.* Chicago: University of Chicago Press.

14. Skolnick, J. (1975). *Justice without trial: Law enforcement in a democratic society.* New York: John Wiley & Sons.

15. Lewis, M. (1989). *Liar's poker.* New York: Penguin.

16. Egan, T. (1991, October 27). Sometimes the disloyal are watched. *New York Times.*

17. Hall, J. L. (2003). *Columbia* and *Challenger:* Organizational failure at NASA. *Space Policy, 19*, 239–247.

CHAPTER 15

Organizations and Society

Learning Objective

To understand how organizations affect society, the issues organizations today raise for democracy and human well-being, and the implications of global organization for the future.

Principles

Organizations affect the social fabric and quality of life of the societies in which they operate. Their impact can be favorable or unfavorable. Society itself may encourage, limit, or otherwise influence the organization's activities.

Organizations have broad social impact through obvious means, including production of goods and services and participation in routine politics. Potentially more important effects occur through mechanisms such as

- Decisions and strategies that, though not intended to affect the broader society, foster important society-wide outcomes
- Attempts by organizations to manage their environment in a manner compatible with their objectives
- Programs conducted for the explicit purpose of social change

Critics have contended that large, formal organizations have weakened community in the United States while adding little economic benefit. However, organizations of a smaller scale do not appear capable of supporting the level of technology and industry on which the world now depends. Internationally, the ability of organizations to direct the thinking and behavior of individuals may have reached its limit.

The Growing Concern With Social Impact

This book has periodically addressed the importance to organizations of matters outside their boundaries. The organizational milieu, as discussed in Chapter 2, includes phenomena such as interpersonal ties and social forces beyond the organization's control. Concerns such as motivation, rewards, and imperative force are not simply matters internal to organizations. Within most organizations, valuation of rewards and acceptance of authority depend significantly on the values, traditions, and institutions of the broader society. Communication across organizational boundaries, addressed in Chapter 10, is vital to many organizations. The broader society's values and culture help lay the groundwork for the ethical challenges discussed in Chapter 14.

Little has been said thus far, however, about how organizations affect the broader society. Outside social forces clearly condition the mechanisms organizations may use to promote cohesion, coordination, and focus among their members. But what impact do organizations have on key dimensions of the surrounding society, such as material well-being, liberty, and democracy?

Until recently, mainstream researchers and commentators paid scant attention to the impact of organizations on society. Today, however, a growing number are contending that the most important questions about organizations concern the impact they may have outside their boundaries. News of large-scale corruption and concern with globalization have underscored the importance of society-wide and worldwide effects.

It is clear that organizations routinely influence the thinking and behavior of people outside their boundaries. Manufacturers, for example, now and then introduce consumer goods that alter the life experience of people worldwide. Inventions such as the automobile, computer, and birth control pill were initially diffused throughout the United States by single, dominant companies, forever changing the way people live. Less arguably beneficial has been the mass marketing of everyday goods such as mouthwash and deodorant.[1] Products clearly destructive of human health such as cigarettes, some critics argue, attained widespread use in the United States only because manufacturers advertised them aggressively.[2]

Effects of government agencies and nonprofit organizations on the thinking and actions of individuals outside their boundaries cannot be ignored. Government agencies affect business activity and professional practice through licensure, regulation, and law enforcement. Agencies concerned with public health attempt to influence the behavior of individuals via publicity campaigns. Nonprofit organizations seek to increase public awareness of issues such as disability, animal rights, and AIDS through advertising, marches, "weeks," and appeals for funds. International agencies such as the European Union (EU) Competition Commission have the power to fine and otherwise punish firms they believe have obstructed the EU's trade liberalization policy.

It is easy to understand why organizations continually attempt to influence the actions of public agencies and officials. Within the United States, organizations such as the National Association of Manufacturers (representing big business), the American

Association of Health Plans (representing HMOs), and the United States Potato Board (representing potato growers) seek to influence government action on behalf of their members. Entities as diverse as major oil companies, labor unions, and wilderness preservation organizations contribute heavily to congressional and presidential candidates in hopes of influencing their decisions when elected. Less familiar, though quite extensive, are attempts by government agencies themselves to influence lawmakers.

The number of organizations whose objectives are largely or entirely political has increased markedly in recent years. By late in the 20th century, no fewer than 2,300 trade associations were actively attempting to influence policy on the national level.[3] Associations representing government bureaucracies to legislators have also proliferated. By the early 2000s, for example, over 300 county, city, and special purpose districts in California maintained lobbies in Sacramento, the state capital.[4]

Many of the resources organizations use to exercise influence beyond their boundaries have no fundamental impact on the broader society. Organizations expend large amounts of money in political activity. But even greater levels of resources are expended on promoting their goods and services to consumers. Advertising expenditures for 2006 were estimated at $286 billion in the United States and $569 billion worldwide.[5] Routine advertising and politicking usually address matters quite narrow in scope. Day-to-day marketing and lobbying leave the basic structure of society intact. Such activities are arguably indispensable for a democratic, free-enterprise society.

But the effects that organizations have on society go well beyond these routine activities. The instances that attract the most attention tend to be negative ones, involving U.S.-based corporations. Tales of excessive corporate power have attained mythic status among social critics. During the 20th century, the United Fruit Company (later Chiquita Brands International) became the "poster child" of alleged U.S. imperialism. For a time, the firm reportedly dominated the Caribbean basin, both economically and politically. So extensively did the company permeate Guatemala's economy, for example, that it operated both the country's railroads and its postal service. Actions by the United Fruit Company are said to have included large-scale bribery of public officials and engineering of periodic regime changes in Caribbean "banana republics."[6] Within the United States itself, sociologists have argued for generations that corporations collude to control American government.[7,8]

The Formal Organization as Villain

Cited early in this textbook (see Chapter 1), the writings of the influential sociologist Charles Perrow[9,10] bring the long-standing concern with adverse corporate influence into broader perspective. Focusing on industrialization in the United States, Perrow traces the rise of the large organization since the early 1800s and cites the importance of corporate advocacy in key legislative and judicial decisions of importance to big business. According to Perrow, the dominance of large organizations (typically major corporate employers) has had many negative consequences for America. These include

- Wage dependence, due to their elimination of small employers and self-employment, and their domination of local labor markets
- Removal of wealth and power from communities and concentration of the same in the hands of corporate executives
- Socialization of people (inside and outside the organization's boundaries) to fit the organization's needs
- Obstruction of the will of the public and its elected leadership
- Replacement of family ties, neighborhood networks, and mutual obligations by relationships within the organization and employee benefits

At the core of Perrow's argument is the assertion that, within organizations, size and resource concentration do not ensure efficiency and productivity. Since the mid-19th century, a limited number of large organizations have replaced a multitude of smaller ones. Traditionally, specialists in industrial organization have interpreted this development as an evolution of organizations capable of achieving economies of scale. But Perrow writes that large, national organizations are in fact no more efficient than local or regional ones. Using examples from the textile and railroad industry, Perrow attributes consolidation to the greedy motivations of industrialists.

Perrow emphasizes that large organizations, today as in yesteryear, have operated in a fashion detrimental to workers and society at large. During the late 19th and early 20th centuries, newly powerful corporations practiced unmitigated exploitation of workers, employing practices such as child labor, extremely long workdays, and insensitivity to safety concerns.

Twenty-first-century organizations appear little better. They have sought to rescind the gains made by workers in an era when unions were stronger than they are today. In the political arena, large organizations oppose worker compensation laws and proconsumer legislation. Many ordinary Americans today hold stock in major corporations. But these small stockholders receive benefits from their investments that are minuscule compared with the gargantuan compensation packages given to high-level executives.

Perhaps the most disturbing part of Perrow's formulation is his assertion that large organizations destroy the democratic community. Financially, they have greater resources than most local governments, and they have the political resources to see their desires realized. The appearance of large retailers such as Wal-Mart in small communities, and the consequent dying out of small businesses, is consistent with this principle.

Perrow asserts that large nonprofits have similar impact on communities. Traditionally, communities conducted their own fund drives and allocated the proceeds to needs they themselves identified. Today, national charitable organizations such as the Red Cross and the American Cancer Society conduct nationally planned fund-raising efforts (often carried out by local individuals) and allocate resources from their central offices.

Researchers who share Perrow's concerns comment that much more needs to be known about how large organizations might collude to control key social institutions.[11] But due to their concern with the internal functioning of organizations, organizational researchers have not focused on this crucial question.

How Organizations Affect Society

That the excesses of formal organizations have abridged the sovereignty of nations and challenged the freedom of Americans is undeniable. Yet the vision of a calculated effort at domination as the driver of organizational influence on the broader society is an incomplete one. Organizations can have important effects on society through a variety of mechanisms. Three illustrative processes are described below. These processes and their outcomes range in scope from barely noticeable to revolutionary.

Inadvertent Social Impact

The decisions made and strategies undertaken by organizations for internal purposes usually have limited importance for society. This is particularly true of organizations of limited scale, such as the small business or local government agency. Repeated decisions and actions by organizations of all types and sizes, though, can have important effects on society over time. Even single actions taken by large organizations for internal purposes, moreover, can have major social impact.

An example of the ultimate effects that small, routine actions inside an organization can have over time concerns the famous "glass ceiling." As described in Chapter 5, the glass ceiling refers to the disinclination in some organizations to admit women into top leadership strata. Although women are approaching numerical equality in such key professions as medicine, they remain thinly represented in corporate executive suites and boardrooms.

This exclusion seems likely to arise from a number of sources. Prior to very recent decades, women have not selected (or been admitted to) university programs in fields leading to top management, such as engineering and accounting. Prejudice among leaders in many organizations has doubtlessly contributed to the exclusion of women from consideration for the top slots.

Neither exclusion from high-mobility career ladders nor conscious prejudice, though, can fully explain today's dearth of women in top corporate executive posts. Many organizations today face pressure to hire and promote women into leadership positions. It seems unlikely that today's male corporate executive, educated in an era of feminist agitation, could have the same level of conscious antifemale bias as did his predecessors.

Rather, an executive today may undervalue female candidates for reasons other than direct antifemale prejudice. Many of today's executives have attained their positions through skills such as abstract thinking, aggressive social behavior, and extreme competitiveness. According to some feminist authors, these constitute primarily "male" characteristics and are not objectively necessary for performing well in top management.[12] A male executive may think himself free of prejudice, then, yet favor candidates for top leadership who possess the capabilities he himself employed in climbing the ladder.

Although explicit antifemale bias may be absent in the case just described, it results in the exclusion of women. As the cycle undergoes successive replication, female leadership models remain absent for future generations.

Another instance of inadvertent social impact concerns erosion of the American middle class through layoffs of middle managers and outsourcing of skilled, lower-level jobs. Business, government, and nonprofits have all carried out processes of these types. Outsourcing has led government to replace career civil service personnel with workers contracted from the private sector. Contract workers typically enjoy less job security and receive fewer benefits. The corporate practice of outsourcing white-collar jobs to overseas firms merely continues the long-term trend to move manufacturing facilities offshore. The social impact of these developments is potentially huge. Economic insecurity and downward social mobility have led to social upheavals throughout history.

"Corporate greed" alone cannot explain the layoffs and outsourcing trend of the early 21st century. Certainly, the new century has seen large increases in executive incomes and widespread job loss among ordinary workers.[13] But business feels intense pressure from consumers for cheaper products and services. Incomes of top government officials have not increased at anything approaching the rate of corporate executives. But taxpayer revolts throughout the nation have pushed these officials to seek means of providing cheaper government. Donors to charitable organizations express discontent about the use of their largess to cover "overhead," a term that includes the salaries of middle managers and the fringe benefits of ordinary workers.

Cutbacks and layoffs are consequences not of a deliberate desire to weaken the middle class, but of responses by individual organizations to market pressures. Neither business nor government desires to create a growing body of insecure, potentially angry men and women in America. Nevertheless, layoffs and outsourcing decisions by individual organizations, taken together over time, have created a major social problem.

Mobility Opportunities Derailed

Economy moves and technological advances have short-circuited a once lively internal labor market in New York's Metropolitan Transit Authority (MTA), which operates the city's famed subway system.

Car cleaners, the lowest-paid job in the system, once had frequent chances to move up to positions such as motorman or tower operator. The system aided employees through a robust training program.

Many fewer opportunities are available today. New technology has eliminated some of the more desirable jobs. In addition, the system has increasingly looked outside its ranks to fill skilled positions.

Like other employers, the MTA has no interest in reducing opportunity at the low-skilled end of the labor force. But its recent actions have had this effect. Details reported by the *Wall Street Journal* apply throughout the U.S. economy:[14]

In the 1980s, the MTA Training Center, housed at a converted elementary school in Brooklyn, bustled with day and night classes. Hundreds of cleaners, security guards, and other entry-level workers passed through each year, some undergoing formal MTA training and others attending seminars to prepare themselves for promotional exams. . . .

Between 1981 and 1991, the MTA offered a promotional exam for car-inspector jobs five times—twice in 1986 alone—and attracted more than 1,500 applicants from its own ranks. Since 1991, the MTA has offered the exam only once, in 1999. . . .

"For too many of our people, entry-level no longer means entry-level. It means dead-end," says Rodney Glenn, director of training for Transport Workers Union Local 100, to which 30,000 MTA employees belong.

 The MTA's move toward hiring people for middle-income jobs who already have qualifications and training mirrors what has happened across America. Traders on Wall Street once started as floor runners out of high school. Newspapers would hire high school dropouts to run sheets of inky carbon paper down to the print shop and later promote them to be reporters. "Macy's used to fill its executive training corps by recruiting stock boys," says Phil Kasinitz, a City University of New York sociologist who studies the working poor. Many of those jobs no longer exist. Over the years, employers have outsourced positions such as cafeteria server, security guard, and janitor that once might have offered a chance to move up.
 Outsourcing and aggressive outside hiring have made many enterprises more efficient and profitable. But these trends raise the risk of workers in low-wage jobs getting trapped there. Annette Bernhardt, a sociologist at New York University Law School, studied the salaries of thousands of workers over nearly 40 years. She found that 12% of workers who started in the labor market in the late 1960s and early 1970s remained stuck in low-wage jobs 10 to 15 years into their careers. But for workers who entered the labor market in the 1980s and early 1990s, that percentage had more than doubled, to 28%.

Unanticipated consequences of organizational actions at times are progressive in nature. The military forces of the United States provide an important example. Since the close of World War II, the United States military services have carried out successive antidiscrimination mandates. Under orders from President Truman, the military services ended racial segregation in the late 1940s; under President Clinton in the 1990s, open discrimination against gays was outlawed. Women now attend elite military academies and attain sought-after positions.

The military services are not known as "liberal" organizations; they carried out antidiscrimination moves because they were ordered to do so by commanders in chief. Still, by allowing traditionally excluded persons to enjoy stable careers and enter leadership positions, which were often continued in civilian life, the armed forces of the United States contributed to progressive social change—however inadvertently.

The above discussion illustrates some of the means by which organizations affect the broader society merely through internal actions and decisions. The actions described here reflected rather than initiated conflicts in American society. Neither the corporation nor the military services invented sexism and racism. But their actions have in one case helped perpetuate and in the other alleviated long-standing social wrongs. Actions by organizations *intended* to have effects outside their boundaries may reflect more direct initiative.

Environmental Management

A second process by which organizations influence the surrounding society may be termed "environmental management." Organizations, particularly large ones, seek to influence aspects of the social environment that are relevant to their objectives. Effort of this kind is most visible when focused on influencing government. Large organizations, and some smaller ones, are continually active in attempting to sway legislation, court cases, and the operating policies of public bureaucracies. Environmental management sometimes takes the form of spearheading change, and at other times of preventing it.

The environmental management process resembles inadvertent social influence, discussed earlier, in one respect: the organizations involved do not deliberately seek to change society at large. Yet, like inadvertent social influence, this mechanism may leave a strong mark on the broader society. Regime change engineered by United Fruit Company (assuming the charges were true) would constitute an example. A business firm of this kind would likely have no interest in changing Guatemalan society *per se*. The firm would only need to install a president favorable to its business interests, and it could easily leave broader social issues (such as church activities and family relationships) untouched. Yet the weakening of the country's political institutions through outside interference could leave a lasting legacy of political instability.

Within the United States, the degree to which corporations are able to control government is uncertain. Two themes have appeared in research on organizations engaged in environmental management. The first, to be referenced here as "coalition dominance," emphasizes the possibility that dominant organizations band together in an enduring relationship. They use this relationship to exercise comprehensive control over government actions relevant to their concerns. In this way of thinking, no single organization may exercise complete dominance. However, a community of interest exists among powerful organizations, which, over time, results in bringing about the actions they desire.

According to some formulations, large corporations dominate American society through coalitions cemented by interlocking directorates and interpersonal ties. In this way, the same individuals may participate in the leadership of several organizations. Informal ties develop among these individuals, which further advance interorganizational coordination. Davis and Mizruchi summarize this outlook as follows:[15]

> In corporate governance, the economic and the social are inextricably linked. Board members are typically recruited from among friends and acquaintances of current directors. Conversely, relations that begin as economic ties often become overlaid with social relations and the resulting social structures shape corporate decision making. Board interlocks, created when two firms share a director, may reflect a number of economic and social influences ranging from co-opting powerful suppliers to extending relations from golf

course to board room. Regardless of their origins, they lend a social organization to the economy that in turn influences economic and political decisions.

Consistent with this thinking is the image of large organizations as members of an exclusive "club," which hammers out political differences in private and acts with little, if any, accountability to the broader society. Jennifer Abbott and Mark Achbar highlighted a similar concern in their 2003 documentary film, *The Corporation*. This film portrayed a world dominated by major firms, whose leaders worked out business plans covering the entire planet in secretive bodies such as the World Trade Association (WTA). In their pursuit of profits, corporations were reported to have taken over the water supplies of impoverished countries and claimed copyright protection over the genotypes of seeds that had supplied food for Third World peasants for perhaps millennia.

An alternative outlook, however, known as "democratic pluralism," sees the world of organizational involvement in politics as less effectively coordinated. This perspective also recognizes that organizations seek to control their environments by participation in coalitions. But this outlook views the coalitions as unstable and ad hoc. The corporations, moreover, do not always control the coalitions, and the ones that include the most powerful corporations do not always win.

To provide detailed insights into the way organizations actually influence their environments, Knock[16] reports research on "lobbying coalitions" that supported or opposed significant pieces of labor legislation during the 1980s. Three legislative measures were studied: a bill raising the federal minimum wage, a bill requiring business to provide family leave to employees, and a bill establishing a special board to inform workers of disease and chemical hazards at the workplace. Participants in the ensuing struggles included proponents such as the American Civil Liberties Union, the National Organization for Women, and a number of key labor organizations. On the opposing side were the National Chamber of Commerce, the National Association of Manufacturers, and the Business Roundtable.

Knock characterizes coalitions of these and other organizations as interorganizational networks that exchanged information and coordinated activity needed for support or opposition. Activities of this kind included research on legislation, contacting public officials, placing and paying for political advertising, testifying at hearings, and organizing letter-writing campaigns and demonstrations. Coalitions were effective because they ensured that the same message was delivered to policymakers repeatedly and from different immediate sources.

Knock's research on coalitions does not suggest the existence of a permanent clique of dominant organizations, a cohesive capitalist class that rules through organizational means, or a dominant labor lobby. In the lobbying contests he followed, pro-labor coalitions won as many rounds as did those dominated by business. Knock's synthesis suggests that coalitions of organizations have a fluid quality. He summarizes the ebb and flow of coalitions during the period he studied as follows:

> Very few prominent coalitions were institutionalized as permanent fixtures on the policy scene.... Most often [collaborating organizations] were constructed as short-term coalitions to fight collectively over a specific

policy event, then to disband after political authorities rendered their decision. Subsequently, new [coalitions] coalesced, composed of different participants lured by the particular policy interests at stake in a new policy proposal.

Deliberate Social Change

Deliberate social change is often striking in speed and scope. Revolutionary parties and rebel armies are the most obvious examples of organizations seeking massive social change. The 20th century furnished examples of revolutionary organizations well known to history, several of which caused extreme suffering for those who came under their rule.

In the best known of these episodes, revolutionary organizations brought about extreme changes in Germany and Russia—many of which, to the relief of people worldwide, proved temporary. Hitler used his National Socialist Party to attain power. In pre-Nazi Germany, the Party formulated and disseminated propaganda, organized youth groups, campaigned in elections, and conducted negotiations with government officials. Through a paramilitary subunit known as the Brownshirts, the Party carried out violent raids against its political opponents. Following his rise to power, Hitler deployed the Party apparatus and the Brownshirts to crush dissident elements in German society.[17] Because all significant government functionaries and army officers were required to join the Party or swear allegiance to it, Hitler was able to use the German government bureaucracy to carry out the Party's social program of totalitarianism and genocide.

Another episode providing stark illustration of the ability of an organization to bring about social change took place in 1917, during a series of revolutionary events in Russia. This organization was the Communist Party of the Soviet Union. Formed prior to the 1917 revolution that overthrew the Russian monarchy, the Party's precursor organization held that only a small, secretive body of dedicated revolutionaries could succeed in the forthcoming struggle for power. Strict discipline enabled the Party to take power after the Czar's fall. Paralleling the history of Nazi Germany, the Soviet Communist Party required key individuals in all social institutions to join, ensuring control by the Party's central decision makers over industry, media, science, the arts, and the military. Party personnel known as *commissars* were installed in factories, military units, and research installations to ensure that activities and communications conformed to the "party line." The Communist Party organization enabled leaders such as V. I. Lenin and Joseph Stalin to control every aspect of Soviet life.[18]

The Nazi and Communist dictatorships well illustrate the ability of organizations to deliberately transform society. Other revolutionary organizations were also effective but significantly more constructive. The Turkish revolution of the early 20th century, which transformed Turkey from a religiously based monarchy to a modern, secular state provides an example.

Turkey fought on the side of Germany and Austria in World War I. Following her defeat in this war, parts of Turkey were occupied by foreign troops. Turkey faced the prospect of being divided into a multitude of separate states, as had been done to Austria. Groups of army officers who organized under the leadership of General

Mustafa Kemal (who was later given the name "Ataturk") deposed the still-reigning sultan, who was willing to see the country divided, and drove out the foreign armies.

Much favor can be found in this revolution. The Ataturk regime established a parliament, ended the dominance of Islamic law, required children to attend secular schools, adopted a Roman script for the Turkish language, advocated Western dress, and eventually gave women the right to vote.[19] A political party spearheaded by the army controlled the republic from its establishment in 1923 until 1950, when an opposition party was legalized and was elected to power.

The Turkish army, however, remained a continuing and powerful force. Still today, this organization considers itself the guarantor of the secular, moderate republic established by Ataturk. Periodically, Turkey has experienced threats from extremists, either leftist or Islamist. At such times, the army has declared martial law, dismissed civilian officials, and promoted formation of a new secular and moderate government. In a strikingly repetitive cycle, the Turkish army dismissed civilian governments in 1960, 1971, and 1980.

The success of Turkey's revolution affected events beyond that country's own borders. Throughout the Middle East, military officers wishing to unseat a reigning monarch looked to Turkey as a model. Engineered by military officers, revolutions and coups in such nations as Egypt gave rise to the secular states that they are today. Decades after these revolutions, the top decision-making bodies in several Middle Eastern countries were still called "Revolutionary Command Councils," the name given by Ataturk to his initial cabinet.

Social change in the United States has seldom, if ever, resulted from efforts of a single organization intent on such an objective. The pluralism that dominates American society helps account for this. The United States has many more separate ethnic and religious groups and followers of distinct lifestyles than the countries described above. Consistent with this picture, networks and coalitions of diverse organizations have been most effective. It is difficult to identify an organization as instigator of the American Revolution, which, in fact, was brought about by a number of independent forces. In any case, organizations in the modern sense were rare during the colonial era.

The movement in the United States to abolish slavery illustrates the manner in which networks and coalitions function as agents of social change. By the middle of the 19th century, the abolitionist movement comprised over 1,000 separate organizations, two political parties, and thousands of independently planned actions, both legal and illegal. The pluralistic nature of American efforts at social change was also noticeable in the 20th-century civil rights movement. In that movement, several large and distinct organizations sometimes collaborated and sometimes acted independently. As the movement matured, tactics changed from disruption to electoral politics,[20] the success of which in the United States nearly always depends on coalition formation.

Direct efforts at social change involve direct interorganizational competition. The years preceding Hitler's rise were marked by street brawls between paramilitary units of the National Socialist Party and armed trade union members and Communists. Prosecution of the Soviet Communist agenda involved bloody confrontations with opposing organizations, a vicious civil war, and wave after wave of purges. In the United States, abolitionists faced harassment and incarceration.

Southern police departments confronted civil rights demonstrators with fire hoses, police dogs, and truncheons. The organizations involved represented directly the underlying social divisions.

Formal organizations have definite impact on the surrounding society. But few, if any, have deliberately, comprehensively, and permanently transformed a society to fit their preferences or needs. It has not been demonstrated that coalitions of large business firms in the United States have been able to control government and policy. Perrow's indictment of large U.S. business organizations in the 19th century, furthermore, is not completely convincing. Large-scale industrialization (necessarily involving large-scale organization) has been a global phenomenon, suggesting that it is not imposed by trickery or force, but embraced for its ability to raise living standards in the long run. Organizations both in earlier eras and today have tried to transform society. In at least one revolutionary situation, that of Germany in 1933, large firms supported the Nazi takeover. But it is difficult to cast today's revolutionary forces as allies of big business. The organizations fomenting insurrection in modern Africa and Latin America, for example, in no way fit this description.

The Multinational Firm: A Case of Management Without Control

Of great concern in the 21st century is the possibility that large organizations operating on a worldwide scale may replace not just communities but entire nations as the key players on the world stage. This issue is a frequent focus of social commentary, analysis, and public protest.[21–23] Of concern has been the possibility that multinational corporations (MNCs) might dominate national economies. In addition, it has been feared that multinational firms will attain political power greater than the nations in which they do business. Thus, world power would no longer be vested in sovereign nations accountable to their citizens. Rather, MNCs whose financing and political power outstripped all but the largest countries would set aside workers' rights, remove environmental safeguards, and undermine national economies. This scenario recalls the United Fruit Company in the last century, re-created on a global scale today.

It is important to exercise vigilance over MNCs. However, a number of considerations raise issues about the likelihood of world dominance. Areas to be taken into consideration include

- The structure of multinational firms, which militates against formation of central decision-making cadres with unlimited power
- The continuing influence of local environments on units of the multinationals
- The relationships among executives at different levels of the MNC
- The dynamics of the global environment

In addition, the possibility exists that there is a fundamental limit beyond which human beings cannot be brought under the direction of a single organization. Examples have appeared throughout this book regarding the limitations of the organizational mechanisms of coordination and cohesion that are at the disposal of a management cadre. Thus, organization on a global scale may itself prove limited.

The possibility of global domination by multinational firms envisages a high degree of centralization within individual organizations and a stable collaboration among major multinationals. One might imagine a CEO at headquarters (HQ) in New York, London, or Tokyo reaching a decision and dispatching messages to subordinate managers throughout the world ordering implementation. Some important evidence suggests that this image might not reflect current reality and may never, in fact, be possible.

The Structure and Dynamics of Multinationals

Although a great deal of variation can be seen in the structure of MNCs, divisionalized arrangements appear to predominate. The structure most frequently observed in MNCs today resembles that described by A. D. Chandler (see Chapter 5). Under this structure, HQ does not make operating or tactical decisions for geographically distant units. These are delegated to division managers. Within this structure, HQ provides capital and makes strategic decisions. Such decisions involve, among other things, whether an overseas division is sufficiently profitable to merit continued investment and whether the division continues to act in a manner consistent with HQ's strategic plan.

Concretely, most MNCs operate as systems of subsidiaries. Headquarters may acquire controlling interest in an overseas firm and transform it into a subsidiary. This procedure enables the MNC to acquire a unit that already has local recognition and a local consumer base. In addition, the MNC acquires a unit that is already in compliance with the country's legal requirements and whose management is already in place. Subsidiaries may also be started from scratch. The largest among MNCs can have over 100 subsidiaries, as is true of Citibank at this writing, with 181 subsidiaries in 181 countries.

Ordinarily, management of the subsidiary is placed in the hands of locals. Cohesion is encouraged by bringing local managers to HQ on multiyear assignment and sending HQ-based personnel to foreign subsidiaries on a rotating basis. Assignments such as these promote networking. They help the foreign managers adopt the culture of the firm as a whole and enable managers from HQ to appreciate the challenges faced by the subsidiary.

Actual participation by HQ personnel in management of the subsidiary may take place in certain instances. Thus, the degree of decentralization in the MNC varies over time.[24] By the same token, managers of the overseas subsidiaries can exercise an important degree of independence from HQ. According to one report, subsidiary managers have been willing and able to significantly loosen their bonds with the multinational.[25] Purchase of a local firm by a multinational, for example, can be reversed. Managers of subsidiaries have raised sufficient capital to buy out the subsidiary from the multinational. In such instances, the multinational's subunit is "de-internationalized."

The structure and associated dynamics of the MNC (see Figure 15.1) is inconsistent with the image of a CEO at HQ autonomously calling the shots. Rather,

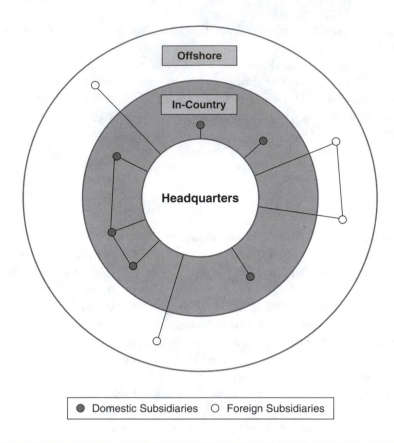

Figure 15.1   Geographic Distribution and Structure in the Multinational Corporation

management at the overseas divisions is capable of exercising important forms of initiative. Not only can managers at subsidiaries challenge HQ, they can utilize ties with other subsidiaries, forming lateral alliances. In addition, the impact of environments in which MNCs operate, both local and global, make push-button control from HQ unlikely.

The Challenge of Competing Mandates

The fact that semiautonomous subsidiary executives must respond to the environments in which they operate creates a continuing challenge to the MNC's integration. *Integration* in this sense means a favorable balance between HQ and subsidiary objectives. Stated otherwise, a well-integrated MNC enables subsidiaries to function effectively in their national environments, while allowing HQ to pursue a global strategy. The most favorable strategies at each level are seldom perfectly compatible.

A classic study by Doz and Prahalad reports a number of difficulties that executives encounter in "reaching an appropriate balance between national responsiveness and multinational integration."[26] For the CEO of an MNC, this requires fostering consensus among managers with multinational and national responsibilities. This task becomes especially difficult in MNCs with numerous subsidiaries.

Balance must be achieved among the concerns of multiple negotiation partners. Maintaining this balance is a continuous challenge, whose particulars are in constant flux. Doz and Prahalad comment: "Very seldom can a clear, exclusive, once-for-all choice between responsiveness and integration be made."

A high potential for conflict and suboptimal decision making thus exists within the MNC. The volume and variety of information reaching HQ defies human analytical capability. Opportunities for self-interest abound, as managers at various levels jockey to promote their unit's well-being or forge a personal career pathway into top management at the HQ. Under such conditions, the firm's CEO serves the MNC best by acting in the manner of a true "executive" (see Chapter 6). Doz and Prahalad remark that "top management should devote more attention to how decisions are made than to what decisions are actually made in the various businesses and countries in which the firms operate." Creating a favorable decision-making process may require applying conflict resolution tools, maintaining open channels of communication, and balancing the power of individual executives at both the HQ and subsidiary level.

It is not surprising, then, that the actual character of the MNC reflects the influences of both HQ and subsidiaries. Almond, Edwards, Colling, et al.,[27] for example, report the "home country," where the HQ is located, attempts to export its structure and practices abroad. Exports of this nature from the United States include the divisionalized structure itself and emphasis on enhancement of stockholder value. U.S.-style management practice tends to be hostile toward collective representation by workers, as embodied in the practice of codetermination (see Chapter 13). U.S.-headquartered MNCs have pushed for policies against discrimination and in favor of diversity. Home country influence is particularly strong when HQ is in a dominant position regarding capital and technology.

Host country influences, however, have often been strong. Many European countries, for example, have laws that make it much more difficult to dismiss an employee than in the United States. Strong European unions have much more influence over establishment and operation of pay grades.

Differences between the home and host countries of an MNC are another dimension of the conflict between global integration and national responsiveness. Just as concerns of subsidiary managers may differ from those of the multinational, local practices sometimes converge and sometimes diverge from those desired by HQ. The oscillation of home and host influences is inconsistent with the notion of a home-country-based boss pulling the strings. Instead, resistance to control seems to be a continual occurrence. As Almond et al. remark,

> Different actors at all levels of the organization will always retain some scope to pursue aims and goals of their own. Even where actors at corporate level issue explicit guidelines or edicts, these may sometimes be circumvented or interpreted liberally [by the subsidiary's managers]. There is, of course, a wealth of evidence from the organizational sociology literature on the space that actors possess within institutional constraints.[27]

It is significant that Almond et al. emphasize resistance to control at the managerial level. Ironically, the same basic phenomenon observed among operatives in American factories appears to take place among high-level international business managers. The widely observed tendency of people at any level to identify and pursue their own goals irrespective of the goals of those above them may constitute the limiting factor in any organization, no matter how local or global.

The Global Environment

It is important to observe in closing that the present global environment of internationalism and free trade did not develop independently of national governments. Rather, this climate was fostered by governments that, like the United States, thought it would be favorable to their national interests. For example, a network of bilateral trade treaties has created conditions favorable to MNCs. Such agreements allow profits earned by subsidiaries to be returned to the home countries without excessive taxation by the hosts. In this sense, the MNC has not superseded the state.

The potential of today's MNCs to increase indefinitely in scope and power must be assessed in the light of other historical periods during which internationalism thrived. Global economic integration is not necessarily permanent. As a reviewer of recent works on globalization has commented,

> The global economy that existed prior to World War I was in many respects more open and borderless than the one that exists today. Even so it collapsed, and in a process that culminated in [very strict tariff legislation in the United States] was replaced by the semi-autarchic closed economies of the interwar years. However securely established it may seem, globalization is not irreversible. Indeed, over time its disruptive effects tend to result in deglobalization.[28]

The "disruptive effects" referred to here include loss of jobs to low-wage countries and dependence on these countries for manufactured goods. States can be counted upon to ensure their own economic stability. If heads of state (or the electorate in democratic countries) believe they are becoming too dependent on imports, they will reduce their involvement in the global economy. Such action by multiple countries could substantially reduce the scope of operation enjoyed by today's MNCs.

Chapter Review and Major Themes

Much research and discussion of organizations has focused on internal processes and ensuring a fit between the organization and its members. But organizations can have far-reaching effects on the surrounding society. These effects can be inadvertent, as organizations change life experience in the surrounding society through the products they disseminate. Changes in society may also occur due to an organization's efforts to manage its environment, for example, by influencing laws and regulations that apply to its business. Finally, organizations can directly seek to bring about social change, as do those with ideological or revolutionary purposes.

Recently, concern has emerged that the essential dynamics of large organizations have come to place individual autonomy, community, and democratic institutions at risk. Recent research on political competition, however, does not indicate that stable coalitions of large business organizations dominate American politics. It is difficult to conceive of a functional substitute for the large formal organization. High productivity may have at one time been attained by networks of small organizations. But industrialization today depends in all countries on large formal organizations.

Critics have raised the possibility that MNCs may come to dominate world politics and economics. Studies of the structures and processes that characterize today's MNCs, however, suggest that this is far from certain. Organization of today's MNCs involves considerable decentralization. Executives of offshore subsidiaries of MNCs sometimes attain substantial independence. Governments, moreover, are likely to protect their sovereignty, taking steps to circumscribe the operations of MNCs should they believe that these organizations challenge their power and security.

The ability of MNCs to achieve global integration depends on the presence of a favorable global environment. Integration, in this sense, involves the MNC's ability to concentrate the efforts of its subsidiaries on global objectives, increase the organization's function, and reduce conflict. As illustrated in Figure 15.2, though, the global environment can have a strong positive or negative effect on global integration within an MNC. The presence of favorable bilateral treaties between home and host countries promotes the MNC's ability to achieve integration. Withdrawal by states of their support of free trade policies would reduce the MNC's ability to operate effectively on a global scale.

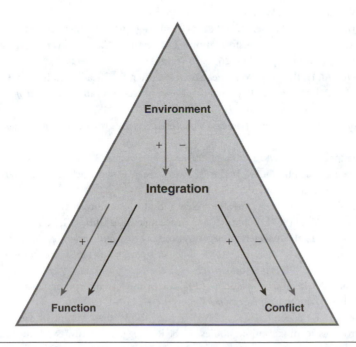

Figure 15.2   Analytical Perspectives Applied to Integration in a Multinational Firm

Discussion Questions

1. Other than producing goods, services, and profits to shareholders, do large business organizations have responsibilities to the surrounding society? What responsibilities can be identified? How should they be fulfilled?

2. Is the dominance of large organizations in the United States today truly detrimental to the well-being of ordinary Americans?

3. Of the theories discussed in Chapter 3, which would best explain the predominance of divisionalized structure within multinational firms?

4. Many nonprofit organizations today are multinational. How similar would you expect their structures to be to those of profit-seeking multinational corporations? What management problems would you expect to be most prominent in them?

5. How can the multinational corporation of today be thought of as an illustration of "management without control"? Can principles observed in the multinational firm be applied to organizations whose operations are entirely domestic?

References

1. Packard, V. O. (1957). *The hidden persuaders.* New York: McKay.
2. Institute of Medicine. (1994). *Growing up tobacco free: Preventing nicotine addiction in children and youths.* Washington, DC: Author.
3. Aldrich, H. E., & Stabler, U. (1988). Organizing business interests: Patterns of trade association foundings, transformations, and death. In G. Carroll (Ed.), *Ecological models of organizations* (pp. 111–126) New York: Ballinger.
4. Greenwald, H. P., Beery, W. L., Pearson, D., Senter, S., Cheadle, A., Nelson, G. D., et al. (2003). Polling and policy analysis as resources for advocacy. *Journal of Public Administration Research and Theory, 13,* 177–191.
5. Elliott, S. (2006, June 29). Forecaster cuts estimate for growth in ad spending. *New York Times,* p. C13.
6. Schlesinger, S. C., & Kinzer, S. (1999). *Bitter fruit: The story of the American coup in Guatemala.* Cambridge, MA: Harvard University, David Rockefeller Center for Latin American Studies.
7. Mills, C. W. (1956). *The power elite.* New York: Oxford University Press.
8. Domhoff, W. J. (1967). *Who rules America?* Englewood Cliffs, NJ: Prentice Hall.
9. Perrow, C. (1991). A society of organizations. *Theory and Society, 20*(6), 725–762.
10. Perrow, C. (2002). *Organizing America: Wealth, power, and the crisis of corporate capitalism.* Princeton, NJ: Princeton University Press.
11. Hennings, C. R., & Greenwood, R. (2002). Disconnects and consequences in organization theory. *Administrative Science Quarterly, 43,* 114–130.
12. Calas, M. B., & Smircich, L. (1994). From "the woman's point of view": Feminist approaches to organization studies. In S. R. Clegg, C. Hardy, & W. R. Nord (Eds.), *Handbook of organization studies* (pp. 218–257). Thousand Oaks, CA: Sage.

13. Philips, K. (1990). *The politics of rich and poor.* New York: Random House.
14. Millman, J. (2005, June 6). Promotion track fades for those starting at the bottom. *Wall Street Journal,* p. 1.
15. Davis, G. F., & Mizruchi, M. S. (1999). The money center cannot hold: Commercial banks in the U.S. system of governance. *Administrative Science Quarterly, 44,* 215–239.
16. Knoke, D. (2001). *Changing organizations: Business networks in the new political economy* (p. 354). Boulder, CO: Westview Press.
17. Shirer, W. L. (1990). *Rise and fall of the Third Reich.* New York: Simon & Schuster.
18. Lincoln, W. B. (1989). *Red victory: A history of the Russian civill war.* New York: Simon & Schuster.
19. Collier, J. F. (1996). Intertwined histories: Islamic law and Western imperialism. *Scandinavian Economic History Review, 5*(1), 1–10.
20. Andrews, K. T. (2001). Social movements and policy implications. *American Sociological Review, 66*(1), 75–97.
21. Vernon, R. (1971). *Sovereignty at bay: The multinational spread of U.S. enterprises.* New York: Basic Books.
22. Korten, D. C. (2001). *When corporations rule the world.* San Francisco: Berrett-Koehler.
23. Chandler, A. D., & Mazlish, B. (Eds.). (2005). *Leviathans: Multinational corporations and the new global history.* New York: Cambridge University Press.
24. Shanley, M. (1996). Straw men and m-form myths: Comment on Freeland. *American Journal of Sociology, 102*(2), 527–536.
25. Griffin, R. (2003). *The loosely bound subsidiary: A case of subsidiary management buy-out.* Sixth McGill Conference on International Entrepreneurship, September 19–22. Montreal: McGill University.
26. Doz, Y. L., & Prahalad, C. K. (1984). Patterns of strategic control within multinational corporations. *Journal of International Business Studies, 15*(2), 55–72.
27. Almond, P., Edwards, T., Colling, T., Ferner, A., Gunnigle, P., Muller-Camen, M., et al. (2005). Unraveling home and host country effects: An investigation of the HR policies of an American multinational in four European countries. *Industrial Relations, 44*(2), 276–306.
28. Gray, J. (2006). The global delusion. *New York Review of Books, 53*(7), pp. 20ff.

Glossary

Administrator. A role whose incumbent advances organizational objectives by implementing internal requirements and procedures, supervising support staff, and dealing on routine matters with outside vendors and agencies.

Authority. A form of imperative force considered legitimate according to the beliefs and values of a social system; the capacity to impel others to set aside personal preferences and judgment about how to behave in a given situation that is voluntarily accepted by those subject to it.

Boundary-spanner. An organizational role whose incumbents either encourage others to communicate outside customary channels or transmit information between individuals and between subunits not normally in direct contact.

Bureaucracy. An organization characterized by features including rules binding on the actions of all members; hierarchical supervision; specialization of personnel; prohibition of personal gain other than fixed salaries; and continuous operation over time.

Channel. A communication pathway that guides the flow of information in an organization.

Charisma (adj. charismatic). Having visible appearance or capacities beyond those identifiable as purely human, often representing the Deity, reflective of His will or power, or expressing the identity, ethic, or aspirations of a people or nation; the basis of *charismatic* authority or leadership.

Circuit. See *Channel.*

Coercion. A form of imperative force under which one actor demands involuntary submission from another and threatens to inflict extraordinary punishment (often including violence) in the event of noncompliance.

Cognitive Dissonance. The presence of contradictory concepts, values, or perceptions in an individual's conscious mind.

Collectivity. A body of individuals directly or indirectly interacting with each other under a durable system of organization, including groups, families, and formal organizations.

Collegial. A classification of organizations whose individual members are not formally subordinated to others for at least some purposes, in which wide participation takes place in at least some decisions, or in which hierarchy plays only a minor role in day-to-day operations.

Community-Based Organization. An organization whose objectives concentrate on protection or betterment of a defined residential community, whose leadership and membership are drawn from the community it serves, and which is accountable (though not exclusively) to that community.

Co-optation. The process by which a dominant leadership structure invites either formal leaders of a less powerful organization or informal leaders in the same organization to cooperate with it in exchange for resources or forbearance from sanctions.

Discipline. n. Habitual, rapid obedience to instructions. v. To apply corrective procedures for disobedience or noncompliance with operating procedures or rules.

Equilibrium. A state of mutual acceptance within an organization in which minimum objectives of all potential adversaries (subunits, role sets, etc.) are being met and challenges to the status quo are discouraged.

Ethics. Obligations of individuals to act toward others in a manner consistent with socially reinforced values.

Executive. A role not involving supervision of operating units, but focusing on the organization's purpose; communication, cohesion, and cooperation among managers; and maintaining the performance of the organization as a whole.

Focal Person. The individual who occupies a role. Synonym for *role incumbent.*

Function. The contribution made by formal organization to the broader society; the contribution made by a role incumbent, subunit, or process to maintenance of the organization or achievement of its objectives.

Goal. A widely recognized, though typically general, purpose toward which an organization aims.

Group. A collectivity comprising a number of people who feel a sense of common purpose or interest, distinguish themselves from people outside the group, and can, when necessary, identify or appoint a leader. Typically, groups arise spontaneously; they seldom have explicit membership requirements or operating procedures. See also *Primary Group.*

Imperative Force. An individual or group capacity for compelling others to set aside personal preferences and judgment regarding action in a particular situation. *Imperative force* is meant to capture Weber's concept of *herrschaft;* it may include power, authority, discipline, or coercion.

Instrumental. A type of reward valued for the purpose of getting something done or pursuing objectives inside or outside the organizational role other than job performance.

Internal Labor Market. The availability of opportunities within an organization in the form of job ladders that provide the means for advancement in the hierarchy, increased income, and secure employment.

Isomorphism. The tendency of organizations with the same objectives or sharing membership in the same organizational field to develop similarities in roles, structure, capacities, and expectations regarding each other's behavior.

Manager. An organizational role including responsibility for the achievements, prosperity, and survival of operating units, participating in setting objectives, and obtaining resources for these units.

Norm. A prescription for action based on values or traditions of a collectivity or society; behavioral standard expected of individuals.

Norm of Reciprocity. A standard of behavior stating that individuals should reciprocate acts of kindness and largess by others, for example, by "giving back" high job performance in exchange for high rewards.

Objective. A specific, often measurable, outcome in whose pursuit organizations allocate their resources.

Operative. Individuals in a work organization who perform routine duties and exercise no supervision of others. In industrial plants, employees who do routine, repetitive, often machine-paced work.

Organization. A body of individuals working under a defined system of rules, assignments, procedures, and relationships designed to achieve identifiable goals. Synonymous with *formal organization.*

Organizational Field. The set of all organizations involved in a particular activity, such as education, health care, or government, whose expectations promote uniformity of structure and process among individual organizations.

Organizational Learning. Lessons from the organization's experiments and ventures, both successful and unsuccessful, that are retained by the organization via absorption into its culture and reflection in its structure.

Organizational Slack. Resources available for discretionary expenditure in an organization, including money, vacant space, and personnel whose time is not fully occupied.

Organizational Structure. A pattern of linkages among roles in an organization.

Patrimonial. A classification of hierarchical organization in which superiors justify their authority over subordinates through claims of personal loyalty, based on grounds including personal favors, family, culture, religion, or history.

Power. A form of imperative force under which an individual or collectivity has the ability, legitimate or otherwise, to force others to act in a manner inconsistent with or contrary to their own judgment, inclination, or will.

Primary Group. A group whose members know each other in great depth through long personal acquaintance, as among people who have grown up in the same neighborhood or worked together for extended periods of time.

Rationalization. The fitting together of resources and activities into a consistent whole for the purpose of achieving objectives; for example, by dividing required operations into routine tasks and arranging these tasks into an appropriate system.

Received Role. The role as perceived by the focal person based on information transmitted by the role set.

Role. What an individual in an organization or other collectivity thinks and does in relation to others; a prescription for recurring behavior interrelated with the activities of others.

Role Ambiguity. Uncertainty by the focal person about his or her duties, place in the organization, and expected contribution to the organization's objectives.

Role Conflict. Perceived inconsistency in role expectations associated with each role occupied by an individual.

Role Expectations. The consensus of beliefs by members of an organization regarding actions and communication behavior expected by the incumbent of a given role; what others expect of the person occupying a role. Often, these expectations mirror those of the broader society.

Role Others. Members of a person's role set.

Role Sending. The process by which members of a role set transmit their expectations to the incumbent (focal person) in a role.

Role Set. The persons with whom an individual interacts in order to fulfill role expectations.

Socioemotional. A type of reward or value from membership in a collectivity consisting of good feelings about the collectivity or its members, including the company of others or encouragement, recognition, or comfort from them. A variety of leadership emphasizing maintenance of the collectivity or subunit through socioemotional means.

Value. The individual's preference for a specific type of conduct, achievement, way of life, or relationship with other people, society as a whole, or the Deity.

Suggested Readings

The following is a brief, annotated bibliography of books and monographs on organizational behavior, theory, and practice. The items cited are an eclectic mix, intended to acquaint the reader with the range of book-length literature in these fields. Some of the works cited (e.g., *Social Psychology of Organizations*) are classics in the field; others (e.g., *Gainsharing and Power*) are more recent, rigorously researched studies with practical implications; still others (e.g., *Zapp!*) are of the easy-to-read, popular management variety. All have their place in helping readers understand and manage organizations.

Allison, G. T. (1971). *Essence of decision: Explaining the Cuban missile crisis.* Boston: Little, Brown.

A detailed account of decision making during an international crisis and examination of the development of "groupthink" in a governmental setting.

Byham, W. C., & Cox, J. (1989). *Zapp! The lightning of empowerment: How to improve productivity, quality, and employee satisfaction.* Pittsburgh, PA: Development Dimensions International Press.

A volume in the easy-to-read, popular management style, this book uses a mythical workplace to illustrate principles of leadership, communication, and team building.

Clark, J. (1991). *Democratizing development: The role of voluntary organizations.* West Hartford, CT: Kumarian Press.

Focusing on nongovernmental organizations (NGOs) in developing countries, this book identifies challenges and solutions with special reference to relationships with governments.

Clegg, S. R., Hardy, C., & Nord, W. R. (Eds.). (1996). *Handbook of organizational studies.* Thousand Oaks, CA: Sage.

Chapters in this edited volume cover specific subject areas in organizational theory, including several with a socially critical orientation, such as feminism and postmodernism.

Collins, D. C. (1998). *Gainsharing and power: Lessons from six Scanlon plans.* Ithaca, NY: ILR Press (Cornell University).

A study of applications of the Scanlon plan for combining group and individual incentives in six organizations, this volume provides practical advice for administering such plans and the type of management practice they require.

Collins, J. C. (2001). *Good to great: Why some companies make the leap—and others don't.* New York: HarperCollins.

Based on a series of well-researched case studies, this book identifies dimensions of leadership, executive ability, strategic planning, and organizational change that have distinguished the most successful business firms.

Daft, R. L., & Lengel, R. H. (1998). *Fusion leadership: Unlocking the subtle forces that change people and organizations.* San Francisco: Berrett-Koehler.

Another book in the popular management style, this volume provides advice on leadership through involvement and collaboration.

Denhardt, R. B., Denhardt, J. V., & Aristigueta, M. P. (2002). *Managing human behavior in public & nonprofit organizations.* Thousand Oaks, CA: Sage.

Widely used as a textbook in public administration, this volume applies basic organizational principles to public and nonprofit settings.

Downs, A. (1967). *Inside bureaucracy.* Boston: Little, Brown.

Concentrating on the Washington, DC, government bureaucracy, this book provides guidelines for success of administrative officials in areas such as cross-checking information from alternative sources.

Dunnette, M. D., & Hough, L. M. (Eds.). *Handbook of industrial and organizational psychology.* Palo Alto, CA: Consulting Psychologists Press.

This volume provides a comprehensive review of psychological principles applied to organizations; chapters cover key concerns such as organizational development and change.

Goleman, D. (1995). *Emotional intelligence.* New York: Bantam Books.

A seminal book on the ability of individuals to achieve empathy with others and the importance of this capability to success in organizations.

Hannan, M. T., & Freeman, J. (1989). *Organizational ecology.* Cambridge, MA: Harvard University Press.

A pioneering work, this book focuses on impersonal forces that shape organizations and influence their entry and exit from the organizational field.

Hickman, G. R. (Ed.). (1998). *Leading organizations: Perspectives for a new era.* Thousand Oaks, CA: Sage.

This book is a set of chapters authored by prominent organizational theorists; it focuses on a potential shift in organizations from hierarchical structures to networks of colleagues and implications for leadership.

Hummel, R. P. (1977). *The bureaucratic experience*. New York: St. Martin's Press.

A study of bureaucracy with special emphasis on bureaucratic culture.

Jablin, F. M., & Putnam, L. L. (Eds.). (2001). *The new handbook of organizational communication: Advances in theory, research, and methods*. Thousand Oaks, CA: Sage.

A well-researched and comprehensive volume, this book contains separately authored chapters on areas such as structure and communication, the external environment, and the effects of new technology.

Katz, D., & Kahn, R. L. (1978). *The social psychology of organizations*. New York: John Wiley & Sons.

This is a well-written and highly comprehensive volume synthesizing experimental studies in social psychology to explain organizational behavior during the classic period of experimental social psychology; the work is limited in that it covers only research completed prior to 1978.

Kets de Vries, M. F. R., & Miller, D. (1984). *The neurotic organization*. San Francisco: Jossey-Bass.

A psychoanalytic approach to organizational behavior, this book applies concepts such as unconscious wishes, transference, and narcissism to the interpretation of relationships within formal organizations.

Meyer, M. W., & Zucker, L. G. (1989). *Permanently failing organizations*. Newbury Park, CA: Sage.

This book examines several organizations that, although they apparently serve the external environment poorly, are able to survive due to the support of a restricted set of stakeholders.

Oster, S. M. (1995). *Strategic management for nonprofit organizations: Theory and cases*. New York: Oxford University Press.

This book applies concepts of strategic management originally developed for profit-seeking organizations to nonprofits; it provides guidelines for successful strategic planning and competition.

Pfeffer, J. (1998). *The human equation: Building profits by putting people first*. Boston: Harvard Business School Press.

An easily comprehensible yet well-researched volume, this book provides a formula for improving human performance, which includes elements such as training, job security, and decentralization of teams.

Powell, W. W., & DiMaggio, P. J. (Eds.). (1991). *The new institutionalism in organizational analysis.* Chicago: University of Chicago Press.

One of the most important contributions to organization theory in the late 20th century, this book expands and updates traditional institutional theory.

Ritti, R. R. (1994). *The ropes to skip and the ropes to know: Studies in organizational behavior.* New York: John Wiley & Sons.

This book presents a fictional story about a young man entering an organization and discovering the secrets that enable it to operate and that contribute to or detract from the success of individuals; basic principles of organizational behavior are illustrated.

Scott, W. R. (1995). *Institutions and organizations.* Thousand Oaks, CA: Sage.

A review and update of institutional theory, this book represents a major contribution to understanding organizations and organization theory.

Shafritz, J. M., Ott, J. S., & Jang, Y. S. (Eds.). (2005). *Classics of organization theory.* Belmont, CA: Wadsworth.

Updated periodically, this book contains short passages from the best-known works in organizational behavior and theory.

Shortell, S. M., & Kaluzny, A. D. (Eds.). (2006). *Health care management: Organizational design and behavior.* Clifton Park, NY: Thomson Delmar Learning.

In this book, well-known writers on organizational behavior and theory apply basic principles to health care settings.

Vaughan, D. (1996). *The Challenger launch decision: Risky technology, culture, and deviance at NASA.* Chicago: University of Chicago Press.

In this well-known study, the author presents a detailed analysis of several agencies and subunits that were given the responsibility of cross-checking the flightworthiness of the space shuttle, and diagnoses the reasons for failure.

Weick, K. E. (1995). *Sensemaking in organizations.* Thousand Oaks, CA: Sage.

This book uses the classical concept of "sensemaking," originating with William James, and applies it through the thinking of a number of other theorists.

Index

About the Author

Howard P. Greenwald, Ph.D., is Professor, School of Policy, Planning, and Development, University of Southern California, and Clinical Professor, Social and Behavioral Sciences, School of Public Health, University of Washington. His academic honors include National Woodrow Wilson Fellow; Special Honors, Committee on General Studies in the Social Sciences, University of Chicago; Special Career Fellow, University of California, Berkeley; and Dissertation Fellow, Manpower Administration, United States Department of Labor. His research interests include organizational behavior and theory, public opinion, survey design and analysis, and program evaluation. He has served as director of USC's Health Services Administration Program, chairman of the Western Network for Education in Health Administration, director of the USC W. K. Kellogg Hispanic Leadership Program, and member of the executive board of the American Society for Public Administration (ASPA) in Sacramento, California. He consults widely for law enforcement agencies, health care providers, foundations, and community groups. His research has been published in *Administrative Science Quarterly, Journal of Public Administration Research and Theory, Public Administration Review, Journal of the American Public Health Association, Milbank Memorial Fund Quarterly,* and other academic periodicals. *The New York Times* and the *Wall Street Journal* have published his opinion pieces. His most recent books include *Who Survives Cancer?* and *Health for All: Making Community Collaboration Work,* coauthored with W. L. Beery.

Play Therapy

Where the Sky Meets the Underworld

of related interest

Play Therapy with Abused Children
Ann Cattanach
ISBN 1 85302 120 2 hb
ISBN 1 85302 193 8 pb

Chain Reaction
Children and Divorce
Ofra Ayalon and Adina Flasher
ISBN 1 85302 136 9

Storymaking in Education and Therapy
Alida Gersie and Nancy King
ISBN 1 85302 519 4 hb
ISBN 1 85302 520 8 pb

Symbols of the Soul
Therapy and Guidance Through Fairy Tales
Birgitte Brun, Ernst W Pederson and Marianne Runberg
Foreword by Murray Cox
ISBN 1 85302 107 5

Approaches to Case Study
A Handbook for Those Entering the Therapeutic Field
Robin Higgins
ISBN 1 85302 182 2

Groupwork with Children and Adolescents
A Handbook
Edited by Kedar Nath Dwivedi
Foreword by Dr Robin Skynner
ISBN 1 85302 157 1

Play Therapy
Where the Sky Meets the Underworld

ANN CATTANACH

Jessica Kingsley Publishers
London and Bristol, Pennsylvania

First published in the United Kingdom in 1994 by
Jessica Kingsley Publishers Ltd
116 Pentonville Road
London N1 9JB, England
and
1900 Frost Road, Suite 101
Bristol, PA 19007, U S A

Copyright © 1994 Ann Cattanach

Library of Congress Cataloging in Publication Data
Cattanach, Ann.
Play therapy: where the sky meets the underworld / Ann Cattanach.
p. cm.
Includes bibliographical references and index.
ISBN 1-85302-250-0 : ISBN 1-85302-211-X (pbk.)
1. Play therapy. I. Title.
RJ505.P6C379 1994
615.8'5153--dc20

British Library Cataloguing in Publication Data
Cattanach, Ann
Play Therapy: Where the Sky Meets the
Underworld
I. Title
616.891653

ISBN 1-85302-211-X (pb)

Printed and bound in Great Britain by
Biddles Ltd., Guildford and King's Lynn

Contents

CHAPTER 1

PLAY
A Mirror into the
World of the Child

Making and Creating a World Through Play

WAS IT NOT AN ILLUSION?
(*Uitoto / Columbia*)

'Nothing existed in the beginning. The Father reached towards an illusion. He encountered mystery. Nothing existed in the beginning...

Nothing was. How to support his dreaming? He spun the dream to a thread and held it. He was the dream's breath containing the emptiness, the illusion. He sought to reach for its base. He felt for its base. Nothing existed in the beginning...

Again the Father sought to reach the base of his dreaming. The father was one with the void and gathered it into his hands. Then he wove the dream thread into the dream. He intertwined them with gum, joining the dream-thread and the dream with the magical gum.

Then he seized the illusion, the base, and he trod upon it. He trod upon it repeatedly. Thus he seized the earth and flattened it. He flattened the dream earth.

Holding the dream, he let spittle flow and more spittle and more spittle. He let it flow from his mouth. Upon this flattened, illusory earth, he fastened the roof of the sky. He grasped his dream and made the blue sky and the white sky.

The maker of narratives sits where the sky meets the underworld. Thus the permission for this story's emergence was given. It was in our being when we were made.'

(Gersie 1992)

This myth powerfully describes a way of realising a world and the fragility and daring of such an enterprise. The process of realising a dream, of making a understandable world from the void, of daydreaming, wishing and wanting, mirrors the process explored by the child in play therapy. When a child first sets out to understand and order their experience, to make their world and make sense of their world through play therapy, there is a moment of beginning, a sense of the void;

'Nothing was. How to support his dreaming?'

The child explores the space in the room, the objects and forms offered by the therapist to help her make a fictional world. How to begin? What to choose? With what monsters and heroes to journey? What kind of world to create? A place which might mirror the world that was, is, or might possibly be in the future. All these worlds are dreams, fictional places explored within the safety of the playing space.

And in this space sit the child and the therapist. The child is the maker of narratives, the player of dramas. The therapist is the audience, listener, commentator and sometime player of dramas with the child. They meet in the playing space, which is the therapeutic space. This is a safe place and an adventurous place, although there are dangerous moments,

'where the sky meets the underworld'

but it should be the place where stories are made and heard, wishes and dreams are made and heard, and the child is respected and not abused.

The child, through play, makes a fictional world as a way to make sense of their real world and the paradox is that the myth-making capacity of the child helps to heal the real hurts experienced. Jane, aged fourteen, abused by a relative since she was a young child wrote:

> 'my life
> is trapped within a maze of mirrors
> Only these mirrors reflect images of the past
> so ugly and distorted
> that no reflection projects the same image…
> When I look in a mirror,
> I often see a bloodstained sky
> and a deadly sunset…
> How wonderful it would be to be free
> to be like a girl called Alice
> and walk through the looking glass.'

Perhaps this is the dream for us all, to be defended for ever from the pain of our experience;

> '"I see nobody on the road" said Alice.
>
> "I only wish *I* had such eyes" the King remarked in a fretful tone. "To be able to see Nobody! And at that distance too! Why, it's as much as *I* can do to see real people, by this light!
>
> All this was lost on Alice who was still looking intently along the road, shading her eyes with one hand' (Carroll 1941)

We must also remember that the world of play, the place where Alice goes, is an attractive device for the abuser of children as well as the abused child.

In his book *Child-Loving*, Kincaid (1992) describes the erotic delight of Alice as being the apparent child who is actually the adult, firmly in the world of power. Alice wants so badly to be grown up, she more or less is grown up now, was probably born grown up. Alice inhabits the world of play through the looking-glass but she is not at home with play and therein lies her erotic attractiveness. Kinkaid observes that we are welcomed into the magic world, enter easily – but find no child at home. Only Alice, the false child, resisting the play, telling us coldly at every turn of the game that we are being silly, that we must wake up, grow up.

What is attractive and elusive about Alice, the powerful adult/child in a playful Wonderland, is attractive and elusive both to Jane, the abused child, who wanted to be in Wonderland, to be a child and play, not to be the adult/child she had to be, and to the pedophile who saw that little girl in Jane and wanted to 'play' to corrupt. So Jane's mirrors now contain images of

> 'a bloodstained sky
> and a deadly sunset...'

and she begins a different, creative journey to find hope and self-affirmation instead of abuse and self-abasement. She mourns the loss of her childhood. Her abuser was found guilty in court and that is a beginning.

Humans as Myth Makers

Vandenberg (1986) describes humans as myth making and believing beings for whom reality is a trusted fantasy. To be human and to live in a meaningful way within a culture requires that we live in and through a very sophisticated, abstract system that is largely imaginary. To be incapable of fantasy is to be barred from human culture. Thus, in fantasy play, children display their human capacity as myth-making beings who create imaginary worlds that structure, energise and give meaning to experience. This close association between play and myth suggests that play therapy can be conceived as a process of providing children with new myths that more directly and successfully address the sources of fear and dread in their lives, and offer new hope. If this view is upheld, then play is a centrally important function in human life. Not only is play a manifestation of myth, it is also, to children, the overt expression of wish and hope, and play therapy is a method for utilising these attributes of play in a healing context.

Yalom (1975) described wish as the impetus for willing and action. He defined wish as the imaginary playing with the possibility of some act or state occurring, which is the first step in the process of willing. Only after wishing occurs can the individual initiate the remainder of the act of willing, commitment and choice, which culminates in action.

Play as a Manifestation of Myth

Sproul (1991), in her Introduction to *Primal Myths,* states that these myths proclaim the relativity of our reality. They express the fact that each thing that has life and being, and the totality of all such things, are limited and conditioned by their opposites: death, non-existence and not being. Myths use symbols and metaphors to make their point concretely. They temporalize and personalize and dramatize the arguments so people will understand.

May (1991) lists four contributions which myths make to our lives. First, myths give us our sense of personal identity; second, they make possible our sense of community; third, they undergird our moral values; and fourth, mythology is our way of dealing with the inscrutable mystery of creation. Sproul (1991) states that creation myths describe the reality of the Universe. A cosmic dance between being and not-being; matter coalescing and disintegrating; suns being born or blowing up; waters solidifying gradually into land or land dissolving into water; new trees growing out of rotting wood of their own kind; generations of people bearing and giving way to the next; and societies, like clusters of cells, growing and dying to others.

Figure 1.1 Island worlds. On this island is Ann, the Mother and Father

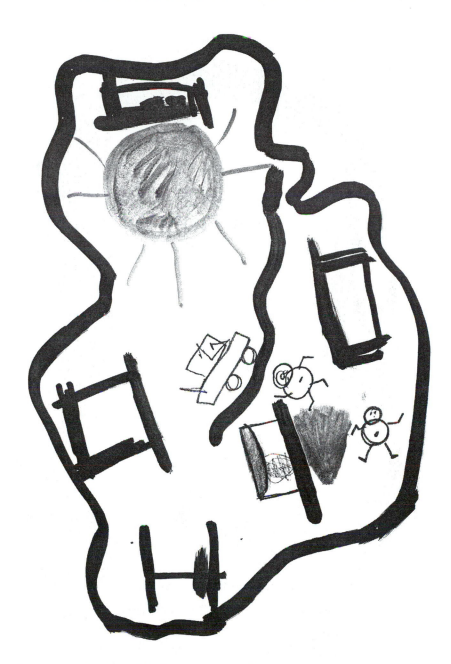

Figure 1.2 Island worlds. Sorting the world

Figure 1.3 Island worlds. Splitting the world

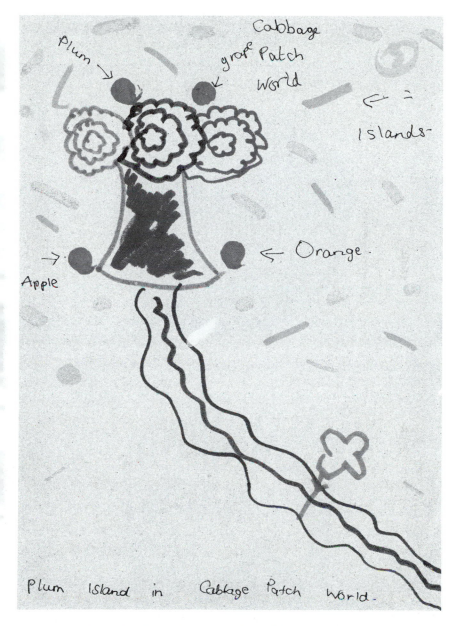

Figure 1.4 Plum island in cabbage patch world

Figure 1.5 The monster who falls on England

Figure 1.6 If I ruled the world

confusion
nervous
happy

Figure 1.7 The world in a face

Creating the Play Therapy World

If creation myths describe the reality of the whole universe, then the worlds the child creates in play are a microcosm of that cosmic dance.

The child and therapist explore those worlds of being and not-being, defining a self to cope with the enormity of the immediate world. Sometimes in those worlds the individual is lost in the ebb and flow. John, aged eight, defined his past world.

'There are two armies fighting, an endless battle, armies
coming and going in ever increasing waves, many soldiers dead
and buried under the earth, nothing but combat. Just rows and
rows of fighting men.'

He said that was what his past felt like, no place for him, but
anyway that's how the world really is. You have only to watch
the news on TV. He thought he existed somewhere in that ebb
and flow, trampled upon, lost, unheard but existing. He described more fully his place in this warring world:

'There was once a world where everybody was fighting. The
baby died because his mother couldn't find her. The mother
was on the back of the dragon. In this world all the animals
stay alive, but the people get dead. They kill each other and
all the animals rescue each other.'

Abigail's worlds shifted and changed many times, a mirror of her real
life moves.

'There was a nice little world. It had a big mountain, lots, lots,
lots of sea but it was all dried up and went for a walk in the
mountain then it went up to Heaven and stayed in Heaven.

The world fell down and it went away because it was too
boring and a new world came and went in a peaceful place,
very happy, not polluted.

Out of the sea came a kind dragon and he sat in a little corner
of the world and if anyone came to destroy it he would blow
them with his fire and take them to the land of naughtiness
and they would get a smack.

The dragon lived in the corner of the world. He was barricaded
in with his friends and lots of trees.

On the other side of the fence the goblins sit there doing their
naughty stuff; swearing and picking their noses.'

A corner of the world, a small place, is easier to contain.

> The world of Abigail is not a secure place, you have to defend your corner. No more moving on, says Abigail, even if now and again you have to go to the land of naughtiness and get a smack.

Singer (1986) states that a central assumption of most play therapy is that children, through make-believe transactions, will reveal either directly or in some symbolic form, their conflicts, unresolved wishes and fears. The research literature on imaginative development supports this view, in the sense that the child will be actively playing and replaying complex environmental issues and trying to cast them into assimilable miniaturised forms in order to reduce negative effects of anger, distress–sadness or shame–humiliation. The nature of the form of imaginative play will depend on the cognitive capacities or levels of imaginative development of the children.

Play Therapy Method: The Creative Imagination

The play therapist needs to offer a suitable environment and stimulation to help the child make and transact imaginary worlds. All creative development begins with play. Erikson (1950) describes three broad stages of development:

Autocosmic: The world of self. The child explores her own body and the body of her mother. A repetition of activity.

Microcosmic: A world of small manageable toys and objects; solitary play, pleasure derived from mastery of toys.

Macrocosmic: The world shared with others.

This is a model similar to that of Jennings (1990), of three evolving developmental stages: from early infant sensation when the child sorts the immediate environment using the senses, through projective play with toys and objects, to the dramatic, social, role-play of children.

Embodiment Play: Being and Nothingness

In the first year of life the infant is involved in a variety of explorations through the senses. She makes sounds, rhythms, marks on food and faeces. She begins to imitate; games of peek-a-boo, hide-and-seek — you don't exist, you do exist. The meaning of mess and the meaning of being and not-being. The great themes of creation myths explored in the microcosm of play.

Embodied play is the beginning of play for the infant and the beginning of play in therapy. We begin to play through sensation and exploration. We start to make the world through sensation, starting from a basic exploration of materials as sensation.

> 'Then he seized the illusion, the base, and he trod upon it. He trod upon it repeatedly. Thus he seized the earth and flattened it. He flattened the dream earth.'

In all creations myths there are descriptions of the time before, the time of nothingness, and then somehow the moment of creation. The nothing before is not nothing; it is the nothing-that-was-not. This sense of creating, beginning to play out of a nothing-that-was-not is a vivid experience when the child and therapist meet.

> In the beginning the world was nothing...

> In the beginning there was chaos...

> At first there was neither earth nor sky...

We begin to explore what was before anything was, when as John described

> 'the mother sat on the dragon's back and the baby died.'

> 'In the beginning the world was darkness...
> In the beginning the world was sludge...
> In the beginning the world was water...
> In the beginning the Unique One dwelt in his shell...'

Sludge, water, slime, sand, shells. These are some of the materials used by children in play therapy, explored for the sensation they create, the way mess can be produced, a re-creation of that pre-verbal universe of the infant. Some children have very limited experience of sensory exploration of their world. Stuck in their push-chair, a bottle stuffed in their mouth which they have to grasp if they are to feed, not allowed to make a mess or explore beyond their pram, the boundaries of their known world are very limited and bodily sensation dulled through lack of use or the pain of abuse.

> Jason, aged ten, had a twin, James, who had a severe learning disability which was not really defined until James was six. As a baby James was difficult and demanding so Jason received little attention from his mother.

> Jason came to play therapy and spent all the ten sessions offered, playing with 'green slime'. He used this slime as 'snot', 'shit', 'sick', and general 'mess'. Some of his explorations were the lavatorial humour beloved by his age group but much of his play was a re-enactment of his infant self.

> I asked him if he intended to continue this play for the ten sessions. He told me that was his intention. He said that when he was a baby nobody had time for him and here he was with me giving him my total attention so he intended to re-create a better infancy. He was sorry if it was boring for me but we did have a lot of laughs and it was important for him and made coping with his brother more bearable.

Children who have never experienced those first infantile explorations can be offered clay, play-doh, bowls of cornflour, bowls of jelly to touch, taste, and explore, as a way to begin their creative life. We must begin at the beginning, start with the sensory world.

Angela Byers, an art therapist, uses embodied play with elderly people with severe memory loss and brain deterioration. She discovered that these sensory explorations were a source of pleasure to her clients and seemed to help them create some order out of chaos and have chaotic thoughts held in place as they were playing. This was a way of containing the chaos, if only for a little while.

Sensory play may remain static or become just part of play therapy, often at the beginning or end of a session, and sometimes the sensory materials can stimulate projective play with the same material. Children often begin to play with 'slime' and then project onto that material symbolic meanings so the stimulation of the material develops into projective play

Rosemary said:

'There was once a piece of slime called Glue Ball. It was not a popular piece of slime, it bounced along slithering every-where, rolling everywhere and was out of control. It also made rude noises.

One day it slithered into a tree and banged his head. The cat chased him round the tree and they began fighting because Glue Ball was always picking fights and tried to control the world.

Glue Ball won the fight and went home well satisfied.'

A Story to Begin

BUMBA VOMITS THE WORLD
Adapted from the Bantu in Zaire

'In the beginning in the dark there was nothing but water. Bumba was alone.

One day Bumba felt a terrible pain. He felt sick, and retched and groaned and strained and sicked up the sun. Then light spread everywhere. The sun was so hot it dried up the water until the edges of the world began to show. There were no living things, just the earth.

Then Bumba sicked up the stars and the moon and there was light at night.

Bumba still felt sick. He strained again and nine living creatures came forth. The leopard, the eagle, the crocodile, the tiny little fish, the tortoise, and Tsetse the lightning, swift and deadly, and then the heron, one beetle and a goat.

Then lastly came men. There were many men.

The creatures themselves made other creatures. The heron made birds, the crocodile made snakes and the iguana. The goat made beasts with horns, the beetle created insects and the tiny little fish all the fish in the oceans and waters.

Of all the creatures only Tsetse the lightening caused trouble so Bumba chased her into the sky.

Bumba showed the people how to draw fire from the trees.

When the work of creation was finished Bumba walked through the villages and said to the people;

"Regard these wonders they belong to you.'"

This story, through the imagery and particular description of creating the Universe, shows the nature of creative, artistic experience. We start with a feeling, sometimes like Bumba, a painful, disturbed, feeling, and from this sensation emerges some form or image which starts the process of creation. Bumba was God, he created a Universe and perhaps the fictional worlds we create in play and the arts are the only worlds where we too can be the ultimate creator.

Projective Play: Making Symbolic Worlds

Projective play can be defined as experiences, feelings, thoughts, wishes, projected out onto toys and media of various sorts, such as sand, paint or water. The child selects toys on which they can project their experiences and then uses these objects to take on roles and relationships which the child wishes to explore. Once the child begins to understand that toys and other media can be transformed to represent actual or imagined experience, then symbolic play begins.

Wilson, Kendrick and Ryan (1992) suggest that symbolic capacity is used in two different ways: first, to transform an event into an objective symbolic representation and second, to transform an inner or outer event into a personal symbolic representation. In the first case the symbols are used to describe facts about events, in the second case a person's feelings about events are given symbolic expression; that is, the symbol is emotive.

Thus, as the child plays, she uses toys to represent her emotions and thoughts symbolically. It is this combination of cognitive sorting of experience and the personal emotional expression of experience which helps the child integrate and make some sense of what has been happening in her particular world.

Many symbols used by the child can have personal meaning and these meanings may not always be communicated to the therapist. Axline (1955) states that too much insistence on finding out may result in a breakdown of communication and rapport.

The importance of symbolic play in therapy with children is that it is the way in which the child can explore experience, safely distanced from their own actual reality. In symbolic play the child creates a fictional world, a space set apart. In this fictional world, free from the constraints of the child's real circumstances and anxiety, where there are no chance accidents or irrelevancies to obscure the logic, the child can develop new meanings free from the constraints of their real circumstances.

In the model of play therapy based on the development of the child's creativity, the therapist helps the child to develop her creative skills so the fictions made can help transform the child's experience. Children often continue to use an image in therapy which has some personal significance but no clarity of meaning. If the therapist helps the child explore and clarify the image artistically, then a satisfying meaning often emerges for the child.

For example, a boy working with the play therapist Brenda Purvey produced a series of images of parrots and all these birds seemed to have powerful, male bodies but very weak wings. Brenda explored the idea of wings, flight and freedom with her client as relevant creative ideas for a boy given too much adult responsibility but little freedom to fly. This helped focus the play, deepening meaning, but staying with the symbol which had most meaning for the client.

Making Art in its broadest sense, be it a story, a drama, an image, is also a satisfying experience and a pleasurable one, however tragic the story. It is important that the child's creativity is respected.

As the child plays, I write their story as they enact or show and tell it to me, then together we experience that magical moment when I read back their creation. This is an important way for me to record the session and to define for the child the importance of their ideas.

Mary, aged eight, neglected and abused.

'"Three pages! Have I really told you three pages?"

"Yes. Shall I read it to you?"

"Yes read it!"'

'Once upon a time there was a country called Sand Land. In Sand Land there lived a mermaid called Ariel and a police car. There are bad people in Sand Land and the mermaid is hiding because they want to kill her.

The soldiers are the enemy. They gather round Ariel and one is very close but when it is dark they can't see her. Ariel sits in the pond which is the sea. She is protected by a fence and trees.

There is a camel and that means the soldiers can't see her. There is a frog in her pool and a tortoise.

There is a mummy and a daddy and they are good. The dolphin can't see her because he is sunbathing.

There is a mouse in another pool so he can't eat Ariel.

The enemy go to sleep, they are lying down. It is night.

Ariel is afraid of people catching her. Then her sister came and said "What's the matter?" "People are trying to capture me," Ariel said.

The people were laughing at Ariel. The baby girl and her brother too. A lady came down and said "Don't be afraid Ariel!"

There are lots and lots of enemy. The mermaids are always scared. "I'll come and eat you if you get in my pond," said the mouse.

Some of the enemy are sleeping, some awake. There was a poisonous hedgehog who was covered up but jumped out and killed the man. Poor man, had to be buried, then the poisonous hedgehog died.

Then the people went away.

The enemy went back home.

Ariel was still crying then she went to sleep and the enemy were happy and the other people were happy for not getting eaten up.

But Ariel is crying and she doesn't know why.

In the end she died of a broken heart and her sister died as well.'

Mediating the Subject and Object World

There is a world of objects, a world out there which exists beyond the individual and independently of her. But there is another world which exists only within the individual. This is the solitary world of the subject, the world of 'I', the world through which the individual experiences her own existence, the inner world of private consciousness. As the individual matures she is faced with the task of finding her way in both of these worlds and of understanding the shifting relationship between the two.

Throughout her story Mary is mediating these two worlds. She uses play objects, small figures and a tray to contain and mediate her worlds. Her inner world of feeling is determined by her experiences in the outside world. Her story symbolically defines some of those experiences but also defines some of her wishes.

A mummy and daddy who are kind, a nice lady, a dolphin, the safety of fences and the safety of hiding. She knows the story of the Little Mermaid so she can let Ariel die in the end, mediating her own despair with her memory of the story. When Mary heard her story she was energised and proud of her achievement. For once she wasn't blamed, called bad, she was Mary and she had a story to tell. She went on to express more optimistic worlds and strategies for mermaids to learn to survive in their blue pool. Her sense of herself became stronger as she learnt to handle that objective world 'out there' which she had created in the sand and through her play. Mary began to assimilate ways of coping with the world outside of herself. In the safety of play she had time away from the pressure of her reality world to develop strategies of dealing with 'the enemy' which she assimilated and began to use.

Erikson (1977) developed this holistic view of play when he argued that play is not only a way of working through traumatic experiences – the wish-fulfilment and sense of hope expressed in children's play could become a prime mover in human development. He stated that the sense of playful renewal present in future-oriented play reinforces children's intrinsic faith in the future of the human race and hopefulness about developing their own personal identities.

Making the Object World

SHELLS WITHIN SHELLS
A Tahitian myth

'For a long time the Unique One lived in his shell which moved round and round in space in the dark.

At last the shell broke open and the Unique One looked outside. "Who is above? Who is below? Who is in front? Who is behind?" Nobody answered. Just the echo of his own voice. He demanded rocks to crawl forth and sand to emerge. Nothing happened. The Unique One became angry.

So he turned over his shell and raised it up to make the sky. Then he slipped out of another shell and made rocks and sand. Then he took his spine for the mountains, ribs for mountain slopes and from his flesh he made the earth and all the creatures of the earth.

The Unique One's head remained sacred to himself and his body remained indestructible.

Later he made gods and much later men.

Everything has a shell like the Unique One. The earth is a shell to water, plants and stones.

Man's shell is woman because it is by her that he is born and woman's shell is woman because she is born of woman.'

Dramatic Play: Understanding the Social World

As the child develops skill in symbolic interaction with external media, dramatic play develops. This usually begins with family play, the re-structuring of real life events, then develops through the enactment of the child's own stories and stories and dramatic material familiar to the child. As the child grows older there is an increase in imaginative play and interactive play, with others taking roles.

To participate successfully in dramatic play also requires the child to develop social skills such as sharing, taking turns, organising the taking of roles and the fictional identities of objects and actions. In play therapy this is negotiated with the therapist, who will take on the roles suggested by the child if appropriate. This should be a safe place to try out social skills and to break rules to test out the safety of the relationship. All play therapists should become familiar with the latest dramatic characters presented in the media. To have such knowledge makes for a street-wise therapist much respected by the client group!

Some media characters move in and out of fashion (thank goodness no more Turtles, fewer wrestlers, for the moment; all difficult roles for an aged therapist!). Others endure in a variety of forms and media. It is interesting to discover where the child first experienced these enduring characters.

Peter Pan and Captain Hook may have been experienced through reading the play, seeing the play, watching the film or watching the cartoon.

> Julian (aged 'very nearly five') and I played Peter Pan and Captain Hook for many weeks. We were cartoon characters and the cartoon form was an important element of the way I had to play my role of Captain Hook. In reality, Julian and his mother had been taken hostage by his father and terrorised for several days. Julian was concerned about how he had behaved under threat. Had he been brave and had he helped his mother? He initiated our play of Captain Hook and Peter Pan. Peter Pan flew around Captain Hook who was unable to capture such a nimble child.
>
>> 'You're much too fast for me Peter Pan', said Captain Hook.
>>
>> 'You don't scare me!' shouted Peter!
>
> We had to be cartoon characters, overbearing and pompous.

This drama and its repeated enactment was re-assuring for Julian, who needed to feel he had done his best against a tyrant. It was his way of relating his inner world to the external environment and coping with the terror.

Role Taking

Landy (1991) suggests that the principle of impersonation lies at the core of the dramatic experience, whether in ritual, play, improvisation or formal theatre. He defines impersonation as the ability of the person to take on a persona or role. This is a paradoxical process involving engagement and separation, taking-on and taking-off, simultaneously existing in the world of me and not-me. In this process, the role-taker becomes the container of two realities, the everyday and the fictional, imaginatively holding them in a paradoxical relationship to one another. Role-taking in this way gives form and meaning to our behaviour.

Julian needed to find a form to express the horror of his experience and the recognition that he had done his best in the circumstances. He could be himself and not himself in the role of Peter
Pan and I could be the container of the terror in my role of Captain
Hook. I realised that in my role I had to make a statement about the
skill and quickness of Peter Pan and define the advantages of being
a young boy. As the monstrous Captain Hook I was defeated but lived
on to fight another day, as inside Captain Hook is also Mr Darling,
a loving though weak father, and to kill Captain Hook is to kill Mr
Darling. The cartoon images were important, as they gave Julian
distance from the actuality of the trauma he was resolving through
his role-taking. The exaggeration of the cartoon characters made it
clear to both Julian and myself that we were playing fictional
characters.

Role-Taking and Role Reversal

For young children, the self and non-self are not differentiated,
leading them to assume that theirs is the only point of view. As
children mature, the self gradually 'decentres' and becomes separated
from the environment. This process of decentration makes it possible
for children to realise that other people can have thoughts and
feelings that are different from their own. Role taking and role
reversal can play an important part in the development of children's
perspective-taking abilities. To re-experience the world from the
others point of view is the very meat of role taking. Justin could
re-experience himself in a stressful situation by taking the role of
Peter Pan. In this he was engaging in a form of re-enactment of his
experience but separated from the actuality or the reality detail of
what happened. Through experiencing me as Captain Hook he could
know the terror of being bullied while still knowing me as his
therapist who had promised to keep him safe in his play.

For children who have been abused by adults it is important that
they can have a means of separating the roles of abused and abuser
so they don't continue to take responsibility for the abuse.

The imbalance of power in abusive relationships can be explored in the playing of both roles. One of the most damaging aspects of the sexual abuse of young children is that at the very time when the child is beginning to walk and to separate from adults to explore the physical world around her, the abusing adult is physically overwhelming her with his body. Many small children tell me that the worst feeling from sexual abuse was the presence of the male body and the feeling of being eaten alive by the physicality of that presence – forever bonded to that body.

How to find a separate self and a separate body after such overwhelming abuse is complex. For some children it is achieved by enacting that enormous monster in the form of a fictional monster, to put him in his place and experience him as separate and different from those he attacks. 'He' of course may be 'she' but the male monster predominates in sexual abuse.

Sutton-Smith (1980) shows that role reversal can foster the sense of autonomy and control in the child. In reality, the child operates from a position of weakness in relation to adults but in role play she can turn the tables on adults. Play then becomes a medium of self-enabling.

Julian could control Captain Hook in his play; in the role of Hook I was often mortally wounded by Peter, only to be rescued at the last minute and cured, usually in some unpleasant way such as having snakes thrown at him. Julian was controlling my destiny in the way that his father had controlled his by threat and the abuse of power, although Julian in play was a more compassionate person than his father in reality.

This kind of role reversal, with the child in control of her own fiction can, for the child, lead to the expansion of a sense of self as an autonomous and functioning person who can influence surrounding events. From this secure position the child can achieve empathy for others.

Acting the World

The child comes to play therapy. We make a world together. It is shared, negotiated, kept safe by the therapist, but belongs to the child.

AN AINU MYTH FROM JAPAN

'In the beginning the world was slush, for the waters and the mud all stirred in together.

All was silence, there was no sound. It was cold.

There were no birds flying in the air. There were no living things.

At last the Creator made a little wagtail and sent him down from his far place in the sky.

"Produce the earth," he said.

The bird flew down over the black waters and the dismal swamp. He did not know what to do. He did not know how to begin.

He fluttered in the water with his wings. He ran up and down in the slush with his feet trying to trample it to firmness. He beat on it with his tail, beating it down and down.

After a long time of treading and trampling, and treading and trampling, a few dry places began to appear in the big ocean.

The wagtail had created earth. The islands of the Ainu. He had created his world.'

CHAPTER 2

PLAY THERAPY
Using The Creative-Expressive Play
of the Child to Heal the Hurt

FINN AND THE DRAGON

'Finn met a dragon once. It was nearly half as big as a mountain. But he had all his men with him and wasn't a bit afraid, so he gave it battle. The head of it was huge, and the mouth of it was gaping open and full of teeth the size of trees. And the tail of it was so high in the air, it was out of sight. And with its tail it could knock a cow or a man over as easy as you like. But it was no match for Finn and his band, though it swallowed them every one. Finn made an opening in the belly of it with his sword, and out he hopped with every man-jack after him. And the brute was that put about it laid down and died. Finn killed that one in Camlough, but sure there were lots of them in them days.'

Creative-Expressive Play

The creative-expressive play described in Chapter 1 is the medium we use to help the child explore when they come to play therapy. This process uses sensory play, projected play with toys and media and dramatic role play to enable the child express creatively the issues they want to bring to play with the adult therapist.

These forms are the child's natural repertoire of playing, and the therapist can offer the child stimulus and materials which will encourage self-expression for the child at an appropriate developmental level.

All these processes are ways of self-expression and we should not encourage the child to 'grow out of' messy sensory play to more structured experiences but to enjoy all forms of playing as pleasurable, or as a means to express what material the child has brought to the session.

Some children stay with certain objects or media throughout their time in therapy, others move freely from one form to another. If the child feels the medium is right for what they want to play, then the choice belongs to the child.

Many children who have been under-stimulated in their early years can become overwhelmed by too much stimulation, so too many media will confuse.

Children in care and others who have lost attachments to adults, or never been attached, sometimes use toys, objects and media as a substitute for human care. This is something concrete to touch, hold, that can't make false promises. The therapist then has the responsibility always to have that object or medium available for the child. The certainty of the presence of an object can be the beginning of trust between therapist and child.

Choices in Playing

Objects-versus-People and Play Patterners and Play Dramatists

Young children have preferences in ways of playing and this is often described in terms of object-versus-people play. Emmerich (1964) observed that some children are more attracted to activities where there is a lot of interaction with people while others prefer solitary activities where the focus of attention is on objects.

Wolf and Gardner (1979) described two styles of symbolic, imaginative play and these were; object-independent fantasy play in which children create imaginary worlds by invoking non-existent events, roles, and props; and object-dependent transformational play in which children create an imaginary world by transforming existing objects and arrangements in the environment. These individual styles seem to be stable across time and are not indicative of particular periods within developmental levels.

Object-dependent play is characterised by children constructing arrangements or patterns with objects and substituting items where actions require props. Object-independent children create stories and play from non-existent elements and can incorporate objects and actual events, changed to be part of their imaginative play. The two styles can be described as play patterners versus play dramatists.

'Patterners' show considerable skill and interest in making patterns, structures and order with objects and materials. 'Dramatists' show a strong interest in human surroundings, what others did, felt and how they could be known. They enjoy games, dramatic play and storymaking.

Imaginative play styles continua

Patterners...............	Dramatists
Visualizers...............	Verbalizers
Configurationalists	Narrators
Object Dependent..........	Object Independent

Louise is a patterner. Trying to make sense of the loss of her brother who is to be adopted and will not return to the family, she constantly makes families, sorting out small family dolls into groups. Each family group is delineated, with its own territory and individual facilities and requirements. The matching of small dolls in each family must be appropriate, by her rules, which cannot be verbalised; they are visual, but clear to Louise. She needs the toys, and she creates patterns and groups with the dolls to help her make sense of her reality world.

Jim is a dramatist. He is in care in a foster family, waiting for a long term placement. He is content where he lives and the family hope, to keep him there, as does his natural mother. Jim remembers the chaos in his natural family when his mother had a violent boy-friend who came to live with them. Jim made up this story and acted it again and again, taking a variety of parts. The roles are ambivalent and there is a bit of the real Jim in every part. He made up the story and began to act straight away; he never used toys or media to stimulate his imagination.

He often tells stories and is now a socially skilled child, negotiating his place with the many other children in the family. He was taught some of these skills by his foster carer; he had wanted to learn because he is sociable. This is his story:

> 'There was once a giant called Anthony, the cold-hearted giant and he lived in the jungle full of tigers, tigers, tigers, and trees that kept falling down. And the giant got angry and died.'

The theme of this story is expanded in the playing. The giant is sometimes like the mother's boy friend who did indeed live in a jungle, as a drug dealer, and often the violence of that way of life entered into the life of Jim, as his home was broken into and damaged. But the foster family is sometimes a jungle where each child has to fight for attention and love with all the other children. School was a jungle for a long time before Jim was accepted. 'Died' has many meanings: a wish that the giant boy-friend really was dead; sometimes the death of anger as the giant/Jim gets the love he craves; sometimes death is separation and the loss of home because the giant/Jim got angry.

All are feeling states that Jim has experienced and through his dramatic enactment he can explore all the ambiguities he feels about himself and the important people in his world. This helps him make sense of his life.

It is important for the therapist to recognise that children will choose to play in a variety of ways and should be encouraged to explore styles of playing which are part of their personal style.

It is also important for the therapist to explore their own personal style and expand their repertoire of styles so they can offer appropriate ideas and stimulation to children. Many therapists feel inhibited when playing dramatic roles and play as an adult humouring the child, instead of finding the artistic truth of the role they are asked to play by the child. Therapists should be trained in improvisation and dramatic play so they can be effective players with the child.

Playing the Memories of the Past

For some children, playing the past is often a theme they wish to explore when they first begin to play. Other children experience the opposite desire and are fearful of their memories. The therapist stands with the child and offers herself as the safe companion for the child's journey, whatever that might be.

The past for many children was chaotic; there was no logic for what happened, no sense to be made of it other than to acknowledge the chaos and confusion.

For some children the present is not yet safe enough and, with no certainty of unconditional love, it is hard to explore rejections experienced in the past, perhaps again to be repeated in the present.

It is important for the children who want to explore what has happened to them that the therapist offers containment for the process. The broad containment of the whole therapy session (see Chapter 4), involves containing the objects and toys in some way, making sure the dramatic play is fictive or transformed so the child has created an imaginary reality which is distanced from the real life and can be owned or rejected by its creator. I always tell children that, when we play, we don't play our own selves. When we make up stories and play, maybe it is someone or something like us but it isn't us. When we play we are making up stories.

Sometimes the beginning sessions take the form of a search for an appropriate fiction or story which will contain and symbolise the past.

Symbols or characters are needed to represent the self; for example, Space Kid, moving from the Good World to the Bad World when

Karate Dad was bitten by the snake, was the symbolic containment for abuse experienced when father had taken heroin.

A baby lost in the world as armies marched backwards and forwards over the ground, the mother flying the dragon that trampled the baby, described a family at war with each other. Amy told many stories about a bleeding snowman, frozen on the inside but bleeding red blood onto the white snow. This snowman was showing its pain to the world. The snowman was strangled by snakes again and again in Amy's stories, which shows what sexual abuse feels like when you are five years old and what it does to your sense of yourself. And this frozen snowman, frozen inside, but clearly shouting his pain as he bled onto the snow, was ignored, and the snakes went on and on. It is important for the therapist to work with the child within the imagery of the story and make resolutions through the story. With Amy, we explored ways in which the snowman might get people to listen to him and ways to trick the snakes. This was difficult.

It is important not to be impatient for happy endings or comfortable resolutions if the child wants to stay with the sadness and the pain. I find children in therapy are very kind and will offer you the comfort of a happy ending if they think that is what *you* need but then their pain goes unacknowledged. It is very important for the child to be able to say

> 'And the mermaid died of a broken heart.'

and have that accepted by the therapist. Very young children, less defended than those with more complex imagery and language, make up stories very similar to their own history. Thus Catherine, aged three, told this story with the dolls:

> 'Once upon a time there were four babies and they were sad because they didn't have enough to eat, they had no dollies.
>
> Mummy was poorly so the ambulance came.
>
> They had a daddy and a mummy who were nice.
>
> The little girl said "I hate you today daddy and mummy. I hate you because you keep shouting, and bossing me about."

The babies are in the car and they get hurt and die because they are naughty. The ambulance came and the baby is dead. All the family is dead.'

Mary began with this story:

'In this family, mum has got lots of kids so she hasn't got time for them all.

Sometimes they go off and play on their own.

Sometimes they be good boys and girls.

Dad said:

"Go to bed now. Come on baby go to sleep."

We put rudie dad in prison because we didn't want the children to go to visit him.'

Anthony, aged five, was traumatised by the death of his mother who was stabbed many times by her assailant. He was unable to mourn his mother or remember the past because of the image of her body and the wounds she suffered. He told me this story:

'Once upon a time there was a skeleton and he was twisted up so he looked as if he was flying. He stood on a knife and flew to Knifeland. Knifeland is orange. The three Drakulas live in Knifeland and they stab people because there are lots of knives in Knifeland.'

Anthony used powerful images but he was able to say that it was just pretend. The reality was too fearful to talk about but it was contained in his drawings and stories. He did a drawing of a house and described it to me;

'There is a house, a tent and a person.

This is Drakula's house. It was thunder trying to knock the house down. He is a duck and this is his house like a castle.

The house is held up by legs. Thunder and rain are getting into the house. The hole is going to be mended but will always be there.

> There is a robber outside the house, he is going to get the bone.
> He won't hurt the dog but he will steal both the bones. He has
> no knife or gun but will steal using his fists.'

Anthony used the cartoon character of Drakula Duck to express his
terror at the attack on his mother. He could acknowledge that

> 'The hole is going to be mended but will always be there'

There was always a dog in his stories and drawings because in reality
the family dog witnessed the attack and dogs in his stories always
saw what was happening.

Perhaps in the same way as the very young child, the adolescent
likes the protection of the image, but the identification is made more
explicit. June, aged 19, made up many stories about a hedgehog
named Hertz. Her first story, called 'The Wicked Witch of Raille-
maule' described the 'wicked witch', the mother and her family and
how the children were changed.

> 'One day, there was a terrible argument and the witch cast
> spells upon her children.
>
> Duncan was turned into a straw in a Vodka bottle, Hertz was
> changed into a hedgehog and Bob was transformed into a
> pogo stick.'

These transformations described how their childhood had disempowered the children. June was very taken by her image of Hertz,
the prickly creature in pain, yet capable of hiding inside a prickly
shell.

Memories of the past can be so painful that they can only be
explored through a fictional creative structure, safely distanced from
actual reality. A story shared and heard by the therapist, with the
images and events explored together by the therapist and child, can
help the child contain the pain. June was so taken by her hedgehog
that she knitted me a very prickly hedgehog and the healing
expanded into laughter. That was also the beginning of her creating
many other idiosyncratic dolls which she was able to sell. And that
did wonders for her self-image.

Sometimes I might suggest a rhyme, a story or image which could be relevant to the child, and here again, a sense of humour can be important.

> 'Jack and Gye went out in the rye,
> And they found a little boy with one black eye,
> Come, said Jack, let's knock him on the head,
> No, said Gye, let's buy him some bread;
> You buy one loaf and I'll buy two,
> And we'll bring him up as other folk do.'

This simple rhyme can help a child acknowledge different kinds of family life and knowing there is a rhyme or story which states this, makes the child feel that they are not alone in what has happened to them. This is a nice rhyme for acting out and can also be used to define the relationship between child and therapist as a nurturing one.

> 'You buy one loaf and I'll buy two,
> And we'll bring him up as other folk do.'

The drawings and text in *Outside Over There* by Maurice Sendak (1985) have a strange, haunting, quality which distances the images in a far-away past. Don't be fooled by the pretty picture on the cover!

It is a strange story about a changeling child and describes a young girl taking adult responsibility for her baby sister who was taken by the goblins in exchange for a baby made of ice. She is helped in her task of rescuing her sister by wearing her mother's rain cloak and hearing her sailor father's advice in a song.

The drawings are powerful for those children who have had to take adult responsibility and lost the chance to be children. Each illustration has its own strong story and can be used as the basis for dramatic play or further story-telling. The power of the illustrations is expressed in a kind of longing and intensity which holds strong resonances for the child. There is also the feeling that, while the child has to do adult things alone, she is symbolically helped by the cloak and the song.

Not Now Bernard (McKee 1987) is a picture book about a child who can't get the attention of his parents even when he turns into a monster. This was great favourite of Jim, who enjoyed the roles of the parents ignoring the child and, in playing, produced accurate portrayals of his mother and his foster carer. He also enjoyed the transformation from boy to monster and the ambivalence of that role.

> '"There's a monster in the garden and it's going to eat me." said Bernard.'

In the book the monster enters the house, and is still called Bernard by the parents. What does it feel like to be a monster on the outside but Bernard, eaten up, on the inside?

And what is it like to be a monster on the outside yet still ignored by those you want most to care for you?

Stories like these are containers, which help the child explore the pain of their past through the form and structure of the stories and illustrations. My pain, yet not my pain. It must happen to other people so I'm not alone.

Playing an Imaginary Past

Sometimes in the safety of the playing space a child might want to enact an imaginary past, with love and warmth she didn't experience in reality. This can often happen when a child has played out memories and terrors of a fearful past or a past without warmth and affection.

The play often begins with toys like baby dolls and feeding bottles and the child and I will share, through story-making or play, a kind of idealised childhood.

Again this is structured in an imaginary mode. We might begin with talk about being a baby and what that means. The baby's need for food, warmth, comfort and love. In this imagined past, the child often takes the role of mother, offering nurture to dolls or soft toys.

This play is not a way to put the child into a helpless, regressed, baby role which would embarrass an older child and disempower her, but is a way to acknowledge the loss of nurture as a baby, a loss which can never be replaced but maybe we can repair. We can play and imagine an idyllic childhood. At this time I often bring books and we look at pictures together and read stories about being a baby.

I usually begin with *Bye Bye Baby* (1989) by Janet and Allan Ahlberg which describes a small baby's search for parents

> 'There was once a baby who had no mummy.
> This baby lived in a little house all by himself.
> He fed himself and bathed himself. He even changed his own nappy.
> It was very sad.'

The baby goes off to search for a mummy then, finally, a daddy. The happy ending is always good for a long sigh of happiness. The baby is assertive, not helpless, and does not want to take responsibility for himself, recognising that that is a job for parents. He says;

> 'I am too young to be doing this.'

It is important that the baby has no sense of guilt about not having parents; it's not his responsibility. It is popular with the child because of the constant repetitions of

> 'I am a little baby... with no mummy, Will you be my mummy?'

and the reply

> 'No, but I will be your cat' or teddy or whatever.

for as the baby searches for his mummy he finds other companions who travel with him. I sometimes use this to express my role with a child, that I won't be your mummy but I will be your play therapist/teddy bear – or however the child describes me.

This theme can produce hope for the child, who is perhaps waiting for a family; to have good companions on the search can mean that you are loved. The cat, the teddy, the clockwork hen, the old uncle; perhaps there is something or someone like that in the life of the child. But nevertheless the central cry of the baby when trouble starts is:

'I WANT MY MUMMY!'

This book expresses with words and illustrations the longing for attachment and, like many of the picture books now available for young children, is so symbolically expressive that it appeals to all ages.

When I was a Baby (1988) by Catherine Anholt describes a very idealised babyhood, but is really popular with young children and gives a sense of continuity, of growing and changing:

> 'I'm not a baby any more.
> Now I'm three, I'm big,'

The Baby Catalogue (1984) by Janet and Allan Ahlberg, for all who are object-dependent, lists everything a baby needs, from clothes to prams to nappies to baths and bedtimes. Painful if you have been deprived of nurture in its object manifestation, but a treasure trove for the child who trusts objects more than people.

Sometimes we have a giggle with *Jojo's Revenge* (Inkpen 1989) when Jojo throws his food about, finally landing on granddad, and *Eat Your Dinner* (Miller 1992), a particular favourite, about Bartholomew, the bear who won't eat his dinner or *Toilet Tales* (Konisglow 1989) and *I Want My Potty* (Ross 1986) about toilet training and who can sit on the toilet.

> 'A seal would be wet and slip off.
> Seals could never use a toilet.'

And Bartholomew again in *On Your Potty* (Miller 1991) saying 'Nah' in the way only a bear can.

All these books are delightful, but for children who have never experienced loving nurture, the warmth is tinged with sadness. Memories of learning to feed and toilet training were often, in reality, scenes of terror and violence when the parent could explode all the self-hatred they felt onto the child for being 'dirty' or 'disgusting'. For the sexually abused young child, this may also have been a time of pain or inappropriate arousal and association.

But there is healing in sharing the fictive experiences of Bartholomew and his companions in children's stories. In that sharing of good times, the child can let go of some of the memories of the bad times and also learn more appropriate meanings about how a baby learns and grows.

Bartholomew's carer, George the bear, is the nicest father figure, most patient and kind. Oh for a dad like that! I often finish with *When Sheep Cannot Sleep* (Kitamura 1986) about a sheep who can't sleep and his journey through the night. He begins with play with other creatures out at night but eventually has a fright when he sees a flight of UFOs in the sky. He runs to hide and finds a house, goes inside, looks around, feeds, bathes and, having nurtured himself, eventually goes to bed.

Then he begins to think. He thinks about all his family.

> 'What were they doing? Were they already asleep?
> His family and friends went round in his head.'

He begins counting them all, before he fell asleep. This is a kind of final acknowledgement that, whatever they were like, whatever childhood you actually had, you can't really forget your family.

Re-Making a World

> 'Tom tied a kettle to the tail of a cat,
> Jill put a stone in the blind man's hat;
> Bob threw his grandmother down the stairs –
> And they all grew up ugly and nobody cares.'

This is perhaps the most difficult task for the child in therapy: how to dare to trust enough to let go of the past and hope for a better future.

Anthony wanted to find ways to lose the image of the stab wounds on his mother's body, to get back to a memory of her as a person, as his mother, so he could mourn her. He made up many stories about skeletons and in talking to me asked me many times how long it would take for his mother to become a skeleton. He gave his own answer and for a long time it was

> 'Not just yet'

Time went by and he played out many things, but often he asked the question and gave the answer 'Not just yet'. Then, about 18 months after her death, he said:

> 'I am asking for the last time; is my mother a skeleton yet?'

and his answer was:

> 'Yes, there is no flesh on the bones. She is a skeleton. She is dead.'

and this was a quiet confirmation which brought him peace. The ritual was ended, he could begin to mourn.

Anthony was settled with a new family who loved him dearly, and now he felt free to talk about his mother and remember the person she was, what she had done for him, how much he had loved her, what fun they had together. He began to mourn her, no longer frozen by the images of her torn body, but able to remember the vibrant person she had been in life. He began to make up stories of living in a caring family and through these stories was able to try out ways of being in his new family.

Many children who have been abused feel so worthless it is difficult to begin to re-make a world where they are other than the victim they perceive themselves to be.

When Jane first began therapy, she drew herself as a scrap car with no door, broken window, no engine, smashed front, and flat tyres. She said there was nothing inside, no petrol and no water, it needed to be towed away. There, in the scrap yard, was a great big metal ball waiting to smash the car. As Jane began to understand that she was not responsible for her abuse she began to change.

Figure 2.1 The wrecked car

Powerful bird and strong if she ever sees the rat again she will hit it and end it. Eagle equals freedom. I would like this to be real.

Figure 2.2 Becoming the eagle

This man is a rat because he is the lowest form of life. Rats carry disease and he gave me part of his disease.
Sewer rat black filthy piece of vermin.

Figure 2.3 Leaving the rat

She drew herself as an eagle and her abuser as a rat. She said 'the eagle is a powerful bird, a strong bird. If ever the eagle sees the rat again he will kill it and eat it, The eagle equals freedom.'

This was a powerful image for Jane, something to hold onto when she felt hatred, rage and humiliation. When she drew the image she wrote

'I wish this could be real'

June's hedgehog, created by her mother, began to change. She wrote her story

HERTZ'S MISSION FOR RECOGNITION

'Once upon a time there lived a lonely and unhappy hedgehog whose prickles were turning inwards. Her heart had been captured, happiness destroyed and identity non-existent.'

Hertz had many adventures, not too many happy endings, but found ways to cope:

'Hertz was in hibernation for a long time and when she awoke she trundled down to her favourite place of tranquillity; the duck pond. She was grimacing at her ugly reflection on the water, when she saw somebody watching her. To her surprise she was the centre of attention to a handsome little frog. Within minutes they were in deep conversation and had made further arrangements...'

Always the morbid sense of humour but always more possibilities to be explored in fiction.

A Story About Future Possibilities

This is based on a story by Terry Jones (1983) from his book *Fairy Tales*. The book is full of magical stories.

Figure 2.4 Hertz's mission for recognition

THE WITCH AND THE RAINBOW CAT

A small girl was walking along the banks of a river when she came across a little house. The house was very small and the girl could touch the roof if she reached up. "Hello, is there anyone at home?" But there was no answer. Now the little girl knew she shouldn't go into a strange house without being invited but she was so curious that she went inside.

Everything was perfect, but half the size of normal things. There was a sitting-room with a fire-place and a mirror over the mantelpiece, and she could see into the mirror perfectly well. But she noticed one very curious thing; the reflection of herself that she saw in the mirror was quite grown-up.

She blinked and stared again. It was definitely her reflection; and suddenly she realised – she was looking at herself as a grown-up woman.

How long she stood there, I don't know, but suddenly she heard the latch on the front door open, and she remembered that she shouldn't be there, so she quickly hid herself behind a little cupboard, feeling very frightened.

She heard the footsteps tapping round the house. The little girl peeped out and saw a little old witch in a green hat and a green cloak, and on her shoulder was a cat that was all the colours of the rainbow.

And the little old witch stopped and looked about her and said; "Who's been looking in my mirror? I can see a child there!"

The witch saw the little girl.

"Who are you?" asked the old witch. "What are you doing in my house?"

"Please," said the little girl, "my name is Rose and I didn't mean any harm."

"Didn't mean any harm? You looked in my mirror" screamed the old witch.

"Oh, please let me go home" cried Rose, "and I'll never come and bother you again."

"No! You've looked in my mirror!" cried the witch. "You'll stay here and be my servant."

The witch locked her in the attic. Poor Rose sat and cried, for she didn't know what she was going to do.

Suddenly, she looked down and saw the rainbow-coloured cat.

"Hello" said the rainbow cat, "You can ask me three questions."

Rose was so astonished to hear the cat talk that she exclaimed: "But how is it you can talk?"

The rainbow cat yawned and replied: "The witch put a spell on me. Two questions left. If I were you, I'd think more carefully about the next."

Rose thought carefully about the next question, and then asked; "Why doesn't the witch like me looking in her mirror?"

"A better question," replied the cat, stretching itself.

"She doesn't like you looking in the mirror because she is the Witch of the Future, and in that mirror she sees the things that are to come. She is the only person that can know these things, and once you know them she'll never let you go. One question left."

"Well, have you thought of your last question?"

"Not yet," replied Rose.

"Very well," said the cat, "I'll wait."

Just then the door flew open and in burst the witch.

"Now," said the witch, "you must start to work for me." And she made Rose scrub the floors from morning till evening.

"You must keep your eyes on the floor so that you don't go looking in my mirror again."

Day after day, week after week, the witch kept her at it until one day, when the witch was out in the forest collecting toads, Rose suddenly felt the rainbow cat rubbing itself up against her leg.

"Well," said the cat, "have you thought of your last question yet?"

Rose said, "I'll ask you my last question tomorrow."

The next morning Rose was scrubbing the doorstep, watching the witch go to the forest, when she noticed a small bird in the garden, with its leg caught in one of the witch's traps.

Rose released the bird and the next moment, she felt something rub against her leg and there was the rainbow cat again.

"Well, have you thought of the last question?"

Just then, the bird flew down and landed on Rose's shoulder and said "I can tell you what to ask."

"Well" said the rainbow cat, "what is your question?"

Rose took a deep breath and then said what the bird had told her: "Tell me, rainbow cat, why can't I choose my own future?"

The rainbow cat looked up and smiled, and his colours all started changing and glowing and spinning round and round. "But you can!" he cried. "The Witch of the Future has no power without her mirror – break that and you are free."

Just then, Rose looked up and saw the witch coming out of the wood towards her. Rose ran back into the little house, took the mirror off the wall and hurled it to the ground so that it smashed into smithereens. Everything went still. Then there was a dreadful scream, and there stood the Witch of the Future, only she looked a thousand years older. The witch stumbled and the wall of the house started to crumble.

Rose ran and didn't stop running until she reached the gate at the bottom of the garden. Then the little house collapsed in a cloud of dust, and an ordinary black cat walked out and rubbed up against her legs.

"Is that you, rainbow cat?" asked Rose. But the cat didn't reply. It simply strolled off into the wood.

And Rose ran home as fast as she could.'

Working with the Story

1. Tell the story up to where the witch sees the image of the girl in the mirror.

2. Ask the child or group to draw pictures of what Rose saw when she looked in the mirror and what the witch saw in the mirror.

3. Continue the story up to the cat's line, 'Very well, I'll wait.'

4. Ask the child or group to write or draw on a piece of paper what the last question might be. Keep the paper safe.

5. Continue the story up to 'scrub the floors from morning to evening.'

6. In pairs, act out the witch and the girl working, with the witch instructing the girl to clean the floors but never look up to see the mirror.

7. De-role from the play and talk about how it felt to be the witch and the girl. What does it feel like never to be allowed to look to the future?

8. Continue the story up to 'choose my own future.'

9. Draw or write three things Rose might want for her future. Share with your partner.

10. Take the two pictures of Rose seen in the mirror and the three things Rose might want for her future. Talk about what you have, with your partner or a small group.

11. Tell the story to the end.

12. Draw a present that Rose might give to the bird. Compare presents with your partner or the group.

This is a playful way to enjoy a story and also to explore what the future might hold for Rose and, paradoxically, for yourself.

All these fictional possibilities, in whatever way they are expressed, be it the clients' own creations or the writings and art of others, offer opportunities to experiment in different ways of being – leaving the past, exploring the future, within the safety of the therapeutic space.

FAIRY TALE

'He built himself a house,
    his foundations,
    his stones,
    his walls,
    his roof overhead,
    his chimney and smoke,
    his view from the window.

He made himself a garden,
    his fence,
    his thyme,
    his earthworm,
    his evening dew.

He cut out his bit of sky above.

And he wrapped the garden in the sky
and the house in the garden
and packed the lot in a handkerchief.

and went off
lone as an Arctic fox
through the cold
unending
rain
into the world.'

(Miroslav Holub. Translated by Ian Miller)

CHAPTER 3

THE ROLES OF THE THERAPIST

This
        silence
vibrating – a
        heart
echoing

    listen

                                        (T. Phillips 1985)

Therapist and Child in the Playing Space

The play therapist and child meet to play and when they play the physical space for play is defined.

This physical space, be it playroom, mat, or a corner of the school library has to be defined, and the boundaries of that space determined. When the physical space is defined by therapist and child then that space is transformed by being named the play space, for in this space we can create illusionary worlds which are aesthetically pleasing.

In this playing space the child can explore an illusionary world free from the constraints of her real circumstances. There are no chance accidents, no obstructions to the creation of this world, and in this play space, the child can develop new meanings for herself, free from the pressures of her own history.

The task of the therapist is to introduce this world and sustain it for the child, to keep the boundaries, to maintain the safety of the playing space.

To sustain this world the therapist needs skill in playing with children. She needs imagination in the choice of toys and objects which will stimulate the child and are appropriate for the themes likely to be presented. She needs skill in taking roles and making dramatic play with the child. She needs to be able to show the child how to gain these skills in play.

Approaches to the Relationship Between Child and Therapist

Yalom

Yalom (1975), describing the role of the therapist in group psycho-therapy, suggests that, underlying all considerations of techniques, there must be a consistent, positive relationship between client and therapist. He states that the patient should be considered a full collaborator in the therapeutic venture.

Child as Collaborator

Yalom was describing the relationship between adult client and therapist, but it is equally important for the play therapist to consider the child as collaborator, and be clear that the therapeutic journey belongs to the child.

If the therapist's role with the child is to facilitate creative play and share in that play when appropriate, then the therapist must create a comfortable relationship with the child, share doubts and uncer-tainties, acknowledge 'scary things'. Yalom calls this 'therapist trans-parency'.

The model of therapist as superior being is not appropriate if we wish the child to explore and make sense of their world through play. Yalom suggests that this is the old authoritarian model of medical healer who has colluded with the distressed human being's wish for succour from a superior being.

When this traditional role is abandoned, the whole process of the therapist/client relationship is demystified, which hastens the autonomy of the client/child.

The child experiences great difficulty in playing in the presence of the therapist if she feels that her play will be dissected by the therapist for some adult purpose which is alien to the child's reason for playing. If this happens, the child finds play difficult because she feels judged instead of supported.

Yalom states that the superordinate principle for successful therapy is responsibility. In work with children, the therapist who is responsible does not present herself as superior being, but someone for whom doubts and uncertainties are acceptable. However, she is aware of the developmental level of the child and takes extra care for the physical well-being and emotional stability of the child.

West

In child-centred play therapy, Janet West (1992) describes four levels of therapeutic interaction.

> Level 1 covers the play therapist's physical presence, non-verbal gestures and simple responsive and reflective statements which simply describe what the child is doing. The main task at this level is to attend and *focus* on the child's communication.

> Level II skills go further to help the child locate statements, actions and feelings and the therapist *reflects* by repetition, paraphrase, summaries and amplification to expand something that has been said or done.

> Level III evokes responses of *third person interpretation* such as 'some little girls, sometimes children feel.'

> Level IV is the area of *direct interpretation*, is usually cautious and is based on what the play therapist sees, deducts or feels. At this level the play therapist takes the child's world into

account but conceptualises differently and tentatively attempts to address what might lie beneath the child's behaviour.

These levels of interaction described by West are present for the therapist who works more directly within the symbolic imagery and dramatic play of the child, as described in this book. In this model:

Level I is the way the therapist establishes the relationship between herself and the child in a social way and keeps the child safe in the playing space.

When meeting and greeting the child this attending and listening is the beginning of the negotiation of what kind of play the child wants.

Level II skills are experienced when the child is making decisions about play and processing stories and other material and the therapist is supporting the shaping of the play.

Level III skills are the core of the processing in an arts therapy model and the exploration of meaning is always through the imaginary characters and play structures presented by the child.

Level IV skills are integrated into Level III skills because the interpretations are made through the images and characters presented in the play, not by reference to the child's reality life.

The world of play creates distance by framing experience in another time and another place. Through the fiction of the play the child tells the truth about her present circumstances, so the therapist frames the interpretations within the fictional world created by the child.

Winnicott

Winnicott (1974) defined the psychic space between child and therapist as a transitional space, like the potential space between child and mother.

He described the development of play as a sequence of relationships with the object world, in which the mother has special roles. She is there to give back what is handed out, to fit in with the baby's play, to be sensitive to children's likes and dislikes and introduce ideas to children that are not their own. A sympathetic adult who can meet those therapeutic needs for the child can facilitate the growth of self. This would suggest that the role of the therapist is to be a nurturing parent and the child's journey is from dependence to separation, through the recognition of what is 'me' and 'not me'.

In the arts therapy model this exploration of what is 'me' and 'not me' is processed in play with objects, especially in sorting and patterning play for example, the play of Louise with small family dolls when she sorted them into groups, each doll's role being defined in that family. And the role play in dramatic play clearly defines these distinctions when the child takes on roles of 'the other', which is the way we learn empathic understanding of what it is like to be 'the other'.

Bowlby

Bowlby's (1969, 1973, 1980) studies of infant–parent relationships provide another model for the process of therapy and the role of the therapist. His theory of attachment is based on four propositions:

1. Proximity-maintenance: to survive an infant needs to maintain proximity to its parent or equivalent adult.

2. This proximity-seeking behaviour requires reciprocal nurturing behaviour from the adult for food, warmth and protection.

3. The child will move towards independence and this means a propensity to explore and use its environment.

4. In order to explore and use its environment, the child will need to develop an internal working model with an accurate enough picture of the outside world and a sense of its own needs, wishes and capabilities.

Each of the components of the model is interdependent, because the operation of one requires the operation of them all. For example, if the care-taking behaviour is good enough, the exploratory behaviour will increase. If the system is in balance the child will be able to explore the environment in safety.

To develop a working model of the environment the internal conditions and capacities which enable perception and learning need to be operating well enough. If that is happening, each experience and exploration is incorporated into the internal working model. This is the foundation of the infant's personality, behaviour and coping mechanisms.

The role of the therapist in this model is an enabling one. It is to be a person who offers consistency and facilitates the explorations required by the child to further develop their internal model of the outside world and a clear sense of their identity in that world. The child will experience distress when the internal model she has developed cannot cope with her existing circumstances.

This model is very potent for the play therapist seeking to develop the child's creative play. The therapist can model a consistent adult who keeps boundaries to care for the child but also offer the chance to explore through the use of toys, objects and dramatic play. These are powerful structures to help the child make some meaning by patterning and creating fictional worlds and, through taking on roles and characters, the child can also develop a clearer sense of identity.

Dramatic play in particular, through the playing of characters, telling their story and making their journeys can help the child understand the feelings experienced by that fictional character who loses someone who is needed to nurture them. But the fictional world is distanced enough from the child's reality to be a safe place in which to explore meaning. In this ambivalent, shifting, world 'me' is 'not me.' The fear of being overwhelmed by feeling can be contained if the therapist has made the boundaries clear.

O'Connor

O'Connor (1991) explores the role of the therapist through his unconventional (i.e., not psychoanalytical) description of the transferences which happen in the play therapy process. The term transference is generally defined as all the emotions, thoughts, and behaviours that either the client or therapist bring to the therapy session, in the belief that no one can isolate herself from her past experience and that every experience a person has in the present is intimately tied to everything that has gone before.

The therapist should be more fully aware of the impact of her past on her present functioning. With awareness should come the ability to use what one has learnt from the past to work in the present. The goal of therapy is to create this sort of awareness in the client.

O'Connor's concept of transference is broader. He regards transference not only as emotions, thoughts and behaviour which the client manifests within the context of the therapeutic relationship, but also as the treatment-related interaction between the child and therapist and the child's ecosystem. That is, transference on the part of the child also occurs when she reacts to events in her ecosystem in a manner consistent with issues occurring in therapy.

In the same way, countertransference refers to the emotions, thoughts, and behaviours that the therapist brings to her interactions with the child's ecosystem, whether it is the child's carers, teachers, social worker, or anyone else. Most play therapists have to be involved with the child's ecosystem and this makes the clarity of boundaries difficult to maintain and very complex.

O'Connor identifies three factors that define the role of the play therapist with her client:

- First, the level of training and expertise that the therapist can offer. The therapist should be aware of the limits of her knowledge.
- Second, the therapist should acknowledge the limits of her time commitment, in that her work will have to be defined by the time she has available.

- Third, the therapist must know her personal limits. It is best if the therapist can define the type of work in which she is comfortable. Whatever she prefers, she must know when to say no.

O'Connor: Three Types of Transference

The therapist should be alerted to three types of transference in which children commonly engage.

At some point in the process the child is likely to develop a parental transference. She may react towards the therapist as the 'good' parent or the 'bad' parent. If the therapy is going well, then the transference is likely to be the 'good' parent. It is important to help the child realise that this is a fantasy and will not become a reality. (The use of the story in *Bye Bye Baby* as described in Chapter 2 shows an appropriate way of helping the child understand the role of the play therapist.)

A second common transference reaction is when the child perceives the therapist as all powerful and able to solve all the child's problems.

The third type of transference concerns the child taking emotions, thoughts, or behaviours out of the therapy space and into the ecosystem. For example, the child who becomes very dependent and clingy in therapy becomes so at home and the child, whose behaviour was already problematic, deteriorates as the therapy continues.

It is important that the therapist actively explains to the child and her carers the underlying needs of the child which stimulate these transferences.

O'Connor suggests that an emphasis on the uniqueness of the play space to the child can be helpful, to create boundaries for the therapy, and in discussion with the carers about ways of coping with the child's behaviour. It is important for the carers to set limits about what is appropriate at home, to help the child differentiate the two environments.

Landy: Transference in Dramatherapy

These descriptions of transferences are interesting to the therapist who uses dramatic play in therapy.

Landy (1992a) states that transference and countertransference define a relationship between two persons in symbolic terms, each person bringing a world containing their past affiliations to that relationship. It is these worlds which are explored together by the client and therapist. The arts therapist uses a variety of symbolic media to explore those worlds.

One of the aspects of playing fictional roles with the child is that she can make transferences onto the characters played by both herself and the therapist, as part of dramatic play. If the child perceives me as the 'bad' mother and asks me to take on the role of witch in Hansel and Gretel then her transference is made overt. But as soon as I take on the role of witch I signal to the child that I am entering into the 'as if' world and taking on a symbolic role. As the child also enters this 'as if' world as Gretel she can express her fear and anger of the witch, safe in the knowledge that it is contained in the fictional world we have created.

Nonetheless, fictional characters contain who we are and who we are not, because it is me, Ann, who plays the role of witch. I accept the role handed to me by the child, who experiences me in that role, then experiences me as Ann the therapist as I unmask myself from the role. I also see the child as Gretel and see her relationship to the witch; then Gretel is unmasked and the child re-appears.

It is important for the therapist who works with creative media not to make assumptions about the roles the child asks her to play. If a child asks me to play a witch, it does not always mean she has made the transference to me as the 'bad' mother. Interpretation of the meanings rests on dangerous ground and can deny all the other symbolic meanings that role has for the child. It is important for the development of the creative imagination to maintain an ambivalence about the meaning of a particular enactment or play. There are many layers to a role and many meanings to a character.

The excitement of creativity lies in the expression of ambiguity and the therapist does not want to model that suffocating, parental certainty about an ultimate meaning, which destroys the layers of meaning which can be attached to the development of a character and the playing of a role. Meanings can change; today the witch is cruel, tomorrow, compassionate.

The Therapist As Actor/Audience: The Dramatic Play of the Child

The relationship of child and therapist is particularly potent when dramatic play is one of the symbolic media used and the therapist is involved either directly in dramatic play or as therapist/audience watching the enactment.

Landy

Landy (1992b), describing the role of the dramatherapist working with individuals, observes that she can becomes an active participant, often playing in role with the client. When the therapist is taking a role in this way it is important while playing to maintain dramatic distance in the construction of the drama. This means a balanced approach in which the individual is capable of feeling, without fear of being overwhelmed by the emotion, and thinking, without fear of losing the ability to respond with feeling.

When the therapist and client take on roles it is the roles which each chooses to play which creates a boundary from the other.

The dramatherapist strives to find a balance between the part of himself that is actor and the part of himself that is therapist/audience. Throughout the playing, the therapist needs to keep an actorly reserve in her therapeutic performance as she strives to find a balance between the part of herself that is actor and the part of herself that is therapist/audience.

These ideas are important for the therapist working with children involved in dramatic play. The role playing will be appropriate to the developmental level of the child and it is important to inform the child when you are about to take on a role, so that the boundary between playing and not-playing is clear. I always tell a child when I have begun to play and when I am stopping. Young children can become confused if these boundaries are not very clearly stated, the start and finish clearly signalled.

An actorly reserve is most important with the child, and the quality of the therapist/actor's performance will be matched to the child's capacity to cope. The child can become confused when the therapist is playing a threatening role if these boundaries of play are not kept very clear, and a subdued witch may be the order of the day. If I feel the child is not clear when I am taking a role I will step out of role and remind the child that I was playing.

> 'I was the witch when I shouted.
> Am I still the witch?'
> or
> 'have we stopped playing?'

I will then respond as the child tells me.

It is important for the therapist to learn skills in drama so that the role playing is real and genuine and not a sort of false role-taking that some adults think children like. You must present your character as having truth. The child will know when you are being truthful and will respond in her playing.

Johnson

David Read Johnson (1992) suggests three roles played by the therapist

1. A social role as the therapist.
2. A dramatic role as a participant in the drama.
3. A transference figure as the client casts the therapist in roles from the client's past life.

While it may be clear to the therapist which of these role she is playing, it is not clear that the child will have the same understanding of these roles. There is clearly an overlap between the dramatic role the therapist might be playing and the transference role. The child may perceive role taking as transference, rather than as dramatic role play. If the child perceives the therapist as a parental figure, for example, she may experience the whole therapeutic interaction as a parental transference, so that the social role, dramatic role and transference roles could merge together for that child. At least the therapist can make it clear when she is 'in role' as a character to make some boundary definition.

Johnson defines some modes of participation by the dramatherapist in dramatic play.

1. As the witness or mirror; the therapist observes the client and then, after play, gives them feedback or mirrors back images or feelings around their work.
    The witness is like a receptacle of the client's images.

2. As director; the therapist sits outside the drama but will be active in setting up scenes, a sort of manager of the play space.

3. As sidecoach; the therapist is outside the drama activity but becomes a voice in the scene itself. The therapist coaches from the sidelines, at times modelling for the client as if she is in the scene. The sidecoach functions is at the boundary of the play space, every once in a while opening the door and making a suggestion.

4. As leader; the therapist as leader participates fully in the group/client activities. No longer on the sidelines, the leader plays and takes on a role in a story. Nevertheless, the leader remains somewhat removed from total participation and attempts to help keep the focus of the client's experiences. The therapist as leader is on the inside of the playspace, encouraging participants to look around and explore.

5. As guide; the therapist can act as knowledgeable guide into the imaginative realm. While similar to the leader, the therapist as guide is allowed a greater degree of centrality

in the imagery of the drama. The guide places himself fully in the framework of the story and the playspace. The guide lives in the playspace and welcomes the client when they knock on the door.

6. As shaman; the therapist as actor enacts the images of the drama while the client watches as audience. The therapist takes the imaginary journey alone, but for them. This mode is characteristic in storytelling and therapist-performances. The client then becomes the witness.

1. Perhaps the most important of these roles for the play therapist working with an individual child is to mirror and witness what the child plays. This is the key role for the play therapist: to acknowledge the child's experience unconditionally.

2. The director role is mainly one of organisation, of keeping the boundaries of the playspace but also helping the child, when asked, with the media and ways to use the media.

3. The sidecoach is a very supportive role with a group of children to encourage self-confidence when playing in the group. The side-coach also helps by skill-sharing with the group. For the individual child the witness role is more supportive, because it doesn't interfere with the omnipotence of the child, who is the controller of the play.

4. The leader role is perhaps an unfortunate term to describe the shared enactments between therapist and child. In play therapy it is the child who will lead the play, not the therapist, although the child and therapist together might resolve problems of how to play a particular moment.

5. The guide suggests that the therapist controls the play space, rather than keeping the space safe, which better describes the function of the play therapist. The space belongs to the child, not the therapist.

6. I would rather call the shaman a storyteller because in play therapy this is more a shared experience. When telling a story or looking at

pictures together, the child and therapist share the journey and the child always wants to participate in the process somehow.

Mitchell

Mitchell (1990) describes a theatre model of dramatherapy. He shows that the dramatherapist helps the client to shift their life problems into a theatrical reality – to catch the image and make it both emotional and cognitive.

He believes it is the function of the therapist to help the clients in a group to use their dramatic skills to release what they themselves aspire to in their life-roles, rather than interpreting, or instructing them about how to inhabit a particular role. It is vital that each client works with her own story, not one imposed by the therapist.

First he teaches the client the process of therapy, the language and method of the dramatherapist. Then he develops character work. Mitchell believes that the artistic process of building a character in itself is rich in therapeutic material. If the therapist transposes a everyday problem into the fictional or mythic dimension of character then the client is involved

- first in a decision making process
- second in so far as the use of the imagination is dramatically and poetically a potent force for healing and
- third in the dynamic process of building the character.

Mitchell puts forward the idea that to create an character and to explore life issues through the character's exploration in a scene, builds in a container that is safe for the client yet at the same time investigates a hot issue.

This is an exciting model for the play therapist working with dramatic play with older children and adolescents, where theatre forms can be explored and texts used to develop character and scene.

Meldrum

Meldrum (1993) also explores a theatrical model of dramatherapy and she defines the role of the therapist as an empathic director. This role is not that of a priest, a mystic healer, a patriarch or a matriarch, but a person with therapeutic and artistic skills and a professional training. She defines these characteristics:

- She should have a through line – not a rigid structure – but she should know what her aims are depending on the nature of the client group or the individual concerned.

- She helps the client to find the character and play the part in interaction with the group or the individual with the therapist.

- She listens to the client – to the texts and the subtexts, to her words and to her silences.

- She gives feedback to the client in a supportive, reflective manner

- She gives the client an empty space to express herself and to help her develop.

- She helps the client shift from everyday reality into dramatic reality and back to everyday reality, to the here and now.

- She recognises the dual role of observer and participator. The therapist guides the client's drama and participates in the drama, acknowledging that we share similar existential issues.

- Her attitude toward dramatherapy acknowledges that therapy is a rational endeavour and encourages the client to collaborate fully in the therapeutic process.

- She encourages each individual to work in a spontaneous and honest way by modelling such behaviour herself.

Conclusions

There are many ways to be a play therapist, not one special way she has to be. The priority is to keep the client safe in the process and this requires a sense of responsibility on the part of the therapist. This sense of responsibility will lead the therapist to training, to have an understanding of the developmental processes of the child in her care and to learn to play in ways which will stimulate the child.

The style of the therapist will depend on the client group, the personality and skills of the therapist, and her level of training. But it is necessary always to be questioning, always remembering that responsibility for the client.

This means that there must be supervision, so the work can be constantly reviewed in the light of the therapist's life experience as well as the child's.

Supervision

Supervision is essential for all therapists and is a professional requirement which the therapist is expected to undertake while they are in practice.

Many arts therapies professional associations have mandatory supervision requirements for recently qualified therapists and requirements for supervision for all therapists in practice.

Supervision is not the same as case management where, for example, the leader of the social services team supervises and manages the work of the team. Supervision can take one of the following forms:

- Regular one-to-one sessions with a supervisor, preferably from the discipline of play therapy.
- One-to-one peer supervision in which the pair alternate roles on a weekly basis or within a session so both deal with the issues of their practice at each meeting.
- Group supervision with a small group and the supervisor, which can be a valuable way to exchange information and

share experiences, although sometimes it becomes a fight to be heard enough during the session.

- Peer group supervision which is usually made up of a group of experienced practitioners from a variety of disciplines who explore issues together from their own perspective; this helps broaden the skills of all the group.

Whatever form it takes, supervision is the place where the therapist explores her play therapy practice. The person being supervised is contained and kept safe, her work is encouraged but she is also challenged and stimulated. Her practice should be explored, inappropriate work challenged, and the therapist confronted. There should be informed discussion between the supervisor and clients about ways of work and the practice of the supervisees developed and deepened.

The pair or group can communicate in a variety of ways. Play and dramatic play can be used from time to time in supervision as a way of exploring the dynamic relationship between the therapist and client, or therapist and supervisor, so that the therapist can gain insight into the processes of their therapeutic interactions.

It is always very stressful for the therapist to hear the pain and suffering expressed by small children; in supervision the therapist can be kept safe in the same way as she has offered safety to her clients. She can share the terror, fear and paralysis. Without this safe place, the burden would be too great and the therapist overwhelmed.

The children in our care have already been abused by a harsh life, so our responsibility is not to add to that abuse. We can only offer the child the safety of that 'empty space', the playing space, to help heal the hurt, if we also have our own safe place to explore our practice and heal ourselves.

CHAPTER 4

STRUCTURING THE PLAY

Lamentation
Nobody loves me,
Everybody hates me,
Going in the garden
To-eat-worms.

Big fat juicy ones,
Little squiggly niggly ones,
Going in the garden
To-eat-worms.

Teasing
I beg your pardon,
Grant your grace;
I hope the cows
Will spit in your face.

Structure of the Therapy

Play is the way children make sense of their world. When we use play as therapy it is important that we offer a safe way and a safe place for the child to play. The safe place is also important for the therapist as the rhymes above will testify!

In my book *Play Therapy with Abused Children* (1992), I described a model of play therapy which focused on the creative elements of play as the healing medium. In this model the centrality of play is acknowledged as the child's way of understanding their world. Play is perceived as a developmental process and the child moves back and forth along this developmental continuum. The basic processes explored in play are sensory play, projected play with objects and toys, and role play developing to dramatic play.

Play is a symbolic process and, as the child creates images, stories, dramatic play and play with objects and toys, the symbolic nature of the play safely distances the child from their reality experiences. Play happens in a therapeutic space, which is a transitional space between the child and therapist, an alternative reality, a place to transcend and transform experience.

In order to offer this experience to the child, the therapist must structure the therapy so that the child is clear about the meaning of play with the therapist, knows the rules, and wants to participate.

Settings and Materials

The Play Space

The play space is a physical space, and also the psychic space which develops between child and therapist.

The physical space can be a play room, if you are lucky, or the corner of the classroom, school library, child's bedroom, the garden shed, the office. Children play in such spaces and are comfortable there, provided the space is contained and customised in some way by player and therapist. My blue mat (1992) is my physical and symbolic space for therapy and when the mat is in place, wherever that might be, then the child and I start to play on the mat.

It is important to be undisturbed in the play space, so a space away from the main hubbub of the building is best and more secure for the child. We play in the hinterland, on the borders of life, we go away, outside, in the attic – away.

Play Materials

The choice of objects and toys will be determined by the needs of the child and the theme of the therapy.

I have described the toys I use for abused children (1992) and for all children there should be materials to stimulate sensory play, figures and objects for scenes and story-making, dolls and puppets to nurture and/or abuse, puppets for storymaking and for dramatic play, clothes, props, boxes and steps for the child to move in and out and up and down.

Sensory Play

The Treasure Basket

Goldschmied (1975) described a treasure basket full of objects with a variety of texture, colour, and weight as a sensory stimulus for the very small child.

She included wooden objects such as rattles, clothes pegs, small boxes, coloured beads on string, objects made of natural materials such as woollen balls, wooden nail brush, shoe horn, natural objects such as fir cones, large pebbles, pumice stone, metal objects such as spoons, keys, whistle, bicycle bell, leather and textiles objects such as leather purse, lavender bags, small teddy bear, and paper objects such as grease proof paper, cardboard boxes.

This is of interest to all children, but for the child not yet ready to play symbolically this can be a good way to begin to explore. It is a real treasure for the child with limited mobility or a child who is unable to attach meaning to objects who can find a comfort in the basket if the contents are kept and the basket always present.

Sand, Water and Slime

Sand and water are basic for the sensory play of the child. My particular favourite messy material is slime, the bane of mother's life but beloved of the child. Bought in tubs, green, red, purple, sometimes fluorescent, this material can depict all the mess and uncontrollable effluence of the human body.

All these sensory materials are used as primitive embodied materials to be stroked, caressed, smoothed out or made rough. With water, there is the pleasure of the feel of it, pouring, splashing and the joy of the flow of it.

Play merges from one form to another and sand and slime in particular often take on symbolic significance for the child and become part of story making. From being messy slime, the material takes on symbolic significance, perhaps depicting the 'mess' that all life seems to be.

Many children still like to work their way into a therapy session by playing with messy materials as they formulate ideas of how they want to play for the major part of the session. The material then becomes a kind of warm-up to stimulate the child, but also to re-establish the relationship between child and therapist, and re-establish for the child their sense of their physical self and the space that self takes up in the play space.

Play with Objects

From sensory play the child can develop what Elinor Goldschmeid calls heuristic play, which describes the child's curiosity and desire to find out for herself what she can do with objects.

Children at this stage are absorbed by putting objects in and taking them out of containers, filling and emptying containers, then placing, pairing and matching, selecting and discarding. For this kind of play the child needs tins and containers of all sizes, cardboard cylinders, and small objects to put in the containers.

This play is important for the child who has not yet learnt to play symbolically but is starting to explore the meaning of objects.

As the child plays, the therapist can watch, and when the child is ready, help them to understand that objects can be used to represent something other than what the are. So a pan can also be a hat and a chain a bracelet.

Symbolic Play with Objects

When children begin to play symbolically and are using toys and objects as a way to project their experiences, it is important to find toys and objects which have relevance to the child in therapy. Children seem to find something in the toy or small figure of the moment which symbolises an aspect of the difficulties the child is expressing in therapy.

When the four turtles were the popular icons for young children, it was interesting to note which of the four characters the child selected, and they were always very clear why they liked one particular character more than the others. The turtles represented the child, who knew what he was like or what he wanted to be like.

There are now a few more female figures who take the heroes' path, a much needed change; although ethnic female heroes are hard to find.

Containing the World

When the child is exploring fearful events in therapy using small toys and objects, it is often useful to contain the figures in some environment to keep the boundary of the play. An adaptation of Lowenfeld's World Technique (1950) is a powerful method to help the child contain and control the 'world' they make.

This technique invites the child to create their 'world' in a sand tray with any materials they choose. The sand tray, she suggested, should be three inches deep, painted blue inside, set on a table waist high to the user. Sand and water were provided.

The toys and objects she suggested were:

> people, divided into types,
> houses, trees, fences,
> animals – wild and tame,
> transport for road, rail, river and sea,
> street signs
> and other small objects.

The Lowenfeld method can be adapted to the circumstances of even the travelling therapist. Trays can be selected from an abundance of blue cat litter trays and small figures carried in bags or boxes.

It is important to keep a record of the 'worlds' created in the tray by the children so I always photograph the completed world.

It is interesting to note that sand in a tray can often lead back to embodied play when the child's world is simply to smooth the sand and make shapes with it in the containment of the tray.

David (aged nine) described his warring world;

> 'There are two armies, Robin Hood and his men and Captain Hook and his men. Robin Hood's men had gone to California to find the dragon. The dragon had had a baby and they were going to take the baby away from the dragon and try to kill the dragon.

> Hook gets hold of Robin Hood's men and all the men are chained to the floor. They are going to hang Robin Hood. The dragon has been caught and is in prison in the torture chamber. The baby dragon is with her and is put on the rack and tortured. If only Megaman was here!'

This was David's world, a sad and bitter place at this time. He wanted it recorded with a photograph.

There are many objects which act as containers for the child. A large cardboard box to contain the child can be a safe place like a den, or a dog kennel, or an unsafe place like the dragon's torture chamber or the fragile house which the fox can;

> 'huff and puff and blow your house down.'

Dolls' houses can contain all the horror or pleasure of a family life which is difficult to understand and death and destruction fly in and out of the doors and windows.

One boy, aged four, endlessly played the house burning down and the fire engine coming to the rescue. The fireman was the rescuer of the family who were unable to keep themselves safe from danger.

Another boy of four, whose mother had attempted to smother him, constantly used the doll's house to contain his re-enactment in a fictional story of a boy who was afraid to sleep at night for fear of robbers.

Castles and forts are fortified containers for the child who needs to defend himself from

'the slings and arrows of outrageous fortune.'

The warring armies slug it out as the hero finds ways to save himself.

The space station, especially the Thunderbirds model at the moment, is quite a magical place where you can go when things are difficult, but also emerge from the safety to cope with the world outside.

Islands, contained by the sea are places to go to rest, although many islands have good and bad sides constantly warring with each other.

Boxes can be artistic containers for older clients. The artist Peter Blake believes that once something is encased in a box it becomes precious. Many artists create boxes either using objects they have made or objects that appeal. Sometimes a theme for the box contains the experience even more clearly, so a box can be made with everything in it beginning with A, or a Peter Pan box, or whatever image or idea appeals – perhaps a box containing a small clock filled with thoughts about time. All these containers have secret places, different levels,

'From the sky to the underworld'

places to hide, places to fear, places for arrivals and departures and places for putting things in and taking things out.

Containers can be objects offered in the play room, but the child may want to create their own castle, island or Thunderbird's space station. For some children the container itself becomes the metaphor. Angela used the metaphor of an island to describe her life circumstances throughout all our meetings.

This was an island she described toward the end of her therapy, separated from her mother who was undergoing psychiatric treatment and separated from her brothers. It was a hard journey, the separation a real punishment.

ANGELA'S ISLAND

'This desert island is about not to be greedy. If you are greedy you get sent to this island.

A man and a lady were sent to the island because they weren't honest. The lady was rich but greedy. She went to market and told the stall holders that her husband was in prison. They gave her food but the Gods saw and punished her and she was sent to the island.

The man did the same, he stole things.

The first island they were sent they had to be slaves and carry coal to the mines to be buried. Some drive tractors but once up there everybody has to dig each day. They beg for rest.

People have to learn their lesson. It's hard work but it's their own fault.

The second island every day it changes. It can get horrible, worse, or better. If the good things happen then working there is nice.

When the sun goes weaker they can stop work.

The island is nicer because they only work 21 hours out of 24.

One day when they have learnt their lesson they can go.

At the moment they can go to their own land to see their relatives but they can't go home.'

The Child as Actor

For the child interested in dramatic play there should be clothes and objects which can be adapted to facilitate play. Hats, bags and suitcases, old curtains to be made into cloaks and costumes. sticks and umbrellas.

The playroom should contain cardboard boxes and other spaces – places bigger than the child, places to hide in and jump out. Perhaps steps, so the child can be the tallest in the room, the 'king of the castle'.

Aqua-paint, a stage make-up with strong, vibrant colours which can be applied with water and fingers, is a material which can be used as a embodied, sensory experience and/or a symbolic process as the child makes marks on their face, using colour to express an image or create a role.

If you haven't the space, then role play can be developed using a tape recorder to dramatise a scene. This scene was played between Liam and myself as he expressed his anger about the 'mothers' he had experienced in his fourteen years of life. He began his scene by making food with slime. He sang as he made the food.

ANTHONY'S SONG

'Making cheese for my mummy, mummy, mummy,
Making cheese for my mummy, mummy, mummy,
Going to poison her, going to poison her,
Going to poison, poison, poison her.
Then she will die, then she will die
Then she will die die die.

Anthony says;
I'm putting the poison in now. Yes I've got to kill her.
She's 'orrible to me.

Mother speaks
Anthony, cheese for your dear sweet mummy.
How kind. Normally you're not such a kind boy. Normally

you're a sloppy horrible child.
Well as you've done something kind I'd better taste it.

Mother spits out cheese.

Boy shoots mother.

Mother says,
You're shooting me you terrible boy. I always knew you were
bad.

Anthony says;
End of Scene 1

Scene 2.
Repeat Scene 1 except making pudding instead of cheese.

Scene 3
Repeat Scene 1 except making dinner.

Then mother says;
You have killed me. The last of your three mothers you terrible
boy.

Anthony shoots with his gun
Then shouts to the gun;
Stop you blasted thing, stop, stop stop.'

Liam found the making and taping of this scene a contained way to
begin to express some of the anger he felt by the treatment he had
received from his natural mother, foster carer and adoptive mother
who had rejected him. His cry of 'Stop' at the end was a cry of pain,
anger and helplessness.

When I played the part of the mother he giggled at my verbal
abuse of the boy Anthony, the first time he was allowed to take
symbolic vengeance for all that hurt.

Liam felt helpless in the care system, as indeed he was, but slowly
and surely he began to fight for his rights.

Mask Make-up and Role

An interesting way to use stage make-up, role play and storymaking was described by Barbara MacKay, who works in Canada. She used this process with adolescents and adults. I have adapted her process for work with my clients.

Introduction

Begin by introducing the process to the client/group. Each person needs a mirror and make-up and the therapist needs a tape recorder.

The process

1. Write down how many roles you have played in your life, for example, son, daughter, student, teacher and so forth.
2. Look in the mirror and explore what you see before you paint your face.
3. Use the make-up to paint your face.
4. When your face is finished look in the mirror and explore what you see.
5. Then the therapist asks the client to tell the story into the tape recorder about what you see on your face.
6. Photograph the image.
7. Place photo and story together.

I have used this structure with individual adolescent clients who enjoy mask-making and role play. It is a powerful medium and the therapist needs to know her client so that trust is established.

Most clients symbolise themselves as a character but some make some kind of self-description such as 'a sad person' or 'helpless'.

The masks can be explored further in role play or the lives of the characters developed in stories. Try it on yourself first to experience the impact!

Making the Contract to Play

Taking a Referral: On Not Changing the Whole World

Perhaps the most important security for a prospective client is the therapist's understanding of the possibilities of play as therapy, the timing of such interventions, and whether such an intervention is appropriate at all.

The therapist needs a case history of the child to be referred and a clear understanding of the present living arrangements of the child. Many children are referred when their current circumstances are very unsafe and other professional workers feel powerless. The child is referred for therapy but the reasons for the intervention are unclear.

If this kind of panic referral is accepted without a careful assessment of the possibilities, then the child will often assume that the therapist will rescue her.

The result can be disaster for the child, which will be interpreted as another rejection by an adult, further confirming a sense of worthlessness.

As well as the life history of the child, the therapist must know who is now caring for the child and what support they will give to the child. It is pointless for the therapist to work with a child and have the carer of the child undermining this work, making for further conflict. The carers should know what goes on in play therapy so they can support the child. The reason for the intervention must also be clear. Why should the child need therapy at this time? The danger is that some professional workers want to use play therapy only as an information gathering process instead of a healing process.

Meeting the Child and Carer and Referrer

It is very important to meet those people who will be involved and responsible for the child while play therapy is in progress. If the parent has asked for the referral, then it is only necessary to see the child and parents, but if the child is in the care system in some way it is important for the social worker to be present with the child's carer so that the plans are clear to everyone.

It is important to find out from each person why they think play therapy would be helpful, especially the child. If the understanding is clear, I then talk to the child in the presence of the adults about what we do in play therapy and ask the child to say if they want to come.

For example, I went to see a family with their social worker who introduced me to the whole family. Then I spoke to Louise, aged six saying that I had heard she was sad because her brother was living with another family and wasn't coming back to live with them.

I asked if she was mixed up and sad about that. Louise nodded. I said I could come and play with her about that if she wanted. I said we might not play about her brother but maybe make up stories about people leaving and not coming back which would help us understand what was happening to her brother and her family.

Louise said she was interested. I then told her how we would play together. We would play in her bedroom and I would bring my special blue mat and bags of toys. We would sit on the mat together and she could look through all the bags and choose the toys she needed. One bag at a time, but we can mix toys from different bags if we want.

We play for one hour each time I come, and I will tell her when the time is nearly finished by saying she has only time to play with one more thing before we finish.

When we sit on the mat to play, Louise can say whatever she likes; nice or nasty things about anybody.

There is a rule, no hitting or fighting with each other and we keep the toys on the mat.

If we don't want to play with the toys, we could draw, make up stories, and act together.

If we acted a story we might use more of the room than the mat but we would go back there when we had finished. At the end of the hour we would fold up the mat.

After we have finished I will talk to your mum to explain how you are feeling. The reason I do that is so that she can look after you and understand how you are feeling.

I won't tell your mum what we have played but just how you might be feeling. If you want to tell mum what you did then you can, of course.

I told Louise that I would come six times and will tell her each time how many more meetings we have to come.

Louise agreed to this; we made the first date and then I showed her the bags of toys in the back of my car.

Initial Assessment

At the first interview or the first play therapy session, if the child is old enough to understand and draw, I ask them to draw a personal shield.

I draw the shield. I say it is like a badge on the school blazer. I divide the shield into six sections.

I ask them to copy the outline of my shield.

I say that when they have drawn the shield I am going to ask them some questions and they are to draw the answers on the shield and then, when it is complete, it will tell their story. After they have finished their drawing I will ask them to explain what they have drawn and I will write their answers on my shield so we will remember its meaning.

I suggest that the child draws the first thing that comes into their head to answer the questions and they can use as many colours as they like to make the drawing.

MY SHIELD

1st Section: What is the best thing that has ever happened to you?

2nd Section: What is the best thing that has happened to your family – any family? (Children in care may have lived in many families.)

3rd Section: What is the worse thing that has happened to you?

4th Section: What do you want most from other people, not your family, but people of your own age? (I usually list a number of possibilities: love, friendship, sex, money, toys, help, fun etc.)

5th Section: If you only had a year to live and all the money you want, what would you do for that year?

6th Section: Now it's your funeral and people are there and they are remembering you; what three things would you like people to say about you? They don't have to be true. If you want I'll write the words for you.

We talk about the drawings and the story in the shield. I give the child continual reinforcement.

Section 1

Often the child can't think of anything good that has happened to her and we share ideas about good times until something is remembered.

Section 2

It is always interesting to hear of good things in the family and which family is selected by the child in care.

Section 3

Some children will define the worse thing that has happened as abuse or a serious difficulty but many children offer a trivial example like 'I got told off by my teacher'.

Section 4

Many children say they want friendship from other people, the drawing of this definition is often interesting, sometimes a very physical expression by abused children, often a confusion between love and sex. Unattached children often choose money or toys as their need, the reliable object, as they perceive it as being the most important exchange.

Section 5 and 6

The way of wording the last two questions is determined by the experience of the child. Clearly the questions are worded in different ways for bereaved children or if I feel the child might be uncomfortable with the notion of death.

In Section 5 the choice seems to be to fight or flight. Staying often requires gifts to set the family right, a house, a car and so forth, and flight to see the world before it is too late.

Only one child has said they would spend the year trying to find a cure for themselves.

Section 6 tells me how the child would like to be seen, although many children are unable to think of three good things they would like people to say.

Good, kind and loving are the most popular words used by abused children.

This chart is a good ice-breaker to start and helps me to understand how the child perceives herself at the moment of drawing.

I reinforce pride in who you are to the child and ownership of the shield as a description of their life. All responses are accepted and acknowledged as important.

Shields

Lloyd, aged ten, adopted into a family who found nurturing very difficult drew the following answers:

Section 1:   Eating bread.
Section 2:   Going to my nannies (adopted family).
Section 3:   New adoptive brother's dreams in bed disturb his sleep.
Section 4:   I want people to like me.
Section 5:   I would spend the year eating food.
Section 6:   I would like people to say I was nice, faithful and clever.

Figure 4.1 Lloyd's shield

Lloyd presented as a thin, weakly boy, but the intensity with which he described his desire for food and bread helped me to focus on his need for nurture. His jealousy of his adoptive brother was about the attention he lost from his parents, who had to attend to the needs of his brother.

Carl, aged seven, was severely physically and sexually abused; he has been adopted for three years.

Figure 4.2 Carl's shield

Section 1:   Being adopted.
Section 2:   My birthdays with my adopted family.
Section 3:   Being hit by mum and dad. (Birth family.)
Section 4:   I want love from my friends, that means kissing.
Section 5:   I would fly round the world with magic wings. I
                    would stop at a train station and feed the cows. I
                    would go to Thorpe Park and Disneyland.
Section 6:   I would like people to think I was funny, a good
                    singer and I could make up stories.

I was interested in Carl's definition of love as kissing and it soon became clear that he was confused about body boundaries. He denied he had been sexually abused for some time until he felt he could trust me.

Carl's sister Amanda, aged ten.

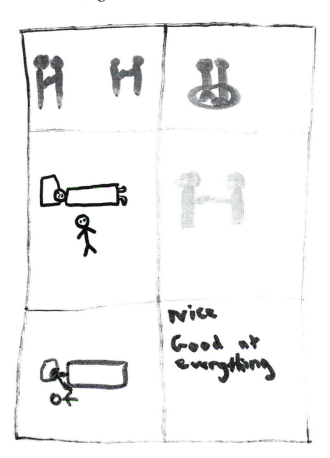

Figure 4.3 Amanda's shield

Section 1:   Mum and dad kissing goodnight.
Section 2:   Going to Butlins with my adoptive family.
Section 3:   Dad touching me in my private parts.
Section 4:   Friendship which means shaking hands.

Section 5:   Try to make myself better. Visit doctors.
Section 6:   Nice, good at everything, clever.

Amanda also had difficulty with body boundaries and ways to express love and affection. She was clear about the sexual abuse but still felt victimised. She was desperate to please.

Jason, whose play was described in Chapter 1.

Figure 4.4 Jason's shield

Section 1:   At Butlins, flooding my brother in the pool.
Section 2:   Holiday in the Isle of Wight.
Section 3:   Chucked in the swimming pool.
Section 4:   I want people to play with me.
Section 5:   Go on holiday in the Outback in Australia.
Section 6:   A good fighter, brainy, a kind of sense of humour.

Jason had this ambivalent attitude about himself and his brother. The best thing he said was doing to his brother what was the worse thing for Jason – being chucked in the swimming pool. He couldn't separate from his brother and his mother wouldn't let him.

Figure 4.5 Paula's shield

Paula, aged 16.

Section 1:   A holiday when I went riding.
Section 2:   When all the family went on holiday.
Section 3:   My dad abusing me.
Section 4:   Friendship.
Section 5:   Buy a house and look after the animals.
Section 6:   Kind, loving person, nice to be with and to have around.

Paula's drawings expressed more ambivalence that her explanations with a lot of confusion about relationships and how they were expressed.

The shields give hints, ideas, feelings, of ways that the therapist might approach the client. Some ideas can be followed through, other ideas are red herrings, some feelings are to be explored 'not just yet.'

And so the work begins.

CHAPTER 5

METHODS AND PROCESSES IN PLAY THERAPY

Creative Free Play

This is perhaps the most often used method in play therapy, when the child is free to play and choose toys, objects and materials for themselves.

This play is structured within the rules described in Chapter 4 and the contract to play made between the child and therapist defines play as a way for the child to make sense of their world. It is most important that the child is clear about the purpose of therapy and has agreed to the contract.

The rules, contract, meaning and boundaries must be very clear even to the smallest child. We must, as therapists, always remember that adults who abuse children also use play as a way to groom a child for abuse and this means that the therapist must think carefully about how a child might interpret what is happening.

There may be much testing of the boundaries at the beginning of play or the child might feel helpless and hopeless and present in a passive way, but the play, or not/play, belongs to the child and is acceptable.

In creative process therapy there is a creative interaction between therapist and child so the therapist can suggest materials and forms of play but accept the child's decision to play or not. For example, many children enter the play space with clear ideas of what they want to do for the whole session, while other children know what they want to play but spend time exploring the possibilities with a variety of objects to discover which is the most appropriate. With these groups, the children have established a relationship of trust with the therapist and may use the therapist to support their play ideas or help resolve creative problems.

Some children are not quite sure what they want to play, or if they dare to play, and here the therapist's role is to reflect back that feeling, and offer creative suggestions only if asked. These are often rejected to test the relationship, and this is accepted by the therapist. It is important, when the child does not feel safe, that the therapist is supportive and quiet and does not overwhelm the child with suggestions and ideas. This can lead to paralysis for the child, and a sense of hopelessness about their own creativity.

When a child becomes engaged in the process, their commitment is very clear. Then the child often enters the room with well thought out ideas of what they want to play and will concentrate intensely for the hour. Stories and play are often repeated and developed with each repetition as the material is integrated.

If the contract to play is open-ended, it is often clear when the process is coming to an end, as the intensity lessens, the play is repeated and integrated, and then the child and therapist begin to reflect on the play they have shared together.

Sally

An example of such a process is Sally, aged eight, who had witnessed the death of her mother, who was stabbed. Play therapy was to help her cope further with that trauma and perhaps to mourn and remember her mother as a person rather than the mutilated body she was as she died.

The play materials she constantly used were slime and play-doh, sometimes small family dolls, and always drawing materials.

The trauma Sally had experienced was intense but she had received expert de-briefing by her psychiatrist about the event of her mother's death which enabled her to make use of play therapy.

There was much negotiation about boundaries at the beginning of the therapy. She wanted to draw pictures on the mat we sat on, so I brought another mat for her to draw on, which she used for that purpose.

Throughout her therapy she wanted the boundaries made clear, especially time boundaries. She always asked how much time she had left and always wanted to win some extra time for herself. I was always very firm to keep the exact time and this had to be to the second.

Figure 5.1 The King of the Jungle

Sally always knew what she wanted to do but sometimes she would begin a drawing or start to play, then find it too overwhelming. Or she would use these snippets of play to test out my acceptance of her and her control over me. She would tantalise, by beginning to draw then stop and divert to some other play. These sudden stops were important, and a mirror of her life.

At the start Sally drew all-powerful, controlling figures: a lion who was king of the jungle, and a fearsome monster who was The Boss. She identified with these controlling figures who ruled the world 'out there', always controlling the chaos. Throughout the therapy she drew horses; at the beginning they were all cut up in pieces, sometimes they were made whole, other times in pieces again. We connected this with a picture by Otto Dix of Baron Munchhausen and his horse, the baron on the horse but the horse cut in two. At the end of the therapy, the whole horse threw me off its back into a pool of blue water surrounded by soft green grass.

Early on she drew a picture of a block of flats and told the story;

THE FLATS

'This is a block of flats. All the flats are nice but it depends if you like heights. There are only nine floors so you don't get scared.

The people who live there can choose their own curtains.

The people can be single people or families

The biggest flat on the bottom floor has four bedrooms, only one reception room.

The studio flats are the smallest.

The flats get massive as you go down.

Nobody at all fights in the flats, just some little boys play silly games.

They are mostly old people who live there. No sexy things, no boy-friends.

The children can come and visit, they are grandchildren and they come in the summer.

Nobody is unhappy because there is a nice path and lots of things to do.

Some flats have really nice things, flowers, vases.

Lots of people want to move in.

There is a satellite dish.

The old people live in Manchester; the children are from London because in Manchester they are in a great big field.

There are two swings, one big, one baby. One small slide that everybody likes and a little roundabout.

The children like the little park, it is small and they can learn to share there.

If they fall off, they have special grass, really soft like a trampoline, and a bouncy castle.

There is a swimming pool leading to a car park because nobody has a car.

There is a very old lady who needs help getting dressed.

She has a bad leg, she broke it. She has swapped flats with another lady because of her leg.

There is a lift, actually three lifts, but nobody likes them.

She is a brown person with orangy hair.

Everybody is jealous.

Another old lady has a wheelchair, she can't walk.

Everybody likes her and everybody else is nice. She is going to get old and tatty like everybody else.'

Sally wanted to explore herself, inside and outside herself. How to find a safe place to live, people to trust, a place to play in safety, to be a child again. These were her preoccupations. Her flat is a safe place, no parents to die on you or leave you, but not a safe place because if all the adults are old, all decrepit, and you can't have one person for yourself then even your therapist

'is going to get old and tatty like everybody else'.

and nobody ever belongs just to you.

But inside these flats, inside the self, there were complications – nine floors, choices but no choices, lots of lifts which nobody uses, lots of unexplored places and unused spaces.

As Sally began to trust me and come to terms with my great age and tattiness, she began a lot of play about the death of her mother. She was unable to talk about this trauma but began to use slime, pretending it was meat, cutting it up into pieces with a toy knife, to make stew. She wrote a story:

THE DINNER PARTY

'This is a dinner party for eight or more. There is a park bench and other people are bringing vegetables. The lady who is giving the party is called Jessica. The husband is a butcher. Jessica is making ham and slicing it. Very fat slices for people who like ham.

Jessica, John, her husband; Joan and Joanna are the friends.

There is a lot of meat.'

She was concerned with the mutilation of the dead body. The rights and wrongs of family relationships which ended in violence. She drew another picture:

THE WHALE

'There is a killer whale and a blue whale.
The killer whale kills the blue whale.
Who is the killer whale?'

Figure 5.2 The Whale

It was important for Sally that I accepted the drawings, the cutting, the meat, that I could cope with the images yet, by making firm boundaries of time and place and the rules of the therapeutic hour, contained the play.

Sally then enacted a death by stabbing, with me as victim, still using the 'as if' mode of dramatic play. After the play, we talked about the nature of such a death and Sally made a personal connection with her own trauma, and acknowledged the loss of her mother, more in silence than words. In the next session, Sally drew two pictures, of a queen and a robot.

Figure 5.3 The Queen

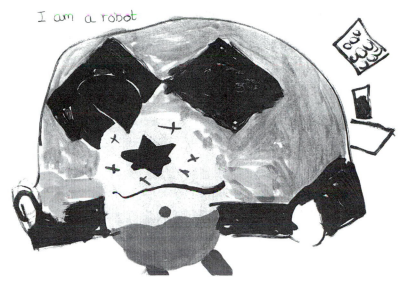

Figure 5.4 The Robot

THE ROBOT AND THE QUEEN

'He is sitting on the queen's sofa in her house.

The queen didn't want a red sofa, she is fed up of red because everything is red, her bed is red and she asked for lots of different colours.

It's very distressing.'

The events surrounding the death of her mother were frequently embedded in her stories and pictures, as in 'The Robot and the Queen'. The sense of alienation which such an trauma brings was explored in stories where the roles of mother, daughter and therapist are enmeshed together and the past and present entwined.

THE BOAT

'The boat is sailing to France carrying people on holiday. The Prime Minister is there, he nearly fell overboard but didn't.

Ann is on the boat, she fell over the edge, and nearly drowned but there was somebody there with a rubber ring which burst, because Ann was so fat and the jelly fish came and stung her.

Ann is holding on to the rope shouting, 'Help, help.'

This diver comes along to rescue her and her clothes fall off.

She runs to her room and she ends up looking like Caesar because she is wrapped in a sheet and has seaweed in her hair.

She didn't want to end up like Caesar, dead. She wanted to go to tea but she had nothing to cover her. She gets some old jeans but they don't fit.

Ann shouts, 'Help, help. I can't get into my pyjamas.'

Her next story was:

ANN ON THE BOAT

'Ann is in her pyjamas after the boat. She has purple cheeks and lipstick because she is embarrassed. She has a teddy under her arm. Everybody is laughing at me because it's a dinner party and only the rich were invited and I wasn't invited. When I turned up they said "Go away, pea brain!" Ann started to cry and threw the teddy at the lady. Ann started to cry and said "I don't like it anymore".'

Sally encapsulated events and feelings from her past life and her present situation into her stories to try to make sense of what had happened in her family. She hated going to places where she was of interest because of what had happened to her mother. 'Ann' becomes 'I' then back to Ann again.

The body is no longer reliable. It is out of control, too fat or too thin and this is dangerous. Clothes fall off and the body is naked, vulnerable. Fat, thin, naked, clothed, especially in pyjamas, all invite danger or death. All explored through play, stories and images.

And, during this time, the horse became whole, then bits of body fell off again, the whole horse could toss the rider from her back into a pond, bodies mended, fell apart then mended again.

Figure 5.5 Ann flying into the pond

Sally began to live with foster carers. We have finished our meetings for the moment. Sally wants to get on with living, enjoy school and make new friends. She struggles on.

The intensity of helping traumatised children is extreme for the therapist, whose prime concern is to keep the safety for the child so they can cope with their distress. The road is long and hard and the therapist needs good supervision.

Figure 5.6 On being haunted

Dramatic Play

Dramatic play can be a part of creative free play as the child takes on roles and makes enactments. The therapist has often to make a judgement about the appropriate form for a child's story and what roles are appropriate for the therapist to play. It is important to create fictional roles and a structure for the play before starting to play.

When I played Captain Hook to Julian's Peter Pan, (Chapter 1), we had prepared the story and structure of the scene and it was clearly a fiction. One Peter Pan enactment was based on this plot, which Julian told to me:

> 'Captain Hook comes at last. Hook is looking for Peter Pan.
> Peter Pan can see the big man's shadow.
> Peter Pan thinks he can fly but his face hits the slime and snow.
> Peter throws the slime and snow out of the window.
> In the end Peter Pan and Captain Hook have a big fight.
> After a long time Peter Pan chops off Captain Hook's wig.
> He has got pretend hair underneath.
> In the end Peter Pan flies home which is like my mum's home.'

It is dangerous for the therapist playing with young children, to jump into a role without preparation, or to play a role not clearly fictionalised. Julian and I sorted out the plot and knew how we would go before we started to play. We had also talked about the sort of dialogue we might use.

Some dramatic play often begins at the start of therapy when the child is testing the boundaries and establishing the relationship.

At this stage many children make food out of play-doh and there is a dramatic enactment of feeding each other. This feeding and exchange of food is not always nurturing, the child often offers poisoned food which might have to be swallowed. Death sometimes ensues, followed by magical re-birth or, sometimes, the recipient of the food does not die but swallows the poison and lives.

Some young children enact this dramatic interchange for many weeks. One girl of four began every play session with the ritualistic exchange of food and a boy of five always offered chips which turned into willies.

These small dramatic exchanges are accompanied by expressions of delight or disgust concerning the nature of the food. The themes are about sharing nurture and the capacity of the therapist to contain the poisoned bits and still be there for the child.

We made Keith's play into a story;

KEITH'S STORY

'There was once a boy who tried to make chocolate cakes for Ann but it turned into slime, a cake slime and nobody would eat it except Ann. She screwed up her face and the slime changed into green jelly but that didn't taste nice so the boy ate it and it was yukky like a slimy monster.

Ann said; "Why are you eating this if it's yukky?"

And the boy said "But it's yummy".

Ann said, "Come off it".

And the boy said "No!"

He had mushed up the slime and he ate it all up in one gulp.

He asked Ann to eat some.

"No thank you!"

So the boy put it back into the pot.

The boy was cross because Ann didn't eat the slime so he threw it at her.

So the boy got some more and made Ann eat it but only little tiny bits.

"It's disgusting" said Ann.

The boy laughed.

He was pretending it was green jelly but he knew really that it was poison.

But Ann didn't die because she can eat poison and still live.

The End of the Story.'

Stimulus for Dramatic Play

Picture Books

Sometimes the dramatic play of young children develops from story telling by the therapist.

GREETINGS AND PARTINGS

A simple picture book such as *Hello, Good-bye* by Lloyd and Voce (1988) describes meeting and parting and has a strong visual impact.

The first picture show a tree in the sunshine, then a bear appears. Then each picture shows the bear saying 'hello' to a variety of creatures. Then it begins to rain and the bear says 'good bye' to all the creatures. The final picture shows the tree saying 'hello' to the rain,

> 'very, very quietly.'

The child and therapist can act the different greetings. It can be a healing process for the child who has experienced 'hello' and 'good-bye' outside their control. The child can act images of meetings and partings which they can initiate. The animals portrayed in the book have very specific characters, quite an amiable bunch!

SELF-ESTEEM

I Want To Be by Tony Ross (1993) is a delightful book about the 'princess', a hero of many of his books. In this story, she is occupied with the idea of growing up and what that means. She asks many people;

> 'What is the best way to be?'

and receives a variety of answers and the most important question which is;

> '... what do YOU want to be?'

The structure of the book is ideal for dramatic play, with the dialogue between the princess and the people she meets who give advice. Lots of role reversal for therapist and child and fun to explore a variety of choices of 'what to be' not given in the book.

THE HERO'S JOURNEY

When The World Sleeps by Cliff Wright (1991) describes in pictures a boy's journey to place the moon back in the sky after it has fallen to earth. The illustrations are strong and often scary and it is no easy task for the boy.

The whole journey could be enacted, or scenes from the journey. There are powerful pictures when the boy places the moon in the branches of a gnarled tree and eventually the tree catapults the moon back into the sky. The moon is powerless outside of the sky but the boy and tree together release the moon from the earth.

The book depicts struggle and determination to complete a task even when it is difficult and frightening. There is much symbolism in the struggle of the boy and the tree together.

Pictures

A single picture or image is a good stimulus for dramatic play or role-taking with older children and adolescents. I collect post cards from art galleries and any image which captures a moment or feeling or a relationship which might encourage dramatic play.

Many Picasso paintings stimulate powerful role-taking, I often use his Minotaur images, and portraits such as 'Head of a Faun' (1937), and 'Portrait of Nusch' (1937) from the Berggruen Collection, to create complex, mirrored characters. I might ask an adolescent exploring the abuser role to imagine they are the character in 'Head of a Faun' or 'Tete d'homme barbu' and make a life history of the character and imagine they are that character and describe themselves in dramatic terms.

The Picasso portrait of the child 'Paolo as Harlequin' (1924) and 'The Artists' (1905) – a portrait of mother and son – can be used for scenes about the nature of childhood. I sometimes use the Paolo painting as an enactment about adults putting children in silly clothes which make them feel stupid and powerless.

The role-taking can be verbal or a physical representation of the painting. This can then lead on to a scene between two people in a painting or two people from different paintings. The meeting of 'The Faun' and 'Nusch', for example.

Otto Dix (1991) painted pictures for all his children, some very frightening images, others funny and charming.

His pictures for his daughter Bettina Dix, show a series of domestic scenes with children and adults and animals which are fun for dramatic family play and he has a powerful painting of Red Riding Hood and the Wolf.

Storytelling and Enactment

Gersie (1983) states that stories communicate what is unknown but, through the very process of storymaking, what is unknown becomes knowable; in the act of naming the unnamed, the object, the experience, the thought not only becomes communicable, it also becomes recognisable. Each story is a journey which indicates movement through time and space. It is a journey with signposts. The skill of the therapist is to find a story which will enhance and enrich the journey the child is already making in play therapy.

Two Stories

NON-VIOLENCE
(Bengali)

'A very wicked snake infested a road and bit everyone who walked by. A holy man was passing by on the road, and the snake rushed at him to bite him. The holy man looked at the snake and said quite calmly, "You want to bite me, don't you? Go ahead".

The snake was shocked by this strange response and was overwhelmed by the gentleness of the holy man. The holy man said "Listen to me dear friend, could you promise me that you won't bite anyone from now on?" The snake bowed to the holy man and agreed. The holy man went on his way and the snake began his new life of non-violence.

Soon everybody in the neighbourhood discovered that the snake was harmless and the boys began to tease him mercilessly. They dragged him around by his tail and threw stones at him. But the snake kept his promise to the holy man.

Fortunately, the holy man came by to see the snake and was shocked to see him so battered and bruised. He asked the snake what had happened and the snake said "Holy man you said I should not bite anyone. But people are so very cruel".

The holy man said "I asked you not to bite anyone. But I didn't ask you not to hiss!'"

The theme of this story is very apt for the angry child who want to find ways to be assertive without being consumed by their own anger. The journey to find a balance has a role-reversal enactment in the snake who begins by being fearful, then experiences being the victim himself.

This theme is very powerful for those veering from abused child to abusing child. To find a way of being out of those roles is a preoccupation in therapy for children who, as children, are still relatively powerless.

The story also describes the victimisation of the snake when trying to change and this is an experience of many children who have become the convenient scape-goat in a family. It is also helpful for the child to play the Holy Man and then the therapist can role-model ways the snake might hiss. Stories have different aspects for whoever is using them. I remember using this story during a training course with experienced therapists and the theme for them, which they explored, was the meaning of the relationship between Holy Man and the snake and the expectations people might have of a person called a Holy Man.

SISTER OF BONES
(*An African story*)

'A family who lived in a dry place had two daughters. There was a lot of work to do where they lived. In the morning cooking, then as the sun got higher there was maize to pound into powder and the yard to sweep. And all the time, other people's children to look after. The hardest work was collecting the water. In the rainy season there was a spring nearby but when it was dry the only place where water could be found was in the river a long way away. To reach the river, and get the water, then return to the village, took half a day.

It was not easy carrying the calabashes of water back from the river. The sun was hot and the wind was dry. For many years it had been the task of the first girl to get the water from the river. The second girl was not nearly as strong, her arms were thin and it was difficult for her to walk long distances. She did most of the work at home, things that didn't require strength.

The second girl felt sad that she was not as strong as her sister but there was plenty of work for everyone in that dry place.

The first girl always fetched water from the same spot. There was a pool and a path leading to the water. Every day the girl came to the pool, filled her calabashes and dipped her hand into the cool water and drank before setting off on the long journey home.

One day as she arrived at the edge of the pool she felt very tired. As she leaned forward to fill the calabashes she became dizzy with the heat and the dryness of the wind, and she fell into the pool.

The river was deep and the girl couldn't swim. She struggled to get to the edge of the river but the current drew her to the centre of the pool. Soon she was in the middle of the river and there she sank with nobody to hear her last cry.

When the first girl had not returned by sunset her father knew something had happened to her. The next morning all the villagers went to search for her. They followed her footprints. When they saw that her footprints didn't come back from the river they knew what had happened. There was great sadness in the family and the village. Everybody had loved the first girl.

Now there was no choice but for the second girl to go and fetch the water. She set off the next morning wondering whether she would be able to carry the heavy calabashes back from the river. She managed the task but felt she would never be able to walk again, although she knew she would have to fetch the water every day until the rains came.

For three days the girl fetched the water from the river and each day it grew harder and harder. On the fourth day she dropped her calabashes by the river and sang the song she had made for her sister. In this song she told how her sister had come to the river and fallen in the water. In that river there were many crocodiles. When they heard the song the crocodiles slipped into the river, and quietly swam closer to the second girl so they could hear the words more clearly. It was a sad song and even the crocodiles felt sorry for her.

After the song was finished the second girl sat on the river's edge to gather her strength. The crocodiles, though. swam into the middle of the river to the place where the first girl had drowned. Then diving down to the bottom of the river they gathered the bones of the first girl and took them to a special rock they know on the other side of the river. There they put the bones together again and made them into a girl again. They carried the girl to the place where the second girl was sitting. and left her there.

When the second girl saw that her sister had come back she sang with joy and kissed her.

"I shall carry your water," the first girl said, "I am stronger."

The first girl carried the calabashes almost all the way back, but just before the village she had to stop and allow the second girl to carry them in.

"The crocodiles will not want me to leave the river now," she said. "I must go back."

From that day onwards, whenever the second girl reached the river the first girl would be waiting for her. She would carry the calabashes for the second girl, singing all the while, telling her sister stories of what happened in the river. The second girl was happy to have her sister back and happy, too, that everybody thought she was strong. She tried to tell her mother and father about her sister but they cried out in anger that her sister was dead.

"She is not" cried the second girl. "Come to the river tomorrow and see for yourself."

The parents went with the second girl the next day and were happy when they saw the first girl waiting by the bank of the river. In gratitude, the father put out some meat for the crocodiles where, he knew the crocodiles like to sit. The crocodiles swallowed the meat in their great jaws and went back to some rocks and watched the family in all its happiness.

This story has many levels, meanings about:

- loss and regeneration
- how we gain strength to do what was thought to be impossible
- being a woman and working for the survival of the group
- self-affirmation
- how to cope
- what to be
- how to gain strength from the one you have lost

- the lost one who can never fully return.

These themes and many more are all part of the healing within this story which can be explored through dramatic play.

How the story is developed dramatically will be determined by the choices made by the child who is using the story. These could be:

- make up a song for the lost sister
- the struggle of the second daughter to carry the pots back and forth, back and forth
- the first sister, reaching out to drink the cool into the river, to drown
- mourning the sister
- how the crocodiles made the girl again after hearing her sister's song
- saying good-bye to the sister who cannot return to the village.

Many themes to be explored in dramatic play.

Time-Limited Task-Based Play

Play therapy can be used effectively to help a client with a particular task, if the task is well defined, and there is a clear agreement between therapist and client about the task and the use of play to help solve a particular problem.

Task-based work should be clear, with the number of meetings stated at the onset of the agreement, then the boundaries of the work agreed.

Sometimes focused work is required because there is limited finance for longer interventions and in those circumstances, the therapist should assess if a short intervention can be effective.

Time-limited and task-based play may still be free play with the therapist's commentary being appropriate for the task; or stories and dramatic play can be focused more directly on the theme with ideas and material from the therapist or the client. So, for a young child who wants to develop self-esteem, I might begin with *I Want To Be* by Tony Ross and then help the child to explore her own answers to that question;

'What do YOU want to be...'

in the time left in therapy.

Free Play Short Term

LOUISE

Louise is five and she has difficulty in accepting that her three-year-old brother is not returning to the family and is to be adopted.

Her mother is supportive of therapy and respects the confidentiality of the play. She also has her own therapeutic support.

I agree to see Louise four times to play how she feels about the loss of her brother. I talk to her about the reason for coming to play with her and she agrees that she wants to sort it all out.

THE FIRST INTERVENTION

We begin by talking about Louise's brother and she said she feels sad and angry that he is not coming back. We sort out the factual information about the reasons for her brother not returning to the family. She thinks it is best for him but horrible for her. She misses him.

She stopped talking and began to play.

She played with play-doh. She said she liked the feel of it. She wasn't going to make anything with it, just touch and feel it and enjoy the colour.

Then she picked up the large bucket of slime and a plastic monster with a large mouth. She put the slime into the mouth of the monster. She made a story

'There was once a monster called Wayne and he was very greedy and he ate piles and piles of green jelly. He got very fat and he was sick. He might have died but he didn't. And when he wasn't eating jelly he was biting people.'

Louise then chose to play with two dolls. I had one, she had the other. She said

'They were good babies and they didn't get into any trouble. They were called Jennifer and Charlotte.

Charlotte has gone to another mummy and Jennifer has stayed with her real mummy.

Charlotte misses her mummy and can't understand why her mummy doesn't want her.

Charlotte misses her sister and her sister misses Charlotte.

Charlotte goes back home and Jennifer goes to another mummy.'

I suggested that perhaps the babies might be getting very cross.

'We aren't parcels, we are people!' I said.

Louise continued the play and story with the dolls being continually passed between us.

'The babies changed mothers again and this time they got really mad with the grown-ups. They smacked people, screamed and they be rude. They swear and it is because they are mixed up.

All the grown-ups are lying to the children and that's what makes them naughty.

So the babies were bathed and changed and went to bed.

The End.'

This story clearly encapsulates the anxieties Louise has about the loss of her brother and her fears for her own security in the family.

Louise can cope with honesty but not the lies of the grown-ups. At the end of the session, I remind Louise that I shall see her three more times and we count this out together. I repeat the reason we are playing together.

The themes expressed by Louise in the first session were explored further and at each visit Louise tells me how many more times she will see me. She plays, we keep the boundaries, and remember the task.

Donald

Donald was three. His father had killed his mother a year before I saw him. He had been taken into care at the time of his mother's death. He had not seen his father since the night of his mother's death and at first he had been told little about what had happened.

It had been agreed that it was appropriate for him to see his father, who was on remand in prison, and I was asked to play with Donald to prepare him for the visit, if he wished to go and see his father.

I saw Donald twice before the visit and once after the visit. When I met Donald, I talked with him, explaining the reason for my visit, and said that we would play together about what had happened with his dad, and to find out if he wanted to see his father.

Donald asked questions about his father, where he was. It was clear he knew that his dad had killed his mother. He said he was very angry with his dad. On my first visit, after talking about his parents, Donald played with finger puppets, using a crocodile and other animal puppets to enact fighting, arguing, and then the crocodile being sent to prison. We talked about prison and enacted a scene when crocodile was in prison and what happened there.

After the session, until my next visit, the foster carers reinforced why dad was in prison, and what happened there.

On the second visit Donald chose the same toys again. We talked as before. Central to the session was the story of the crocodile.

SNAPPY THE CROCODILE

'One morning, Snappy the crocodile was getting out of his bed and he thought he would play a trick on turtle. "Put your head in my mouth." The turtle got ate up.

The crocodile did it again and again until one day the crocodile met a really big monster (Mr Punch) who got his hat with the bell and shot it at the crocodile.

But crocodile went on eating people, and more people have been eaten by crocodile and more people got fooled by him.

The next day, the man (Mr Punch) came again and ate crocodile for his dinner.

One day the police came and got the crocodile out of his mouth and he was squashed up like a ball.

The police put the crocodile in jail and he stayed there for ever and ever.

He was put into the right shape again and he promised not to bite anyone ever gain.'

Again we enacted the jail and what happened to the crocodile there.

Donald visited his father in prison. When I saw him after the prison visit, he talked about his father, how angry he was with him, but how happy he was to see him again.

In his play, Donald had expressed some of the fear he felt about his father being a great consuming monster. This monster had mysteriously disappeared, his mother had mysteriously disappeared, people talked and whispered but Donald wasn't clear about what had happened and was he next?

Donald showed great relief after he had seen his father and realised he was alive. He could ask questions and receive a reply which made sense. It's a beginning.

Conclusion: Two Stories

TORTOISE, MEN AND STONES
(A Nigerian creation myth)

'God created the tortoise, men and stones. Of each he created male and female. He gave life to tortoises and men, but not to stones. None could have children, and when they became old they did not die but became young again.

The tortoise, however, wanted to have children, and he went to God. God said

"I have given you life, but I have not given you permission to have children."

But the tortoise came to God again to make his request and finally God said

"You always come and ask for children. Do you realise that when the living have had several children they must die?"

But the tortoise said

"Let me see my children and then die." Then God granted his wish.

When man saw the tortoise had children, he too wanted children. God warned man, as he had the tortoise, that he must die. But man also said

"Let me see my children and then die."

That is how death and children came into the world. Only stones did not want to have children, and so they never die.'

A story for the therapist:

THE MOTHERLY ELEPHANT
(*American?*)

'There was once a kindly elephant who accidentally stood upon a hen. She was much distressed, especially when she looked down and saw all the little chickens running about, cheeping.

"Poor little creatures. I will be a mother to them."

And gathering the chickens tenderly underneath her, she sat down upon them.'

CHAPTER 6

WORK SETTINGS FOR PLAY THERAPISTS

There are many settings in which play therapy is an appropriate intervention to help children and adolescents. As society begins to acknowledge the abuse of children and understand the needs of children experiencing difficulties of some kind, we need to be able to communicate and help children in ways with which they are comfortable and can really express how they feel.

If play is the child's natural medium of expression, then therapeutic help can best be offered in this medium. It is comfortable and familiar for the child and less anxiety-provoking than other forms of communication.

The work settings where therapists can help children most effectively at present are social services, education, hospitals and clinics.

Play Therapy in Social Services

Child Protection is the area in social services where the majority of therapy will be productive, although therapeutic help for children with learning disabilities or in residential care can be appropriate.

Investigative Interviews

In the field of Child Protection, interventions are in the area of *treatment* for children which would take place *after* the investigation of abuse.

Interviews with children about the possibility of abuse are investigative by nature and, although play materials may be used to assist the child and it is hoped that the interview will be therapeutic, it is not within the remit of the play therapist.

Disclosures in Therapy

Clearly, some children do disclose further abuse during the course of therapy and this has to be appropriately reported to the Child Protection Team. The contract between the child and therapist at the beginning of therapy should include the agreement that any such disclosure will have to be reported. This contract is most important because the child will know that disclosures cannot be kept confidential, and this leaves the decision to tell or not to tell with the child.

It is important to tell all children, including the youngest. I usually say something like

> 'If you tell me that a grown-up has done something bad like hurting you or something rude or sexy, then I shall have to tell your social worker or you can tell your social worker, or we can do it together. We will talk about it first and decide how we will tell, but we will have to tell.'

This part of the contract is for all play therapy work, not just in social services, because children do disclose abuse in other work settings.

Initial Contract

This initial contract will explain the reason for the therapy, which is not to find out about the abuse but to help the child come to terms and make some sense of what has happened. The other rules explained in Chapter 4 will be part of the contract.

Waiting for Court

Therapy undertaken with children who are waiting for court can present difficulties as it is importance not to influence the evidence which a child is to give in court.

However, the symbolic nature of children's play and adolescent imagery, especially after serious abuse, when the child needs to find a way of expressing abuse but distanced from the actuality of their own life experience, makes the problem minimal.

In therapy, the child or adolescent wants to explore what it felt like, not the actual evidential detail.

The therapy can also help the child develop self-confidence to make an appearance in court less traumatic.

The therapist is also available and, it is hoped, has developed a relationship with the child so that, after the court case, she is available to support the child or adolescent and help integrate that experience.

Many court cases are anything but supportive of the abused person, who is further disempowered by the ferocity of questioning from barristers and the whole nature of the court setting. Many children are not believed by adults in court, which is very hard to bear, and seems like being abused again. In these circumstances the child begins to doubt the validity of their very existence.

If social workers need training to interview children who have been abused, then it is even clearer that barristers need training in questioning children and adolescents in court, so that they do not forever damage the child's sense of identity and self-esteem.

Organisation for Play Therapy

It is important in a social services setting to organise carefully which clients are accepted for play therapy. It is difficult to maintain the neutrality required as a therapist if you are known to the child as their social worker, who has the power to make decisions which might totally change the future living circumstances of the child. The social workers I have trained take referrals for play therapy from other social workers on their team, so they are not therapists to their own clients.

They are able to set aside time for their work as play therapists, so role confusion does not arise for them or their clients and this has worked successfully.

Short Term Interventions

Short term interventions can help a child sort out their feelings about a particular event, as in the case of Louise and the loss of her brother, described in Chapter 5.

Preparation for Permanency and Post-Adoption

Part of the task of preparing the child for permanent placement can be undertaken using play therapy. Sometimes therapists are asked to help a child resolve the loss of the natural family before the child goes on for adoption. If a new family has been found for the child, then some issues of separation can be explored, but the child who has been removed from their natural family and has not yet found another permanent placement is not safe enough to deal with such an enormous loss.

There is sometimes a sense in social work that, once these losses have been explored in therapy, that is the end of the matter. Like a tick on the six-monthly review sheet of life; once done, never repeated!

The therapist can help the child to come to terms with some of the events of their past, perhaps to understand what happened to them, but she cannot 'magic' away pain and hurt for a child who has experienced such devastating loss and trauma.

When abuse has occurred, the child often takes responsibility for that abuse and then responsibility for the family breakdown, so the loss of family is not only distressing but also perceived as the child's responsibility.

These feelings do not change quickly. Carl, aged seven, whose shield was described in Chapter 4, adopted for three years, told me that, although he knew in his head that he wasn't responsible for being abused, inside his body he did feel responsible and that feeling wouldn't go away. It was always there, no matter what he did.

He drew a picture of his new family. None of the females had arms.

Above in the sky were birds planes, rain. He said you never knew when the rain would rain on you, the birds would shit on you and the planes would bomb you.

Figure 6.1 You never know when...

He has carried the fear from his natural family to his adopted family because he feels he is responsible for what happened so he can't stop it happening again.

Working with children in adoptive placements can help the child become part of the new family and, it is hoped, maintain the placement.

Kath Donaldson, a play therapist and family placement worker, undertook play therapy with a nine-year-old child called Janine to help settle her in her adoptive placement.

Session Five explored the theme of nurture.

> 'At the beginning of Session Five, Janine asked me if I had any paints and brushes. I said the only paints were finger paints and showed her. She began tentatively painting the sky with one finger and then said "I've gone wrong, want to start again".
>
> I said "You could start again or look carefully at the picture and imagine what it could be". She liked this idea and saw a dolphin.
>
> This led to another expression of Janine's nurturing. She outlined the dolphin with the blue and then put red paint quite lavishly over the blue.
>
> This was blood.
>
> The dolphin was hurt and needed help.
>
> Janine placed a piece of plain paper on top of the dolphin – pressed down and lifted it off.
>
> The blood had come off – the dolphin was getting better. Janine repeated this.
>
> She then changed to yellow and said this was bandages and plasters.
>
> The pressing down of the second picture was repeated. I said "Thank goodness there is someone who will help heal him and make him better".

She then took all the baby dolls out and said they were in hospital. She named them all and then herself and me. This meant we could get into role and not be ourselves, which felt good. The dolls were undressed and looked at for hurt places: then powder and lotion was put on them. Janine used the bottles, dummies and feeder cups. She gave them medicine too. In turn she made each one better.

Janine filled a baby's bottle with water and fed me. This felt really bold. She then tentatively fed herself and by this time we were both laughing.'

Kath's observations of the session were

1. The strength of the nurturing theme both with the dolphins and the dolls.

    Kath felt that the need for nurture was acknowledged but perhaps Janine has to sacrifice parts of herself to get the nurture she wants.

2. Dolphins and the sea are potent personal metaphors and are constantly featured in the therapy.

3. The dolls could have been Janine in the past. That is, they were looked at to see if they had any hurt places.

Residential Settings

If the therapist is working in a residential setting, it is important to discuss what is happening with all the workers involved with the child, so that everyone has the same information to help the child. All too often, a child in residential care will try to split the carers and, if the lines of communication are poor and the messages inconsistent, this can all too easily be accomplished.

Yiota Antonopoulou is a play therapist working in Athens and she described an intervention with M, a child of seven years, who had been neglected by her parents and placed in the custody of a residential centre by the social welfare centre and the juvenile court.

Before Yiota began therapy she had many meetings with the staff and throughout her intervention with M she communicated with the social workers, care workers, and psychologists so there was no confusion about what was happening.

M was developmentally delayed and it was not known if this was the result of her living conditions or inherited from her mother. It was hoped to rehabilitate M with her mother if support was available, but this was not known at the time of the intervention. Yiota undertook ten play therapy sessions with M. This is a description of part of Session Five.

> 'I begin. I say "I am Yiota" (I want her to say I am M). She says it twice with pleasure. At the same time we clap hands. Then I say "I feel fine"
>
> "I don't feel" she says, disturbed.
>
> I continue, "I want that we have a good time to-day".
>
> "I want to play" she says laughing. Straight away she continues "I want my pistol".
>
> She takes two little boxes with jelly in them and puts the pistol into it, takes it out, then places little men in it and says they are having a bath.
>
> Shaking the jelly, she throws it on the carpet exploring like a young child.
>
> She puts the jelly back in the boxes. She says she is good at closing boxes well.
>
> She takes out the baby dolls.
>
> She finds dressing the doll difficult. She wants me to help her dress the doll.
>
> At this point I say to her that she is capable of dressing the doll on her own as she wishes and the best way she can.

I tell her that whoever is playing on the mat can make the baby suck its dummy, drink from the bottle or do anything else one wishes without anyone saying it is good or bad.

She is very satisfied and fits the baby's bonnet on the baby's bottom...

At the end of the session she does everything she can to go beyond the time limit. She gathers up angrily.

Then I suggest for an ending the "I am, etc." "I am M" she says laughingly, "I have a lot of books". She is calm and cheerful once more.

I tell her there are five more sessions remaining.'

This play is very typical of a developmentally delayed child, neglected by her family, then placed in care.

The desire for nurture shown in the play with dolls, the search for approval from the therapist, the limited sense of self

"'I don't feel" she said,'

and the fear of loss, as typified by the difficulties with endings.

Yiota wrote some interesting observations about her time with M and working in a residential setting.

'My experience with M was significant and fulfilling.

My contact with a neglected and deserted child together with my contact with the institution, is for me a first time situation...

I gained a lot of experience from the whole procedure. Even the closest connection which existed with different persons, such as the social worker, the teacher and the child nurses, helped me to find my place, to see my own feelings towards the child and the institution and to set my terms.

Regarding the play therapy; first of all, the boundaries maintained throughout the programme were necessary in a relationship with such a child.

M was living within the vague and dim environment of the institution, was struggling to make a workable relationship with me as well as with the play objects. It was very difficult for this child to understand the real active connection involving two different personalities when conversing. The 'I am' game helped her differentiate the therapist from herself.

The maintenance of the boundaries of the play, the permissible position of the child during the hour of play omnipotence, the control and handling the situation of freedom of expression without translation, restriction or criticism, helped her to put things in order, to realise her existence and to begin to differentiate from the objects.'

School Settings

School can be an appropriate setting for play therapy if the therapist is not involved with the child in any other role in the school. There should be a clear understanding in the school about the function a therapist might have in the organisation. I have worked with groups of first year students in secondary school who found it difficult to adjust to the change from small primary school to large secondary and felt lost and overwhelmed by the change. This work is described in my book *Drama for People with Special Needs* (1992).

Special Educational Needs

Sally Meyer, a play therapist, works in special education and here describes an intervention with Mark, aged 12, who has a form of cerebral palsy affecting all four limbs. At the time of the intervention, Mark was undergoing tests in hospital and he used part of this play therapy session to explore his hospital visit.

'Mark had been sorting a Play mobile hospital.

He kept one piece of equipment – the lights from the operating table – but told me to put the rest in the box. He wanted to use it to show me the brain scan in hospital.

He then wanted to use the house to act out his experience at the hospital. He chose figures to represent a boy, who was placed on the top floor of the house, a mother and a father who were put on the ground floor.

A ghost with a kind of laser arrived in the house. He wanted to hurt the boy. The ghost went downstairs and killed the mum and the dad although mum came alive again.

(The part of the play about the mum and especially the dad seemed to be about Mark's family relationships. His parents were divorced.)

Mark then turned to me and asked me who I thought he was today. He drew my attention to his leather jacket He gave me a phonetic clue, "t" and "tor" I guessed Terminator.

I asked him of he would like to tell me about the Terminator (a film character, half man half metal).

I suggested he write a story about the character. He was very emphatic that this was Terminator 2 not Terminator 1, because 2 was good and had been programmed not to kill.

Terminator 2

Terminator 2 was programmed by John Conner not to kill. He is good and not like the last one.

The first sight of Terminator 2, there was a lorry and there was a bolt of lightening and then the Terminator was there and then he looked around and saw a pub and he went in and saw a man and said "I need your bike, your shoes and your gun".

The man said "You forgot to say please!"

The man pushed his cigarette at the Terminator, but as he was made of metal inside, he swung the man round into the kitchen and then beat up the rest. He'd won the bike, the shoes and the gun.

I said we didn't have any more time, but that we could continue next week. At the very end of the session he stretched out his hand, which he called a ghost hand, scooped up the ghost figure and said

"You didn't say please."

This seemed a very empowering way to finish; he felt strong enough to tackle the ghost himself.'

Sally's comment about the image of the Terminator.

'The Terminator seemed to contain so many connections for Mark. It is a character without a disabling history – he just arrives out of nowhere.

He knows what he needs and he is able to ask for it very directly.

The bike, the shoes and the gun have symbolic meaning for Mark in terms of speed, walking and power.

Just as the Terminator is part metal, so Marks legs are his wheelchair.

Dealing with the invasive, frightening ghost at the end by saying "You didn't say please," was perhaps his chance to express some anger towards all those people in his life who don't consult him about things that affect him.'

This intervention with Mark helps him cope with the difficulties he is experiencing. If he has the opportunity to use play therapy for this purpose then he will have more emotional energy left to cope with learning at school, so the educational value of this therapeutic space is evident.

Play Therapy in Hospitals and Clinics

Child Psychiatry Clinics

Child and family guidance clinics use play therapy as an appropriate intervention in their work with children experiencing a variety of difficulties.

Such clinics are usually part of the Child Psychiatric Service, run by multi-disciplinary teams including social workers, psychologists, clinical nurses, child psychiatrists, and other therapists.

The teams usually take referrals from general practitioners, social services, and paediatric departments, and self-referrals from families. The remit is to help families, using the skills developed by the specialisms of the team.

In such settings, play therapy is part of a team approach and could be used as part of family therapy or as an individual referral when the team sees play as the appropriate form of therapy. Such an intervention would start at the referral meeting when a case is discussed and team members decide on ways of working with that family. There would be an initial family meeting with all family members and the professional workers who have accepted the case.

At this meeting the family define the difficulties as perceived by all family members. From that meeting a plan is made by the workers and with the agreement of the family, a therapeutic programme set up.

The play therapist might be working individually with the children, or one particular child, perhaps occasionally seeing the sibling group. Then there might be meetings with the whole family, from time to time, to assess progress and define future plans.

Play therapy for the whole family can be another mode of intervention as part of a systems approach to family therapy. Watching a family build a kite together or make a family den and play together can clearly show how members of the family group communicate with each other. Dramatic play with family pairs and triads using play texts can also explore the nature of family dynamics.

Play Therapy in Hospital

Play therapy with children in hospital can be an effective way to help the child understand some of the treatments which they have to cope with during the course of an illness. If a child is an in-patient, one of the task-based functions of a play therapist might be to help the child cope with treatment procedures by playing what is to happen. Much of this work will be shared with the child's parents to help empower the whole family.

One of the most complex tasks, only undertaken by a skilled therapist, is to communicate with the child who is dying. This is a most complex task, to be available, but not to impose upon the child and family, to empower the family yet help the child who wants to express thoughts and feelings about death and dying.

Irene Manatakis is a play therapist working in Athens in a hospital team which treats cancer in children. She describes her relationship with Dina, a 14-year-old girl who was suffering from acute leukaemia. Irene had met Dina when she first became ill, then again, nearly a year later, when she was re-admitted to hospital. Irene writes:

> 'When Dina was re-admitted into hospital, I felt extremely bad. Her severe condition upset me a great deal. Physically, she was unrecognisable; she was thin, pale and very angry.
>
> Each time I visited her, I looked into her eyes and saw all that anger, anger and despair; anger towards everything and everyone and I saw how right she was to feel that way. I acknowledged her anger.
>
> Dina was aware of her situation; she knew how serious things were; consequently she was very angry when everyone was trying to assure her that everything was going to be all right instead of telling her the truth.
>
> At the same time she was negotiating her very own feelings; the acceptance of her situation which developed in due course...'

Irene brought Dina the pictures she had drawn the first time they worked together and Dina asked for them to be hung in her hospital room.

> 'I saw Dina every day. I asked her whether she wanted to draw again and she replied "yes," but she didn't know what to draw. I suggested that she drew the way she conceived her illness. She burst out laughing and then asked whether I was kidding. She asked me
>
> "What should I draw, a big, black worm? I'd rather not. Leave me with some paper and crayons and I'll draw something at some point in time."
>
> I agreed, telling her that she knew best. She laughed and said "Of course."
>
> The following day I enter her room and found a drawing waiting for me. She gave it to me with all the delight a child carries when it gives someone it loves a present.
>
> I asked whether she wanted to discuss it and she said "What's there to discuss? It is a beautiful valley with flowers."
>
> "I agree."

Figure 6.2 The valley with flowers

That evening Dina had a relapse. Her lungs started to collect fluid and made it difficult for her to breathe. In the morning when I went to the hospital, first thing I asked was how Dina was doing. They informed me that she was better. I went and saw her. She was extremely exhausted. I sat next to her.

The next day a second drawing was waiting for me.

Figure 6.3 Children climbing up to Heaven

She said that when children are playing and are having a good time it is as if they are climbing up to heaven. She added that the truth was when she was drawing the picture, she hadn't really thought about it in those terms, but that is how it turned out to be.

I said I hadn't noticed that the children were ready to fly away together with the kites.

She asked me "Interesting don't you think so? In this drawing
the flowers are less, there is no sun nor hills, just the sky. The
kites are what prevail in the drawing. The one child on the left
is drawn in black pencil."

Figure 6.4 The island

The following day a third drawing was awaiting me. I told her
that this time I would appreciate a story about this interesting
island with the incredible trees. Willingly, she gave me a
positive answer.

The drawing depicts a deserted island. It's not a beautiful
island; on the contrary it looks dry.

However, it is in a way beautiful, because it is a rare island
inhabited by birds and animals that exist nowhere else on
earth.

It has rare plants and flowers. All strange species and plants
here are in harmony.

I asked her whether people know of this island.

She replied that it is known to them, nevertheless they fear it, for it is guarded all round by sharks and other dangerous sea animals so that people who are not supposed to come to the island do not come and harm the environment.

That is why people are afraid to come all the way here and discover the truly rare treasures of the island.

I asked her what the trees stood for at the very top of the island.

She said they were two palm trees. The big tree stood for a wise woman who was gifted with patience, love and knowledge. Due to its size, and position, it could see and hear what was going on, on the island and in the other world. It helps the smaller tree and advises it.

"What does it advise the younger tree?" I asked her.

"Not to be afraid of the animals that are guarding the island," she said. "Besides, they cannot reach it now; the dangerous animals respect it, for it has become one with the environment which they are protecting. On the contrary, they are protecting it now – they don't want to harm it."

"Is there anything else the big tree could be telling the small tree?" I asked.

"Yes, it could be telling the small tree to look carefully on the island for new species – either plants or animals. Each time it would look without fear, it would discover something new. It would be able to feel the beauty of harmony the island carried."

I asked her whether the trees could stand for people.

She replied that they could.

"And who would these people be?"

"The small tree could be me."

"Do you want to add anything else to your drawing now you are the young tree?"

"I'd add a boat somewhere far in the sea filled with people."

"And what would you have liked to tell them?"

"I'd tell them not to be afraid of my island"

"How would you tell them?"

"I'd send them a message with one of the birds that fly in the sky."

"Will you be happy if those people get your message?"

"Yes, I would, very much, as a matter of fact. You see there's peace on my island and many treasures. They mustn't be afraid of the animals. The animals harm only bad and mean people."

"Who would you say the big tree represents?"

"I told you, a wise woman who knows how to listen and love. A woman who has a lot of courage and who loves children very dearly."

I spoke to Dina's parents, who seemed to believe that their daughter was looking so much better that she might overcome the illness.

I told them she may only seem better; therefore, perhaps it would be a good idea that her brother and sister visit her at the weekend.

Her parents agreed and indeed her brother and sister came and saw her that weekend.

Monday morning at 10.30, Dina died due to a sudden haemorrhage.

She didn't suffer, it all happened very quickly.

Her parents told me how right I was to have suggested that her brother and sister came to see her, for Dina had a great time with them and felt extremely happy that the family were all together again.

When her father and the children said good-bye to Dina that Sunday evening, she looked so well and happy that her father couldn't believe that she had died when they announced it to him. He called the hospital again to make sure that no mistake had been made and that he had heard well.'

Irene's Observations

'When Dina was on the support machine and the doctors were checking how it was functioning, while I stood there holding the cassette I had brought her, I felt Dina saying,

"Let them do what they are doing. As soon as they're are gone we will do our thing."

Even though death was there for a fact, even though she had undergone such hardships, Dina was playing, as if she were two different people, one body.

One lying in bed surrounded with problems and doctors watching over her and another one which went out for a walk, listened to music, drew, played with her doll, made jokes and was always in such a good-natured joking mood.

I dare say that Dina died happy. She was in no pain and in two minutes everything was over, whereas, she could have suffered if she had died due to her difficulty in breathing.

She died, however, of a haemorrhage – a death far easier and less painful.

I came to think how natural my communication with Dina had become.

I detached myself from my invisible machine of guilt, fear and obligation which I had imposed on myself, in order to be an impeccable professional.

Without my friend Margarita's supervision, I may not have had this experience.

Without my play therapy training and my becoming sensitive and aware of the children's drawings, I wouldn't have been able to pick up and understand whatever messages I got from Dina and, therefore, help her come out with these feelings, live with them and share them; live one side of herself and live it well.

I think of the daily significant and insignificant deaths that we have; how many losses – and at the same time how many gains – a life experience which makes life itself so valuable.

Last Story

THE CHAMELEON AND THE LIZARD
(Central Africa)

'When Death first entered the world, men sent the chameleon to find out the cause. God told the chameleon to let men know that if they threw baked porridge over a corpse, it would come back to life.

But the chameleon was slow in returning and Death was rampant in their midst, and so men sent a second messenger, the lizard.

The lizard reached the home of God soon after the chameleon.

God, angered, by this second message, told the lizard that men should dig a hole in the ground and bury their dead in it.

On the way back, the lizard overtook the chameleon and delivered his message first, and when the chameleon arrived, the dead were already buried.

Thus, owing to the impatience of man, he cannot be born again.'

CHAPTER 7

THE ADULT PLAYGROUND

'If all the year were playing holidays
To sport would be as tedious as to work.'

(*I Henry IV*)

I suppose I have a really loose interpretation of 'work' because
I think that just being alive is so much work at something you
don't always want to do. Being born is like being kidnapped.
And then sold into slavery. People are working every minute.
The machinery is always going. Even when you are asleep.

Warhol: *From A To B And Back Again*

Play and Work

Our ideas about what is play and what is work are complex. This is
perhaps linked with how we view the concepts of child and adult
and the meaning given to us as children about play. Both Freud and
Piaget have argued that the growth of reason results in the disap-
pearance of play as a factor in thought. Freud (1960) claimed that
play in young children is brought to an end by the strengthening of
a factor that deserves to be described as the critical faculty, or
reasonableness.

Piaget (1962) suggests that overt make-believe play goes underground and becomes internalised. This happens when assimilation
and accommodation become more differentiated and integrated,

creating a more stable cognitive structure, and play becomes more adapted to realistic goals and activities. Vandenburg (1986) states that this is not so. He suggested that the myths and fantasies of childhood are not eroded by the onset of logic and reason; rather they are replaced by more sophisticated adult myths about the importance of logic and reason. This in turn has led to the myth that adults have no myths.

He suggests that the motivation that pushes fantasy inwards has more to do with embarrassment. The development of cognitive skills, that allow for the internalisation of fantasy also allows for the internalisation of an external audience. We develop a capacity to evaluate our behaviour from the perspective of this imaginary audience and so acquire a capacity for embarrassment. We become more aware and also less bold.

The message for the child is always to 'grow up'. 'Don't show me up' we say. Childishness is frowned upon; to be grown up is the ideal. To be grown-up is a serious business, grown-ups don't play, grown-ups work. Play is for babies.

And yet in growing up, taking responsibility and power, how we yearn for that other world of play. But if *we* can't have it, then we encourage the child to grow out of it so *she* can't have it. To do so we find reasons to denigrate play or place it firmly in the realm of the child.

The Neverland: Peter Pan the boy who plays for ever

Kincaid (1992), writing about the erotic child and Victorian culture, explores growing up. He argues that Freud (1960) reduced all play to wishing and wishing to one simple wish, to be grown up. Freud constructs a single restrictive story, the child plays at one thing and for one reason; and that is how you must see it. Telling the story in this way allows us to use the child's own activities to gain what we want, for the child to be an adult-in-training. But that is not what we really want, because the child functions as a mirror for us, a complex mirror, yielding distanced views of desirable otherness.

Kincaid describes Peter Pan in the play by Barrie as the most alluring of Others, with no interest in imitating the grown-up, with no need of anyone outside himself.

The dynamism of Peter Pan is directed only towards having fun, towards inconsequential play. This playing forms most of the action of Peter Pan and most of the appeal of the drama. It is not simply that Neverland is set up and equipped with all the apparatus necessary for fantasy play; it is that Peter manages to conduct the adventures so that they are repeatable and yet infinitely variable. His life is centred in play and thus naturally works to perpetuate that play, to keep things going. If it looks as though he possibly might win, he simply changes sides. Peter's position on all matters is dictated by this form of being; play does not serve other ends, but acts as the centre, to explain and allow all else. Even death will be 'an awfully big adventure' – one more way to play.

Play and Culture

Huizinga (1949) suggests that play is a function of culture proper and not simply as it appears in the life of the animal or the child. Play is a special form of activity; it is significant and has a social function. Far from being an occasional interlude, an activity marginal to man's history and culture, play is the determining characteristic of human sensibility.

He considered that modern civilisation has separated play from life. It is no longer part of every man's cultural activities but is relegated to sport and similar occupations which are isolated from the fabric of the process of living.

Scheueri (1986), examining some phenomenological aspects of play, says that what our language calls play is a typical form of movement which can be characterised by a handful of qualities. Play is

- an effortless movement of an up and down, a to and fro
- free from external restraints

- exciting and attractive in itself because of its inner tensions, ambiguity and openness
- fulfilled in presence with a tendency to infinity
- distant from usual reality on a figurative or symbolic level.

Play and games are an opportunity to free ourselves from the compulsions and pressures of life and to abandon ourselves to the mood of 'playfulness'.

But at the same time they have their own reality and objectivity, with special laws and challenges. The special quality of play phenomena depends on their double-faced character. They challenge both activity and contemplation, the doing itself changing into happening that occurs on its own account.

Only if we want it, if we are able to respond, if we are in earnest with it and take it seriously as distinct reality, play becomes an area of irreplaceable experiences and impressions which enrich out lives.

Babcock (1978), an anthropologist, contends that many of the described characteristics of play in modern society are actually terms for what is feminine. Play, like womanhood, is a limited or marginal area of life. It is defined in our masculine dictionaries as:

- trivial
- frivolous
- immature
- childlike
- narcissistic
- nonsensical
- free
- unreal
- unnecessary
- disorderly
- indiscreet

- fluid
- open

All of these terms contrast with the seriousness of the male order of political and economic life, from which she concludes that play and recreation, to which men have access and women largely do not, is in a large part a magical projection of what men think of, and represents men wearing the costumes of women in a kind of magical sphere to which women do not have access.

This is an interesting contention, especially when we consider the venom of some church men confronted with women priests, or the lack of leading roles for women in the theatre. How jealous men become when women try to regain their own playing sphere!

The Play Therapist at Work – Playing

It would seem that the sphere in which women are allowed to play is with children. Then play can be properly marginalised as something in which women and children participate. The danger for play therapists who use play as 'work' is the feeling that they have to surround playing with lots of logic and reason to prove that play is 'serious'. (Read this book!) I wish I could count how many times a man has made some detrimental remark, picking up one of my toys:

'I wish *I* could play all day! You get paid for this?'

then goes back to his desk and his computer on which *he* 'plays' all day.

However, when that man picks up my toys, he plays for quite some time and there is a feeling that he wants to get back in touch with a lost part of himself but is afraid to acknowledge that longing in the adult world. Then it is quite a struggle on my part to get my toys back again as the fun of playing takes hold.

I have great admiration for the men who are play therapists, who can acknowledge and utilise that relationship with a child and who do not abuse that relationship.

What is not recognised, because it is unbearable, is that children experience pain and terror and sadness and that is what is played in therapy. It is much easier for adults to marginalise, patronise play than acknowledge the pain of children.

Or perhaps childhood was such a fearful experience for the adult, both man and woman, that they can only defend themselves from that pain by being 'adult' and denying the playful side of their nature.

The Play Therapist at Work – Not Playing

It is important for the play therapist to take a firm stand about the importance of the work in the hierarchy of the institution in which she works. The therapist represents the viewpoint of the child and is one of the key people who can mediate the child and the adult world. This is a critical role for the therapist and she must represent the views of the child to the best of her ability.

This is the function of the therapist working with the child's ecosystem to represent the child within the child's world. There are many stresses to this role.

The ambiguity of being patronised by a judge who believes the adult myth that he deals in logic and reason as he sits there in his wig and gown, never ceases to amaze me.

Playing in the Adult World

The need to play, to finds release from the tensions of the world about us, is critical for humans. People *must* play and we all find ways to do so. While play itself is a phenomenon, the descriptions of the meanings of play are bound in the rhetoric and culture of the observer and researcher, so my descriptions of play in the adult world are bound by the ideologies which imbue my work as a play therapist. My interest in adult play is to examine ways in which adults explore those creative and developmental processes of embodiment, projection and role in my particular culture.

Embodiment Play

> 'Day after day I look in the mirror and I still see something –
> a new pimple. If the pimple on my upper right cheek is gone,
> a new one turns up on my lower left cheek, on my jawline,
> near my ear, in the middle of my nose, under the hair on my
> eyebrows, right between my eyes. I think it's the same pimple,
> moving from place to place. If someone asked me "What's your
> problem?" I'd have to say "Skin".'
>
> Warhol: *From A to B and Back Again*

THE BEACH

Perhaps the ultimate place for embodiment play is the beach, with
sand, sea and the presentation of the body on the beach. All the play
of the infant is present here, making a small world for yourself on
the sand with clear territorial boundaries. The equipment for nurture:
towels, creams for sun protection, food, drink. Even the clothing for
the beach, in particular male swim wear, is reminiscent of the nappy
of the small baby. Lying on the sunbed or in the pocket of sand
created just for you by the form of your body, then the immersion
into the sea. A totality of embodiment experience.

BODY PAMPERING

There is much adult play around the care and pampering of the body.
The sauna, steam bath, aromatherapy, massage, reinforce the sensory
state of the body and the space the body takes up in the world.

A visit to the hairdresser; washing hair, the smell of the shampoo
and conditioner, all the processes of cutting, shaping colouring,
curling, done as the client looks at their image in the mirror. The
whole ritual of care offered by the hairdresser. The cup of coffee,
the expensive magazines to read, all feed into the sense that we are
important and worthy of love.

THE FAIRGROUND

Then 'All The Fun of the Fair' – the sense of putting the body in danger. There is no feeling like the terror of the roller-coaster, the slow haul up to the top of the climb when we see the world around us, for one second powerful, then the terror of that pause before the rush of fear as the body becomes paralysed by the speed of the descent. A metaphor for the body in life like nothing else.

And the hall of mirrors to show us a body we dare not see, but so ritualised and distanced that we laugh and bear the pain.

Projective Play

'I'd rather have jewelry.' B said.

'Why?'

'Because a diamond is forever,' B said.

'Forever what?'

Warhol: *From A to B And Back Again*

ADULT TOYS

Much play in the adult world is about collecting and possessing objects. These objects become containers for the adult's images of themselves or what they would like to be. The car, the phone, the computer, while ostensibly used for work, are really the play toys of adults. These toys also define the owner's status to the outside world.

COLLECTIONS

Perhaps play patterners grow up to become collectors, forever arranging and changing their collections. What adults choose to collect is often rooted in childhood memories. I remember at one time I had a collection of Victorian dolls; the fragility of their china heads was a constant source of worry to me. My mother came to visit and asked me if I had ever forgiven her for breaking the head of the china doll I had as a child. I looked at her blankly. I had forgotten about that doll.

Then the memory flooded back: a large Victorian doll, given to me by a kind friend of my mother's. She was a women who had always had time for me as a child and had taught me many things about the countryside when we first came from the city. Then my mother breaking the doll's head during one of her cleaning bouts and her guilt about it. The replacement head was a grotesque creation, the best my mother could do in war-time. I never played with the doll again.

When my mother reminded me of that loss I gave up my collection. My mother had acknowledged her responsibility for the loss of my doll and I didn't need to worry about keeping fragile dolls safe anymore.

But play with objects is fun and the collector can express much through her collections. The objects and images which we use to make our worlds have a playful significance and are a meaningful way of expressing that world. We also move towards other people who share some of the feelings we have about certain objects and play with them by trading objects and showing off what we have got.

This kind of collecting can be a way of being able to play which was not possible as a child. The adult with a complex miniature train system is making up for a lost childhood, but there is no reason why creating a complex railway world should not be the creative task of an adult.

THE SAFETY OF OBJECTS

For many people, much of this playfulness with objects is rooted in the childhood feeling that objects are more reliable that people and perhaps communication with others can only be achieved through talk about the objects, avoiding direct intimacy.

It is fascinating to listen to conversations between people on short wave radio; men sitting in their little radio shacks at the bottom of the garden, talking to people they will probably never see, talking with the intensity and passion of the truly committed. A paradoxical world, disembodied voices, yet the safe place for some to express their passion for their objects of desire.

THE DANGER OF OBJECTS

Perhaps another feeling about playing with objects is that you can take them to pieces and if they do go wrong they can probably be put right. The tension of play with a newly bought electronic gadget which can either work magic or blow up and crash your world is a thrill not to be missed.

Who can deny the delights of play with a computer? I have a deep emotional relationship with my spellchecker, I talk to it, I perceive it as a kindly gnome, but I also know that there is a dragon in the machine which can support my creativity or crash the lot in a second. The tension this induces is play indeed. A game of magical skill and as I write this I am tempting the dragon!

THE CAR. AN OBJECT OF DESIRE AND COMBAT

And finally, the car, that symbolic object of desire, into which the owner projects all sorts of creative and destructive feelings. The car is a clearly defined world and, like a womb, enfolds the occupant within a shell. The danger of play in a car is clear: watch the adolescent car thief, watch the combat between drivers. A mild mannered person changes into a life-destroying maniac. The car as projective object also shows the interaction between projective play and role-taking. It is not in the use of the car as an object to express identity which is dangerous, but the use of the car as a chariot of war in a competitive race. This could be linked with the male-oriented interest in competitive games where there is no concept of collaboration but where all are supposed to be equal before the laws of action.

Perhaps we should re-define all circular motorways like the M25 as gladiatorial battle grounds and offer them to the world as symbolic war-zones!

Role Play and Enactment

> 'The acquisition of my tape recorder really finished whatever emotional life I might have had, but I was glad to see it go. Nothing was ever a problem again because a problem just meant a good tape, and when a problem transforms itself into a good tape it's not a problem any more. An interesting problem was an interesting tape. Everybody knew that and performed for the tape. Better yet, the people telling you the problems couldn't decide anymore if they were really having the problems or if they were just performing.'

> Warhol: *From A to B And Back Again*

Life as a performance has been explored in recent times by a variety of experts including sociologists, psychologists and anthropologists. These explorations analyse two kinds of life performances: social performances and cultural performances.

Turner (1987) states that if man is a sapient animal, a toolmaking animal, a self-making animal, a symbol-using animal, he is no less a performing animal and in performing he reveals himself to himself. This can be in two ways: the actor may come to know himself better by acting; or one set of human beings may come to know themselves better through observing and/or participating in performances generated and presented by another set of human beings. Goffman (1959) described social performances as the presentation of self in everyday life He explored this presentation through a conceptual framework called role theory in which everyday encounters were termed performances.

During these performances we make roles or we can break roles and in so doing gain acceptance or otherwise from those who observe.

Play for some in adult life can involve us in extraordinary enactments which we do regard as play, even though they might take place in a work setting.

I remember being told by a learned professor that, to get what he wanted from a meeting, he organised a long and dreary agenda, extended the meeting for as long as possible, then brought his request into 'any other business' when everyone was so tired and hungry they would agree to anything to get home.

Everyone at his meetings clearly knew what he was doing, a simple enough ploy to be transparent, but for him, the ambiguity, inner tensions and openness which was present during the meetings, created a playground out of the committee room. This was his playground and he was at play. Many people conduct their professional life as a form of play, from power dressing in imitation of the latest soap on TV... to using the portable phone to attract attention as you cut into the traffic on the motorway. Making life a competitive sport and using role only for power.

Cultural performances involve varieties of ritual, festival, carnival, theatre, film, ceremonial, enactment. It is here that the adult plays in the roles of actor/participant or audience/observer.

Turner (1987) states that one of the best ways we learn by experience is through our 'performative genres'. These cultural performances belong to the 'subjunctive' mood, that is, they express supposition, desire, hypothesis, possibility, and in this way ambiguity reigns. People and public policies may be judged sceptically, vices, follies, stupidities may be satirised. These performative genres occupy a liminal frame which he defines as a ritual associated with the passage from one human state or status to another. For example, rituals which mark a whole group's passage from one culturally-defined season to another, or the collective response to hazards – either natural or man-made disasters. Rituals of this kind have their liminality in public places. The city squares are not abandoned but transformed and everything is switched into the subjunctive mood for the specific period of time. As I write, the streets of Notting Hill in London are transformed for the Carnival.

Turner goes on to say that within the liminal frame, new subjunctive, even ludic structures, are then generated with their own grammars and lexica of roles and relationships. Jennings (1992) argues that dramatic rituals are about consciousness-raising – about empowerment. People need empowerment against the wrath of the gods, or to alleviate the dangerous malady, or to procreate or to be a successful cultivator or business person.

So as you enter the Carnival spirit, dance your Morris dance, shout support for your local football team, play Hamlet, watch Coronation Street, or light a candle to

'Light a light to light a life'

you are in touch with that essential human need to play.

Stories for the Adult Playground

It is important to stay playful if we wish to lead a creative adult life, so find your way to play and be inventive. Start here, read some stories just for fun.

An Embodiment Story

THE WITCHBALL
(*Hillbilly – USA*)

'Once there was a poor boy who wanted to marry a girl, but her folks didn't want him. His grandma was a witch, an' she said she'd fix it up. She made a horsehair witchball, and put it under the girl's doorstep. The girl came outside, passin' over the witchball, an' went back in the house. She started to say somethin' to her mother, an' ripped out, an' every time she spoke a word, she'd rip out. Her mother told her to stop that or she'd lick her. Then the mother went out for somethin', an; when she came back in, she broke wind, too, every time she spoke. The father came in an' he did the same thing.

He thought somethin' was the matter, so he called the doctor, an' when the doctor come in over the doorstep, he started to poop with every word he said, and they were all atalkin' an' apoopin' when the old witch came in an' told them God had probably sent that on them as a curse because they wouldn't allow their daughter to marry the poor boy. They told her to run an git the boy, cos he could marry their girl right away so god would take the curse off them. The ole witch went an' got the boy, an' on her way out, she slipped the witchball out from under the doorstep. The boy an' girl got married an' lived happy ever after.'

Stories about Objects

A RIDDLE

'In marble halls as white as milk,
Lined with a skin as soft as silk,
Within a fountain crystal-clear,
A golden apple doth appear.
No doors there are to this stronghold,
Yet thieves break in and steal the gold.

Answer. A hen's egg.'

THE GLASS BALL
(British)

'There was once a woman who gave a beautiful glass ball to each of her daughters. The girls loved to play with these delicate balls, throwing them to each other, but one day, while they were playing, one tossed her glass ball over the wall into the next garden. This garden belonged to a fox. He was not a sociable fellow, he never talked to his neighbours.

The girl was very much afraid of the fox, but she went to his door and knocked, and the fox came to the door, and said she could have her glass ball back, if she would serve him as his housekeeper for one year.

Unwillingly, she agreed, but the fox made her very comfortable and happy until one day he said to her, "I am going away, and until I come back there are five things you must not do. You must not wash up the dishes, sweep the floor, dust the chairs, look into the cupboard, nor look under my bed."

The girl promised, but when the fox had gone, she began to wonder why he had given her such strange orders. So she washed up the dishes to see what would happen, and at once a great bag of copper fell down in front of her. Then she swept the floor, and down fell a great bag of silver. So then she dusted the chairs, and down came a bag full of gold. She looked in the cupboard, and there was her glass ball. At last she went upstairs and under the fox's bed lay the fox!

Terrified she ran downstairs and out of the house, until she came to a lane. At the top of the lane she met a horse and said to it,

> "Horse of mine, horse of mine,
> If you meet a man of mine,
> Don't say that I've passed by."

And the horse said, "I will not".

Further on she met first a cow, then a mule, then a dog, and a cat and an owl, and to each of them she said the same thing. and they gave her the same reply.

The fox was following close behind and he said to the horse,

> "Horse of mine, horse of mine,
> Hast thou met a maid of mine?"

And the horse said, "She's just passed by,"

The cow, the mule, the dog, the cat, and the owl all gave the same answer.

"Which way did she go?" said the fox to the owl.

"You must go over that gate and across the field, and behind the wood you will find her," replied the owl.

So the fox ran off, but neither he, nor the girl, nor the glass ball have ever been heard of since.'

Stories about Roles

BRING ME FOUR
(a Story from India)

'One day Akbar said to Birbal, "Bring me four individuals: one, a modest person; two, a shameless person; three, a coward; four, a heroic person—

Next day Birbal brought a woman and had her stand before the emperor.

Akbar said, "I asked for four people, and you have brought only one. Where are the others?"

Birbal said, "Refuge of the World, this one woman has the qualities of all four kinds of persons."

Akbar asked him, "How so?"

Birbal replied, "When she stays in her in-laws' house, out of modesty she doesn't even open her mouth. And when she sings obscene insult-songs at a marriage, her father and brothers and husband and in-laws and caste-people all sit and listen, but she's not ashamed. When she sits with her husband at night, she won't even go alone into the storeroom and she says 'I'm afraid to go'. But then, if she takes a fancy to someone, she goes fearlessly to meet her lover at midnight, in the dark, all alone, with no weapon, and she is not at all afraid of robbers or evil spirits."

Hearing this Akbar said, "You speak truly," and gave Birbal a reward.'

FATHER AND MOTHER BOTH 'FAST'
(Hillbilly – USA)

'Oh yes. Well a fella stayed with a girl, and by and by he went to his father and he said, "Father, I'm going to marry that girl". He says, "John, let me tell you – I'se fast when I was young, and that girl's your sister."

Well, he felt bad and he left her. By and by, he picked up another one, and he stayed with her for a while, and he went to his father and he said, "Father I'm going to marry that girl," He said, "Johnny, I was fast when I was young – that girl's your sister."

Felt awful bad and one day he's sitting up by the stove and his mother said, "What's the trouble?" He said "no nothing" She said, "There is something I want to know what it is. Why did you leave that girl the first one, and you left the second one?" "Well" he said, "Father told me he was fast when he was young, and they's both my sisters". Says she, "Johnny, I want to tell you something. I was fast when I'se young, and your father ain't your father at all".'

On Being a Creative Play Therapist

First, we have to accept the child, as she is, not how she might, be or how somebody else would like her to be. Carolyn Cassady described her relationship with Neal Cassady, the 'prophet' of the Beat generation, the 'holy con man with the shining mind' in Jack Kerouac's *On The Road*.

In a newspaper interview (The Independent 21 August 1993) she said:

> 'He'd never known loyalty in love. His horrific childhood of emotional and physical neglect with a drunken father had crippled the adult man. Because he thought himself so value-less, he gave himself away. He'd never known unconditional love...

I started by trying to mould him.

In the end, after 25 years, I finally learnt to love him as he was.'

We offer our acceptance of the child and we can offer the child our skill and companionship as a playing partner. We must be a creative player and constantly renew our own pleasure in play in the adult world to replenish our resources so we have something to offer to the child.

And so we end where we began:

MAKING THE WORLD
(North American – Salishan-Sahaptin)

'The Chief above made the earth. It was small at first, and he let it increase in size. He continued to enlarge it, and rolled it out until it was very large. Then he covered it with a white dust, which became the soil.

He made three worlds, one above another – the sky world, the earth we live on, and the underworld. All are connected by a pole or tree which passes through the middle of each.'

'I had a boat, and the boat had wings;
And I did dream that we went a flying
Over the heads of queens and kings,
Over the souls of dead and dying,
Up among the stars and the great white rings,
And where the moon on her back is lying.'

M.E. Coleridge.

References

Ahlberg, J. and Ahlberg, A. (1984) *The Baby's Catalogue*. Harmondsworth: Penguin Books.

Ahlberg, J. and Ahlberg, A. (1989) *Bye Bye Baby*. London: Heinemann.

Anholt, C. (1989) *When I Was A Baby*. London: Heinemann.

Axline, V. (1955) 'Play therapy procedures and results,' *American Journal of Orthopsychiatry, 25*, 618–626.

Babcock, B. (1978) (ed) *The Reversible World*. Ithaca, NY: Cornell University Press.

Beier, U. (1966) (ed) *The Origin of Life and Death*. Oxford: Heinemann.

Bowlby, J. (1969) *Attachment and Loss, Vol. 1 Attachment*. London: Hogarth Press.

Bowlby, J. (1973) *Attachment and Loss, Vol. 2 Separation*. London: Hogarth Press.

Bowlby, J. (1980) *Attachment and Loss, Vol. 3 Loss*. London: Hogarth Press.

Briggs, K.M. (1970) (ed) *A Dictionary of British Fairy Tales*. London: Routledge and Kegan Paul

Carroll, L. (1941) *Alice In Wonderland: Alice Through The Looking Glass*. London: Macmillan.

Carter, A. (1992) (ed) *Second Virago Book of Fairytales*. London: Virago.

Cassady (1993) Love letters from a bent jailbird Sandra Berwick, *The Independent 21 August*.

Cattanach, A. (1992) *Drama for People with Special Needs*. London: A & C Black.

Coleridge, M.E. (1957) In W.H. Auden and J. Garrett *The Poets Tongue Anthology*. London: G. Bell and Sons.

Dix, O. (1991) *Children's Album.* (edited by D. Gleisberg). Leipzig: Edition Leipzig.

Emmerich, W. (1964) 'Continuity and stability in early social development'. *Child Development, 35,* 311–332.

Erikson, E. (1950/63) *Childhood and Society.* New York: W.W. Norton.

Erikson, E. (1977) *Toys and Reasons.* New York: W.W. Norton.

Freud, S. (1960) *The Standard Edition of the Complete Psychological Works of Sigmund Freud. Vol. VIII.* (edited by J. Strackley). London: Hogarth Press.

Gersie, A. (1983) 'Storytelling and its links with the Unconscious.' *Dramatherapy: Journal of BADTh, 7,* 7–12.

Gersie, A. (1992) *Earthtales.* London: The Merlin Press.

Goffman, E. (1959) *The Presentation of Self in Everyday Life.* New York: Doubleday Anchor Books.

Goldschmied, E. (1975) 'Creative play with babies'. In S. Jennings (ed) *Creative Therapy.* London: Pitman and Sons.

Holub, M. (1970) 'Fairy tale'. In G. Summerfield (ed) *Junior Voices.* Harmondsworth: Penguin Books.

Huizinga, J. (1949) *Homo Ludens.* London: Routledge and Kegan Paul.

Inkpen, M. (1989) *Jojo's Revenge.* London: Walker Books.

Jennings, S. (1990) *Dramatherapy with Families, Groups and Individuals.* London: Jessica Kingsley Publishers.

Jennings,S (1992) 'The nature and scope of dramatherapy', In M. Cox (ed) *Shakespeare Comes To Broadmoor.* London: Jessica Kingsley Publishers.

Johnson, D.R. (1992) 'The dramatherapist "in role"'. In S. Jennings (ed) *Dramatherapy Theory and Practice 2.* London: Routledge.

Jones, T. (1983) *Fairy Tales.* London: Penguin Books.

Kincaid, J.A. (1992) *Child-Loving.* London: Routledge.

Kitamura, S. (1986) *When Sheep Cannot Sleep.* London: A and C Black.

Konisglow, W. von. (1989) *Toilet Tales.* Toronto: Annick Press.

Landy, R. (1991) 'Role as a primary bridge between theatre and drama therapy.' *Dramatherapy Journal of BADTh, 13,* 1, 4–11.

Landy, R. (1992a) 'Introduction to special issue on transference/countertransference in the creative arts therapies'. *The Arts in Psychotherapy, 19,* 5, 313–315.

Landy, R. (1992b) 'One-to-one: the role of the dramatherapist working with individuals'. In S. Jennings (ed) *Dramatherapy Theory and Practice 2.* London: Routledge.

Lloyd, D. and Voce, L. (1988) *Hello, Goodbye.* London: Walker Books.

Lowenfeld, M. (1979) The World Technique. London: Allen and Unwin.

May, R. (1991) *The Cry For Myth.* New York: Norton and Co.

McCall Smith, A. (1989) *Children of Wax.* Edinburgh: Canongate Publ.

McKee, D (1987) *Not Now Bernard.* London: Arrow Books.

Meldrum, B. (1993) 'A play of passion. A theatre model of Dramatherapy.' Paper presented at The Institute of Dramatherapy Summer School.

Miller, V. (1991) *On Your Potty.* London: Walker Books.

Miller, V. (1992) *Eat Your Dinner.* London: Walker Books.

Mitchell, S. (1990) 'The theatre of Peter Brook as a model for dramatherapy.' *Dramatherapy Journal of BADTh, 13, 1,* 13–17.

O'Connor, K.J. (1991) *The Play Therapy Primer.* New York: Wiley.

Phillips, T. (1985) *The Heart of a Humument.* Stuttgart: Hansjorg Mayer.

Piaget, J. (1962) *Play, Dreams and Imitation in Childhood.* New York: Norton.

Ramanujan, A.K. (1991) (ed) *Folktales from India.* New York: Pantheon Books, Random House.

Ross, T. (1986) *I Want My Potty.* London: Collins Picture Lions.

Ross, T. (1993) *I Want To Be.* London: Anderson Press.

Scheueri, H. (1986) 'Some phenonenological aspects of play'. In R. Kooij, and J. Hellendoorn (ed) *Play, Play Therapy, Play Research.* Lisse: Swets and Zeitlinger, BV.

Sendak, M. (1985) *Outside Over There.* Harmondsworth: Penguin Books.

Singer, J.L. (1986) 'The development of imagination in early childhood: foundations of play therapy'. In R. van der Kooij, and J. Hellendoorn (ed) *Play, Play Therapy, Play Research.* Lisse: Swets and Zeitlinger, BV.

Sproul, B.C. (1991) *Primal Myths*. San Francisco: Harper Collins.

Sutton-Smith, B. (1980) 'Piaget, play and cognition revisited'. In W. Overton (ed) *The Relationship Between Social and Cognitive Development*. New York: Erlbaum.

Turner, V. (1987) *The Anthropology of Performance*. New York: P.A.J. Publishers.

Vandenberg, B. (1986) Play, myth and hope. In R. van der Kooij and J. Hellendoorn (ed) *Play, Play Therapy, Play Research*. Lisse: Swets and Zeitlinger BV.

Warhol, A. (1975) *From A to B and Back Again*. London: Cassell and Co.

West, J. (1992) *Child-Centred Play Therapy*. London: Edward Arnold.

Wilson, K., Kendrick, P. and Ryan, V. (1992) *Play Therapy*. London: Balliere Tindall.

Winnicott, D.W. (1974) *Playing and Reality*. London: Tavistock.

Wolf, D. and Gardner, H. (1979) 'Style and sequence in early symbolic play'. In M. Franklin and N. Smith (ed) *Symbolic Functioning in Childhood*. Hillside, NJ: Erlbaum.

Wright, C. (1991) *When The World Sleeps*. London: Random Century Children's Books.

Yalom, I.D. (1975) *The Theory and Practice of Group Psychotherapy*. New York: Basic Books.

Subject Index

Name Index